A HISTORY
OF THE NATIVE PEOPLE OF CANADA

VOLUME I (10,000 – 1,000 B.C.)

by J. V. WRIGHT

Mercury Series
Archaeological Survey of Canada
Paper 152

Published by
Canadian Museum of Civilization

© Canadian Museum of Civilization 1995

CANADIAN CATALOGUING IN PUBLICATION DATA

Wright, J. V.
A history of the Native people of Canada.
Volume I (10,000–1,000 B.C.)

(Mercury series, ISSN 0316-1854)
(Paper/Archaeological Survey of Canada, ISSN 0317-224;
no. 152)
Includes an abstract in French.
Includes bibliographical references.
Issued also in computer file (diskettes and CD-ROM)
This is the first of 3 volumes.
ISBN 0-660-15951-1

1. Native peoples – Canada – History.
I. Canadian Museum of Civilization.
II. Title.
III. Series.
IV. Series: paper (Archaeological Survey of Canada);
no. 152.

E78.C2W74 1995   971'.00497   C95-980241-X

 PRINTED IN CANADA

Published by
Canadian Museum of Civilization
100 Laurier Street
P.O. Box 3100, Station B
Hull, Quebec
J8X 4H2

Senior production officer: Deborah Brownrigg
Cover design: Ashton Station Creative Group Inc.

Front cover: The early 17th century fragment of a stone
smoking pipe from Ontario represents an exceptional
example of the skill of the Huron artisan.

Back cover: Dated to 2,250 B.C., the ivory maskette
from Devon Island, Northwest Territories is believed to
portray a tattooed woman.

OBJECT OF THE MERCURY SERIES

The Mercury Series is designed to permit the rapid
dissemination of information pertaining to the disciplines
in which the Canadian Museum of Civilization is active.
Considered an important reference by the scientific community,
the Mercury Series comprises over three hundred specialized
publications on Canada's history and prehistory.

Because of its specialized audience, the series consists largely
of monographs published in the language of the author.

In the interest of making information available quickly, normal
production procedures have been abbreviated. As a result,
grammatical and typographical errors may occur. Your indulgence is requested.

Titles in the Mercury Series can be obtained by writing to:

Mail Order Services
Canadian Museum of Civilization
100 Laurier Street
P.O. Box 3100, Station B
Hull, Quebec
J8X 4H2

BUT DE LA COLLECTION

La collection Mercure vise à diffuser rapidement le résultat de
travaux dans les disciplines qui relèvent des sphères d'activités
du Musée canadien des civilisations. Considérée comme un
apport important dans la communauté scientifique, la collection
Mercure présente plus de trois cents publications spécialisées
portant sur l'héritage canadien préhistorique et historique.

Comme la collection s'adresse à un public spécialisé, celle-ci
est constituée essentiellement de monographies publiées dans la
langue des auteurs.

Pour assurer la prompte distribution des exemplaires imprimés,
les étapes de l'édition ont été abrégées. En conséquence,
certaines coquilles ou fautes de grammaire peuvent subsister :
c'est pourquoi nous réclamons votre indulgence.

Vous pouvez vous procurer la liste des titres parus dans la
collection Mercure en écrivant au :

Service des commandes postales
Musée canadien des civilisations
100, rue Laurier
C.P. 3100, succursale B
Hull (Québec)
J8X 4H2

Canadä

DEDICATED TO THE MEMORY OF THE ANCESTORS

OF THE NATIVE PEOPLE

PREFACE

The purpose of this volume and its two sister volumes is to provide a wide readership with information on the history of the native people prior to the dislocating incursions of Europeans into the territory now known as Canada. Unlike most history books that are drawn from written documentary evidence the volumes are based upon archaeological evidence as there are no pre-European written records. It is a history built upon the minute fragments of evidence that have survived normal decay and other natural processes. It is, thus, a woefully incomplete history reliant upon such remains as broken stones tools, discarded food bones, and the vague traces of dwellings. The great innovators, healers, warriors, and leaders in this history are all unknown as are the majority of the significant events which would have been of vital importance to the people at the time. This admittedly inadequate archaeological history is, however, the only history that exists for the more than 12,000 years that the ancestors of the native people occupied Canada prior to its colonization by Europeans. Even given the severe limitations of the archaeological record, evidence of human cultural ingenuity, perseverance, commerce, and religion still manages to express itself despite the passage of thousands of years. It is this human experience which these volumes attempt to outline.

Years of working as an archaeologist for the Canadian Museum of Civilization and its progenitors, the National Museum of Man and the National Museum of Canada, convinced me of the need for an archaeological history of the native people of Canada. Many people have a strong interest in the archaeology of the land they live on even when most of the archaeological record pertains to unrelated cultures. It appears that, for many people, the past record of humanity has a universal appeal which overrides more parochial concerns such as whether the archaeological evidence is directly related to one's immediate ancestors. There is also a need to make available to the native people of Canada a synthesis of the archaeological record left by their ancestors. This is particularly so as native people continue to recover from the devastating impact of European disease and the occupation of their former lands and attempt to negotiate agreements that will provide them with a viable economic land base. In deliberations of land-claim cases litigation is frequently concerned with who were the original occupants of the disputed lands. In addition to the written historical records, the oral traditions, and the ethnographic and biological affinity evidence provided by cultural anthropologists and physical anthropologists, respectively, is the archaeological record which can extend the historical time depth of human occupation of a region many thousands of years back into the past. Such evidence can be used to good purpose in a court of law. Once, when ordered to appear in a land claim case as an expert witness, I heard argument by the Crown that natives did not use minerals or forest products until the coming of Europeans and, thus, had no particular claim to these resources even if their land claim should be upheld. This argument was countered with archaeological evidence of a trade in copper, silver, exotic minerals, and marine shells that criss-crossed the country thousands of years prior to the appearance of the first Europeans and by an estimate of how many tens of thousands of cedar posts were used in the construction of even a relatively small two acre native village. This kind of knowledge is generally unknown to the public, including native people. I still recall the surprise and delight of a group of native craftsmen to whom I had just presented a talk when they learned for the first time that their far distant ancestors had once fashioned tools and ornaments of native copper and silver and, thus, they could legitimately include metal work within their craft productions.

To aid access to a wide range of information the volumes are organized in a fashion that hopefully permits convenient reference. An art historian interested in the decorative motifs used more than 4,000 years ago in the Ottawa Valley can refer to the <u>Cosmology</u> section of the appropriate chapter. A medical historian researching pre-European occurrences of spinal tuberculosis or other pathologies can look for the information in the <u>Human biology</u> sections. A metallurgist writing a book on the history of mining in Canada can include the 7,000 years that native miners worked the Lake Superior copper deposits by referring to the <u>Technology</u> section of the pertinent chapter. Most archaeological information is published in technical articles and manuscripts not readily available to the non-specialist. These volumes make this information available to the broadest possible audience and attempt to present it in as digestible a form as possible. In the effort to achieve this goal I could be accused by some of my colleagues of intellectually `clear-cutting´ the forests of archaeological minutiae. Archaeology tends to be a geographically parochial discipline made up of many regional specialists who focus on a province or, more often, a portion of a province. In order to provide a nation-wide synthesis it has been necessary to force these regional chronologies and their associated taxonomies into a rational national framework. Undoubtedly academic toes have been trod upon. Archaeologists, however, are a generous and flexible group and it is trusted most will judge that the goal of the volumes justifies the freedoms taken with more regionally focused interpretations. To reach a wide audience it has been necessary to make complex issues appear simple, to limit discussion of archaeological controversy to the core issues, and to organize bodies of information into somewhat artificial systems such as settlement patterns and subsistence when, in truth, all of these systems would have been intimately interrelated. Statements are supported by references. Readers requiring the evidence upon which conclusions are based or who need more detailed information on any particular matter are advised to use the references.

The volumes are unapologetically descriptive outlines of the culture history on the native people of Canada as discernible by archaeological methods. Many scientific disciplines pass through an initial descriptive phase and only in time achieve a higher analytical phase. Archaeological interpretation, however, cannot be based solely upon the scientific method. In fact, the majority of archaeological evidence is particularly perverse when attempts are made to mathematically manipulate it in order to arrive at probability statements. Analytical rigour is absolutely necessary in archaeology but it must be applied within a framework controlled largely by human cultural accommodations to their environments. It is this human factor which constrains archaeology from too closely mimicing many of the analytical methods of disciplines such as biology and other sciences. It is simply a case of whether the rule of genetics or the rule of culture is the dominate organizing force within a scientific discipline and, in the case of archaeology, culture is clearly the dominate force.

J. V. Wright,
Curator Emeritus,
Canadian Museum of Civilization,
Hull, Québec.   March, 1995.

AVANT-PROPOS

Cet ouvrage et les deux autres qui l'accompagnent ont pour but de renseigner le grand public sur l'histoire des autochtones avant les incursions perturbantes des Européens, qui eurent lieu entre le XVIe et le XIXe siècle, dans le territoire qui porte maintenant le nom de Canada. Contrairement à la plupart des manuels d'histoire qui se fondent sur des écrits, ces volumes ont été rédigés à partir de documents archéologiques puisqu'il n'existe aucun document écrit remontant à la période préeuropéenne. Cette histoire est élaborée à partir des fragments des vestiges qui ont survécu à la décomposition et aux autres processus normaux de destruction. Comme elle dépend de restes tels que des outils en pierre taillée, des os provenant de déchets alimentaires et de vagues vestiges d'habitations, cette histoire est malheureusement bien incomplète. Tous les grands innovateurs, guérisseurs, guerriers et dirigeants y demeurent inconnus tout comme la plupart des événements qui ont eu une importance vitale pour les habitants de l'époque. Cette histoire archéologique quoique bien médiocre est cependant la seule qui couvre les 12 000 ans au cours desquels les ancêtres des autochtones occupèrent le Canada avant la colonisation par les Européens. Mais, même avec les limites des documents archéologiques, des preuves de créativité culturelle, de persévérance, de commerce et de religion, ont survécu à l'épreuve du temps. C'est cette expérience humaine que ces volumes ont tenté d'ébaucher.

Mes nombreuses années de travail comme archéologue pour le Musée canadien des civilisations et pour ses précurseurs le Musée national de Canada et le Musée national de l'Homme m'ont convaincu de la nécessité d'une histoire archéologique des peuples autochtones du Canada. Nombreux sont ceux qui s'intéressent à l'archéologie de leur coin de planète même quand les données archéologiques concernent des cultures qui leur sont complètement étrangères. Il semble que l'intérêt de beaucoup d'individus pour l'histoire de l'humanité dépasse certaines préoccupations bornées qui voudraient que les données archéologiques aient un rapport direct avec les ancêtres immédiats. Il est aussi important que les autochtones puissent avoir accès à une synthèse des documents archéologiques laissés par leurs ancêtres, d'autant plus qu'ils continuent à se relever des effets dévastateurs des maladies importées par les Européens et de l'occupation de leur territoire et qu'ils essaient de négocier des ententes pour obtenir des assises territoriales viables. En plus des documents historiques écrits, des traditions orales autochtones et des preuves d'affinités ethnographiques et biologiques avancées par les anthropologues culturels et physiques, ce sont les documents archéologiques qui peuvent faire remonter l'histoire de l'occupation humaine d'une région de plusieurs milliers d'années. On peut utiliser une telle preuve en cour. Un jour je dus comparaître en tant qu'expert dans une cause de revendication territoriale J'ai alors entendu la plaidoirie de la Couronne qui insinuait que les autochtones n'utilisaient ni minéraux ni produits de la forêt avant la venue des Européens, qu'ils n'avaient donc aucun droit sur ces ressources même si leur revendication était accueillie. La défense a riposté en donnant des preuves archéologiques qu'il y avait des échanges de cuivre, d'argent, de minéraux exotiques et de coquillages marins, d'un bout à l'autre du pays, des milliers d'années avant l'arrivée des premiers Européens, et en estimant combien de dizaines de milliers de poteaux avaient été utilisés dans la construction de villages autochtones, même d'assez petits qui ne dépassaient pas deux acres. Le public, y compris les autochtones, ne connaît pas ces faits. Je me souviens de la surprise et de l'enchantement d'un groupe d'artisans autochtones lorsqu'ils apprirent pour la première fois que leurs ancêtres éloignés utilisaient des outils et des ornements en cuivre natif et en argent. Ils pouvaient donc légitimement inclure le travail des métaux dans leurs productions.

Les volumes sont agencés pour pouvoir y référer facilement. Un historien d'art, qui s'intéresse aux motifs décoratifs d'il y a plus de 4 000 ans dans la vallée de la rivière des Outaouais, peut consulter la section «Cosmology» du chapitre approprié. Un historien de la médecine qui recherche le nombre de cas du mal de Pott ou autres maladies avant l'arrivée des Européens peut trouver des renseignements dans la section «Human biology» de chacun des chapitres. Un métallurgiste qui trace l'histoire de l'exploitation minière des métaux au Canada peut inclure les 7 000 ans pendant lesquels les mineurs autochtones ont exploité les dépôts de cuivre du lac Supérieur; il trouvera les renseignements pertinents dans la section «Technology» des chapitres appropriés. La plupart des renseignements archéologiques ont été publiés dans des articles techniques et dans des monographies qui ne sont pas à la portée des profanes. Le présent ouvrage rend cette information disponible et accessible au plus grand nombre possible de lecteurs. Certains collègues pourraient même m'accuser d'avoir fait «de la coupe à blanc» dans les forêts de la précision archéologique pour atteindre mon but. L'archéologie a tendance à être une discipline de clocher regroupant des spécialistes régionaux qui restreignent leurs recherches à une province ou, plus souvent, à un secteur de province ou à une époque. Afin de pouvoir faire une synthèse à l'échelle du pays, il a fallu modifier certains éléments des chronologies régionales ainsi que les noms donnés aux formations culturelles. Les théoriciens se sont sans aucun doute fait marcher sur les pieds. Les archéologues cependant forment un groupe généreux et flexible et je suis assuré que la plupart d'entre eux considéreront que le but visé justifiait les libertés que j'ai prises en spécialisant les travaux par régions. Afin de toucher un plus grand nombre de lecteurs, il a fallu simplifier les questions complexes, limiter aux problèmes de fond les discussions autour des controverses archéologiques et agencer l'information dans des systèmes quelque peu artificiels, comme les types de peuplement et la subsistance, quand on sait que ces systèmes étaient en fait interdépendants. Les lecteurs qui auront besoin de connaître les fondements des conclusions ou qui auront besoin de renseignements plus détaillés sur certains sujets devraient consulter les ouvrages de référence.

Ces volumes tracent les grandes lignes de l'histoire culturelle des peuples autochtones du Canada telles que les méthodes archéologiques ont permis de les distinguer. De nombreuses disciplines scientifiques passent à travers une phase initiale descriptive pour parvenir avec le temps à une phase analytique supérieure. L'interprétation archéologique toutefois ne peut pas se baser uniquement sur une méthode scientifique. En fait, les documents archéologiques sont iniques en eux-mêmes si on essaie de les manipuler mathématiquement pour avancer des probabilités. La rigueur analytique est essentielle en archéologie, mais elle doit être appliquée à l'intérieur d'un cadre composé en grande partie des adaptations culturelles des humains à leur environnement. C'est ce facteur humain qui empêche l'archéologie d'imiter de trop près les méthodes analytiques d'autres sciences, comme la biologie par exemple. À l'intérieur d'une discipline scientifique, prédomine une force organisatrice qui peut être les lois de la génétique ou de la physique ou encore les règles de la culture. Dans le cas de l'archéologie, la culture est nettement la force dominante.

J. V. Wright
Conservateur émérite
Musée canadien des civilisations
Hull (Québec)   Mars 1995

PERIOD III (4,000 - 1,000 BC)

CHART

TABLES

COLOUR PLATES

BLACK AND WHITE PLATES

MAPS

FIGURES

CHAPTER 1

INTRODUCTION

When Europeans explored the Western Hemisphere in the late 15th to 17th centuries they found all regions, from the Arctic to the southern tip of South America, occupied by other human beings. The societies of these people ranged from that of simple hunting bands to complex priest-emperor ruled city states and empires with elaborate ceremonial architecture, evolved agriculture based on a wide range of domesticated plants, astronomy, calendric systems, mathematics, and writing. Explanations for the presence of the people of a hemisphere, which had unexpectedly intruded itself between Europe and China, abounded and in the vast majority of cases were flagrantly Eurocentric. Indeed, rather than Indians and Inuit being the occupants of the Western Hemisphere, the "...major actors seem to be Vikings, Phoenicians, Irishmen, Egyptians, Welshmen, the Lost Tribes of Israel..." among others (McGhee 1989: 164). Fray José de Acosta's astute observation in AD 1590 that the Indians descended from hunters who had entered North America from Asia was the exception to the rule. This European biased view of the pre-European human history of the Western Hemisphere is still prevalent. Text books on Canadian history focus on the last 350 years and, in general, have ignored the preceding twelve millennia of native history. The reason for this situation is that Western Hemisphere native peoples were not literate with the exception of parts of Mexico and Central America. Even in these instances, literacy was limited to the ruling classes who were quickly eliminated by their European conquerors along with most of their written documents.

Fortunately for the history of the preliterate societies representing the majority of the history of Homo sapiens the essential difference between humans and other animals is that humans possess culture which permits them to manipulate their environments for their own well-being. This manipulation involves tool making, dwelling construction, the manufacture of clothing, and the endless array of `artifacts´ which have permitted a semi-tropical species to occupy every environmental zone on the planet. Humans are also universally concerned with their origins and their ultimate place in the cosmos and, thus, in addition to the secular artifacts and features there are structures and objects which relate to cosmology, such as special cemeteries, temple mounds, various stone cairn structures, and religious art and artifacts. Many of these cultural manifestations survive the passage of time and through the methods of the discipline of archaeology can be used to reconstruct long vanished cultures.

Although archaeological data and methods are quite different from those of the discipline of history, having more in common with the natural sciences, archaeology nevertheless shares with history the goal of attempting to record and understand the human past. Until recently history has tended to focus upon written documents pertaining to great people and great events whereas the nature of most archaeological evidence insures a more mundane form of reconstruction relating to human technology, subsistence, settlement patterns, cosmology, and human biology. Only in rare instances can the methods of archaeology catch even a brief glimpse of the impact of a powerful individual or group and, even then, only in respect to sudden changes in the recognized cultural patterns. In this respect, archaeological reconstructions of human history prior to written records lack the personal and grand event dimensions of historical reconstructions based upon written documents. Needless to say, great leaders, innovators, and intellectuals existed and great events occurred but given the limitations of archaeological methods, their impact upon the archaeological record would generally be undetectable. And, as a result, "...a great deal of the texture of history - the interplay of human personalities - is lost and that we will never be able to know how an ancient people felt about their world and themselves" (Willey 1966: 2).

What follows is the history of the preliterate societies of what is now Canada as deciphered by archaeology. The central purpose of this and subsequent volumes is to provide a reference source to the archaeological evidence pertaining to the 12,000 years of human history in Canada prior to the arrival of the Europeans, excluding the brief 11th century Norse probes westward from Greenland.

Volume I examines the evidence from 10,000 to 1,000 BC. During these 9,000 years a number of major environmental and cultural changes took place. Dramatic geological and environmental changes were associated with the ablating continental glaciers at the end of the Pleistocene (Pielou 1991; J. Ritchie 1987). Other significant natural occurrences ranged from a period of intermittent dry climate between 6,000 and 2,000 BC, which had an impact upon the plant and animal communities and the human occupants of the Plains and adjacent regions, to the 5,500 BC explosion of Mt. Mazama in Oregon which deposited volcanic ash over a wide area of southwestern Canada. After 4,000 BC environments became increasingly stable. The most striking single cultural achievement during the 9,000 years under consideration in this volume was the apparently sudden occupation of North America by Palaeo-Indian culture and the occupation of South America by Palaeo-Indian culture equivalents. The colonization of an entire hemisphere was a unique human accomplishment. Another significant cultural happening was the regional cultural differentiation from the relatively homogeneous Palaeo-Indian culture base, a process that was to continue to the time of European contact. Some of the other developments were as follows: a new weapon system called a spearthrower appears to have been invented around 8,000 BC in what is now the southeastern United States but took 3,500 years to diffuse to Alaska and the Yukon; the human occupation of the last major habitable region of the world, exclusive of parts of Oceania, took place around 2,000 BC when Early Palaeo-Eskimo culture spread across the Canadian Arctic and into Greenland; complex ceremonialism appeared by 5,500 BC in the form of burial mounds on the northshore of the Gulf of St. Lawrence while by 3,000 BC large stone cairn structures, popularly called `medicine wheels´, appear on the Plains to initiate a 5,000 year old ceremonial tradition; by 5,000 BC the native copper of the Upper Great Lakes region was being mined and fashioned into tools and ornaments; from 2,000 to 1,000 BC communally operated bison pounds and jumps, which permitted the slaughter of large numbers of animals, become increasingly common on the Plains; approaching 1,000 BC there is evidence of increasing wealth and resource acquisition along the West Coast which would lead eventually to social stratification; and also towards the end of this period there is increasing evidence across most of Canada of expanding trade networks moving goods such as exotic cherts, marine shell ornaments, obsidian, and copper over distances sometimes exceeding 1,500 km.

Even within three large volumes the attempt to provide a general outline of native history prohibits substantive consideration of most issues. Yet, the equivocal nature of much archaeological evidence guarantees that a healthy amount of differing opinion and controversy exists. To accommodate this problem in the most economic manner I have extensively used references to direct the reader concerned with specifics to the evidence that my generalizations are premised upon. As the purpose of the volumes is to provide a general reference source to native culture history other considerations are not addressed in detail. The history of archaeological research in Canada, for example, is already available in outline form (Noble 1972; Wright 1985). There is also a history of the development of archaeological thought and theory (Trigger 1989). Manuals are available which describe archaeological field excavation and recording procedures (Fladmark 1978). The analytical methods and the theories underlying most archaeological interpretation could well constitute a volume in itself and it is recommended that the reader consult Chapter 1 in Jennings (1989) and the review of Renfrew and Bahn (1991) for succinct and well illustrated summaries. In addition, throughout this and subsequent volumes, a variety of laboratory techniques will be briefly described and references provided. While the volumes are specifically concerned with the land mass that now constitutes Canada, pertinent information from the adjacent United States of America and Greenland is used, particularly during the earlier periods when archaeological data are more limited and the earlier cultures more widely distributed.

Archaeological taxonomy and nomenclature as they pertain to broad cultural patterns are poorly developed in Canada. Archaeological terms tend to be regional in nature and based upon differing criteria rather than being broadly equivalent and systematic. There is the problem that archaeologists must base their classifications, for the most part, upon technology which means they are forced to establish their nomenclatures long before the desirable evidence is at hand. By the time sufficient evidence does become available to establish more accurate classifications, the earlier descriptive units have acquired a certain sanctity through use and familiarity and are extremely resistant to change. Throughout this work I have made a number of `culture´ name changes that I know will be unpopular with some archaeologists. Such changes are regarded as essential, however, in order to accommodate the scope of the work. For example, the earliest unequivocal evidence of people in the Western Hemisphere was first found at Clovis, New Mexico. The distinctive style of fluted projectile point found at this site has been used to identify a Clovis culture. Later descendants, who manufactured different styles of the fluted projectile point, have been referred to as Folsom culture or by other regional names. These manufacturers of the culturally diagnostic fluted point are currently referred to as Early Palaeo-Indians. Their descendants in the west have been described under a number of culture names centred around the word `Plano´ or collectively as Late Palaeo-Indian while in the east the equivalent developments have been referred to as Archaic. In this study Palaeo-Indian culture incorporates Clovis culture (early) and Folsom and other regional related developments (late) and treats Plano and early Archaic cultures as equivalent western and eastern developments out of western and eastern manifestations of late Palaeo-Indian culture.

Archaeological classifications of cultures are faced with a unique problem; they have to avoid the error of mixing the variables of time and cultural content (Childe 1935; Stoltman 1978). Time has been

A

B

C

BLACK AND WHITE PLATE I: EARLY NATIONAL MUSEUM OF CANADA ARCHAEOLOGISTS

A.   Dr. Diamond Jenness when he was a member of the Canadian Arctic Expedition (1913-1916). Noted for his ethnological and applied anthropological work, Dr. Jenness also made significant contributions to archaeology. For example, he was the first to recognize Palaeo-Eskimo culture from Arctic collections in the National Museum of Canada. His book "Indians of Canada", first published in 1932, is still a basic source of information on the native people of Canada. Dr. Jenness received many honours during his lifetime including having a major peninsula on the west coast of Victoria Island in the Northwest Territories named in his honour by the Canadian Permanent Committee on Geographical Names.

B.   Dr. Harlan I. Smith carrying plaster of paris casts of petroglyphs, probably in the Bella Coola region of British Columbia, 1922. Dr. Smith worked mainly in British Columbia. In addition to archaeological research, he was involved in programmes to preserve totem poles and to encourage the use of West Coast native motifs in commercial design.

C.   Mr. William J. Wintemberg examining Roebuck site pottery, 1932. Self-trained, Mr. Wintemberg's research was largely carried out in eastern Canada. He is best known for his detailed archaeological reports on a number of Ontario Iroquoian village sites. These reports are still major reference sources many years after their publication.

     The highest honour the Canadian Archaeological Association can bestow in recognition of contributions to Canadian archaeology is called the SMITH-WINTEMBERG AWARD. All three researchers spent most of their professional careers employed by the National Museum of Canada, now the Canadian Museum of Civilization. (Canadian Museum of Civilization negative numbers 51236, 55792, and 76087, respectively).

organized into the following absolute time periods across Canada: Period I (10,000 to 8,000 BC); Period II (8,000 to 4,000 BC); Period III (4,000 to 1,000 BC); Period IV (1,000 BC to AD 500); and Period V (AD 500 to European Contact). While the periods are absolute brackets of time they are not entirely devoid of content significance as they incorporate broad environmental and/or cultural factors that characterize the country as a whole. Period I, for example, incorporates the rapidly changing environments associated with the demise of the last major glacial episode and the appearance of the earliest unequivocal evidence of people south of the ice masses. Relative to the final time period, European contact in Canada is a sliding scale with frequent contacts recorded along the east coast around the beginning of the 16th century (McGhee 1991) while the latest direct contacts in the far northwest occurred only towards the end of the 19th century.

Within each of the time periods, cultures are described beginning in the east, advancing westward and, thence, to the north and then back to the east to initiate the next time period. As most of the archaeological cultures of Canada correlate with major environmental-physiographic zones, such as the Plains or the Canadian Shield, culture names, as much as possible, have been selected to reflect this fact. Further, continuity through time of a culture in any particular region is identified by the adjectives Early, Middle, and Late, relative to the absolute time periods. These cultures, set geographically into major environmental zones, provide the spatial dimension. The description of each culture is then organized under the following sections: précis; cultural origins and descendants; technology; subsistence; settlement patterns; cosmology; external relationships; human biology; inferences on society; and limitations in the evidence. Such an arrangement provides simple and consistent reference points for both archaeologists and non-archaeologists alike. One could, of course, debate the ordering of the aforementioned units. Other approaches with somewhat different emphases, for example, could view the human ecosystem as being composed of the following subsystems: environment; subsistence; technology; population; and social organization (Stoltman and Baerreis 1983). The focus of the latter approach was upon the interplay of culture and environment and the need to appreciate an interacting data matrix if cultural change is to be understood. While I am in accord with such an integrated approach to archaeological and environmental data, I find a combination of time units (absolute periods) and form units (cultures), each made up of a number of identified systems, to be more appropriate to the generalist task at hand. As the systems within any culture are interdependent, it follows that a certain amount of repetition is inevitable. Hopefully such repetition will contribute to clarity. For the reader with specific concerns, such as Cosmology, the large and often dull Technology sections can simply be avoided. A geologist writing a history of the mining of metals in Canada, however, would be ill-advised to ignore the Technology sections of certain chapters.

The word `culture´ is used as a general label to encompass the evidence pertaining to a pattern of broadly shared behaviour as expressed in technology, subsistence, settlement patterns, and cosmology practices. Such `cultures´ are only held together by the loose glue of current archaeological evidence and are most certainly not inscribed in stone. Any single culture, as used in this work, would have been composed of many independent societies. More regionally focused studies could certainly be subdivided into a number of archaeologically `related´ cultures.

The volumes represent a relatively detailed synthesis of the pre-European history of the native peoples of the land mass now called Canada. This land mass is not only environmentally and physiographically complex but has changed dramatically through time. North of Toronto 11,000 years ago, for example, early hunters shared the open lichen woodlands with caribou herds, grizzly bears, Arctic fox, California vultures, mammoths, and mastodons. As has been noted, archaeological cultures correlate with major environmental zones. Given that with a few late exceptions the entire 12,000 year archaeological record pertains to hunting societies it should not be surprising that the various environmental zones, with their different plant and animal communities, conditioned distinctively different human adaptations. It is these regional adaptations which permit archaeologists to differentiate past cultures from one another. Such cultures, however, are crude approximations of the societies that once existed. Numerous independent bands of hunting peoples, often with regional cultural characteristics of their own, are all subsumed under the rubric of a particular culture. It will be noted that with increasing cultural regionalism through time, there is an increase in the numbers of identified archaeological cultures.

Writing such a synthesis is not as much a personal endeavour as a participation in a process contributed to by generations of scholars. The subject matter can be compared to an ever-changing kaleidoscope of interplay between developing regional cultural traditions and the cross-cutting influences of technological and intellectual diffusion. Like history based upon written documents, however, archaeologically based history should be rewritten every generation lest it becomes a series of anecdotes. Any archaeological synthesis must also be done with sensitivity to the caveat that, "The rationalists' outlook upon the universe as a mechanistic, cause-and-effect system which can be subjected to analysis may seem to offer a comprehensive explanation of the practices of primitive people. However, these people perceived the world as working according to principles which would be quite alien to us" (Haack 1987: 139).

It is a common human misconception that the landforms and plant and animal communities around them are timeless and unchanging. Physical and biological change are continuous processes but are so gradual that during an individuals' lifetime there is a perception of stability. All scholarly disciplines whose subject matter spans time, such as geology, biology, and archaeology, must be cognizant of the changes that have taken place over the millennia. It would be fruitless for an archaeologist, for example, to do the following: seek 8,000 to 7,000 BC sites in the central interior of Québec or along the present shorelines of the Upper Great Lakes; look for 5,000 BC sites along most of the current coastlines of Hudson Bay; and survey for 9,000 BC sites in much of southern Manitoba, adjacent Ontario or the Cordilleran of British Columbia (see McAndrews et al. 1987). The nature of the plant communities at any point in time is also critical to understanding the behaviour of people. Plant communities determine the nature of the animal communities which are dependant upon them. Human beings relied upon both plant and animal foods and particularly the latter. Any impact upon the plant community would have a direct effect upon the availability or abundance of animals. A climatically induced contraction of the Grassland and Parkland vegetation provinces, for example, would lead to a contraction of the bison herds following pasture. Human predators dependant upon the bison for much of their food and other requirements, such as sleeping robes and tent covers, would be forced to respond accordingly.

For those readers interested in the methods used in the reconstruction of past environments and the identification of climatic change the following references and their bibliographies are recommended: Harington 1980; 1981; 1983; 1985; Harington and Rice 1984; Pielou 1991; and J. Ritchie 1987. The book by E. C. Pielou is written with a clarity particularly suited to the novice venturing into the complex field of the proxy evidence used in environmental reconstructions.

The increase in the body of archaeological evidence through time is apparent in the fact that Volume I covers a time span of 9,000 years while the remaining two volumes address approximately 1,500 years each. Volume II, which covers the time period from 1,000 BC to AD 500, describes the following cultures: Late Maritime; Late Great Lakes-St.Lawrence; Late Eastern Shield; Early Western Basin; Late Western Shield; Late Plains; Late Plateau; Late West Coast; Late Northwest Interior; and Middle Palaeo-Eskimo. Covering the period from AD 500 to European contact, Volume III considers the following: Proto-Maritime Algonquian; Proto-St. Lawrence Iroquois; Proto-Ontario Iroquois; Proto-Northern Algonquian; Late Western Basin; Proto-Plains; Proto-Interior Salish; Proto-West Coast; Proto-Southern Athapaskan; Proto-Northern Athapascan; Late Palaeo-Eskimo; and Proto-Inuit. As the culture names of the final volume indicate, an effort has been made to link the archaeological sequences with either major language families or with an environmental region inhabited by speakers of a number of different languages. Summaries of ethnographically recorded cultures for many of the native people of Canada are available in Jenness (1932), Kehoe (1981), and McMillan (1988).

It is necessary to make my theoretical orientation explicit as it is very much a part of this personal view of the history of the native people. Regarding culture change, which is so critical to archaeological interpretation, I favour regional biological and cultural continuity responding to the diffusion of technology and concepts rather than to cataclysmic population replacements. Hunting peoples around the world have tended to treat warfare as an activity they simply cannot afford to indulge to any extent without placing their families and communities at risk. For most hunting societies, the economic base simply did not exist which would have permitted the use of aggression to acquire the territories of their neighbours. As with all statements about people there are exceptions. The replacement of the Late Palaeo-Eskimos by Proto-Inuits appears to have been the result of a technologically superior group pushing another out of the resource-rich areas necessary for survival in the harsh Arctic environment. By 3,000 years ago and probably longer, the processing and storing of the seasonally abundant food resources of the West Coast provided an economic base capable of supporting both warfare and the acquisition of wealth. The foregoing examples, however, were exceptions to the rule that inter-group hostilities were not a major factor in cultural change. When a new projectile point variety suddenly appears in a region, for example, it is interpreted as evidence for the diffusion of a new facet of weapon technology rather than being indicative of an invading population, particularly when the rest of the technology, the subsistence, settlement patterns, and cosmology systems in the area remain unchanged. Relative to methodological orientation, rather than relying upon selected `diagnostic´ traits to reconstruct culture history, reliance is placed upon a quantitative and qualitative approach which incorporates not only the total technology but also all of the other cultural systems which are detectable by archaeological means. This approach includes the evidence relating to human biology as provided by the discipline of physical anthropology. It is this interwoven mass of data pertaining to technology, subsistence, settlement patterns, cosmology, other aspects of culture, and human biology which constitutes the core of the cultures described in the volumes.

It cannot be overemphasized, however, that each of the cultural systems, such as technology, are isolated only for purposes of ease of reference. In reality, all of these descriptive units once were integral parts of a cultural whole. The availability of data will, of course, determine the relative validity of the cultural constructs and this is directly related to the quantity and quality of published reports and notes. With reference to chronology, primacy is given to stratigraphy and other geological and cultural factors which isolate components over an excessive reliance upon radiocarbon dates, particularly when the dated samples are drawn from questionable archaeological contexts.

Radiocarbon dates have been calibrated for fluctuations in the atmospheric production of the radioactive carbon isotope, carbon 14, using the calibration tables produced by Klein et al. (1982). The tables are derived from the radiocarbon dating of individual tree rings of bristle cone pine trees, which had been absolutely dated by the dendrochronology method as far back as 7,240 years ago. Dates earlier than this 7,240 year limit will be generally given in radiocarbon years indicated by the symbol BP (Before Present, specifically before AD 1950). Such dates are 800 or more years earlier when given in calendar years. There are more recent dendrochronology based calibrations of radiocarbon dates (Stuiver and Pearson 1986; Stuiver and Becker 1993) but the ranges provided in Klein et al. are adequate expressions of calendrical accuracy given both the limitations of the radiocarbon method and the nature of most archaeological contexts for datable materials. A brief review of the range of factors which should be taken into consideration relative to radiocarbon dates can be found in Browman (1981). Radiocarbon dates, their + and - ranges, laboratory numbers, the material dated, and other factors, including the calendrical range represented by each radiocarbon reading, were amassed for each cultural unit as an aid in transforming the radiocarbon dates into the `years ago´ or BC/AD date estimates used throughout the text. Rather than subject the general reader to table upon table of detailed information on numerous dates and in recognition of the unavoidable incompleteness of such tables, references are provided for those readers who wish the detailed information. The calendrical dates represent approximations of the actual range of years given in the calibration tables. For example, a radiocarbon date of 5,000 BP +/- 100 has a calibrated range of 3950 to 3640 BC but in the text, when referring to the site from which the date was obtained, it will be given as 3,800 BC or rounded as an average of other pertinent dates. Thus, each date actually falls into the middle of an age spread and should be treated as an approximation. Some archaeologists will take exception to this procedure on the grounds that it may leave readers with a false sense that the dendrochronology corrected radiocarbon dates represent actual absolute dates rather than median extrapolations from statistical probability age ranges. A far greater risk is to confuse and bore the general reader with the many qualifications necessary in any evaluation of radiocarbon dates. It is assumed that the average reader will recognize that the dates provided in this work are approximations whose usefulness is in the area of relative chronology rather than absolute chronology. Traditional documentary history is characterized by absolute calendrical dates such as the day, month and year of a coronation ceremony. The dating of sites occupied prior to the arrival of literate recorders, except where direct dendrochronology (tree-ring) dating is possible, are very much approximations with their value lying more in the realm of their relationship to earlier and later approximations. Such relative dates are most definitely general and not specific chronological indicators.

Archaeological evidence across the country is uneven. Rising sea levels which submerged much of the archaeology of the Maritime provinces, for example, are only partially compensated for by the rising lands of the northshore of the Gulf of St.Lawrence that elevated ancient sites above the sea. Fluctuating water levels of the ancestral Great Lakes have covered large segments of the archaeological record. In geologically stable regions, such as the Upper St.Lawrence Valley, for 9,000 years people occupied the same site locations resulting in the thorough mixture of the shallow archaeological deposits. This has often led to the questionable procedure of isolating components from the mixed deposits on the basis of typology. Acid soil conditions throughout the Canadian Shield have destroyed most bone placing constraints on both technological and subsistence interpretations. Many of the early archaeological sites of the Plains have either been destroyed by erosion or buried under many metres of sediments. Much of the native history of the Plateau suffers from essentially the same problem as the Upper St.Lawrence River Valley in that people tended to occupy the same sites over many years. West coast archaeology, like that on the east coast, must contend with isostatic and eustatic forces affecting land submergence and emergence. Most of the archaeology in far northwestern North America suffers from the absence of bone, the simple nature of the stone tool kits, the thin populations represented, and severe component mixture at seasonally productive sites which were used over and over again for millennia. Arctic archaeology, like that in most of the Subarctic and the mountainous regions, is impeded by the problems of operating with field crews in isolated regions and difficult terrain. On the other hand, certain regions accommodate the needs of archaeological research. The Plains, for example, is blessed with generally good bone preservation and an abundance of stratified sites. The relative paucity of sites and enormous spaces of the Arctic is compensated by the generally thin plant cover, which makes aerial survey for sites a practical consideration. The interconnecting waterways of the Canadian Shield have always been the major communication routes, whether in a liquid or a frozen state, and thus permit some prediction regarding site locations. Major contrasts exist between regions such as the Upper St.Lawrence Valley-Lower Great Lakes where commercial and urban destruction of the archaeological record has been massive and the Subarctic and Arctic where caribou, wolves, muskoxen and bears roam in sight of the archaeology crews. But as the Baie James Project illustrates, the north is quite vulnerable to massive modification. A final factor affecting the archaeological data base is the degree of archaeological activity in any particular region. Naturally, more archaeological work tends to be done in proximity to the institutions of higher learning in the major urban centres or adjacent to convenient road networks. Publication of archaeological evidence has been a problem. As much as possible, I have avoided referencing unpublished government documents, theses, unpublished papers in the possession of the author, and papers presented at professional meetings. Such documents are often difficult, if not impossible, to obtain. In the future, it is anticipated that the development of electronic data bases will do much to rectify the problem of availability of archaeological information.

Before proceeding to Chapter 2 a review of the archaeological evidence prior to 12,000 years ago is in order. The evidence is limited, equivocal and, therefore, controversial (Dillehay and Meltzer 1991; Dincauze 1984; Meltzer 1989a; 1993; Morlan 1988; 1991). The nature of the pre-15,000 BP evidence from the Western Hemisphere stands in curious contrast to the relatively clear evidence of early human settlement of Australia and the initial occupation of northeastern Asia (Jelinek 1992). Relative to pre-20,000 BP evidence, either in eastern Beringia or in the Western Hemisphere proper, there is also the problem that the earliest acceptable evidence of people in northeastern Asia is 25,000 BP at the earliest and pertains to cultures with an Upper Palaeolithic technology. It is a fundamental premise that people out of Asia colonized the Western Hemisphere. This premise is founded upon both biological and anthropological evidence. Homo sapiens does not appear to have adapted to the rigorous environmental conditions of northeastern Asia until around 40,000 years ago (Grayson 1988: 113; Muller-Beck 1982). The earliest generally accepted archaeological evidence from Western Beringia (Eastern Siberia) pertains to the Diuktai culture, which is dated to 18,000 BP (Aikens 1990; Dikov 1978; Morlan 1987; Yi and Clark 1985). The Diuktai culture assemblage is usually regarded as being ancestral to Northwestern Palaeo-Arctic culture dated to 10,500 BP in Alaska although a Palaeo-Indian culture ancestry has also been claimed (Mochanov 1969). It should be cautioned, however, that considerable regional and temporal variation exists within "...a cultural horizon with wedge-shaped microcores and bifacial points extended from the Yenisei to Hokkaido and from the Huanghe Valley to the Northwest Territories of North America in terminal Pleistocene times" (Pei 1985: 14). There are a number of problems with what would otherwise appear to be a neat lineal progression of people and their cultures from Western Beringia to Eastern Beringia and thence to the Western Hemisphere. First, the Northwestern Palaeo-Arctic culture in Alaska has been recovered stratigraphically above an earlier assemblage apparently lacking microblade technology and dating to approximately 12,000 BP (Powers and Hoffecker 1989). Second, the evidence from the Bluefish Caves site in the northern Yukon raises the possibility of a much earlier appearance in Beringia of the microblade-burin technology typical of the Northwestern Palaeo-Arctic culture (Morlan and Cinq-Mars 1989). Third, the 12 dates on what appear to be human altered proboscidean (mammoth and/or mastodon) bones from the Old Crow River in the Yukon, range from 28,750 to 39,500 BP with an average of 33,382 BP (Morlan et al. 1990: Table 3). We are, therefore, faced with the paradox of having evidence of people in Eastern Beringia as early as the earliest evidence from northeastern Asia and a microlithic industry possibly dating as early as the earliest evidence from Eastern Siberia. Certainly there are such gaps in the archaeological records of both eastern Asia and adjacent North America that these paradoxes should not be surprising.

The evidence of people in the Yukon Territory as early as 40,000 BP is based upon modified proboscidean bones which were redeposited by sedimentary processes in the Old Crow River Valley (Cinq-Mars and Morlan n.d.; Morlan et al. 1990). Considerable effort has been directed towards differentiating between bone modification resulting from natural processes, such as animal trampling, violent depositional forces, and scavenger breakage, and bone purposefully modified by humans in the process of marrow extraction, butchering, or tool production (Bonnichsen and Sorg 1989). The sequence of events required to modify the proboscidean long bone cores from Old Crow would appear to defy non-human processes but there are other problems with these data in addition to their recovery from non-archaeological contexts. Cut marks on a number of the early bones suggest the use of stone tools yet very few such tools have been recovered from the same sedimentary deposits. Arguments for differential sedimentary deposition of bone and stone are not convincing (Morlan 1980: 235). Also, it is most perplexing that given the harsh, largely treeless environment of the time (Hopkins et al. 1982), there appears to be a total absence of burnt bone from these same deposits although the practice of using bone as fuel was a common archaeological phenomenon across the Arctic and Subarctic. On the other hand, a proboscidean bone core was dated 23,600 BP at the Bluefish Caves site (Cinq-Mars 1990) along with evidence of butchering on megafauna bones dating from 25,000 to 10,000 BP. At least part of the lithic

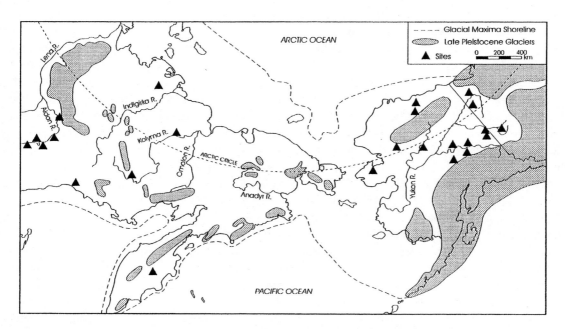

FIGURE 1: BERINGIA AT THE HEIGHT OF THE LAST GLACIATION 20,000 YEARS AGO   The dotted lines indicate the original coastline of the Beringia land mass and provide an impression of the breadth of the landmass which once joined the continents. Early archaeological sites are shown as triangles. The majority of the sites indicated for Eastern Beringia, in what is now Alaska and the Yukon, pertain to Northwestern Palaeo-Arctic culture. (Adapted from Morlan, 1987: Fig.1 by Dr. Richard E. Morlan, Archaeological Survey of Canada, Canadian Museum of Civilization).

---

assemblage is believed to be associated with the bone materials (Ibid 23, 25: footnote). While the association of the archaeological tools and debris with the megafauna remains at Bluefish Caves has been questioned (Dixon 1985: 86, 89-90), microflakes and modified bone occur throughout the deposits along with the megafauna remains. The deposit and presumably its contents, accumulated over a period of 15,000 years between 25,000 and 10,000 years ago (Cinq-Mars and Morlan n.d.). In addition to the dated mammoth bone core (Black and White Plate II) and a matching flake, a modified caribou bone, believed to have functioned as a flesher, provided a date of 24,800 BP. Of significance is the fact that the proboscidean core-flake technology at this site bears such a close resemblance to the re-deposited, core-flake technology in the Old Crow Valley. If a cultural-historical connection existed between the upland and lowland evidence it would suggest that people had adapted to northern latitudes by 40,000 BP. This early position runs contrary to the evidence from adjacent Asia which indicates the area was not occupied until people with an Upper Palaeolithic tool tradition appeared around 25,000 BP (Jelinek 1992).

The evidence from both secondary and primary deposit sites in the northern Yukon is still too limited to close the book on controversy. It is of sufficient credibility, however, that one is advised to keep an open mind and should the Eastern Beringia evidence be eventually vindicated to marvel not at the perversity of the archaeological record but at the faith archaeologists have placed in such a paucity of evidence from as massive and complex a landmass as Beringia. The recent discovery of microblades directly below a mammoth tusk in a stratum dated to 11,700 BP at the Swan Point site in northern Alaska (Mason 1993) is a classic case in point where a single piece of new evidence has the potential to markedly alter current culture history reconstructions. The latter relates to the proposition that the Nenana complex of central Alaska, which lacks microblades and burins, (Powers et al. 1990; Powers and Hoffecker 1989; Powers 1990) represents the earliest technology to enter the region to be followed by a technology characterized by microblades and burins. The proposition appeared to be on firm grounds in terms of stratigraphy, archaeological context, and chronological placement. Dated to between 11,800 and 10,500 BP, the Nenana complex consists of triangular and lanceolate projectile points, gravers, flake knives, and a range of scrapers. Relative to the maximum date, it is pertinent to note that the Nenana Valley was likely uninhabitable prior to 12,000 BP. Assemblage similarities are seen with pre-11,000 BP Siberian sites. It has been suggested that Beringia was not settled until between 15,000 and 13,000 BP (West 1981) or 25,000 to 18,000 BP (Powers 1990: 59) and that the initial migration likely originated from the Far East rather than the Siberian interior (Powers and Hoffecker 1989: 284). The hypothesized initial penetration of the Western Hemisphere by the ancestors of the Nenana complex is regarded as also being ancestral to Palaeo-Indian culture. Occurring stratigraphically above the Nenana complex and dated to 10,500 BP is a microblade dominated assemblage with Siberian Diuktai culture affiliations (Anderson 1980; Dumond 1977; West 1981). Referred to in this work as Northwestern Palaeo-Arctic culture, it is considered to be the product of a second major Asiatic immigration into the Western Hemisphere and the one which gave rise to the Eyak-Athapascan language family. As pointed out by Morlan and Cinq-Mars (1982: 380), however, rather than wave migrations of large numbers of peoples, movements more likely involved the gradual shifting through time of hunting ranges by small bands which maintained communications across Beringia. Further, biological evidence (Ossenberg n.d. - see the Human biology section in Chapter 2) suggests that the split between Athapaskan-speakers and other Indians, as well as Eskimos, was not as sharp as was once believed. There is also the likelihood that the microblade technology, which differentiates Northwestern Palaeo-Arctic culture from the preceding Nenana complex, represents a diffused element of technology within the Beringian communication network rather than being the product of a discrete new population movement. The late temporal placement for this microlithic culture in Alaska is, of course, at odds with the earlier dates for a similar assemblage from the Bluefish Caves site in the Yukon and now with the recent date from the Swan Point site in Alaska itself. If the microflake concentration at the former site is associated with the microblade cores, microblades, burins and burin spalls, then a date of 13,500 BP would pertain.

As is the case with the archaeological evidence from Beringia, there is controversy concerning the nature of the plant and animal communities. One view is that a steppe-tundra, capable of supporting a large, diverse mammal assemblage, existed (Guthrie 1982) while the contrary view interprets the evidence between 30,000 and 14,000 BP to indicate a relatively impoverished, patchy herb tundra (J.Ritchie 1984; Ritchie and Cwynar 1982). Unlike earlier, more favourable environments, this period was probably characterized by polar desert conditions with dry, sunny summers, dry, windy winters, and limited snow

BLACK AND WHITE PLATE II: PROBOSCIDEAN (MAMMOTH OR MASTODON) BONE CORE FROM THE BLUEFISH CAVES SITE, YUKON TERRITORY   Both the bone core and a flake which had been struck from it are believed to be the work of human hand. Virtually identical specimens have been recovered from Palaeo-Indian sites where flakes struck from such cores were used as cutting tools. The core is dated to 23,600 BP. (Photograph courtesy of M. Jacques Cinq-Mars, Archaeological Survey of Canada, Canadian Museum of Civilization)

cover (Schweger et al. 1982). The incomplete plant cover would have consisted of a low vegetation nearly devoid of trees. These patchy plant communities supported a depleted version of the preceding period, namely mammoth, bison, horse, caribou, mountain sheep, saiga antelope, and musk-ox. Between 14,000 and 13,000 BP sudden climatic change resulted in a rapid elevation of sea levels and an increase in birch reflecting a wetter and warmer climate which persisted for 5,000 years. It was during this period that both the mammoth and the horse disappeared.

While a number of archaeologists would argue for a much earlier human presence in the more southerly latitudes of the Western Hemisphere (Bonnichsen and Young 1980; Bryan 1969; 1978), it currently appears that the immediate ancestors of the Palaeo-Indian people represent the initial human migration to the south from the deteriorating environment in Beringia. Two obvious questions are when and how? With reference to the `when´, most archaeologists believe that the distinctive weapon tip of Palaeo-Indian culture was invented south of the ice masses and only subsequently penetrated north as far as Alaska. As Palaeo-Indian culture has been dated to approximately 12,000 years ago, it logically follows that their pre-fluted point ancestors must have existed for some time south of the ice masses in order for the point style to be invented and to diffuse north as environmental conditions ameliorated. Evidence of pre-fluted point sites south of the glaciers, excluding equivocal claims (Lynch 1990; Morlan 1988), is quite limited. If, however, as is speculated here, a small number of people managed to work their way to the south shortly before 15,000 BP they could have formed the nucleus of Palaeo-Indian culture and been the innovators of the distinctive point style. Given the massive alterations to Late Pleistocene landforms, detecting the archaeological evidence of small, mobile groups of hunters across a dramatically altered landscape can be understandably difficult. An alternative hypothesis proposes that the fluted point was developed in Eastern Beringia from whence it was carried through the corridor between the Continental Ice Sheet and the Cordilleran Ice of the Rocky Mountains to be widely adopted by already resident populations (Morlan and Cinq-Mars 1982: 380-381). There is currently no evidence of early fluted projectile points in Eastern Beringia except from the controversial Putu site (Alexander 1987) which has probably been too readily dismissed.

The 14,000 to 14,500 BP levels of the stratified Meadowcroft Rockshelter site in Pennsylvania is the best example of a probable ancestral Palaeo-Indian site (Adavasio et al. 1988: 58). These levels produced an assemblage which included a small, laterally ground triangular projectile point, flake knives, gravers, and a side scraper (Adavasio et al. 1978: 644) although the claim for a microblade technology is rejected. Another possible candidate for a pre-Palaeo-Indian culture site is level 10 of the Fort Rock site in Oregon (Bedwell 1973). A date of 13,200 +/- 720 BP was associated with a basally thinned and laterally ground small triangular projectile point, a graver on a biface, a range of end, side and combination scrapers, a graver on a flake, a flake knife, and a mano. While the archaeological context of this assemblage and the dated charcoal appears to be sound, it is hazardous to place too much weight on a single date. At the Shriver site in Missouri an assemblage consisting of such tools as side, flake, and end scrapers, burins, biface knives, a chopper and pick, were found stratigraphically under a late Palaeo-Indian culture occupation (Reagan et al. 1978). Stratigraphic, geological, pedological, and thermoluminescence testing suggested a date of more than 15,000 BP. Finally, there is the Manis Mastodon site in Washington. The remains of a mastodon with a possible bone projectile point lodged in a rib, rested on an organic mat dated to 12,100 +/- 310 BP (Runnings et al. 1989: 264; also see Gustafson et al. 1979). Bison and caribou remains were also associated. It is worth drawing attention to the similarity of the stone tool assemblages from the Meadowcroft Rockshelter and Fort Rock sites to that of the Nenana complex of central Alaska which is regarded as being related to Palaeo-Indian culture (Powers and Hoffecker 1989).

In addition to the issue of when the first people penetrated the Western Hemisphere there is also the question of how. Given the glacial conditions and environments of the Late Pleistocene period there are only two plausible routes, through an ice-free corridor along the eastern flank of the Rocky Mountains or by water transport following a chain of refugia along the west coast. With reference to both routes northern hunters, with their intimate knowledge of animal behaviour including bird and other animal migratory habits, would have known land existed to the south although not necessarily how far.

The ice-free corridor route is the older of the two hypotheses and is still generally the most

COLOUR PLATE I: BERINGIA 15,000 YEARS AGO A family greets the hunters returning to camp. The geographic and environmental setting is based, in part, on evidence from the Bluefish Caves site even though such a site was more likely used by one or two foraging hunters rather than as a camp for an entire family. While the reconstruction portrayed is speculative, remains of extinct Late Pleistocene animals, such as horse and mammoth, were found at the site. Given the rigorous climate at the time, it is reasonable to assume that tailored skin clothing was essential for survival as well as a wide range of other cold climate cultural adaptations. It is further inferred that it was just such small groups of highly mobile big game hunters who gradually spread out of Asia into Beringia and eventually pioneered the human settlement of the Western Hemisphere. (Painting produced by Vidéanthrop Inc., Montréal, under contract with the Canadian Museum of Civilization. The painting was done by M. François Girard based upon sketches containing scientific and composition requirements compiled by M. Marc Laberge and the author; as with subsequent colour plates the original coloured version is provided on diskette and CD-ROM.)

favoured. Despite intensive and focused research (Ives et al. 1989), however, this route has still not been demonstrated to be that followed by the earliest hunting bands into the heart of the continent. The earliest archaeological evidence in the corridor dates to 10,500 BP and more likely represents a late northward thrust long after the initial occupation of the Western Hemisphere. In the portion of the corridor from the Athabasca River Valley to Montana a cold, dry tundra prevailed between 24,000 and 11,400 BP with birch and poplar/aspen appearing at the end of the period (Schweger 1989: 498). As early as 14,000 BP environmental conditions in the corridor had ameliorated somewhat and would have been more favourable for migrants than the preceding 6,000 years (Ives et al. 1989). There is also evidence that the Laurentide and Cordilleran ice sheets did not coalesce until 15,000 BP, if then, suggesting the existence of a corridor into the interior of the continent from the north between 45,000 and at least 15,000 BP (Bobrowsky and Rutter 1990). The main point to make relative to the corridor is that throughout much of the period it was believed to be open it constituted 2,000 km of hostile, barren country. A secondary consideration, but one of vital importance to archaeology, is the probability that any human movement through the corridor was likely to have been quite rapid, leaving little archaeological trace. On the other hand, if Late Pleistocene caribou herd behaviour was similar to that of today then the elevated, dry, harsh climate of the corridor would have been ideal as seasonal calving grounds and could have led to both the northern and southern portions of the corridor attracting large herds during the warmer months of the year. Such a hypothesized rich seasonal animal resource could have resulted in substantial sites. Geological evidence suggests that the high terraces of the corridor were likely uninhabitable in contrast to the alluvial fans (Levson 1990) but if the caribou calving grounds hypothesis has any validity it will be necessary to reconstruct Late Pleistocene land forms in the corridor in order to predict where early archaeological sites would most likely be encountered.

A west coast migration route used by sea-faring people who exploited coastal refugia (Figure 2) was first suggested by Knut R. Fladmark (1979) and while feasible between 15,000 and 10,500 BP (Luternauer et al. 1989), like the corridor hypothesis, lacks concrete evidence. Indirectly supporting the hypothesis is the present linguistic diversity of the West Coast which contrasts with the much simpler linguistic situation to east of the Continental Divide. This linguistic diversity has been explained as a product of early peoples occupying the refugia (Rogers et al. 1990) although there are a number of major theoretical problems with the proposition. A fundamental assumption of the coastal route hypothesis is that the migrating people were proficient maritimers in possession of sophisticated watercraft. While evidence of watercraft rarely survive in the archaeological record, the foregoing assumption is, in all probability, correct even if the coastal hypothesis is not. In northern latitudes, in particular, the rich maritime animal resources must have been a strong attraction for any hunting peoples. Certainly it is inconceivable that Palaeo-Indian culture people could have functioned in the rapidly changing Late Pleistocene environments without some form of watercraft and, indeed, settlement pattern evidence indicates islands were often exploited (Storck 1979). The single greatest weakness with the coastal hypothesis is that it is difficult to test due to post-glacial submergence of the coastal refugia. Similarly, any east coast Late Pleistocene archaeological evidence is `out to sea´ (Porter 1988: Fig.5). In regions such as the Vancouver area, where sea levels between 10,000 and 11,000 BP approximated today's levels, there is no evidence of Palaeo-Indian culture (Roberts 1984: 15). There is also the problem of how maritime adapted people could get south of the frozen Alaska Peninsula much less survive on the hostile refugia (Reanier 1990). The limited evidence for Palaeo-Indian culture in the Pacific Northwest and its lateness (Meltzer and Dunnell 1987) suggests that the ancestors of these people did not arrive in the region as accomplished maritimers. The fact that the earliest recognized colonists survived in the rapidly changing environments of the glacial-interglacial transition is proof enough that they were superb generalists and opportunists capable of rapid adaptive cultural adjustments. As such, these earliest people could have possessed both maritime and interior adaptive strategies and, thus, been able to accommodate either or both interior and coastal migration routes. At this point, however, neither of the two routes into the Western Hemisphere has been demonstrated. What can be demonstrated is that around 12,000 years ago people were widespread in the interior of the continent. It must be cautioned that the `burst´ of Palaeo-Indian culture upon the scene

12,000 years ago may be more apparent than real. The archaeological visibility of Palaeo-Indian culture is very much keyed to the distinctive lanceheads which, in various forms, were used for approximately 1,000 years. Indeed, the majority of Palaeo-Indian sites have been dated by these projectile point `index fossils´ rather than by datable samples recovered from good archaeological contexts. Theoretically earlier sites lacking such a convenient `index fossil´ cannot be typologically dated and thus cannot be given a cultural assignment. The major Palaeo-Indian sites tend to be kill sites in the west, where large animals were killed and butchered, or seasonal residential sites in the east, often associated with stone quarries and lacking bone preservation. In addition to the limitations in the archaeological record there are the considerable difficulties in attempting to comprehend the unique event of the human occupation of an entire hemisphere with its great diversity of physiography and environments. The occupation and exploration of the Western Hemisphere by Palaeo-Indian culture and its derivatives must be accorded respect as one of the greatest accomplishments in the history of our species.

It is speculated that the earliest evidence of people spreading throughout the Western Hemisphere is around 15,000 BP with conclusive evidence currently limited to 12,000 years ago. Archaeological, physical anthropological (Turner 1983), linguistic (Greenberg et al. 1986), and genetic evidence (Williams et al. 1985) has been used to argue for three major migrations from Asia into the Western Hemisphere. While controversy exists regarding the specific timing of these events, one sequence has been suggested as follows: the first migration between 30,000 and 15,000 years ago involved the Palaeo-Indians whose descendants would constitute the vast majority of the native peoples of the Western Hemisphere; a second migration between 15,000 and 10,000, gave rise to the members of the Eyak-Athabascan linguistic family and probably some of the current linguistic isolates such as Haida and Tlingit; and a third migration between 9,000 and 6,000 years ago resulted in the historic members of the Eskimo-Aleut linguistic family (Turner 1983). The more than 1,000 languages spoken in the Western Hemisphere at the time of European contact have been divided into three major groups, Amerind, Na-Dene, and Eskimo-Aleut (Greenberg et al. 1986). These large groupings of language families are stated to exhibit closer relationships to different Asiatic groups than to one another suggesting that the three groupings reflect three distinct migrations with different Asiatic origins (Ruhlen 1990). Amerind, representing the first migration, accounts for the majority of the language families in the Western Hemisphere. Most Western Hemisphere linguists reject this tripartite division of languages. Both human cranial discrete trait studies (Ossenberg n.d.) and aspects of the archaeological evidence, caution that this currently favoured three sequential migrations theory may be a bit too facile. The nature of human migrations into the Western Hemisphere will be considered in greater detail in Chapter 2. For a current and succinct review of the pre-Palaeo-Indian evidence from the Western Hemisphere and an assessment of the archaeological, linguistic, physical anthropological, and genetic evidence as they pertain to Asiatic origins and the three migration hypothesis see Meltzer (1993). An annotated bibliography of late Quaternary studies in Beringia is also available (Beaudoin and Reintjes 1994).

As this synthesis involves large segments of time and space considered within variable and changing environments it is only natural that it be general in scope. Archaeological syntheses will vary according to their geographic focus and intended audiences. The audience I am addressing is anyone who, for whatever reasons, has an interest or a need to know something about the 12 millennia of human history

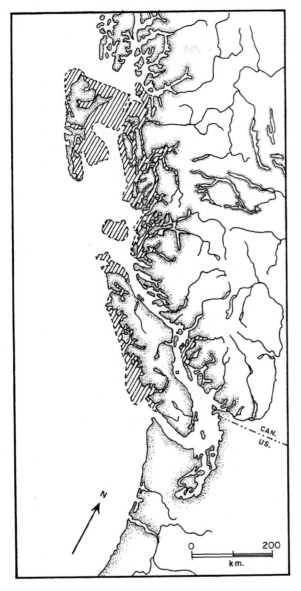

FIGURE 2: COASTAL REFUGIA ALONG THE WEST COAST AT THE END OF THE PLEISTOCENE

The oblique lines demarcate areas less than 100 m below present water levels which were likely exposed land between 10,000 and 9,000 BC. If the coastal hypothesis of human migration into the Western Hemisphere is correct such land areas, now submerged beneath the sea, would have represented the most likely `stepping stones´ to the south. Refugia refer to regions isolated by glaciers but where plant and animal species survive to eventually colonized land as it was released by the ice. (Adapted from Luternauer et al. 1989: Fig.1; drawn by Mr. David W. Laverie.)

in this country prior to the arrival of the Europeans. Archaeological syntheses are an important part of the process of advancing our knowledge of past societies. However, the attempt to bind an array of facts and propositions of variable conviction and theoretical rigour into some form of cohesive system assures that all syntheses are premature and, thus, vulnerable to error. While a synthesis by a single scholar has the advantage of consistency, it will suffer from the single scholar's understandably uneven background in the mass of archaeological data which underlies all regional archaeological sequences. A synthesis by a group of scholars, on the other hand, possesses the advantage of tapping the intimate knowledge of a group of regional specialists but suffers from not infrequent contradictions and unevenness of presentation. Such drawbacks stem from the wide range of theoretical, methodological, and analytical proclivities of individual archaeologists. I am fully aware that the present synthesis will have warts. Since it is not encyclopedic in the sense of blindly accepting regional interpretations of the archaeological record it is almost certainly going to be controversial. To use an analogy, throughout the volumes I have been striding into large, local herds of sacred cows and, on occasion, taking my boots to them. I accept the ever-present danger that some of these herds, if not all of them, also contain bulls and that I will, on occasion, get gored. The process, however, should be constructive in helping to prepare the way for a new and better synthesis which will eventually be replaced by the next and so on ad infinitum.

This is probably the appropriate place to note that I have little patience with much that has recently posed as archaeological theory, particularly in North America. This is not to denigrate the role of theory in any quest for knowledge. Theories must be substantiated by details but details are of limited use if they are not conceptually part of theory. There has been an unfortunate tendency, however, to create theoretical cul-du-sacs and then place these creations in opposition to one another. Or put another way, "We are now becoming scientific by changing the definition of science rather than the nature of archaeology" (Dunnell 1982: 4). An example of the ongoing acrimony involves the relative value of a processual approach (based on systems theory which attempts to view archaeological data as a body of complex, interconnected elements that interact in complex ways with one another within a whole cultural system or entity) and a normative approach (based on the assumption that archaeological evidence is patterned as a result of culturally approved behaviour). Neither position is necessarily in opposition to the other. Relative to the nature of archaeological evidence, the latter approach is the more pragmatic but the former approach seeks an ideal worth striving for relative to the new insights it may provide. I have absolutely no difficulty in applying both processual and normative orientations to archaeological interpretations. The goal is information, not theoretical one-up-manship. I have attempted to adhere to an inclusive intellectual approach to the subject matter of archaeology which accommodates, among other things, the following quotations: "We must, so far as we can, reconstruct the actual history of mankind, before we can hope to discover the laws underlying that history" (Boas 1898: 4); and "Given the vagaries, fortuities, and complexities that are present in any record of a mute past, modesty is always a becoming stance for the archaeologist" (Willey and Sabloff 1974: 211). In an otherwise favourable review of Bruce Trigger's book `A History of Archaeological Thought´(Dunnell 1991) exception was taken with the observation that archaeology is a patchwork affair (Trigger 1989: 88). I concur with this `patchwork´ analogy and would suggest that it is a more accurate characterization of archaeological evidence than some theoretical square peg crammed into an unaccommodating factual hole. Tongue in cheek it may be suggested that such an `unscientific´ perception of archaeological data is trending towards chaos theory with its non-linear dynamic systems and elements of randomness (Stewart 1989). At the risk of playing the role of the Devil's advocate, I would suggest that it is difficult to envision a grand theory of culture which could be applied to archaeological evidence for if one accepts the definition of a theory as an assumption based upon principles independent of the phenomenon under investigation then the uniqueness of human culture results in an epistemological parameter which is incapable of accommodating an all-encompassing theory of culture. The foregoing observation will only pertain, of course, until that time when the stories of the T.V. series `Star Trek´ become fact rather than fantasy.

This work is an outgrowth of a recent effort by archaeologists to communicate archaeological information to a wide public. The organization has been influenced by the Canadian Prehistory Series of the Canadian Museum of Civilization (Fladmark 1986; MacDonald and Inglis 1976; McGhee 1976; 1978; Tuck 1976; 1984; and Wright 1972; 1976; 1979), and, in particular, by Volume I of the Historical Atlas of Canada (Harris and Matthews 1987). A number of syntheses published by provincial agencies, ranging from pamphlets to books, are also available; British Columbia - (Bunyan 1978), Alberta - (Helgason 1987), Saskatchewan - (Epp and Dyck 1983), Manitoba - (Pettipas 1983), Northern Ontario - (Conway 1981, Dawson 1983), Southern Ontario - (Ellis and Ferris 1991), and Québec - (Ministère des Affaires culturelles 1986). The introductory sections of North American archaeological syntheses (Jennings 1989; Willey 1966) represent useful digests of archaeological method, theory, and pertinent cultural and environmental information. Also of value are the archaeological, physical anthropological, linguistic, and ethnographic summaries in Volumes 5, 6, 7, and 15 of the Handbook of the North American Indians (Damas 1984; Helm 1981; Suttles 1990; Trigger 1978). Only through greater public understanding and appreciation will the rich archaeological heritage left by the ancestors of the native peoples of Canada be recognized as an essential part of our national heritage, to be cherished and respected. At this point in our history, when the native peoples of Canada and elsewhere in the world are gathering political strength and asserting their rights, it is important that the dominant society have some appreciation of the history of the first people. It is also necessary that the newcomers become aware of the tragedy which struck the native peoples during the 16th to 19th centuries of our era. It is estimated that throughout this period native populations suffered a 90 percent population reduction due to introduced microbes. This massive loss of life, which particularly struck the old and the young and, thus, eradicated the wisdom of the past and the hope of the future, was then exacerbated by the irresistible pressure of an invading culture with a superior technology and state political organization (Diamond 1988). The wonder is not that so many native cultures disappeared but rather that so many survived. It has been astutely noted concerning the total imbalance of reciprocity in the respective impact of Europeans and natives upon each other that "...the loss of 80% of the North American large mammal fauna at the end of the Pleistocene, and the difficulty of domesticating the survivors, played a large role in creating the strategic imbalance. Not just because native Americans then had few animals for transport and protein (page 28), but because as epidemiologists have shown many infectious diseases (especially those that devastated native Americans) co-evolved with animal domestication. That alone speaks loudly for why the 15th century invasion was one way, native Americans had no diseases in exchange, and why in 1987 the Smithsonian was anticipating the Columbus quincentenary and not the millennium of the Iroquois Confederacy" (Meltzer 1990: 390).

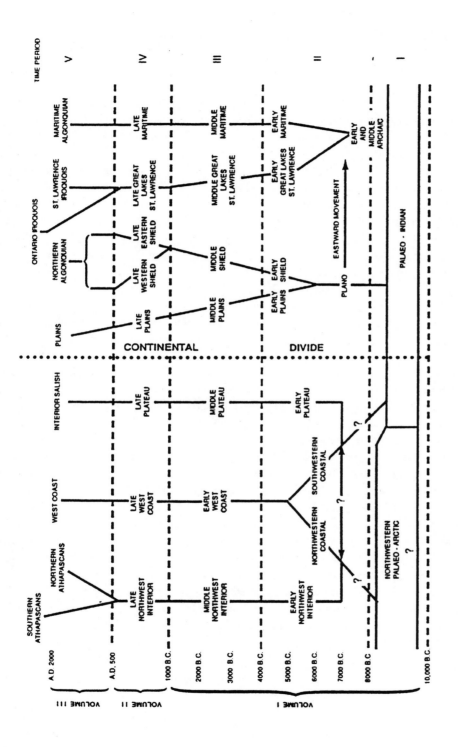

CHART 1: A SCHEMATIC AND SIMPLIFIED CHRONOLOGY OF THE ARCHAEOLOGICAL HISTORY OF CANADA The chart, which does not include the Palaeo-Eskimo and Proto-Inuit cultural developments, is intended to assist the reader in following the geographic and temporal relationships of the various cultures described in the chapters. The five time periods are demarcated from one another by dashed lines while the segments of time involved in each volume are indicated on the left. Geographically, the chart is oriented with East to the right and proceeds across to West on the left.

PERIOD I

(10,000 TO 8,000 B.C.)

CHAPTER 2

PALAEO-INDIAN CULTURE

Précis:

The colonizing of the Western Hemisphere by people with a Palaeo-Indian culture and its derivatives was a truly momentous accomplishment. In the history of <u>Homo sapiens</u> it falls into the same record of achievements as the population movements which occupied Europe and Asia and reached Australia between 30,000 and 40,000 BP (Jelinek 1992). Just as the magnitude of the colonizing event was unique so are some of the characteristics of Palaeo-Indian culture. Analogies with historically documented hunting peoples are not totally appropriate given the nature of some of the Palaeo-Indian cultural systems, particularly the maintenance of technological continuity over enormous distances. Such an ability must reflect social systems that operated on a scope beyond our historically recorded comparisons. These systems initially functioned within a wide range of changing and highly variable Pleistocene environments. What follows, therefore, must be prefaced with the caveat that just as the rapid spread of Palaeo-Indian culture throughout the Western Hemisphere was unique so are the problems of explaining the phenomenon. In the archaeological history of the Western Hemisphere only the Early Palaeo-Eskimo culture occupation of the High Arctic and Greenland around 2,000 BC is comparable albeit on a reduced scale.

This chapter follows Dr. James B. Griffin's recommendation that the term Palaeo-Indian be restricted to the users of the distinctive fluted spear head, the hallmark artifact of Palaeo-Indian culture (Griffin 1977: 10). Thus, Plano culture, which developed out of late Palaeo-Indian culture in the west, is not referred to as Late Palaeo-Indian contrary to current practise. The Plano cultures of the west and the Archaic cultures of the east were equivalent developments. The exclusion of Plano cultures from the Palaeo-Indian designation and their treatment as a western equivalent of Archaic in the east represents a more coherent classificatory arrangement.

Despite the fact that between AD 1895 and 1932 there were a number of reported associations of extinct bison remains with stone tools on the Plains (Rogers and Martin 1986) the evidence was not generally accepted by archaeologists until the advent of radiocarbon dating (Wilmsen 1965). A number of archaeologists began to change their minds, however, in 1925 when stone spear heads associated with the bones of extinct bison at a site near Folsom, New Mexico were excavated by archaeologists (Figgins 1927). The distinctive style of spear head uncovered at this site was subsequently recognized as being widely distributed east of the Rocky Mountains in the United States and Canada (Cotter 1937). Sites producing such points often contained evidence of geological and environmental conditions significantly different from the present and with the advent of radiocarbon dating were consistently dated between 11,500 and 10,500 BP. Because this wide-spread culture has been firmly dated and stratigraphically appears to represent the first human occupation many archaeologists accept it as the earliest unequivocal evidence of people in the habitable portions of North America exclusive of Beringia. Initially defined in the central Plains, the earliest and most wide-spread manifestation is called Clovis while later expressions of the culture are referred to as Folsom. There is, however, no gap between the radiocarbon dates of early (Clovis) and late (Folsom) Palaeo-Indian culture (Haynes 1984). At the Lindenmeier site in Colorado both early and late styles of fluted spear points were recovered in association along with unfluted points (Wilmsen and Roberts 1978). It is apparent that there is a cultural continuum from early to late Palaeo-Indian culture marked by increasing cultural regionalism through time. This regionalism is sufficiently pronounced in western and eastern North America that many archaeologists believe western-derived terms like Clovis and Folsom are being over-extended when applied to Palaeo-Indian assemblages east of the Mississippi River (Deller and Ellis 1992).

In this study Clovis, Folsom, and related eastern classifications, are subsumed under the category `Palaeo-Indian culture´. The term `culture´ is used as a label to describe a broadly shared, predominantly technological, cultural pattern (Frison 1983; Haynes 1980; MacDonald 1983; Wilmsen 1965; Wormington 1957). The spread of Palaeo-Indian culture coincided with the massive environmental changes that accompanied the end of the Pleistocene period; changes related to climate, vegetation, hydrology, erosional-depositional cycles, and animal extinctions and population densities. Palaeo-Indian people encountered unique environments, consisting of mosaics of plant communities which have no direct parallels today, as well as glacial ice and associated water bodies, and a range of fauna that included species such as mammoth, horse, camel, and large extinct varieties of bison. At the end of the Pleistocene plant communities changed rapidly and a number of the large fauna, both prey and predator, became extinct. The role played by Palaeo-Indians in these extinctions is still being debated. There is evidence that Palaeo-Indian culture established the base from which most later regional cultures developed with Archaic cultures evolving in the east and Plano cultures in the west.

Cultural origins and descendants:

If Palaeo-Indian technology is accepted as a derivative of the Upper Palaeolithic technological tradition of northern Asia, as would appear to be the case, then pertinent to the occupation of the Western Hemisphere is the fact that Upper Palaeolithic sites dating to 25,000 BP currently represent the earliest evidence of humans in northeastern Asia (Jelinek 1992). With reference to the likelihood of a relationship between Palaeo-Indian culture and the Nenana complex of Alaska it has been noted that "With the exception of the different point forms, the Nenana Complex tool kit is typologically similar to the Clovis tool kit" (Powers 1990: 57). It is also pertinent that the technologies of the Nenana complex and the Northwestern Palaeo-Arctic culture are very similar when the microblades and burins of the latter are excluded. Evidence of a Palaeo-Indian migration through either the Rocky Mountain corridor or along the West Coast is currently lacking although the former hypothesis is regarded as the more likely one. People probably penetrated south of the ice masses by 15,000 BP, as indicated at sites such as the Meadowcroft Rockshelter and Fort Rock. The spread of people into the new lands resulted in a common technological horizon across most of the habitable regions of North America and also spread, in derivative forms (Bird 1946), throughout much of South America. Regional differentiation from this common cultural base took

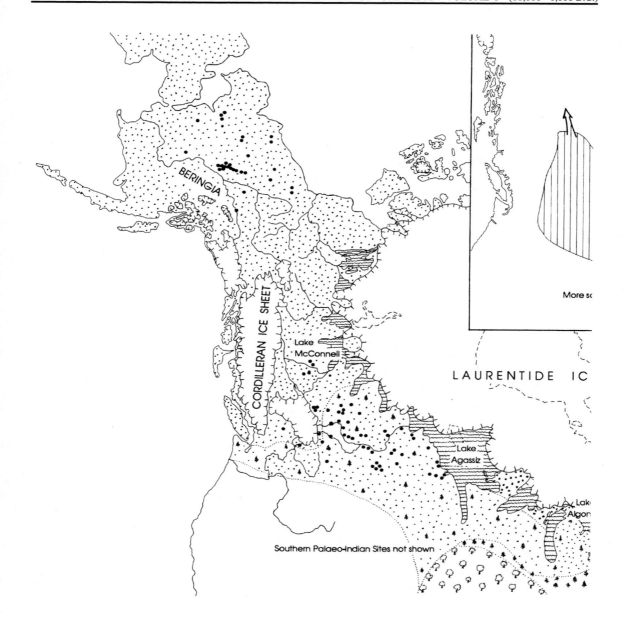

MAP I: DISTRIBUTIONS OF PALAEO-INDIAN AND PLANO CULTURES   In addition to showing physiographic features and major plant communities through time. It was within these dramatically different Canada, Volume I, From the Beginning to 1800. R. Cole Harris, editor, and Geoffrey J. Matthews, carto-

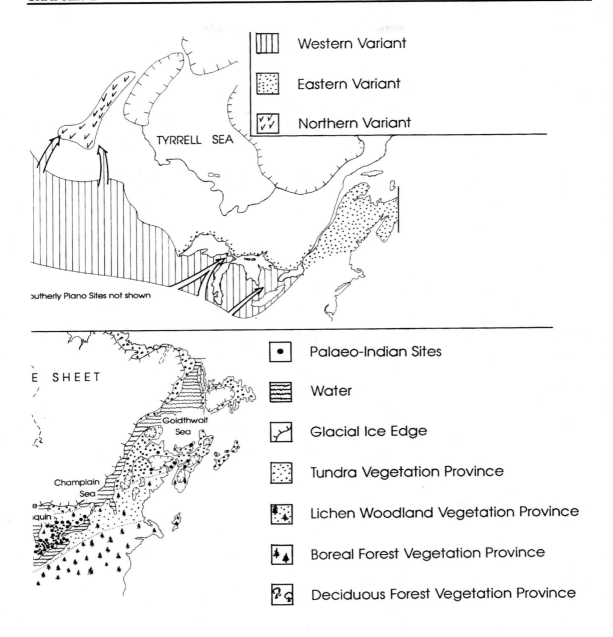

the geographical distributions of Palaeo-Indian and Plano cultures, Map I provides an impression of the changing environments that the earliest people lived. (Adapted, in part, from Plates 2 and 5 of the Historical Atlas of grapher/designer. University of Toronto Press. Drawing by Mr. David W. Laverie.)

place relatively quickly as bands of hunters adapted to the different and rapidly changing environments in which they found themselves.

There is much debate concerning where the fluted spear head was first developed (Clark 1991a; Morlan 1991). If Palaeo-Indian culture spread south out of Beringia then the earliest dated sites should be in Alaska and the Yukon. With the exception of the Putu site in Alaska (Alexander 1974; 1987), the earliest dates all come from sites to the south of the ice mass. This has led to the suggestion that either the fluted spear heads were developed in the interior of the continent and were then introduced to the north (Wormington 1957: 109) or that the northern and southern point styles are unrelated (West 1981). Thus, there are the three options of northern, southern, or independent development of the fluted point. Although the southern option currently appears to be favoured, the evidence is simply too limited to discard a northern origin at this time. Given the attributes of the point style in question, independent invention in both the north and the south would appear to be the most unlikely option.

The sudden appearance and homogeneity of the chipped stone tool kit of early Palaeo-Indian culture across North America and its rapid differentiation into regionally distinctive technologies over a period of one thousand years is one of the most persuasive arguments for the absence of an earlier human occupation. Despite the suggestion that Palaeo-Indian technology may have spread by diffusion to a number of different populations already present south of the ice (Bonnichsen and Young 1980; Morlan and Cinq-Mars 1982: 380-381) the shared characteristics of the assemblage appear to be too many to be explained as a product of diffusion. In this regard, it appears that Palaeo-Indian technology "...was spread by a colonizing population that maintained a specific cultural identity" (Storck 1988: 243). Although it has recently become popular to treat Palaeo-Indian culture technological homogeneity as a myth and to emphasize regional variability (Ellis and Lothrop 1989: xx) the matter is relative and the similarities of early Palaeo-Indian culture across North America cannot be denied.

The rapid spread of Palaeo-Indian culture has been attributed to an abundance of unwary, relatively uniformly distributed large game animals (Haynes 1982; Kelley and Todd 1988) and the absence of other human competitors. The lower seasonal extremes of the Late Pleistocene would have permitted the existence of broad expanses of diverse plant and animal communities now isolated by seasonal climatic extremes (Guthrie 1984). As increasing seasonality placed stresses on animal and plant species, Palaeo-Indian culture hunters had the option to respond to game depletion by shifting either territory or food resources or use a combination of these options. In this respect, Palaeo-Indian culture appears to have been uniquely adapted to exploiting terra incognita as well as a wide range of resources in occupied territories. Evidence of the spread of colonizing bands from the west is apparent in the fluted points manufactured from a distinctive Wisconsin quartzite that have been found in Indiana and Ohio up to 900 km to the east. There is the problem of whether such finds represent the product of eastward shifting migrations or a reflection of broadly based networks of social interaction (Tankersley 1989: 270) or both.

It was in early Palaeo-Indian culture times that the spread into new lands would have been accomplished. Ignoring for the moment the possibility of a veneer of people being present two to three thousand years prior to the archaeological visibility of Palaeo-Indian culture (Agenbroad 1988), it can be suggested that the 1,000 years it took to reach Tierra del Fuego on the southern tip of South America would have involved annual southward shifts of 16 km (Kelly and Todd 1988: 234). This is also a time when a number of megafauna extinctions took place that some have directly attributed to human hunting (Martin 1973) although the palaeontological evidence would suggest that the path to extinction, induced by climatic and environmental change, began 18,000 years ago (Meltzer and Mead 1983) and that people may simply have administered the coup de grâce to certain species (Grayson 1988; Jelinek 1967). For an overview of the factors underlying recent animal extinctions see David A. Burney (1993).

Until recently all radiocarbon dates were based on the method of measuring the rate of decay of beta particles of the unstable isotope carbon 14 (beta method). A more recent method, which can measure carbon samples as small as a few milligrams, involves the use of accelerator mass spectrometry (AMS) where individual C14 atoms are directly measured. Readers requiring the specifics on individual radiocarbon dates from Palaeo-Indian sites, such a laboratory number, whether a bone date was based upon the apatite or collagen fraction, if correction for C13 fractionation was made, what half life was used, and a number of other factors, can consult the references of the following sites: Alberta - a combination of 3 AMS dates and 2 beta particle dates from a single living floor feature at the Vermilion Lakes site ranged from 10,270 +/- 100 to 11,000 +/- 480 BP with an average of 10,626 BP (Fedje 1986) but no diagnostic implements were recovered; British Columbia - three bone samples from the Charlie Lake Cave site ranged from 10,380 +/- 160 to 10,770 +/-120 BP with an average of 10,533 BP (Fladmark et al. 1988); Nova Scotia - 13 charcoal dates from the Debert site ranged from 10,128 +/- 275 to 11,026 +/- 225 BP with an average of 10,590 BP (Meltzer 1988); Idaho - four bone samples from the Wasden site ranged from 9,735 +/- 115 to 10,910 +/-150 BP with an average of 10,315 BP (Miller 1989); Maine - an AMS charcoal date of 10,200 +/-620 from the Michaud site (Spiess and Brush 1987) and 6 charcoal dates from the Vail site that ranged from 10,040 +/- 400 to 11,120 +/- 180 BP with an average of 10,518 BP (Meltzer 1988); Montana - a 10,600 +/- 300 AMS bone date from the Anzick site (Taylor et al. 1985: 138); New Hampshire - a charcoal date from the Whipple site of 11,050 +/-300 (Meltzer 1988); South Dakota - a bone date and an organic sediment date from the Lange/Ferguson site of 10,730 +/- 530 and 10,670 +/- 300 BP, respectively, (Hannus 1989); and Alaska - a charcoal date from a Putu site hearth feature of 11,470 BP +/- 500 (Alexander 1987). Other dates from the Putu site are excluded on the grounds of questionable archaeological context.

The two major post-Palaeo-Indian culture developments in North America took place in different areas. On the Plains and adjacent regions changes in tool technology led to the Plano cultures whose settlement and subsistence patterns, however, remained essentially the same as that of their predecessors. To the east of the Mississippi River, technological changes led to the Archaic cultures but, once again, at the early stages of development changes in both settlement and subsistence patterns appear to have been minimal. The land mass that is now Canada was on the northern periphery of these developments. This northerly location in the east, with its inferred persistence of caribou herds, permitted the maintenance of earlier hunting practices that are reflected in the unbroken narrow band of Plano culture occupation that extended from the Plains to the Maritime provinces. Cultural regionalism in the east appears to have been contemporary with Folsom (late Palaeo-Indian) in the west and consisted of the Parkhill complex centred on the Great Lakes, the Cumberland complex in the upper Mississippi drainage, the Debert/Vail complex in the Maritimes and northern New England, and other developments in the southeastern United States and southern New England (Deller and Ellis 1992: 137).

Technology:

There are a number of good descriptions of the Palaeo-Indian chipped stone tool kit. The classic study of the Shoop site in Pennsylvania pertains to early Palaeo-Indian (Witthoft 1952; reanalysed by Cox 1986) while the Hanson site in Wyoming is a late Palaeo-Indian site (Frison and Bradley 1980). The description of the stone tool industry at the Thedford II site on Lake Huron and the patterning of lithic reduction (Deller and Ellis 1992) is an excellent analytical study illustrating the kinds of information that can be derived from sites disturbed by ploughing. A general consideration of Palaeo-Indian technology in North America is also available (Gramly 1990). The wide distribution of early Palaeo-Indian technology must have involved some form of poorly understood mechanism that resulted in an exceptional degree of technological sameness over great expanses. In a relatively short period of time, however, the technology takes on an increasingly regional character. The tool kit consists primarily of chipped stone fluted spear heads and knives, bifacial and flake knives, a range of scraper forms, gravers, burin-like tools including wedges or pièces esquillées, spoke-shaves, drills, and rough stone items such as hammerstones, choppers, and anvils (Gramly 1982; MacDonald 1968; Storck 1979; Wilmsen and Roberts 1978). There is a progression of tool use with `worn out´ end scrapers being recycled into gravers and then into wedges (Gramly and Funk 1990). With reference to the wedges, use-wear studies indicate that they were neither wedges nor bipolar cores but rather functioned as burins to fashion tools of wood and bone by slotting and planing (Meltzer 1988: 42). A characteristic of Palaeo-Indian culture stone working technology was its efficient use of biface preforms to produce a readily transportable and multi-purpose chipped stone tool kit (Kelly and Todd 1988).

Natural pigments were occasionally used such as red ochre (Lahren and Bonnichsen 1974) and graphite nodules (Grimes et al. 1984). The most common tool encountered, as in all stone tool-using cultures, is the stone flake that upon being detached from a core is razor sharp and capable of performing a wide range of cutting, scraping, slotting, and puncturing functions with no or little further modification (see Storck and Tomenchuk 1990). Even rare tool varieties are of potential significance to culture historical reconstructions. The large quartzite plane tool (called a core tool) from the Charlie Lake Cave site in British Columbia (Fladmark et al. 1988: 377-378) bears a remarkable resemblance to tools from the Nenana complex Walker Road site in Alaska (Powers et al. 1990: 42) and could be a distant echo of a past technological relationship. If the assemblage from the Putu site in northern Alaska represents a single component the following traits are part of the Palaeo-Indian tool kit in northern Alaska and presumably the adjacent Yukon: fluted, lanceolate, and triangular (Chindadn) projectile points; burins and gravers, including gravers on bifaces; large biface knives; wedge-shaped microblade cores, microblades, `blades´; and utilized flakes (Alexander 1987: 44). Such an assemblage would represent an amalgam of Palaeo-Indian and Northwestern Palaeo-Arctic culture technologies and contradict the dual migration hypothesis involving an initial migration to the Western Hemisphere of people lacking microblade technology followed by microblade using people.

There is a major difference between most Palaeo-Indian culture sites in western North America and eastern North America. In the west, where bone tends to be preserved, many of the major sites represent kill-butchering locales. In the east bone preservation tends to be non-existent and most major settlements were seasonal residential sites situated at or near sources of high quality stone. Such sites invariably contain considerable evidence of stone tool manufacturing. A west and east dichotomy of kill-butchering sites versus stone tool manufacturing sites is an over simplification as a wide range of activities would have been performed at sites in both regions. This is reflected by the fact that the stone tool attribute trends through time are similar in both the west and the east (Cox 1986: 13). In addition to the recovered tools, it can be inferred that people could not have functioned in the late Pleistocene environment without some form of portable water transport (canoe) or snow-ice transport (sled-toboggan) (Deller and Ellis 1991). In most instances direct evidence of such essential   elements of technology will never be recovered and their presence must be inferred from settlement pattern distributions and environmental reconstructions. Exceptions, however, are always the rule. A number of bone rods from the Richey Clovis Cache in Washington State have been speculated to represent shoes that were once attached to the bottom of wooden sled runners (Gramly 1993: 59). The presence of dogs or, more accurately, wolf-dog hybrids in the late Palaeo-Indian component of the Agate Basin site in Wyoming (Walker and Frison 1982: 125) raises the possibility of dog cartage although such dogs were more likely employed as aids in the hunt.

Although `blades´ are frequently attributed to the Palaeo-Indian chipped stone technology (Frison 1978; West 1981) in the majority of instances it would be more accurate to classify these items as `linear flakes´ as they generally lack multiple arrises on their dorsal faces that would indicate the detachment from cores specifically designed for blade production. In other words, there appears to have been little effort in the literature to distinguish between blades struck from specially prepared blade cores and linear flakes with a single longitudinal arris. Many of the so-called `blades´ possess extensive lateral edge retouch that has obliterated the original flake form. Such retouched linear flakes incorporated a medial arris for tool strength but should not be confused technologically with blades struck from cores specifically fashioned for the production of numerous blades. In some instances,the definition of blade´is so inclusive as to be meaningless as a classificatory unit (Goebel et al.1991; Powers 1990:59). Most lithic assemblages in the Western Hemisphere would contain blades under such broad criteria. Matters have been further confused by an unquestioning acceptance of the association of the blades from the Blackwater Draw site in New Mexico with the Palaeo-Indian occupation (Jennings 1989: 87; Willey 1966: 39) even though the blades in question were not recovered in a clear archaeological context (Green 1963). Blades have not been found associated with the many thousands of Palaeo-Indian culture stone tools excavated under good context controls (Meltzer 1988: Table VI). An exception to the foregoing may be the early Palaeo-Indian quarry-workshop sites in Kentucky (Gramly and Funk 1990; Sanders 1990) where bonafide conical cores and multi-arris blades and tools made from blades were being produced. This, however, may be an isolated instance related to the nature of the chert cobbles that facilitated a specialized technology. It would appear that the desire to have a Eurasian, Aurignacian lithic industry represented in the earliest unequivocal archaeological industry in the Western Hemisphere has led to the acceptance of the linear flakes of Palaeo-Indian culture as true blades (Alexander 1974; Aikens 1990: 13 and 22). At the very least, researchers should be more explicit regarding their classificatory criterion otherwise there will be a danger of people `talking past one another´.

Bone tools, while rare due to unfavourable soil conditions, tend to be of limited variety. Awls, scrapers, fleshers, points, bone needles, some with eyes, cut and incised plaques, and spear foreshafts are among the more common implements (Frison and Standford 1982; Haynes 1980; Lahren and Bonnichsen 1974; Wilmsen and Roberts 1978). A fossilized bone foreshaft, found at a depth of 2.4 m while digging

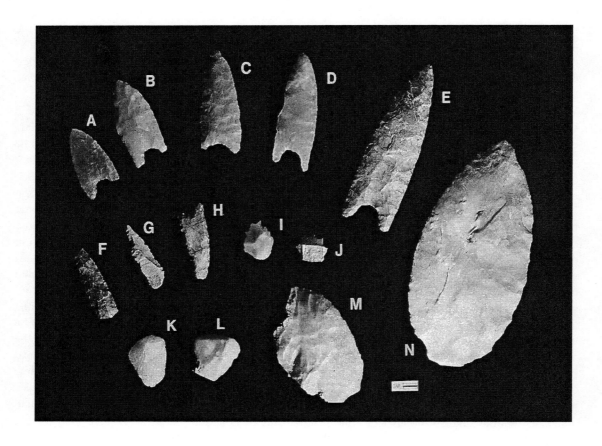

COLOUR PLATE II: PALAEO-INDIAN CULTURE TOOLS FROM THE DEBERT SITE, NOVA SCOTIA A range of the distinctive fluted spear heads (A to E), drills (F and G), a multi-purpose cutting tool (H), gravers (I and J), scrapers (K and L), and knives (M and N) are shown. All are manufactured from a colourful chalcedony found in the nearby Minas Basin of the Bay of Fundy. Original colour only on diskette and CD-ROM. (Reproduced from Keenlyside 1984)

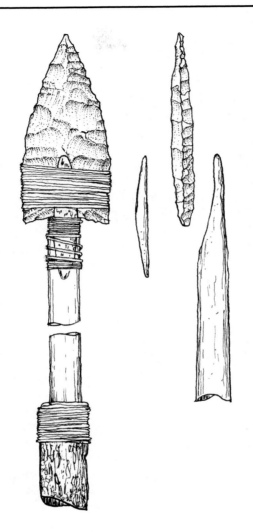

FIGURE 3: PALAEO-INDIAN CULTURE WEAPON SYSTEM This reconstruction of how Palaeo-Indian hunters hafted their chipped stone spear heads to the spear shaft is based upon the recoveries of sections of bone foreshafts. Upon thrusting a spear into a large animal the stone piercing tip and the attached bone or ivory foreshaft would remain in the wound and detach from the wooden spear shaft. Such a composite spear system would permit the spear shaft to be quickly rearmed with new weapon tips already lashed to their foreshafts allowing a number of strikes to be made in rapid succession.(Adapted from Lahren and Bonnichsen 1974, Figure 3. Drawing by Mr. David W. Laverie)

a water hole in southeastern Saskatchewan (Black and White Plate III), was manufactured from proboscidean bone (Wilmeth 1968). Very simple bone implements have only been recently recognized. At the Wasden site in southern Idaho, the typical stone tool assemblage was recovered in association with mammoth bone reduced both for marrow extraction and as raw material for tools (Miller 1989). Thick cortical bone was specifically selected and reduced to bone flakes in a patterned fashion with many of the flakes exhibiting use-wear suggesting their use as expedient knives. Bone choppers were also present. Of significance is the mammoth core-flake technology at the mammoth kill Lange/Ferguson site in South Dakota (Hannus 1989: 406). The technology bears a striking resemblance to that of the Bluefish Caves site as well as recoveries from the Old Crow River basin (Cinq-Mars 1990; Morlan et al. 1990) in the northern Yukon Territory. Heavy mammoth bone cleaving tools and flakes derived from shoulder blades and longbones were also found. In lieu of bone preservation, some speculations are possible regarding bone technology on the basis of the nature of the stone tools. At the Putu site in Alaska, for example, both the unusually limited vista of the site for big game hunters and the domination of the tool kit by `blades´, burins, and gravers led to the suggestion that the major site activity was the fashioning of antler into tools (Alexander 1987: 42).

The stone tips with which stone age hunters frequently armed their weapons appear to have been objects of particular significance. Not only did they function as the piercing tip of the spear but also as knives to judge from use wear studies (Cox 1986: 111; Gramly 1993). Although the form and specific characteristics of these artifacts vary through both time and space changes were generally slow and the point styles widespread within general cultural groupings. For this reason weapon tips (spears, darts, and arrow heads) are very useful to archaeologists in identifying specific cultures. This is particularly true for Palaeo-Indian culture with its distinctive fluted spear heads. It should be noted, however, that at sites such as Debert in Nova Scotia (MacDonald 1968) as many as 20% of the spear heads were basally thinned rather than actually fluted (Keenlyside 1985) and a number of the spearheads from the late Palaeo-Indian Hanson site were not fluted (Frison and Bradley 1980). There has been considerable speculation whether such points tipped spears that were thrust into the prey rather than being hurled. Although points lodged in animal bones would permit a calculation of the angle of penetration only one such clear instance is recorded. In this case a bison at the Lindenmeier site in Colorado appears to have been dispatched with a thrusting spear (Wilmsen and Roberts 1978: 172 and 176). It has been recorded at mammoth kills (Haury 1953; Sellards 1938) that spear thrusts were directed at the base of the skull, "...the angle and place of penetration was about the same in each case, from the upper right side of the elephants and at the base of the skull, the spot on the elephant's anatomy where the spinal cord was most vulnerable" (Haury 1953: 7). The association of points with the pelvic girdle and hind leg bones also suggests ambush from the rear while associations with the spinal column and the rib cage could represent coup de grâce thrusts (Haury et al. 1959: Table 1). There are other lines of indirect evidence which suggest that the fluted points were hafted to thrusting spears. Based on butchering and lancing experiments on dead circus elephants (Huckell 1979; 1982) the most vulnerable area of a mammoth, which was taxonomically closely related to modern elephants, would have been the belly. There are a number of historic records of native African elephant hunters belly wounding elephants from ambush and then following them until they collapsed (Johnson, Kawano and Ekker 1980). The belly region of a mammoth or any game animal would not be accessible to a thrown spear except under most unusual circumstances. The presence of bone spear foreshafts, to which the stone tips would have been hafted, indicates that the spear was a composite weapon with a detachable foreshaft and tip (Figure 3.). At the Anzick burial site in Montana the ten bone foreshaft crossections ranged from 15 to 20 mm in maximum width and 11 to 14 mm in minimum width (Lahren and Bonnichsen 1974: Table 1) with averages of 17.9 mm and 12.5 mm, respectively. These measurements closely match the 15 mm by 12.5 mm crossection dimensions of the fossilized foreshaft from southeastern Saskatchewan (Wilmeth 1968) and are similar to the size range of the foreshafts from Blackwater Draw Locality 1 site (Sellards 1952). Such a weapon system where the spear shaft could be rapidly rearmed and multiple strikes made in quick order would appear to be more suitable to a thrusting spear than a throwing spear. The bone foreshaft composite weapon system may even have been a special adaptation to the

BLACK AND WHITE PLATE III: FORESHAFT MADE FROM ELEPHANT BONE
While digging a waterhole in southeastern Saskatchewan a farmer found this bone implement. A recent analysis of the internal structure of the bone suggested that it had been obtained from a limb bone of an extinct elephant. Another quite different type of implement from Manitoba, which was believed to have been also manufactured from elephant bone (Leechman 1950), has since proven to be moose bone that dated to the last 1,000 years (Buchner and Roberts 1990). These two events illustrate how ongoing research on museum specimens can both generate new information and correct past misinformation. (Reproduced from Wright 1976: Plate 9)

hunting of dangerous prey such as mammoth and bison. This speculation is based upon evidence that spear heads were sometimes hafted directly to wooden spear shafts. At the Vail site in Maine, stone dart heads narrower than 24 to 25 mm were discarded while points marginally wider were still used suggesting that the wooden spear shafts were from 24 to 25 mm in diameter. Such a diameter is more in accord with ethnographically recorded thrusting spears than with lighter throwing spears that have smaller shaft diameters (Gramly 1984: 113).

Around 8,000 BC in eastern North America notched varieties of stone weapon tips replaced the fluted points. On the Plains and Intermontane area 2,000 years later the lanceolate derivatives of fluted points were similarly replaced by notched points. Such relatively sudden and wide-spread replacements are not likely the result of stylistic whim and more probably represent the adoption of a new weapon system that had obvious advantages over the older thrusting spear. The new weapon system is inferred to have been the spearthrower, a device that permits light spears to be thrown with greater force, distance and accuracy than is possible by the arm alone. This discussion of thrusting spears versus throwing spears may strike some readers as being overly long. The importance of such innovations, however, cannot be overemphasized. Hunting peoples relied upon their knowledge and weapons to survive. Any new weapon system which offered obvious advantages in hunting and defence would likely be promptly adopted. Yet such changes in the technology are extremely difficult for archaeology to recognize as the product of technological diffusion. Geographic regionalism was well advanced by late Palaeo-Indian times as hunting bands adapted to different environmental zones and as the Late Pleistocene climate progressively ameliorated. It is proposed that the adoption of the spearthrower at this time resulted in changes in technology and other cultural systems that have created a false impression of a cultural hiatus between Palaeo-Indian culture and subsequent regional cultures. The archaeological record from stratified sites bridging this period and the analysis of the tool technology, settlement patterns, and subsistence

COLOUR PLATE III: A MASTODON HUNT 11,000 YEARS AGO Two Palaeo-Indian hunters prepare to ambush a juvenile mastodon. The scene is set north of what is now the city of Toronto. In the background is the broad expanse of glacial Lake Algonquin, now shrunk to the Georgian Bay of Lake Huron. A California condor flies overhead. Among the other inhabitants who shared this open lichen woodland with the first human occupants of the interior of North America were caribou, Arctic fox, grizzly bear, and mammoth. Based upon knowledge of the Palaeo-Indian weapon system, the evidence from contemporary mammoth kills, and historically documented records relating to the spearing of elephants in Africa, it is speculated that the hunters would have `gut- wounded´ the young mastodon and then followed at a safe distance until it succumbed to its wounds and was abandoned by its mother. The detachable weapon tips and foreshafts carried in the bag, could be used to rapidly rearm the spear shaft thus permitting a number of successive spear thrusts. (Painting produced by Vidéanthrop Inc., Montréal, under contract with the Canadian Museum of Civilization. The painting was done by M. François Girard using sketches and technical information compiled after close collaboration between M. Marc Laberge and the author; the original coloured version is provided on diskette and CD-ROM)

---

do clearly indicate cultural continuity from Palaeo-Indian culture to subsequent regional cultures (Coe 1964; Frison and Bradley 1980; Gardner 1977).

Subsistence:

The migratory habits of big game animals, such as bison and caribou, would insure that the Palaeo-Indian hunting bands were highly mobile. As it was a time of rapidly changing environments, people would have had to be flexible in responding to changes in the availability of food. They would also have to be able to cope with sudden emergencies such as the possibility of the now extinct 1,000 kg giant short faced bear (Voorhies and Corner 1986) or sabre tooth cat wandering into camp. Having once had a very large Barrenground grizzly bear rise up on his hind legs to scrutinize me from a distance of 100 feet, I can empathize with the feelings of people under such circumstances. What I am unable to assess is the degree of advantage provided by my rifle over the Palaeo-Indians spears and intimate knowledge of bear behaviour.

During the Late Pleistocene, the cool and wet conditions of southwestern North America contrasted with the semi-open boreal parklands of the Plains and the Northeast and the mixed hardwood and softwood forests of the Southeast. A key subsistence factor in both the west and the east would have been the availability of large herd animals. In the Northeast, for example, it is inferred from site locations and the extant environmental conditions that caribou likely were the major prey (Fitting, DeVisscher and Wahla 1966; Gramly 1982; MacDonald 1968). Further south, factors such as variable topography and environmental instability would have tended to encourage a broad subsistence base over a highly specialized one focused on a single species (Grimes et al 1984). This is not to suggest that a herd animal such as elk would not have been important during a segment of the annual subsistence rounds. It simply means that in lieu of substantial herds of large ungulates, the subsistence pattern to the south was likely finely tuned to a wider range of available resources.

Controversy has surrounded the issue of whether humans were a factor in the extinctions at the end of the Pleistocene. It has been suggested that the extinctions were most likely related to climatic change that resulted in increasing seasonality and less biotic variability and, thus, habitat (Lundelius 1988). Undoubtedly Palaeo-Indian hunters did hasten a process of natural extinction (Agenbroad 1988; Jelinek 1967; Martin (1973) but it is worth noting that 103 mammal species became extinct between 12,000 and 14,000 years ago (Lundelius 1980: Table 1) just prior to the appearance of Palaeo-Indian culture. Of the 35 genera that became extinct at the end of the Pleistocene, 22 dated to the 12,000 to 10,000 BP period. Some of these genera had already been markedly reduced by 12,000 years ago (Grayson 1987). Only seven genera have unquestionably been dated to the 12,000 to 10,000 BP period - Camelops (camel), Equus (horse), Mammut (mastodon), Mammuthus (mammoth), Nothrotheriops (ground sloth), Smilodon (sabre tooth cat), and Tapirus (tapir). Such findings raise problems relative to both the suddenness of the extinctions and the respective roles of climatic change and the appearance of humans. The three most common extinct megafauna to be associated with Palaeo-Indian culture sites, exclusive of extinct varieties of bison, are mammoth, horse, and camel in that order. The vast majority of the evidence comes from the Great Basin and the southwestern United States (Grayson 1984: Table 2; 1987; 1988: 155) thus presenting a limited picture derived from areas where both kill-butchering sites and good bone preservation are common. Certainly such evidence is rarely encountered east of the Mississippi River (Adovasio et al. 1988). For example, although mastodon remains in direct association with Palaeo-Indian culture tools have not been found in Southern Ontario, 60% of fluted points with known locations are found in the same areas as the mastodon, some of whom were contemporary with humans (Jackson 1987). While a fluted point was found with mastodon remains at the Hiscock site in western New York State, the mixed nature of the deposits has raised questions regarding an association (Laub 1990: 117). The presence of presumed cut marks on one mastodon bone at this site and a mastodon bone date of 10,500 BP do heighten the probability of an association and it has even been speculated that some human scavenging took place (Gramly and Funk 1990). This probability has been reinforced by the recent recognition of possible human modification of mastodon ivory and ribs (Dr. David Steadman, New York State Museum: personal communication, November, 1994). Despite the foregoing there undoubtedly has been too much of an emphasis upon Palaeo-Indian culture people as specialized megafauna hunters. It would be more appropriate to say these people possessed a highly adaptive and flexible hunting strategy finely tuned to all resources which included the ability to dispatch large and potentially dangerous species.

The spread of Palaeo-Indian culture into an unoccupied hemisphere demanded an exceptional degree of mobility. As a colonizing population, it was essential to rapidly acquire an intimate knowledge of both the inorganic and organic resources of new territories. The exploitation of high quality cherts, a chipped stone technology based on bifacial preforms which could be transformed into a number of tool varieties, the limited use of caves and rockshelters or of food storage, have all been cited as facets of this unique adaptive pattern (Kelley and Todd 1988). It is an overstatement, however, to suggest that, "Generalized knowledge of animal behaviour, rather than place-specific knowledge of habitat may have been the key to Paleoindian survival in the changing late Pleistocene environment" (Ibid: 239). Almost certainly both factors were at play and increasingly so as the hemisphere became occupied. At the Shawnee-Minisink site in Pennsylvania (McNett 1985), for example, plant materials associated with the Palaeo-Indian culture occupation were chenopodium, hawthorn plum, blackberry, acalypha and minor amounts of amaranth, buckbean, grape, hackberry, smartweed, and watercress (Dent and Kauffman 1985). Plants at this site were an important diet supplement, providing a high carbohydrate source of energy as well as concentrated Vitamin C from plants such as hawthorn plum. Fish remains were also recovered. At the Wasden site in southern Idaho (Miller 1989: 382) mammoth, bison, pronghorn, dire wolf, fox, fish, reptiles, amphibians, birds, small mammals, and snails were recovered from the Palaeo-Indian culture occupation although some of the smaller animal remains likely came from owl pellets. The range of food resources exploited by Palaeo-Indian people was, of course, determined by the environmental zones occupied. It is likely that Palaeo-Indians were neither big game specialists (Stoltman and Baerreis 1983) nor generalists (Meltzer 1988) but rather relied upon a combination of both orientations as circumstances dictated. Palaeo-Indian sites in Canada would have occupied mainly Lichen Woodland or Tundra vegetation provinces (McAndrews et al. 1987; Roberts et al. 1987). The only two species identified at the early Palaeo-Indian culture Udora site in Southern Ontario were caribou (Rangifer tarandus) and Arctic fox (Alopex lagopus), both primarily tundra and lichen woodland species (Spiess and Storck 1990).

Bone does not survive well on Palaeo-Indian sites in eastern North America except in the south and, therefore, subsistence practices must be inferred from indirect evidence. The problem with drawing inferences from site locations alone is that such locations may simply represent the largest aggregates of people during one segment of their seasonal rounds, such as locations favourable for intercepting migrating caribou (Jackson 1990a). Sites once near the coast are likely under the Atlantic Ocean due to rising sea levels (Edwards and Emery 1977). Evidence of the association of Palaeo-Indian people with mastodon remains in the east is limited (Graham et al. 1981; Laub 1990) and often indirect (Fisher 1984; Garland and Cogwell 1985; Shipman et al. 1984). There is, however, a correlation in the concentrations of mastodon and mammoth remains and the distribution of fluted points, including a common northern boundary, which suggests the likelihood of megafauna hunting in the east given the demonstrable contemporaneity of some of these remains (Mason 1981: 98-99). Since most of the early excavations of mammoth and mastodon remains were not carried out by trained people, the evidence of an association with humans may well have been over-looked. The recent reinvestigation of a 1897 mastodon discovery in southwestern Wisconsin, for example, suggests that a fluted spear head was associated with the remains (Mason 1981: 101).

Bone preservation on the Plains and the Great Basin is relatively good thus permitting direct observations regarding subsistence practices. Most of these data pertain to `kill sites´ and can present a biased impression of the entire subsistence base. On the basis of such sites it has been suggested that the early Palaeo-Indian hunters (Clovis) were mammoth hunters while their descendants (Folsom) were bison hunters (Eiseley 1955). The proposition of single species specialization through time on the Plains appears to be too simplistic. Mammoth kills have particularly attracted the attention of both archaeologists and the public. Mammoth would certainly have been more available early in the period and particularly in the southwest where the contraction of water bodies would have tended to concentrate the herds. Most museum artist reconstructions of early Palaeo-Indian hunters attacking mammoths depict a direct confrontation. It has even been suggested that entire family groups of mammoths were killed during such envisioned frontal assaults (Saunders 1980). A less dramatic but safer procedure would be for individual animals to be `gut-wounded´ from ambush and then trailed until they became incapacitated by their wounds; a common technique practiced by native African elephant hunters (Johnson, Kawano, and Ekker 1980). The location of Palaeo-Indian mammoth kill sites in once aqueous environments supports the gut wounding hypothesis as wounded animals would eventually seek out water. This could also account for the `multiple kills´ at sites that were once water holes and where sequential kills accumulated rather than representing single mass killings of herds. There is evidence of a mired mammoth (articulated foot elements) at the pond-bog, kill-butchering site of Lange/Ferguson in South Dakota (Hannus 1989). At the Colby site in Wyoming, two bone caches, one used and the other not, contained portions of six mammoths, five of them immature. Each cache would have represented several hundred pounds of meat (Frison 1978). This suggests, contrary to Kelley and Todd (1988: 238-239), that storage of seasonally abundant resources was practiced although a ceremonial function of these caches has also been suggested (Frison 1978: 109).

The population increase of bison around 11,000 BP correlates with the expansion of the short-grass prairie and the extinction of competitors such as mammoth, horse, and camel (Guthrie 1980). It is in late Palaeo-Indian times that bison herds, particularly females and their calves, were driven into natural impoundments such as arroyos or dunes or over cliffs (Frison 1980). Such herd hunting techniques would permit the storage of large winter stocks of meat and fat.

Blood residues preserved on stone tools (Loy 1987) have provided direct evidence of animals that had been killed and butchered. Such residues from the East Wenatchee site in central Washington State included human, bison, cervid (caribou, moose, elk, deer), and rabbit (Gramly 1991). As there was no sera for sloth, camel, or mastodon, the presence of these genera could not be determined. The residues came from knives and a graver. With reference to the human blood, any archaeologist who has experimented with the manufacturing and use of stone tools knows that self-inflicted wounds are an all too common occurrence.

Settlement patterns:

Allowing for a settlement pattern sampling bias where sites in the west are mainly kill-butchering sites while those in the east are seasonal residential sites associated with stone tool manufacturing, there are two aspects of settlement patterns to be considered. First, there is the manner in which people seasonally distributed themselves across the landscape and, second, there is the patterning of the actual dwellings and associated features encountered on sites. The changing environments of the Late Pleistocene required an exceptional degree of flexibility in subsistence practices and, thus, settlement strategies. While the majority of Palaeo-Indian sites relate to the seasonal rounds of territorial bands, "...it is likely that different sets of land-use patterns were involved during the process of colonization and, later, during the process of `settling-in´" (Storck and Von Bitter 1989: 187). Initial colonization was probably a combination of free-wandering (Beardsley et al. 1956) and incremental expansion determined by local circumstances rather than being one or the other. Given the unique nature of Late Pleistocene environments it should not be surprising that human adaptation to that environment(s) would also be "... unique or at least unusual in the human record" (Storck and Von Bitter 1989: 189).

The relationship of archaeological sites to Late Pleistocene landforms, such as the ancient beaches of glacial lakes, can be used as a geological dating method (Storck 1982). As has been stressed, environmental conditions at this time period were quite different from the present in terms of climate, hydrology, plant and animal communities and landforms. Subsequent erosional-depositional cycles, particularly on the Plains and in northwestern North America, have modified landforms and, in the process, destroyed an unknown number of early archaeological sites. In the east, the submergence of a large portion of the Atlantic coastal plain by the rising sea levels at the end of the Pleistocene and early Holocene has undoubtedly inundated many sites. The early Palaeo-Indian Bull Brook site in Massachusetts, for example, was located between 10 and 15 km from the Atlantic (Gramly and Funk 1990: 15) at the time of occupation and it would be surprising if coastal resources had not been included in the seasonal rounds. Evidence indicates Palaeo-Indian people occupied every habitable area of North America although the penetration west of the Rocky Mountains appears to have been both weak and late. While the density of Palaeo-Indian archaeological sites is greatest east of the Mississippi River, the more severe erosional-depositional cycles in the west and northwest have undoubtedly masked an appreciation of the original settlement patterns. Another difficulty in interpreting Palaeo-Indian settlement patterns is the necessity to reconstruct the ancient landscapes in order to have an appreciation of the quite different world within which the Palaeo-Indian people lived. This is well illustrated in Plate 3 of the Historical Atlas of Canada, Volume I (Roberts and McAndrews: 1987) which illustrates Palaeo-Indian settlement patterns and their relationship to stone quarry sources in what is now the western and central portions of Southern Ontario. Fluctuations in the water levels of the ancestral Great Lakes have resulted in sites adjacent to what is now Lake Huron being isolated some distance back from the present lake while sites once along the shores of Lake Erie and Lake Ontario are now under water. Indeed, at this time, the City of Ottawa was beneath the waters of an intrusion of the Atlantic Ocean called the Champlain Sea that was home to baleen whales, beluga, harbour porpoise, seals, marine fish like capelin and marine shellfish (Harington 1978: 16-20). Evidence suggests that at this time one or two bands occupied the southern margins of glacial Lake Algonquin from spring to fall and then shifted 185 km to the southwest for the winter (Roosa 1977; Storck 1979; 1982). Small hunt camps, such as Sandy Ridge and Halstead, located adjacent to Rice Lake, contain predominantly Fossil Hill chert obtainable 160 km to the northwest suggesting the existence of an eastern band of Palaeo-Indian people (Jackson 1990a). Band size has been inferred to have been between 45 and 75 people (Roosa 1977a). Seasonal band movements probably were made in conjunction with caribou migrations to northern calving grounds and then to southern wintering ranges. In the process of this annual cycle, the chert deposits at Fossil Hill, near present Georgian Bay, were exploited. An understanding of the southern settlement distribution is constrained by the fact that sites along the Lake Erie and Lake Ontario shores are now underwater. Interior sites removed from the major glacial lake shorelines tend to be situated in areas with water, on knolls and ridges with broad vistas, and in a topography that favoured opportunities to ambush game. Such sites are now situated on well-drained soils adjacent to mucklands (Jackson and McKillop 1987). The importance of topography to Palaeo-Indian culture settlement patterns for game channelling, ambush, and vistas cannot be overemphasized. A number of presumably cold weather Palaeo-Indian sites were also oriented for protection from wind while gaining maximum exposure to the sun. At the Debert site in Nova Scotia, highlands to the north and, to a lesser extent, the west, provided some protection while permitting a broad view of the landscape to the south and east, a situation that would favour late fall caribou interception (MacDonald 1968: 119). In contrast, the 19 cultural debris concentrations at the Fisher site, strung along the shore of glacial Lake Algonquin for more than 55 acres, suggest the use of lakeshore topography for observation and interception (Storck 1984).

In eastern North America, Palaeo-Indian sites have been classified as quarry-workshop sites, habitation sites, kill-butchering sites, burial or cache sites, and stray point sites (Gramly and Funk 1990). Quarry-workshop sites, such as the West Athens Hill site in New York (Ritchie and Funk 1973), are characterized by a dominance of chipping detritus and evidence of preform manufacture whereas habitation sites produce a wider range of tool types, evidence of tool resharpening, and only minor evidence of primary tool production. Features can also be anticipated at the latter site type. All of these site types, except the stray points category, are generally found in close proximity to one another. There is evidence that the West Athens Hills site also functioned as a look-out hunt camp. Even killing-butchering stations, such as those at the Vail site in Maine, are located only a short distance upwind from the habitation site (Figure 5). Rather than site settlement types the total variety of site function within a region of utilization at a single point in time would probably represent a more appropriate, albeit idealistic, classification system. It has been observed that the location of the habitation site was almost certainly a secondary consideration relative to the positioning of the interception sites (Gramly and Funk 1990). It was a combination of factors; game behaviour, topography relative to stalking and ambushing potential, availability of water, chert and other resources, prevailing winds, proximity to alternative or later seasonal resources, supernatural considerations, and very likely other factors, which determined occupation of a certain region at a particular time. Probably for these reasons, "Predicting the locations of fluted point Paleoindian encampments is more an art than a science" (Ibid: 12). Added to the complications of reconstructing the Pleistocene physical surroundings in order to see through Palaeo-Indians eyes, are the difficulties of determining whether site size was a product of length of occupation, multiple seasonal use, or group size.

In eastern Canada and adjacent areas to the south, it has been suggested that caribou were the major prey animal (MacDonald 1968). It will be appreciated that the reconstruction of topography and the nature of the plant and animal communities of the period (Karrow and Warner 1990), including inferences relating to ancient caribou herd movements, are extremely complex matters. Despite limited recovery of caribou remains (Fitting, DeVisscher, and Wahla 1966; Funk et al 1969; Storck 1988) the likely importance of caribou receives support from settlement pattern characteristics. Viewed from the perspective of occupation in an open spruce-tundra setting, certain site locations would favour the interception of migrating caribou herds. At the Vail site in Maine (Gramly 1982; Gramly and Funk 1990) the habitation site and what are interpreted as contemporary kill sites, are located on opposite sides of the river, a situation suggesting the probable use of watercraft to spear animals at water crossings. Watercraft were of vital importance to the success of historically documented caribou hunters, such as the Inuit and the Chipewyans (Jenness 1932). The S-bend in the steep-sided river valley at the Vail site would have assisted in detecting and ambushing herd animals such as caribou. Not only did the kill sites contain complete spearheads but also tip fragments that, in a number of instances, were fitted to the discarded base fragments found at the habitation site some 200 m away (Figure 5). Similarly, Palaeo-Indian site locations along the strandline of glacial Lake Algonquin (Storck 1982) appear to be situated at vantage points for sighting and ambushing caribou herds. The location of sites on islands also indicates the use of watercraft as resources on such locations were likely only available during seasons of open water. Major waterways appear to have been important areas of exploitation and travel (Ritchie 1965) and particularly at the juncture of streams with rivers (Gardner 1983). Given the surface water conditions in Late Pleistocene times, it would be difficult to conceive how people could have survived without some form of watercraft. Unfortunately there is very little chance of evidence for watercraft surviving in the archaeological record and yet the likely existence of perishable items, such as watercraft, toboggans, and snowshoes, must have been critical factors in Palaeo-Indian mobility.

On the Plains and Foothills of Canada there is limited evidence of Palaeo-Indian culture except in Alberta and adjacent portions of British Columbia (Fladmark 1981). Occupation of the Sibbald Creek site (Gryba 1983) in the Foothills of Alberta begins with Palaeo-Indian culture and continues virtually unbroken to the time of European contact. Such continuity of occupation on the protected south side of a high knoll overlooking a broad meadow suggests that the site function had not changed significantly over many thousands of years. Palaeo-Indians also occupied the Peace River region of British Columbia (Fladmark 1982; 1986). The stratified Charlie Lake Cave site was situated at a probable bison water crossing. To the north, in the Yukon and Alaska, Palaeo-Indian culture sites tend to be concentrated along the Yukon River drainage and northward (Clark 1991: Figs. 1 and 2). A number of these sites are associated with siliceous deposits and contain abundant evidence of stone tool manufacturing (Bowers 1982; Clark and Clark 1983; Dixon 1975). The obsidian of the Batza Téna site in central Alaska, which was exploited by Palaeo-Indian culture people, was subsequently visited by cultures right up to the time when stone tools were replaced with European introduced substitutes (Clark and Clark 1993). In fact, in the local Koyukon Athapaskan language Batza Téna means `obsidian trail´.

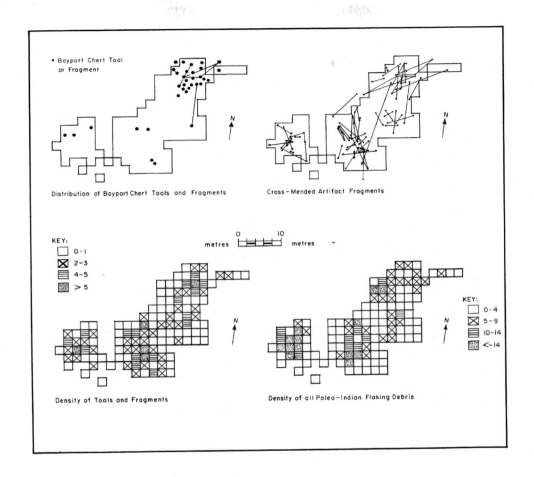

FIGURE 4: THEDFORD II SITE FLOOR PLANS Excavation floor plans from this Palaeo-Indian site in Southern Ontario consider four different aspects of the distribution of cultural debris: the occurrence of Bayport chert from the Saginaw Bay area of adjacent Michigan; the original locations of artifact fragments subsequently glued together; the concentration of artifacts; and the concentration of chipping detritus. These data not only suggest the existence of three distinct living floors and a tertiary activity area but also indicate that the people responsible for the northernmost living floor were apparently in closer contact with people in Michigan than the other occupants of the site. Such detailed recording in the field is the only way, in most instances, that the flimsy dwellings of the highly mobile Palaeo-Indian families will be recognized in the archaeological record often disturbed, as in this case, by ploughing. (Adapted from Deller and Ellis 1992: Figs.73, 74, 76, and 83. Drawing by Mr. David W. Laverie.)

The tracing of siliceous materials recovered from archaeological sites to their geological deposits by petrographic and chemical means in eastern North America (Deller and Ellis 1992a) suggests that the northern caribou hunting bands of the Lichen Woodland vegetation province were more mobile than their cousins in the deciduous forests to the south. Habitation site distances from quarry sources are as follows: the Crowfield site in Southern Ontario - 100 to 200 km; the Debert site in Nova Scotia 50 to 100 km; and the Parkhill site in Michigan - 160 km. With few exceptions, the more southerly sites exhibit more localized exploitation of lithic resources (Ellis 1989: Table 6.1; Meltzer 1988: Table IV; 1989: Table 2.2). Distance of sites from quarry sources in the Great Lakes region decreases through time with the earliest Palaeo-Indian bands exploiting more distant quarries (Wortner and Ellis 1993: 9). Even though the nearby Onondaga and Collingwood cherts of the Niagara Escarpment dominated at the early Palaeo-Indian Gainey site in Michigan, the abundance of Mercer chert from 380 km to the southeast suggests that at least certain Palaeo-Indian culture bands utilized territorial ranges in excess of the 5,000 to 6,000 square kilometres maximum recorded ethnographically (Deller 1989: Table 8.4; Ellis 1989: 161). As the Gainey site is an early Palaeo-Indian site, this occurrence of exotic cherts could simply reflect an initial colonization from the south. In contrast, the chipped stone from the Shoop site in Pennsylvania was predominantly Onondaga chert whose deposits are situated more than 300 km to the north (Cox 1986; Witthoft 1952). The combination of exotic cherts in the cache feature of the Lamb site in New York (Gramly and Funk 1990: 8; Gramly 1988) and its association with two living floors characterized by poor quality chert even though excellent bedrock chert deposits existed only a short distance to the north, has been interpreted as evidence of an initial colonizing population unfamiliar with the lithic resources of the region.

On the Plains, considerable mobility can be inferred for the Palaeo-Indian bands where exotic lithics were obtained from sources as far away as 300 km (Haynes 1982: 392). As has been noted a number of times, Palaeo-Indian settlement pattern strategy was keyed to high quality siliceous deposits as well as game availability (Clark and Clark 1975). There is also some suggestion that certain stone varieties were selected for aesthetic reasons (Haynes 1980; Dennis Stanford: Smithsonian Institution, personal communication). The predominant use of a particular variety of stone on most Palaeo-Indian sites may even represent an expression of territorialism whereby the distinctive stone acted as a kind of band badge of territorial identification (Ellis 1989). In both the east and the west, Palaeo-Indian culture concentrated on exploiting high quality cryptocrystallines, usually from one or two quarries, to produce their portable chipped stone tool kit (Goodyear 1989). Quartzites of variable quality were also exploited (Curran and Grimes 1989: 50-51). Contrary to Ellis (1989), many later cultural groups, such as Middle Maritime culture, elements of Late Great Lakes-St.Lawrence culture (Meadowood), and Late Plains culture (Besant), also specialized in the exploitation of specific distant lithic sources.

The dwellings of Palaeo-Indian people appear to have been simple structures of a size that would suggest single nuclear families. Although diagnostic artifacts were not recovered from the living floor excavated in the lowest level of Locality A of the Vermilion Lakes site in the foothills of Alberta (Fedje 1986), the five dates from the feature, averaging 10,626 BP, suggest a Palaeo-Indian culture authorship. The validity of the dates is supported by the presence of the remains of unusually large mountain sheep believed to be Late Pleistocene precursors of the present Ovis canadensis (Ibid: 94). The living floor, demarcated by a central hearth and lithic debris and charcoal concentrations, was roughly 3 m in diameter. At the Thedford II site in Ontario (Deller and Ellis 1992; Ellis 1989: 162) living floors were spaced between 5 m and 15 m apart and may even have been arranged in a circular pattern (Figure 4). At the Udora site, also in Ontario, 2 m to 6 m diameter concentrations of chipping detritus and artifacts, spaced

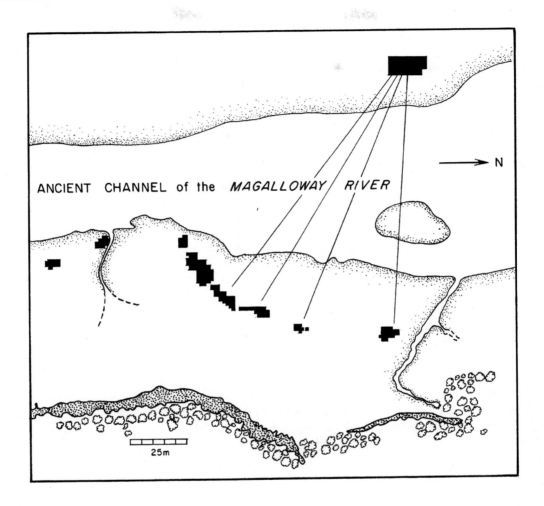

ANCIENT CHANNEL of the *MAGALLOWAY RIVER*

→ N

25m

FIGURE 5: VAIL SITE SETTLEMENT PATTERNS The Figure illustrates the relationship between the habitation site and a `kill site´ at the Vail site in northern Maine just south of the Québec border. The habitation area occupies the west bank of the Magalloway River while the kill site is on the opposite bank. Connecting lines indicate where spear tip fragments from the kill site have been fitted onto spear base fragments from the habitation site 175 to 200 m away. When weapon tips were broken during the killing of game, the base portion of the stone spear head would be brought back to camp in the spear shaft where it would be detached and replaced with a new stone tip. The Vail site situation is a good example of why archaeologists should ideally examine a large area as an exploitation region within which a number of different activities may have taken place rather than simply focusing on one activity such as habitation settlement. (Adapted from Gramly 1984: Fig.4. Drawing by Mr. David Laverie).

3 m apart, suggested a series of individual living floors (Storck 1988). The 6m by 8m living floor at the Adkins site in northwestern Maine (Gramly 1988; Gramly and Funk 1990: 14) has been estimated to house from 6 to 8 adults with a 1.5 m by 2 m debris-free area likely reserved for sleeping. Similarly, an oval structure 7.3 m by 3 m in Virginia raises the possibility of multi-family dwellings (Gardner 1977). At sites such as Debert in Nova Scotia (MacDonald 1968), it is believed that the living floors represent single occupations by large number of families rather than being the product of sequential seasonal occupations. This proposal finds support in both the lack of overlap between living floors and the number of mended specimens connecting different living floors (Grimes et al 1984; Speiss 1984). Multiple seasonal occupations of such sites, however, cannot be ruled out on the basis of the present settlement pattern evidence, particularly if there was a cultural inclination not to reoccupy former living floors. Evidence from the Vail site in Maine indicates that at least one area was occupied at least twelve different times by two family groups (Gramly 1985). Here living floors ranged from 3 m to 4 m in diameter. Such living floors tend to be similar to one another, consisting of either general camp refuse or stone tool reduction debris. The recovery of numerous discarded spear base fragments indicates the repair of weapons, an activity most likely performed at the base camp.

In the more northern regions of eastern North America the proposal that sites represent single large aggregations of people rather than multiple, seasonal occupations, implies the coalescence of the entire band or even a number of bands. Such large gatherings are historically documented to have taken place where pounds had been constructed to entrap and snare caribou. The co-operative effort required to exploit herd animals may explain the existence of certain large sites both on the Plains and in the northern woodlands of the east. While the general absence of storage pits on these sites suggests that winter storage of food was unimportant (Ellis 1989:160) or impractical given the unstable Late Pleistocene environment, caches of frozen caribou at a site such as Debert would leave no archaeological trace. In fact, most ethnographically recorded food storage methods in northern Canada would leave little or no archaeological record. As a rule, archaeological evidence of food storage is scarce throughout the archaeological record of Canada until relatively late times. There is also the evidence of the use of food caches at Palaeo-Indian sites such as Vail and Adkins in Maine (Gramly 1982: 61 - 62; 1988: Fig.11; Gramly and Funk 1990: 14) and at the Colby site in Wyoming (Frison 1976).

Cosmology:

As used in this work, cosmology refers to features and objects, whether a monument or a motif on an artifact, which are believed to relate to a past people's effort to place themselves in an advantageous position relative to a mysterious and powerful universe. The word is used in preference to the term `religion´ as it better accommodates an animistic and individualistic system of beliefs. Beliefs of a universe controlled by the omnipresence spirit power in animals, plants, rocks, the sky, the water, etc., and of which humans were an integral part, appear to be universally held by hunting populations. Individual spirit powers can be good or evil or, more often, indifferent to humans. It was of utmost importance, however, for people to acquire power in order to prosper in a world permeated with spirit power. Food acquisition, health, weather, and any other factor bearing on human existence, involved spirit forces which had to be contended with using a combination of personal spirit power, adherence to taboos, offerings,

BLACK AND WHITE PLATE IV: ARTIFACTS FROM A LATE PALAEO-INDIAN CEREMONIAL FEATURE ENCOUNTERED AT THE CROWFIELD SITE, SOUTHERN ONTARIO The feature in question was a pit containing a mass of chipped stone objects, most shattered by heat. Interpreted by the excavators as a cremation burial from which all bone somehow disappeared, it is viewed here as either a ceremonial votive offering or a burial that once contained uncremated individual(s) whose remains were subsequently dissolved by acid soils and the passage of time. Late style fluted spear points are in the upper row with another two spear points and a backed knife in the middle row and a biface sample, two scrapers and a graver in the lower row. (Collection loaned to the Archaeological Suvey of Canada, Canadian Museum of Civilization for photography and replication by Dr. Chris Ellis, Department of Anthropology, University of Western Ontario, London, Ontario)

shaman assistance, and, most important, prayer. It is likely that these historically documented views of hunting people around the world existed among people from earliest times.

Very few examples of Palaeo-Indian cosmology have been discovered in North America. An exceptional example from Canada is a pit feature at the Crowfield site in Southern Ontario (Deller and Ellis 1984). The feature consisted of a 1.5 m diameter pit containing approximately 4,500 heat fractured portions of more than 200 chert implements as well as some tools that had not been exposed to fire. Fluted points, gravers, scrapers, knives, and drills were included in the cache (Black and White Plate IV) and had been manufactured from three different varieties of Southern Ontario cherts. The style of the fluted spear points indicate that the feature dates toward the end of the Palaeo-Indian culture. Although believed by the excavators to represent the remains of a cremation, the total absence of carbonized human remains makes this interpretation suspect. There is no doubt, however, that the feature reflects some significant ceremonial act. If it had been associated with uncremated bodies, acid soils would have long ago destroyed all traces of the remains. The possibility of the feature being a votive offering required by some unknown event cannot be excluded.

Burial and/or cache sites are known from Montana, Idaho, Colorado, Washington, and New York. The Anzick site in Montana (Lahren and Bonnichsen 1974) contained two human subadults who were placed in a small rockshelter, covered with red ochre, and richly provided with grave offerings. Unfortunately the entire site was destroyed by heavy equipment during the construction activity that resulted in its discovery. Grave offerings numbered over 100 items of which the distinctive spear heads, chipped stone knives, and bone foreshafts were the most common finished tools. There is evidence that the bone foreshafts were `killed´ or purposefully broken (Robson Bonnichsen: Oregon State University, personal communication), a not uncommon animistic practice intended to release the spirit of the tool in order for it to accompany the spirit of the dead person. The collagen portion of a bone sample from this site was dated by the radiocarbon accelerator mass spectrometry technique to 10,600 +/- 300 BP (Taylor et al. 1985). The site in Idaho, which was exposed by ploughing, produced of a range of artifacts stained with red ochre, including biface knives, projectile points, two scrapers, and backed knives and a spokeshave and a flake knife (Butler 1963). A site in Colorado contained of a cache of a dozen spear heads, all manufactured from Texas chert obtained 500 km to the southeast (Dennis Stanford: Smithsonian Institution, personal communication). The Richey Clovis Cache in the East Wenatchee site in central Washington consisted of a cache that had been placed in a 1.1 m by 1.5 m shallow pit 50 cm beneath the surface (Gramly: 1993). Exclusive of flakes and bone fragments, the cache contained 14 projectile points and fluted knives, 8 biface knives, 7 point preforms used secondarily as knives, 4 side scrapers, 3 linear flakes, 3 chipped adzes, 2 gravers, 2 flake knives, a large blank, and 14 bone rods. The rods, manufactured from elephant limb bones, averaged 25 cm in length and had both ends bevelled by grinding. It has been speculated that the rods constituted 7 paired items that, when lashed together, made two rods 1.4 m in length. Such rods could have been attached to the wooden runners of a hand-pulled sled. It is further speculated that the sled was 1.5 m long, 1.0 m wide and 25 cm high (Gramly 1993: Fig.C, 59). The survival of the bone items and absence of human remains clearly indicates the feature was not a burial. Objects were apparently placed in an open pit that was then provided with a perishable covering since there is evidence that wolverines entered the pit and chewed on the bone shafts. While it has been proposed that this feature represented a cache that was not retrieved by its owners, it is difficult to accept that all the people who knew of the cache would have perished in some catastrophe or that subsequent visitors to the site would not have retrieved its contents. It is possible that this feature was some form of votive offering required by an unknown ceremonial circumstance. To the east, at the single component early Palaeo-Indian Lamb site in western New York State (Gramly and Funk 1990), a plough disturbed cache of large fluted spearheads, fluted knives, and bifacial preforms, was recorded. These pristine items were manufactured of exotic cherts obtained from Ohio, Indiana, Kentucky, and even North Dakota 1,800 km to the west. It has been speculated that the items represent grave offerings placed on the surface or in a shallow grave.

Several other fragments of evidence are suggestive of activities relating to cosmology. It has been speculated (Frison 1978: 109) that one of the mammoth bone caches at the Colby site in Wyoming may have represented some form of ceremonial structure. This inference is based on the fact that the cache was not opened and that a mammoth skull had been placed on top of the bone pile. It has also been speculated that the emphasis upon colourful stone for projectile points in Palaeo-Indian culture relates to prey-hunter ritual relationships (Haynes 1982: 387). Bison bones painted with red ochre from the Shearman site in Wyoming (Frison and Stanford 1982) must have symbolized some unknown ritual activity. There is the unique occurrence of a quartzite cobble with a ladder-design petroglyph etched into it that was recorded at the West Athens Hill site in New York State (Ritchie and Funk 1973). It has been suggested that such geometric `pebble art´ had genealogical meaning and had their origins in the Upper Palaeolithic of northern Europe and Asia (Carpenter 1988: 795). It will be recalled that Palaeo-Indian culture appears to have been derived from an Upper Palaeolithic technological tradition. Whether the incised bone plaques from the late Palaeo-Indian Lindenmeier site in Colorado (Wilmsen and Roberts 1978: Fig.128b) were of ritual significance or simply gaming tokens is unknown. The same observation pertains to the incised bone fragments from the same site and the late Palaeo-Indian occupation of the Agate Basin site in Wyoming (Frison and Stanford 1982: Fig.2.114). Historic documentation suggests that such simple motifs are often symbolic and can represent abstract portrayals of such things as ancestor figures (Carpenter 1986). Pigments, such as pyrolusite, graphite, limonite, hematite and magnetite, while not common, are widespread and possibly had symbolic powers that contributed to ritualistic requirements (Gramly 1990: 37). Finally, there are the miniature points from the Fisher site that had been manufactured from the channel flakes of normal sized spear heads (Storck 1994). Such points are widespread, occurring from the Rocky Mountains to the Atlantic coast, and may have functioned as hunting amulets. Miniature copies of weapons are rare within the archaeological record of Canada, the only other occurrence known to the author being in Middle and Late Palaeo-Eskimo culture.

Palaeo-Indian people appear to have believed that all things, animate (animal and plant), inanimate (rock and artifacts) as well as natural phenomena (wind and water), possessed spirits and, thus, introduced to the Western Hemisphere the animistic belief system that characterized all of the native peoples of Canada at the time of European contact. They also introduced the tradition of placing red ochre with the deceased. A unique cosmological trait was the practice of making votive offerings of large numbers of stone and bone tools, sometimes covered with red ochre.

External relationships:

Relationships with Northwestern Palaeo-Arctic culture are considered in chapters 1 and 3. As this category relates to relationships between different contemporary cultural groups it is not pertinent to Palaeo-Indian culture that is regarded as the first unequivocal evidence of human occupation in the Western Hemisphere exclusive of Beringia. Some archaeologists will take exception to this stance but, "Whatever the ultimate judgement on pre-Clovis may be, Clovis people became the first American culture to become widespread and to achieve an archaeological visibility" (Agenbroad 1988: 72).

Human biology:

Human dental and skull morphology and genetic characteristics, and the evidence of historical linguistics and archaeology have been used to support the proposal of three major migrations to the Western Hemisphere (Greenberg et al. 1986). The populating of the Western Hemisphere was likely a more complex matter (see the **Human biology** section in Chapter 3) and the three migration hypothesis has increasingly come under attack (e.g. Crawford 1992). Now mitochondrial DNA (deoxyribose nucleic acid) variation studies suggest that the first migration, which is equated with early Palaeo-Indian culture, is represented in present populations by as few as four primary lineages (Schurr et al. 1990). Unlike nuclear DNA, which represents the combined male and female genetic material, mitochondrial DNA is only inherited from the female so any changes to this DNA must be the product of random mutations. As a rapid rate of evolutionary change to mitochondrial DNA, resulting in a range of genetic differentiation, permits discrimination between closely related human populations, radiating female lineages can be traced. Comparison of the Pima of the southwestern United States, the Maya of Central America, and the Ticuna of South America, indicated a common genetic female ancestry for four basic lineages. "Amerindian individuals with the four mt DNA haplotypes have interbred since the ancestral Paleo-Indian population became isolated in the New World some 12,000-20,000 years ago, yet after over roughly 500-1,000 generations this population still maintains all four haplotypes at virtually complete linkage disequilibrium" (Ibid: 619). It is also suggested, relative to Siberian and Amerindian populations, that as the mitochondrial DNA variation data base increases it may be possible to determine if multiple or single migrations were involved. At this early stage in mitochondrial DNA research there is considerable argument as to whether or not mitochondrial DNA mutates at a steady rate and can, therefore, be treated like a chronological clock (Shreeve 1990).

It does not appear that the remains of the two subadult humans from the Anzick site in Montana (Lahren and Bonnichsen 1974) have been studied by physical anthropologists. The only other pertinent human remains are the relatively uninformative finger bone and skull fragment from the 12,500 BP level of the Meadowcroft Rockshelter site in Pennsylvania (Adovasio et al. 1988). The appearance and general health of these first people was probably similar to that of their immediate descendants.

Inferences on society:

Archaeological evidence permits some tentative inferences regarding the social organization of past societies. Given the nature of archaeological information, however, such glimpses of society are incomplete and speculative. Settlement pattern evidence suggests that the societies making up Palaeo-

Indian culture were based upon the nuclear family, a number of which would have coalesced into a band for at least a portion of the year. Such band concentrations appear to have been larger where a co-operative effort was required to exploit herd animals such as bison and caribou. Most of the large sites in the northern region of eastern North America, believed to be caribou procurement stations, appear to represent occupations by a regional band. A degree of band territoriality may even be reflected in the preponderant use of regional cherts as a band social marker (Ellis 1989: 154). At least two bands appear to have exploited southwestern Southern Ontario (Roberts and McAndrews 1987). Similarly, in New York State the different geographical distributions of exotic cherts, such as Upper Mercer and other Ohio cherts, Normanskill from the Hudson Valley, and Pennsylvania jasper, has led to the speculation that three bands occupied the State (Gramly 1988a: 269-270) although whether bands or groupings of blood related regional bands are involved is not known. It is speculated that labour intensive seasonal activities involving the construction of caribou impoundment traps would have required some form of central authority. Such authority, albeit temporary, would have been necessary to achieve the co-operation of everyone in order to insure the winter supplies of meat, fat, hides, and other animal products. The specific characteristics of social organization would, of course, vary with circumstances such as the game being sought. It can be anticipated that when a mammoth was killed the entire band and probably other bands within communication range would congregate at the kill. Even so, many such mammoth kills were only partially used (Haynes 1980) suggesting the human populations were too small to totally process the meat before putrification led to abandonment of the carcass.

With reference to such societies it has been suggested that the women were "... the primary conduit of interband exchange" (Snow 1980: 141) as individual bands were likely exogamous. Thus, marriages had to be contracted between bands rather than within a single band. Stone scrapers, for example, are inferred to be a tool used by women and the high frequency of scrapers manufactured from exotic chert sources at the Thedford II site in Ontario has been interpreted as evidence of wives, along with their personal tool kits, joining their husbands' band (Deller 1989: 218). On the other hand, projectile points, believed to be used by men, also were frequently manufactured from non-local cherts but in this instance they have been interpreted as a medium of exchange between bands (Snow 1980; Hayden 1982). There is obviously a long way to go before such social inferences can be demonstrated. Periodic gatherings of related bands likely account for some of the larger archaeological sites such as Bull Brook in Massachusetts where an aggregation of as many as 225 people has been proposed (Snow 1980: 146). Such band gatherings can be regarded as tribes that represent "...the greatest extension of population throughout which there is sufficient intermarriage to maintain many-sided social communication" (Helm 1968: 118). Within such a network of neighbouring territorial bands, interrelated by female marital bonds, trade items might better be regarded as evidence of gift exchange rather than economics. Female mobility would tend to maintain a significant degree of cultural homogeneity over a large area as was the case with the historically documented northern Algonquian-speakers of the Canadian Shield (Wright 1981). In sum, there appears to be general agreement that these people were organized into bands composed of a relatively small number of nuclear families that interrelated with neighbouring bands for the purpose of acquiring wives and, on occasion, carrying out large cooperative hunting exercises. Intra-band relationships would also act as a form of life insurance involving mutual support, such as when the fall hunt failed for one band it could rely on help from blood-related neighbouring bands. In addition to adult female mobility between bands, it can be suspected that a high value was placed on individualism thus permitting considerable mobility of individuals and families between bands as well.

Limitations in the evidence:

Archaeological evidence is always incomplete. Given this constraint, the evidence upon which the Palaeo-Indian culture is based is surprisingly good considering the effects of Late Pleistocene environmental change and the passage of time. Undoubtedly this happy circumstance has arisen from an archaeological interest in `Early Man´ studies. The limited remains from most Palaeo-Indian camp sites have tended to discourage systematic excavation thus restricting investigation to major kill or habitation sites. Most of the excavated evidence on Palaeo-Indian culture comes from eastern Canada, Southern Ontario in particular. Increasing attention to the Foothill region along the eastern flank of the Rocky Mountains, however, will very likely correct this imbalance. Past field and laboratory methods have been found wanting as has the lack of "...a standardized system of terminology..." (Gramly and Funk 1990: 22). Certainly the absence of bone preservation in many areas of North America has restricted information on both the technological and subsistence facets of the culture. A major gap in archaeological knowledge pertains to the origin and spread of Palaeo-Indian culture. If the fluted spear point is a Western Hemisphere innovation we must know where and when it was developed in order to trace its diffusion and/or spread by Palaeo-Indian colonizers. The relationship of Palaeo-Indian culture in Beringia to the contemporaneous Northwestern Palaeo-Arctic culture must be clarified. And on origins, the whole troublesome issue of the initial occupation of the Western Hemisphere by either pre-Palaeo-Indian cultures or Palaeo-Indian culture people is still a long way from being resolved to everyone's satisfaction. The cultural mechanisms underlying the rapid spread of Palaeo-Indian culture, resulting in a relatively homogeneous cultural base across much of North America, require continuing investigation as do the processes leading to the different regional developments from the shared ancestral base. The factors involved in these continent-wide changes and the rapidity with which they took place are still poorly understood. A serious limitation is the lack of evidence relating to human biology, particularly for the early Palaeo-Indian culture populations. Such evidence would permit physical anthropologists to glean vital population and racial information. By 8,000 BC, the process of cultural differentiation across North America permits the identification of a number of descendant cultures that, with the exception of Northwestern Palaeo-Arctic culture, are the topics of the Period III chapters. No subsequent culture in North America would ever approach the geographical distribution and cultural homogeneity of Palaeo-Indian culture. It was a unique culture that expedited a unique event, the occupation of virtually all of the habitable regions of an entire hemisphere.

CHAPTER 3 ————————————————————————————
NORTHWESTERN PALAEO-ARCTIC CULTURE

Précis:

The earliest securely dated archaeological sites in eastern and western Beringia involving Yukon/Alaska and eastern Siberia, respectively, fall between 10,000 and 14,000 BP (Morlan 1987). For 10,000 to 15,000 years prior to 14,000 BP a harsh Arctic environment existed and it has been suggested that Beringia may have been uninhabitable (Fladmark 1983: 22-23; Schweger et al. 1982: 439). Between 10,000 and 8,000 BC and probably earlier, an Asiatic-derived Upper Palaeolithic culture spread across much of the unglaciated territory of Beringia in Alaska and the Yukon. Originally called the American Palaeo-Arctic tradition (Anderson 1970) the name has been changed in this work to reflect more accurately the culture's geographical position in the Western Hemisphere. Technological similarities between Northwestern Palaeo-Arctic culture and Siberian assemblages have encouraged even more inclusive designations such as the Siberian-American Paleo-Arctic tradition (Dumond 1977) and the Beringian tradition (West 1981). Also in common use is the term Denali complex (West 1967). Possessing a technology characterized by specially prepared microblade cores, microblades, burins, and few bifacial tools, Northwestern Palaeo-Arctic culture may be regarded as the eastern expression of a circumpolar Eurasian technological tradition (Larsen 1968: 71-75). Its close relationship to Siberian cultures (Anderson 1980; Mochanov 1973; 1978; Powers 1973) should not be surprising. Beringia was more a part of Asia than America, representing an extension of the Asiatic steppe tundra to the glacial ice of the eastern Yukon and southern Alaska. Most excavated Northwestern Palaeo-Arctic sites are in Alaska where the earliest evidence dates around 10,500 BP although there are a number of earlier dates whose veracity is questioned (Anderson 1984). The earliest site in the northern Yukon to produce microblades and burins has been estimated to have a minimum date of 10,000 BP and, on the basis of a range of archaeological and environmental evidence, could be earlier than 13,500 BP (Cinq-Mars 1979; 1990). These age estimates pertain only to the Northwestern Palaeo-Arctic culture materials and not to potentially earlier evidence of human activity at the site (see Chapter 1).

Cultural continuity from Northwestern Palaeo-Arctic culture in Alaska has been traced to approximately 6,000 BC with events up to 4,600 BC being poorly understood (Anderson 1984). By the end of Period I (8,000 BC) microblade technology had spread south into southeastern Alaska (Ackerman 1980), down the Pacific coast, and possibly eastward along the Yukon coast. Given the diversity of environmental and physiographic zones occupied the descendants of the Northwestern Palaeo-Arctic culture appear to have possessed both maritime and interior adaptations (Fladmark 1983).

While Northwestern Palaeo-Arctic culture has been interpreted as the intrusion of a new Asiatic population (Greenberg et al. 1986) which absorbed an earlier Nenana-Chindadn population and its derivatives, it more likely reflects the diffusion of microblade technology into Beringia and its adoption by earlier people (Goddhardt 1990: 267). This scenario assumes that pre-microblade people actually settled eastern Beringia first and that the Upper Palaeolithic derived Palaeo-Indian and Northwestern Palaeo-Arctic cultures are not technologically and biologically related; an assumption that is far from being demonstrated. It is inappropriate to view the migratory behaviour of these small bands of northern hunters as similar to the mass movements of later Asiatic pastoralists. Their territorial movements were not only generational and, therefore, incremental (Morlan 1987: 267-268) but would have taken place within a far flung communication network (Morlan and Cinq-Mars 1982). Under such circumstances the spread of innovative technologies could potentially be quite rapid. Migration into Beringia was more likely a matter of `dribbles´ rather than `waves´ and would have involved many back and forth movements rather than single-minded eastward thrusts.

The chipped stone technologies of Palaeo-Indian culture and Northwestern Palaeo-Arctic culture appear to be essentially the same except for the microblade industry of the latter. Even this qualification is in doubt if the association of fluted points and microblades at the Palaeo-Indian Putu site in northern Alaska proves to be valid (Alexander 1987). Others, however, have argued that the two assemblages are technologically distinct (Dixon 1985: 54) and unrelated (Haynes 1982). Beyond the issue of the technological relationship between the Nenana complex and the related Chindadn complex (McKennan and Cook 1968) and Northwestern Palaeo-Arctic culture is the evidence that both cultures occasionally occupied the same sites (Powers and Hoffecker 1989) suggesting a similar way of life. Further, as will be outlined in the section on **Human biology**, genetically based discrete human cranial attributes can be interpreted as evidence of a biological relationship between these two early populations. Contrary to the currently popular view of two migrations involving a culture with a bifacial industry followed by a culture with a microblade industry, the evidence from the Diuktai culture in Siberia and the early evidence from the Bluefish Caves site in eastern Beringia does not support the technological distinctiveness of the two industries nor the chronological priority of one over the other. The recent discovery of microblades in a 11,700 BP level of the Swan Point site (Mason 1993) reinforces the above. In addition, bifacial tools and microblades are more often than not found together (Morlan 1987). Any assessment of the archaeological evidence from Beringia at this time must be cautious given its impoverished nature. The limited and equivocal nature of the evidence is undoubtedly responsible for current divergent archaeological opinion.

Cultural origins and descendants:

Pertinent to the debate of whether two discrete migrations are represented by the Northwestern Palaeo-Arctic culture and the Nenana-Chindadn complex with its Palaeo-Indian culture affiliations is the observation that when the microblade technology is excluded from the former the technologies of the two cultures are essentially the same (Powers and Hoffecker 1989; Powers 1990). The parallels consist of triangular and lanceolate projectile points, gravers, flake knives, and side and end scrapers. This

BLACK AND WHITE PLATE V:　AERIAL VIEW OF THE BLUEFISH CAVES SITE, YUKON TERRITORY　The deposits in the Bluefish Caves site are unique in northwestern North America in that they constitute 25,000 years of in place accumulation. In addition to the archaeological evidence is the sedimentological record, the palynological evidence left by tree pollens as well as actual plant fragments, and the palaeontological remains. All of these data sets are extremely relevant to the archaeological evidence. Allowing for some disturbance of the primary deposits, evidence of Northwestern Palaeo-Arctic culture falls between 10,000 and 13,500 BP (Cinq-Mars 1990: 20-21). Earlier but more controversial evidence occurs in lower levels. Whether one accepts or rejects these early dates for microblades and burins depend upon one's assessment of the extent of post-depositional disturbance at the site and the association of the stone tools with the Late Pleistocene environmental evidence. The two arrows in the lower left hand corner of the picture indicate the mouths of Cave 1 and Cave 2. (Reproduced from Cinq-Mars 1979: Fig.2 with the permission of Jacques Cinq-Mars, Archaeological Survey of Canada, Canadian Museum of Civilization)

---

technology can be traced back to pre-11,000 BP Siberian sites (Mochanov 1978; 1980; Powers and Hoffecker 1989: 284) and, with reference to the microblade industry in particular, to the Diuktai culture of Siberia (Anderson 1980; Dumond 1977; West 1981). For a succinct and critical evaluation of the archaeological evidence from Beringia see Morlan (1987).

According to the sequential migration hypothesis the initial movement of the Nenana-Chindadn complex ancestors into Beringia took place between 18,000 and 25,000 years ago (Powers 1990: 59) while the subsequent Northwestern Palaeo-Arctic culture is dated to 10,500 BP. As has been noted, however, this chronological sequence of events is at odds with the earlier evidence for microblade technology at the Bluefish Caves site in the Yukon (Cinq-Mars 1990; Cinq-Mars and Morlan n.d.) as well as new discoveries in Alaska (Mason 1993). There is also the issue of whether a microblade industry was associated with the 11,000 BP (Chindadn complex) Healy Lake site occupation (McKenna and Cook 1968) and the Palaeo-Indian Putu site in northern Alaska (Alexander 1987). It appears that a dual migration into Beringia of a Nenana-Chindadn complex (Palaeo-Indian culture) followed by the Northwestern Palaeo-Arctic culture is too facile. Incremental band population movements, spanning a considerable time period, resulting in a widely dispersed and sparse population that maintained close cultural and biological ties with one another is a more likely scenario. If their chipped stone tool kits varied seasonally, regionally, and/or temporally, all exacerbated by the whims of archaeological recovery, it may have been sufficient to create a false impression of a bifacial tool - microblade tool dichotomy.

The earliest stratum at the Dry Creek site in the central interior of Alaska, dated to 11,000 B.P, lacked evidence of a microblade technology while the overlying stratum, dated to approximately 10,500 BP, contained living floors both with and without microblades (Powers 1978; Powers, Gutherie, and Hoffecker n.d.;Powers and Hoffecker 1989). This whimsical occurrence of microblades is not uncommon in the archaeological record of northwestern North America raising doubts concerning the relative value of this single facet of technology in the reconstruction of culture history. At the Healy Lake site, in the same general vicinity as the Dry Creek site, there is controversy whether the microblades and burins from the earliest deposits, dated to 11,000 BP, were in their appropriate context or whether they were intrusive from later occupations (Dixon 1985; Dumond 1977). For some archaeologists the absence of microblades from some early components but their presence in subsequent occupations of the same site has suggested that two unrelated cultures are involved; an early culture characterized by the manufacture of bifacially flaked triangular projectile points and knives and a subsequent, unrelated culture that emphasized the use of microblades and burins. Given the sparseness of the data it might be suggested that the presence or absence of microblades could be fortuitous and related to different seasonal and functional activities at sites and not necessarily reflect the actual existence of two distinct cultures (Morlan 1987). Similarly, the relationship of fluted points in Alaska and the Yukon to a culture characterized by a bifacial tool technology or a culture characterized by a microblade technology or both is in a very confused state (Clark 1984). At the Putu site fluted projectile points were recovered with microblades (Alexander 1974; 1987) although the association has been questioned by many archaeologists. This rejection may have as much to do with the parsimony of the current bifacial/ microblade dichotomy as it does with depositional problems at the Putu site. Certainly the Diuktai culture of Siberia, dated as early as 18,000 BP and which all researchers accept as being ancestral to Northwestern Palaeo-Arctic culture, is characterized by both a bifacial industry and a microblade industry as well as a cobble tool industry (Morlan 1987: 279).

At the stratified Akmak site in northwestern Alaska (Anderson 1970; 1980) cultural continuities from Northwestern Palaeo-Arctic culture could be traced from approximately 10,000 BP to 8,000 BP. A similar continuity was noted at the Dry Creek site (Powers and Hoffecker 1989: Table 1) while in central Alaska such continuities have been traced to 5,000 BP (Dixon 1985). Not all researchers concede a technological relationship between the Nenana-Chindadn complex and the Northwestern Palaeo-Arctic culture (Haynes 1982: 395). Others see a common technological heritage (Clark 1984; West 1981). Cultural continuities lead to a coastal adapted culture (Northwestern Coastal culture) and an interior adapted culture (Early Northwest Interior culture) (Powers 1990: 60) in Period II. Relative to the coastal adaptation, the Palaeomarine tradition of southeastern Alaska, dated between 9,000 and 4,500 BP (Ackerman et al. 1979; Davis 1990: 197-198), with its wedge-shaped microblade cores, cobble tools, notched scrapers, gravers and burinated tools, most probably represents a coastal development out of Northwestern Palaeo-Arctic culture. The evidence for the gradual spread of microblade technology down the west coast from the north to the south is supported by radiocarbon dated sites (Carlson 1990: 67).

Technology:

Small, wedge-shaped microblade cores and their microblade byproducts are the most common items, aside from unmodified flakes, in the Northwestern Palaeo-Arctic tool kit. In lesser frequencies are linear flakes, burinated flakes, biface knives, lanceolate and triangular projectile points, cobble spall flakes, side and end scrapers, hammerstones, anvilstones, and some rough flaked items (Powers and Hoffecker 1989: 273). Unretouched flakes at Dry Creek II accounted for 90% of the 28,881 recovered items while microblades represented only 6% of the total. At the Bluefish Caves site (Cinq-Mars and Morlan n.d.; Jacques Cinq-Mars: Archaeological Survey of Canada, personal communication) microblades, wedge-shaped microblade cores and core rejuvenation tablets, burinated flakes, burin spalls and flakes are believed to date between 10,000 and 13,500 BP if not earlier. Some of the flakes from the upper deposits also appear to have been detached from bifacial tools (Cinq-Mars 1979).

The technological traits which Northwestern Palaeo-Arctic culture shared with the Diuktai culture of Siberia are as follows: a range of highly specific traits involving wedge-shaped microblade core production, reduction, and rejuvenation; microblade mid-sections with blunted backs for inserting into bone or wooden weapon shafts and handles; large core tools; the presence of the Levallois core technique; large ovate biface knives among other forms; burins with striking platform preparation involving unifacial retouch; and large linear flakes modified into scrapers and other tools (Anderson 1970; 1980: 237). Not all sites contain all of the preceding traits but the microblade wedge-shaped cores, microblades, burins, and generally some form of evidence of bifacially flaked tools are present in even small collections. Microblades functioned as lateral inserts in slotted antler, bone, or wood spear tips (Morlan 1987: 281) but the organic portion of such weapons tips rarely survive. Even given the precise procedures involved in the production of microblades, the erratic occurrence of the industry is such that it has restricted utility in culture historical reconstructions (Morlan and Cinq-Mars 1982: 373-374). At the NkTj-1 site in the Mackenzie Delta region of the Northwest Territories, for example, microblades and burins were recovered from the surface of a Late Pleistocene river channel. Such items could either pertain to Northwestern Palaeo-Arctic culture or subsequent cultures or both (LeBlanc 1991: 67-68). As was noted in the consideration of Palaeo-Indian culture technology the term `linear flake´is preferred to `blade´. While clear and definable production procedures pertain to the microblade industry, the same cannot be said for the so-called `blade´ technology. Linear flakes were produced in a more informal manner from a wide range of core varieties and, thus, are extremely difficult to categorize in a systematic fashion (Gotthardt 1990: 239).

SITE	BP DATE	LAB NO.	MATERIAL	REFERENCE
ALASKA				
Akmak	9,857+/-155	K1583	bone	Anderson 1984
Dry Creek II	9,340+/-195	S12329	charcoal	Powers & Hoffecker 1989
	10,690+/-250	SI1561	"	
Healy Lake	11,090+/-170	GX1341	bone	McKennan & Cook 1968
Mt. Hayes III	10,150+/-280	UGa572	soil charcoal	Morlan 1987
Putu	11,470+/-500	SI2382	charcoal	"
Swan Point	11,700 ?	?	?	Mason 1993
YUKON				
Bluefish Caves	12,210+/-210	RIDDL277	bone	Cinq-Mars pers.comm.
Engigstciak	9,400+/-230	RIDDL319	"	Cinq-Mars et al 1991
	9,870+/-180	RIDDL362	"	"
	9,770+/-180	RIDDL281	"	"

TABLE 1: EASTERN BERINGIAN RADIOCARBON DATES PERTINENT TO NORTHWESTERN PALAEO-ARCTIC CULTURE The RIDDL dates from the Bluefish Caves and Engigstciak sites are all AMS dates. RIDDL277 dated the collagen fraction of a butchered caribou bone recovered from a level containing microflakes. Situated near the Yukon coast (MacNeish 1956), the Engigstciak site dates were based on bison bone from a feature which only produced non-diagnostic chipped stone items. All of the Alaskan sites contained both bifaces and microblades although only microblades were found under the mammoth tusk in the lowest deposit of the Swan Point site. It should be noted that the single date for the Chindadn complex from the Healy Lake site was obtained on the apatite component of bone that has a history of producing erratic dates. The Palaeo-Indian Putu site, with its fluted points and microblades, is included in the Table to emphasize the possibility that Palaeo-Indian and Northwestern Palaeo-Arctic cultures are related.

Tables such as the foregoing were created for each culture considered in these volumes. When radiocarbon dates were 7,240 BP or younger they could be calibrated into calendar years (Klien et al. 1982). In the above instances, however, all of the dates are earlier than the earliest bristle cone pine tree ring dendrochronology dates that permitted the conversion of radiocarbon years into calendar years in the first place. In recognition of the many variables, physical and contextual, which can affect each radiocarbon date and the ongoing dating process that would make any table of dates incomplete in short order, it was decided, with the above exception, not to produce such tables but instead to provide references in each chapter to guide the interested reader to some of the literature containing the details on the pertinent radiocarbon dates.

It has been suggested that the bow and arrow was extant at this early period. Sandstone shaft abraders from the Akmak site (Anderson 1970: 51), dated to approximately 10,000 BP, have concavities adapted to 9 mm diameter shafts, a measurement that corresponds closely with the average diameter of ethnographic wooden arrow shafts (Wright 1994: Fig.4). Of course, it is possible that small diameter foreshafts were part of a composite spear weapon system. The lower levels of Trail Creek Caves on the Seward Peninsula (Larsen 1968), believed to date to 9,000 BP, produced both microblades and small antler weapon tips of arrow size with inset slots apparently cut to receive microblades. If the bow and arrow technology was introduced into the Western Hemisphere in Northwestern Palaeo-Arctic culture times then it was soon discarded not to be reintroduced from Asia until around 2,000 BC.

One of the arguments that has been used to support the proposition that an earlier biface technology was replaced by a microblade technology has been the absence of bifacial projectile points at some Northwestern Palaeo-Arctic culture sites. It is reasoned that such sites, using microblade inserts in bone or wooden weapon tips, would not have required the bifacially flaked stone weapon tips. There has been a tendency, however, to over-emphasize the temporal and cultural significance of microblades that persisted in an erratic fashion into the Christian era in areas of both Alaska and the Yukon and generally in association with bifacial tools.

Subsistence:

Although most Northwestern Palaeo-Arctic culture sites either lack or have poor bone preservation, their locations suggest that caribou was of paramount importance. As with all hunting peoples, however, all available food resources would have been exploited as indicated by the bones of small mammals and birds from the 11,000 BP Chindadn level of the Healy Lake site. At the Bluefish Caves site, with its excellent bone preservation, caribou was the dominant large animal. Horse, mammoth, elk, saiga antelope, and bison were also present but it is not always clear how many of these remains represented the results of human predation as opposed to the activities of other predators (Cinq-Mars 1979). An instance of excellent archaeological context at the Swan Point site in northern Alaska, where microblades were found directly under a mammoth tusk (Mason 1993: 24), would suggest that mammoth were being still hunted around 11,700 BP. As a rule the faunal remains from Northwestern Palaeo-Arctic sites pertain to extant Holocene species even if these animals no longer occupy the region today. The presence of certain species is also an indicator of the environment that once existed. The bison and elk remains from the Dry Creek site, for example, suggest the presence of remnant grasslands. A similar environmental situation must have existed during the occupation of the lowest level of the Engigstciak site near the Yukon coast (MacNeish 1956) where bison as well as caribou and muskox remains were recovered.

Settlement patterns:

The majority of Northwestern Palaeo-Arctic sites appear to be temporary hunt camps (Anderson 1984: 82) which functioned as look-outs and processing stations. A site like Akmak, on the other hand, was likely a major base camp where a wider range of activities took place (Anderson 1970). Bluefish

BLACK AND WHITE PLATE VI: ARTIFACTS FROM THE BLUEFISH CAVES SITE Estimated to date between 10,000 and 13,500 BP, microblades and microblade cores are shown in the upper row and a number of burin varieties in the bottom row. These two artifact categories are most typical of the stone tool kit of Northwestern Palaeo-Arctic culture. Bifacial trimming flakes from the site indicates that bifacially chipped tools were also part of the kit. All of the above items were manufactured from chert resembling chert common on sites over 100 km to the north (Cinq-Mars 1990: 20, footnote 8). (Photograph courtesy of Jacques Cinq-Mars, Archaeological Survey of Canada, Canadian Museum of Civilization)

Caves site, located on the end of a bedrock ridge overlooking a river valley, would be a typical instance of a temporary camp albeit used on numerous different occasions. In the Nenana Valley of central Alaska the settlement pattern model for both Northwestern Palaeo-Arctic culture and the Nenana-Chindadn complex proposes that hunting groups moved upriver into the foothills in the summer-fall following game seeking pasture. Sites are situated on south facing, elevated river terraces with good views of the valley and adjacent to fresh water. In winter it is speculated that people shifted into the lowlands following the herds (Powers 1985: 2).

Both of the Dry Creek site occupation levels had two activity areas, one on the bluff edge and the other a short distance back from the edge (Powers 1978). Such a settlement pattern may reflect different activities, such as tool manufacture or repair on the bluff edge while scanning the valley for game while the dwellings were situated back from the bluff out of view. Certainly the description of the living floors from Level II, consisting of a debris scatter of tools, chipping detritus, and bone fragments, is reminiscent of the structures of Palaeo-Indian culture. These debris concentrations ranged from 2 m to 4 m in diameter with some being suggestive of single family dwellings. Hearths were not clearly defined and the various concentrations varied in content and raw materials suggesting sequential occupations over time (Powers and Hoffecker 1989: 276). The occupations also produced some evidence of bone being used as fuel and of possible fat extraction by breaking and boiling bones. If, as suspected, the dwellings were skin tents erected on frozen ground or turf little else could be expected to survive in the archaeological record.

Cosmology:

There is currently no archaeological evidence from Northwestern Palaeo-Arctic culture which can be related to cosmological beliefs. Given the limited data involved and the general scarcity of such evidence from archaeological sites such a situation is not surprising. At a speculative level it could be suggested that an animistic belief system, not unlike that described for Palaeo-Indian culture, would have prevailed.

External relationships:

The relationship between the Nenana-Chindadn complex and Northwestern Palaeo-Arctic culture was considered in **Cultural origins and descendants** as was the relationship of the latter culture to Siberian sites. It is of note that at the 10,000 to 9,000 BP Groundhog Bay site on the southern Alaskan coast (Ackerman et al. 1979) Mt. Edziza obsidian from 300 km to the southeast and 150 km inland was recovered (Fladmark 1985: 13) suggesting either a very early exploitation of interior resources in northern British Columbia by the coastal descendants of Northwestern Palaeo-Arctic culture people or the existence of a trade network between the interior and the coast.

Human biology:

Although no Northwestern Palaeo-Arctic culture skeletal remains have been identified recent studies of cranial discrete traits of later populations are pertinent to the issue of biological relationships (Ossenberg n.d.; Szathmary and Ossenberg 1978). The application of a Mean Measure of Divergence statistic to the frequencies of 25 nonmetric human cranial traits suggested the following: Aleuts are more closely affiliated with Indians, particularly Athapascans, than with Eskimos indicating that the division between Aleut-Eskimo and Indians is not as sharp as once thought (Laughlin et al. 1979: 98); Aleut-Eskimo and northwestern Indian groups all resemble Chukotkans of northeastern Siberia closer than other northeastern Asians; the two major subclusters of, first, Aleut/Na-Dene and Algonquian- and Siouian-speaking Plains groups and, second, Eskimo, including both Inupiaq and Yupik speakers, represent two separate migrations; the first migration of the Aleut/Na-Dene/Plains subcluster is attributed to

Northwestern Palaeo-Arctic culture (Palaeoarctic), which dispersed from southwestern Alaska; and during their expansion they absorbed elements of an earlier migration. The importance of the evidence derived from the relatively stable human cranial discrete trait data is that it raises the possibility that both the Palaeo-Indian culture and the Northwestern Palaeo-Arctic culture peoples were biologically related. Northwestern Palaeo-Arctic culture has generally been attributed to the migration of the Eyak-Athapascan (Na-Dene) speakers (Greenberg et al. 1986). From an archaeological perspective, the relationship of Siouian and Algonquian-speakers on the Plains to both the Na-Dene and Aleut can be best explained if, at one time, Palaeo-Indian and Northwestern Palaeo-Arctic cultures were biologically related (Morlan 1987: 297).

Inferences on society:

Settlement pattern evidence indicates the existence of small hunting bands composed of a number of nuclear families. There is some evidence of an association with high quality siliceous deposits but not to the extent noted for Palaeo-Indian culture where such deposits acted as a major focus in the seasonal rounds. Most of the Palaeo-Indian fluted points from Alaska, for example, were manufactured from Batza Téna obsidian (Clark and Clark 1975; 1993). It can be speculated that the hunting of large herd animals, including some extinct Pleistocene species, required close co-operation at the band level. To survive in such a harsh environment some degree of inter-band sharing of food would also have had a survival advantage. Since these bands were small and likely patrilocal where the wife moved to the husband's community, it follows that wives would have been obtained from neighbouring bands thus establishing a network of blood-related bands. The nuclear family would have been the most important single social unit and both individuals and families probably could move relatively freely from one band to another. Female mobility related to inter-band marriage can be expected to have had a linguistic and cultural levelling effect.

Limitations in the evidence:

Over large areas of Alaska and the Yukon archaeological sites are buried under water, loess, pluvial and fluvial sediments or destroyed by erosion, and what survives is subjected to ongoing cryoturbation (disturbance by freeze-thaw cycles) and bioturbation (disturbance by animals, including people, trees, etc.). As Figure 1 showing the original Beringian coast line indicates, it is now impossible to assess the possibility of an early maritime adaptation in the area. The nature of the technology, with its microblades and burins, remained relatively unchanged for thousands of years making separation of very early sites from much later materials difficult or impossible unless recovered in a datable context. The major limitation, of course, relates to the massiveness of a Beringian landscape and the paucity of the archaeological evidence. Until the latter is substantially increased conflicting interpretations will continue to be the rule.

PERIOD II

(8,000 - 4,000 BC)

CHAPTER 4 —————————————————————

EARLY AND MIDDLE ARCHAIC COMPLEXES

Précis:

A number of poorly known Period II cultural complexes are distributed from the east coast to the Great Lakes. The evidence is so incomplete that it is premature to apply specific cultural names and, thus, the use of the word `complex´. As late as 1983 the 10,000 to 8,000 BP portion of a chronological chart of the archaeology of eastern North America referred to `traces´ of Early Archaic followed by `poorly known´ bifurcated base points. For the Upper Ohio Valley, the Niagara Frontier of New York, and Southern Ontario, the chart is a blank between 6,000 and 3,000 BC (Funk 1983: Fig.8.1). Regardless of the limitations in the archaeological evidence it is of critical importance to attempt to understand the interregnum (Mason 1981) which existed between late Palaeo-Indian culture and the more complete archaeological record beginning about 4,000 BC. By convention (Fowler 1959), the Archaic assemblages of this period have been subdivided into Early Archaic (8,000 to 6,000 BC) and Middle Archaic (6,000 to 4,000 BC). In late Palaeo-Indian culture as 10,000 BP was approached tool kits became increasingly elaborate and the spearheads thinner and more carefully manufactured. After this time the technology differentiates into a number of regional complexes that are subsumed under the broad categories of Archaic and Plano in the east and the west, respectively. In eastern Canada these regional developments out of late Palaeo-Indian culture are categorized as Eastern Early Archaic, Central Early Archaic, Western Early Archaic, and Southern Early Archaic. Middle Archaic is so poorly known in Canada that it can be summed up in a précis.

The reasons for the paucity of archaeological evidence are many. With the exception of the northshore of the Gulf of St.Lawrence, where coastal uplift has raised sites well above sea level, many of the likely site areas occupied lands now either submerged beneath the waters of the Atlantic and Great Lakes or destroyed or buried by erosional and depositional processes. Environmental change and cultural events have further complicated the situation. Plains-derived Plano culture 9,000 years ago extended eastward as far as the Atlantic following a narrow belt of Lichen Woodland and Boreal Forest (McAndrews et al. 1987), apparently exploiting caribou herds expanding into lands recently released by the glacial ice and the receding water levels of the Great Lakes. To the south of Plano culture, in the eastern Great Lakes region, an indigenous development out of late Palaeo-Indian culture is referred to as Central Early Archaic or the Hi-Lo complex. Around 9,500 BP there appears to be an actual population penetration into Southern Ontario by the Southern Early Archaic complex. There is evidence of direct contacts between the Plano culture and some of these Early Archaic complexes. Settlement pattern distributions also suggest that the Central Early Archaic complex was a contemporary of Plano culture. It was into this complex region of environmental and cultural diversity that the spearthrower weapon system was introduced from the south. Southern Ontario was in the centre of these events. To the north, earlier Palaeo-Indian hunting practices were retained by Plano culture hunters. To the south, the northward expanding deciduous forests with their increasing numbers of plant resources such as nuts and berries, expanding fish resources, and a broad range of game animals, required somewhat different adaptive systems. Along the northshore of the Gulf of St.Lawrence in Québec and Labrador, on the other hand, an early maritime adaptation permitted a continuity of settlement pattern and subsistence through thousands of years. Of all the Early Archaic complexes in Canada the Eastern Early Archaic complex is best known but information is steadily increasing relative to the Southern Early Archaic complex. Middle Archaic, represented by the two thousand years from 6,000 to 4,000 BC, is even less well known than the complexes of the Early Archaic. In addition to the submergence of sites beneath rising water levels there is a serious identification problem. Middle Archaic materials picked up from the surfaces of ploughed fields are simply not recognized as being early as many of the tools resemble much later archaeological styles. And yet, it had to be from this amorphous base that the cultures of Period III developed around 4,000 BC.

Unlike their late Palaeo-Indian culture ancestors, the stone knappers of the Early Archaic complexes tended to rely more upon local stone. In contrast to the earlier attention to core and preform production and reduction procedures, Early Archaic people used a wide range of core varieties in quite variable fashions. There appears to have been little of the Palaeo-Indian culture concern with the curation of stone. The major goal of the stone knapper appears to have been to produce simple flakes as expedient tools to be quickly discarded when they became dull. Exotic stone does occur but it is less frequent and obtained from closer sources than was the case with Palaeo-Indian culture. New technological traits appear, such as ground stone adzes in the Eastern Early Archaic and Southern Early Archaic complexes, and stone tubular spearthrower weights in the latter. Characteristic of all of the complexes are the stone tips with which they armed their weapons. It would appear that sometime around 10,000 BP some ingenious individual in what is now the southeastern United States invented a new and superior weapon system. The spearthrower was a device that used the same principle as that applied to the hand basket throwing device of the Basque ball game of jai alai or pelota. In the spearthrower instance, the propelling device permitted a spear to be thrown with greater force and accuracy than was possible by hand alone. The new weapon system spread rapidly throughout most of the Western Hemisphere and particularly so throughout eastern North America. The thin, symmetrical spear heads of late Palaeo-Indian were replaced by the thick and often asymmetrical Early Archaic notched, stemmed, and lanceolate points. It is suspected that the dramatic change from late Palaeo-Indian culture lithic tool production procedures relates directly to the introduction of the new weapon technology in conjunction with changing environmental requirements.

Little direct evidence of subsistence practices exists. Settlement pattern distributions indicate that the Eastern Early Archaic complex people seasonally exploited maritime resources. Similarly, the association of Central Early Archaic complex sites with ridges and lakeshores suggests that caribou were still an important game animal. There is evidence for increasing reliance upon plant foods by the Southern Early Archaic populations but how much this characterized sites south of the Great Lakes as opposed to sites in Southern Ontario is not yet clear. As the deciduous forests, with their populations of deer, turkey,

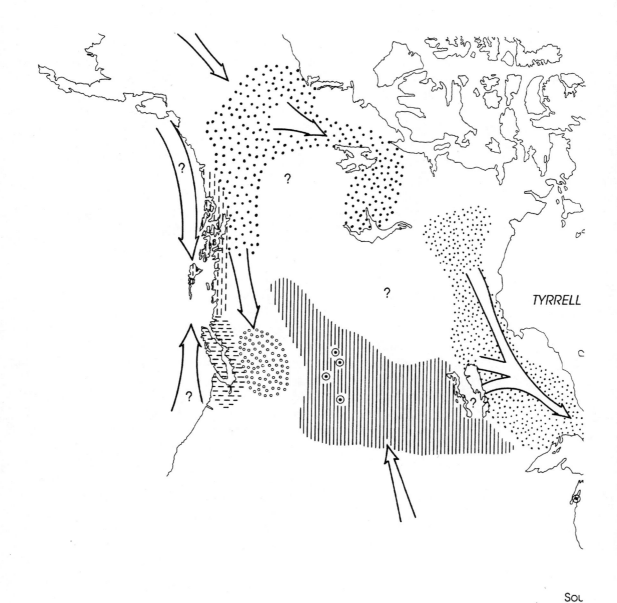

MAP II: CULTURAL DISTRIBUTIONS, 8,000 TO 4,000 BC Map II is intended to act as a geographic reflected in this Map in contrast to Map III which presents the much better understood cultural distributions (Drawing by David W. Laverie).

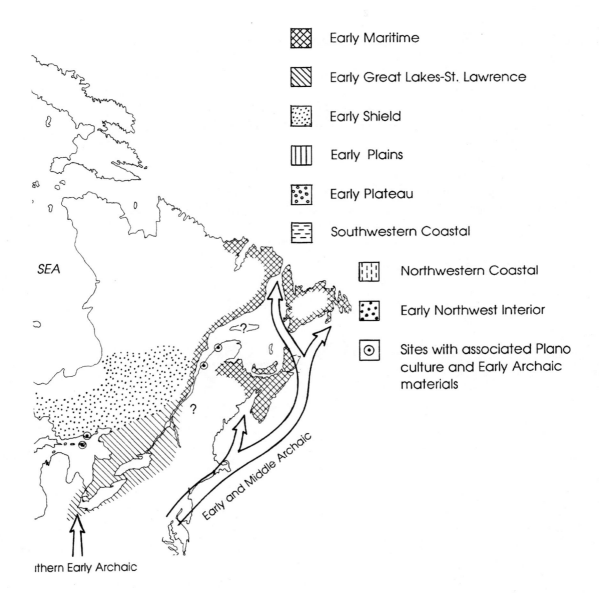

guide to the distributions of the cultures discussed in Period II. The patchy archaeological evidence is clearly of Period III (4,000 to 1,000 BC). Adapted from Plate 6 of the Historical Atlas of Canada, Volume I

and other more southerly species, spread northward at the expense of the Boreal Forest and Tundra vegetation, with their caribou and other northern species, adaptive systems were forced to change. The disappearances of Plano culture and the Central Early Archaic complex, for example, were more likely the result of necessary adaptive changes, including major changes in the stone tool kit, rather than being due to physical replacement by encroaching southerners.

Nothing is known regarding either cosmology or human biology in the Early Archaic and Middle Archaic complexes of Canada. With reference to external relationships, there is evidence that southern contacts were maintained by colonizing groups like the Southern Early Archaic complex. Direct evidence exists of contacts between Plano culture people and Western Early Archaic complex and Southern Early Archaic complex peoples. The proximity of different groups to one another in the Great Lakes region during this period would have made culture contact situations inevitable. Cultural distributions would also have accommodated diffusion of both technology and ideas as witnessed by the spread of the spearthrower and possibly the gill net. It can only be speculated that these societies were composed of nuclear families organized into bands and that intermarriage with adjacent bands would have been the norm.

As information on Early Archaic complexes is limited the descriptive procedure applied to most of the cultures will be abbreviated as dictated by the evidence.

EARLY ARCHAIC COMPLEXES

EASTERN EARLY ARCHAIC COMPLEX

Cultural origins and descendants:

Eastern Early Archaic complex has been called Late Palaeo-Indian (Renouf 1977: 35) and either Paléoindien or Archaïque inferior (Taillon et Barré 1987: 198, 234). The designation `Palaeo-Indian´ or `Paléoindien´ explicitly accepts a tentative hypothesis that the assemblage had its origins in late Palaeo-Indian culture (McGhee and Tuck 1975: 118). The link with Palaeo-Indian culture is based upon both projectile point morphology and chronological considerations. First, the triangular projectile points (Figure 7) are interpreted as descendant forms of Palaeo-Indian weapon heads (Keenlyside 1985; 1985a). Second, the complex occurs on the higher strandlines elevated by coastal uplift and has radiocarbon dates approaching 9,000 BP. However, the majority of dates from both Québec and Labrador provide readings around 7,000 BP (McGhee and Tuck 1975; Renouf 1977; Taillon et Barré 1987). Thus, "Serait-il possible que les dates de 8855 et 8600 ans BP des site Pinware et Cowpath soint trop anciennes?" (Groison 1985: 131), particularly as both the Pinware and Cowpath dates were obtained from scattered charcoal and, in the latter instance, lacked clear cultural association in contrast to the dates from the stratified EiBg-7e site near Blanc-Sablon. If, as it would appear, the Eastern Early Archaic complex dates closer to 7,000 BP than 9,000 BP then one would have to accept a 3,500 year transitional period from Palaeo-Indian culture to the Eastern Early Archaic complex. A cultural transition that represents nearly twice the entire time span of Palaeo-Indian culture is a dubious prospect.

Another hypothesis proposes that Early Maritime culture developed out of the Eastern Early Archaic complex (McGhee and Tuck 1975: 118; Tuck 1977). The nature of the technological remains from the strandlines at differing elevations support this proposal. Eastern Early Archaic materials occur on the highest beaches. On the next highest beaches a similar assemblage is encountered which includes points with diminutive contracting stems resembling, in many respects, the earlier triangular points (Groison 1985; Levesque 1980; McGhee and Tuck 1975; Renouf 1977). A radiocarbon date of the latter assemblage from the Templier site at Blanc-Sablon provided a chronologically sequential reading of 6,215+/-70 BP (Groison 1985: 131; Roger Marois, Archaeological Survey of Canada, Canadian Museum of Civilization, personal communication). Further, if the 7,000 BP dating of the Eastern Early Archaic complex is accurate then it would make the complex coterminous with Early Maritime culture with its stemmed projectile points, polished stone gouges, semi-lunar knives, and bayonets. Given the frequent difficulty of establishing good archaeological contexts for charcoal from many sites along the northshore of the Gulf of St.Lawrence the chronological sequence of sites indicated by the beach elevations probably reflects a more accurate picture of technological change in the region. This change would suggest an in situ transition from the Eastern Early Archaic complex into Early Maritime culture.

Technology:

Only stone tools have been found on Eastern Early Archaic complex campsites. Manufactured mainly from local quartzite cobbles, the tool kit consists of triangular projectile points with basal thinning and edge grinding, abundant small end scrapers sometimes with graver spurs, side scrapers, retouched flakes, biface knives, wedges probably used as burins, hammerstones, and a possible ground stone adze (Groison 1985; McGhee and Tuck 1975; Renouf 1977). In the Eastern Early Archaic complex, as in most other Early Archaic technologies, the heating of igneous and metamorphic cobbles, either to form the `hot plate´ of a roasting hearth or to boil water, is in frequent evidence and, in this respect, differs markedly from the preceding Palaeo-Indian cooking practices.

Subsistence:

Eastern Early Archaic complex subsistence practices must be inferred from settlement pattern evidence as little in the way of bone has survived. The region would have been available to caribou and other animals as early as 10,000 BP and by 7,000 BP tundra was widespread with a narrow band of Lichen Woodland vegetation occurring along much of the northshore (McAndrews et al. 1987). It can be inferred that caribou, black bears, and wolves would have been among the larger land animals occupying the region. Caribou, of course, would have been the land resource of greatest value to hunters. Small campsite locations on beaches between bedrock headlands indicate a seasonal orientation to the rich maritime resources. Late winter to early summer would be the most bountiful time to be situated on the coast. Easily captured harp seals would have been available as well as enormous schools of spawning salmon and capelin. The latter species strand themselves in uncounted thousands on the spawning beaches and are often preserved naturally by the sun and wind. All that would be needed to harvest them would be a basket. Presumably in this dried state, the fish could be stored for later consumption. Paradoxically, as the bones were almost certainly eaten along with the flesh, one could not expect to recover remains of the species that could well have been the major reason for locating camps on beaches. Similarly, there would be no archaeological record of the consumption of seabird eggs, crabs or squid. Such is the nature of the archaeological record. Large sea mammals would also have been captured or scavenged. In the lowest level of the EiBg-7e site near Blanc-Sablon, Québec, for example, walrus bone was recovered. While walrus are extremely dangerous to hunt in the water they can be captured with relative ease on land (Dumais et Rousseau 1986: 81).

Settlements patterns:

Evidence from the coasts of Labrador (McGhee and Tuck 1975) and Québec (Groison 1985; Levesque 1980) indicates the use of small campsites, probably representing only a few families. Numerous such campsites, however, could have been occupied at the same time and have represented a substantial population. Harp seal, salmon, capelin, and other species would be available from late winter to early summer as well as caribou escaping the insects of the interior during the summer. It would be a logical inference that these people possessed some form of watercraft although no direct evidence has survived the passage of time.

At the EiBi-5 site a 3 m diameter living floor was demarcated by chipping debris, charcoal, a central hearth, and artifacts typical of the 7,500 to 6,500 BP occupation (Beaudin et al. 1987: 131). Generally, however, evidence of living floors is lacking suggesting that dwellings were flimsy affairs that left little archaeological trace.

Most evidence pertaining to the Eastern Early Archaic complex comes from the north coast of the Gulf of St.Lawrence. Little evidence along the Atlantic coast to the south can be anticipated as a sea level rise in excess of 30 m would have destroyed the majority of early coastal sites in the Martime provinces. A possible exception to the foregoing is the lowest occupation level of the severely eroded Jones site on the coast of Prince Edward Island that is regarded as the source for a series of possible transitional Palaeo-Indian to Eastern Early Archaic projectile points (Keenlyside 1985: 123).

External relationships:

Eastern Early Archaic complex lithic materials along the northshore of the Gulf of St.Lawrence are of local origin and are not indicative of distant contacts. If the polished stone adze from the Pinware Hill site on the Labrador coast (McGhee and Tuck 1975) is actually associated with the Eastern Early Archaic assemblage then it would suggest southern influences. One is left with the strong impression that the colonizing bands of the Eastern Early Archaic complex were a relatively isolated population.

Inferences on society:

It is speculated that the major social unit of Eastern Early Archaic society was the nuclear family. Not only would a number of these families constitute a band but it is probable that the band was exogamous and marriages had to be contracted with neighbouring bands. Thus, a string of blood related bands would have been distributed along the northshore of the Gulf of St.Lawrence and elsewhere and provided an important safety net.

Limitations in the evidence:

Unlike most regions of the Gulf of St.Lawrence and the Atlantic coast, where early sites on the coast have been subjected to heavy erosion and inundation, coastal uplift along the northshore has isolated sites on elevated beaches. In this respect there is some reason for optimism that continuing work along this coast and in specific areas of the Maritime provinces will eventually lead to a better understanding of the nature of the Eastern Early Archaic complex. It is unlikely, however, that we will ever attain much of an appreciation of the bone technology or direct evidence of subsistence practices given the acid soils.

CENTRAL EARLY ARCHAIC COMPLEX

Cultural origins and descendants:

The Central Early Archaic complex or, as it is generally known, the Hi-Low complex, is found in Southern Ontario between Lake Erie and the southern reaches of Lake Huron with a minor extension along the northshore of Lake Ontario (Ellis and Deller 1982; Roberts 1985; Wright 1978). It is also found in adjacent Michigan, Ohio, and New York, being particularly common in southeastern Michigan and northwestern Ohio (Stothers 1982). The Central Early Archaic complex is regarded as the product of in situ change from a late Palaeo-Indian cultural base. There is a classificatory problem, however, which needs to be addressed. Some who see a relationship between the Central Early Archaic complex and Palaeo-Indian through a transitional phase call Holcombe after a site in Michigan (Fitting et al. 1966), classify the Central Early Archaic or Hi-Low complex as Late Palaeo-Indian (Ellis and Deller 1990). While agreeing with the transition, the complex is classified as Archaic on the grounds of a dramatic change in the nature of the weapon system; a technological change which has been generally used to differentiate Palaeo-Indian from Archaic in the east. This change in weapon systems dramatically altered the nature of the stone projectile points.

The Central Early Archaic complex represents a northern version of the Dalton transition from Palaeo-Indian to Archaic described for the southeastern and midwestern United States (Ellis and Deller 1990). These widespread and contemporary technological changes relate to the innovation and spread of the spearthrower sometime between 10,500 and 10,000 BP; an event that, given the importance of projectile form to archaeological classification, has had a dramatic impact on the classification of local archaeological assemblages. Unfortunately no undisturbed Central Early Archaic complex site has been discovered. Virtually all of the material has been recovered from the surface of ploughed fields and, as such, there are no radiocarbon dates. A level from an Ohio rockshelter that produced a Southern Early Archaic complex occupation in association with what appear to be Central Early Archaic projectile points did, however, provide a radiocarbon date of 9,480 +/- 160 BP (Brose 1989). The fate of the Central Early Archaic complex is unknown although it is likely its people adopted the tool kit of the intrusive Southern Early Archaic complex after 10,000 BP.

Technology:

Although no undisturbed Central Early Archaic complex sites are known from Ontario, at the Welke-Tonkonoh site near London it was assumed that a distinctive white Haldimand chert was only used by the Central Early Archaic complex occupation of the multi-component site (Ellis and Deller 1982). If this assumption is correct then point preforms, backed biface knives, end and side scrapers, and gravers were part of the tool kit. The distinctive lanceolate, basally thinned, basally and laterally ground projectile points were also reworked into end scrapers, drills, and gravers. What is needed to clarify the nature of the Central Early Archaic complex are excavatable sites with good archaeological contexts.

Central Early Archaic projectile points are markedly different from late Palaeo-Indian points. These differences are attributed to the former functioning as javelin heads propelled by a spearthrower as opposed to the latter handheld thrusting spears. Late Palaeo-Indian culture spearheads from the Crowfield site are extremely thin, ranging from 3 to 5.5 mm in thickness (Deller and Ellis 1984: 441). The later (10,000 > BP) Holcombe lanceolate points, which are inferred to be the immediate ancestor of the Central Early Archaic complex points, are also generally less than 5 mm in thickness. In contrast, Central Early Archaic complex projectile points range in thickness from 6.5 to 11.0 mm with a mean of 8.2 mm. Add to this the distinctive Early Archaic projectile point attributes of blade bevelling and edge serration and a high frequency of asymmetrical outlines, and the impression is inescapable that a major new kind of weapon system has been introduced. The high instance of blade bevelling on these points probably relates to other functions such as their secondary use as knives for butchering game (Ellis and Deller 1990: 57).

Subsistence:

There is increasing evidence that the view of a big game rich, tundra-spruce parkland of Palaeo-Indian times being replaced around 10,000 BP by a resource impoverished boreal forest (Fitting 1968; Ritchie 1969) is not an accurate reconstruction. Forests, particularly in the area occupied by the Central Early Archaic complex, appear to have been more mixed with significant deciduous elements (Ellis et al. 1991: 25). While the local environment was undoubtedly impoverished relative to that further south, there was the likelihood that proximity to the Lichen Woodlands to the north compensated somewhat by providing access to caribou. No faunal remains have been recovered from Central Early Archaic complex sites.

Settlement patterns:

Settlement pattern evidence indicates the existence of a mixed hunting, fishing, and gathering economy. Sites tend to be situated on well drained, elevated locations facing south and overlooking poorly drained areas adjacent to small streams thus reflecting a previous Palaeo-Indian culture settlement pattern. Site locations on ridges and ancient shorelines have been interpreted as evidence for the maintenance of the previous pattern of intercepting caribou (Ellis and Deller 1990; Roberts 1985: 110). Given the lower waterlevels of the Great Lakes during this period many, if not most, Central Early Archaic complex sites are underwater and particularly the spring to summer fishing sites at the mouths of rivers and streams (Figure 6). The concentration of sites along the northshore of Lake Erie suggests this was the heartland of the complex or, at least, the favoured winter interior hunt camp locale. If the `white chert´ reported from the Welke-Tonkonoh site (Ellis and Deller 1982) is, indeed, a variant of the Haldimand deposits 200 km to the southeast then the dominance of Ontario and Michigan cherts (Ibid: Table 4) would indicate a local population rather than an intrusive one. Evidence of the Central Early Archaic complex along the northshore of Lake Ontario (Roberts 1985) and the southeastern Lake Huron Basin (Deller et al. 1986: 6) is so sparse one might suspect the region was once shared with the more northerly Plano culture and was perhaps only sporadically exploited.

External relationships:

Although direct evidence is lacking, settlement pattern distributions and age estimates suggest that the Central Early Archaic complex was a contemporary of Plano culture to the north and east (Ellis and Deller 1990: 61). Such a situation would account for both the weak northern and eastern distribution of the complex. The points attributed to Plano culture associated with the 9,500 BP Southern Early Archaic complex occupation of the Squaw Rockshelter site in Ohio (Brose 1989) look more like Central Early Archaic complex (Hi-Lo) points.

Limitations in the evidence:

The rising water levels of the Great Lakes (Karrow and Warner 1990) would have drowned the majority of Central Early Archaic complex sites. In addition to this major limitation is the total absence of excavatable components that would permit an accurate assessment of the nature of the tool kit as well as provide information on site features, evidence of trade, and material for radiocarbon dating. Until such sites are located the Central Early Archaic complex will remain a tentative construct based upon inferred projectile point form changes through time.

WESTERN EARLY ARCHAIC COMPLEX

Cultural origins and descendants:

The Western Early Archaic complex in Ontario may not even represent a complex but rather the diffusion of a broad, side-notched projectile point style from the south to more northerly Plano sites. The point style in question (Figure 7) is dated to 10,000 BP in Illinois and West Virginia (Broyles 1971; Fowler 1959), 9,000 BP in Alabama (DeJarnette et al. 1962), between 10,000 and 8,000 BP in Missouri (Logan 1952; Crane 1956: 666-667), and 8,500 BP in Iowa where they were associated with extinct bison (Agogino and Frankforter 1960). Such early dates make the point style a contemporary of Plano culture. As in the case with the Central Early Archaic complex, these projectile points reflect the spread of the spearthrower weapon system. It is speculated that as the northern examples are usually manufactured from local stone their appearance represents the diffusion of technology from the south rather than an actual population intrusion of southerners. If this assumption is correct, it would mark the beginning of the technological transformation of Plano culture in the north into the subsequent Early Shield culture.

Technology:

If the broad, side-notched lanceolate projectile points of the Western Early Archaic complex, with their generally concave bases and basal and lateral grinding, do represent the adoption of the spearthrower technology by northern Plano culture people then no other items of technology need be expected. This would appear to be the most parsimonious interpretation of the evidence at this time. There is some descriptive utility in retaining the complex construct, however, until the evidence becomes clearer, particularly as early looking side-notched points have been recovered from the surface of sites in Southern Ontario lacking a Plano culture association (Ellis et al. 1990; Wright 1978).

Subsistence and settlement patterns:

As all of the distinctive Western Early Archaic complex projectile points have been recovered from Plano culture sites in the Upper Great Lakes (Buckmaster and Paquette 1988; Fox 1975; Greenman and Stanley 1940; Lee 1957; Mason and Irwin 1960) it follows that evidence pertinent to the above systems be considered in the Plano culture chapter.

Cosmology:

At the Renier site in northeastern Wisconsin a fire-fractured, side-notched projectile point was found in a Plano culture cremation burial containing an abundance of fire-fractured Plano culture implements (Mason and Irwin 1960). A cache or burial from the Gorto site (Buckmaster and Paquette 1988) in Michigan contained a mixture of large side-notched points and Plano culture points. The feature involved is estimated to have been 1.8 m in diameter, was associated with two 10 cm diameter post holes (markers?), and contained 86 projectile points and point fragments including 14 Plano point styles and

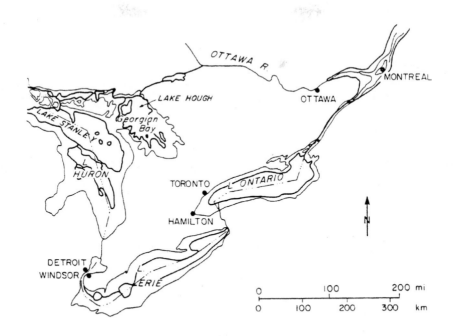

FIGURE 6: GREAT LAKES LOW WATER LEVELS AT 10,000 BP The thicker lines indicate water levels at 10,000 BP while the finer lines demarcate current water levels. As hunting peoples tend to congregate along the margins of large bodies of water from spring to fall, it can be seen how much of the archaeological record pertinent to the Central Early Archaic complex and other Early Archaic complexes is now drowned. (Reproduced from Karrow and Warner 1990: Fig.2.11 with permission of Mr. Neal Ferris, Occasional Publications Series Editor, London Chapter, Ontario Archaeological Society, London, Ontario.)

4 large, side-notched points. The remaining points consisted of fire-fractured fragments although there was no direct evidence of fire. In a number of respects, the feature resembles one discovered at the late Palaeo-Indian culture Crowfield site (Deller and Ellis 1984). Most of the projectile points, both Plano culture and Western Early Archaic complex, were manufactured from the distinctive Hixton quartzite of southwestern Wisconsin. Three of the side-notched points also had been fashioned in the distinctive manner of the Plano culture stone knappers while the sole chert specimen possessed the characteristic Early Archaic bevelled blade attribute (Buckmaster and Paquette 1988: 115). The attributes of the side-notched points from this feature suggest the involvement of both the processes of stimulus diffusion and direct cultural contact between Plano people in the north and Early Archaic people in the south.

External relationships:

A key issue to be determined is whether the Western Early Archaic complex is an actual complex in Canada or simply a single diffused element of technology. The latter would appear to be the case relative to Plano culture in the Upper Great Lakes but there are Early Archaic side-notched points a short distance to the south that could have entered parts of Canada as part of an assemblage.

Limitations in the evidence:

Unlike the situation with the Central Early Archaic complex, most of the evidence pertaining to the Western Early Archaic complex in the Upper Great Lakes was recovered during archaeological excavations. Materials came from either Plano culture quarry sites or ceremonial features. Between 9,000 and 8,500 BP the lower water levels of the Great Lakes assures that much of the pertinent information is either destroyed or underwater. Side-notched lanceolate projectile points with concave bases, basal thinning and grinding have a long history in eastern North America and more sophisticated attribute studies will be necessary in order to isolate the earliest representatives from later look-alikes.

SOUTHERN EARLY ARCHAIC COMPLEX

Cultural origins and descendants:

This widely distributed cultural complex, embracing much of the United States east of the Mississippi River (Coe 1964; Broyles 1971), reached as far north as the northshores of the Lower Great Lakes and, in particular, Lake Erie (Ellis et al. 1990; 1991; Wright 1978). While considerable archaeological information pertinent to this complex is available south of Canada, the nature of its penetration to the north is still poorly known and, thus, the designation `complex´ is retained until the northern tier of the Southern Early Archaic is more fully understood. When Early Archaic is referred to in the literature it generally pertains to one of the several time segments of the Southern Early Archaic complex.

The Southern Early Archaic complex developed out of a Palaeo-Indian cultural base through a transitional stage known as Dalton (Coe 1964; Tuck 1974). The Dalton complex, however, is absent from Southern Ontario where the Central Early Archaic complex appears to be a northern contemporary and equivalent. Penetration of Ontario probably involved both an actual intrusion of people as well as a technological acculturation of the local Central Early Archaic complex people.

Throughout eastern North America the Southern Early Archaic complex is perceived as a number of cultural time horizons that are characterized by distinctive projectile point styles. Progressing from early to late these projectile point styles are side-notched forms (10,000-9,500 BP), corner-notched forms (9,500-

9,000 BP), and bifurcated base forms (9,000-8,000 BP). Transecting the horizon point style changes is a continuity of cultural development (Tuck 1974) and radiocarbon dates from southern sites are accepted as being applicable to similar materials in the north (Ellis et al. 1991: 24). Evidence of the early side-notched point horizon in Southern Ontario is equivocal except to the northwest where the point style appears to have been adopted by local Plano culture peoples. There is abundant evidence for both the corner-notched and the bifurcated-base point horizons in Southern Ontario and particularly in southwestern Southern Ontario (Ellis et al.1990; 1991; Wright 1978). It is assumed that it was from this Early Archaic base that subsequent Middle Archaic complexes developed to provide the cultural base for the much better understood cultures of Period III.

Although the Southern Early Archaic complex was relatively peripheral to Canada the impact of its technological innovations and adaptive patterns upon the northern hunting bands, in conjunction with the continuing northward spread of the deciduous forest, appear to have been both massive and ultimately pervasive. The formative processes underlying the genesis of the Southern Early Archaic complex is a matter of some dispute. Dumont (1981) has suggested that a changing forest, involving a high percentage of pine, resulted in a reduced biomass and thus forced a major subsistence shift that transformed the Palaeo-Indian culture hunters into Early Archaic hunters, fishermen, and gatherers. Such an environmental/cultural correlation encounters difficulties, however, when it is appreciated that the pine forests did not attain an ascendant position in northeastern North America until a thousand years after the transition of Palaeo-Indian into Early Archaic (Richard 1985; Trubowitz 1979: Fig.1).

Technology:

The two most important technological innovations associated with the Southern Early Archaic complex are the spearthrower and the gill net (Dumont 1979: 41). Not until 8,500 BP, however, do changes in the plant and animal communities due to warming trends favouring the expansion of the hardwood forests result in major changes to either the tool kit or the adaptive system (Gardner 1977: 258). Given its northern location these changes can be expected to have been less dramatic in Southern Ontario and environs.

The hallmark of the Southern Early Archaic complex is a series of projectile point styles (Figure 7) which are culturally diagnostic even when removed from an archaeological context. With few exceptions (Lennox 1993) sites in Southern Ontario producing the distinctive projectile point styles also contain later occupational material making it difficult to determine what the total tool kit looks like. Related sites to the south have produced other tools in good context that include chipped and ground celts in Pennsylvania by 9,000 BP (Michels and Smith 1967) and in New York and New Jersey by 8,000 BP (Dumont and Dumont 1979; Ritchie and Funk 1971). The relative homogeneity of cultural remains from the surface collected Nettling site near the northshore of Lake Erie (Ellis et al. 1991) has led to its treatment as a single component. In addition to the distinctive early projectile points other items from this estimated 9,500 to 9,000 BP site consist of the following: biface knives and preforms; retouched flakes; and end scrapers. Minor items include drills, saws, side scrapers, chipped and ground celts, rough stone objects such as choppers, hammers, and anvilstones, and ground stone tubular spearthrower weights. Over half of the assemblage was composed of biface knives and preforms while another 25 percent was made up of projectile points, retouched flakes, and a distinctive form of end scraper. As with all Early Archaic complexes, in contrast to the preceding Palaeo-Indian culture, there was a heavy reliance upon expedient flake tools struck from a variety of core forms. This technological change from a highly standardized core-preform-reduction pattern to a much less systematic one (Ellis et al. 1991) had a major impact upon the appearance of the overall tool kit.

What appears to be a single component Southern Early Archaic complex site in Southern Ontario, even though disturbed by the plough, produced mainly scrapers represented by end, side, and random flake scrapers, biface reduction fragments, projectile points and rarer items like drills, burins, and a distinctive form of lenticular unifacially and bifacially flaked tool (Lennox 1993). In addition to the foregoing this 8,300 BP site contained many utilized flakes. Of interest was the fact that the majority of the scrapers were manufactured from Kettle Point chert situated 120 km to the west (Janusas 1984) even though the material had an overall sparse occurrence on the site. Such a situation indicates that the value of certain chert varieties for certain tool functions was clearly recognized.

Subsistence:

The relative scarcity of Early Archaic sites in northeastern North America, including the northern range of the Southern Early Archaic complex, has been attributed to the dominance of a resource-poor pine forest (Fitting 1968; Ritchie 1969: 212-213), particularly between 10,000 and 9,000 BP (Funk 1979). The increasing evidence of people after 9,000 BP is correlated with the northward spread of the deciduous forests accompanied by cultures with appropriate adaptive systems. While an ecological factor may be partly responsible for the limited evidence of human occupation during this period other factors, such as the destruction and submergence of sites, a settlement patterns record that pertains mainly to winter settlement, and the inability of archaeologists to recognize much of the pertinent technology removed from a datable archaeological context, would all reduce the archaeological visibility of people at this time (Dincauze and Mitchell 1977). Also, a substantial portion of the northern margin of the region was already occupied by Plano culture hunters adapted to the tundra/lichen woodland and boreal forest latitudinal vegetation belts.

There is some agreement that the northern limits of favourable habitat for the Southern Early Archaic complex was the oak forest ecotone (Dincauze and Molholland 1977: 450; Funk 1979). A deciduous forest containing an abundance of deer, elk, bear, and turkey as well as nut trees (Funk 1979: 25) could have provided the economic base for some population increase. Such a proposal, however, would have only marginal pertinence to Canada. It has even been speculated that the Southern Early Archaic complex exploitation of Southern Ontario may have initially been a seasonal event (Ellis et al. 1991).

Settlement patterns:

Southern Early Archaic complex materials in Ontario are frequently found on the same sites once occupied by Palaeo-Indians and the clusters of remains suggest both groups were carrying out similar activities at small hunt camps (Ellis and Deller 1991a). The Nettling site is situated beside a dry creek 5 km from the current Lake Erie shore (Ellis et al. 1991). Lithics from the site consist of a high percentage of Ohio varieties such as Pipe Creek chert, 175 to 200 km away, and Upper Mercer chert, 300 km away, suggesting an actual migration of people from Ohio into Ontario. While the Ohio cherts were from primary deposits, the local Onondaga-Selkirk chert was derived from secondary sources, probably from along the Lake Erie shoreline. Finished tools were generally manufactured from Ohio cherts while primary manufacturing focused on the local cherts. These data have been taken as evidence of a seasonal exploitation of the site by Ohio residents (Ibid: 25) but, if this were the case, contemporary and related Ohio sites with exhausted tools of Ontario chert varieties should be expected. The interpretation favoured here is that the Nettling site represents an actual penetration of Southern Early Archaic complex people into Southern Ontario. The single component Kassel base camp site is situated in an interior uplands setting adjacent to wetlands. Covering approximately 100 square metres, the site is located 800 m from an apparently contemporary kill (?) site only 25 square meters in size (Lennox 1993).

Cosmology and Human biology:

There is no information on either cosmology or human biology from Southern Ontario. Further south, however, quartz crystals from the Southern Early Archaic complex levels of the Rochelein site in northern New Jersey and other sites in the upper Delaware Valley (Dumont and Dumont 1979) are speculated to have functioned as `magico-religious´ objects (Kraft 1975: 21). Further afield in Arkansas, a `boneless´ cemetery produced diagnostic projectile points along with chipped and ground stone adzes, adze blanks, end scrapers, sandstone abraders, and other items arranged in linear east-west configurations that have been interpreted as extended burials from which all of the bone has disappeared (Morse 1982).

External relationships:

Southern Early Archaic complex materials have been stated to be associated with Plano culture at the Squaw Rockshelter and the Aurora Run Rockshelter sites in Ohio dating prior to 9,000 BP (Mason 1981: 116). The `Plano´ points from the former site, however, would appear to relate more closely to the Central Early Archaic complex (Hi-Lo). The contemporaneity of the Southern Early Archaic complex with Plano culture to the north has been used to explain the restricted distribution of the former in Southern Ontario (Ellis et al. 1990; 1991).

Limitations in the evidence:

With the exception of the Eastern Early Archaic complex along the northshore of the Gulf of St.Lawrence archaeological information on Early Archaic sites in Canada has been drastically curtailed by the rising waters of the Great Lakes and other water bodies, the scarcity of excavatable sites, and the problems of isolating the appropriate assemblages from multi-component sites. Water level fluctuations, however, must be recognized as the single most limiting factor. The low water phase of Lake Ontario between 10,000 and 5,000 BP (Karrow et al. 1961), for example, means that all Early and Middle Archaic lakeside sites are now underwater. This situation is particularly serious given the fact that settlement pattern distributions in the area indicate an orientation towards the lake (Roberts 1985: 121). Thus the entire summer to fall settlement pattern record of occupation of major fishing base camps at the mouths of rivers and streams and at narrows has been eradicated.

MIDDLE ARCHAIC COMPLEXES

Précis:

The time period between 6,000 and 4,000 BC that incorporates the Middle Archaic is essentially an unknown entity in large areas of eastern North America. In stark contrast, along portions of the New England coast (Dincauze 1976) and the northshore of the Gulf of St.Lawrence, events during this period are relatively well known. In the interior, however, there is a virtual archaeological void. Added to the problem of drowned shoreline sites in the Great Lakes and Lake Champlain regions, interior sites are extremely difficult to distinguish from much later sites. As such, if specimens are not recovered from datable archaeological contexts they are not generally recognized as being early.

There is some limited evidence of a coastal stemmed projectile point horizon (Dincauze 1976), dated in New England between 8,000 and 7,000 BP, penetrating into the interior of the Lower Great Lakes and the Upper St.Lawrence Valley (Ellis et al. 1990; Wright 1978). Around 6,500 BP there is also some evidence of the beginnings of a transition into Early Great Lakes-St.Lawrence culture. By and large, however, archaeological evidence between 8,000 and 6,000 BP is extremely sparse. As noted, this is mainly due to the fact that archaeologists are unable to distinguish pertinent materials from much later tools. Such a proposition receives support from the evidence from the John's Bridge site in northwestern Vermont (Thomas and Robinson 1980). This site, dated to 8,000 BP, produced side- and corner-notched points, bifacially flaked knives including hafted varieties, a range of scraper forms, gravers, large tabular knives or choppers, abraders, graphite nodules, and a drill. If recovered from a ploughed field, most regional archaeologists would likely have classified these materials as post-dating 4,000 BC. A personal examination of the mixed archaeological deposits from sites in the Lake St.Francis expansion of the Upper St.Lawrence River revealed the presence of virtually identical varieties of projectile points to those excavated under controlled conditions at the John's Bridge site suggesting that the assemblage may be more widely distributed but simply not recognized for what it is. The John's Bridge site also contained hearths and deep pits. A scatter of lithic debris in association with a hearth of calcined bone and pits is inferred to represent a living floor (Thomas and Robinson 1980: 123-125).

Given the limitations in archaeological evidence pertinent to the two millennia prior to 4,000 BC it is probably best not to belabour the issue further. Suffice to observe that the much better known cultural developments of the subsequent Period III in the interior of eastern North America owe their existence to a number of amorphous complexes subsumed under the rubric `Middle Archaic´.

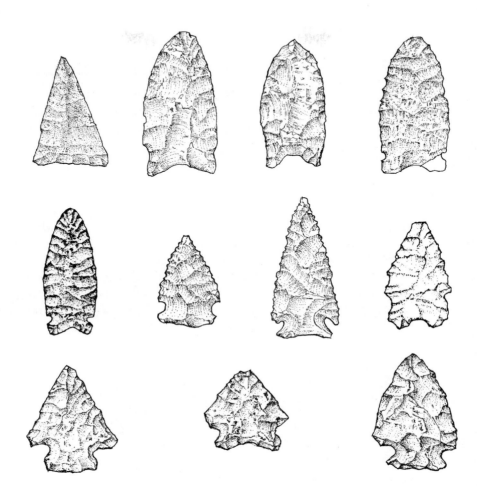

FIGURE 7: **EASTERN, CENTRAL, WESTERN, AND SOUTHERN EARLY ARCHAIC AND MIDDLE ARCHAIC PROJECTILE POINT STYLES** In the upper row a typical Eastern Early Archaic complex point style is followed by two Central Early Archaic and a Western Archaic complex examples. Another Western Early Archaic complex point from the Sheguiandah site on Manitoulin Island associated with the Plano culture occupation is shown to the left side of the middle row. The three points to the right are typical Southern Early Archaic complex forms while the last three points in the lower row are Middle Archaic complex specimens from the John's Bridge site in northwestern Vermont. (Drawn by David W. Laverie - Scale 1:1.3)

CHAPTER 5

EARLY MARITIME CULTURE

Précis:

Early Maritime culture developed out of the Eastern Early Archaic complex in the maritime regions of the Gulf of St.Lawrence and probably the Maritime provinces around 6,000 BC. Coastal submergence has destroyed the archaeological evidence along the coasts of the Maritime provinces while the rising coast of the northshore of the Gulf of St.Lawrence has elevated the earliest sites on the highest ancient beachlines above the present sea level. Early Maritime culture developed into the Middle Maritime culture of Period III (4,000 to 1,000 BC). Prior to 4,000 BC, Early Maritime people spread north to the central Labrador coast and there is tentative evidence that they also penetrated up the St.Lawrence River as far as Ontario. The sites along the Upper St.Lawrence River, however, are characterized by mixed cultural deposits that include contemporary Early Great Lakes-St.Lawrence culture materials. As both cultures shared certain elements of technology it has been difficult to isolate one from the other. There is currently a difference of opinion of whether the Period II materials near the embouchure of the Saguenay River into the St.Lawrence and immediately upriver represent Early Maritime culture (Maritime Archaic) or Early Great Lakes-St.Lawrence culture (Laurentian Archaic) (Plumet et al. 1993; Wright: 1994).

Early Maritime culture people were capable maritime hunters who also exploited land resources such as caribou. A chronology based upon elevated marine strandlines and radiocarbon dates has outlined a local sequence of development characterized by changing projectile point styles and other artifact categories. The occurrence of ground stone axes, gouges, lances, projectile points, and knives, is suggestive of southern influences. A significant addition to the weapon system is the earliest evidence in the Western Hemisphere of the toggling harpoon. Settlement pattern distributions indicate that Early Maritime culture societies were composed of small family groups who coalesced into bands during the portion of the yearly rounds spent on the coast. Marriages were likely contracted with neighbouring bands resulting in a broad social network of blood related families. One of the most striking features of Early Maritime culture is the construction of complex burial mounds. Such mounds represent the earliest evidence in Canada to date of monumental construction. It is suspected that the special need for cooperation among maritime hunters may have led to some degree of ranking although the ranking was likely personal rather than hereditary as well as being temporary. The possibility of some form of social ranking in the society is also inferred from the organization and cooperation required by mound construction.

Cultural origins and descendants:

The Eastern Early Archaic complex was ancestral to Early Maritime culture in the Gulf of St. Lawrence and probably the Maritime provinces. It has been suggested that Early Maritime culture received significant influences from the 6,000 BC Atlantic Slope Macrotradition (Dincauze 1976: 140; also see Brennan 1974 and Funk 1978) but the evidence is not particularly compelling (Renouf 1977) although it is probable that the ground stone tool component of the technology does reflect southern influences (Petersen 1991: Table 7). As much of the coast between the Gulf of St.Lawrence and the New England states has been submerged beneath the waters of the Atlantic it is particularly difficult to assess suspected north-south relationships. The chronological sequences along the northshore of the Gulf of St.Lawrence and north to the central Labrador coast demonstrate that Early Maritime culture developed directly into the Middle Maritime culture of Period III. Coastal uplift, resulting in a significant degree of isolation of cultural components on elevated strandlines, has provided archaeologists with an exceptional opportunity to study sequential changes in technology and other cultural systems.

Information on some of the radiocarbon dated sites pertaining to Early Maritime culture can be found in the following references: Québec - Lavoie (Plumet et al. 1993); Templier (Taillon et Barré 1987); Labrador - Barney, L'Anse Amour, Arrowhead Mine, Fowler, L'Anse Amour 10, 5-3d, and 5-3c (Fitzhugh 1975; McGhee and Tuck 1975); and Forteau Bay 1 and 3, Nukasusutok 5, Gull Arm 1, and Cut Throat 2 (Fitzhugh 1978). Radiocarbon dates from the Barney, Arrowhead Mine, and Juniper sites in the Strait of Belle Isle that were based upon scattered charcoal in poor context are rejected in favour of dates recovered from discrete features.

Technology:

Information on the technology of Early Maritime culture comes mainly from the northshore of the Gulf of St.Lawrence in the Strait of Belle Island region of Labrador and Québec (McGhee and Tuck 1975; Levesque 1980; n.d.). An exception to the foregoing statement is the Lavoie site (Archambault 1987; Plumet et al. 1993) situated downriver from Tadoussac. This 4,000 BC site produced side-notched and stemmed chipped projectile points, ground slate points and semilunar-shaped knives, choppers, bifacially flaked knives, abraders, polished stone axes and gouges, plummets, and wedges. Approximately 1,000 years earlier at the Koliktalik 1 site near Nain on the central Labrador coast nipple based projectile points, end scrapers, abundant wedges, ground slate semilunar knives and ground stone gouges, chisels and celts, including double-bitted forms, were recovered (Fitzhugh 1978). Also on the central Labrador coast in Hamilton Inlet is the 4,500 BC Black Island Cove 1 site (Fitzhugh 1975). Here, chipped stemmed projectile points, biface knives, wedges, chipped and ground celts, ground slate points and knives, flake knives, hammerstones, scrapers, and red ochre nodules are reported. The central Labrador coast assemblage compares closely with materials from the northshore of the Gulf of St.Lawrence. It is in this latter region, however, that the clearest evidence of technological change through time has been obtained (Levesque 1980; McGhee and Tuck 1975; Renouf 1977).

The earliest tools of Early Maritime culture consist of contracting stemmed projectile points with lateral grinding and often slight blade edge serration, bifacial knives, end scrapers, flake scrapers, wedges, hammerstones, hematite paintstones, and polished stone gouges. This basic tool kit, with certain minor modifications, continues to be used into later times with drills and ground slate projectile points, lances, and semilunar knives being added. Throughout a technological sequence of some 2,000 years projectile points, biface knives, and random flake scrapers predominate. Igneous and metamorphic cobbles, heated to boil water or roast food, are also a common occurrence. The heating and sudden cooling of such cobbles result in very distinctive fracture patterns not duplicated by nature. Another characteristic of the Early Maritime culture tool kit is a heavy reliance upon local stone, particularly quartzite and quartz, with little evidence of the use of imported stone.

As a rule, bone does not survive on Early Maritime culture sites. An exception was the L'Anse Amour burial mound site where the boulders capping the mound contributed to the preservation of the bone grave offerings. This accident of preservation revealed an elaborate bone industry. Bone implements consisted of conical socketed projectile points, a stemmed point, an antler paint grinder-applicator, a pendant, a two-hole flute, and particularly significant, a toggling harpoon head and an ivory hand toggle (McGhee and Tuck 1975: 87-92; McGhee 1976). To the best of my knowledge, the toggling harpoon represents the earliest example of its kind in the World. Unlike harpoons that are fixed into a spear shaft, the toggling harpoon upon impact detaches from the tip of the spear shaft but remains attached to a hand-held line. After penetrating the hide of a sea mammal the line comes under tension and the toggling harpoon head `toggles´ into a horizontal position under the hide of the prey making it almost impossible to be dislodged from the wound. The toggle handle would be held by the hunter to control the line until the prey weakened and could be drawn into spear or club ranges for `le coup de gra•e´. Such a technological innovation, particularly if supported by line floats, would permit the capture of large sea mammals at sea and markedly reduce the risks in hunting a dangerous animal like the walrus. The ivory hand toggle as well as the flute, the pendant, and the antler pestle-paint applicator were all decorated with horizontal lines of short parallel incisions. The occurrence of dog remains at the Lavoie site (Plumet et al. 1993) raises the likelihood of the use of this domesticated animal in hunting and possibly as a draft animal.

Subsistence:

Although acid soils rarely permitted the survival of bone, the fact that the majority of recorded sites are located along the coast indicates that maritime resources were seasonally important. The site distribution also suggests that the coastal portion of the seasonal round was the time when the largest aggregations of people took place. It is only from fall to early winter that marine resources are scarce on the coast and during this period Early Maritime culture hunters likely moved into the interior to obtain caribou for meat and hides. On the assumption that animal behaviour patterns were similar to that of today, harp, hood, ringed, and bearded seals would be available in late winter as would the once extant walrus herds. From December to June, harbour and grey seals, porpoise, and small whales would be present. In June, the arrival of the enormous caplin schools would bring codfish and other predators close to shore.

FIGURE 8: TYPICAL EARLY MARITIME CULTURE PROJECTILE POINTS The two projectile points, manufactured from local quartzite and quartz cobbles, were recovered from elevated marine beachlines in the Strait of Belle Isle region of southern Labrador. (Drawings by David W. Laverie. Scale 1:1.3)

Spawning salmon and sea trout as well as nesting seabirds would add to the rich resources of the area. The nutritional importance of caplin and other animals that leave no trace in the archaeological record such as squid, lobster, and crab, will never be known. The fact that most major archaeological sites along the northshore of the Gulf of St.Lawrence are situated on sand beaches between bedrock headlands suggests that caplin, who use such beaches during spawning, may have been a major attraction to the coast.

Bone refuse recovered from Level III of the Lavoie site indicated that seal were the major prey. Next in frequency was beaver followed by smaller quantities of bones identified as red fox, porcupine, dog, and whale including beluga. Minor traces of moose, hare, caribou, deer, weasel family, and black bear are also recorded (Plumet et al. 1993: Tableaus 55 et 56). Birds were important at this site representing 7.9% of a sample dominated by mammals and particularly seal (91.8%). Fish only represented 0.3% of the total sample but the fragile nature of all the bones recovered from the site and the fact that the occupation was on an active beach lacking plant cover may have contributed to their poor survival in the archaeological deposits. The presence of dog bone fragments suggests that dogs were occasionally used as food.

With reference to the Strait of Belle Isle region on the northshore of the Gulf of St.Lawrence, it has been speculated that Early Maritime culture people retired to the interior in the fall and early winter for the caribou hunt, returning to the coast in late winter-spring for the harp seal and fishing and open-water and/or ice-edge hunting (McGhee and Tuck 1975: 120). Certainly the toggling harpoon, toggle handle, and the presence of a walrus tusk in the L'Anse Amour burial mound points to ice-edge and/or open water hunting of a large and dangerous animal. Towards the end of Period II direct evidence of subsistence in the form of calcined seal, caribou, and bird remains occurs.

Settlement patterns:

Sites along the northshore of the Gulf of St.Lawrence tend to be located on sandy beaches between bedrock headlands. Few discrete features have been recognized on these sites suggesting that dwellings were both flimsy and probably disturbed by subsequent seasonal occupations. There is also the possibility that camps were situated on active beaches lacking vegetative cover such as noted at the Lavoie site (Plumet et al. 1993). At one site the concentrations of cultural debris tended to be a few meters in diameter (McGhee and Tuck 1975: 36), possibly representing the remains of single family dwellings.

Prior to 4,000 BC, some of the bands from the northshore of the Gulf of St.Lawrence moved north to occupy most of the Labrador coast. This event correlated with a major increase of Arctic shrubs such as alder, willow and dwarf birch around 4,500 BC that would have provided people with firewood and material for tools (Short 1978). While the northern-most forays likely represented seasonal events, the central portion of the Labrador coast and the adjacent interior could have supported people throughout the year. In this region settlement on the outer coast at sites such as Koliktalik 1 favoured locales with sand beaches and protected coves (Fitzhugh 1978: 79). Sites also tended to be situated on the eastern shore of islands and headlands with an unobstructed view of the sea or near the mouths of deep bays. Some of the large sites may have been seasonal base camps from which small groups of hunters could range out. As further south, features are rare consisting of shallow pit hearths filled with fire fractured rock. Circular pit houses three to four meters in diameter, dug into cobble beaches, are believed to date between 5,000 and 4,000 BC (Fitzhugh 1984). This age estimate, however, is based upon both the elevation above the present sea level and hypothetical considerations of house form development. Such circular to oval structures, representing single family dwellings, are recorded in clusters of up to three.

The seasonal cycle on the central Labrador coast appears to have involved a movement to the larger sites on the outer islands in the spring in order to intercept the northward migrating harp seal. Other sea mammals, such as walrus, as well as sea birds would also have been available. In the summer, small groups would disperse to the surrounding islands and bays to exploit local resources, to trade, and visit. In the fall, the caribou hunt would be followed by the harp seal hunt along the adjacent mainland (Fitzhugh 1978).

Most Early Maritime culture sites represent late winter to summer camps distributed along the coasts and are presumed to have functioned as base camps from which small groups of hunters ranged out over their hunting territories. Some sites where quartzite and quartz cobbles were available would permit the replacing of the worn-out elements of the tool kit. Evidence from the Lavoie site has led to the suggestion that it was essentially a seal butchering locale (Plumet et al. 1993: 144). The absence of scrapers and drills at this site, used as evidence to support this special function, is not convincing as the occurrence of these tool categories in Early Maritime culture around 4,000 BC is quite erratic (McGhee and Tuck 1975). Of course, the authors of the Lavoie site report attribute the site to Early Great Lakes-St.Lawrence culture (Laurentian Archaic) and not Early Maritime culture. If the people occupying the site were indeed seasonal visitors from far up the St.Lawrence River the total absence of exotic stone is curious as one would expect such travellers to bring their home territory tool kit with them rather than rely upon local resources.

Cosmology:

The 7,500 BP L'Anse Amour burial mound in southern Labrador (McGhee and Tuck 1975; McGhee 1976) is currently the earliest elaborate mortuary structure in Canada (Colour Plates IV and V). The one meter high mound consisted of two layers of cobbles, averaging 10 kg in weight, which covered an area approximately 8 m in diameter. An abrader and a chunk of quartz had been placed in the centre of this cobble mound covering. Under the lower cobble layer a cist composed of vertically set bolder slabs was encountered and extended to a depth of 1 m below the surface of the mound (see Harris and Matthews 1987: Plate 15, upper right corner). Some form of decomposed organic matter and a hearth with some fishbones was all that was found in the cist except for red ochre that had been sprinkled around its edge. At 30 cm below the cist an extended subadult was found lying on its stomach with a large rock slab placed across the lower back. Two ceremonial hearths demarcated by charcoal stains one meter in diameter were present on either side of the body. The body was oriented with the head to west and faced north with the arms at the sides. Grave offerings consisted of the following: a sprinkling of red ochre over the back of the head; an unworked walrus tusk near the head; a cluster of four chipped projectile points or knives, three socketed bone points, and a stemmed bone point immediately to the west of the skull; two stone points or knives at one shoulder and a biface knife between the legs; two graphite paintstone nodules stained with red ochre and a decorated caribou antler paint pestle/applicator formed a cluster at the waist; a bone pendant, a bone whistle or flute, a few fragments of bird bone, and a bone toggling harpoon head were placed under the chest; and under the pelvis a decorated antler toggle was encountered. A boulder had been placed to one side of the body and some antler and quartz chunks on the opposite side. Scattered charcoal particles demarcated a grave pit five meters in diameter. Although in a state of poor preservation it was possible to determine that the subadult was between 11 and 13 years of age (McGhee and Tuck 1975: 93-94).

Tumulus II near Blanc-Sablon in adjacent Québec is another mound which is likely as early or earlier than the L'Anse Amour mound despite its 3,500 BP radiocarbon dates (Levesque 1980: 157-158; Taillon et Barré 1987). The mound measured 8.5 m in diameter and rose 1.4 m above a rectanguloid cist 2.1 by 2.4 m dug 1 m into the sterile beach sand. Construction had consisted of digging the cist and lining it with vertical stone slabs. The body or bodies, assumed to have been totally dissolved by acid soils, would then have been placed in the chamber along with the grave offerings. Then the top of the cist was capped with cobbles, a layer of sand was mounded over the cist and the surrounding area to be capped with a layer of boulder slabs and the process repeated once again (see Figure 23 in Chapter 14). It is the typological characteristics of some of the grave offerings that suggest the mound was an early feature (Fitzhugh 1980: 158). Although these materials have never been described they included full-grooved polished stone gouges and nipple based projectile points (personal examination courtesy of René Levesque, St.Foy, Québec). Similar points from the nearby Templier site have been dated to 5,000 BC.

Both the single burial in the L'Anse Amour mound and the limited holding capacity of the Tumulus II mound cist suggest that these features were of special ceremonial significance and not the standard method of burying the dead. The fact that such mound features, representing a considerable span of time, have been found along the coast of the Strait of Belle Isle and north to the central Labrador coast, indicates

COLOUR PLATE IV: A VIEW OF THE EARLY MARITIME CULTURE L'ANSE AMOUR BURIAL MOUND ON THE SOUTH COAST OF LABRADOR The mound with its capping layer of boulders is seen here after it was restored to its original form following excavation. (Reproduced from McGhee 1976)

that the belief system that required their erection was both persistent and widespread. Due to the overlying caps of cobbles at the L'Anse Amour mound, which protected bone from normal soil acidity, archaeologists have also had their first glimpse of the elaborate bone technology of Early Maritime culture. The use of red ochre and quartz chunks in the mound ceremony are of unknown symbolic significance. While it can be speculated that the central purpose of the mound ceremonialism probably related to establishing a favourable position within the all powerful supernatural world that surrounded people, we will never know the details of the ceremonialism nor why, in the case of the L'Anse Amour mound, a twelve year old child was the centre of focus. For a fictious but imaginative reconstruction of the events surrounding this mound see McGhee (1976). It is likely that such mounds acted as territory markers that would be respected by members of other bands.

A feature discovered at the Arrowhead Mine site on the southern Labrador coast may indicate a more common method of disposal of the dead. At this site a pit 30 cm in diameter and 20 cm deepcontained six crude bifacial preforms, two polished stone full-grooved gouges, and a projectile point, all covered with red ochre (McGhee and Tuck 1975: 36-37). The feature probably represents a grave where the remains have been totally destroyed by acid soil.

External relationships:

Early Maritime culture sites characteristically lack evidence of external trade. The dominant use of local quartzite cobbles is suggestive of either isolated populations not involved in a broad exchange network or which had not yet located major local sources of high quality siliceous stone. The probability that the ground stone tool elements of the technology represent southern ideas that diffused northward has already been commented upon. Some of the projectile point forms and attributes like blade edge serration are also reminiscent of more southerly Early Archaic points. There does appear to have been a prolonged relationship with Early Great Lakes-St.Lawrence culture. While the probable boundary between these two contemporary groups was likely a short distance upriver from Québec City (Côté 1987), characteristic Early Maritime culture projectile points have been recovered from mixed multi-component sites along the 200 km section of the St.Lawrence River between Trois-Rivières and Cornwall (Lueger 1977; Marois 1987; Wright: 1994). As both cultures shared many of the same ground stone tools and as there are certain similarities in their side-notched projectile point styles, there has been difficulty isolating the two cultures from one another in the mixed archaeological deposits of the upper St.Lawrence River. On the admittedly tenuous basis of projectile point typology contacts between the two cultures could have taken place as early as 6,000 BC and continued for more than four millennia. If current evidence is correct and there was a major technological transfer of ground stone tools from Early Maritime culture to the interior Early Great Lakes-St.Lawrence culture (Tuck1976a: 116-117) such a culture contact situation would not likely have been one-sided even though reciprocity from the interior has not been recognized in the archaeological record.

The similarity of the small quartz end scrapers of both the Eastern Early Archaic complex and Early Maritime culture to specimens from the Brigham site in central Maine has been noted (Petersen et al. 1986: 10). In addition to the end scrapers, the occurrence of polished stone celts from the 7,450 +/- 440 BP dated stratum of this site raises some interesting considerations as do the ground slate points from the nearby Sharrow site associated with a 6,320 +/- 110 BP date (Petersen and Putnam 1987). While the Maine dates on ground stone tools are similar to those from the north the likelihood of a northward spread of stone grinding is tentatively supported by the occurrence of ground stone celts and spearthrower weights at the 9,500 BP Nettling site near Lake Erie (Ellis et al. 1991). Whether the fashioning of tools by grinding diffused down the St.Lawrence River or along the Atlantic coast or both is difficult to assess at this time. Paradoxically, with reference to the St.Lawrence route, ground stone tools such as gouges, semilunar knives, and ground slate lances and points are significantly earlier in the Gulf of St.Lawrence than equivalent material in the lower Great Lakes suggesting diffusion upriver rather than the reverse (Tuck 1976a: 116-117).

`A´

`B´

COLOUR PLATE V: THE L'ANSE AMOUR BURIAL AND SOME OF THE GRAVE OFFERINGS
View `A´ shows the twelve year old child that was buried under the mound. The individual was placed in an extended position on its stomach; a most unusual burial position. Grave offerings are shown in place as well as the stone slab over the back. Photograph `B´ illustrates some of the bone implements that were placed with the deceased. On the left and the lower centre are two bone points. In the upper centre is the oldest known toggling harpoon in Canada. On the right is a highly ornamented ivory toggling handle. (Reproduced from McGhee 1976)

Across the Canadian Shield from Québec to Manitoba a limited number of full-grooved polished stone gouges and ground slate lances have been found to the west of the Early Maritime culture distribution (Wright 1972a). Such typologically early tools could have been acquired by Early Shield culture (Chapter 8) from either Early Maritime culture or through Early Great Lakes-St.Lawrence culture intermediaries. The probability that the tools in question are quite early is not only suggested by their dated contexts along the coast but by the possible association of a gouge with the dated human remains from a site in Northern Ontario. Red ochre burials destroyed during the construction of an airfield on the Wapekeka Indian Reserve 600 km north of Thunder Bay, have provided AMS dates of 7,080 +/- 90, 6,800 +/- 90, and 6,630 +/- 90 BP (Hamilton 1991). The sparse evidence does suggest that Early Maritime culture had relationships with both Early Shield culture and Early Great Lakes-St.Lawrence culture as well as people to the south along the Atlantic coast.

Human biology:

All that can be said concerning the subadult found in the L'Anse Amour mound is that the individual stood 150 cm in height, its sex cannot be determined, and discrete traits suggest it was "...apparently an American Indian" (Jerkic 1975: 93-94).

Inferences on society:

Early Maritime societies would have consisted of small populations of related families organized into regional bands. Individual relationships were likely egalitarian albeit with some age and possible gender ranking. The cooperative effort that is often required of sea mammal hunters to be successful in the killing of large and dangerous sea mammals, however, may have required authority to be at least temporarily vested in the band leader or, more likely, boat captain. Similarly, the labour involved in the construction of burial mounds suggests a level of social organization not usually associated with hunting societies. Individual family mobility provided by watercraft in conjunction with a leader's knowledge of boatmanship, the sea, and his `hunting luck´ could have contributed to families being attracted to the leadership of specific individuals whose personal prestige would then be enhanced. Such status, however, would have been based upon abilities or, more accurately, perceived power, and not blood and thus would have been vested in the individual and not his family line or other kinship unit. If, for example, the individual's `luck´ changed he would probably be abandoned in favour of a more successful band leader or boat captain.

Limitations in the evidence:

The greatest single limiting factor in the evidence was rising sea levels that destroyed or submerged contemporary sites in the Maritime provinces and the New England states. If the northshore of the Gulf of St. Lawrence and the Labrador coast had been similarly submerged archaeology would know virtually nothing of this thriving maritime culture that occupied the region for so many thousands of years. This is particularly so given the concentrated settlement on the coast. Interior hunt camps must still exist and it can only be hoped that the interior tool kit of Early Maritime culture did not differ too dramatically from the sea mammal hunting tool kit. Functional differences in tool kits appear to have been insignificant among the hunting populations in Canada.

Another major limitation in the evidence pertaining to Early Maritime technology is the near total absence of bone due to acid soils. Such a limitation forces inferences on subsistence to be drawn from the settlement pattern distributions. Fortunately, the special conditions of the L'Anse Amour burial mound permitted a glimpse of the elaborate bone technology. The general lack of skeletal remains also frustrates efforts to glean information on population relationships and other biological considerations.

More detailed qualitative and quantitative descriptions of the respective technologies of Early Maritime and Early Great Lakes-St.Lawerence cultures are required in order to distinguish between the two. There has been a tendency for archaeologists to look to the interior of the continent for comparisons rather than the east coast and this has led to probable erroneous cultural assignments (Badgley et Boissonnault 1985; Plumet et al. 1993). This problem of cultural identification has been compounded by the generally hopelessly mixed multi-component sites of the upper St.Lawrence River.

CHAPTER 6
EARLY GREAT LAKES-ST. LAWRENCE CULTURE

Précis:

Given the limited information on Early Great Lakes-St.Lawrence culture all comment can be confined to a précis. The somewhat cumbersome name `Great Lakes-St.Lawrence´ is intended to identify the Lake Erie, southern Lake Huron, Lake Ontario, and the St.Lawrence valley upriver from Québec City as the region occupied by this culture. It is a region of lowlands flanking the Canadian Shield to the north. The vegetation province during the latter part of Period II was Great Lakes-St.Lawrence Forest except for a significant portion of western Southern Ontario where a Deciduous Forest prevailed (McAndrews et al. 1987). Not only does this region today contain the richest farmlands of Ontario and Québec but it is also the area of most dense human population. The proposal of an Early Great Lakes-St.Lawrence culture is more a working hypothesis than a demonstrable entity. In fact, the formulator of the concept of the Laurentian Archaic, here referred to as Great Lakes-St.Lawrence culture, would restrict its application to Period III (4,000 to 1,000 BC) (Ritchie 1971). While the archaeological evidence for a pre-4,000 BC Early Great Lakes-St.Lawrence culture is weak, there is a basis for the assumption that such a culture construct will eventually be demonstrated. This assumption is premised on the following: the association of broad side-notched projectile points (Figure 9) with sites dated to approximately 5,500 BC (Funk 1965; Wellman 1974); the existence of earlier Middle Archaic complex sites in the region that shared certain chipped stone traits with Early Great Lakes-St.Lawrence culture (Thomas and Robinson 1980); and the fact that the much better known Middle Great Lakes-St.Lawrence culture of Period III must have developed out of a local ancestral population as evidence of a population intrusion is absent. Thus, the Early Great Lakes-St.Lawrence culture or, as it is also known, Proto-Laurentian, developed in situ from a Middle Archaic culture base (Funk 1988: 17). Pertinent sites in New York State, dated between 5,500 and 5,000 BC, contain broad side-notched projectile points, end and side scrapers, biface knives, and rough stone tools but appear to lack ground stone implements (Funk 1988: 26). This simple chipped stone tool kit is widely distributed in eastern North America. As has been noted, within this distribution "...rigid boundaries cannot be drawn for archaeological cultures or complexes" and "In the absence of important geographic or ecological barriers to movements of traits and peoples, individual traits generally vary independently in frequency and distribution outside the territory where the clusters were first observed by archaeologists" (Funk 1988: 34). Like the preceding Middle Archaic complex, the chipped stone tool kit of Early Great Lakes-St.Lawrence culture is not distinctive from that of the early portion of Middle Great Lakes-St.Lawrence culture. Some of the regionally distinctive ground stone celts, knives, points, lances and plummets were likely adopted late in Period II. As others have noted (Funk 1988; Tuck 1976), the diagnostic ground stone tools of Middle Great Lakes-St.Lawrence culture appears to have actually been adopted from Early and Middle Maritime culture in the Gulf of St.Lawrence. Thus, contrary to the poor typological visibility of the simple and widespread chipped stone technology of Early Great Lakes-St.Lawrence culture, the addition of the regionally distinctive ground stone tool categories to Middle Great Lakes-St.Lawrence culture technology permits cultural identifications even when materials are removed from an archaeological context. It is probably for this reason that recognized evidence of Early Great Lakes-St.Lawrence culture is so sparse in contrast to the abundant evidence of their descendants who adopted ground stone tools. This difficulty has been further compounded by the fact that many Early Great Lakes-St.Lawrence culture sites are submerged beneath the waters of the Great Lakes and Lake Champlain and are either destroyed by erosion or deeply buried by sedimentary processes. Problems relating to cultural identifications based upon a limited number of `distinctive´ traits instead of the dominant, albeit simple, tool kit will be considered in greater detail in the discussion of Middle Great Lakes-St.Lawrence culture in Chapter 15.

An accidentally discovered burial probably pertains to Early Great Lakes-St.Lawrence culture (Katzenberg and Sullivan 1979). The buried individual was a male over 50 years of age who had been placed on his back in a tightly flexed position in a grave on the south slope of a small hill west of Toronto. Some missing hand and foot bones and teeth suggest that the body was in an advanced state of decay prior to burial, possibly due to death in the winter when frozen ground forced a temporary scaffold burial. In life the individual stood 169 cm (5' 6.5") in height and was moderately broad headed with a high cranial vault. This particular skull shape is comparable to a number of Archaic populations in the following Period III (Pfeiffer 1977). Evidence of disease was restricted to the common maladies of age, namely osteoarthritis of the vertebral column, the upper limb, the foot, and the clavicle and advanced dental attrition leading to some peridontal infection of the surrounding jaw bone. A radiocarbon date of 5,910+/-165 BP, which calibrates to between 5215 and 4450 BC, places the burial within the time period under consideration. Non-perishable grave offerings were lacking and, therefore, a cultural identification of the burial was not possible.

An important discovery at the stratified Sharrow site in central Maine has ramifications for Early Great Lakes-St.Lawrence culture. Some of the charcoal floated from site features for radiocarbon dating was submitted for botanical examination which identified squash rind (Cucurbita sp.) ((Petersen 1991: 141-143). The radiocarbon date of 6,320 +/- 110 BP from the feature containing the squash remains calibrates between 5,535 and 5,005 BC (Klein et al. 1982). An AMS date on a 0.2 mg sample of the squash rind provided a date of 5, 595 +/- 100 BP or 4,870 to 4,400 BC (James B. Petersen: University of Maine, Farmington, personal communication, 1992). The earlier date is likely the more accurate given the small sample used in the AMS date. Only in Illinois have dates associated with squash been earlier (Asch and Asch 1985). The Sharrow site squash represents the earliest evidence of plant cultivation in northeastern North America. Stratigraphy at the site was excellent thus limiting the possibility of the squash being introduced into the feature by accident. Carbonized squash seeds have been recovered from sites in Michigan and Ohio adjacent to Southern Ontario that date to 500 BC. Carbonized squash is very fragile and does not survive well in archaeological deposits. Even its recovery from the Sharrow site was accidental in that samples of charcoal were being collected for radiocarbon dating. Given the Period II

FIGURE 9:   A PROBABLE EARLY GREAT LAKES-ST.LAWRENCE CULTURE PROJECTILE POINT   This point from near Cornwall on the upper St. Lawrence River was not recovered from a datable context but is believed, on typological grounds, to pertain to Period II.   Most such specimens are recovered from the surfaces of ploughed fields. (Drawing by David W. Laverie, Scale 1:1.3)

dates on squash cultivation in Illinois and Maine there is a possibility the cultigen was also cultivated by Early Great Lakes-St.Lawrence culture people in Canada, particulary in the western portion of Southern Ontario where the Deciduous Forest vegetation province of 5,000 BC (McAndrews et al. 1987) would have been most conducive to incipient horticulture. There is increasing evidence that long before the development of full-blown agricultural economies Archaic peoples were far advanced in experimenting with plant domestication.

It is unfortunate that so little is known of this critical period in the Great Lakes and St.Lawrence Valley region. Suffice to repeat that Early Great Lakes-St.Lawrence culture suffers from the same lack of typological visibility as its Middle Archaic complex predecessor. It was from this archaeologically ephemeral cultural base, however, that the much more detailed archaeological record of Period III must have been derived.

CHAPTER 7

PLANO CULTURE

Précis:

The name 'Plano' derives from the fact that the culture was first recognized on the Plains. In part, the name is a misnomer as Plano culture extends from the Southern Plateau of British Columbia to the Atlantic coast and from Keewatin District in the Northwest Territories to the Gulf of Mexico. Moreso than the Early Archaic complexes of the east, Plano culture's occupation of a number of markedly different environments mimics that of its Palaeo-Indian ancestors. The core area of the culture, however, was the Plains and whether Plano culture is found on the Gaspé coast of Québec or the Barrengrounds of the Northwest Territories, its origin was originally the Plains. Although Plano culture incorporates a number of regionally different assemblages these are all held together by a highly distinctive method of chipping stone. The technological change from late Palaeo-Indian culture to early Plano culture on the Plains involved a dramatic change in projectile point form with the rest of the stone tool kit, settlement patterns and subsistence characteristics remaining unchanged. It is speculated that the change in projectile point style relates to a change in the weapon system (Frison 1990: 22), possibly the replacement of the split shaft hafting method by a socketed hafting system. Whatever the changes in the weapon system, the new point styles were rapidly adopted across the Plains and adjacent regions. These changes in point form took place shortly before 10,000 BP, a time when the spruce forests were being replaced by grasslands with an intervening parkland belt (Epp and Dyck 1983: 66; J. Ritchie 1976).

The Canadian Plains represent the northern portion of the Central Plains of North America and the northern Plano culture bands participated in the cultural developments of this extensive region. It is therefore possible to draw upon a substantial body of information from the northern Plains of the United States. There is evidence that the spread of some elements of early Plano culture into the Plains of Canada was from the south. This is seen in the abundance to tools manufactured from distinctive stone varieties whose geological sources are to the south (Ebell 1980: 18). Early Plano culture occurs south of the North Saskatchewan River in Saskatchewan and in the foothills of the Rocky Mountains north to the Peace River Valley of Alberta and adjacent British Columbia. At this time, most of Manitoba was still covered by Glacial Lake Agassiz and associated glacial ice (Buchner and Pettipas 1990: Fig.6).

The regions occupied in the west were the grasslands and parklands that were most attractive to the bison herds. Around 9,000 BP the retreating glaciers and associated lakes permitted the expansion of plant and animal communities to the north and the east. In these newly released regions caribou would have replaced bison as the major prey animal. An eastward population shift along a relatively narrow corridor between the glacial ice and lakes to the north and the expanding Early Archaic complexes to the south, eventually would reach the east coast. There was also a possible western penetration over the Rocky Mountains into the Southern Plateau (Fladmark 1986: 24; Stryd and Rousseau n.d.) but the nature of the occupation is still unclear.

Plano peoples, both on the Plains and in adjacent regions, adopted cultural traits of eastern Early Archaic origin, particularly projectile point styles. These technological changes have provided archaeologists with a basis for establishing a number of regional cultures east of the Continental Divide during the late portion of Period II. On the Plains the bison hunting way of life persisted whereas both the Eastern and Northern variants of Plano culture changed subsistence and settlement patterns, as well as their technologies, in response to markedly different environmental conditions. The development of a widely distributed Plano culture into two later regional cultures, Early Shield and Early Plains, appears to have been realized by the processes of changing technologies, such as the adoption of the spearthrower, and adaptation in the north and the east to the Lichen Woodland and Boreal Forest environments (McAndrews et al. 1987).

Cultural origins and descendants:

The cultural antecedent of Plano culture was late Palaeo-Indian culture on the Plains. Its descendants were Early Plains culture of the Grasslands, Parklands and Foothills and Early Shield culture of the Lichen Woodlands and Boreal Forest of the Canadian Shield and its margins. The latter developments are recognizable around 8,000 BP. Many archaeologists believe Plano culture extended into the Yukon and western Northwest Territories as well as Alaska although both the technological and chronological evidence for such a population incursion is weak. Given the extensive territory and variable environments involved, Plano culture will be considered within Western, Northern, and Eastern subareas. A questionable Northwestern subarea will also be examined.

WESTERN PLANO:

As Western Plano was ancestral to both the Eastern and Northern Plano geographical variants it will be considered first and in greater depth than the others. Most archaeologists regard early Western Plano culture as having descended from late Palaeo-Indian (Folsom) culture (Frison and Stanford 1982: 367; Irwin and Wormington 1970: 25; Irwin-Williams et al. 1973). Strong continuities are apparent in the technology, subsistence, and settlement patterns. Both stratigraphy and radiocarbon dates reinforce the sequential relationship of early Western Plano to late Palaeo-Indian culture.

Perhaps more than in any other region in North America projectile point styles on the Plains have dictated cultural assignments and temporal placements. This emphasis upon projectile point styles has been encouraged by sudden changes in projectile point form. As there is no evidence of population replacement to account for these widespread and synchronous changes in point styles, diffusion of technology would seem to be the most likely causal factor. It is speculated that such projectile point style changes relate to improvements in the re-arming capabilities and possible penetration characteristics of the composite thrusting spear. While differing in a number of important respects, Plano culture projectile points retain the symmetry and precision of chipping found in late Palaeo-Indian culture. The introduction of the spearthrower around 8,000 BP transformed Plano culture on the Plains into Early Plains culture.

In many parts of the northern Plains the earliest Plano culture projectile point style, a lanceolate form called Agate Basin after a site in Wyoming, was replaced by stemmed point varieties called Alberta, Scottsbluff, and Eden. Other than some increase in the numbers of specialized stone tools the remainder of the tool kit remained basically unchanged as did the subsistence and settlement patterns. Lanceolate point styles, superficially similar to the earlier Agate Basin point type, continued to be used in the Foothills and reappeared on the High Plains during late Plano culture times between 9,000 and 8,000 BP. It is at this time that cultural regionalism becomes increasingly apparent, a development that was probably accelerated by a time transgressive climatic event called the Altithermal or Hypsithermal, dated in Alberta on the basis of water level fluctuations in lake basins between 9,000 and 6,000 BP (Schweger et al. 1981). This period of intermittent hot, dry summers and cold winters would have reduced water availability and forage, forcing bison into higher latitudes and river valleys along with their predators including people. By approximately 8,000 BP late Plano culture materials are found in direct association with notched projectile points of southern and eastern origin (Doll 1982; Forbis 1968). In the Plains of the United States such notched points replaced the lanceolate varieties by 8,500 BP (Wheat 1972: 158) suggesting there was a gradual advance northward of the new projectile point form. Shortly after 8,000 BP notched projectile points totally replaced the lanceolate forms on both the Plains and the adjacent Foothills of the Rocky Mountains. It has been argued with some justification that these notched projectile points represent the first evidence of the introduction of the spearthrower onto the Plains (Reeves 1983: 36). This proposition is supported by the appearance of distinctive eastern Early Archaic projectile point attributes, such as the blade bevelling of the transitional Pryor Stem points of Montana/Wyoming dated between 8,500 and 7,500 BP (Frison 1978:37).

A decline in the craftmanship of stone chipping, an increase in the varieties of points, and a decrease in the use of exotic stone are significant traits that accompany the transformation of Plano culture into Early Plains culture. In attempting to explain the greater stylistic homogeneity of Plano culture relative to the succeeding Archaic stylistic heterogeneity, it has been suggested the latter was a product of decreasing social interaction (Hayden 1982). A contrary view is that there has been an over-emphasis on Archaic technological heterogeneity on the Plains. Also, the so-called decline in projectile point `craftmanship´ likely relates to the different functional requirements of dart heads for spears propelled by a spearthrower as opposed to the stone tips of hand thrusted weapons.

There is currently a debate regarding the nature of Plano cultural development on the Plains. Although there is both stratigraphic and technological evidence of cultural continuity from early to late Western Plano involving a sequence of projectile point style changes, progressing from Agate Basin to Hell Gap to Alberta to Scottsbluff and Eden (Cody) and terminal Plano lanceolate varieties (Frison 1978;

Irwin-Williams et al. 1973), a number of archaeologists regard the Agate Basin-Hell Gap and Alberta-Cody units as partially contemporary and competing populations or traditions (Buchner and Pettipas 1990; Dyck 1983; Pettipas and Buchner 1983). In the Waterton Lakes National Park in the Foothills of southwestern Alberta a site dated to 8,000 BP produced Agate Basin points associated with Scottsbluff and Southwestern Coastal culture (Cordilleran) varieties. Exotic stone indicated contacts with Montana and Wyoming, the northern Alberta Rockies, and the interior of British Columbia (Reeves 1975: 245). It has been suggested than an Agate Basin variety of Western Plano moved into the Rockies and gave rise to a population distinct from the Southwestern Coastal culture to the west and the Cody Complex on the Plains to the east (Reeves 1975; Swanson 1962). The proposition has received support from the Wyoming evidence (Frison et al. 1986). On the other side of the Plains in Manitoba, it has been proposed that Agate Basin-Hell Gap (early Western Plano) spread into the province following the expanding grasslands and bison herds between 10,000 and 9,500 BP but were displaced by Alberta-Cody (late Western Plano) hunters who were following other northward shifting bison herds responding to reduced forage caused by a warming trend between 9,000 and 8,500 BP (Pettipas and Buchner 1983). The descendants of the original Agate Basin-Hell Gap population were then pushed into the forests of the Canadian Shield and to the north into Keewatin District in the Northwest Territories. Unfortunately the uncritical application of the term `Agate Basin´ to a wide range of lanceolate point forms has led to the suggestion that Agate Basin is common to a number of different regions including the Foothills of the Rockies, the McKenzie District of the Northwest Territories, and the western margins of the Canadian Shield. There is relatively good stratigraphic and radiocarbon evidence throughout the northern Plains for the priority of early Western Plano, characterized by Agate Basin and Hell Gap type projectile points, relative to late Western Plano with its Alberta and Scottsbluff/Eden projectile points. At this point in time the stratigraphic evidence is favoured over a loose application of typological evidence. Thus, the early and late Western Plano units are regarded as sequential entities rather than contemporary competing populations.

NORTHERN PLANO:

Northern Plano represents an off-shoot of Western Plano that adapted to the resources of the boreal forest/lichen woodland/tundra vegetation provinces. The move to the north may have been encouraged by the availability of caribou herds and a decreasing predictability of the bison herds reacting to Altithermal climatic fluctuations. This adaptation did not necessarily represent a simple switch from bison to caribou as presumably from earliest times caribou were exploited by the more northerly hunting bands. The transition from the Plains to the northern environmental zones produced significant changes in the technology (Wright 1976) and ultimately the transformation of Northern Plano into Early Shield culture (Wright 1972).

EASTERN PLANO:

Eastern Plano was another off-shoot of Western Plano that spread eastward as far as the Atlantic.

To the north, the Eastern Plano culture distribution was constricted by both glacial lakes and ice. To the south it was constricted by Early Archaic people and the expanding deciduous forests. Evidence of Eastern Plano culture in the states of New York and Vermont is limited (Funk 1983) except close to the St.Lawrence River (Ritchie 1944: Plate 115, figs.13-15; 1953; 1965). The Boreal Forest and Lichen Woodland vegetation provinces appropriate to caribou were also compressed into a narrow east-west corridor (McAndrews et al. 1987) that correlated relatively well with the distribution of the majority of Eastern Plano sites. Although minor elements of Western Plano culture did penetrate Southern Ontario from the Ohio Valley, the major thrust to the east was along the northern margin of presumed caribou habitat. This penetration to the east, however, appears to have involved a small population that retained its cultural identity for only a short period of time.

As was the case with Northern Plano, the transition from Plains bison hunting to the resources of the boreal forest/lichen woodland would have initially been a matter of emphasis rather than substantive change. Technological change required by the forest-tundra adaptation and the adoption of the spearthrower from Early Archaic neighbours, as evidenced by the direct association of notched points with Plano point varieties (Buckmaster and Paquette 1988; Greenman and Stanley 1940; Lee 1957; Mason and Irwin 1960; Storck 1978; 1982: 13), led to the transformation of Eastern Plano into Early Shield culture and possibly, to a lesser degree, Early Great Lakes-St.Lawrence culture.

NORTHWESTERN PLANO?:

While bona fide Western Plano projectile points have been recorded as far north as the Peace River Valley in Alberta and British Columbia (Fladmark 1981; Wormington and Forbis 1965) the presence of Plano culture in the McKenzie River Valley, the Yukon, and much of Alaska (Roberts et al. 1987) is debatable. The delicate collaterally and diagonally flaked northern points in question bear only a superficial resemblance to southern Plano projectile point varieties and tend to date much later in time. Better evidence will be required to resolve the controversy but at this time the northwestern lanceolate points appear to represent an independent northern development that had little or nothing to do with Plano culture.

Western Plano culture radiocarbon dates in Canada generally fall between 8,500 and 7,500 BP (Doll 1982; Driver 1982; Meyer 1985; Quigg 1976; Reeves 1975; Vickers 1986; Wilmeth 1978) and between 10,500 and 8,000 BP further south (Frison 1978; Husted 1969; Irwin-Williams et al. 1973; Schneider 1985). It should be noted that the late Boss Hill site dates (Doll 1982) pertain to the transition from Plano culture to Early Plains culture. Dates from both the Fletcher site (Quigg 1976) and the Niska site (Meyer 1985) are regarded as being too late. An AMS date of the Eastern Plano Cummins site, situated on a Glacial Lake Minong elevated strandline overlooking Lake Superior, provided a reading of 8,480 +/- 390 BP although the ancient beach on which the site is located has been geologically dated to 9,500 BP (Julig 1984: 93). The projectile point styles from the site are more in accord with the AMS reading than the geological beach dating. This particular site was occupied on a number of occasions by Plano culture people and the extent of the time depth present is still unclear. A small charcoal sample from the Eastern

Plano culture site of Sainte-Anne-des-Monts on the Gaspé coast provided a reading of 5,960 +/- 100 BP (Benmouyal 1987) which is at odds with the geologically dated 8,000 to 9,000 BP elevated strandline on which it sits (Dumais et Rousseau 1985). Dates between 7,500 and 8,000 BP from the related Rimouski site further west along the Gaspé coast (Chapedelaine et Bourget 1992) are more in accord with the expected time frame. A 9,500 BP date from the Weirs Beach site in New Hampshire was associated with stone tools regarded as being Plano culture on the basis of the flaking technique (Bolian 1980: 124). The only radiocarbon date from a Northern Plano site pertains to the Grant Lake site in Keewatin District of the Northwest Territories (Wright 1976). The reading of 7,220 +/- 850 BP, however, has an unacceptably large +/- span.

Technology:

On the Plains, projectile point styles or types are heavily relied upon for cultural identifications and temporal placements. As a result, a series of point type names has become intimately associated with certain time and space dimensions of Plano culture. Such an approach has an undeniable utility and certainly in many instances the projectile point styles do appear to reflect reality in terms of time and space. Not infrequently, however, this point type `index fossil´ approach encounters difficulties due to inaccurate point type identifications and the fact that, in some instances, later point varieties can mimic earlier ones. Taxonomic weaknesses have led to errors in identification which express themselves in both cultural distributions and age estimates. Some projectile point types are better than others in terms of their diagnostic value and some archaeologists are more precise in their use of the type concept than others. Despite the foregoing problems, projectile point styles are the most sensitive indicators of change through time in contrast to the rest of the tool kit that is relatively undifferentiated. Aside from assemblages recovered in clear archaeological contexts, there are limited alternatives to this heavy reliance upon one element of technology. The hazards inherent in such an interpretive dependency can only be reduced by an emphasis upon projectile point type descriptions drawn from collections whose temporal placement is controlled by stratigraphy and dates.

WESTERN PLANO:

Early Western Plano is characterized by a point type called `Agate Basin´ which, along with a subsequent variety called `Hell Gap´, date between 10,500 and 9,500 BP. There is good stratigraphic, radiocarbon, technological, settlement and subsistence evidence for accepting the origin of early Western Plano culture in the preceding Palaeo-Indian (Folsom) culture. Some Agate Basin points even retain basal thinning scars which could be classified as flutes (Agogino 1970; Wright 1976: Plate VII, fig.2). The abrupt change in point style from the thin, fluted late Palaeo-Indian point to the relatively thick lanceolate Agate Basin point has been attributed to a technological innovation of the thrusting spear. Experimentation with socket hafted Agate Basin points and evidence of their use in bison corrals and traps suggest the weapon tips armed thrusting spears (Frison 1987: 333-341). While the Agate Basin point style is widely

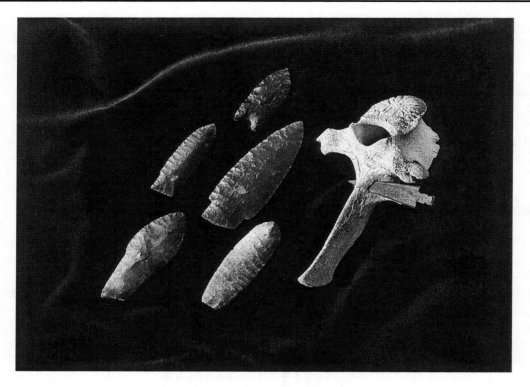

COLOUR PLATE VI: WEAPON TIPS OF THE PLAINS The two specimens in the lower left corner are early Western Plano culture point types, Hell Gap to the left and Agate Basin to the right, while the two points above them are late Western Plano culture types, Eden to the left and Scottsbluff to the right. Above these is a Period III Middle Plains culture point. The bison vertebra with the iron arrowhead lodged in it illustrates the continuity of bison hunting on the Plains. All of the chipped stone specimens are plastic replicas of the original southern Saskatchewan specimens residing in the Royal Ontario Museum. Such replicas are useful in research as well as exhibits vulnerable to damage. Except for weight, the replicas are indistinguishable from the originals. The points were all manufactured from North Dakota Knife River chalcedony. (Reproduced from Wright 1974: Plate 4)

distributed in the Plains, Foothills, Parklands, and eventually the Boreal Forest, Lichen Woodland, and Tundra regions of Canada, the distribution of the Hell Gap variety is more restricted and is probably best regarded as a regional point variety largely restricted to the Plains.

Around 9,500 BP stemmed lanceolate points, called Alberta points, appear and survive in modified forms called Scottsbluff and Eden until 8,000 BP. These point styles are not always temporally discrete and Alberta points, for example, can be found in association with the generally earlier Hell Gap point style (Wormington and Forbis 1965: 22). The Scottsbluff and Eden points of late Western Plano were replaced around 8,000 BP by a range of lanceolate point styles such as Frederick, Browns Valley, and Jimmy Allan.

These, in their turn, were quickly substituted for the notched points of eastern and southern derivation which initiates Early Plains culture. Most researchers on the Canadian Plains have accepted the view that the notched points reflect the introduction of the spearthrower that replaced the earlier thrusting spear (Reeves 1969; 1983). There is still controversy, however, surrounding the issue of distinguishing between stone weapon tips which armed thrusting spears as opposed to spearthrower propelled missiles (Vickers 1986: 53). The preceding discussion of projectile point types on the Plains has been necessary as they are critical to cultural classifications and the reconstruction of local culture history. Sudden changes in point styles would not have been a product of whimsy or fad. One can suspect when dealing with hunters that a change in point style reflects the adoption of some pragmatic innovation to the all important weapon system. Such weapon systems were composite entities and archaeologists only see the piercing stone tip of the spear or javelin shaft. An alternative explanation to account for sudden and widespread change in weapon tips is population replacement; a proposition that is difficult to accept given the economic base of the people under consideration.

Throughout 2,500 years, from 10,500 to 8,000 BP, the non-projectile point technology is characterised by only minor changes. The basic tool kit consisted of chipped biface knives, a range of scraper varieties, drills, spokeshaves, hammerstones, choppers, and gravers. There is also some tenuous evidence for a presence of a prepared core-blade technology (Ebell 1980; Irwin and Wormington 1970; Nero 1959) although in too many instances the `blades´ lack cultural association and are simply inferred to be early (Schneider 1982; Stoltman 1971). A macroblade technology, currently restricted to the Peace River area of northern Alberta, may pertain to Western Plano (Le Blanc and Wright 1990). Minor traits are the secondary use of broken projectile points as burins and knives (Ebell 1980) and the occurrence of sandstone shaft abraders (Dick and Mountain 1960; Wheat 1979). Through time in Western Plano culture there is an increase in the popularity of end scrapers and specialized stone tools including spoke-shaves and certain varieties of knives (Irwin and Wormington 1970). Despite some changes, the stone tool kit from Palaeo-Indian culture to the end of Western Plano culture is characterised by an "...underlying unity" (Ibid: 24). The bone technology includes eyed needles (Irwin-Williams et al. 1973), the use of bison femur, tibia, and humerus limb bones as expedient butchering tools (Frison 1974: 51-57; 1978: 167), and probable projectile points (Frison and Stanford 1982: 172).

NORTHERN PLANO:

Although the projectile points of Northern Plano are indistinguishable from the Agate Basin point type of early Western Plano much of the rest of the tool kit is quite distinctive. The chipped and polished stone adzes, chithos, wedges, saws, linear flakes, graver-on-a-point, and scraper-knives of Northern Plano appear to be absent from early Western Plano culture. There are also frequency differences between the classes of tools, their relative sizes, and the degree to which broken projectile points were re-used as burins (Harp 1961; Wright 1976). Further, the use of heated stones in food preparation in Northern Plano contrasts with the general absence of evidence of this procedure in both Western and Eastern Plano. Minor elements that appear in the south but are absent in the north are bi-pointed projectile points and large side scrapers whose working edge converges to a point. While some of the technological differences between

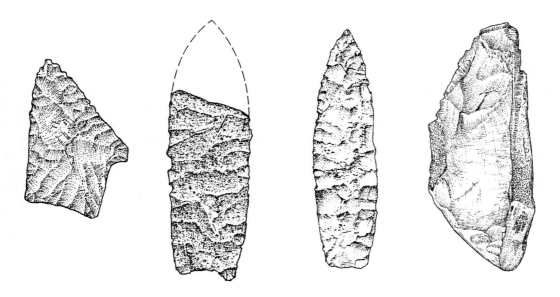

FIGURE 10: MISCELLANEOUS PLANO CULTURE IMPLEMENTS   In the upper left is the distinctive `Cody Knife´ frequently found on late Western Plano culture sites. Beside it is a late Eastern Plano culture point form encountered in the Upper Great Lakes region. Next are a Northern Plano culture point and an associated chipped and ground stone adze. (Drawn by David W. Laverie Scale: variable)

Northern Plano and Western Plano sites may be the result of comparing habitation camp sites in the north to kill sites in the south, there do appear to be a number of distinctive differences between the tool kits of the caribou hunters of the north and the bison hunters of the south. Presumably much of the technological differences stem from the need for Northern Plano people to adapt to a forest-tundra seasonal round. While it cannot be demonstrated, it is difficult to conceive how hunters could function in such a setting without the use of canoes and snowshoes/toboggans or their equivalents. No trace of bone technology has survived the acid soils of the north.

It has been proposed that changes in the tool kit in response to survival in the Boreal Forest, Lichen Woodland, and Tundra contributed to the formation of Early Shield culture (Wright 1976: 91-93). This transformation is most clearly seen in the western portions of the Boreal Forest-Canadian Shield (Buchner 1981; 1984).

EASTERN PLANO:

Most of the major Eastern Plano culture sites, such as Cummins (Dawson 1983; Fox 1975; Julig 1984; n.d.), Brohm (MacNeish 1952), Sheguiandah (Lee 1957); George Lake (Greenman and Stanley 1940), Sainte-Anne-des-Monts and Cap-au-Renard (Benmouyal 1976; 1987) are situated at sources of siliceous stone suitable for fashioning into tools. There is abundant evidence of stone tool manufacture. Even the large 1,250 square metre Rimouski site, which was removed from any known local source of suitable stone, produced abundant evidence of stone tool production (Chapdelaine et Bourget 1992). Here the tool kit was dominated by biface knives, utilized flakes, end and side scrapers, and projectile points with limited numbers of drills, preforms, and abraders (Ibid: Tableau 2). Allowing for the possibility that stone tool kit rejuvenation activities at most Eastern Plano culture sites may have affected the appearance of the assemblages, both the stone chipping techniques and many of the specific tool forms clearly relates Eastern Plano to Western Plano. At a more regional level, however, it may develop that the Eastern Plano culture sites of the St.Lawrence River and eastward are sufficiently distinct from contemporary sites along the northshore of the Upper Great Lakes to warrant a separate designation. There appears to be a greater time depth represented at the latter sites but it is not possible to isolate the various Plano culture components and thus the relationship between the western and eastern aspects of what is here lumped under Eastern Plano culture is still poorly understood. There is some evidence that cultural developments along the northshore of the Upper Great Lakes were somewhat different from what was taking place along the southshore. This is particularly apparent during late Plano culture times when sites such as Renier in Wisconsin (Mason and Irwin 1960) and Gordo in Michigan (Buckmaster and Paquette 1988) are most closely affiliated with the late Western Plano culture sites of the Plains. While the projectile points of Eastern Plano culture have most often been compared to early Plains varieties such as Plainsview and Agate Basin (MacNeish 1952; Dawson 1983) such attributions over-extend the type concept (Doyle et al. 1985). Sites along the northshore of the Upper Great Lakes and down the St.Lawrence Valley to the Atlantic Ocean most often produce a distinctive Eastern Plano point variety (Wright 1979; 1982) which cannot be equated directly with Western Plano culture point types. What shared projectile point attributes that do exist, such as the delicate and highly controlled parallel and oblique flaking, suggests a relationship to terminal Plano culture 9,000 to 8,000 BP lanceolate projectile points on the Plains; an observation that is in agreement with the eastern radiocarbon dates and geological age estimates. This observation also pertains to certain related materials from adjacent northern Minnesota (Steinbring 1974) and Wisconsin (Salzer 1974).

Whether Eastern Plano people entered Southern Ontario from along the northshore of the Upper Great Lakes or via the west end of Lake Erie or both is still not clear (Deller 1976; Ellis and Deller 1990; Storck 1982). The occupation of Southern Ontario appears not only to have been limited but also largely confined to the west of Toronto and to the north of the contemporary Central Early Archaic complex (Hi-Lo). The assignment of some surface collected points from Southern Ontario to Plano culture is also questionable (see Deller 1979: figs 9 and 10; Stewart 1984: fig.5). Current evidence would suggest that the major Plano culture eastward thrust was along the northshore of the Upper Great Lakes into the St.Lawrence drainage system, a distribution pattern that correlates closely with the Tundra Woodland and Boreal Forest vegetation provinces (McAndrews et al. 1987).

Although the association of many Eastern Plano culture sites with quarry locations has possibly biased comparisons with sites not heavily involved in stone tool production, it has provided vital information on the processes involved in the manufacture of chipped stone tools. At the Cummins site on the northshore of Lake Superior the taconite jasper deposits may have been exploited for 2,000 years (Dawson 1983). Careful baking of the jasper thermally altered the stone crystal structure thus improving flaking qualities. Such treated cores, blocks, and large flakes were then subjected to edge preparation prior to being flaked into the final desired forms. Although the assemblages from sites such as Cummins, Sheguiandah, and Ste.Anne-des-Monts are dominated by cores, preforms, and general chipping detritus, tool manufacture was not the sole activity and it can be assumed that the finished tools, many manufactured from non-local stone, were used in hunting and domestic activities carried on in conjunction with the production of tools and preforms. Such tools include projectile points, biface knives, flake knives, drills, and end and side scrapers (Benmouyal 1987; Chapdelaine et Bourget 1992; Dawson 1983: Fig.3) although the evidence for burins (Julig 1988) is questionable in lieu of use-polish studies. Burinated projectile points are, however, occasionally encountered on Eastern Plano culture sites (e.g. Thompson Island site: personal examination) but not nearly in the frequency found on Western Plano and, in particular, Northern Plano sites. A distinctive characteristic of the Gaspé sites is the manufacturing of fine collaterally flaked knives with one extremity fashioned into a drill (Benmouyal 1987) or the modification of projectile points into drills (Chapdelaine et Bourget 1992).

Implements such as choppers and chipped adzes with triangular crossections on Eastern Plano culture sites in the Lake Superior region have been interpreted as forest adaptations that eventually led to Early Shield culture (Dawson 1983). Similar adaptations were taking place in southeastern Manitoba (Buchner 1981; 1984) and to the south in northern Wisconsin (Salzer 1974). The 8,000 BP Sinnock site on the east side of the Winnipeg River in Manitoba (Buchner 1981; 1984) is regarded as a transitional site from Plano to Early Shield culture and will be considered in detail in Chapter 8.

Subsistence:

Generalizations regarding Plano culture subsistence practices are complicated by the wide range of environments that were occupied. In the Foothills of the Rockies, for example, elk, sheep, and goats along with the seasonal exploitation of bison would have been important while on the Plains the bison was the primary prey. To the north, caribou was the most important prey and to the east bison would have quickly given away to caribou. In the Lower St.Lawrence River Valley sea mammals and other marine resources were probably at least seasonally exploited. The preceding comments give short shrift to a number of periodically important mammal species, such as hare, as well as fish, birds, molluscs, and plant foods. Direct evidence of subsistence in the form of discarded food remains from Plano culture sites in Canada, however, is rare. The bison remains from the late Western Plano Fletcher site in southern Alberta (Forbis 1968) is one of the rare exceptions. All of the recovered carbonized caribou bone from the Northern Plano Grant Lake site was required to provide a single radiocarbon date using the beta method (Wright 1976). Under the circumstances, inferences concerning Plano culture subsistence in Canada must be based upon settlement pattern evidence and from extrapolation to sites south of the border.

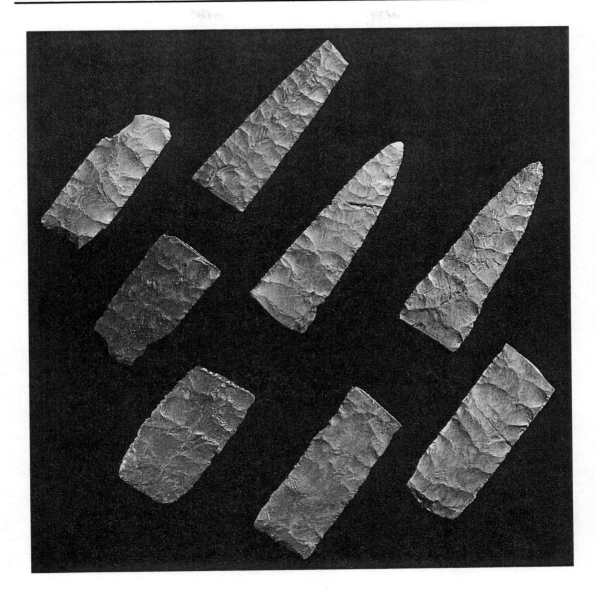

COLOUR PLATE VII: EASTERN PLANO CULTURE POINT FRAGMENTS The above specimens were recovered from islands in Lake St.Francis, a widening in the St.Lawrence River where the borders of Québec, Ontario, and New York converge. The extremely fine workmanship and the overall form attributes are typical of the easternmost Eastern Plano culture points. To date, this culture represents the earliest evidence of human occupation of the St.Lawrence Valley. (Reproduced from Wright 1979: Plate 3)

The use of natural traps to kill large numbers of bison was first recorded for late Palaeo-Indian culture and continued as a major strategy of Western Plano culture hunters. It is probable that the herd entrapment hunting method has been overemphasized relative to single animal kills given the greater archaeological visibility of the former. Historical documentation, bison behaviour studies, and butchering evidence from sites, suggests that the communal bison hunt was a late summer to fall activity whose central purpose was to acquire a large stock of meat and grease for winter consumption (Frison 1974: 109-110). Large numbers of people, working in close co-operation, were required to insure the success of a communal hunt. While natural bison herd traps, such as arroyos (Wheat 1972) and sand dune basins (Frison 1974) do occur in the archaeological record, the recognition of other historically recorded natural traps such as snow drifts and thin ice on rivers and lakes, defies archaeological identification. At the late Western Plano Horner site in Wyoming, some form of constructed corral or "other artificial structure" was apparently used as part of the trap (Frison 1983: 117). There is some evidence for the use of the surround and drive tactic to force a herd into a natural trap (Wheat 1972). The large numbers of people required to effectively initiate the `controlled stampede´ of the surround and drive method would have also been required to process the large numbers of carcasses before spoilage set-in. It is probably a valid assumption that much of the meat was dried in the sun or over fires. Such a process not only inhibits spoilage but also reduces volume in a ratio of 5:1, an important consideration for pedestrian people. Evidence of bone marrow extraction (Meyer 1985: 32) may indicate that bone grease was rendered for mixing with dried and pounded bison meat to produce pemmican. It is difficult to conceive that the elaboration of techniques of bison herd slaughter did not correlate with efficient meat preservation techniques (Wheat 1972). At the fall to early winter Horner site in Wyoming, for example, it has been estimated that 200 bison were killed (Frison 1978: 181). Carcasses were generally butchered into units, such as legs and spinal columns, with complete disarticulation and breaking of marrow bones being common. Mandibles were also removed to extract the tongue and render the rich fat content of the jaw bone. Tail bones were missing as they would have been removed with the hide.

While winter food storage of bison meat was undoubtedly critical to survival during the most difficult time of year, the archaeological refuse left at kill and processing sites has very likely masked the importance of other animals as well as gathered foods. Metates and manos, generally associated with the grinding of plant foods, have been recovered from Western Plano sites in Wyoming (Frison 1978: 353) although it should be cautioned that such implements have been historically documented as being used for pulverizing dried meat. At the transitional Western Plano/Early Plains Boss Hill site, choke cherry seeds (Prunus virginiana) were recovered along with bison, elk, fox, badger, beaver, muskrat, hare, duck, geese, fish, and possible dog remains (Doll 1982). It is an unfortunate fact that the importance of plant foods in the diet will always be difficult to evaluate even when the use of the flotation method to recover charred plant materials becomes a more widely adopted field procedure. The wide range of species at Boss Hill site reflect its location in the ecotonal Parklands. Pulverized bison bone at this site also suggested the production of bone grease. Another contemporary transitional site, the Hawkwood site in southwestern Alberta (Vickers 1986: 47), produced only bison remains.

With reference to the subsistence of the Northern and Eastern Plano peoples, direct evidence is almost entirely lacking. Northern Plano summer sites overlook caribou crossings or are associated with caribou trails within dendritic esker systems which both channel the herds and provide numerous ambush opportunities. Such subsistence inferences based upon site locations and topography, however, provide no insights into the importance of musk-ox or water fowl or to what extent the rich and generally predictable lake trout and grayling fish resources were exploited. Encampments in the caribou wintering grounds in the Lichen Woodland and Boreal Forest probably relied to some extent upon stored meat from the late summer and fall hunt. The probability of large caribou herds in the wintering grounds would have warranted the construction of pounds and, if successful, permitted the aggregation of relatively large human populations at a single locale. Complex factors determining the location of a winter pound would make the archaeological location of such sites extremely difficult. If the pound was not successful, the dispersal of small family groups across the land would be the alternate survival strategy. Such sites would be even more difficult to locate than the hypothesized pound sites.

Major Eastern Plano culture sites are generally located near siliceous deposits suitable for the manufacture of chipped stone tools. Presumably local foods were available while people attended to the annual task of rejuvenating the tool kit. It has been assumed that caribou were a major prey of Eastern Plano hunters but this is undoubtedly an oversimplification. Caribou herds would permit large aggregations of people, particularly if pounds were in use. Animal resources such as moose and beaver would call for a more dispersed settlement pattern. Fish resources in the Upper Great Lakes at this early period were likely limited and relatively unimportant. Further east, into the St.Lawrence Valley, riverine resources could have been important as suggested by site locations on islands. Further downriver marine mammals and fish would have been available.

New analytical methods are partially overcoming the usual lack of faunal remains from Eastern Plano culture sites. At the Cummins site near Thunder Bay, Ontario, blood protein residues on stone tools have been identified to the family level by a process called cross-over electrophoresis (Newman and Julig 1989). Positive test results suggest the presence of bison, porcupine, rodent (muskrat, beaver, etc.), cervid (caribou, moose, elk, etc.), lynx, and human. The presence of bison blood protein residues on the stone tools from the Cummins site is particularly significant as it indicates the animals were either locally available or were within ready reach of the band during a portion of its seasonal rounds. At 9,000 BP the Cummins site was situated in the Boreal Forest but only a relatively short distance from Lichen Woodland, Parkland, and Deciduous Woodland vegetation provinces (McAndrews et al.1987). The proximity to the Parkland and its adjacent Grassland vegetation province almost assures that the western flank of the Boreal Forest in which the Cummins site was located was seasonally penetrated by bison. The presence of lynx and muskrat or beaver suggests the use of snares and dead-fall trapping. As anyone who has attempted to fashion stone tools knows cutting oneself is an inherent hazard, thus the presence of human blood on chipped stone tools should come as no surprise.

Settlement patterns:

WESTERN PLANO:

There is limited evidence of Palaeo-Indian culture on the Canadian Plains. When the northward advancing grasslands gradually replaced the earlier spruce forest around 10,000 BP (J. Ritchie 1976) Western Plano culture appears on the scene. While the direct descendants of northern Palaeo-Indian people must be represented in the Western Plano populations of Canada there does appear to have been an influx of southern bands. This is suggested by the abundance of exotic cherts from southern geological sources such as the Knife River chalcedony of North Dakota. Contacts to the south, particularly with Montana and North Dakota, were maintained into late Western Plano culture times (Meyer 1985: 32-33). Western Plano culture followed a Palaeo-Indian settlement pattern strategy that survived until Europeans destroyed the bison herds. During winter, populations settled into the forested valleys, foothills, and parklands with their dried meat supplies. Communal bison hunting and individual stalking of animals resulted in both large aggregations of people and dispersed populations depending upon the fortunes of the hunt. In spring, populations would shift to the edges of the valleys seeking drier site conditions and to take advantage of the increasing sunlight. Both communal hunting and the stalking of bison would be practiced as dictated by weather conditions. In summer, with a bountiful supply of water in the sloughs, the open Plains could be exploited and bands would leave the protection of the forests. Small dispersed groups of hunters could take advantage of irregular topography to stalk bison. It is also likely at this time that band gatherings for social and ceremonial purposes took place. By fall the water supply on the `High´ Plains had disappeared initiating the gradual shift to the winter camp sites during which time the major bison communal hunt and the processing of winter provisions were the primary activities (Vickers 1986: 7-8).

The influence of topography and weather on the seasonal round cannot be over-emphasized. The former can be so important that at sites like Sibbald Creek in Alberta an unbroken occupation from Palaeo-Indian to the European contact period is represented (Gryba 1983). When considering Plano culture and other early cultures on the Plains there is the difficulty of reconstructing the original landscape. During the Altithermal, an intermittent period of dry, warm climate beginning in some regions as early as 9,000 BP (Schweger et al. 1981), a complex series of depositional and erosional cycles markedly modified the physical geography. It would appear that the impact of these processes and their local character has been underestimated. There is also increasing recognition of some of the hazards involved in using a general climatic episode to interpret certain facets of Plains culture history (Wilson 1983: Figs. 77 and 79). Periods of warm, dry climate across the Plains would dry-up water supplies and reduce bison forage forcing the herds to higher latitudes or into the major drainage systems. Herd adjustments to climatically induced changes in water and forage availability would, of course, have a direct impact upon human settlement. Increasing availability of big game animals in the Foothills, the Barrengrounds, and the margins of the Canadian Shield, in conjunction with drought on the Plains, led to the eventual permanent occupation of these adjacent environmental zones. The greatest degree of band mobility appears to have occurred on the Plains (Reeves 1974). Exotic lithics from the Agate Basin site in Wyoming, for example, included an abundance of North Dakota chalcedony situated 800 km to the northeast and Flat-Top chert 400 km to the south (Frison and Stanford 1982: 367). The former high quality chert was abundant on the early Western Plano Parkhill site in southern Saskatchewan (Ebell 1980; Nero 1959). Late Western Plano tools of this material have even been found in the Peace River region of northern British Columbia (Fladmark 1981), a distance of nearly 1,800 km.

The mobile small family groups of Western Plano culture must have left innumerable campsites. In addition to hunting camps there would have been root or berry or possibly lodge pole gathering camps, camps seeking protection from severe winter weather and other camps situated for maximum exposure to the late winter sun. These only represent some of the possible camp functions, functions that are directly related to settlement pattern distributions. As can be appreciated, most of these camps would be small and, thus, of low archaeological visibility. An unusual stilling of the wind during the height of the mosquito season would probably be sufficient reason for a temporary change in settlement pattern strategy but such a move would severely test the capabilities of archaeology to follow. The identification of small campsites is rare. The majority of excavated Western Plano culture sites on the Plains are either large kill sites (Frison 1978: 13) or sites near good quality stone for fashioning into tools (Irwin-Williams et al. 1973) and, thus, archaeology is obtaining a very incomplete view of the annual seasonal round of settlement.

The recognition of dwellings on Western Plano sites is rare and it can only be assumed that flimsy lean-to or other structures were used which left little archaeological trace. Lodge structures ranging from 2 m to 4 m in diameter,demarcated by post moulds, were recorded at the Hell Gap site in Wyoming (Irwin-Williams et al. 1973). Although the lodge floors did correlate to some degree with cultural debris there were no discernible features such as hearths or pits. Lines of cobbles tentatively identified as weight stones to hold down the tent covering of a wind-break were recorded for two sites in southern Manitoba (Buchner 1981; Haug 1981). At the Niska site in southern Saskatchewan (Meyer 1985: Fig.10) debris was concentrated around a hearth floor that suggested a possible structure measuring 4 m by 2 m. Such small dwellings would have sheltered one or possibly two nuclear families.

NORTHERN PLANO:

The major Northern Plano sites in the tundra are associated with caribou crossings. Suitable stone for fashioning into tools was usually locally available in the form of high quality quartzite cobbles in glacial outwash deposits. Site concentrations reflect an interception strategy between the more northerly calving grounds of the caribou herds and their southward migration routes to the wintering grounds in the forests (Gordon 1975). Such interception locations would have been occupied only during the summer. Sites invariably provide or have access to uninterrupted vistas of the surrounding countryside and, in particular, the crossing areas that can involve several miles of river. No information exists relative to winter settlement but based on the practices of historically documented caribou hunting Indians the winter pattern could range from major population gatherings at large communal caribou pounds to individual families scattered across the land as predicated by caribou availability. Either type of archaeological site would be difficult to locate across the enormous tracts of the Lichen Woodland and Boreal Forest. A bog or stream, for example, is not only habitable in the winter but, in the latter instance, possess certain advantages such as an unhindered transportation network over frozen water.

BLACK AND WHITE PLATE VII: THE GRANT LAKE SITE, KEEWATIN DISTRICT, NORTHWEST TERRITORIES This major Northern Plano culture site on the Dubawnt River is situated at the foot of the high esker knob in the background. The irregular configuration of the esker forces caribou to follow specific paths thus providing hunters with excellent stalking and ambush cover. Quartzite cobbles in the esker deposits provided ready raw material for tool production. (Reproduced from Wright 1976a: Figure 1)

Northern Plano lodges at the Grant Lake site in the Keewatin District of the Northwest Territories (Wright 1976) consisted of 4.3 m to 5.2 m diameter tent floors demarcated by the weight stones that held the base of the skin tent covering. In one instance a hearth floor was situated in the northern half of the structure with another hearth immediately outside (Figure 11). There is some suggestion at this site that the lodge entrances faced north providing the best view of the esker ridge used by migrating caribou. Technological variability and differing varieties of chipping detritus from the individual lodge floors at the Grant Lake site indicate that the dwellings were the product of different seasonal occupations and do not represent a single large camp. Northeast of the Grant Lake site on the Thelon River drainage a rectangular house floor 3.7 m by 2 m was recorded at a site overlooking Schultz Lake (Harp 1961: 18). The structure is interpreted as a 3-sided lean-to or wind-break shelter.

EASTERN PLANO:

Northern Plano and Eastern Plano were off-shoots of Western Plano culture. The off-shoots then developed in response to different environments and eventually were transformed sufficiently to taxonomically justify the establishment of new cultural names. One of the clearest examples of this cultural transition is found in southeastern Manitoba. The Sinnock site and related sites along the east bank at narrows in the Winnipeg River have been interpreted as bison crossing-kill sites with associated processing, tool repair and other camp activities (Buchner 1984; Pettipas and Buchner 1983: 443). Sites were used for only a short period by a few families during the fall when bison would be leaving the Grasslands to seek protection in the then extant Parkland and Lichen Woodland vegetation provinces. Sites were situated downwind of crossing herds. As the animals began to emerge from the river they would have been vulnerable to attack. With the draining of Glacial Lake Agassiz an abundance of forage and water

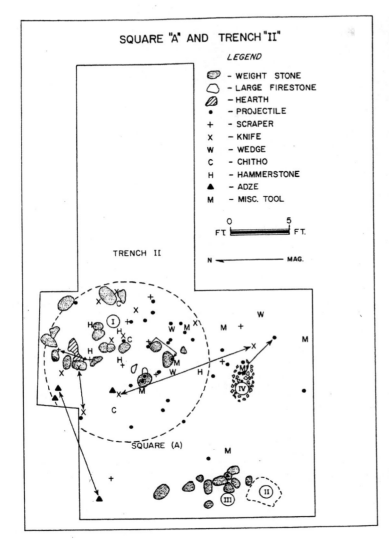

SQUARE "A" AND TRENCH "II"

LEGEND

⬭ – WEIGHT STONE
◯ – LARGE FIRESTONE
▨ – HEARTH
• – PROJECTILE
+ – SCRAPER
X – KNIFE
W – WEDGE
C – CHITHO
H – HAMMERSTONE
▲ – ADZE
M – MISC. TOOL

0   5
FT ▰▰▰▰▰ FT.

N ◄──────── MAG.

TRENCH II

SQUARE (A)

FIGURE   11:   A NORTHERNPLANO CULTURE DWELLING   A number of features were encountered at the Grant Lake site on the Dubawnt River that are interpreted as living floors. In this floorplan of one such feature the large rocks functioned as weight stones around the margin of a skin tent cover but were knocked out of place when the tent was dismantled. A hearth floor, demarcated by carbonized caribou bone, charcoal, and other debris, was surrounded by artifacts and other evidence of activity that collectively suggested a structure over 4 m in diameter.   Connecting arrows indicate where broken tool fragments have been glued back together. There is   tentative evidence that the entrance of the structure faced north permitting occupants to observe caribou approaching along the esker knob and its associated ridges. Feature IV is probably an associated exterior hearth composed of fire fractured rock while Feature III could simply represent displaced weight stones. Feature II was a charcoal concentration   unrelated   to   the dwelling. (Reproduced from Wright 1976a: Figure 2)

would have made southern Manitoba attractive to bison, particularly during periods of drought (Pettipas and Buchner 1983: 444). For the rest of the year the resources of the forests would have been available to these people who, on the basis of technology and settlement patterns, appear to be in the process of a cultural transformation from a grassland to a forest adapted culture. This transformation was sufficiently advanced that the 8,000 BP Sinnock site will be considered in Chapter 8 on Early Shield culture.

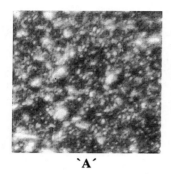

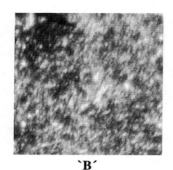

`A´                                                              `B´

COLOUR PLATE VIII: PETROGRAPHIC AND CHROMATIC FINGER PRINTING   Photograph `A´ is a polarized microphotograph of a petrographic thin-section taken from an Eastern Plano culture projectile point recovered from an island site in the Upper St.Lawrence River, Québec. Photograph `B´ is the same kind of photograph but of a specimen from an Eastern Plano site on the Gaspé coast 880 km downriver. Petrographically and chromatically the two photographs match suggesting that the point recovered from a site near the city of Cornwall in Ontario was manufactured from Gaspé chert. The sites in the Lower and Upper St.Lawrence River all produced very similar looking points. This evidence indicates that at an early time period people were ranging over extensive reaches of the St.Lawrence River. They must have possessed adequate water-craft and thus likely the technological equipment to exploit both riverine and maritime resources. (Adapted from Wright 1982: Figure 1)

Most Eastern Plano culture sites recorded to date were involved in the seasonal manufacture of stone tools at quarry sites (Julig et al. 1989: 297). Needless to say such sites would have acted as base camps for other activities such as hunting and gathering. A series of sites on elevated 9,500 to 8,000 BP ancient lake strandlines along the northwestern shore of Lake Superior are associated with the outcrops of the Gunflint Formation (Dawson 1983; Fox 1975; Julig 1984; n.d.). At some sites removed from the raw material, such as the Brohm site (MacNeish 1952), there is evidence of tool curation (Julig n.d.). On other sites, like the Biloski site, the primary focus appears to have been on the production of preforms to be manufactured into finished tools somewhere else (Hinshelwood and Webber 1987). Some limited exotic stone, particularly Hixton quartzite from west-central Wisconsin (Julig et al. 1989), was recovered from the stratified Cummins site and indicates contacts with southern Plano culture bands.

Other Eastern Plano culture sites, exclusive of the scattering of Plano point varieties found mainly in southwestern Southern Ontario (Ellis and Deller 1990),provide further insights into the settlement pattern system. Small fishing and hunting campsites located on islands in the Upper St.Lawrence River would have been most likely occupied from spring through to fall. The finger-printing of a stone specimen (Wright 1982) (Colour Plate VIII)from one of these sites to a Gaspé quarry site 880 km downriver (Benmouyal 1976; 1987) suggests the people possessed efficient water-craft. This is also indicated by the abundance of apparently eastern Gaspé cherts on the Rimouski site (Chapdelaine et Bourget 1992: 28) which would have been more convenient to transport by water than land. In fact, the locations of most Eastern Plano culture sites supports the probability of water-craft being an essential element of technology. Under the circumstances, riverine-oriented and even maritime-oriented settlement patterns of Eastern Plano should not come as a surprise. Recent evidence from Maine further indicates the hunting of caribou in highland regions (Doyle et al. 1985). In consideration of the fact that Eastern Plano extends from eastern Manitoba to the Atlantic Ocean it should be expected that a wide range of settlement pattern strategies will appear in response to the varied opportunities represented within this extensive region. Information on Eastern Plano dwellings is lacking. At the Ste.Anne-des-Monts site on the Gaspé coast, however, concentrations of cultural debris are suggestive of dwellings about 3 m in diameter (Benmouyal 1987: Figs. 11 and 23).

Cosmology:

Evidence relating to Plano culture cosmology is about as limited as it was for Palaeo-Indian culture. In north-central Colorado a young woman had been placed in a flexed position into a red ochre lined burial pit. The body was then sprinkled with ochre and provided with offerings consisting of chipped preforms, scrapers, a hammerstone, a problematical ground stone object, utilized flakes, cut animal ribs, and perforated elk incisors (Breternitz et al. 1971). Subsequent to covering the body with red ochre, animal remains were cremated and the contents of the fire deposited in the grave. None of the grave offerings are diagnostic of Plano culture but a date of 9,700 BP suggests an early Western Plano assignment. An extended burial in Browns Valley, Minnesota (Jenks 1937) contained knives and projectile points typical of terminal Western Plano culture and likely dates to around 8,000 BP (Johnson 1969: 6). At Green Bay on the west side of Lake Michigan in Wisconsin a cremation burial richly provided with grave offerings was discovered (Mason and Irwin 1960). The offerings had been shattered by exposure to fire and were mixed with fire-fractured rock fragments and calcined human bone suggesting the remains and the offerings had been removed from the crematorium and deposited in the grave pit. Grave offerings included late Western Plano style points (Scottsbluff and Eden), knives and scrapers, and a single Western Early Archaic complex side-notched point. A cache of late Western Plano culture style projectile points, many of Hixton quartzite from southwestern Wisconsin, and Western Early Archaic Complex side-notched points found near Marquette, Michigan may represent the remains of a grave where all bone material has disappeared. Regardless of its specific function the Gorto site was clearly some form of ceremonial feature. The 1.8 m diameter pit with its two 10 cm diameter post moulds (markers?) contained 86 projectile points and point fragments, many fragmented by fire (Buckmaster and Paquette 1988). Like the Renier site in Wisconsin the majority of the points were of the Scottsbluff type. There were also four large side-notched points associated, three manufactured from Hixton quartzite flaked in the distinctive Plano culture style. Such points are likely the product of stimulus diffusion when the spearthrower technology was adopted by Plano culture people but the side-notched points were, with the exception of the side-notching, fashioned in traditional Plano culture fashion. The single chert side-notched point, in contrast, was typical of Early Archaic points and included distinctive Archaic attributes such as a bevelled blade (Buckmaster and Paquette 1988: 115). The Gorto site stands as an exceptional example of technological diffusion and adoption from one cultural group to another.

Pertinent information on Plano culture cosmology from Canada is even more limited than the foregoing. At the Cummins site on the northshore of Lake Superior some scattered calcined bone was all that survived of a cremation burial destroyed by sand quarrying activities. An AMS date from Atomic Energy of Canada of these remains gave a reading of 8,500 BP that is in agreement with some of the late style Plano points from the site.

Although the evidence is limited, it can be speculated that the in-flesh, articulated burials accompanied by red ochre and grave offerings of Palaeo-Indian culture persisted into Plano culture. Cremation burial appears for the first time in late Plano times, at least in Eastern Plano culture. There is also the possibility that some of the caches of chipped stone preforms found along the northshore of Lake Superior (Julig et al. 1989) actually represent grave offerings from burials where all bone has been dissolved. The `killing´ of grave offerings at the Renier site in Wisconsin and the Gorto site in Michigan by exposing them to fire exhibit continuity with the deliberate breaking of grave goods at the Palaeo-Indian Anzick site in Montana (Lahren and Bonnichsen 1974) and the fracturing of offerings by fire and percussion at the late Palaeo-Indian culture Crowfield site ceremonial feature in Southern Ontario (Deller and Ellis 1984). Such practices suggest that animism was an essential element of the spiritual belief system. It has been suggested that the aesthetic nature of Plano culture exquisitely controlled flaking of "...semi-gemstone materials..." extends beyond the functional requirement of weapon tips (Hayden 1982: 114) and that somehow these traits relate to hunting success and, thus, represent some form of hunting magic.

External relationships:

The transformation of Plano culture into Early Plains and Early Shield cultures is attributed to a single event, adoption of the spearthrower weapon system. This device, which first appears about 10,000 BP in the southeastern United States, permitted a javelin to be propelled through the air with greater force and accuracy than a hand-held spear. Throughout most of North America the spearthrower either replaced the thrusting spear or, further north where the lancing of herd animals was still productive, was added to the weapon system. The spearthrower would reign supreme until the diffusion from Asia of the bow and arrow weapon system around 2,000 BC. While the spread of the spearthrower across North America was rapid there are a series of time clines as it diffused from its centre of origin. By 8,000 BP or slightly earlier Plano culture began to adopt the spearthrower and, thus, initiate the transformation into a number of regional cultures frequently referred to as `Archaic´. Others have argued that in addition to the change in the weapon system additional technological innovations such as stone boiling, gathering of cereal crops, development of new fishing methods, more efficient sleds and canoes, and the domestication of the dog, in conjunction with major climatic changes that impacted upon subsistence practices, were responsible for the transformation from Plano to Archaic (Hayden 1982: 119). Many of the preceding technological `innovations´, however, were already part of Plano culture technology and others either have not been or cannot be recognized in the archaeological record. The evidence that climatic change had a significant impact upon subsistence and settlement pattern practices on the Plains during Early Plains culture times is also not as apparent as was once thought. In essence, there does not appear to have been a dramatic change during the transformation from Western Plano culture on the Plains to Early Plains culture. As argued here, a single major element of technological transfer was involved and, therefore, it should not be surprising that people who adopted the spearthrower would retain most of their former cultural hardware and practices. An issue to be resolved is to what extent this technological transfer was a product of direct contact between Early Archaic complexes and Plano culture peoples or a process of cultural diffusion from the more easterly bands of Plano peoples to the westerly ones. The spearthrower probably spread from band to band by the processes of both direct and indirect diffusion. The diffusion of new weapon systems, such as the spearthrower and the bow and arrow, appear to initially involve a strong adherence to the original form of the technology being adopted. In other words, the new weapon system is taken in the form received and is rigorously replicated in that form. It is only after some familiarity with the new contrivance that regional modifications alter the adopted technology to the point where it eventually bears little resemblance to the original introduced technology. Perhaps this initial conservatism relates to the critical importance of weapon systems to hunting peoples. This is also reflected in the retention of the earlier weapon system for a period after the adoption of the new system. If the single side-notched projectile point at the late Western Plano Fletcher site in southern Alberta is associated, as it would appear (Forbis 1968; Meyer 1985: 30-31), the adoption of the new weapon system may have initially been quite hesitant.

While the spread of the spearthrower throughout Plano culture on the Plains most likely involved a process of east to west to north diffusion from Plano culture band to Plano culture band, in Eastern Plano culture the contact with Archaic peoples was probably more direct. It would appear that contacts between the Western Early Archaic complex and Eastern Plano culture would have been quite probable given their geographic proximity. Evidence exists in the form of Western Early Archaic complex projectile points or point attributes being found in direct association on late Plano sites (Buckmaster and Paquette 1988; Greenman and Stanley 1940; Lee 1957; Mason and Irwin 1960; Storck 1978). It is likely going to require a major finger-printing of exotic lithics from Eastern Plano culture sites and contemporary Early Archaic complex sites to determine the extent of direct contacts in the north-south relationship between these two groups.

There has been some suggestion of an association between Western Plano culture and Southwestern Coastal culture (Cordilleran) in the Foothills of southern Alberta (Reeves 1974) although the evidence is not sufficient to evaluate at this time. Also, the suggestion that certain projectile point styles in the southern Plateau of British Columbia were the product of stimulus diffusion from late Western Plano sites to the east (Sanger 1970: 119) is not convincing.

There is the matter of Plano culture in the western Mackenzie District of the Northwest Territories and parts of the District and Alaska (Roberts et al. 1987). The original proposal that Plano culture spread into these northwestern regions of North America to form one of the early cultural horizons was made by Richard S. MacNeish (1964). A number of archaeologists have accepted the proposal (Millar 1981). Others regard the materials in question as having no relation to Plano culture. In one of the latest synthesis of the archaeology of northwestern North America there is some confusion regarding the role of Plano culture as either an indigenous entity or an intruding entity. In this work (Clark 1987) a hypothetical construct called `Cordilleran´ is used to account for early non-microblade cultural expressions including

Palaeo-Indian. The confusion comes where a particular site, the Acasta site, is treated as both a phase of Northern Plano (Ibid: Table 5.2) and a part of the Cordilleran construct (Ibid: 152). As was noted earlier, the materials from northwestern North America equated with Plano culture materials to the south bear only a superficial similarity, generally date too late to be related to Plano culture, and are most likely the product of a northern development that has no relationship whatsoever to Plano culture.

Human biology:

There is no data from Canada. Plano culture physical remains from Minnesota and Colorado have been incorporated into a recent study that lends support to the evidence of affinities between early North American and Asiatic populations with regard to certain craniometric dimensions (Steel and Powell 1992).

Inferences on society:

As with Palaeo-Indian culture, Plano culture consisted of nuclear families organized into bands. Families would periodically coalesce into the band at a favourable time of the year for communal hunting or the rejuvenation of exhausted stone tool kits. Inter-band solidarity would likely have been reinforced by ceremonies and, in particular, by establishing kin relationships through marriages. While it has been suggested that band interaction was probably more heavily based upon the principle of resource failure insurance than wives (Hayden 1982: 118) the two factors are inseparably linked with the blood relationship establishing the right to help from blood relatives during time of need. Historically documented information on roughly equivalent societies suggest that Plano culture was probably patrilineal with descent being traced through the male line and patrilocal where the wife went to live in the household of her husband. Territoriality was likely well established but the mobility of females between bands would have created a sense of kinship across territories and, thus, permitted some degree of inter-band mobility not totally dependant upon marriage. Families of a band with an unsuccessful hunt leader, for example, might abandon their leader and join a neighbouring band. This kind of mobility, however, was likely constrained by the fact that the men, as hunters, required an intimate knowledge of the game resources of their territory and the assistance of male kin and other band members in the hunt and other ventures. The responsibilities of women, which essentially involved the camp and its immediate environs, would have permitted them greater mobility at the inter-territorial and inter-band levels than their male counterparts. Indeed, it has been suggested that female mobility (verilocal) and band exogamy (marriage only outside of the band) is reflected in the fact that the only exotic stone material at the transitional Sinnock site in southeastern Manitoba were scrapers, an inferred woman's tool (Pettipas and Buchner 1983: 447).

In the Plains, the Foothills, and the forest-tundra of the north and the east, Plano culture populations would have been dispersed as family or small groups of families for most of the year due to the seasonal

BLACK AND WHITE PLATE VIII: PROJECTILE POINTS FROM THE RIMOUSKI SITE, QUÉBEC
Both the late radiocarbon dates and the appearance of side-notching on some of the projectile points from this Eastern Plano culture site suggest that the site occupants were in the process of adopting the spearthrower weapon system from Early Archaic people to the south. It is speculated that with the incorporation of the spearthrower and other southern traits Eastern Plano culture technology was so transformed that it disappeared as an archaeologically recognizable entity. (Reproduced from Chapdelaine et Bourget 1992: Planche 2 with permission of Professeur Claude Chapdelaine, Département d´anthropologie, Université de Montréal)

distribution of resources. On the Plains the major fall communal bison hunt was the most likely period for the gathering of the band or, in some instances, even more than one band. Conversely, although it cannot be proven, the hunters of the north and the east could well have congregated into their largest social units in the winter around successful caribou pounds.

Limitations in the evidence:

The greatest limitation in the evidence pertaining to Plano culture is the scarcity of excavated sites.

The forces of erosion, deposition, and water level fluctuations have destroyed or hidden from view an unknown number of campsites. Across most of the area occupied by Plano culture land forms have changed to the point where using the present topography as a strategy for locating sites is often fruitless. Prior to archaeological survey it is necessary that geological and environmental reconstructions be formulated for each particular region and time period. Few archaeologists possess the scope of knowledge necessary to control all of the pertinent geological and biological factors. While an interdisciplinary approach is most likely to succeed, it is often both difficult and expensive to arrange for a group of specialists to focus their research on a single problem.

Archaeological visibility of small, special purpose campsites is another problem. The bulk of the excavated knowledge of Plano culture comes from kill-butchering sites on the Plains and from quarry sites in the east, the same pattern as noted for Palaeo-Indian culture. There is, thus, good reason to suspect that only a very incomplete outline of the annual seasonal round has been uncovered.

Inappropriate archaeological taxonomic constructs have inhibited the application of the comparative approach. Even though Plano culture had the same ancestral roots as the Early Archaic complexes of the east and was a contemporary it has been designated `Late Palaeo-Indian´ as if its relationship to `Early Palaeo-Indian´ (Palaeo-Indian culture in this work) was somehow different and special. Archaeological classification frequently suffers from geographically constrained nomenclatures established early in the science on limited evidence that then become entrenched in the literature through familiarity of use and, thus, resistant to change. Given the national scope of the present work it has been necessary for taxonomic consistency to break away from some of these earlier classifications no matter how beloved. This is why the term `Plano´ has been excluded from `Palaeo-Indian´, which is restricted to the manufacturers of the distinctive fluted projectile point that established the cultural base for a number of different subsequent cultures including Plano culture.

Another problem that is particularly applicable to Plano culture is the frequent use of poorly defined projectile point types to reconstruct culture history. Too often lanceolate points from the surface of sites are equated with Plano culture. Erroneous type classifications lead to erroneous temporal and cultural identifications. The malady is then compounded by a heavy reliance upon secondary sources rather than going to the primary data to critically assess the evidence. Simplistic cultural identification criteria, such as projectile point outline, should be replaced with the use of a constellation of morphological and metrical attributes that have originally been defined from assemblages in good, dated archaeological contexts. Without such criteria the erroneous typing of surface specimens will continue to insert misinformation into the archaeological record. It is a promising sign that the seriousness of the problem involved with the misuse of projectile point types as cultural and temporal `index fossils´ is increasingly being recognized (Ellis and Deller 1986: 54-55; Martijn 1985; Stothers 1991: 211) as is the need to confirm such identification with other evidence such as culturally distinctive reduction processes identifiable in the chipping detritus (Stewart 1991).

CHAPTER 8

EARLY SHIELD CULTURE

Précis:

The sparse information on Early Shield culture can all be considered in a précis. As was the case with the neighbouring Early Great Lakes-St.Lawrence culture, Early Shield culture is more a working hypothesis than a clearly demonstrable culture. It is an unavoidable fact that the incremental nature of archaeological research often requires the formulation of premature cultural constructs, particularly when attempting to draw together widely scattered bits of information to form some kind of coherent picture. The demonstration, rejection, and, most certainly, modification of the working hypothesis presented here rests with the recovery of more substantial evidence at some future date. The fact that a hypothesis can be proposed is based upon certain threads of evidence whose degree of validity will eventually be testable. In attempting to construct a synthesis of this nature the interweaving of cultures representing working hypotheses with more substantial cultural classifications is unavoidable.

The basis for suggesting the existence of an Early Shield culture between 8,000 and 4,000 BC is certain technological characteristics and trends which suggest the development of such a culture from a late Eastern and Northern Plano cultural base (Buchner 1981; 1984; Wheeler 1978; Wright 1972; 1976). It is speculated that this culture occupied the western portion of the Canadian Shield as it became habitable after glaciation. There are also a number of early radiocarbon dates from Ontario and Manitoba. This has led to the proposition that "The Shield Archaic evolved from a late Palaeo-Indian (Plano tradition) cultural base in the eastern Northwest Territories and probably the western portions of the Boreal Forest-Canadian Shield" (Wright 1972: 69). Technological trends apparent on Northern Plano sites in Keewatin District have added support to the hypothesis (Wright 1976: 91-93). Firmer evidence comes from the Sinnock site in southeastern Manitoba that was situated in the Parklands between the Boreal Forest and the Grasslands at the time of its occupation (Buchner 1981: 1984; Wheeler 1978).

The 8,000 BP Sinnock site has been interpreted by its excavator as a Western Plano (Agate Basin) site in the process of adapting to a forest environment (Buchner 1984). While agreeing with the site's transitional position the use of the term `Agate Basin´ to describe the projectile points is an over-extension of point typology. In terms of knapping attributes as well as other discrete attributes, the majority of the points do not correspond with the Plano culture pattern and it is for this reason that the site is being considered in this chapter rather than Chapter 7. The differing opinions of whether the site is a Plano culture site or a derivative Early Shield culture site emphasizes its transitional character. Whether the site is regarded as terminal Plano culture or initial Early Shield culture site is a taxonomic issue revolving around the question to what degree a culture's technology must change before the establishment of a new cultural designation has some utility. While such transitions are generally regarded as a product of local Plano culture bands adopting the spearthrower technology, as indicated by notched projectile points, the Sinnock site lacks notched points suggesting that the adaptation to a forest environment took place, in some instances, prior to the introduction of the new weapon system. It is worth noting, however, that side-notched projectile points associated with Sinnock site type materials are recorded from other sites in the same general region (Buchner 1981: 99). In fact, such early appearing side-notched points are relatively common in the Shield country of southeastern Manitoba (Buchner 1982; Steinbring 1980).

In order of frequency the stone tool kit at the Sinnock site was composed of biface knives, some quite large, scrapers including scraper planes and end and side scrapers, a wide range of lanceolate points that are relatively crude in terms of flaking when compared to late Plano points, distinctive chipped adzes with triangular crossections, flaked choppers with ground bits, uniface knives, and minor frequencies of spokeshaves, denticulates, abraders, and perforators (Buchner 1984: Table 4). Proposed evidence of a microblade technology is not convincing. Use-wear studies suggest the chipped and ground adzes were used as both picks and maddocks as well as adzes. The characteristics of the chipping debris indicate that preforms were brought to the site where they were fashioned into finished tools. There is also evidence of a tempering pit where stone cores would have been baked to alter their crystal structure and improve the chipping qualities of the materials to be fashioned into tools (Ibid: 72-77). The minor amounts of exotic stone from the site, represented by Knife River chalcedony, Swan River chert, and possible Gunflint Formation taconite (Ibid: 41), provide evidence of wide ranging contacts to the south, west, and east, respectively.

The Sinnock site is situated on the east bank of the Winnipeg River at narrows likely to have been used by bison moving off the Plains in the fall to seek the protection of the woods. Related sites duplicate this settlement pattern. Occupational debris on the two terraces differ with much workshop debris and evidence of weapon repair on the upper terrace in contrast to the high frequency of broken point tip fragments on the lower terrace nearer the water. It would appear that the upper terrace was used as a look-out and campsite location while the lower terrace was the area where fording bison became vulnerable along the sticky clay bank as they attempted to exit the river and were dispatched and butchered. Poor bone preservation characterized the site but bison remains were identified. It is also worth noting that the site was situated downwind from fording bison coming from the opposite bank.

Proceeding to the east, a slotted antler preform associated with a simple stone spall tool was recovered from Glacial Lake Agassiz II deposits in the Rainy River region of southwestern Northern Ontario. The antler provided a date of 7,800 BP (Kenyon and Churcher 1965). Neither artifact is culturally diagnostic but the agreement between the radiocarbon date and the geological context in which the tools were found suggest a possible Early Shield culture assignment (Figure 12). While the identification of the antler section as moose (_Alces alces_) is favoured it is also tentatively suggested that it may pertain to the extinct elk-moose _Cervalces_ (Ibid: 245-246). From the standpoint of archaeological visibility the two artifacts were accidentally exposed 3.7 m (12') beneath the surface by a gravel pit excavation.

At the Foxie Otter site on the Spanish River drainage, which flows into the northshore of Lake Huron, a charcoal sample from a pit containing only flakes provided a reading of 7,670 +/- 120 BP (Hanks 1988). Detailed distributional and attribute analysis of the chipping detritus from the site suggested that the greywacke flakes in the feature and those from the site in general pertained to an early occupation and was distinct from later occupations. On the basis of assumptions relating to material used and knapping procedures, large bifacially flaked tools and an end scraper are believed to be associated with the radiocarbon date. Though such large bifaces would normally be classified as preforms, residue analysis indicates that they had been used in butchering and cutting meat (Broderick 1988: 201). It appears that large bifacial forms need to be looked at more closely before they are treated as objects intended for eventual tool production rather than being tools in their own right. It has been suggested that while "...large bifacial tools are not restricted to the Early Archaic, they are certainly a significant indicator of it" (Hanks 1988: 74). Here the `Early Archaic´ is equated with Early Shield culture. A chipped and ground adze with a triangular crossection from another nearby site may pertain to the same early occupation of the Foxie Otter site as there are reasons to believe these tools span the transition from Plano culture to Early Shield culture. Such tools are widely distributed in the western Canadian Shield (Buchner 1984; Fox 1977: 4-5).

Another Early Shield culture component is the O.S.A. Lake site overlooking Georgian Bay in Ontario (Storck 1974). The site was discovered during a survey focusing on 7,000 to 8,000 year old strandlines looking for archaeological sites of a similar antiquity. Thought to be a single component, the site produced preforms, biface knives, flake scrapers, a side-notched lanceolate projectile point of early form, a chipped adze with a ground bit, a side scraper, and a graver as well as abundant bifacial core reduction debris. It is speculated that the bit ground bifacial knife or adze is an early trait that, along with the notched points, were diffused to the north from Early Archaic complexes to the south.

During the construction of the airplane landing strip at the Wapekeka Reserve 600 km north of Thunder Bay, Ontario several burials stained with red ochre were exposed and subsequently reburied in the Wapekeka Band cemetery. When work continued and encountered more human remains funding was raised in order to conduct a detailed archaeological survey and assessment of the site (Hamilton 1991). While excavation and survey did recover some scattered human bone and stone tools all the materials occurred in disturbed contexts. The application of modern analytical methods of analysis to some of the human bone fragments from the site stands as an exceptional example of how much information can be gleaned from a minuscule amount of material. In this particular instance, the evidence would appear to pertain to Early Shield culture. Descriptions from workmen suggest that the burials were probably articulated and buried in an extended position. An examination of the handful of human bone fragments that had not been reburied suggested that three children, ranging from approximately 5 to 14 years of age, were involved. Except for two instances of severe hypoplasia, evidence of pathology was absent. Hypoplasia appears as a horizontal groove in the teeth and is indicative of severe physiological stress in early childhood between two and four years of age. With hunting peoples such stress is usually caused by malnutrition. Preliminary carbon isotope examination of bone samples produced intriguing results.

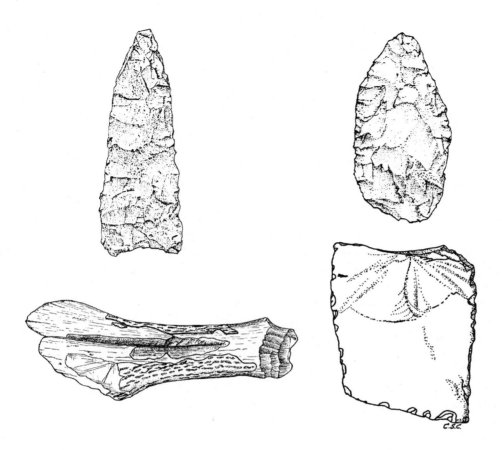

FIGURE 12: PROBABLE EARLY SHIELD CULTURE IMPLEMENTS The lanceolate point on the upper left is believed to pertain to this culture on the basis of attributes that appear to be transitional from Plano culture to Early Shield culture. The biface knife in the upper right is the most characteristic all-purpose tool to be recovered from Early Shield culture sites but lacking recognized diagnostic attributes cannot be identified as such outside of a dated context. Large biface knives have been recovered from a level of the Migod site in Keewatin District dated just prior to the end of Period II (Gordon 1976: 51). The bottom row shows a stone spall tool to the right and an associated worked section of antler recovered from the Rainy River region of Northern Ontario. While neither item is culturally diagnostic their recovery from Glacial Lake Agassiz II deposits and a 7,850 BP radiocarbon date suggest they may pertain to a transitional phase of Early Shield culture out of Plano culture.   (The large flake chopper is reproduced from Kenyon and Churcher 1965: Figure 1 with the permission of Dr. C.S. Churcher, University of Toronto, and the remaining tools were drawn, or in the case of the worked antler, redrawn by David W. Laverie. Scale is variable.)

Before proceeding it is necessary to briefly outline the stable carbon isotope method. Different plants have different photosynthetic pathways whereby the stable or non-radioactive carbon isotopes of C12 and C13 are fractionated in different ways resulting in different ratios of the two isotopes. Plants with a photosynthetic pathway called C3, which predominate in temperate and northern environments, discriminate against C13 while C4 plants, which are found most commonly in desert or dry environments, do not discriminate against this stable carbon isotope. Further, there are differences in carbon isotope ratios of organisms from the atmospheric versus the marine carbon-dioxide reservoirs (Chisholm et al. 1983) as determined by terrestrial C3 plants and by dissolved carbonates in salt water (see Katzenberg 1992). Marine animals, unlike most northern land animals, record a C4 pattern of C13 fractionation. This process affects humans whose diet includes a significant percentage of marine animals whether they be fish or seal (see Chisholm et al. 1982).

The Carbon 13 ratio of the bone samples from the Wapekeka Burial site suggest that marine food sources were important whether derived from anadromous fish, which travel from salt water to fresh water in order to spawn, or from direct exploitation of the littoral resources of the Tyrrell Sea, an early enlarged version of present day Hudson Bay. Determination of the ratio of Nitrogen 15 in the bone samples from this site are now underway as a check on the validity of the Carbon 13 evidence. Nitrogen 15 is more abundant in marine environments than terrestrial environments.

Three AMS dates were also obtained on bone from the Wapekeka Burial site. The surprisingly old dates were as follows: 7,080 +/-90 BP; 6,800 +/-90; and 6,630 +/- 90 that calibrate (Klein et al. 1982) to 6,385 to 5,480 BC, 6,035 to 5,355 BC, and 5,840 to 5,265 BC, respectively. At the time of its occupation the burial site was situated in a boundary area between the Boreal Forest and the Lichen Woodland vegetation zones and was only a short distance south of the Tyrrell Sea (Hamilton 1991: Fig.8), a fact that helps explain the staple isotope evidence for the consumption of marine animals. In addition to the isotope evidence and the early radiocarbon dates, another surprise consisted of the recovery of a full-grooved polished stone gouge, the only diagnostic tool found at the site. Unfortunately like all the other evidence it had been disturbed by the bulldozers and, therefore, cannot with certainty be associated with the burials. Full-grooved gouges are diagnostic of the later portions of both the Early Maritime culture and Early Great Lakes-St.Lawrence culture sequences and continue into the following middle development of these two cultures. While such gouges are rare in the Canadian Shield they do occur as occasional finds across northern Québec (Laliberté 1978), Northern Ontario (Wright 1972a), and into adjacent southeastern Manitoba (Buchner 1982) and Minnesota (Johnson 1969). Their presence likely reflects early trading relationships of Early and/or Middle Shield culture people with either Maritime or Great Lakes-St.Lawrence cultures. Given the antiquity of gouges and, specifically the full-grooved gouge, the specimen recovered at the Wapekeka Burial site could have been associated with the burials and, thus, the early dates. Given the available evidence, the hypothesis is reasonable that the people who occupied this recently deglaciated region may have originated from a late Plano culture base in the Lake Superior region who shifted northward with the expanding plant and animal communities following the retreat of the glacier and its associated waterbodies (Hamilton 1991: Fig.26).

The limited evidence pertaining to Early Shield culture should not come as a surprise. The dramatically fluctuating water levels of the Upper Great Lakes during this time period (Prest 1970: Fig XII-16) means that many sites are now situated on elevated standlines in the heavily forested hinterlands of the Upper Great Lakes. Given the proximity of the Tyrrell Sea, glacial ice and associated lakes to the north it can also be inferred that much of the area was likely in various stages of biotic recovery and were not particularly richly endowed with food resources, a factor guaranteeing small human populations. An equally important limiting factor is the simple nature of Early Shield culture technology that, for the most part, cannot be identified outside of a datable archaeological context. It is unknown, for example, how many of the bifacially flaked preforms and knives from major quarry sites along the northshore of the Upper Great Lakes pertain to Early Shield culture. Certainly large preforms similar to those recorded at the Foxie Otter site (Hanks 1988) are abundant at quarry sites like the Sheguiandah site on Manitoulin Island (Lee 1957). If the hypothesis is correct that the transformation of late Plano culture in the Canadian Shield region into Early Shield culture essentially involved a change in projectile point styles related to the adoption of the spearthrower and the appearance of other traits, such as flaked adzes with ground bits, accompanied by a dramatic change in stone knapping techniques, then the assemblage will be very difficult to recognize from later materials unless recovered in a datable context. Small sites with a generalized stone tool kit occurring on mixed multi-component sites are usually impossible to either isolate into distinctive cultural components or date. The O.S.A. Lake site (Storck 1974) is a fortunate exception to the foregoing. Projectile points similar to the early side-notched projectile points forms found in association with late Plano culture sites (Buckmaster and Paquette 1988; Greenman and Stanley 1940; Lee 1957; Mason and Irwin 1960) do occur on multi-component sites in the Canadian Shield (Wright 1972a: Plate VI, Figs. 1 and 9, Plate XIII, Fig.5). The fact that early ground stone tools, such as the gouge and the lance, have been recovered from sites like the Fretz site (Ibid: Plate XII) also suggests that some of the projectile points from this site are likely early. As has been suggested by others, however, (Hanks 1988; Stewart 1991; Storck 1974) increasingly sophisticated analytical techniques are going to be required to recognize and isolate the early occupational debris from later materials. For example, an AMS date of a sliver of wooden spear shaft from a conical copper projectile point from South Fowl Lake on the Ontario - Minnesota border just west of Lake Superior provided a radiocarbon date of 4,800 BC (William Ross, Ministry of Culture, Tourism and Recreation, Thunder Bay - personal communication 1994 and Beukens et al. 1992). The date raises the possibility that the working of native copper in the area was considerably earlier than originally believed. In stark contrast to the paucity of hard evidence on Early Shield culture is the rich archaeological data during Middle Shield culture times (4,000 to 1,000 BC). It is also possible to `down stream´ from the earliest components of Middle Shield culture sites like the Migod site (Gordon 1976) in order to acquire insights into what the technology of the later portion of Early Shield culture must have looked like. Until more Early Shield culture sites are excavated, however, the construct will have to remain as a parsimonious but largely untested hypothesis.

CHAPTER 9

EARLY PLAINS CULTURE

Précis:

Early Plains culture pertains to a segment of time extending from 8,000 BP to 4,000 BC. The reader will recall that the calibration tables used in this work (Klein et al. 1982), which permit the expression of radiocarbon years in calendar years, only extend as far back as 7,240 BP and, thus, the preceding BP to BC age range. In terms of the cultural chronologies of the Northern Plains this period has been referred to either as a cultural hiatus or any of the following: Middle Prehistoric (Early II); Plains Archaic (Early); Middle Plains Indian; and Middle Prehistoric (Early) (Walker 1992: Fig.18).

Around 8,000 BP the exquisitely flaked terminal Plano culture lanceolate and stemmed projectile points were replaced with notched and, less frequently, lanceolate and stemmed projectile points lacking the distinctive flaking technique. The dramatic change in projectile point styles occurred across the Plains of North America and extended into the adjacent Foothills of the Rocky Mountains. Equivalent changes in settlement patterns, subsistence, and the remainder of the technology, except the stone knapping procedures, are not evident. This suggests that the change in projectile point styles was a product of diffusion which also affected many aspects of the older stone working techniques. Increasingly the appearance of notched points is being interpreted as evidence of the diffusion of the spearthrower weapon system (Buchner 1980: 20; Vickers 1983: 62) rather than as evidence of a migration of people onto the Plains (Gryba 1976: 92; Husted 1969: 88). The chronology of radiocarbon dates from sites producing early notched points suggests the spearthrower was invented somewhere in what is now the southeastern United States around 10,000 BP. If, as current evidence would suggest, these notched points represent the introduction of the spearthrower into the Plains and adjacent regions then Early Plains culture is simply the continuation of the earlier Plano culture with the addition of a new but important element of technology. As it is necessary for archaeologists to organize time and space in relationship to cultural events, the appearance of the notched projectile point provides an appropriate horizon style. It is almost certain that the replacement of the thrusting spear by the spearthrower was a longer and more complex process than is currently envisioned.

There is considerable difficulty in recognizing the antiquity of many of the early notched projectile point forms when they are removed from a datable context. Thus, their use as `index fossils´ for typological cross-dating is fraught with risks, especially given the evidence of considerable projectile point form variability within single components (Gryba 1980; Schroedl and Walker 1978). Matters have not been particularly helped by a host of regional type names (Mummy Cave, Bitterroot, Mount Albion Corner-Notched, Gowen Side-Notched, Salmon River Side-Notched, Hawken Side-Notched, Blackwater Side-Notched, etc.) whose temporal and spatial significance are still unclear (Vickers 1986: 59) and whose cavalier application to culture history reconstructions has done more to confuse than clarify. While there has been a recent effort to establish objective criteria for classifying such projectile points (Walker 1992: 132-142) it remains to be seen how a mathematically-derived discriminant function classification system will be accepted by Plains archaeologists. Regardless of these difficulties, it is apparent that Early Plains culture established the cultural base for the Middle Plains culture of Period III.

A significant episode on the Plains at this time was a prolonged period of intermittent dry, warm weather called the Altithermal or Hypsithermal. The period of significant drought occurred between 9,000 and 6,000 BP (Anderson et al. 1989: 528; Schweger et al. 1981: 581). It is critical to note, however, that the climatic severity of warm temperatures and dryness was definitely regional in character (Anderson et al. 1989). In fact, there is so much palaeoenvironmental evidence of regional variability that the Altithermal concept simply cannot be used as a chronological marker. There has been sufficient misuse of the concept as a widespread climatic phenomenon that it has been recommended that the term be abandoned (Schweger 1987: 374-375). There is also an increased scepticism regarding any one to one relationship between climatic episodes and human responses. The most accepted current view is that the shortgrass Plains was sporadically occupied throughout the period of the Altithermal. It is probable that small and widely distributed populations were involved and that during times of severe drought in certain regions people simply shifted into marginal areas following the game. Such occupations would have been centred in the major river valleys. While there is still considerable controversy regarding both the dating and the severity of this climatic event (Buchner 1980; Vickers 1986) it must be acknowledged that its impact upon people can only be eventually determined through archaeological and not palaeoenvironmental evidence (Vickers 1986:58).

The impact of the Altithermal on the hunting bands of the Plains, of course, related to its effect upon browse and water availability and, thus, the movements and concentrations of the bison herds (Buchner 1980). A drier and warmer climate would have favoured grasslands over forests and, thus, the grasslands and their dependent bison herds would have expanded northward and particularly towards the northeast. Even as the grasslands expanded at the expense of the forests, however, the density of browse and its quality would have been reduced by drought. Drought conditions would have tended to force the herds into the major river valleys and marginal parklands and forested regions where sufficient water and browse were available. Forested oasis in the grasslands, such as the Cypress Hills which straddle southern Alberta and Saskatchewan, would also have provided refuge for the herds as well as their human predators. Added to the climatically induced environmental changes and their effect upon the herds and, thus, human settlement patterns and the difficulty of recognizing Early Plains culture technology from surface sites, were erosional and depositional cycles which either deeply buried or destroyed sites (Vickers 1986: 49-51; Wilson 1983). This seriously reduced archaeological visibility has severely limited archaeological reconstruction of Early Plains culture lifeways (Dyck 1983).

An important natural event, occurring at 6,600 BP (5805 to 5250 BC), was a volcanic explosion in Oregon which covered much of southern British Columbia, southern Alberta, southwestern Saskatchewan, and the adjacent states with a geologically recognizable and datable volcanic ash fall (Black and White Plate IX; Bobrowsky et al. 1990). Known as the Mazama ash fall or tephra, the deposit acts as an important geological and archaeological horizon time marker in the respect that remains either below or above the ash lense must date earlier or later than the ash.

Cultural origins and descendants:

Early Plains culture is regarded as having its origins in the preceding Plano culture although a number of archaeologists favour the proposal that an actual population replacement took place on the Plains at this time (Forbis 1992; Gryba 1980; Husted 1969; and, with qualifications, Reeves 1990). Whether advocating a continuity or a replacement hypothesis, most archaeologists would agree that the transformation involved in the replacement of Plano culture by Early Plains culture is most strikingly evident in the adoption/appearance of the spearthrower weapon system. The replacement of the Plano culture lanceolate and stemmed projectile points by notched points was thought in some areas to have been a sudden event (Frison 1978) although it has recently been suggested the process may have taken as long as 1,000 years (Doll 1982: 107). Allowing for the spotty nature of the archaeological record, it would appear that the replacement of the thrusting spear by the spearthrower was a relatively rapid event across the Northern Plains. There is general agreement that it was from an Early Plains culture base that Middle Plains culture, as expressed in the Oxbow complex, developed about 4,000 BC (Walker 1992).

Aside from the dramatic changes in projectile point form and chipping procedures applied to stone tools, there appears to be technological continuity from terminal Plano culture into Early Plains culture. At the stratified Mummy Cave site in northwestern Wyoming (Husted and Edgar n.d.; McCracken et al. 1978), for example, it is noted that other than the replacement of Plano culture projectile points by side-notched forms around 7,500 BP the rest of the assemblage "...shows little or no significant change from those of earlier levels" (McCracken et al. 1978: 24). A close relationship between late Plano culture and Early Plains culture is also supported by the occurrence of the two distinctly different point styles together on a number of surface sites (Doll 1982: 84-86) as well as their direct association at excavated sites in Alberta such as Boss Hill, Fullerton (Doll 1982), Hawkwood (Van Dyke and Stewart 1985), and Fletcher (Forbis 1968). It must be cautioned that the cultural transformation of Plano culture into Early Plains culture was undoubtedly a more complex matter than the simple adoption of notched projectile points. The projectile point attributed to the 8,500 BP occupation of the DjPo-47 site in the Crowsnest Pass of Alberta, for example, (Driver 1982) closely resembles a point style from the latest 8,000 BP `Plano´ level of the Medicine Lodge Creek site in Wyoming which occurred above the Early Plains culture Pryor Stemmed point level (Frison 1978: Fig. 2.4,c). Cultural continuity from Early Plains culture into Middle Plains culture (Oxbow complex) is apparent in both the respective technologies and general lifeways (Reeves 1973: 1245; Walker 1992: 144). In fact, Oxbow style projectile points were directly associated with the Early Plains culture assemblage at the Gowen 2 site in Saskatoon (Walker 1992: 131).

Recent annotated compilations of radiocarbon dates and associated information are available in published form (Morlan 1993; Walker 1992: Appendix 1). The reader is cautioned, however, that the calendrical dates provided in the Walker reference were obtained by the questionable method of subtracting the radiocarbon readings from AD 1950.

Technology:

While it has been suggested that the Middle Prehistoric Period of the regional Plains chronology, which begins with Early Plains culture as used in this work, was marked by "The diversity of species taken, the common use of coarse local lithics, the shallow hearth associations with fire-broken rock, and, in particular, the corner-notched points..." (Meyer 1983: 248), the data are simply too limited at this time to accept certain of these traits as being particularly distinctive of Early Plains culture. The basal level of the Boss Hill site (Doll 1982) with its associated late Plano culture and Early Plains culture projectile points produced abundant random flake scrapers along with bifacial knives, end scrapers, cobble chopper and spall tools, wedges, hammerstones, anvilstones, possible grinding stones, and a spokeshave-graver. The rare bone items all appear to have been expedient tools with little evidence of extensive modification. The Hawkwood site on the outskirts of Calgary contained at least four components relevant to Early Plains culture (Van Dyke and Stewart 1985). The basal level, dated to 8,000 BP, produced side-notched projectile points and a stemmed point in association with a late Plano culture point. Also associated were bifacial knives, cobble chopper and spall tools, and random flake scrapers. The level directly above, dated to 7,000 BP, lacked diagnostic projectile points but contained biface knives, scrapers, cobble spall tools, and a cobble chopper. Level 3, beneath the Mazama ash layer and thus dating sometime prior to 6,600 BP, contained an assemblage similar to Level 2 but with numerous random flake scrapers and cobble spall tools. The final pertinent level occurred above the Mazama ash layer and produced side-notched projectile points, biface knives, wedges, a large number of cobble spall tools and moderate numbers of random flake scrapers. An Early Plains culture 7,000 BP component at the stratified Stampede site in the Alberta portion of the Cypress Hills (Gryba 1976) contained a small sample of side-notched points, biface knives, random flake scrapers, a drill fragment, and fragments of a bone needle (Figure 13). An Early Plains culture occupation represents the initial occupation of the Head-Smashed-In buffalo jump site. In addition to the notched projectile points, this occupation also contained a single biface knife and abundant local quartzite cobble spall tools likely used as knives and choppers in the butchering process (Reeves 1978: 164).

The Gowen sites, inside the city limits of Saskatoon, were accidentally discovered during construction work. The two sites, separated by 70 m, were likely contemporary and represent short term occupations where the major activities were butchering of bison and hide preparation (Schroedl and Walker 1978; Walker 1992). These sites are the most extensively excavated and described Early Plains culture sites on the Canadian Plains. Random flake scrapers, projectile points, end scrapers, and `gouges´ dominated the tool kits, representing 74.5% and 82.6% of the artifact samples from the Gowen 1 and Gowen 2 sites, respectively. The gouge, not to be confused with the polished stone gouges of the east, appears to be a distinctive tool of Early Plains culture, at least at the Gowen sites. They are generally triangular shaped quartzite spalls with a steep scraping face at the base of the triangle and, most characteristic, a convex cortex spall surface on the ventral face of the tool. They may have been used for heavy duty scraping work, particularly involving wood and bone. As the cortex is the most durable portion of quartzite cobbles it makes sense that edges were used as the cutting portion of the tools. Less frequent tool categories consisted of projectile point preforms, hafted bifaces, biface knives, side scrapers, uniface knives, gravers, drills, spokeshaves, anvils, and hammers (Walker 1992: Table 11). The two samples of stone tools from the adjacent sites were very similar to one another with a high coefficient of similarity of 166.7. A coefficient of 200.0 indicates identical comparative units in contrast to totally different comparative units which would have a 0.0 coefficient (Brainerd 1951). Bone tools consisted of a tube, retouched expedient knives, awls, possible birdbone beads, flakers, and an ochre grinder or applicator. Rock cobbles cracked by being exposed to fire were common.

Surface collected projectile points from southern Manitoba have been related to Early Plains culture (Gryba 1980) but no excavated evidence is currently available. In adjacent northwestern Minnesota relatively extensive excavations were carried out at the Itasca site (Shay 1971). Although there is a possibility of some component mixture the 7,500 BP occupation of the site produced, exclusive of preforms and chipping detritus, the following items: end scrapers; notched and trianguloid projectile points; flake knives; and minor frequencies of biface knives, cobble choppers, side scrapers, drills, gravers, hammerstones, grinding stones, hematite nodules, and a native copper fragment. No bone tools are reported. If the copper fragment dates to 7,500 BP it would represent the earliest evidence of copper working, exceeding that of Early Shield culture situated in the copper producing region by 1,500 radiocarbon years.

Exclusive of the projectile points and probably the `gouges´ it would be difficult on technological grounds to identify the remainder of the tool kit as being distinctive of Early Plains culture. With reference to the projectile points, a chronological sequence of five Early Plains culture notched point types have been established using objective criteria (Walker 1992) and may permit the separation of Early Plains culture point varieties from later forms, particularly the Besant point type which became popular during Period IV. It is also of note that while relatively good bone preservation characterized all of the foregoing sites, there is little evidence of a highly developed bone tool industry. This would mirror the situation noted with the preceding Plano culture.

Subsistence:

In response to the suggested appearance of `Archaic´ foragers on the Plains during the Altithermal it has been commented that "... I doubt if a concept of a forager adaptive strategy is applicable then, if at any time, in the Northern Plains" (Reeves 1973: 1246). Given the paucity of evidence of change in the Northern Plains from an economic base centred on the bison there is every reason to reject the evolutionary stage implications frequently associated with the term `Archaic´ (for a discussion of this issue see Forbis 1992). Excavated Early Plains culture sites in Canada are dominated by bison remains. The long stratigraphic sequences at the Stampede, Hawkwood, and Head-Smashed-In sites suggest a continuity of this focus upon the bison. Despite claims to the contrary (Buchner 1980), there is no strong evidence, at

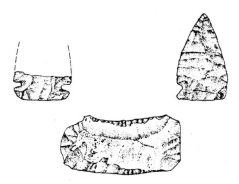

FIGURE 13:   EARLY PLAINS CULTURE IMPLEMENTS The side-notched point fragment, the probable knife with a single notch, and the side scraper were all found in the lowest recorded level of the Stampede site in southern Alberta. The level was dated to 6,000 BC. (Drawn by David W. Laverie Scale 1:1.3)

least on the Canadian Plains, of a subsistence change from the earlier emphasis upon bison to a more diffuse exploitation of a wider range of food resources. This does not mean that a range of foods would not have been exploited depending upon season and opportunities but simply that bison appear to have been the mainstay of Early Plains culture subsistence.

At the Hawkwood site in Calgary (Van Dyke and Stewart 1985: 36-37) and the Gowen sites in Saskatoon (Schoedl and Walker 1978; Walker 1992) bison was the dominant prey although Canid and Chenopodiaceae, possibly lambs quarters, are also recorded from the latter sites and deer, canid and elk from the four Early Plains occupations of the former site. Bison represented 95% of the faunal remains from the Gowen 1 site. Despite the highly fragmented nature of these remains the detailed study of the bison radial carpals permitted the inference that bison from the Gowen sites were cows and calves while at the contemporary and nearby Norby bison kill site the fragmented remains pertained to bulls which were probably killed after being driven into snowdrifts (Morlan 1992). Bison and elk represented the major food animals at the Stampede site (Gryba 1976). Although elk, fox, badger, beaver, bear, dog, muskrat, rabbit, hare, ducks and geese, and even fish remains were found at the Boss Hill site in central Alberta (Doll 1982) bison constituted the most important single prey animal. One can anticipate a somewhat different focus by hunters in the Foothills. At the DjPo-47 site there is evidence of communal hunting of Bighorn sheep by 8,500 BP (Driver 1982). It is problematical, however, if this occupation pertains to terminal Plano culture or Early Plains culture. At the Itasca site in northwestern Minnesota, while bison was most important, turtle and fish were also represented as well as acorns, hazel nuts, and berries (Shay 1971: 64).

In Wyoming extinct species of bison were killed by Early Plains culture hunters in an arroyo trap around 5,000 BC (Frison 1978: 44). The fact that the initial use of the Head-Smashed-In buffalo jump site pertains to Early Plains culture (Reeves 1978: 159) indicates that even more sophisticated methods of mass bison entrapment may have been developed by this time. The ability to process the large quantities of meat resulting from kills of bison herds is indicated by the faunal remains of both the Gowen sites and the Hawkwood site where extensively pulverized bone suggests grease rendering of marrow bones, a historically documented process in the production of pemmican. As a rule, faunal analysis of Early Plains culture sites has been plagued by the fact that the bones are invariably broken into very small fragments. There is merit in the suggestion that part of the scarcity of large bones may also be the result of dogs, wolves, and other scavengers removing such bones from the sites (Forbis 1992: 54). Wolf, coyote, dog and/or dog-wolf hybrid remains, for example, are reported from the Gowen sites.

It has been speculated that the communal hunting of bison may have become more practical as bison evolution from earlier, larger forms like <u>Bison</u> <u>antiquus</u> to <u>Bison</u> <u>occidentalis</u> resulted in <u>Bison</u> <u>bison</u> (Forbis 1992: 41-44). The plausibility of the assumption, however, is directly related to the accuracy of palaeontological projections of earlier bison herd sizes and behavioural traits, a risky business at the best. The suggestion that pronghorn antelope, which are more adaptable to dry conditions than bison, may have been a major Altithermal prey animal (Ibid: 40) has not yet been born out by the Canadian evidence.

Settlement patterns:

Early Plains culture occurs in different environmental zones such as the Plains, the Foothills, and the Parklands. The hypothesis that the grasslands of the Plains were largely abandoned in favour of peripheral environmental regions during the Altithermal (Mulloy 1958: 208) still finds acceptance among some archaeologists (Forbis 1992). Not only is it now known that the Altithermal was not a synchronous event across the Plains (J. Ritchie et al. 1983) but geological considerations suggest that during this period many sites on the Plains have either been destroyed by erosion or buried by sedimentary processes (Reeves 1973; Wilson 1983) thus adding to the impression of a cultural hiatus. The inability to identify most of Early Plains culture technology removed from a datable context has further exacerbated the recognition of Early Plains culture sites. A cause and effect scenario that Altithermal drought forced bison and their human predators into less severely impacted regions like the Foothills, Parklands, and major river valleys (Buchner 1980) suffers from a number of methodological limitations (Vickers 1986) as well as being largely based on the negative evidence of identifiable sites. On the other hand, there is evidence which supports the drought hypothesis in respect to, at least, a partial abandonment of the grasslands.

The Hawkwood site, situated near the edge of an upland overlooking a major river valley, occupied partially protected depressions just back from the escarpment edge. An 8,000 year sequence of occupation is represented at the site. Hearths and large quantities of burned bone, consisting predominantly of bison limb elements, were recovered from the lowest occupation. The presence of these selective bison parts suggests that the site was situated near an undiscovered kill/butchering site. There is evidence that the area was occupied from winter to early spring. Some tenuous evidence of stone-weighted lean-to shelters exists. Most of the stone used to manufacture tools was local in origin although a few flakes of Montana chert were recovered from the component under the Mazama ash layer (Van Dyke and Stewart 1985: 62-63). The Boss Hill site (Doll 1982), located at the foot of a hill in the Parklands of central Alberta, is associated with a seasonally dry pond and is interpreted as a late summer to fall campsite. Two hearths are recorded although fire-cracked rock appears to have been rare. All of the stone used for tool manufacture was of local origin. In contrast to the preceding sites, the Gowen sites in Saskatchewan (Schoedl and Walker 1978; Walker 1992) are located 70 m apart on a terrace of the South Saskatchewan River in the grasslands. On the basis of similarities in the tool kits and the raw materials exploited, it has been inferred that the two sites were probably contemporary and represent a short occupation focusing on butchering and hide processing. A late summer occupation is suggested. Features consisted of circular hearths and pits containing burned and highly fragmented bison bone. Some of the small pits lacking evidence of intense fire may have been smudge pits to ward off biting insects. An interesting feature at the Gowen 2 site was a hearth-pit associated with four concentrations of burned and raw bone fragments that are likely the remnants of a grease rendering process related to the production of pemmican (Walker 1992: 117-118). Other features consisted of a concentration of fractured chert pebbles associated with a stone anvil and hammer and four post moulds demarcating an area 2.7 m by 3.2 m that may have represented a dwelling of some sort.

While the drier conditions which prevailed at certain times during the Altithermal undoubtedly affected bison herd concentrations, particularly during summer and fall, and would have required appropriate adjustments by hunting bands, these adjustments would have been periodic. Like most hunting peoples, flexibility would have been essential to survival. The continuity of settlement reflected in the thousands of years of occupation represented at stratified sites such as Sibbald Creek, Hawkwood, Stampede, and Head-Smashed-In indicates that there was considerable subsistence-settlement pattern stability despite periodic drought conditions. The decrease in the use of exotic stone in Early Plains culture may suggest some increasing degree of regionalism in contrast to the preceding Plano culture although current data are too limited to properly assess the matter.

The presence of dog or dog-wolf hybrids at the Gowen sites and other sites suggests the possibility that the dog travois was in use at this early period. It has been historically documented that Plains dogs attached to this simple cartage device could drag up to 75 pounds and cover between 8 and 10 miles a day (Forbis 1992: 45). Mobility has always been important on the Plains and if, as it would appear, food resources were on occasion more `patchy´ during the drought episodes of the Altithermal then dog transportation of household goods would have provided a definite adaptive advantage.

Cosmology:

Information on Early Plains culture cosmology in Canada, or elsewhere for that matter, is lacking. If the assumption of direct cultural continuity from Plano culture to Early Plains culture and, thence, to Middle Plains culture is valid it can be inferred that bundle, `in flesh´, and cremation burial with grave offerings and the use of red ochre were characteristic of the mortuary system. The only possible fragments of direct evidence pertinent to Cosmology come from the Gowen sites and consist of a fragmented bone tube, which could have been a shaman `sucking tube´ and a natural `stylized bison effigy´ in bitumen (Walker 1992: 95). Fossils and other natural objects which resembled bison probably relate to the historically documented `iniskim´ or buffalo stones used as medicine for `calling´ bison (Verbicky-Todd 1984: 12-22, 220-224).

External relationships:

The contemporaries of Early Plains culture were Early Shield culture to the east, Southwestern Coastal culture (Cordilleran) and Early Plateau culture to the west, and Early Northwest Interior culture to the north. To date, there is little evidence of contact evident in the distributions of exotic stone identifiable to geological source. The minor amounts of Knife River chalcedony from North Dakota at the Gowen sites (Walker 1992: 65) likely reflects trade between the various bands making up Early Plains culture. There is evidence that during Early Plains culture times stone tool manufacture was more heavily based on local resources than during the preceding Plano culture times. The single copper fragment from the Itasca site in Minnesota would indicate eastern contact with Early Shield culture people.

Human biology:

Evidence pertinent to human biology is currently lacking.

Inferences on society:

If speculation regarding the level of social organization required to successfully maneuver bison herds over cliffs is accurate (Reeves 1983: 188) and, if the Early Plains culture presence at the Head-Smashed-In bison jump site does relate to the use of the `jump´, then Early Plains culture bands were capable of forming temporary intra-band cooperatives. As the earliest claim for the use of `buffalo jumps´ pertains to Early Plains culture (Reeves 1978) it would indicate that these people were the first to achieve this level of social organization. One site, however, does not constitute a pattern and with the sole exception of the Head-Smashed-In site there is little evidence of communal bison hunting. Other than the foregoing possibility there does not appear to be any significant difference in the social organization of Early Plains culture and the preceding Plano culture. This is supported by the similarities in subsistence and settlement patterns. An apparent increase in regionalism, as reflected in the use of local rather than exotic stone for tools, could indicate decreased mobility on the Plains as a result of the periodic droughts creating a patchwork of habitable game `oasis´ across the Grasslands rather than representing any particular trend towards more restricted social contacts.

Limitations in the evidence:

The most obvious limitation in the evidence is the paucity of excavated sites. With reference to the postulated hiatus during the Altithermal it has been appropriately observed that "...the lack of evidence of human occupation is a result of sampling, geological variables and nonrecognition of the artifact types in surface collections" (Reeves 1973: 122). Given the combined effect of sedimentary erosion and burial it is likely that the evidence will remain weak when compared to that of later human occupations. If, as would appear to be the case, many Early Plains culture sites would have been closely associated with major river systems with their water, browse, and bison, then sites would have been even more vulnerable to the processes of erosion and burial by the combined alluvial (river transported deposits), colluvial (deposits resulting from the combined actions of slope angle and gravity), and aeolian (deposition by wind) processes. The Gowen 1 site, for example, was buried under more than a metre of sediments. Even sites adjacent to lakes and ponds would be obscured from the eyes of archaeologists. Reductions in lake levels during peak arid periods would have resulted in Early Plains culture occupations on lake margins which are now underwater as a result of the return to normal water levels (Schweger and Hickman 1989). The geological reconstruction of earlier landform configurations would provide archaeology with a necessary tool to predict the potential locations of Early Plains culture sites buried deeply beneath sediments (Walker 1992; Wilson 1983). The application of more sophisticated analytical techniques to the classification of projectile points (Walker 1992) and other tool categories and the achievement of greater classificatory consensus would also assist in distinguishing between the surface remains of Early Plains culture and later occupations (Ronaghan 1986: 331-333). This, in turn, would provide archaeology with a more balanced view of the distribution and relative frequency of Early Plains culture sites on the Plains and adjacent regions. Simplistic use of projectile point typologies for cross-dating (for a brief critique see Ronaghan 1986: 313-315) have already added much confusion regarding the distribution and age of Early Plains culture. In the 2,000 BC Middle Plains culture component of the Crown site near Nipawin on the Saskatchewan River in Saskatchewan, for example, a single `alien´ side-notched projectile point was attributed to the Early Plains culture Mummy Cave complex (Quigg 1986) rather than considering a far more parsimonious and temporally appropriate association with very similar and contemporary Middle Shield culture projectile point forms from northern Manitoba sites only 500 km to the northeast on the Churchill River (Dickson 1980).

CHAPTER 10 ———————————————————————

EARLY PLATEAU CULTURE

Précis:

In the first synthesis of the archaeology of a portion of the Southern Plateau (Sanger 1969; 1970) it was proposed that people with a Southwestern Coastal culture (Cordilleran) moved into the area from the south around 9,000 BP. Their tool kit consisted of bipointed projectile points and knives, linear flakes, cobble core and spall tools, and distinctive concave-faced end scrapers. Microblade technology was absent. This initial occupation was then replaced by the Nesikep tradition (Early Plateau culture) with its microblade technology and notched projectile points. The Nesikep tradition was believed to have moved south from the central interior of British Columbia around 7,500 BP. The evidence supporting an initial occupation by Southwestern Coastal culture was equivocal at the time of this first synthesis and still is. By 11,500 to 10,500 BP glacial ice had disappeared from the Southern Plateau and grasslands-sagebrush occupied the valley bottoms with trees on the uplands and valley sides. Warmer and drier conditions began by 10,500 BP and lasted until 6,500 BP (Stryd and Rousseau n.d.). Evidence for even a limited occupation by Palaeo-Indian culture or the ambiguous Stemmed Point tradition at this time is still not convincing. Some evidence for a penetration by Plano culture from the east is apparent but it was weak and concentrated in the southeastern portion of the Plateau. As detailed archaeological reports become available it may develop that the Kootenai region of the southeastern Southern Plateau was closely affiliated with the Plains at this early time period. Others would argue for a pre-Mazama ash fall occupation by the Stemmed Point tradition (Goatfell complex) with origins in the Columbia Plateau and the Great Basin (Choquette 1987a: 330).

In another synthesis (Fladmark 1982: 112) it is argued that there is no solid evidence for an initial occupation by Southwestern Coastal culture people and that the assemblage which had been earlier attributed to this culture actually dates to Period III (4,000 to 1,000 BC). Further, it is proposed that the earliest occupation actually was represented by people with a microblade technology who moved up the Fraser River from the coast rather than out of the central interior. "The prior occurrence of microblades on the Northern and Central Northwest Coast suggests that this technology may have originally penetrated the southern British Columbia Interior from the west, rather than southwards from the Yukon" (Fladmark 1982: 128). This hypothesized population movement has been correlated with the expansion of salmon spawning ranges into the interior (Carlson 1979: 222-223; 1990: 66). The most recent synthesis (Stryd and Rousseau n.d.) proposes that the earliest occupation was by a number of different cultures represented by Palaeo-Indian, Stemmed Point, Northwestern Coastal (Early Coastal Microblade), and Southwestern

Coastal (Cordilleran or Old Cordilleran) cultures. The phase regarded in Sanger's synthesis as the earliest occupation is now treated in Stryd and Rousseau as a late penetration from the coast into the interior beginning near the end of Period II (4,250 BC).

The problem faced by all of the preceding syntheses relative to the initial occupation of the Southern Plateau is that a human antiquity in the interior equivalent to that of other regions has generally not been demonstrated by either excavation or radiocarbon dating. In lieu of direct evidence, hypotheses have been supported by typological cross-dating using a number of tool varieties which are now known to have limited diagnostic value (Stryd and Rousseau n.d.). Recent evidence (Rousseau 1991) indicates that the first significant occupation of the Southern Plateau probably came from the northern interior and involved a culture whose tool kit was dominated by a microblade technology. The earliest occupation of the multi-component Landels site by Early Plateau culture has been dated to 8,500 BP. The date is contemporaneous with the Gore Creek human remains discovered a short distance to the east on the same drainage system. No artifacts were found with this adult male who died accidentally in a mudslide. Solid carbon isotope analysis, however, revealed that his consumption of marine foods, such as anadromous salmon and steelhead, was relatively insignificant. Such evidence compromises the proposition that microblade technology was introduced into the interior from the west by coastal people following the expanding spawning ranges of salmon. Further, evidence of a specialized microblade technology on the Southern Coast is absent (Fladmark 1982: 112). Thus, the chronology of syntheses relating to the earliest occupants appears to have come full circle and returned to an early hypothesis which stated that the microblade users who occupied the Southern Plateau originated in the northern interior (Borden 1975). This would imply a close relationship between Early Plateau culture and Early Northwest Interior culture. There is also no reason to assume that the 8,500 BP date from the Landels site represents the earliest evidence of the peopling of the Southern Plateau. Certainly prior to 9,000 BP the region was available for colonization (McAndrews et al. 1987).

Cultural origins and descendants:

The original classification of Early Plateau culture, called the Nesikep tradition, treated it as a cultural composite composed of influences and people coming from different regions. This cultural amalgam was thought to have involved a movement of people out of the north with a microblade technology who adopted projectile point styles derived from or influenced by Plano culture to the east and woodworking tools from some unspecified place of origin (Sanger 1967; 1970). It was further hypothesized that these people replaced a resident Southwestern Coastal culture population but, as has been noted, the evidence in support of this earlier occupation is still equivocal. Some suggestive evidence, however, does exist. In the Alberta Foothills, for example, lanceolate and bipointed projectile points resembling Southwestern Coastal culture point forms have been recovered in association with dates of 9,500 BP (Fedje 1986: 31-34). Similarly, in the lower levels of the Sibbald Creek site (Gryba 1983: 64-65) a number of bipointed and lanceolate projectile points were recovered. The bipointed points have been attributed to either the Plano culture Agate Basin and Hell Gap point types (Fedje 1986: 31) or the Stemmed Point tradition (Carlson 1988: 320). None of these points, except for a single possible exception from the Sibbald Creek site (Gryba 1983: Figure 28, d), can be attributed to Plano culture and the existence of a Stemmed Point tradition is still to be demonstrated. The possibility that bipointed and lanceolate projectile points, with unremarkable chipping characteristics, existed in the Southern Plateau at an early date and spilled over into the Foothills of Alberta is an option which should be kept open at this time.

Early Plateau culture origins have been attributed to the interior adaptation of Northwestern Palaeo-Arctic culture in northwestern North America (Early Northwest Interior culture) (Sanger 1970). Sanger's Nesikep tradition, here referred to as Early Plateau culture, was thought to represent the early culture history of historically documented interior Salish-speaking peoples, such as the Shuswap and Thompson. Others (Stryd and Rousseau n.d.) regard Early Plateau culture as a non-Salishan people who were replaced by the Salishan Sqlelten tradition as it advanced up the Fraser River from the coast shortly before 4,000 BC. The association of the Sqlelten tradition with the Salish-speaking peoples encountered in the region by Europeans is based upon subsequent cultural continuities. Evidence supporting a cultural discontinuity between Early Plateau culture and the following Sqlelten tradition, however, is lacking. First, there are a number of technological continuities which span the transition. Second, two innovations at the time likely have created an archaeological impression of population replacement. These cultural changes were a seasonal subsistence-settlement pattern focusing upon salmon and the introduction of the spearthrower. While Fladmark (1986: 46) would attribute a date of 8,000 BP to the first appearance of the spearthrower in the interior it can be argued that the earliest evidence of this weapon system is to be seen in the thick, side-notched projectile points of the Lochnore phase (Stryd and Rousseau n.d.) which was in place prior to the end of Period II. This would suggest the diffusion of the spearthrower from the Plains and Foothills of the east or, less likely, the Columbia Plateau. Once again, the evidence is sufficiently equivocal that the possibility of an in situ development of Early Plateau culture into Middle Plateau culture rather than a cultural replacement should not be dismissed prematurely (Rousseau 1991: 7-8).

Despite controversy regarding who occupied the Southern Plateau first and from where, there is general agreement that little contact existed between the Fraser and Columbia rivers at this early period (Carlson 1988: 322; Sanger 1967: 194). The Columbia Plateau was occupied by an extension of the Desert culture of the Great Basin whereas the Southern Plateau occupation was mainly a product of coastal, northern, and eastern populations and influences.

Early Plateau culture radiocarbon dates extend beyond the calendrical calibration tables (Klien et al. 1982) to approximately 8,500 BP and range up to calibrated dates of 4,000 BC (Cybulski et al. 1981; Rousseau 1991; Sanger 1967; 1970; Stryd and Rousseau n.d.).

Technology:

If Early Plateau culture was, in fact, related to Early Northwest Interior culture then the earliest expressions of the culture in the Southern Plateau should be most similar to assemblages encountered in the north. Unfortunately the evidence is too limited to test for such a relationship. Over time it can be expected that, given the isolating effect of mountain ranges and drainage divides, regional variants of the culture would develop (Fladmark 1982: 125). The assemblage from the earliest level of the stratified

Landels site (Rousseau 1991) consisted of microblades, utilized flakes, an amorphous `uniface´, and a core. The 7,500 BP Drynoch Slide site, whose 20 m overburden of slide debris has defied excavation (Black and White Plate IX) produced microblades, unifacial flake tools, and a single bifacial knife or projectile point (Stryd and Rousseau n.d.). At the 5,500 BC Lehman II site corner-notched projectile points, some with serrated edges, predominated although side-notched points were also present. Other tools consisted of microblades struck from wedge-shaped cores, hafted scraper-burins on side or corner-notched bifaces, amorphous bifacially flaked knives, end scrapers, cobble core tools and abundant flake scrapers (Sanger 1970). The 4,250 BC Nesikep Creek VII occupation contained triangular, corner-notched, and basal-notched projectile points, microblades, amorphous bifacially flaked knives and flake scrapers, cobble core and spall tools, red and yellow ochre, bone awls, needles, beads, beaver and marmot incisor tools, antler wedges, and a pendant (Sanger 1970). It was around this time that the method of cooking food with heated rocks appears to come into use (Fladmark 1986: 51).

Through time microblades decrease in importance and the tool kit becomes increasingly varied. By the end of Period II microblades disappear (Stryd and Rousseau n.d.) but most of the other elements of the tool kit continue into Period III. Around this same time, the exceptionally well made expanding stemmed, barbed, concave based, laterally and basally ground, and basally thinned projectile points are replaced with thick, bipointed points. This abrupt change in point styles has been interpreted as evidence of a population replacement (Stryd and Rousseau n.d.) although the introduction of the spearthrower would represent a more parsimonious explanation, particularly as other elements of the technology and the culture as a whole remain unchanged.

Subsistence:

Little direct evidence is available regarding the subsistence practices of Early Plateau culture. Both the 8,500 and 7,500 BP occupations of the Landels site appear to have focused on deer hunting although a range of animals were likely taken as indicated by the muskrat remains from the lowest deposit (Rousseau 1991). At the 7,500 BP Drynock Slide site, elk, deer, and fish are reported (Stryd and Rousseau n.d.) and while the fish remains have been reported as salmon (Fladmark 1986: 42) there appears to be some question regarding the certainty of this identification (Stryd and Rousseau n.d.) . Certainly from 7,000 BP to Period III (4,000 to 1,000 BC) deer, elk, small game, fish, and likely plants, were of importance with no strong evidence of a special focus on salmon (Stryd and Rousseau n.d.). The preceding generalization is upheld at both the Lehman II and Nesikep VII occupations were the faunal evidence was dominated by deer with little evidence of fish (Sanger 1970).

Settlement patterns:

Most Early Plateau culture sites are situated on tributaries and springs back from the main river (Sanger 1970: 113). Sites tend to be repetitively used and, as a result, stratified sites representing a considerable passage of time are not uncommon. The sheltered location of the Lehman site in a creek

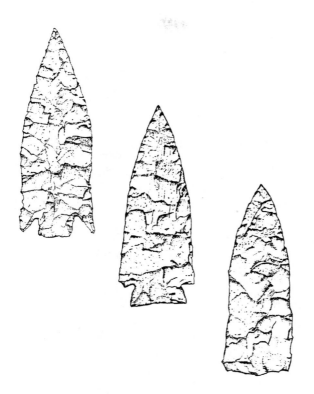

FIGURE 14: EARLY PLATEAU CULTURE IMPLEMENTS   The thin, carefully flaked corner-notched and triangular points were associated with microblades in the 4,500 BC level of the Nesikep Creek site on the Fraser River. To the right is an illustration of a microblade core and dorsal and lateral views of a microblade with their descriptive terms. (Reproduced from Sanger 1970: Figures 24 and 26 with permission of Dr. David Sanger, University of Maine at Orono. Drawn by Mr. David W. Laverie.   Scale of projectile points ca. l:1.3.)

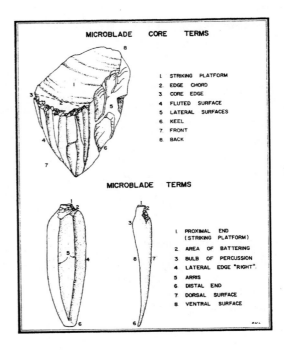

MICROBLADE   CORE   TERMS

1. STRIKING   PLATFORM
2. EDGE   CHORD
3. CORE   EDGE
4. FLUTED   SURFACE
5. LATERAL   SURFACES
6. KEEL
7. FRONT
8. BACK

MICROBLADE   TERMS

1. PROXIMAL   END
   (STRIKING   PLATFORM)
2. AREA   OF   BATTERING
3. BULB   OF   PERCUSSION
4. LATERAL   EDGE "RIGHT".
5. ARRIS
6. DISTAL   END
7. DORSAL   SURFACE
8. VENTRAL   SURFACE

valley may suggest a winter occupation. The Nesikep Creek site, on the other hand, is exposed to the elements and was probably occupied during the warmer months of the year. Recoveries from the Landels site, situated in a tributary valley of the Thompson River, indicate that it functioned as a base camp for deer hunting and the processing of meat and hides. To date, fingerprinting of lithics in the Southern Plateau has revealed little evidence of trade in exotic materials (Fladmark 1986: 49).

Cosmology:

The occurrence of red and yellow ochre pigments may relate to cosmological beliefs or simply be cosmetics. Such `cosmetics´, however, would likely have had some kind of symbolic significance. Equally tenuous is a cache from the Nesikep II component consisting of projectile points in a pristine, unused condition, red ochre, marmot incisors, an antler projectile point and possible needle, scrapers, and miscellaneous bird bones (Sanger 1964). There is, of course, no way of knowing whether this cache was a votive offering or simply a cached tool kit that, for whatever reasons, was never retrieved.

External relationships:

In the southeastern portion of the Southern Plateau a scattering of points recovered from surface sites have been attributed to Palaeo-Indian, Plano, and Southwestern Coastal cultures as well as the yet to be adequately described Stemmed Point tradition (Stryd and Rousseau n.d.). The preceding cultural assignments are based upon a very general application of typological crossdating that, as has been pointed out on a number of occasions, can be a hazardous method of reconstructing culture history. While Plano culture hunters did cross over the Continental Divide into the Southern Plateau, the nature of this penetration will have to await additional evidence. The suggestion of a Palaeo-Indian presence is unconvincing. There is also a problem with the identification of Southwestern Coastal culture based, as it is, upon surface collected bipointed projectile points that are known to be also present in Period III. An early penetration of people using bifacially flaked bipoints is tentatively suggested by evidence from the Alberta Foothills (Fedje 1986; Gryba 1983; Reeves 1974: 10).

The Southern Plateau was strategically situated to interrelate with the Plains to the east, the Great Basin to the south, the Pacific coast to the west, and the northwestern interior of North America to the north (Stryd and Rousseau n.d.: Figure 1). To date, however, the evidence is simply too sparse to even speculate on the relationship of Early Plateau culture with its neighbours. A programme of fingerprinting exotic stone tools and flakes, as well as other items, would likely alter the current picture.

Human biology:

A young man who perished in a 8,250 BP Gore Creek mudslide has contributed considerable information to the early history of the Southern Plateau (Cybulski et al. 1981). Though cranial remains were absent physical anthropology has been able to provide a sketch of the appearance of this early individual. He was of tall and slender build but with powerful lower limbs in contrast to the physical characteristics of the coastal dwellers of a later period. Tests relating to the fact that marine and terrestrial sources of protein in human diets can be differentiated by the stable carbon isotope ratios in human bone (Chisholm et al. 1982; Tauber 1981) revealed that the individual had eaten little marine protein such as would be found in anadromous fish like salmon and steelhead. This, of course, raises the question of how far anadromous fish were penetrating the interior at this time. Stable carbon isotope ratios in the bones of later populations in the same region certainly indicate that salmon were important in the diet (Chisholm et al. 1983). Although this individual has been tentatively attributed to Plano culture (Fladmark 1986: 24) the equivalent radiocarbon date from the Landels site (Rousseau 1991) would suggest that he was a member of Early Plateau culture. The Landels site is only 120 km to the west of the Gore Creek site (Rousseau 1991).

Inferences on society:

Nothing can be said regarding Early Plateau culture society other than to speculate that these early hunting people were likely organized into patrilineal and patrilocal bands. Female mobility, as a requirement of intermarriage with neighbouring bands, likely prevailed and would have contrasted with the more local residence of males. This speculation is premised upon the need for hunters to be intimately familiar with the resources of their local hunting territories. Hunting also demanded the cooperations of male kinsmen. The core social unit would have been the nuclear family within which individuals would have possessed considerable autonomy including the option of changing allegiance from one band to another.

Limitations in the evidence:

There is a serious lack of excavated evidence relevant to Early Plateau culture. Paucity of evidence has contributed to conflicting culture historical reconstructions reliant upon typological cross dating. The debate surrounding issues such as whether people moved from the interior to the coast, from the coast to the interior, or if the interior and coast were essentially independent of one another at this early period, are direct products of limited evidence. There have also been questionable extrapolations from archaeological evidence outside of the Southern Plateau. The Marmes Rockshelter in southeastern Washington, for example, is frequently referenced as an 11,000 BP site pertinent to early developments in the Southern Plateau. Of the seven radiocarbon dates from unit I of this site (Rice 1972: 31, Table 3) six were run on shell whose capacity to incorporate old carbonates has long been known to provide older than true dates. The single charcoal date of 8,700 BP was in agreement with only one of the shell dates and is more likely an accurate age estimate for the unit 1 component.

The difficulties of attempting to reconstruct the culture history of Early Plateau culture have undoubtedly been exacerbated by the fact that the small and mobile groups of people involved left little evidence of their passing. Many elements of their tool kit were retained into Period III making the separation of Early Plateau culture technology from later cultures difficult if not impossible. Given the nature of the topography and resultant sedimentary processes, erosion and burial of sites have also conspired to either destroy or hide an already limited archaeological record (Black and White Plate IX).

`A´

`B´

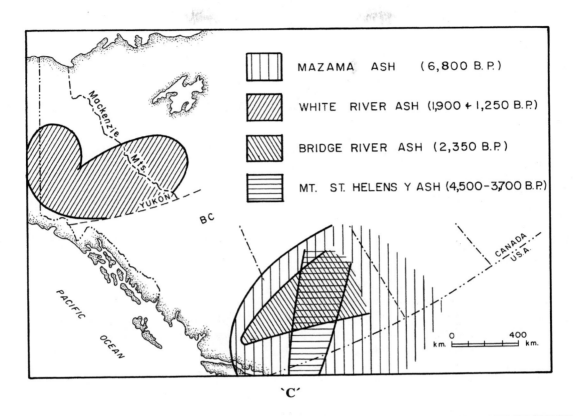

MAZAMA   ASH   (6,800 B.P.)

WHITE   RIVER   ASH (1,900 + 1,250 B.P.)

BRIDGE   RIVER   ASH   (2,350 B.P.)

MT.   ST.   HELENS Y ASH (4,500-3,700 B.P.)

`C´

BLACK AND WHITE PLATE IX: THE DRYNOCH SLIDE SITE AND VOLCANIC ASH HORIZON MARKERS   Photograph `A´ of the Drynoch Slide site illustrates the difficulty of excavating some Early Plateau culture sites even when they are located. The 20 m of sedimentary deposits which cap the human occupation has defied archaeological excavation methods and resources. Exposed by a highway cut, the archaeological deposits are capped by an airborne volcanic ash deposited over the site at 6,800 BP. The arrow indicates the location of the archaeological stratum and the automobile in the centre of the picture provides scale.

Photograph `B´ is a close-up view of the band of whitish Mazama volcanic ash which covered the wind-blown sands containing archaeological remains. (Photographs courtesy of Dr. David Sanger, University of Maine at Orono)

Figure `C´ demarcates the four major volcanic ash plumes or tephra deposits in Canada and provides their dates. Such volcanic airborne ash deposits are extremely useful to archaeologists as they act as datable horizon markers. If, for example, charcoal for radiocarbon dating had not been available at the Drynoch Slide site archaeologists would still have known that the archaeological deposits were older than the stratigraphically more recent Mazama ash. (Adapted from Bobrowsky et al. 1990: Figure 6. Drawn by David W. Laverie.)

CHAPTER 11

SOUTHWESTERN COASTAL CULTURE

Précis:

The term `Southwestern Coastal culture´ is used instead of previous terms, such as Old Cordilleran culture (Butler 1961; Fladmark 1982; Matson 1976), the Pebble Tool tradition (Carlson 1983; 1990), and the Olcott complex (Nelson 1990), in order to accommodate the geographic-habitat based culture nomenclature followed in this work. Less frequently used other names for the culture under consideration are Early Lithic culture (Mitchell 1971) and the Protowestern tradition (Borden 1975). There is a controversy whether Southwestern Coastal culture and its contemporary along the coast, Northwestern Coastal culture, represent geographic variations of a single culture or were two distinctly different cultures, one that originated from Palaeo-Indian in the south and spread north along the coast while the other, an off-shoot of Northwestern Palaeo-Arctic culture in Beringia, spread southward down the coast. There is also the debate whether Southwestern Coastal culture was an interior culture that moved to the coast or was a coastal culture that spread up the major river valleys into the interior or alternatively, possessed both maritime and interior adaptations. Evidence relating to this initial human occupation of the southern coast indicates that a sophisticated maritime adaptation was in place by 10,000 BP.

A resolution of the controversy surrounding the origin(s) and relationships of Southwestern Coastal culture and Northwestern Coastal culture are critical to any appreciation of the formation of West Coast culture. Some regard the Palaeo-Indian derived transitional cultures in the Great Basin- Columbia-Snake River region as being unrelated to contemporary developments along the coast to the north and, in particular, on the lower Fraser River (Carlson 1988: 322). Others regard Southwestern Coastal culture as being part of a broad cultural differentiation from Palaeo-Indian culture into a number of geographically confined and regionally distinctive cultures (Willig and Aikens 1988: Table 3). While it does appear that cultural developments in southern British Columbia were distinct in a number of important respects from those of the Columbia Plateau of Washington, Oregon, and Idaho, the area still appears to have participated in a widely distributed technological pattern. South of British Columbia various dimensions of this technological pattern have been classified as the San Dieguito horizon (Aikens 1978), the Western Pluvial Lakes tradition (Bedwell 1973), and the Stemmed Point tradition (Carlson 1983). The central issue is whether Southwestern Coastal culture shared its origins with other regional cultures that developed out of a Palaeo-Indian cultural base or whether it was a product of a southward movement of people down the coast of British Columbia from the North Pacific. Evidence relating to a sophisticated large sea mammal hunting capability and, more tentatively, the historic linguistic diversity of coastal British Columbia has been used to support the northern origin hypothesis. At this point in time a southern origin of Southwestern Coastal culture (Borden 1975) would appear to be more probable.

Within Southwestern Coastal culture technology the bifacially flaked bipointed projectile point is regarded as the major diagnostic artifact of "... an unspecialized hunting-gathering culture which appeared on the scene in the Pacific Northwest at or near the end of the Late Pleistocene. This culture, which I shall now refer to as the Old Cordilleran culture, appears to have been a widespread, basal culture in the area, ranging from the maritime province of the Puget Sound southward to the Northern Great Basin and eastward into the Columbia Basin, and possibly into eastern Idaho" (Butler 1961: 63). Butler regarded Old Cordilleran culture as a contemporary of Palaeo-Indian culture although sites generally date from 10,000 to 8,500 BP or later. Much of the difficulty in attempting to demonstrate the distribution of Southwestern Coastal culture can be attributed to its relatively simple tool kit containing artifact categories that are also found in much later cultures. The assemblage consists primarily of cobble core and spall tools and bipointed projectile points and knives, none of which are necessarily diagnostic of an early time period. The situation is then compounded by the scarcity of excavated sites and discrete components. Ground stone implements are either absent or rare as are bone implements. The few bone implements from the Glenrose Cannery site in the Fraser Delta (Matson 1976), for example, consisted of a single fixed barbed harpoon and a number of antler wedges, the latter being suggestive of wood-working. Evidence to the south in Oregon does indicate that the spearthrower may have been in use at this time.

Faunal evidence from coastal sites indicates a seasonal round that exploited both terrestrial and maritime resources but made relatively little use of intertidal food sources such as shellfish. The Bear Cove site on the north end of Vancouver Island (C. Carlson 1979), for example, contained high frequencies of dolphin, porpoise, and sea lion, thus providing strong support for the proposal that Southwestern Coastal culture possessed sea-worthy watercraft and the technology and knowledge necessary to capture large sea mammals. In contrast, in the Fraser River Canyon the location of the Milliken site suggests that salmon were captured in the rapids using some form of dip-net (Borden 1961). Given the complex nature of the topography of coastal British Columbia and its highly variable resources it is likely that the adaptive strategy of Southwestern Coastal culture was fine-tuned to all available foods, maritime and terrestrial. Even the limited evidence of the use of intertidal resources could prove to be more a product of limitations in archaeological sampling and preservation than any culturally motivated indifference to the rich resources of this ecotone. The suggestion that a diffuse adaptive subsistence system prevailed rather than a focal one is also supported by the highly variable settlement patterns which involved the utilization a number of different environmental niches. Site locations range from sea mammal hunting and fishing camps situated on exposed coastal beaches to interior riverine locations adjacent to rapids with their seasonal migrating salmon. Features of any kind at these campsites are rare and tend to have been disturbed or, in many instances, probably destroyed by flood waters or ocean storms.

The impression that Southwestern Coastal culture in southern British Columbia involved small populations of mobile hunting and fishing bands is certain to have been heightened by the processes of sea-level fluctuations, tectonic forces, and soil erosion and deposition that have either destroyed sites or markedly reduced their archaeological visibility. At 8,000 BP, for example, the high tide along the south coast was between 10 m to 15 m lower than present and did not reach its present level until shortly before the end of Period II (Mathews 1979). Many Southwestern Coastal culture ocean beach campsites during this time period would, of course, have been destroyed or drowned.

Cultural origins and descendants:

Controversy exists regarding the origin of Southwestern Coastal culture. The controversy centres on whether the culture developed out of Palaeo-Indian culture and then advanced northward along the coast and into the interior or whether it branched off from Beringian cultural roots and expanded southward with a technology pre-adapted to the exploitation of maritime resources. While recognizing the equivocal nature of the evidence, it would appear that two populations are involved, one advancing northward along the coast (Southwestern Coastal culture) and the other advancing southward (Northwestern Coastal culture) (Borden 1975). Pertinent to the debate is the proposition that northern people were possibly on the coast as early as 14,000 BP (Fladmark 1982: 104, 117) despite the absence of direct evidence earlier than 10,000 BP. Such an early human presence is unlikely given the environmentally hostile conditions of the Alaska Peninsula and the few coastal refugia at this time (Mathews 1979; Renier 1990). The basis of the early origin hypothesis is that late Palaeolithic people (Diuktai culture) in Beringia, possessing a maritime adaptation, moved south along the coast at a very early date but the migration hasn't been discovered as most of the evidence is now underwater (Borden 1975; Carlson 1990: 66-67; Davis et al. 1969: 76-77; Fladmark 1982: 118; 1990). A Beringian origin for a potentially early cobble tool complex on the Queen Charolotte Islands and other coastal areas is currently favoured by a number of archaeologists (Carlson 1990; Fladmark 1979; 1990; Hobler 1978). Cobble choppers, flakes, and cores at the Skoglund's Landing site on the Queen Charlotte Islands, geologically estimated to be as early as 10,000 BP (Fladmark 1982: 105), would fall into the same time period as similar materials from the Namu site on the Central Coast. However, this still begs the question of whether the cobble tool technology spread from the north or from the south along the coast or from both directions. The debate is further complicated by the fact that the northern and southern technologies possess much in common with the distinctions between them being primarily the presence of microblade technology to the north and a bifacial technology to the south. Bifacial flaked tools, however, are not totally absent to the north. In addition, there is controversy whether Southwestern Coastal culture had an initial interior adaptation and only acquired maritime skills later or had an original coastal adaptation and spread into the interior along with the expanding spawning ranges of salmon (Carlson 1979: 222-223; 1990: 66). At this writing, it would appear that Southwestern Coastal culture, as its name implies, was essentially a coastally oriented culture with the capability of exploiting land resources.

A parsimonious origin hypothesis suggests, "...that the San Dieguito-like complexes are derived from Clovis antecedents..." (Aikens 1978: 148) and that the bipointed and stemmed projectile points of an extensive area of northwestern North America are the geographic equivalents of the Early Archaic point styles of eastern North America. In this hypothesis Southwestern Coastal culture developed out of a Palaeo-Indian cultural base, evolved a maritime adaptation and advanced northward along the coast. An equivalent early penetration of the interior cannot be demonstrated at this time. The foregoing does not deny that the developmental path taken along the British Columbia coast and the lower Fraser River was different in a number of respects (Carlson 1988) from developments in the Great Basin-Columbia Plateau region (see Willig and Aikens 1988: Table 3). An expanded programme of fingerprinting exotic lithics to source would certainly be a useful method to assess the southern versus northern origins of Southwestern Coastal culture as well as its coastal versus interior associations.

Southwestern Coastal culture radiocarbon dates range from 8,000 BP to the end of Period II on the South Coast (Borden 1975; C. Carlson 1979; Carlson 1979; Matson 1976) and from 9,000 BP to the end of Period II in the Fraser Canyon (Borden 1975; Eldridge 1981). At the stratified Namu site on the Central Coast dates range from nearly 10,000 BP to 4,000 BC (Carlson n.d.). Microblades appear in the Namu site sequence around 8,000 BP and are regarded as a diffused element of technology from Early Northwest Interior culture. They are not construed as evidence for the appearance at the site of either Early Northwest Interior culture or Northwestern Coastal culture.

Cultural continuity from Southwestern Coastal culture into Period III (4,000 to 1,000 BC) can be recognized in a number of regional phases or phase clusters (Charles, Mayne, St.Mungo and Eayem). At the stratified Milliken and Esilao sites in the Fraser Canyon cultural continuity appears to incorporate approximately 6,000 years (Borden 1975: 72).

Technology:

The wide range of animals exploited by Southwestern Coastal culture would suggest the existence of a substantial perishable technology such as watercraft, nets, snares, etc. (Matson 1988). Very little other than the chipped stone tools, however, have survived the passage of time and the normally acid soils. One component of the stone technology, the cobble core and cobble flake tools, has been the subject of considerable discussion. These multi-purpose chopping, scraping, and cutting core-flake expedient tools were manufactured from suitable cobbles readily available along the entire coast (Fladmark 1986: 29-30). An assemblage on the lower Fraser River, referred to as the Pasika complex, was originally believed to represent a widespread Pleistocene age cobble tool industry devoid of bifacially flaked tools (Borden 1969). Subsequent research has indicated that these tools can be relatively recent and, indeed, that cobble tools occur throughout the archaeological record of southern British Columbia and are not culturally diagnostic (Grabert 1979; Haley 1983). On the other hand, if the geological age estimates of 10,000 to 11,000 BP for certain raised marine beaches on the lower Fraser River are correct then the dates probably also pertain to the associated water-tumbled cobble tools (Fladmark 1986: 30). In addition to the cobble core and flake tools other common elements of the tool kit are bipointed and bifacially flaked projectile points and knives, a wide range of scraper forms including end and side scrapers, and linear flakes (Borden 1979). Contracting stemmed points, polished stone tools, and possible burins are rare occurrences (Borden 1960; 1961; 1975; Matson 1976). Red ochre nodules are also found on the lower Fraser River sites. After 5,500 BC there is an increase in the numbers of abraders which may indicate the increasing importance of bone implements fashioned by grinding (Fladmark 1986: 39).

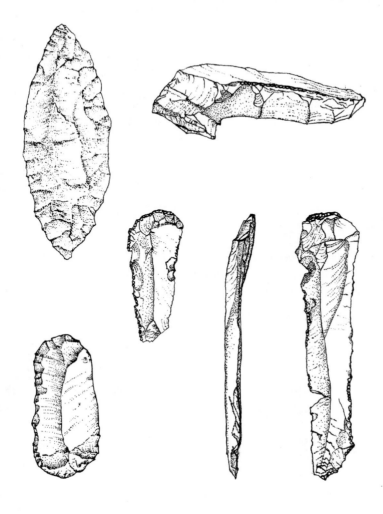

FIGURE 15: SOUTHWESTERN COASTAL CULTURE IMPLEMENTS The bipointed projectile point/knife and scraper on the left were recovered from the lowest level of the Milliken site in the Fraser Canyon. Situated to the right of the aforementioned artifacts is a core striking platform remnant and below a scraper manufactured on a linear flake and a linear flake showing both dorsal and lateral views. The latter specimens came from the undated lowest level of the Lochnore Creek site in the Southern Plateau.The relationship between Early Plateau culture and Southwestern Coast culture is still unclear. (Linear flakes and core fragment drawings reproduced from Sanger 1970: Figure 35 with permission. Drawings by Mr. David W. Laverie Scale l:1.3)

Of the 614 tools from the lower level of the Glenrose Cannery site on the Fraser River Delta (Matson 1988) 44% were cobble tools, predominantly unifacially flaked. Other tools consisted of bipointed projectile points, a single stemmed point, bipointed knives, abundant random flake scrapers, a few abraders, a number of antler wedges, and some other bone tools. At the Bear Cove site on the north end of Vancouver Island frequencies of stone tool varieties were as follows: cobble core tools (48%); cobble spall tools (35%); bifacially flaked tools (6%); and some miscellaneous items such as hammerstones, possible netsinkers, and a few bone items (C. Carlson 1979: 183). The abundance of porpoise, northern fur seal, and sea lion at this site implies the existence of efficient sea-going watercraft and a sophisticated large sea mammal hunting technology. Exclusive of debitage, the Southwestern Coastal culture components of the stratified Namu site on the Central Coast, ranging from 10,000 BP to the end of Period II, contained cobble tools, bipointed projectile points, bifacial knives, choppers, flake scrapers, hammerstones, microblades, macroblade cores and blades, edge ground cobbles, abraders, and a grooved bola stone, among other items (Carlson 1979: Table 1). The grooved bola stone is of particular interest as it closely resembles forms from a 8,000 BP salmon fishing component at the Five-Mile-Rapids site on the Columbia River in Oregon (Cressman 1960).

Over the 3,000 years of Southwestern Coastal culture occupation of the Glenrose Cannery site there is little evidence of technological change (Matson 1976: 283). Within a similar time span at the upriver Milliken site, the upper levels contained more cobble tools, smaller projectile points, and minor new traits such as gravers, spokeshaves, and stone wedges (Borden 1960; 1961; 1975). There would appear to have been a conservative adherence to a basic tool kit over a long period of time.

Subsistence:

The people who first occupied the coast of British Columbia were capable of exploiting both marine and terrestrial resources (Carlson 1990). The differences between sites, such as the Glenrose Cannery site and the Bear Cove site, likely reflect different facets of the seasonal round. At the former site the importance of elk/deer, seal, canids (dog?), salmon, sturgeon, flounder, and eulachon contrasts with the heavy reliance on sea mammals (dolphins, porpoise, sea lion, fur seal) and rockfish at the latter site (Matson 1976; C. Carlson 1979). Intertidal resources, such as the bay mussel, were also being exploited at the Glenrose Cannery site raising the probability that the scarcity of such evidence on other Southwestern Coastal sites is more likely an archaeological sampling problem than evidence of an avoidance of the rich littoral resources. Within any balanced coastal-interior exploitation pattern considerable seasonal and geographic variability can be anticipated.

Juvenile elk and deer, seasonal growth rings that can be determined from the shell valves of shellfish, and the presence of salmon as the most important fish at the Glenrose Cannery site (Matson 1976) all suggest a summer to fall occupation. Throughout the 3,000 years of Southwestern Coastal culture occupation of this site there appears to be little change in the exploitation of marine and terrestrial animals although fewer birds appear in the later deposits. Paradoxically, at the Milliken site with its total absence of bone preservation cherry pits (Prunus demissa) were preserved by accidental charring. This accident underlines the likelihood that plant foods would have been seasonally important and were probably dried for winter consumption as a food rich in vitamins. The cherry pits also indicate a late summer occupation which is in agreement with the inferred salmon fishing activity at the site (Borden 1975). As has been noted (Carlson 1990: 64), the only explanation for locating a site in a steep canyon must have been because of the advantages such a locale provided to intercept the salmon runs.

Although the evidence bearing upon the subsistence practices of Southwestern Coastal culture is limited, it is sufficient to suggest that the foundation of the Northwest Coast subsistence pattern were being established at this early time period. Only the limited evidence of the utilization of intertidal resources, which is probably more a product of archaeological sampling rather than any Southwestern Coastal culture gastronomic inclination, and a less focused specialization on specific species such as salmon, would appear to differentiate the subsistence rounds of these first occupants of the South and Central coasts of British Columbia from that of their descendants. Stable carbon isotope analysis of bone samples from the rare burials dated to the end of Period II at both the Pender Island site and the Namu site suggests that 90% of the protein in the diet of these individuals came from marine sources (Carlson 1990: 65).

The evidence of cultural continuity and conservatism seen in the lithic technology might suggest that these generalized coastal/interior hunting and fishing bands were in equilibrium with their food resources and, therefore, had no need to increase the productivity of the food supply. Such a proposition is unlikely. It is difficult to conceive of a people who were capable of taking large sea mammals on the high seas with an archaeologically invisible technology being incapable of appreciating the benefits of other resources such as those occupying the rich intertidal zone. The picture of the subsistence rounds is still woefully incomplete but it is sufficient to suggest that "...all or most of the fundamental technological and economic basis for Northwest Coast culture may always have been present, from the very first occupation of the region" (Fladmark 1982: 132).

Settlement patterns:

Southwestern Coastal culture settlement patterns are highly variable. Sites on the coast or deltas tend to be situated beside small freshwater streams (C. Carlson 1979; Matson 1976). The marine mammal hunting camp in Bear Cove is located in a small cove facing west onto a large bay suggestive of a summer occupation, an interpretation supported by the faunal remains. Local beach cobbles were the major material used for stone tool production although a few obsidian flakes of unspecified origin were also recovered (C. Carlson 1979). Like the Bear Cove site, the Glenrose Cannery site on the Delta of the Fraser River lacked discernible features or even activity areas (Matson 1976). Exotic shell species at this site, however, indicate contacts to the south. At the Milliken site in the Fraser Canyon post moulds and hearths were recorded although no pattern could be determined (Borden 1961; 1975). Of significance was the recovery of obsidian identified as coming from an Oregon quarry 700 km to the south. In the same region, a 2.0 m by 1.5 m ovate feature 1.0 m deep at the DiRi-14 site has been interpreted as a possible storage pit (Eldridge 1981: 96). On the rugged Central Coast the Namu site is situated at a river mouth facing the open Pacific Ocean except for a screen of offshore islands (Carlson 1979). Bone preservation in the lowest deposits was poor but it is suspected the prey species would have been similar to those of the later occupations. These contained "Salmon, seal, sea lion, bear, beaver, deer, canid, mustellidae (mink, weasel, marten, river otter), delphinids, and porcupine..." (Carlson 1979: 220). Regardless of the subsistence focus of the earliest occupants of this site with its virtually unbroken 11,000 years of occupation, people could not have reached the area without watercraft, much less have survived (Ibid).

As this short section on settlement patterns indicates, knowledge of Southwestern Coastal culture is dependant upon a limited number of excavated sites. Fortunately, in terms of information, the sites have all presented somewhat different facets of the settlement pattern.

Cosmology:

There is no information on Southwestern Coastal culture cosmology although the ochre nodules and powder from some sites may have had some unknown symbolic significance.

External relationships:

The most critical external relationship to determine is if "The Central B.C. coast was the meeting ground of the early Pebble Tool and Microblade Traditions, and the Early Period there represents a blending of their technological aspects" (Carlson 1979: 225) or whether the Southwestern Coastal (Pebble Tool Tradition) and Northwestern Coastal (Microblade Tradition) cultures are actually a single culture onto which certain traits were grafted (Carlson 1990; Fladmark 1982). With some reservations, the earlier view of two cultures being involved, one originating in the south and the other in the north is adopted here. A corollary to the eventual resolution of this matter will be the determination if these early cultures, Southwestern and Northwestern Coastal cultures, were only coastally oriented or whether they both possessed broad adaptive systems that exploited interior resources as well. There is also the issue of whether the interior adaptations of Early Plateau culture and Early Northwest Interior culture were sufficiently different from some of their contemporaries on the coast to be readily distinguished from one another.

Human biology:

Nothing can be stated regarding human biology for Southwestern Coastal culture for, as has been noted, "With the possible exception of one or two individuals, human remains and mortuary sites are unknown prior to 3500 BC" (Cybulski: 1994: 76).

Inferences on society:

It is a reasonable speculation that Southwestern Coastal culture consisted of a number of independent bands, each composed of groupings of self-sufficient families who likely traced their descent through the male line. Neighbouring bands would be related through a marriage system that required wives to move to their husband's band. Considerable individual choice would have characterized the social system. It is probable that extra-ordinary power was temporarily allocated to certain individuals under special circumstances such as to the captain of a vessel hunting large sea mammals on the open sea. An animistic view of the world, in which personally acquired power through prayer, fasting, and taboo adherence, likely prevailed. When coping with any one of the host of animate and inanimate spirit powers exceeded individual capabilities then the exceptional powers of shamans could be solicited.

Limitations in the evidence:

Archaeological evidence is always confined by the facts of preservation that usually permit the survival of a very limited portion of the technology and other facets of culture. The vast majority of cultural remains are perishable except under the most exceptional circumstances. In this regard, evidence pertinent to Southwestern Coastal culture is exceptionally limited resting as it does upon a few major site excavations and widely distributed surface collections. Fortunately, the excavated sites have all been situated in somewhat different locales thereby providing archaeologists with some appreciation of cultural variability. Also, like Early Plains culture, not only is the technology difficult to attribute to a particular culture when removed from a datable archaeological context but the land surfaces originally occupied have often been destroyed, buried, submerged, or otherwise affected in ways that make archaeological detection difficult or impossible. Relative to this last problem "...the earliest portions of all coastal cultural sequences are now effectively lost to us, hidden up to several hundred meters high along the rugged forested slopes of the inner mainland coast, or as much as 100 m below the modern ocean surface along the outer coast" (Fladmark 1990: 184). Black and White Plate X and Figure 16 help illustrate the nature of the archaeological visibility problem at one Southwestern Coastal culture site.

BLACK AND WHITE PLATE X: THE 1961 MILLIKEN SITE EXCAVATION IN THE FRASER CANYON, BRITISH COLUMBIA, UNDER THE DIRECTION OF THE LATE CARL BORDEN (Courtesy of the Laboratory of Archaeology, University of British Columbia. Photo by Peter Holburn)

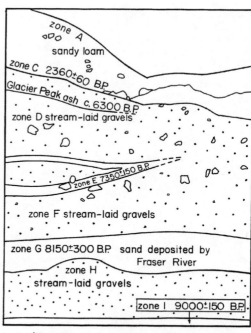

25' PROFILE of FRASER CANYON SITE

FIGURE 16:   SCHEMATIC PROFILE OF THE MILLIKEN SITE, FRASER CANYON The lowest stratum of this 7.6 m archaeological excavation profile, dated to 9,000 BP, was represented by a Southwestern Coastal culture occupation. Such sedimentary deposition along this portion of the salmon rich Fraser River have undoubtedly obscured much of the evidence of the earliest human occupations of the region or has destroyed it outright through erosion. (Adapted from Borden 1961: Figure 1. Drawing by Mr. David W. Laverie.)

CHAPTER 12 —————————————————————————————

NORTHWESTERN COASTAL CULTURE

Précis:

The divergent views regarding the origins of Southwestern Coastal culture and Northwestern Coastal culture were considered in the preceding chapter. Among the options, the view favoured here follows an earlier hypothesis (Borden 1975) whereby two distinct cultures, one of southern origin and the other of northern origin, were involved in the initial coastal settlement of British Columbia (for a discussion see Fladmark 1982: 117-118).

Northwestern Coastal culture, a regional development from the Northwestern Palaeo-Arctic culture of Period I, appears along the North Coast of British Columbia and adjacent Alaska between 10,000 and 9,000 BP, reaching the Queen Charlotte Islands by 7,500 BP if not before. The maritime adaptation of this culture may have developed along the now submerged coastline of southern Beringia (Aigner and DelBene 1982). It is proposed that the southward movement along the coast was roughly coeval with a similar interior movement by the related Early Northwest Interior culture people of Period II. These two adaptations, coastal and interior, are believed to have quickly differentiated from one another (Carlson 1990: 68).

Erosional and depositional forces in conjunction with fluctuating sea levels have complicated the search for early Northwestern Coastal culture sites and as a result the construct is based upon limited evidence. The mainland portion of the North Coast was subjected to more dramatic sea level fluctuations than the Queen Charlotte Islands and sea level did not stabilize until 5,000 years ago (Fladmark et al. 1990). As a result, all of the evidence from the North Coast of British Columbia comes from the Queen Charlotte Islands. Between 7,000 and 2,500 BC sea levels around the Queen Charlotte islands were approximately 15 m higher than at present and it has been along the ancient elevated beaches where most sites have been located. Intertidal water-tumbled flakes, cobble tools, and even a microblade core, could possibly pertain to an occupation as early as 10,000 BP (Hobler 1978). Reworked beach gravels at the Skoglund's Landing site, containing cobble tools and cores, may date to 9,000 BP. As noted in the **Cultural origins and descendants** section of Chapter 11, these findings could suggest the existence of a cobble tool industry and even microblade technology on the Queen Charlotte Islands at an early period (Fladmark et al. 1990: 231).

Northwestern Coastal culture technology is dominated by microblades and, on occasion, macroblades that are differentiated from microblades by widths of 10 mm or more. These narrow flakes with prismatic and triangular crossections were struck from specially prepared cores. Sections of the resulting microblades would have been used as inserts to arm wooden or bone lances, knives, and other composite tools. Microblade technology represents the most economic use of stone ever developed by stone age people. Ubiquitous cobble core and spall tools are also well represented.

Site locations on outer islands and the limited recovered faunal materials indicate that these people must have been superb mariners. No traces of watercraft have survived in the archaeological record but presumably such vessels were sufficiently substantial to navigate the dangerous waters of the North Coast and yet were portable enough to be lifted manually out of the water. It is speculated that the boats would have been sheathed in skins rather than bark and commodious enough to accommodate extended family groups. It is most unlikely that archaeology will ever be able to discover this essential element of Northwestern Coastal culture technology. There is a basis for optimism, however, that some insights into the large sea mammal hunting gear will eventually be unearthed on those sites with bone preservation. The technological elements of Northwestern Coastal culture that have survived in the archaeological record stand as a humbling example of the chasm separating the archaeological record of technology from what must once have existed.

Cultural origins and descendants:

Northwestern Palaeo-Arctic culture and its microblade technology have been traced from 10,000 to 8,000 BP and later in interior Alaska at sites such as Akmak (Anderson 1980) and Dry Creek (Powers and Hoffecker 1989). Earlier evidence has been recovered from the Bluefish Caves site in the northern Yukon (Cinq-Mars 1990) and from recent excavations at the Swan Point site in northern Alaska (Mason 1993). Although contested (Haynes 1982: 395), a number of archaeologists regard Northwestern Palaeo-Arctic culture as a development out of the Nenana-Chindadn complex that was also related to Palaeo-Indian culture (Clark 1984; West 1981). Northwestern Palaeo-Arctic culture was ancestral to a coastal adapted culture (Northwestern Coastal culture) and an interior adapted culture (Early Northwest Interior culture) (Powers 1990: 60). It is possible that both of these adaptations and their respective `cultures´ are simply expressions of a single culture with a very flexible adaptive system. Only additional evidence will resolve this matter and, for the moment, the coastal and interior adaptations will be treated as separate cultural entities.

Names of cultures equivalent or related to Northwestern Coastal culture are the broadly conceived Microblade tradition (Carlson 1990), the Anangula complex in the Aleutians (Aigner 1978; Dumond et al. 1976), the Palaeomarine tradition in southeastern Alaska (Ackerman et al. 1979; Davis 1990: 197-198), and the Early Coastal Microblade tradition of the coast of British Columbia (Fladmark 1982: Fig.6). Dated sites range from 9,000 to 5,000 BP and thus extend through most of Period II and into Period III. The cultural affiliation of Level III of the Ground Hog Bay site in southeastern Alaska (Ackerman et al. 1979), with its 10,000 BP date, is still uncertain as only a couple of biface fragments, a scraper, and some flakes were recovered (Carlson 1990: 67). Radiocarbon date distributions indicate a spread of microblade technology down the coast from the north to the south (Carlson 1990: 67). In this study, the appearance of Northwestern Coastal culture on the Queen Charlotte Islands and adjacent Alaska is regarded as the product of the initial colonization of the area by people. The occurrence of microblade technology further south on the Namu site of the Central coast is interpreted as a product of diffusion from the interior to the Southwestern Coastal culture early occupants of the site. With reference to the initial colonizing of the North Coast it is pertinent to note that the earliest evidence of plant communities establishing themselves after glaciation in southeastern Alaska only predate the earliest archaeological evidence by 1,500 years (Ackerman 1988: 177). Regarding the issue of where Northwestern Coastal culture on the North Coast of British Columbia and adjacent Alaska actually originated most archaeologists believe that it represents a southern extension of more northerly maritime adapted people colonizing new lands (Clark 1983a). Others would disagree and suggest the culture originated in the interior of Alaska and then penetrated to the coast (Henn 1978). The latter view follows an earlier proposed movement from the interior to the coast (Borden 1975) and may still be a viable option (Ackerman et al. 1979: 206), particularly given the fingerprinting of obsidian from Northwestern Coastal sites to interior geological deposits such as those on Mt.Edziza. As in many instances of archaeological interpretation it may not be an either-or situation but rather one where both coastal and interior elements interacted. Given the specialized nature of a maritime adaptation, however, Northwestern Coastal culture and its southward penetration along the British Columbia coast must have been predominantly a coastal phenomenon.

It has been suggested that the maritime adaptation of Northwestern Coastal culture took place between 11,000 and 10,000 BP along the now submerged south coast of Beringia and/or the northeastern coast of Asia (Aigner and DelBene 1982: 65). This development would have been contemporaneous with a Late Pleistocene interior adaptation which eventually gave rise to Early Northwest Interior culture. The Anangula site, near the western end of the Aleutian chain, is critical to an appreciation of this maritime adaptation and will be considered in some detail.

The Anangula site, dated between 9,000 and 8,000 BP, and subsequent cultural developments in the region are speculated to have led directly to the historically documented Aleuts (Aigner and DelBene 1982). Such a proposal would establish Eskimo-Aleut speakers in the eastern Bering Sea region at a very early time period and would presuppose that other language families shared the same basic technology with roots going back to Northwestern Palaeo-Arctic culture. For example, it has frequently been suggested that the related Early Northwest Interior culture was carried south through the interior by Athabaskan-speaking peoples (Borden 1975; Carlson 1979; Dumond 1974). Such propositions overextend the capabilities of linguistic scholarship to control chronology. At the best, speculations concerning early language family associations with archaeological assemblages should be treated as operating hypotheses requiring considerable testing and confirmation by a range of different disciplines. On firmer ground, albeit based on indirect evidence, is the obvious necessity for these early maritimers to have possessed sophisticated watercraft along with the technology to capture large mammals at sea. While direct evidence of watercraft is not likely to be recovered from archaeological sites, the location of sites and faunal recoveries all point to an efficient maritime adaptation where such elements of technology would have been absolute necessities. Settlement pattern evidence from the Anangula site revealed the existence of a village of between 75 and 125 people occupying some 20 to 30 semi-subterranean houses. These single family ovate-shaped dwellings measured 6 m by 3 m to 4 m, contained hearths, storage pits, and other features

(Aigner and DelBene 1982:50). The distribution of cultural debris in and around houses was indicative of specific activities such as stone tool manufacture immediately outside of the dwellings. Unfortunately poor bone preservation provided little direct evidence of the animals hunted and their relative importance to the villagers. The Anangula site technology is dominated by a range of tools manufactured from blades struck from prepared cores as well as a variety of scrapers but totally lacks bifacially flaked implements. Other artifacts, such as stone bowls, ochre grinding palettes, shaft abraders, and anvilstones provide the basis for suggesting a regional continuity with subsequent cultures (Ibid: 54).

It would appear from the community settlement pattern evidence at the Anangula site that a considerable degree of social complexity had been achieved in the southern Bering Sea at an early date. Presumably the Northwestern Coastal culture people who appeared on the northern coast of British Columbia around 10,000 BP, shared, to some degree, in this rich social structure as well as the highly developed maritime technology. The prevailing view that Northwestern Coastal culture people then advanced up the major rivers into the interior of British Columbia (Carlson 1990; Fladmark 1986) has not been demonstrated. Instead there is evidence suggesting that microblade technology moved southward through the interior to reach the Southern Plateau.

With reference to descendants, there has been a highly speculative suggestion of a language-technology correlation that associates Northwestern Coastal culture with the historic speakers of Tlingit, Haida, and Athabascan (Carlson 1983). On considerably safer grounds it has been noted that on the Queen Charlotte Islands Northwestern Coastal culture (Moresby tradition) appears to carry through into Period III (4,000 - 1,000 BC) (Fladmark et al. 1990: Table 1).

Radiocarbon dates from the Queen Charlotte Islands Lawn Point and Kasta sites range from 7,400 BP to just prior to Period III (Carlson 1990) while dates from adjacent southeastern Alaska range from either 9,000 BP or, less certainly, 10,000 BP to 4,750 BC (Ackerman 1974; Ackerman et al. 1979; Davis 1990).

Technology:

Microblades struck from specialized cores are characteristic of Northwestern Coastal culture. On the Alaska Peninsula in the 9,000 BP Narrows phase (Henn 1978) microblades and macroblades were associated with a range of core varieties. By 8,000 BP in the same region the distinction between microblade and macroblade core varieties disappears (Dumond 1981) mimicing a situation noted at the Anangula site in the Aleutian chain. Situated on the Alaskan Panhandle near Sitka the stratified Ground Hog Bay site deposits ranged in age from 10,000 BP to 2,500 BC. The lowest stratum produced little cultural material that included biface blade fragments but no microblades. The following occupational level contained both microblades and macroblades, the former being 10 mm or less in width. Scrapers, flake tools, choppers, notched scraping tools, bifacially flaked preforms, hammerstones, and cobble spalls were also present (Ackerman et al. 1979: 201). While the obsidian microblade cores were based upon pebbles and resemble northern forms (Ackerman 1974: 7) the macroblade cores were manufactured from local

FIGURE 17: A RECONSTRUCTION OF MICROBLADE PRODUCTION USING SPECIALIZED CORES
The drawing by artist Jaclynne Campbell of Simon Fraser University illustrates a possible method of locking the microblade core between two pieces of wood preparatory to striking off the microblades. Methods of fitting the microblades into wooden handles to produce sharp edged knives are shown at the bottom of the Figure. (Reproduced from Fladmark 1986: Plate 8 with the permission of Dr. Knut R. Fladmark, Simon Fraser University)

argillite/andesite. The ready availability of stone suitable for chipping likely explains the abundance of heavy cores and choppers rather than being indicative of a distinctive technology. At the nearby Hidden Falls site, dating to 9,000 BP, a microblade assemblage was recovered in association with scrapers and pebble choppers.

On the Queen Charlotte Islands microblade cores, macroblades cobble core and flake tools, and amorphous flake scrapers were dated to 7,500 BP (Fladmark 1982:109). This assemblage represents the earliest `well documented´ cultural evidence on the North Coast (Fladmark et al. 1990). Despite the total absence of bifacially flaked tools the assemblage resembles those from sites in southeastern Alaska immediately to the north (Ackerman et al. 1979). The ubiquitous cobble core and flake expedient tools used in scraping, cutting and chopping functions and as cores from which to detach sharp flakes are unlikely to be identifiable to a specific culture. The appearance of abraders around 4,000 BC, however, may indicate the increasing importance of a ground bone tool industry despite the lack of bone preservation at the sites in question (Fladmark et al. 1990: 231).

Subsistence:

A shell midden composed mainly of clams and mussels was excavated at the 8,000 BP Chuck Lake site in southeastern Alaska. Fish remains were also abundant with other vertebrates, such as seal, sea lion, deer/caribou, beaver, canid, and birds, being less so (Ackerman 1988: 184; Davis 1990: 198). Ninety-five percent of the faunal remains were derived from marine sources. The presence of the shell midden also suggests that the absence or scarcity of shellfish remains at other Northwestern Coastal culture sites may be a product of either poor preservation or cultural practices affecting the discard of shell refuse. Settlement pattern distributions of sites along beaches and at river mouths on the Queen Charlotte Islands would support the suspected importance of intertidal and estuarine resources such as shellfish (Fladmark 1982: 110). The reliance upon food from the sea is similar to that noted for Southwestern Coastal culture at sites such as Namu (Carlson 1979) and Bear Cove (C. Carlson 1979). In the latter instance, marine food consumption was calculated between 85 and 95 percent (Ackerman 1988: 184).

Settlement patterns:

The characteristics of sites on offshore islands are indicative of small, marine oriented and highly mobile maritime populations (Fladmark 1982: 108). It follows that "If one uses a coastal migration route for the initial settlement of the northern part of the Northwest Coast, then a model of temporal priority for island populations would be likely. Mainland settlement would be a later development with the exploitation of salmon resources a major component of local population aggregation" (Ackerman 1988: 185-186). Sites situated along coastal and estuary beaches were frequently subjected to disturbance by wave action indicating the occupation of active beaches. At the Ground Hog Bay site a protecting reef could have provided safe anchorage again emphasizing the maritime nature of the settlement patterns (Ackerman 1988: 175). Sites also tend to provide broad vistas of ocean straits and bays. Simple hearth floors, devoid of fire shattered rock, have been identified on the Queen Charlotte Islands (Fladmark 1970; Fladmark et al. 1990) but structural features are absent. A rare feature from the 7,000 BP component of the Lawn Point site on the Queen Charlotte Islands was a cache of eleven freshly struck microblades which were never retrieved by their owner (Fladmark 1986: 34). Pertinent to population dispersal and culture contact situations is the identification of the obsidian from the Ground Hog Bay site as having originated on Mt.Edziza 220 km up the Stikine River from the coast or 250 km as the crow flies from the Ground Hog Bay site (Ackerman et al. 1979).

Cosmology:

There is no evidence pertinent to **Cosmology** unless the microblade cache from the Lawn Point site represents some form of votive offering or even offerings placed in a grave from which all other evidence has vanished rather than being an unclaimed cache.

External relationships:

There is considerable debate regarding the origins of Northwestern Coastal culture. The relationship of the occupants of the coast to those in the interior is also a matter of continuing discussion. From the perspective of this work the contemporary neighbours of Northwestern Coastal culture would be Southwestern Coastal culture on the Central and South coasts and Early Northwest Interior culture in the northern interior.

Microblade technology suddenly appears as an added cultural element to the tool kit of the Southwestern Coastal culture occupation of the Namu site around 8,000 BP (Carlson 1979; n.d.). Given the sophisticated maritime adaptations of both Southwestern Coastal culture and Northwestern Coastal culture it would be reasonable to assume that the microblade technology arrived on the Central Coast via diffusion along the coast from the north. The microblades at the Namu site, however, were manufactured from interior obsidian (Carlson 1979). This could suggest a trade relationship with either Early Northwest Interior culture in the interior or the possibility that Southwestern Coastal culture people made periodic trips to the interior to collect obsidian. Once again, the question is raised of how distinct Northwestern Coastal culture and Early Northwest Interior culture really are from one another. Another option would be that if the microblade technology diffused from Northwestern Coastal culture to Southwestern Coastal culture a need was created for the high quality stone required by microblade production and thus encouraged the establishment of a trade relationship with Early Northwest Interior culture people or actual quarrying expeditions from the coast into the interior. Given the nature of the evidence all of these options are feasible. There is also the evidence of Mt.Edziza obsidian on Northwestern Coastal sites in southeastern Alaska. As has been noted in other instances, the fingerprinting of exotic lithics to their geological sources will be critical to any understanding of the nature and direction of such relationships.

Human biology:

No data.

Inferences on society:

While the usual speculations regarding the social structure of early hunting societies, such as being composed of nuclear families organized into patrilineal and patrilocal bands with intermarriage throughout a network of neighbouring bands, probably applies, an additional facet may be pertinent to the social structure of Northwestern Coastal culture. A maritime adaptation to the varied and rich resources of the coast would have differentiated these maritime societies from their interior neighbours. The complex settlement pattern of the 9,000 to 8,000 BP Anangula village site is a reflection of a relatively developed social organization (Aigner and DelBene 1982). A need for centralized authority during navigation of ocean going watercraft and the cooperative hunting of large sea mammals on the high sea could have resulted in a degree of social ranking, albeit likely temporary. In other words, the captain of a vessel may have been assigned special authority over his crew while at sea.

Limitations in the evidence:

The major limitation in the archaeological evidence pertaining to Northwestern Coastal culture is its scarcity and often equivocal nature. Erosional forces and, in particular, the submergence and/or emergence of former shorelines have either destroyed or hidden a large portion of the archaeological record. For a brief outline of the variable nature of sea level changes along the coast at this time see Fladmark (1986: 27-28). It is also probable that the populations involved were quite small further reducing the degree of archaeological visibility.

There has been a tendency for archaeologists working along the northern Pacific coast to espouse either-or scenarios to explain their data and support various origin hypotheses. These stances have tended to divide along lines of the coast versus the interior. Matters have then been further complicated by the temptation to equate interpretations with the historic linguistic diversity of the West Coast. Given the equivocal nature of the actual evidence and the very questionable control linguistics has over chronological projections involving millennia, it would more appropriate at this time to keep one's interpretive options open. Instead of adhering to one origin hypothesis to the total exclusion of another, for example, it may be well to assess a number of options and balance these options relative to different processes such as population movements and diffusion. This, of course, does not mean that archaeologists should not favour a particular point of view or hypothesis but rather that alternative possibilities should be continually reassessed in order that matters do not become `etched in stone´. It may even develop that the either-or scenarios currently being debated will eventually turn out to be simply two dimensions of a single cultural process such as an adaptive system that was capable of exploiting both maritime and interior resources.

CHAPTER 13
EARLY NORTHWEST INTERIOR CULTURE

Précis:

Early Northwest Interior culture is a tentative cultural construct. It could even be called a classificatory `catch-all´ bred of archaeological desperation. The nature of the archaeological evidence makes it difficult to determine if there is one or two or more distinct cultures in the region. A range of factors have coalesced to insure an exceptional poverty of clear archaeological evidence. Early Northwest Interior culture may have been initially represented by a technology with bifacially flaked tools but lacking a microblade technology called Northern Cordilleran (Clark 1991). Microblade technology was adopted later from the west, except in the northern Yukon where it was probably present at a very early date (Cinq-Mars 1990). There is the problem of whether the movement of microblade technology out of Alaska into the Yukon Territory, the western portion of Mackenzie District of the Northwest Territories, and northern British Columbia, represented an actual movement of people bearing a distinctive culture or was simply microblade technology being adopted by indigenous populations. There is the additional problem of whether, in many instances, the absence of microblade technology reflects specific site function where microblades were not required rather than evidence of a culture lacking microblade technology. As has been aptly noted "...the logical and probable existence of Northwest Microblade tradition sites without microblades is an insidious problem inasmuch as identification of this tradition is dependent on the recovery of microblades or cores" (Clark 1987: 167). The mixture of traits also causes classification problems. The Tuktu complex of the Brooks Range of northern Alaska (Campbell 1962) "...could be classified as early Northern Archaic, as a regional form of the Northwest Microblade tradition, or as a later development out of Denali and the Paleo-Arctic tradition ..." (Clark 1981: 113). Certainly the almost whimsical presence and absence and disappearance and reappearance of microblades throughout much of the archaeological record of the region would suggest that this particular element of technology can be quite untrustworthy as a cultural diagnostic (Clark 1983: 11; Morlan and Cinq-Mars 1982: 373). On the other hand, the complex demands made on the tool manufacturer during the production of microblades, not to mention their associated composite tool organic hafting elements, would imply that the knowledge to produce microblades must have been a highly integrated element within a culture's technology. Following a personal inclination to favour diffusion as a major cause of cultural change rather than population replacement in northern environs, a scenario that envisions an initial occupation of the region by the Northern Cordilleran complex, with its Nenana-Chindadn complex/Palaeo-Indian relationships, onto which microblade technology was grafted at a later date, is favoured albeit with some trepidation. In this respect the Northern Cordilleran complex would represent the earlier manifestation of Early Northwest Interior cultural development while the microblade component would represent a later attribute of the same culture. These developments carried into Period III. While it would have been a simpler matter to have argued for the existence of an early culture lacking microblades (Northern Cordilleran complex) followed by a replacing microblade culture (Northwest Microblade complex) neither the limited evidence nor the economic foundations of these early northerners support such a descriptively convenient sequence population and cultural replacement.

Given the paucity of evidence for Early Northwest Interior culture no attempt will be made to generalize about the various cultural subsystems in the précis. Certainly a major factor in this scarcity of information is that "With a few exceptions, archaeological sites in the western Subarctic are either small and sparse or involve shallow multiple occupations, often over large areas, that are disturbed and mixed through frost action" (Clark 1981: 107). The situation has then been compounded by a virtual lack of bone preservation and a not particularly distinctive chipped stone tool technology.

Cultural origins and descendants:

Much discussion has revolved around the origins of the first people to enter northwestern North America. Presumably these people would have represented the ancestors of those who eventually breached the Pleistocene barriers and colonized an entire Hemisphere. Under the circumstance, this section will be larger than in most of the preceding chapters.

It is speculated that a population related to the Nenana-Chindadn complex and ultimately Palaeo-Indian culture initially occupied areas of northwestern Canada and adjacent Alaska. Such people would have represented Period I populations who had remained in the area and expanded as land was progressively released by the retreating glaciers and bodies of meltwater. The proposition that the earliest occupation consisted of Plano culture intrusions from the Grasslands to the south (MacNeish 1964; Millar 1981; Noble 1981) was considered and rejected in Chapter 7. Other researchers have substituted the hypothesis of an occupation by pre-microblade Plano culture people with the proposition that a Northern Cordilleran complex, descendant of the Nenana-Chindadn complex, represented the earliest population in the region (Clark 1981; 1983; Clark and Morlan 1982; Irving and Cinq-Mars 1974; Morlan and Cinq-Mars 1982). The appearance of microblade technology, however, is then regarded as evidence of an intrusive population (Clark and Morlan 1982: 36) albeit it is cautioned that "...microblade technology might not be identifiable with a single cultural tradition or period" (Clark 1982b: 7). Still, a technology based upon microblades as opposed to one based upon bifacially flaked tools is interpreted as a "...technological cleavage..." indicative of separate people (Clark 1991: 40; 48). The dichotomy between distinct ` biface´ and `microblade´ cultures with presumed biological and/or linguistic dimensions in northwestern North America is rejected here although most other researchers support such a view. A significant number of technological elements were shared by microblade complexes and the Northern Cordilleran complex. In addition, there is the problem to what degree microblade versus bifacial technologies are actually being detected in the chipping detritus of sites in lieu of diagnostic tools. Such rejectage from stone tool manufacture frequently contains informative waste fragments such as bifacial trimming flakes. At this point in time, the evidence for the diffusion of microblade technology from its Asiatic homeland into northwestern North America is a more compelling scenario than the alternative of cultural invasion and replacement. In this respect, "...the spread of ideas concerning microblade production and composite tools occurred independently of a human migration, and these elements were essentially added to the technology of the groups already present in the interior Northwest" (Gotthardt 1990: 267).

A charcoal date from the JcRw-3 site in the Fisherman Lake region of extreme southwestern Mackenzie District of 8,700 BP is probably pertinent to Early Northwest Interior culture but the cultural association of the date is uncertain. In the basal deposit of the Canyon Creek site in southwestern Yukon Territory a charcoal date of 6,000 BC was associated with a limited number of artifacts but no microblades (Workman 1978: 407-409). The three stratigraphic levels of the MfVa-9 site in the Rock River region of the northern Yukon Territory produced a combined charcoal sample that dated 7,580 +/- 420 BP placing it beyond the range of the calibration tables in Klien et al (1982). Despite the large standard deviation of this reading, the date is important as the associated assemblage not only resembles materials from the Acasta Lake site to the southeast but also contained possible microblades (Gotthardt 1990: 34-36). The Acasta Lake site southeast of Great Bear Lake in the Mackenzie District (Noble 1971; 1981) provided dates ranging from 6,000 to 5,400 BC. The only radiocarbon dated Early Northwest Interior culture site in Canada with a definite microblade assemblage is the Moosehide site on the Yukon River in the Yukon Territory. The date of approximately 4,500 BC falls near the end of Period II. During Period II evidence of a significant presence of microblade technology in the Yukon and the western Mackenzie District is generally late (Clark 1983b: 4, Fig.5).

The antiquity of microblade technology is currently under debate. As noted in Chapter 1, evidence from the Bluefish Caves site in the northern Yukon Territory would suggest the technology may have been present in eastern Beringia by 13,000 BP and possibly as early as 18,000 BP (Cinq-Mars 1990: 25, footnote) along with bifacially flake tools as indicated by the presence of bifacial reduction flakes. Also pertinent is the presence of microblades in the earliest deposit of the Healy Lake site (McKennan and Cook 1968) and the Palaeo-Indian Putu site (Alexander 1987). The general rejection of the association of microblades with the early dates from these two Alaskan sites may well turn out to be in error. Recent support for an early appearance of microblade technology comes from the 11,700 BP dated stratum of the Swan Point site in northern Alaska where microblades were recovered directly under mammoth tusk (Mason 1993). Early dates on microblade assemblages from other Alaskan sites, such as 10,500 BP from Dry Creek II and 10,000 BP from Mt.Hayes III, support the suggestion of an early western and northern presence of the technology. An assemblage characterized by "Wedge-shaped microblade cores; blocky rotated blade and microblade cores; microblades and blades; core tablets; burins struck from flakes; burin spalls; elongate bifaces; scrapers; straight, concave, and convex base projectile points; spokeshaves..." (Dixon 1985: 53) persisted in the central interior of Alaska to approximately 3,500 BC. Cultural continuity into Period III is also apparent in the Yukon Territory complexes, such as Pointed Mountain and Little Arm (MacNeish 1964; Millar 1981; Workman 1978). It is commonly accepted that around the end of Period II throughout much of northwestern North America Early Northwest Interior culture people were replaced by another population advancing out of the south (Anderson 1984; Workman 1978). It is believed that these intruders, referred to as the Northern Archaic complex, possessed a diffuse economy adapted to the expanding coniferous forests as opposed to the focused economy of the people they replaced. Mackenzie Valley sites, however, possess both microblades and burins as well as the so-called diagnostic side-notched projectile points of the Northern Archaic, thus supporting an earlier proposal that the indigenous culture was an amalgam of traits coming from different regions (MacNeish 1964). The proposition of an intrusion of a `Archaic´ economic system into the region has been justly questioned inasmuch as the perceived dichotomy between Early Northwest Interior culture and the Northern Archaic complex may be "...no more than the diffusion of a few isolated technological traits..." (Morrison 1987: 67). The appearance of side-notched projectile points at this time likely reflects the continuing diffusion of the spearthrower weapon technology from its 10,000 BP centre in southeastern North America. Many of the distinctive traits of Early Northwest Interior culture, such as wedge-shaped microblade cores and their associated products, transverse burins and burin spalls, and scrapers, were recovered from the 2,500 BC Bezya site in northeastern Alberta (Le Blanc and Ives 1986) indicating the exceptional conservative nature of a tool kit which persisted for more than 6,000 years. Technological continuity is also supported by settlement pattern evidence which indicates that Period II and Period III peoples occupied the same sites, presumably for the same reasons.

Technology:

        Although suspect due to the large standard deviation, the 7,500 BP date from the MfVa-9 site in the northern Yukon (Gotthardt 1990) is currently the earliest date from an Early Northwest Interior culture site in Canada. The three components of the site produced a lobate stemmed projectile point, biface knives and preforms, linear flakes struck from generalized cores, a range of notched, burinated, and scraper tools made from linear flakes, and possible microblades (Ibid: 34-36). A distinctive tool variety, the transverse burin (Figure 18), was also found on other Rock River sites. The major activity at the Rock River sites was the manufacture of tools from the argillite bedrock with the result that there is a strong quarry factor reflected in the assemblages. There is also evidence of cultural mixture. The transverse burin appears to have been in use from 10,500 BP to 3,250 BC and occurs in assemblages both with and without microblades (Clark 1983b: 3). Convex based lanceolates points from the Rock River sites were manufactured in a fashion similar to that of the lobated stemmed projectile points and are likely part of the same assemblage. As a whole, however, the tool kit, as with others in the northwestern interior, is "...characterized by relatively low levels of standardization" (Gotthardt 1990: 270) with many expedient flake tools that were quickly discarded after use. The 7,000 BP basal deposit of the Canyon site in the southwestern Yukon only produced two bipointed, bifacially flaked projectile points, one of them possibly burinated, a biface or preform fragment, and a possible bone awl (Workman 1978: 407-409).

        It has been estimated that microblade technology first entered northern British Columbia around 9,000 BP (Smith and Harrison 1978; Smith and Smith 1982: 254). This early estimate was based on the obsidian hydration dating method that often provides unreliable results (Fladmark 1982: 125). Evidence in the form of a microblade technology in Early Plateau culture dated to 8,500 BP, and a date of 8,000 BP from the Southwestern Coastal culture occupation of the Namu site on the Central Coast of British

Columbia where the microblades were manufactured from interior obsidian, would suggest an early penetration of microblade technology from the north following the Cordilleran trough rather than entering the interior from the coast. Further east Early Northwest Interior culture, that appeared suddenly on the Barrengrounds of the Mackenzie District around 5,750 BC, disappeared leaving no apparent descendants (Noble 1981). On the other hand, the culture history of Period II is poorly known throughout the entire Great Bear Lake region (Clark 1987: 152-153).

In the Barrengrounds to the southeast of Great Bear Lake in Mackenzie District excavations were carried out around a large quartzite glacial erratic that had served as a source of raw material for tool manufacture (Noble 1971; 1981). Bipointed, side-notched bipointed, lobate based and convex based lanceolate projectile points, bipointed and ovate biface knives and preforms, a range of scraper varieties including large end scrapers, scraper planes, retouched flakes, spurred gravers, spokeshaves, `bladelike flakes´, cores, rare wedges, a drill and an abrader were recovered. Also present in the assemblage were the distinctive notched transverse burins that were, however, manufactured from chert rather than the local quartzite. While the majority of the materials from the Acasta Lake site appear to pertain to an Early Northwest Interior culture occupation lacking microblade technology there was some component mixture. The fact that the site primarily functioned as a place to rejuvenate the chipped stone tool kit using the large quartzite boulder erratic as a source of material must also be taken into consideration when assessing the size and form of many of the implements. Materials from sites in the Fisherman Lake region of the southwestern Mackenzie District, estimated to date between 9,000 and 7,000 BP, have been compared to the assemblage from the Acasta Lake site (Millar 1981). Included among the items present are bipointed, lanceolate, stemmed, and trianguloid projectile points, a range of biface knives including asymmetrical forms, large end scrapers and amorphous flake scrapers, a range of burin varieties, gravers on end scrapers and flakes, cobble choppers, hammerstones, and abraders.

When microblade technology is added to the Early Northwest Interior culture tool-kit earlier traits such as generalized cores from which linear flakes or blades were struck, notched transverse burins, burinated broken projectile points, large end scrapers, biface knives, gravers, including the multiple spurred variety, lanceolate and bipointed projectile points, and rare large rough stone implements, persist (Workman 1978). Microblade mid-sections were sometimes modified along one edge to assist in fitting them into composite tools made from bone, antler, and presumably wood.

The historical reality of cultural traditions based upon certain major stone tool categories, such as microblades, burins, and projectile points, has been recently questioned (Gotthardt 1990: 53-54). Instead of a reliance upon `morphological typology´ it is argued that greater attention should be directed to issues like expediency versus curation and formality versus informality within the total tool kit. While the detailed quantification and qualification of all available evidence, including reduction, modification, use, and discard patterns, is a laudable and necessary procedure, it must be cautioned that relative to assemblage integrity sites such as those in the Rock River region also suffer from the chronic problem of mixed cultural deposits.

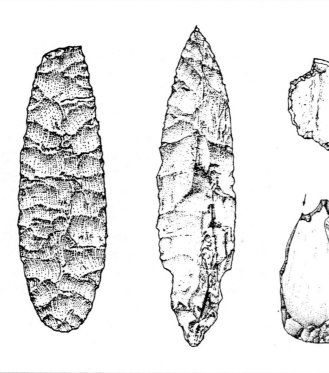

FIGURE 18: EARLY NORTHWEST INTERIOR CULTURE IMPLEMENTS From left to right are a 6,000 BC bipointed projectile point from the base of the Canyon site in the southern Yukon followed by a typical `Acasta´ type point and a transverse notched burin from the 5,500 BC Acasta Lake site southeast of Great Bear Lake in the Mackenzie District and, below the burin, an undated but probably early combination burin and end scraper from northwestern Alaska. The Acasta point could be characterized as a side-notched bipointed projectile point. (Drawn by Mr. David W. Laverie. Scale variable but all considerably less than natural size).

Subsistence:

The fact that mountain goat, caribou, muskox, mountain sheep, and moose are all of Asiatic origin and appear to have entered the Western Hemisphere with humans would suggest that they were important elements in the human diet (Workman 1978:58). It has been assumed that the marked reduction of grazers, such as bison, horse, and mammoth in northwestern North America by 10,000 BP was a result of shrinking grasslands in conjunction with increasing human predation (Hopkins 1967). Such a proposition, however, does not account for the demise of the mammoth and the horse and the subsequent success of the bison.

The passage of time over much of northwestern North America has eliminated the direct evidence of subsistence in the form of discarded food bones . As a result, site location is usually relied upon to infer subsistence. A few exceptions to the foregoing do exist. Bison remains were recovered from the Canyon site (Workman 1978: 409) but it was not possible to determine if they pertained to an extinct subspecies. The range of species was much larger at the Acasta Lake site and consisted of caribou, black bear, beaver, hare, eagle, and fish, a combination that would indicate a fall occupation. It is probable that Early Northwest Interior culture subsistence gradually became more diffuse as opposed to the earlier reliance upon bison and caribou. Given the varied topography of the Cordilleran physiographic region and its wide range of faunal resources it is reasonable to suspect that a variety of animals were exploited with concentrated seasonal focus upon certain specific species. Of potential importance relative to food storage was the discovery of pulverized and calcined caribou bone at the 8,000 BP Kobuck site in west central Alaska. This occurrence may indicate the practice of rendering fat from bone for later consumption (Anderson 1984).

Settlement patterns:

In the northern Yukon Territory the distribution of sites suggests a focus in the uplands at caribou interception points. Sites provide broad vistas and are generally situated near streams (Gotthardt 1990). No doubt the siliceous argillite in the Rock River area also influenced site location. This upland settlement distribution has also been equated with bison hunting (Irving and Cinq-Mars 1974). Site distributions in the southern Yukon are similar to those to the north in that they are often situated along ridges that provide good vantage points for sighting game. The Canyon site in the southwest Yukon is a deeply stratified site on a bluff overlooking a river (Workman 1978: 134-135). A hearth floor surrounded by chipping detritus suggests that it represented a small, transitory campsite.

Referred to locally as Acasta culture, the most easterly expression of Early Northwest Interior culture is found from the Great Bear Lake region almost to the Arctic coast (Clark 1987; Harp 1958; Noble 1971). An occasional diagnostic projectile point has even been recovered as far east as the central Keewatin District of the Northwest Territories (Wright 1972: Plate VII. fig.16). Sites are generally situated on eskers with broad vistas. A major attraction to the Acasta Lake site was the large quartzite boulder erratic from which raw material was obtained for tool manufacture. Situated on a lake, the site occupied a gully in the side of an esker near the aforementioned quartzite glacial erratic. The 105 excavated pit hearths averaged 0.3 m in depth, had fire-reddened margins, and contained an abundance of quartzite chipping detritus and artifacts. These features have been interpreted as baking ovens where the quartzite was slowly heated to improve its flaking qualities. Pit hearths were arranged into five or six clusters that formed rings with each cluster being between 2.4 m to 3.4 m in diameter and containing from 15 to 25 hearths (Noble 1981: 98). The overlapping of a number of the pit features clearly indicated sequential use of the site.

In west central Alaska the Kobuk site, situated on a major river and dated between 8,500 and 8,100 BP, had cultural debris concentrated for 1.4 m around central hearths suggestive of 2.8 m diameter single family dwellings (Anderson 1984: 82).

Cosmology:

No data.

External relationships:

Early Northwest Interior culture was contiguous and contemporary with Northwestern Coastal culture to the west, Southwestern Coastal culture to the southwest, Plano culture to the southeast, and Early Plateau culture to the south. Territories to the north and northeast were unoccupied at this time.

A relationship with both Northwestern and Southwestern coastal cultures has been suggested by the presence of interior obsidian on coastal sites. The differentiation of Early Northwest Interior culture technology from those of the coastal cultures, however, is far from clear. Some archaeologists regard the spread of microblade technology throughout the interior as a product of population movements that displaced earlier peoples (Clark 1991: 40) while others interpret the appearance of the technology as evidence of diffusion from the northwest (Gotthardt 1990). The latter interpretation is the more probable and best accommodates the sudden appearance of microblades in Southwestern Coastal sites on the Central coast although in this instance the direction of diffusion would have been westward from the interior to the coast. As an introduced element into the interior the appearance of microblade technology does not necessarily imply a transfer of technology from one unrelated population to another. As noted in Chapter 2, the technology of the supposed pre- or non-microblade Nenana-Chindadn complex in Alaska possessed a significant number of correspondences with the subsequent Northwestern Palaeo-Arctic culture except for the microblades. Even this exception is far from clear given early dates on microblades and their possible association with both the Chindadn complex Healy Lake site (McKennan and Cook 1968) and the Palaeo-Indian culture Putu site (Alexander 1987). Thus, there is the possibility of an early cultural and biological stratum in northwestern North America that has been blurred in the archaeological record by the appearance and/or wide adoption of an Asiatic microblade technology. It has been suggested that by 4,000 BC there is a clear differentiation of the coastal and interior microblade-using cultures (Dumond 1984: 73). Fingerprinting of exotic lithics, obsidian in particular, would appear to be the most direct method of determining the nature of interaction between peoples along the coast and in the interior.

While a number of archaeologists (MacNeish 1964; Millar 1981; Noble 1981) have argued that Plano culture played a fundamental role in the formation of Early Northwest Interior culture there is growing opinion that the relationship has been based upon very tenuous technological and chronological evidence (Clark 1991). With Plano culture being well represented in the Peace River Valley of northeastern British Columbia (Fladmark 1981) it would be surprising if contacts with Early Northwest Interior culture had not existed. Direct evidence in terms of either excavated sites or finger-printed exotic lithics, however, is lacking.

An association between Early Northwest Interior culture and Early Plateau culture is purely speculative. An earlier hypothesis of a southern movement through the Cordilleran would appear to best fit the available evidence. With the exception of the Bluefish Caves site in the northern Yukon (Cinq-Mars 1990), microblade producing sites in the Southern Plateau of British Columbia have dated earlier (Stryd and Rousseau n.d.) than sites in the southern Yukon and adjacent Northwest Territories (Clark 1991). Given the early dates for microblade sites in northern Alaska and the overall paucity of information at this time period, however, there is every reason to keep one's options open. If a north to south movement down the Cordilleran is a viable hypothesis then the earliest sites in the Southern Plateau should theoretically produce a percentage of northern exotic lithics, particularly as microblade technology requires high quality stone.

Human biology:

No data.

Inferences on society:

It is speculated that the social organization of Early Northwest Interior culture would have been similar to that of the historically documented Athapascan-speaking peoples of the region. This implies that "The vagaries of food supply in these regions caused frequent dispersals and reunions of the aborigines. Now they wandered in individual families, now in small groups of three or four families together. At another time all the families in a district would combine into a definite band at some favourite fishing or hunting ground, and several bands generally united for a few short days each year to trade and hold festivities" (Jenness 1932: 119-120).

Limitations in the evidence:

The nature of the remains from most sites in northwestern North America creates serious problems for archaeological interpretation, a fact reflected in the number of controversial issues and   the `muddled´ character of much of the evidence presented in this Chapter. Sites often are spread over large areas as veneer deposits that defy component separation or even a context for radiocarbon samples. Many sites were reoccupied seasonally for thousands of years. The impact of bioturbation (biological disturbance caused by tree falls, bears digging out gophers, etc.) and cryturbation (disturbance caused by freeze and thaw cycles to sedimentary deposits) on the archaeological deposits have then further mixed the sparse evidence. The difficulty of isolating components carries the corollary of a limited number of trustworthy radiocarbon dates. Added to the problem of trying to isolate components is the simple nature of the stone tool kit and its conservative persistence over time. And, given the generally acid soils resulting in an absence of bone, analysis is usually limited to the chipped stone portion of the technology. All of these serious limitations occur within a vast and physiographically complex region that has always supported very small and mobile human populations. At a site such as NkIj-1 (Le Blanc 1991), with its microblades, early appearing burin forms, large biface knives, lanceolate and side-notched projectile points, it is impossible to determine how many components and years of occupation are represented. Such situations have forced too great a reliance upon typological cross-dating with all of its potential hazards (Gotthardt 1990: 43-44).

The aforementioned limitations in the evidence are particularly disruptive as they pertain to a region critical to the understanding of the initial human colonization of the Western Hemisphere. Given its theoretical importance and the limitations in the archaeological evidence it is perhaps not too surprising that numerous conflicting hypotheses not only exist but are likely to continue to exist for some time.

PERIOD III

(4,000 TO 1,000 B.C.)

PROLOGUE TO PERIOD III

By 4,000 BC climatic and environmental conditions across most of Canada were similar to the present time. Sea levels approached their current positions and remnants of the glaciers were limited to the High Arctic and alpine settings. Forests west of Hudson Bay extended further north but cooler and wetter climate after 2,000 BC forced the tree line as much as 300 km south of its present location. Geographical stability favoured the survival of increasing numbers of archaeological sites.

In most areas the process of cultural regionalization continued apace. The most dramatic single human accomplishment of the period was the colonization of the High Arctic and Greenland by Early Palaeo-Eskimo culture beginning around 2,500 BC. This migration constituted the last human occupation of a major geographical region in the world exclusive of the settling of Oceania. Elements of Early Palaeo-Eskimo culture would eventually reach northern Saskatchewan, Manitoba, Québec, the Labrador coast and the northshore of the Gulf of St.Lawrence as well as the Island of Newfoundland. In these more southerly regions culture contacts would have been made with a number of different Indian cultures. Less dramatic population movements were represented by the Middle Maritime culture expansion to the north coast of Labrador and onto the Island of Newfoundland and the Middle Shield culture occupation of the increasingly habitable regions of the Canadian Shield, penetrating to the Labrador coast and the northshore of the Gulf of St.Lawrence by 2,000 BC.

There was an increase in the communal hunting of bison and the production of pemmican on the Plains while in the Southern Plateau by 2,500 BC semisubterranean pit house villages were being established at favourable salmon fishing locales. Early Northwest Coast culture settlements became increasingly sedentary with villages being characterized by large shell middens. Towards the close of Period III along the west coast the first indications of the development of socially ranked societies can be detected. Elaboration of mortuary ritualism is apparent across the entire country. Shortly before the close of Period III the bow and arrow technology appears for the first time. This technology was apparently introduced from Asia by Early Palaeo-Eskimo culture and diffused, via the High Arctic, down the Labrador coast to the St.Lawrence River and into the eastern Canadian Shield and, thence, westward.

Of the 9,000 years considered in Volume I the 3,000 years of Period III only represent a third of the total yet constitutes more than half of the Volume text. This situation reflects a massive increase in the amount and variety of archaeological evidence. While population growth and the release of new lands from glacial ice and associated water bodies undoubtedly accounts for some of the increase in archaeological sites, the major factor must be the reduced intensity of the processes of erosion and deposition and of the submergence of ancient land surfaces occupied during Period III. This increase in the body of archaeological information continues into Period IV and Period V. Indeed, so much so that separate volumes were required for each of these periods.

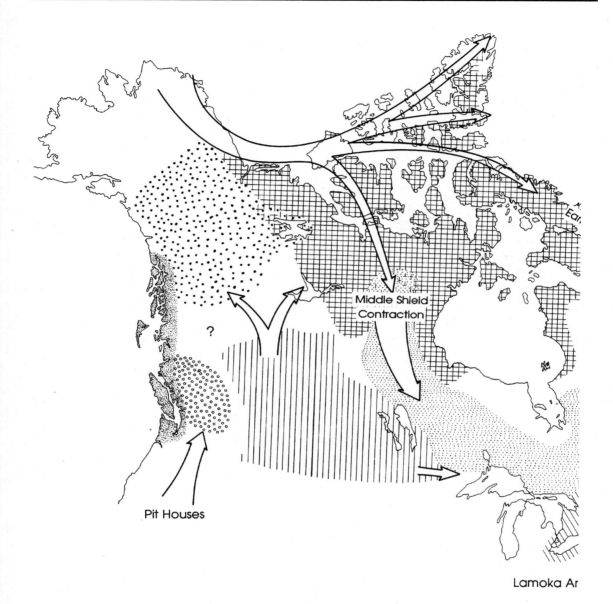

MAP III: CULTURAL DISTRIBUTIONS, 4,000 TO 1,000 B.C. The map is intended to act as a modifications, from Plate 7 of the Historical Atlas of Canada, Volume I. Drawn by David W. Laverie.)

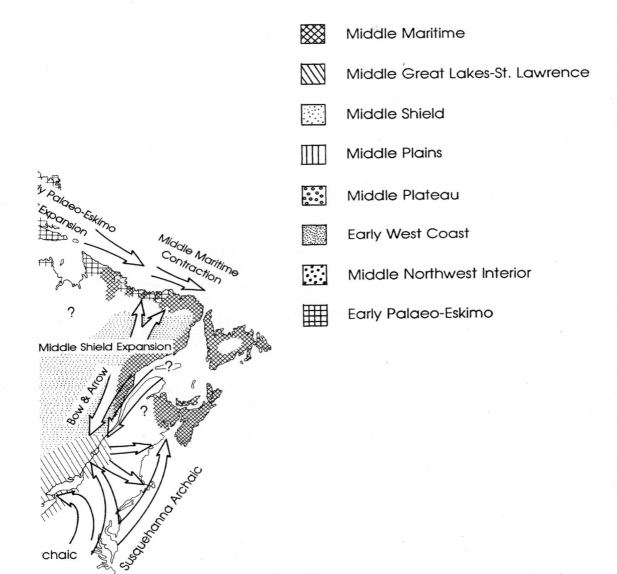

Middle Maritime

Middle Great Lakes-St. Lawrence

Middle Shield

Middle Plains

Middle Plateau

Early West Coast

Middle Northwest Interior

Early Palaeo-Eskimo

simplified, geographical guide to the distribution of Period III cultures. (Adapted, but with considerable

CHAPTER 14 ———————————————

MIDDLE MARITIME CULTURE

Précis:

The existence of a distinct east coast maritime adapted Archaic population was first proposed by Douglas Byers (1959) and was subsequently classified as the Maritime Archaic (Tuck 1971; 1976a). A substantial antiquity attributed to Maritime culture (Early, Middle, and Late), first suggested by Elmer Harp's work on the southern coast of Labrador (Harp 1963), has since been confirmed (Fitzhugh 1972; McGhee and Tuck 1975). There has been some dispute regarding the cultural integrity of an archaeological manifestation distributed from northern Maine to the northern coast of Labrador and from the Island of Newfoundland up the St.Lawrence River to Québec City. The acknowledged regional variations within this extensive cultural distribution would not appear to be sufficient to warrant multiple cultural classifications at this time. Two factors bear on the extensive distribution of Middle Maritime culture that do not apply to most land based hunters and gatherers. First, an exceptional degree of mobility can be achieved with seaworthy watercraft where the problem of portability of possessions is markedly reduced. Second, while the regions occupied span four major vegetation provinces (McAndrews et al. 1987), the marine resources throughout the entire area are essentially the same or have equivalents such as walrus hunting to the north and swordfish hunting to the south. With some regional variations the most important marine and land animal foods would have consisted of seal, walrus, whale, marine and anadromous fish, shellfish, beaver, bear, sea birds, caribou, deer, and moose. Archaeologically invisible but likely of great significance would have been the enormous schools of spawning capelin and smelt, as well as squid, crab, and lobster.

Even given the shared marine resources, to regard the varied ecological regions occupied by Middle Maritime culture as being the homeland of a homogeneous culture would be an over-simplification. Significant regional variations of the culture are represented along the northshore of the Gulf of St.Lawrence of Québec and adjacent Labrador and its east coast, the Island of Newfoundland, the Maritime provinces and adjacent Maine, and the St.Lawrence Estuary. To an as yet undetermined degree, this regionalism is a result of the variable archaeological evidence. It is only at the beginning of Period III that the `Great Hiatus´ of cultural evidence in the Maritime provinces following Palaeo-Indian culture ends (Tuck 1984). Another factor pertinent to the visibility of Middle Maritime culture is past local conditions as they pertain to changes in sea levels, tidal amplitudes, and ancillary effects. At 4,000 BC, for example, the geographical appearance of certain regions were strikingly different with Prince Edward Island still being attached to the New Brunswick and Nova Scotia mainland. Labrador and the adjacent portions of

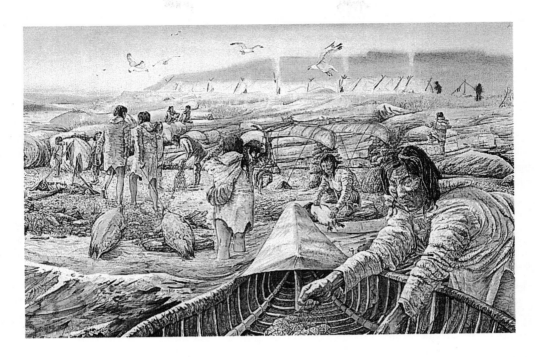

COLOUR PLATE IX: MIDDLE MARITIME CULTURE HUNTERS RETURNING TO A SUMMER CAMP This reconstruction, set on the Labrador coast at 2,000 BC, shows the hunters unloading seal, now-extinct great auks, and gull eggs from their skin-covered ocean going watercraft. In the background is the communal dwelling while on the beach other skin canoes are secured against the wind and elevated on stone cairns to keep their skin coverings out of reach of hungry dogs. Herring gulls wheel overhead while around the head of the man in the foreground is a ubiquitous swarm of blackflies. (Painting produced by Vidéanthrop, Inc., Montréal under contract with the Canadian Museum of Civilization. The painting was done by M. François Girard based upon sketches containing scientific and composition requirements compiled by M. Marc Laberge and the author; as with subsequent colour plates the original coloured version is provided on diskette and CD-ROM.)

coastal Québec are undoubtedly the best known region due to focused archaeological research and the emerging coastline that has isolated sites on elevated strandlines. The Island of Newfoundland, with few exceptions, has not been subjected to as concerted a research effort and also suffers from coastal submergence that would have drowned most sites dating prior to 3,000 BC. Recent research in the St.Lawrence Estuary of Québec has only produced a limited number of substantive archaeological reports. The emerging coasts of this region, with its well demarcated and geologically dated Goldthwait/Champlain Sea strandlines, holds great promise. The generally acid soils of much of the region and a tendency for sites to have a strong stone tool manufacturing element, however, have complicated the comparative process. In both the Maritime provinces and adjacent Maine coastal submergence and erosion between 8,000 and

3,000 BC has undoubtedly been the single greatest limiting factor. Paradoxically, there is relatively abundant information on Middle Maritime culture mortuary practices from this region. The boneless `Red Paint´ cemeteries of Maine attracted much attention and speculation at the turn of the century (Moorehead 1922; Willoughby 1935). Despite regional cultural variability the evidence from technology, cosmology, subsistence, and settlement patterns suggest the existence of a number of independent societies who shared a more or less common culture distinct from that of their neighbours. Cultural correspondences over such a broad and variable region are likely due to the interrelated factors of a shared technology, a similar way of life, interlocking trade networks, a common cosmological view, and the mobility of marriageable females within a framework of exogamous, patrilineal hunting bands. Of primary importance relative to cultural similarities would have been the maritime transportation system. Some researchers will probably regard a construct such as Middle Maritime culture as being premature and would argue that it is too heavily based upon shared mortuary practices (Sanger 1973: 106).

A factor that has confused efforts to isolate a distinctive Middle Maritime culture has been a certain amount of trait-sharing between the coastal Middle Maritime culture and the interior Middle Great Lakes-St.Lawrence culture (Laurentian Archaic). Traits such as ground stone gouges, ground slate points, bayonets, and semilunar knives, and plummets were, due to the historical development of archaeological research in eastern North America, first established as the diagnostic traits of the interior culture (Ritchie 1944). Subsequently it has been demonstrated that most of these particular traits date earlier from coastal sites (Harp 1963; McGhee and Tuck 1975) and were only adopted later by interior peoples. In addition to sharing most major categories of ground stone tools contacts between Middle Maritime culture and Middle Great Lakes-St.Lawrence culture are suggested by the mixture of the distinctive projectile point styles of the two cultures, as well as other chipped stone tools, on sites in the St.Lawrence River between Québec City and the Ontario border. In Maine and adjacent New Brunswick, Middle Great Lakes-St.Lawrence sites in the interior are but a short distance from contemporary Middle Maritime culture coastal sites. Evidence of trading relationships can be seen in the occurrence of what are most likely Lake Superior copper tools on coastal sites and walrus ivory and Labrador quartzite implements on sites in the Lower Great Lakes and Upper St.Lawrence Valley region (Wright 1994). Despite the cultural homogenizing impression created by certain shared ground stone tool categories, the overall technology of Middle Maritime culture is quite distinct from that of their interior neighbours (Bourque 1975; Carignan 1975; Fitzhugh 1972; McGhee and Tuck 1975; Wintemberg 1943).

Middle Maritime culture ceased to exist as a traceable entity on the north side of the Gulf of St.Lawrence and the Island of Newfoundland shortly after 2,000 BC. An exceptional series of events took place at this time that likely account for the disappearance. Along the northern Labrador coast the closing of the Altithermal climatic episode between 2,000 and 1,500 BC and the onset of cooler weather may have had a delterious affect upon the northernmost Middle Maritime culture colonists. It has been noted that the spread of Middle Maritime culture in Labrador and Newfoundland correlated with a period of warm and stable climate (Fitzhugh 1978). Another critical factor would have been the roughly synchronous appearance of two alien cultures along portions of the coast. Early Palaeo-Eskimos began forays down the Labrador coast from the north around 2,250 BC (Fitzhugh 1985a) while Middle Shield culture interior hunters appeared on the central and southern coasts at roughly the same time (Nagle 1978). Of the two intrusions the appearance of Middle Shield culture people was likely the most disruptive event and probably contributed along with climatic change to the eventual abandonment of the north side of the Gulf of St.Lawrence by Middle Maritime culture people. It is speculated that the Middle Shield culture occupation of the mainland interior with seasonal forays to the coast inhibited Middle Maritime culture people from obtaining their annual supply of caribou skins required for clothing. While maritime foods were probably capable of supporting the sustenance needs of these people it would have been difficult, if not impossible, to survive in the northern climes without access to the insulating qualities of caribou skin clothing. Although it has been proposed that the Middle Maritime culture people on the Island of Newfoundland eventually developed into the historically documented Beothuk (Tuck 1976a) a more likely proposition is that periodic failures of essential seasonal prey species to appear resulted in a number of human extinctions on the Island including late Middle Maritime culture (Tuck and Pastore 1985).

Another combination of natural and cultural events appears to have had a similar impact upon some of the Middle Maritime culture occupants of the Maritime provinces and adjacent Maine shortly before 1,500 BC. After 3,000 BC increases in tidal amplitudes would have mitigated against the abundance of swordfish, an important element in Middle Maritime culture subsistence in the region, but would have favoured an increase in soft shell clams (Sanger 1975:61). The cooling climate around 1,700 BC would also have had an unfavourable impact on the deer populations upon which the Middle Maritime people relied. For a neighbouring culture to the south, the Susquehanna Archaic, these changes favoured their subsistence pattern and they appear to have actually occupied Maine and a section of adjacent New Brunswick. This cultural replacement, initiated by changing environmental conditions that favoured one cultural adaptation over another, is also seen as having established the cultural base for the Algonquian-speaking peoples encountered by Europeans (Sanger 1975: 69-72). While most of Maine and a portion of adjacent New Brunswick appear to have been occupied by the Susquehanna Archaic people from the south, the remainder of the Maritime provinces was not affected. Although the evidence is equivocal, it appears that indigeneous Middle Maritime culture peoples continued to occupy most of the Maritime provinces and developed into the subsequent populations (Late Maritime culture). The rapidity and nature of the cultural changes, however, have obscured the evidence of cultural continuity (Tuck 1975a; 1984).

At this stage of research in the St.Lawrence Estuary little can be stated regarding the fate of the Middle Maritime culture population although there is evidence of Middle Shield culture people from the northern interior exploiting the coast along the northshore (Chevrier 1978). Further, the Gaspé appears to have been at least partially abandoned after the Plano culture occupation (Benmouyal 1987). At a speculative level it is suggested that Middle Shield culture bands adopted a seasonal pattern of exploiting maritime resources along portions of the northshore of the St.Lawrence Estuary, particularly near the mouths of the major rivers that would have acted as the transportation routes between the interior and the coast. An early development of this pattern appears to have provided these people with sufficient maritime skills to account for their sudden and persistent appearance along the northshore of the Gulf of St.Lawrence and the Labrador coast around 2,000 BC.

Cultural origins and descendants:

The origins of Middle Maritime culture are rooted in the Early Maritime culture of Period II. Evidence from the northshore of the Gulf of St.Lawrence suggests cultural continuity (Fitzhugh 1978; Tuck 1975a) with subsequent regional differentiation between southern Labrador/Québec and northern and central Labrador. Around 3,000 BC, however, there appears to have been a temporary intrusion of Middle Maritime people from the northshore of the Gulf of St.Lawrence onto the central Labrador coast at Hamilton Inlet (Fitzhugh 1977). A contraction of northern and probably central Labrador Middle Maritime culture populations to the Gulf of St.Lawrence at 2,000 BC appears to have submerged the former regional differences between the two areas. The southward contraction not only correlates with deteriorating climatic conditions but also with the intrusion onto the coast of Early Palaeo-Eskimo culture from the north (Cox 1978) and Middle Shield culture from the interior (Nagle 1978). Middle Maritime culture along the northshore of the Gulf of St.Lawrence and the Labrador coast disappears after 1,500 BC.

The Island of Newfoundland was apparently not colonized by Middle Maritime culture until 3,000 BC with the migrating population likely crossing at the Strait of Belle Isle between Labrador and Newfoundland and/or the Cabot Strait between Cape Breton and Newfoundland. Earlier sites, however, may be submerged beneath the sea. These first people to settle the Island of Newfoundland may have orginated further up the Gulf of St.Lawrence in Cape Breton and the St.Lawrence Estuary below Québec City. There are a number of shared technological traits between these two regions including a distinctive prepared core macroblade tradition (Carignan 1975; and personal examination of Canadian Museum of Civilization collections from Tadoussac, Québec). An intensive occupation of the Island of Newfoundland by Middle Palaeo-Eskimo culture around 1,000 BC suggests the former Maritime culture occupants had disappeared by this time. Whether Palaeo-Eskimo culture contributed to the demise of the original occupants or whether they simply occupied abandoned territory is uncertain. It has been speculated that the Middle Maritime culture settlers of the Island of Newfoundland may have suffered extinction as the result of a natural disaster involving the precarious food-cycle (Tuck and Pastore 1985), a fate eventually shared by their Middle Palaeo-Eskimo culture successors. Middle Maritime culture populations along the northshore of the St.Lawrence Estuary were eventually displaced from their territory by Middle Shield culture populations from the northern interior who were progressively developing a seasonal round that incorporated the resources of the coast.

The lower level of the Lavoie site near the mouth of the Saguenay River was examined during Period II in Chapter 5. It is given additional consideration here as there could be problems with the early radiocarbon dates (Plumet et al. 1993: Tableau 3, 40) associated with artifacts that typologically pertain to Period III rather than Period II. The earliest occupation of the site is attributed to Great Lakes-St.Lawrence culture (Laurentian Archaic) on the basis of ground slate projectile points and ulus, side-notched projectile points, polished stone axes and adzes, and plummets (Archambault 1987: 108; Plumet et al. 1993: 78). Not only do all of these traits also occur in Middle Maritime culture (e.g. see Carignan 1975) but a number of the specific attributes of some of the specimens, such as the polished slate stemmed and barbed points, compare more closely with eastern coastal specimens than equivalent weapon tips from the interior (Snow 1980: Fig. 5.3). As the cultural distinction between Maritime and Great Lakes-

St.Lawrence assemblages in the St.Lawrence Estuary and elsewhere has presented difficulties it was decided that a brief comparative exercise may be of some use to those concerned readers. The tool kit from Level III of the Lavoie site (Plumet et al. 1993: Tableau 13) was compared with those of the early Middle Great Lakes-St.Lawrence culture (Laurentian Archaic - Vergennes phase) KI site in northern Vermont (see Chapter 15, Table 2) and the 3,750 to 2,250 BC Middle Maritime culture Level 2 of the Beaches site on the Island of Newfoundland (Carignan 1975). The KI site is situated in the St.Lawrence River drainage system near the southern end of Lake Champlain 550 km to the southwest of the Lavoie site while the Beaches site is more than 1,000 km to the east of the Lavoie site. Applying the coefficient of similarity comparative process to the formal tool categories of the respective assemblages, where a figure of 200 indicates the two compared units are identical while a figure of 0 denotes total dissimilarity of the compared units, produced the following results: Lavoie and KI - 52.0; KI and Beaches - 59.2; and Lavoie and Beaches - 91.6. Arriving at coefficients of similarity involves the use of percentages and the percentages derived from the 157 specimens from the early Beaches site occupation were as follows: preforms - 41.4; biface knives - 23.6; macroblades - 13.4; random flake scrapers and a single end scraper on a macroblade - 11.5; chipped and ground projectile points - 2.5; ground slate preforms - 2.5; hammerstones - 1.9; and single specimens of 0.6 each of a celt, abrader, gouge, uniface knife, and a quartz crystal (extracted from Carignan 1975). A relatively high occurrence of preforms at both the Lavoie and Beaches sites have undoubtedly contributed to the higher coefficient. Also pertinent to the relationship between the Lavoie and Beaches assemblages is the possibility that the distinctive macroblade technology described from the latter site may be present in the former site (see Plumet et al. 1993: Planche 1: c; Planche 3: A; Planche 6: B and C). This possibilty is heightened by the identification of a macroblade technology in a sample of chipping detritus from the nearby Tadoussac site (personal examination by the author of collections from Tadoussac in the Canadian Museum of Civilization with confirmation by Dr. Robson Bonnichsen while he was a visiting scientist with the Museum). Regardless of what eventual relationship is established between the Lavoie site and its neighbours, the preceding suggests that establishing a cultural assignment on the basis of artifact categories used by both Maritime and Great Lakes-St.Lawrence cultures is not an appropriate procedure and that more detailed comparative analytical methods are necessary.

If the descendants of Middle Maritime culture survived the combined natural and cultural disruptions between 2,000 and 1,000 BC it would have likely been in the Maritime provinces and possibly the adjacent Gaspé coast. Unfortunately the destruction of most coastal sites in the Maritimes due to a submerging coastline and the difficulty of arriving at a cultural assignment of the limited remains from the quarry workshops of the Gaspé (Benmouyal 1987) has resulted in conflicting interpretations. There are two contradictory origin hypotheses concerning the subsequent populations of the Maritime provinces. Tuck (1976a; 1984) has proposed that the Middle Maritime culture populations of the Maritime provinces were forced to adapt to rapidly changing environmental conditions where swordfish hunting, for example, was replaced by shellfish gathering. It is argued that these changes had such a dramatic impact upon the technology and other cultural systems that they have masked the cultural continuity to a later culture. On the other hand, Sanger (1973; 1975) would favour an in situ origin in the Maritime provinces and adjacent Maine from an early penetration of the interior mixed-hardwood forest adapted Middle Great Lakes-St.Lawrence culture (Vergennes phase of the Laurentian Archaic) to the coast. It was this population that was eventually replaced by Susquehanna Archaic people advancing along the coast from the south. The late Susquehanna Archaic population would have thus established the cultural base for subsequent archaeological developments leading to the Micmac, Malecite, and Passamaquoddy Algonquian-speakers documented in the historic European records.

There are two problems with the preceding discontinuity hypothesis. First, while the archaeological evidence is clear that the Susquehanna Archaic culture appears suddenly along coastal Maine and the southern edge of New Brunswick, there is no evidence of the culture occupying the rest of the Maritime provinces. Second, rather than being an `either-or´ situation regarding Middle Great Lakes-St.Lawrence culture or Middle Maritime culture on the coasts of Maine and New Brunswick both cultures appear to be present but with Middle Great Lakes- St.Lawrence culture being limited to a relatively early phase (Vergennes) and to the interior while Middle Maritime culture was restricted to the coastal regions. As has already been noted, part of the problem has been the use of traits such as stone gouges, ground slate points, bayonets, and semilunar knives and plummets as specific cultural indicators when both Middle Great Lakes-St.Lawrence culture and Middle Maritime culture shared these traits.

The stratified Turner Farm site off the central coast of Maine (Bourque 1975) contained a series of components dating between 4,000 and 2,000 BC. The latest occupation pertained to the intruding Susquehanna Archaic while an intermediate component, dated to 3,000 BC, related most closely to Middle Maritime culture. Similarily, the 2,000 BC Stanley site on an island 12 miles off the coast of Maine (Sanger 1975: 62) contained an abundance of swordfish remains and had its closest technological correspondences with Middle Maritime culture. On the other hand, the major occupation of the stratified Hirundo site, situated part way into the interior of Maine on a river with access to the coast, pertained to an early phase of Middle Great Lakes-St.Lawrence culture. This early cultural phase appears in both the hinterlands of Maine and at least the southern regions of New Brunswick as well as further south into New England where it did extend to the coast (Ritchie 1969).

While a continuity hypothesis for Middle Maritime culture descendants throughout most of the Maritime provinces and likely portions of the Gaspé is favoured it is admitted that the evidence it equivocal. There are, however, a number of cultural correspondences between Middle Maritime culture sites on the Gulf of St.Lawrence and the Island of Newfoundland with those in the Maritime provinces and northern Maine, such as Rattlers Bight, Port au Choix, Cow Point, Turner Farm, and Nevin which suggest the entire coastal region was once occupied by a related population (Tuck 1984).

Middle Maritime culture radiocarbon dates from the northshore of the Gulf of St.Lawrence and the eastern Labrador coast range from 4,000 to 1,500 BC (Fitzhugh 1975; 1978; Wilmeth 1978). The Neskuteu site, the only dated possible Middle Maritime culture site from the interior of Quebéc, dates to 3,750 BC (Pilon 1982). Sites on the Island of Newfoundland have been dated from 3,500 to 1,500 BC (Rutherford et al. 1984; Wilmeth 1978). Dates from the Cow Point Cemetery site in New Brunswick were 2,250 BC (Wilmeth 1978). Finally, if one accepts the Lavoie, Du Ruisseau, and Delacroix sites in the St.Lawrence Estuary as being either Middle Maritime culture sites or closely related, then the dates range from 4,250 to 2,000 BC (Taillon et Barré 1987).

Technology:

As with the other cultural systems, information on the technology of Middle Maritime culture is uneven. Coastal submergence and emergence were the two most critical factors affecting the availability of evidence. A general absence of bone preservation and the frequent existence of stone tool workshop situations, particularly in the St.Lawrence Estuary, has also exacerbated efforts to qualify and quantify the technology and its regional expressions. The potential to obtain information from interior sites has been limited by the occupation of most of the interior regions by either Middle Great Lakes-St.Lawrence culture or Middle Shield culture. Despite such limitations in the evidence and the apparent existence of a number of regionally distinct tool kits, certain categories of implements do extend from Labrador to Maine and up the St.Lawrence River. Ironically, the traits most often identified as diagnostic are among the least diagnostic as they were shared with Middle Great Lakes-St.Lawrence culture to the west. These traits are the polished stone gouges, the ground slate dart heads, bayonets, and semilunar knives or ulus, and the stone plummets. Under the circumstances, the most appropriate way to proceed is to consider Middle Maritime culture technology from the following regions: the northshore of the Gulf of St.Lawrence and Labrador: the Island of Newfoundland; the Maritime provinces and adjacent Maine; and the St.Lawrence Estuary.

I. The Northshore of the Gulf of St.Lawrence and Labrador:

The most complete archaeological record is available from this region with its emerging coastlines. Evidence of Middle Maritime culture in the Québec portion of the coast is most apparent between Blanc Sablon and Natashquan but does occur as far west as Tadoussac at the mouth of the Saguenay River (Archambault 1987; Chevrier 1978). In Labrador it has been demonstrated that the technology of the northern and central coast becomes increasingly differentiated from that of the southern coast after an initial expansion northward. Technological uniformity, however, was re-established prior to 2,000 BC (Fitzhugh 1978). Between 4,750 and 3,250 BC along the east coast of Labrador tapered stemmed projectile points, small flake points, wedges, ground slate ulus, the use of red ochre and rare bipointed and stemmed knives as well as ground stone celts, knives, and points are among the traits recorded (Fitzhugh 1972; Tuck 1982). Predominantly local stone was used to manufacture tools although as early as 4,750 BC the Ramah quartzite deposits of northern Labrador were being exploited. Prior to 2,000 BC there was a flourescence of objects manufactured from soapstone including pallets, plummets, and pendants with geometric designs (Fitzhugh 1985a). By 2,500 BC in northern Labrador nearly 80% of the tools were manufacture from non-Ramah quartzites and only 20% from the high quality Ramah quartzite yet 500 years later the percentage use of these quartzite varieties has reversed to itself to 9% and 91%, respectively. The `northern branch´ of Middle Maritime culture in Labrador is viewed as being distinct from a `southern branch´ situated to the south of Hamilton Inlet. The southern branch is characterized by "...large broadly side-notched or expanding stemmed projectile points, leaf-shaped bifaces, occasional end scrapers and other unifaces and `linear´ or `blade-like´ flakes..." (Tuck 1982: 205). Celts, gouges and ground slate points are also present from sites dated between 3,250 and 2,500 BC (McGhee and Tuck 1975). An intrusion of this `southern branch´ north to the Hamilton Inlet region between 3,000 and 2,500 BC has been recorded

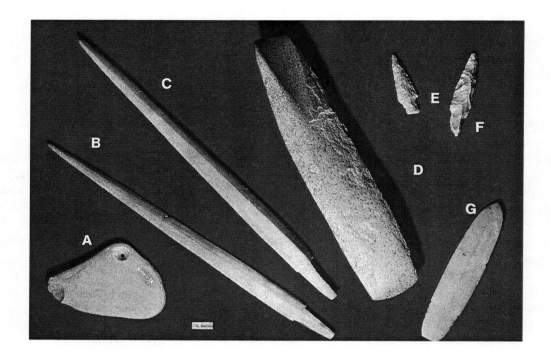

COLOUR PLATE X: MIDDLE MARITIME CULTURE STONE TOOLS FROM THE COW POINT CEMETERY, NEW BRUNSWICK   Proceeding clock-wise are a drilled possible whetstone (A), ground slate bayonets (B and C), a polished stone gouge (D), chipped projectile points (E and F), and a ground slate spear. (Reproduced from Keenlyside 1984: Colour Plate III.)

at the Black Island 2 site (Fitzhugh 1975). The intrusive nature of this occupation is reinforced by the fact that all of the tools were manufactured from a felsite foreign to the area.

With the expanding use of Ramah quartzite around 2,500 BC along the entire Labrador coast and west at least as far as Natashquan opposite Anticosti Island, chipped stone tools achieve a greater symmetry of form (Tuck 1976). Of greater technological consequence is the suggestion that contacts between the northern Middle Maritime culture bands and the southward advancing Early Palaeo-Eskimo culture led to the exchange of the bow and arrow from the latter in return for the toggling harpoon from the former (Fitzhugh 1972: 141; Tuck 1976: 54). None of the late northerly Middle Maritime culture sites, however, have produced projectile points bearing any resemblance to contemporary Early Palaeo-Eskimo points. Such points, however, do appear in Middle Shield culture suggesting these people may have been responsible for the spread of the bow and arrow technology to the west after they had received the innovation from Early Palaeo-Eskimos on the Labrador coast.

All researchers in this region have used elevated strandlines as a relative dating method of archaeological sites (Fitzhugh 1972; Levesque 1980; McGhee and Tuck 1975) as have archaeologists in the St.Lawrence Estuary (Archambault 1987; Dumais et Rousseau 1985). On the not always valid assumption that people would camp no further from the active beach than necessary, it follows that the earliest sites will occur on the highest strandlines with sites becoming increasingly recent as they approach the active beach at present sea level. The weakness of this dating method is the fact that all of the progressively elevated strandlines would have been available for occupation by later people who wished to camp on a raised beach for reasons that could range from relief from insects to obtaining a broader view of the sea. Despite this weakness and the frequent evidence of component mixture involving different time periods on the same strandline, the beach elevation relative dating method does work more often than not.

II. The Island of Newfoundland:

Middle Maritime culture on the Island of Newfoundland exhibits similarities with the previously mentioned `southern branch´ of Middle Maritime culture along the northshore of the Gulf of St.Lawrence. As the two regions are only separated by the narrow Strait of Belle Isle a relationship should not be too surprising. Similarities between sites such as Graveyard in Labrador (McGhee and Tuck 1975) and the Beaches in Newfoundland (Carignan) are side-notched and expanding stemmed projectile points, a range of biface knife forms, retouched flakes, linear flakes or macroblades struck from prepared cores, and other items. At the Beaches site the stratified deposits, dating from 3,750 to 2,250 BC, had been partially destroyed by coastal submergence. In addition to the notched and stemmed points, scrapers, ground slate points, gouges, celts, plummets, and abraders were recovered. Of particular note was the prepared core -macroblade technology which exhibits striking parallels with macroblades recovered from a site in the Tadoussac area. This correspondence highlights similarities with sites in the St. Lawrence Estuary. Similarities also exist with the Pittman site (Linnamae 1975) but, like the situation at Tadoussac, some of the resemblances may be a product of similar stone tool production procedures.

The importance of the bone technology has been obscured by poor bone preservation. If the bone assemblage had survived at the Beaches site (Tuck 1976) it would probably have resembled that of the burial site at Port au Choix (Tuck 1976a). The latter site, on the west coast of Newfoundland, produced an exceptional glimpse of Middle Maritime bone technology. Bone items included in the recoveries were toggling and fixed barbed harpoons, projectile points and bayonets, leisters, whale bone harpoon lance foreshafts, barbed bird darts, beaver incisor knives and chisels, awls, eyed needles - some with eyes less than 0.5 mm in diameter suggesting the use of caribou sinew as thread - and, less common, effigy bird heads, an ivory dagger and antler sheath, caribou scapula scrapers, beamers, effigy hair pieces, a caribou metapodial needle case, whistles, pendants, a modified wolf maxilla, probable medicine bundles containing the remains of animals, and numerous other items. Dog burials were also present with two of the four burials occurring in a single grave. Ground slate bayonets, gouges, celts, slate weaving shuttles, a side-notched and a stemmed projectile point, quartz, amethyst, and calcite crystals, and natural zoomorphic stones were among the stone items. One of the most striking objects was a stylized stone killer whale effigy. Shell beads and pendants were also present. Indirect evidence of clothing was preserved in the form of sewing tools, a hooded garment outlined by periwinkle shell beads, possible caps and capes of great awk (Pinguinus impennis) skins retaining the beaks, and various probable amulets and charms sewn onto clothing as well as shell beads and skate teeth. The closest similarities with the foregoing assemblage are found at the Nevin site in Maine (Byers 1979) in the form of the specific attributes of harpoon foreshafts, barbed points, harpoons, bird darts, daggers, etched motifs on certain bone objects, needles with cut eyes, modified beaver incisors, perforated teeth of seal and other mammals, and a number of more minor traits (Tuck 1976a: 110).

III. The Maritime Provinces and Adjacent Maine:

Few Middle Maritime culture habitation sites have been located in the Maritime provinces where coastal submergence- erosion has been particularly severe (Simonsen 1979). The limited number of formal tools from the Geganisq workshop site on Cape Breton Island in Nova Scotia (Nash 1978) exhibit parallels with Middle Maritime culture remains from the Beaches site on the Island of Newfoundland (Carignan 1975). Of critical importance are the results of excavations along the coast of Maine. The 3,250 BC middle component of the stratified Turner Farm site (Bourque 1976) produced plummets, gouges, swordfish harpoon foreshafts, and chipped stemmed projectile points. Approximately 1,000 years later, the Stanley site, situated 12 miles off the coast, contained stemmed projectile points, gouges, adzes, plummets, a ground slate projectile point and a possible bone harpoon foreshaft (Sanger 1975: 62). At the Nevin site (Byers 1979) the disturbed nature of the multi-component deposits overlying the cemetery and its grave offerings made accurate association difficult but pertinent implements would appear to include plummets, iron pyrites fire-making kits, ground slate points and bayonets, a gouge and adze, bone beamers, eyed needles, awls, modified beaver incisors, harpoon foreshafts manufactured from swordfish bills, swordfish bill lances, moose cannon bone daggers with elaborate etched designs, perforated canine teeth, and other minor bone items including a cut and drilled human humerus.

In the Ellsworth Falls sequence in Maine (Byers 1959), extending from 2,500 to 1,750 BC, the following artifact trends were recognized: chipped stone tools become increasingly common at the expense of ground slate points and rods; gouges increase in abundance as do stemmed and corner-notched projectile points; and plummets remain constant but bolas stones are restricted to the earlier portion of the sequence.

IV. The Estuary of the St.Lawrence River:

The Lavoie site, a short distance downriver from the mouth of the Saguenay River, was considered in Chapter 5 even though the most reliable radiocarbon date from Level III extended into Period III. In addition, the side-notched and stemmed chipped points, barbed ground slate points and ulus, polished stone celts, and plummets could pertain to Middle Maritime culture technology rather than Early Maritime culture. On the elevated strandlines at Tadoussac a number of workshop stations have been recorded (Wintemberg 1943). As well as an abundance of chipping detritus from one site, bipointed projectile points, bifacial quadilateral and semilunar knives, chipped and ground adzes, ground slate rods, a prepared core-macroblade technology and, less common, ground slate points, adzes, plummets, and gouges were recovered. The presence of full grooved gouges suggest some time depth as do the high elevation of the standline on which the site was located. Traits, such as the ground slate rods, could indicate an antiquity of 2,500 BC as do a number of correspondences with similarily dated sites along the northshore of the Gulf of St.Lawrence. Polished stone rods, however, appear to date to the beginning of Period III at Middle Great Lakes-St.Lawrence culture sites such as the KI site in Vermont (Ritchie 1971a) and may represent an interior trait that diffused to the coast. Some carbonized seal bones from the site at Tadoussac as well as from the nearby Lavoie site indicate that the technology was capable of exploiting marine resources. In his report Wintemberg (1943: 340) suggested a relationship between the Tadoussac site and the `Red Paint´ burial complex of Maine that a number of researchers would now attribute to Middle Maritime culture.

The situation in the Gaspé is difficult to interpret at this time. The region was largely abandoned after the Eastern Plano culture occupation (Benmouyal 1987). While two charcoal samples from a hearth at the Du Ruisseau site (Taillon et Barré 1987: 131), attributed to a cultural category called the `gaspésienne ancienne´, date to 2,500 BC there is simply too little artifactual material that can associated with either the dates or the gaspésienne ancienne construct. Lanceolate, stemmed, triangular, and side-notched points, biface knives, side scrapers, flake knives, planers, and possible end scrapers are noted (Benmouyal 1987: 365-366).

As has been commented upon a number of times, there has been some difficulty distinguishing Middle Maritime culture technology from Middle Great Lakes-St.Lawrence culture technology. The difficulty is a result of reseachers using artifact categories shared by both cultures as cultural diagnostics of the interior Middle Great Lakes-St.Lawrence culture. Cultural identifications so arrived at are then supported by a highly generalized treatment of certain projectile point types. In the St.Lawrence Estuary relationships have generally been sought to the west rather than the east. What is required in order to distinguish between the technologies of these two adjacent and contemporary cultures is a complete qualitative and quantitiative consideration of the artifactual remains as well as attribute analysis of shared artifact categories such as ground slate projectile points and plummets. Negative or rare trait characteristic of the two cultures should also be considered such as the presence of drills and atlatl weights to the west and bipointed biface knives and notched flake points to the east. When the total technologies are considered there appears to be little difficulty in isolating Middle Maritime culture assemblages from that of their neighbour to the west.

Subsistence:

Given the general absence of bone preservation much of the information on subsistence practices of Middle Maritime culture must be inferred from site locations. An exception to this rule is along the coast of Maine where relatively good bone preservation exists. Another exception is the Port au Choix site on the west coast of the Island of Newfoundland where sea shells incorporated in the sand neutralized the normally acid soils. As with the section on `Technology´, the major regions of the Middle Maritime culture distribution will be considered separately.

I. The Northshore of the Gulf of St.Lawrence and Labrador:

Settlement pattern distributions suggest a subsistence pattern centred on seasonally available maritime resources. The seasonal round likely involved seal hunting on pack ice and/or landfast ice in the late winter to early spring, sea mammal hunting, fishing, birding, including the gathering of eggs and moulting birds, and berry gathering in the summer, and inland caribou hunting in the fall. With variations relating to species availability and ice-conditions, the aforementioned pattern appears to have prevailed in all regions of Middle Maritime culture. To the south, deer/moose and swordfish hunting would have been the approximate equivalents of caribou and walrus hunting in the north.

Marine resources are more stable and, thus, dependable than land resources (Fitzhugh 1972). While the greater predictability of marine resources would undoubtedly have been important to the subsistence strategies of Middle Maritime culture this fact should not be overemphasized. The need to acquire hides for clothing, sleeping robes, and tent covers during the interior fall caribou hunt was likely of greater importance than the caribou meat itself. Survival would have been dependant upon a balanced utilization of both maritime and inland resources.

Climate, through its effect upon currents and wind, can determine the drift pattern of pack ice and thus the availability of such critical food sources as harp seal. Similarly, forest fires, freeze-thaw cycles, heavy snow on grazing grounds, wet -cold weather during the calving season, and other natural disasters could have a sudden impact upon the availability of caribou. During unpredictable shortages of critical prey species Middle Maritime culture hunters must have had to rely upon alternative food sources such as fish. In can be anticipated but not demonstrated with archaeological evidence that the preservation and storage of foods during periods of abundance for winter consumption played a critical role in the annual subsistence strategy.

Along the coasts of the northshore of the Gulf of St.Lawrence and Labrador all species were not to be found in all areas. Smelt currently only reach as far north as Hamilton Inlet (Scott and Scott 1988: 153). Other resources do not appear to have been exploited, such as the blue mussel, soft-shell clam, and ground fish. Shellfish may have been looked upon as a starvation food and people may not have possessed the technological capability to exploit deep-water ground fish such as cod. Alternatively, the evidence for the taking of these species may simply not have survived in the archaeological record. Given the general lack of bone preservation, it is impossible to assess the importance of the aforementioned species or large sea mammals like the walrus, which would have been abundant along the coast at the time. Even with bone preservation, evidence of important species like capelin, smelt, squid, crab, and lobster cannot be expected to survive in an archaeological context.

The limited faunal remains from the Rattlers Bight site at the entrance to Hamilton Inlet on the central Labrador coast, consisted of harp, harbour, and ring seal and birds with some evidence of walrus and a limited number of land animals including caribou, black bear, otter, hare, beaver, and muskrat. This mix of species suggests a spring to fall occupation (Fitzhugh 1978). On the northern Labrador coast at site Q on Rose Island the stratigraphic occurrence of both Middle Maritime culture and Early Palaeo-Eskimo culture suggests, in lieu of bone preservation, that these two unrelated cultures followed a similar subsistence round during at least part of the year (Tuck 1975).

It has been suggested that Middle Maritime culture on the Labrador coast was displaced by Early Palaeo-Eskimo culture and not an inability to adapt to environmental change (Fitzhugh 1972). While the intrusions of Early Palaeo-Eskimo culture onto the northern coast and Middle Shield culture onto the central and southern coasts were undoubtedly factors in the local demise of Middle Maritime culture, the role of environmental change in this dramatic population shift cannot be totally ignored. At the time when Middle Maritime culture disappeared, at least from the northern and central coast of Labrador, for example, the Early Palaeo-Eskimo intruders also contracted back to the north suggesting some problem with the accessibility of food.

II. The Island of Newfoundland:

It has been speculated that the migratory habits of the limited number of marine and terrestrial species on the Island of Newfoundland and the "...lack of `fall-back´ resources within a simple ecosystem" (Tuck and Pastore 1985: 79) contributed to periodic human extinctions in the past. Middle Maritime culture disappeared from the Island's archaeological record after 1,500 BC with no clear evidence of a contemporary replacing population. Seal and, in particular harp seal, were probably the single most important Island resource and yet it is a resource that can become unavailable during the migration period due to perverse currents and winds. Site locations on the Newfoundland coast and the high frequency of seal pup remains indicate that harp seals were hunted on the ice. As has been historically recorded, even a short period of off-shore winds can drive the pack ice, along with the seals, out to sea where they would not be available if the whereabouts of the ice could not be determined. All of the other major prey species, such as caribou, salmon, capelin, and sea birds are also migratory and although they do periodically congregate in enormous numbers it is only for short periods. Nothing is known of Middle Maritime culture food storage capabilities and, thus, the ability to fully exploit these periodic episodes of plenty as insurance against want during the winter months. Ethnographic analogy based upon the historically documented Beothuck of the Island of Newfoundland, who did possess a sophisticated food storage technology (Howley 1915), would not be appropriate for these people appear to be a relatively late Algonquian-speaking population incursion from the mainland across the Strait of Belle Isle. Caribou in the interior would have been an alternate prey but if their numbers had been severely reduced by an ice storm during calving several years earlier their availability could be limited. While in most years the food resources of the Island of Newfoundland would have been sufficient to support the human population it would only take a single occasion of unfavourable circumstances to severely test human survival. That said, the evidence from the graves of the Port au Choix site suggests that all available food resources were being exploited. Among the animal remains recovered from this site were seal, walrus, caribou, beaver, fox, marten, geese, ducks, terns, swans, great auk, wolf, black bear, and polar bear (Tuck 1976; 1976a).

III. The Maritime Provinces and Adjacent Maine:

All of the direct information on subsistence from this region comes from sites along the coast of Maine. By the beginning of Period III there is evidence from the Gulf of Maine of increasing biological richness and diversity of marine resources (Sanger 1988). The seasonal round consisted of maritime hunting and fishing in the summer, spring and fall fishing, and hunting in the interior during the winter (Bourque 1976: 25). At the Turner Farm site around 3,250 BC swordfish, deer, and seal were the major food animals. Shellfish appear at this site as early as 4,000 BC and were also an important food item at the nearby Nevin site (Byers 1979). Scallop draggers working in 7.6 m of water off the Maine coast retrieved a number of artifacts, such as a polished slate ulu, along with large oyster shells from a now drowned channel. This suggests the existence of an early submerged shell midden (Speiss et al. 1983: 93). The accidental discovery of the 3,250 BC Boylston Street Fishweir in Boston (Johnson 1949; Byers 1959: 242) raises the possibility of the existence of an early littoral fish capturing technology along the coast. Unfortunately evidence of weirs is generally either destroyed by erosion or hidden under meters of sediment.

One of the striking characteristics of sites such as Turner Farm (Bourque 1976; 1976a), Nevin (Byers 1979), and Stanley (Sanger 1975), is the abundance of swordfish remains as well as implements fashioned from swordfish bills. Presumably the method of capturing swordfish was to stalk a surface basking animal and dispatch it with a lance used in conjunction with a toggling harpoon. Such a hunting procedure, operating from relatively small watercraft whether bark canoes or dugouts, would be fraught with danger as swordfish will frequently turn on attacking boats with potentially lethal consequences.

An interesting hypothesis suggests that by 2,000 BC rising sea levels and tidal amplitudes in the Gulf of Maine and the Bay of Fundy had affected major changes in marine ecology. Cooling water temperature accompanying these changes would have been unfavourable to swordfish but favourable to shellfish such as the soft shelled clam. These changes, accompanied by the southward expansion of the conifer forest, that would have been detrimental to deer populations, correlate with the disappearance of Middle Maritime culture and its replacement along coastal Maine and the immediately adjacent New Brunswick coast by the Susquehanna Archaic culture with its shellfish and small fish based subsistence pattern.

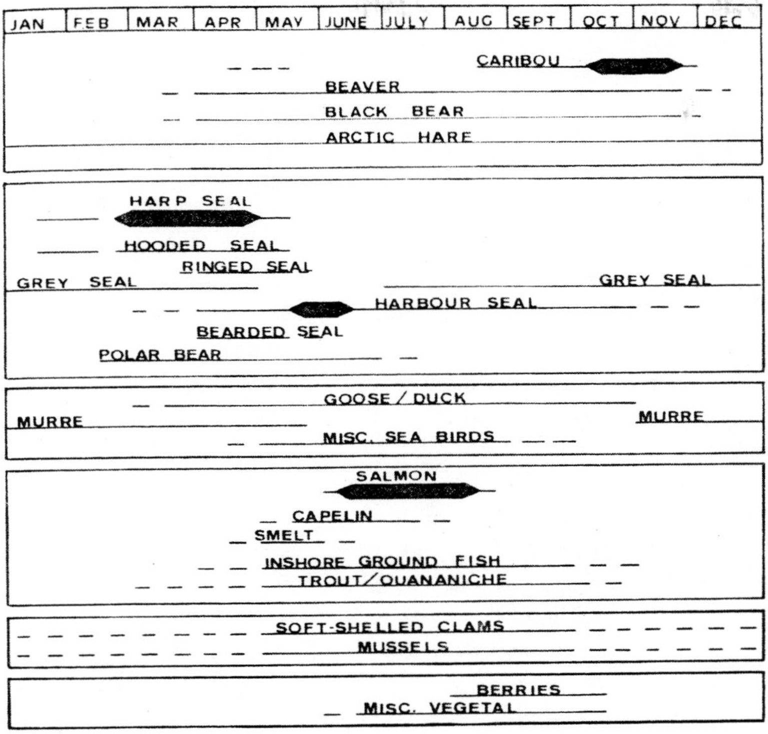

JAN	FEB	MAR	APR	MAY	JUNE	JULY	AUG	SEPT	OCT	NOV	DEC

CARIBOU

BEAVER

BLACK BEAR

ARCTIC HARE

HARP SEAL

HOODED SEAL

RINGED SEAL

GREY SEAL   GREY SEAL

HARBOUR SEAL

BEARDED SEAL

POLAR BEAR

GOOSE / DUCK

MURRE   MURRE

MISC. SEA BIRDS

SALMON

CAPELIN

SMELT

INSHORE GROUND FISH

TROUT / OUANANICHE

SOFT-SHELLED CLAMS

MUSSELS

BERRIES

MISC. VEGETAL

FIGURE 19: SEASONS OF FOOD AVAILABILITY ON THE ISLAND OF NEWFOUNDLAND The dependency of people on a limited number of seasonally available animals may have left them vulnerable when the expected animals did not appear and may even account for the sudden disappearance of Middle Maritime culture and some subsequent cultures from the Island. (Reproduced from Tuck and Pastore 1985: Figure 1 with permission)

IV. The Estuary of the St.Lawrence River:

Little direct evidence exists regarding subsistence practices of Middle Maritime culture people in the St.Lawrence Estuary. Seal bones have been recovered from the Lavoie site (Archambault 1987) and another site in the Tadoussac area (Wintemberg 1943). It can only be assumed from the site locations that the rich marine resources, ranging from beluga to a variety of fish and littoral species, were exploited as well as available terrestrial resources including seabird rookeries. Evidence of Middle Maritime culture as far up the St.Lawrence River as Cornwall, Ontario would indicate that the Upper St.Lawrence River was also utilized, albeit likely on a sporatic basis and with some kind of understanding with the resident Middle Great Lakes- St.Lawrence populations.

Settlement patterns:

I. The Northshore of the Gulf of St.Lawrence and Labrador:

As with the other cultural systems of Middle Maritime culture settlement pattern information is most complete from Labrador and adjacent Québec. Particularly detailed information is available for the portion of the Labrador coast extending north from the entrance to Hamilton Inlet.

An important consideration regarding the occupation of the Labrador coast was the location of the Ramah quartzite deposits in northern Labrador. The appearance of this high quality distinctive stone on archaeological sites towards the end of Period II (Fitzhugh 1978) points to the early colonization of the entire coast. Major use of the deposits, however, was between 2,500 and 2,000 BC (Gramly 1978; Lazenby 1980). This semi-transluscent quartzite, often called chert, was traded as far south as Florida (Fitzhugh 1972: 40) as well as appearing in the Middle Maritime culture cemeteries and sites of northern Maine (Smith 1948: 34-37). In the latter instance the Ramah projectile points (Snow 1980: Figs. 5.12 and 5.13) are of a late northshore of the Gulf of St.Lawrence style raising the issue of whether they represented objects of trade or direct evidence of contacts between the Middle Maritime populations of the two regions. Specimens and flakes of this distinctive stone also occur as far up the St.Lawrence River as Cornwall, Ontario (Wright 1982; 1994).

Ramah quartzite veins occur in the bedrock as stratified layers 40 to 50 cm thick. The material appears to have been simply levered out of the badly fractured and jointed veins by the Middle Maritime miners although cobble hammerstones were also used. At one grouping of quarry sites it was estimated on the basis of careful survey that "...at least two million large-sized pieces of worked stone may be viewed there. This quantity, however, is minor in comparison with the masses of material north of Hilda's Creek where at least 20 to 40 million items are present" (Gramly 1978: 39-41). Although it took some time to develop (Tuck 1975), an extensive trade network in this material appeared after 2,500 BC. It has been speculated that the superior working qualities of Ramah quartzite changed the appearance of the chipped stone tools by permitting the production of thinner projectile points and knives with flat crossections, longer stems, and greater symmetry (Tuck 1976). While differences in stone quality has frequently been evoked to explain characteristics of chipped stone tools such propositions have never been convincingly demonstrated. To the contrary, there are many instances where stone knappers have produced totally controlled flaking patterns on what would appear to our novice eyes to be very intractable materials. The quartzite Plano culture points of Keewatin District are a case in point (Wright 1976a).

Prior to Period III large sites were established on the outer islands off the central coast of Labrador. Such sites were likely occupied in the spring in order to intercept the northward migrating harp seal as well as exploit other seal species, walrus, and bird resources. The sites are associated with sandy beaches and protected coves along the east sides of islands and on headlands suggesting that both boat landing convenience and vantage points overlooking expanses of sea were important considerations for base camps. In the summer small hunting parties could fan-out from the major base camps to exploit a range of resources as well as to trade and make social contacts with other families. In early fall the caribou hunt, presumably some distance into the interior, would provide additional meat and the critically important hides. This hunt would be followed by a late fall seal hunt after which people moved into the protected interior for the winter (Fitzhugh 1978).

Certain Middle Maritime culture house structures do not accommodate anthropological generalizations regarding the usual dwelling size of northern hunting bands. On the elevated boulder beaches of the Aillik site north of Hamilton Inlet a chronological sequence of house structures has been recorded (Fitzhugh 1984). On the highest beaches are oval and rectangular structures ranging from single room 3 m by 2 m structures to a two compartment dwelling excavated 25 cm into the cobbles and surrounded by 15 cm high walls. The compartments were separated by a low ridge of boulders. On progressively lower and more recent beaches, longhouses with four to ten individual dwelling segments were recorded. One house, deeply excavated into the beach cobbles, measured 28 m by 4 m. Post supports and hearths occurred at regular intervals inside the house walls while 10 small exterior cache pits were adjacent to the individual house partitions. All of the longhouses were oriented parallel to the beach. Little refuse was associated with these multi-family dwellings as most objects would have trickled down through the cobble interfaces.

In the Hamilton Inlet region proper rectangular structures with two or three hearths were present by 3,750 BC. Of significance is a 50 m long house with 12 hearths dated to 3,000 BC (Fitzhugh 1985: 49) that contained artifacts typical of the `southern branch´ of the northshore of the Gulf of St.Lawrence and Labrador indicating similar structures were used in both subregions.

The Nulliak site, near the northernmost distribution of Middle Maritime culture on the Labrador coast, contained at least 15 longhouses. While it is unlikely that all of these houses were occupied at the same time it is probable that the individual segments within each house were occupied by contemporary family groups. This would imply that a 10 segment longhouse could have housed as many as 40 people and a 20 segment dwelling twice that number. Such congregations of people suggest entire hunting bands lived communally under a single roof for at least part of the year. Hearths in each cubicle were spaced 3.5 m apart and contained points, red ochre, flake and biface knives, soapstone pallettes, plummets and pendants. Celts and ground slate tools and flake points were rare occurrences. Debris common to each hearth generally consisted of a few projectile points or biface knife fragments, one or two soapstone items, the odd celt, 5 to 10 utilized flakes, and several hundred small pieces of chipping detritus, all suggestive of brief occupations. Camp debris was absent outside of the houses although meat caches, burials, and caribou fences appear to be associated with the longhouses. Large hearths or food-roasting platforms between 1.8 m and 2 m in diameter with associated cultural debris are also recorded in the region (Tuck 1975). The large hearths occur on late winter to early summer sea mammal hunting sites (Ibid: 99) taking advantage of winter landfast ice and spring to summer drift ice.

To summarize, the following house structure sequence has been proposed: by the end of Period II pit houses and the 8 m long, two segment rectangular houses disappear and are replaced by 12 m to 16 m long, 3 to 4 segment houses; by 3,250 BC houses are lengthened from 25 m to 30 m and contain up to 7 segments; at 2,750 BC houses reach 50 m in length with 12 to 13 segments; and between 3,000 and 2,250 BC houses reach their greatest lengths of between 60 and 100 m and incorporate between 20 and 25 segments (Fitzhugh 1985). The progressive lengthening of structures and the increase in the number of living cubicles reflects increasingly larger social groupings. The nature of the cultural debris within each family cubicle suggests the houses were occupied by egalitarian families.

The abandonment of the Labrador coast by Middle Maritime culture correlates with a cold period between 2,500 and 2,000 BC and the southward expansion of Early Palaeo-Eskimo culture (Fitzhugh 1972; 1984). To judge from the similar site locations of these two cultures they would have been in direct competition for the marine food resources. A curious settlement feature has emerged from this culture contact situation. The Early Palaeo-Eskimos appear to have bypassed the northern Saglek region to establish a salient in the Nain-Okak region of the central Labrador coast even though small contemporaneous Middle Maritime culture campsites still occupied the outer islands to the north. It appears that the Middle Maritime culture bands retained control of the Hebron-Ramah area and its Ramah quartzite deposits and transported the stone around the Nain-Okak region to the northshore of the Gulf of St.Lawrence. Although only separated by 45 km these two cultures occupied their respective salients for several hundred years and at the same time maintained contact with home territories to the north and the south, respectively. It has been suggested that the large longhouses in the northern Middle Maritime culture salient reflect short term occupations by large populations required to maintain an `expeditionary procurement system´ that involved central coast groups making forays to the north coast for Ramah quartzite and possibly caribou in the summer (Fitzhugh 1985). It appears that these multi-band summer economic ventures required a formidable force in the face of possible opposition from Early Palaeo-Eskimo culture peoples. Exceptional mobility is not only reflected in the continued use and trade in Ramah quartzite but also the neutron activation studies of soapstone implements from the Hamilton Inlet region that suggests the raw materials were obtained from Okak and Davis Inlet of the Labrador coast as well as L'Anse aux Meadows on the Island of Newfoundland (Fitzhugh 1985a).

Survey in the interiors of Labrador and Québec has produced only minimal evidence of exploitation by Middle Maritime culture hunters (Samson 1978; 1978a). If the coastal populations were exploiting the interior caribou herds on a regular seasonal basis then one would expect to encounter extensive evidence at major caribou crossing locales similar to those found in the Barrengrounds of Keewatin District in the Northwest Territories. Such is not the case suggesting that the interiors of Québec and Labrador were only sporadically exploited. In addition, "Pollen data indicate persistence of glacial ice in the interior of Labrador and northern Quebec until c.5500 B.P. Subsequent environmental disruption caused by rapid uplift, ice-dammed lakes and later, alder thickets, may have made the interior plateau of marginal human value until after 5000 B.P." (Fitzhugh 1975: 137). The presence of Ramah quartzite at Indian House Lake in the interior of Québec does indicate contacts with the Labrador coast (Samson 1978). Sites generally consist of 4 m to 6 m diameter concentrations of debris lacking hearths and situated on exposed look-out points, apparently representing very transitory camps. It is possible that at the time of the occupation of the Labrador coast by Middle Maritime culture there were significant caribou herds adjacent or within close proximity to the coast thus reducing the need to push far into the interior.

Paradoxically, two of the best described Middle Maritime culture dwellings are from Indian House Lake 175 km west of the Labrador coast (Pilon 1982). Two oval to rectangular structures, demarcated by weight stones and overlooking the surrounding country were recorded. Formal artifacts were sparse but chipping detritus abundant, including Ramah quartzite. The most common artifacts were large, local quartzite flakes that were used and then discarded. Artifacts and debris were concentrated around red ochre stained areas in the central depressions interpreted as hearths. Based on the configuration of the weight

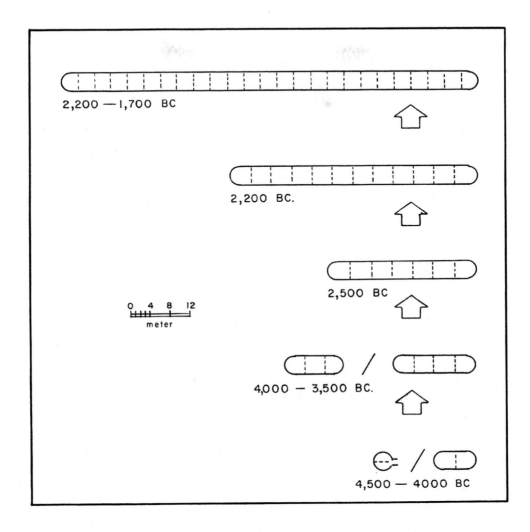

FIGURE 20: A SCHEMATIC AND TENTATIVE DEVELOPMENTAL SEQUENCE OF MIDDLE MARITIME CULTURE HOUSE STRUCTURES ON THE LABRADOR COAST Of importance to an understanding of social structure in Middle Maritime culture is a sequence of house structure changes through time that suggest a change from nuclear family dwellings to increasingly larger multi-family dwellings. It is likely, however, that such multi-family dwellings were occupied only during a portion of the year and that the changes in dwelling size do not reflect a significant and permanent change in social structure. (Adapted from Fitzhugh 1985a: Figure 1. Drawing by Mr. David W. Laverie.)

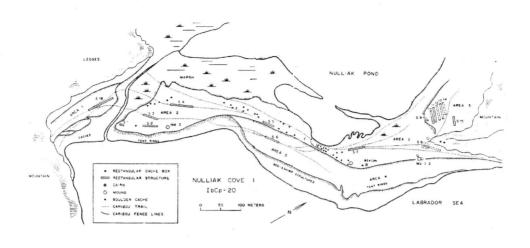

`A´

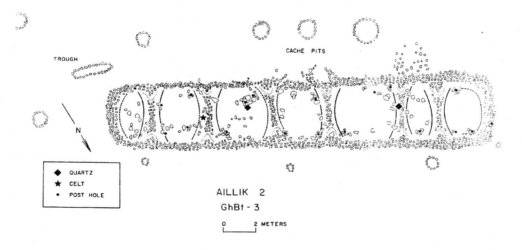

`B´

FIGURE 21:   MIDDLE MARITIME CULTURE SETTLEMENT PATTERNS ON THE LABRADOR COAST In view `A´ the Nulliak Cove site occupation is strung along the elevated beaches between the sea and a freshwater pond. In addition to longhouse structures are two forms of stone caches, a cairn, burial mounds, and even caribou fence lines. `B´ illustrates some of the detail of the largest of the house structures at the Aillik 2 site. (Reproduced from Fitzhugh 1984: Figures 4 and 3, respectively, with permission.)

stones, debris, and interior features, structure 1 would have been a 6 m by 5 m dwelling with the following characteristics: an entrance facing north; a meat processing and storage area by the entrance; a work area around the hearth; and a sleeping area at the back of the structure. The adjacent house structure 2, that is believed to have been occupied at the same time, was constructed in a similar fashion (Figure 22). Of the two radiocarbon dates from house structure 1 the earlier date of 3,750 BC would be more acceptable than the 2,000 BC date on the admittedly questionable grounds that by the latter date the area would have been occupied by Middle Shield culture hunters (Chapter 16). On the other hand, if bipointed biface knives are not a valid basis for distinguishing Middle Maritime culture from Middle Shield culture then the 2,000 BC date may be accurate and the houses actually pertain to a Middle Shield culture camp whose occupants were already in contact with the northern coast of Labrador. While the cultural evidence is equivocal, a Middle Maritime culture authorship of these features is favoured at this time. Other sites in the Indian House Lake region do clearly indicate the presence of Middle Maritime culture hunters (Samson 1978; 1978a). The location of the Neskuteu site on the west side of Indian House Lake and the probable route from the coast up the Kogaluk River to a chain of connecting lakes would suggest that some form of portable watercraft were used to reach the site. Although a winter occupation has been proposed for these interior sites (Conrad 1972) the fact that game would be most abundant and in prime condition from the end of summer to the early fall, points to this season as the most likely time of the occupation. Given the rugged nature of the route from the coast and the difficulty of transporting heavy loads, it may even be speculated that such forays were specifically intended to obtain prime caribou skins to meet clothing and bedding needs. Meat would have been of secondary importance unless it was dried to increase its portability as well as preservation.

II. The Island of Newfoundland:

The Island of Newfoundland has been regarded as a cultural refuge (Fitzhugh 1972: 193) and, therefore, one would expect its closest relationship with the northshore of the Gulf of St.Lawrence. This would appear to have been the case from the initial 3,750 BC occupation of the Island via the Strait of Belle Isle until the disappearance of the northeast coastal settlements around 1,500 BC (Tuck and Pastore 1985). The maintenance of mainland contacts is indicated by the presence of animals remains not indigenous to the Island, such as moose and fisher, at the Port au Choix site (Tuck 1976a: 81) and exotic lithics. At the Beaches site no features or activity areas were recognized (Carignan 1975). The location of the site overlooking Bonavista Bay with access to two rivers, would suggest that sea mammal hunting and salmon fishing were important. The paucity of settlement pattern evidence from the Island of Newfoundland is a direct reflection of the general scarcity of Middle Maritime culture habitation sites.

III. The Maritime Provinces and Adjacent Maine:

On the basis of evidence from sites in Maine the Middle Maritime culture occupation of the Maritime provinces is believed to have centred on the coast for most the year with the focus on sea mammals, fish, birds, and possibly shellfish with deer, moose, or caribou hunting in the winter (Tuck

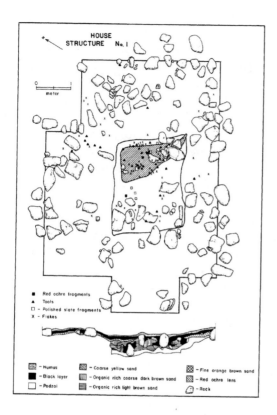
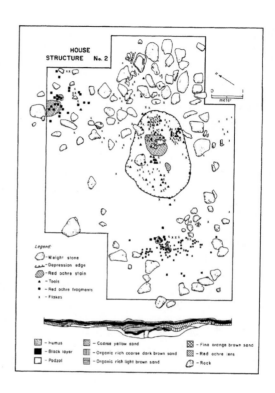

FIGURE 22: TWO MIDDLE MARITIME CULTURE (?) DWELLINGS AT THE NESKUTEU SITE, QUÉBEC   Situated in the interior of northern Québec on Indian House Lake 175 km from the Labrador coast such semi-subterranean dwellings may have been typical of seasonal interior fall caribou hunt camps. (Adapted from Pilon 1982: Figures 4 and 5, respectively. Drawn by Mr. David W. Laverie.)

1984). Given the mast forests between 3,500 and 1,750 BC in Maine and the Maritimes deer were most likely more important than either moose or caribou. Further, as deer are carriers of a neurotropic nematode (Parelapostronqulus tenuis) their presence would likely exclude the other cervids that were more vulnerable to the infection (Sanger 1975: 68). There is no evidence of dwellings and the 3 m to 6 m diameter clearings in the shell midden at the Turner Farm site could have served either as work areas or house floors (Bourque 1976). An impressive demonstration of the capability of Middle Maritime culture seafarers is apparent in the occupation of the Îles de la Madeleine (McCaffrey 1986). This island cluster in the Gulf of St.Lawrence is 100 km from the nearest land in Cape Breton and Prince Edward Island. Exotic siliceous slate from the Madeleine's have been fingerprinted to Cape Breton (Ibid: 134).

IV. The Estuary of the St.Lawrence River:

It has been speculated that a pattern of seasonal coastal exploitation, in conjunction with movements up the major rivers into the interior, prevailed in this region (Archambault 1987: 111). Unfortunately the lack of archaeological reconnaissance in the interior does not permit testing of the hypothesis. Even on the coast archaeological evidence is sparse suggesting only brief seasonal forays. Given the evidence of Middle Shield culture hunters in the Saguenay and Lac Saint Jean area (Chapdelaine 1984: 99) as early as 3,500 BC it is likely that the coastal Middle Maritime culture occupations represented seasonal extensions from further east along the northshore.

Cosmology:

At the turn of the century the `boneless´ cemeteries of Maine attracted considerable attention (Moorehead 1922; Smith 1948; Willoughby 1935). Relationships with these cemeteries were noted with sites as far away as Tadoussac, Québec (Wintemberg 1943: 340). Some archaeologists, including myself, believe that the cemeteries represent one facet of the elaborate mortuary system of Middle Maritime culture. Cemeteries and other elements of culture pertaining to cosmology will be considered within the four geographic regions of the Middle Maritime cultural distribution.

I. The Northshore of the Gulf of St.Lawrence and Labrador:

As noted in Chapter 5, the ceremonial mound features of this region are unique. It has been speculated that the mounds were the product of "...a society whose existence was so precariously dependent upon natural phenomena beyond its control that its concern with the supernatural was perhaps greater than that of other societies whose relationships with nature was less precariously balanced" (Tuck 1978a: 73). As a corollary to the preceding quotation is the proposition that the florescence of burial practices throughout Middle Maritime culture after 2,500 BC relates to anxiety over changing environmental conditions and the incursions of other cultures into traditional territory (Middle Shield culture, Early Palaeo-Eskimo culture, and Susquehanna Archaic culture). Be that as it may, the evidence does indicate that the mounds are early and currently restricted to the northshore of the Gulf of St.Lawrence and Labrador. Though the mounds were ceremonial monuments that could include human remains they obviously were not the standard method by which Middle Maritime culture buried their dead. This was done in cemeteries that have been dated as early as 3,500 BC. By 2,500 BC the mortuary complex reflected in the cemeteries achieved cult proportions across the entire region from Labrador to Newfoundland and the Maritimes to Maine. Unlike the mounds, in the majority of instances these `sacred places´ were not directly associated with habitation sites.

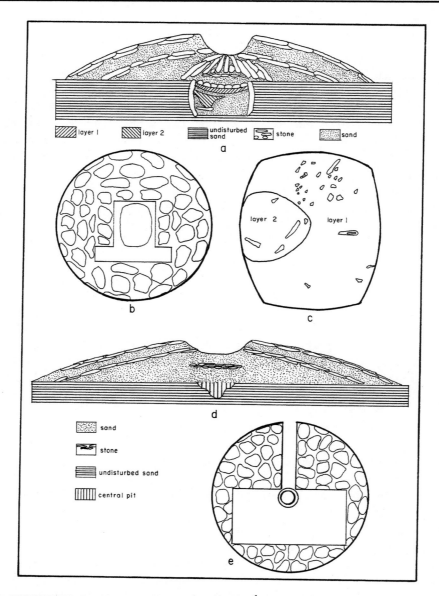

FIGURE 23: THE BURIAL MOUNDS AT BRADOR, QUÉBEC   There is a problem with the dating of one of these mounds. Tumulus II (a, b, and c) contained tools that typologically should date around 5,000 BC but the mound produced an unacceptably late date. Tumulus I (d and e), in contrast, produced radiocarbon dates of approximately 1,500 BC that are in agreement with the associated projectile point styles. The variability in the construction of the two mounds presumably relates to changing practices associated with the passage of time. Neither mound has been fully described but Tumulus II had some skull fragments associated with the grave offerings in the uppermost layer of the flagstone crypt (Levesque 1980: 158). (Adapted from Levesque 1980: 156-162. Drawn by Mr. David W. Laverie.)

Two mound features have been excavated in the Brador area of the northshore of the Gulf of St.Lawrence in Québec (Levesque 1980). Tumulus II consisted of a 9 m diameter and 1.3 m high mound with a central crypt and two mounded layers of large flagstones separated by layers of sand. A radiocarbon date that calibrated to AD 250 is not only at odds with the dating of Middle Maritime culture but also with the stone tool offerings discovered in the mound. These items occurred in two superimposed layers and consisted of nipple based triangular points, including an edge serrated specimen, large end scrapers, small biface knives, full grooved stone gouges, and a celt blank. Such an assemblage of implements typologically cross-dates somewhere between 5,750 and 5,000 BC and, thus, the mound would be contemporary with the Period II 5,500 BC mound in nearby Labrador (McGhee 1976). Tumulus I, of similar form and size to Tumulus II, produced two stemmed projectile points and an adze and two radiocarbon dates of 1,500 and 1,750 BC. The dates are in agreement with the estimated age of the associated projectile point style. Given the early dates for the L'Anse Amour mound in Labrador and the equally early typological estimate of Tumulus II and the late, even terminal, dates for Tumulus I, it can be suggested that such ceremonial structures were an important element of Middle Maritime culture religion in the region for approximately 4,000 years.

The burial pattern along the central and northern Labrador coast consists of an early phase represented by rare mound burials situated in imposing settings, containing single individuals, and requiring considerable group effort in their construction (Fitzhugh 1978). A second, later phase is represented by cemeteries with cobble/boulder coverings over graves and an abundance of grave offerings. Continuity in burial practices is seen through time. The ages of the mounds between 4,750 and 2,500 BC are somewhat less than that on the south coast. At the Nulliak site on the northern Labrador coast (Fitzhugh 1981) one of the two burial mounds produced a native copper pendant while the other contained a number of Ramah quartzite tools, large sheets of mica, and ground stone celts. On typological grounds these northernmost Middle Maritime culture mound features should date to 2,500 BC. On the central Labrador coast, at the Ballyrack site in Nain, one mound feature was composed of a surface boulder pavement 5 m in diameter that was superimposed over a conical pit filled with sand and boulders, biface knife fragments, flakes of Ramah quartzite, and red ochre. In the bottom of the pit, 1 m below the surface of the ground, a flexed burial covered in red ochre was encountered. In the second mound at the same site the 4 m diameter boulder pavement occurred over a subsurface oval ring of boulders that covered an oval pit containing a biface knife, scrapers, red ochre and charcoal while a number of bipoints and small celts had been deposited on the surface around the mound. A stone slab feature adjacent to the mound contained Ramah quartzite, quartz, and a style of projectile point that would date around the end of Period II (Fitzhugh 1978).

A series of features in southern Labrador, consisting of red ochre deposits containing artifacts, likely represent graves in which all bone has dissolved. This interpretation is reinforced by the linear arrangement of implements occurring in a number of concentrations a few meters in diameter as well as the high proportion of ground stone tools and the scarcity of general camp debris. One such feature consisted of a patch of red ochre stained sand containing celts, a gouge, stone tool blanks, and an abrading stone (McGhee and Tuck 1975). They have been dated to 3,750 BC.

In the Hamilton Inlet area, a cemetery at the major base camp site of Rattlers Bight contained 1 to 1.5 m diameter bark lined pits covered with rock slabs. Many of the graves were marked on the surface with boulder grave stones. Graves were tightly clustered and frequently overlapped one another indicating sequential use. One grave had rock lined sides and contained the remains of a dog. Grave offerings consisted of plummets, chipped semi-lunar knives, abraders, cut mica, stemmed Ramah quartzite projectile points, ground slate points, celts and gouges, Ramah quartzite and soapstone blanks, sheets of native copper and, in one instance, a walrus skull and probable ivory adzes (Fitzhugh 1976). Most of the grave offerings, while of the same form as those from the adjacent habitation site, tended to be larger and better finished suggesting specific manufacture as grave inclusions. Further, most of the offerings were purposefully broken or `killed´ in order that the spirit of the implement might accompany the soul of the deceased. Such practices are relatively clear evidence of an animistic belief system where all matter and phenomenon are believed to possess spirits. This would include animals, the wind, water, rocks, etc. Although bone preservation was largely non-existent at this cemetery, the grave pit outline configurations suggested flexed and/or bundle burials as is the case with other `boneless´ graves in Middle Maritime culture cemeteries. In fact, one bundle burial was actually preserved. Radiocarbon dates from the Rattlers Bight cemetery range from 3,500 to 1,750 BC and approximately duplicate the dates from the associated habitation site. The dates suggest that the site and cemetery were used seasonally over a period of approximately 2,000 years.

The engraved soapstone pendants from some Middle Maritime culture sites in northern Labrador may have had ritualistic significance (Fitzhugh 1985a). Regarded as pendants, such objects could also have functioned as fish and squid jigging lures given both their form attributes and ethnographic analogy (Willoughby 1935: 302, Fig.143; for a discussion of the function of plummets see Clermont 1987). The pendants generally possess edge notching and a great variety of designs. They also appear to be essentially unfinished. Their spatial distribution in the longhouses suggests that they were individual personal items subject to daily use and breakage.

II. The Island of Newfoundland:

Information on Middle Maritime culture mortuary practices on the Island of Newfoundland is limited to the fully described Port au Choix site (Harp and Hughes 1968; Tuck 1976a) and the undescribed Curtis site (MacLeod n.d.). The Port au Choix site on the west coast of the Island contained three cemeteries spanning the period from 3,000 to 1,500 BC (Figure 24). Adult burial position was usually flexed although bundle burials and partially disarticulated burials also occurred. Infants and young children were often buried in an extended position on their backs. The probability that the site was a sacred place is supported by the fact that human remains in various states of decomposition had been brought to the locale for final burial. Evidence of an associated habitation site was lacking. General characteristics of the burial site were as follows: all sexes and ages were represented; relative to the cardinal points there was no particular orientation of the bodies; red ochre was always used to line the grave pit and to cover parts of the body; rocks and boulders frequently capped the graves, presumably functioning as grave markers; there was some evidence of grave offerings being broken or`killed´; there was no relationship between abundance and types of grave offerings and sex or age except that shell pendants were most commonly found with infants and young children; and the peripheral cemeteries appear to have been used several centuries after the use of the main cemetery was discontinued. Some evidence of individual family burial plots occurred in the main cemetery and may represent lineages or clans (Kennedy 1981: Fig.3, 19). Features found at the same level as the graves consisted of hearths, presumably ceremonial in function, a cache of iron pyrites, seal bones, whale bone planks, and a stone pavement not unlike the one described from a site in northern Labrador (Fitzhugh 1978: 82-83).

All the graves were richly provided with grave offerings that included tools, weapons, ornaments and probable amulets. Small quartz pebbles of unknown significance occurred with most burials. Other objects presumed to symbolize magical powers consisted of bird bills and feet, a cut and ground wolf maxilla, a range of mammal teeth, claws, and skulls, natural zoomorphic stones, and quartz, calcite, and amethyst crystals. Among some of the exceptional recoveries were the following: a possible hooded garment outlined by periwinkle beads; dog burials as grave offerings including one killed by a blow to the head; effigy pendants and combs, particularly of birds including the extinct great auk; a perforated human collar bone that equates with a cut and perforated human humerus from the Nevin site in Maine; and the grave of a possible woman shaman (Tuck 1976a: 136-137). The twelve most common categories of grave offerings were shell beads, pebbles, skate teeth beads, bird parts, mammal parts, crystals, needles, pins and pendants, concretions, worked beaver incisors, toggling and barbed harpoons, and barbed points. Of the 34 species of bird represented among the animal remains there were only a single terrestrial species and several raptorials and a passerine, the remainder were aquatic or semi-aquatic species (Tuck 1976: 60-70). Among the mammal remains seal and red fox were the most common marine and land animals, respectively. A number of objects were found in clusters suggesting that they were originally contained in bags (Ibid: 60). As will be noted in Chapter 15, Middle Great Lakes-St.Lawrence culture shared the practice of depositing the parts of animals with their deceased kinsmen. Whether these animal remains related to lineage totems or to the power inherent in a particular animal or portion of its anatomy is unknown. Of particular interest from Port au Choix was the occurrence of inverted human figurines (Ibid: Fig.26, 190). Similar bone or ivory figurines occur in Palaeo-Eskimo, Inuit, and Early West Coast cultures. They have also been recorded from Palaeolithic sites in Eurasia where it has been speculated that they represented deceased ancestors whose function was to act as amulets to protect the living (Carpenter 1988: 499). Additional information on the grave contents of the Port au Choix site can be found in the section on **Technology**. It can be readily appreciated how little would have survived at this site if the typical acid soil situation had prevailed.

The Curtis burial site near Twillingate on the northeast coast of Newfoundland has been dated between 2,000 and 1,500 BC. The deep, boneless red ochre filled grave pits contained a rich array of stone grave offerings, particularly ground slate bayonets (Wilmeth 1978: 158) but a detailed published description of the site is not available. A red ochre stained quartz crystal from the Level 2 occupation of the Beaches site (Carginan 1975) likely had symbolic significance as did similar crystals from the Port au Choix graves. Quartz crystals, a metaphor for `Light´, were believed to have magical powers by many native peoples in eastern North America (Hamell 1983: 15).

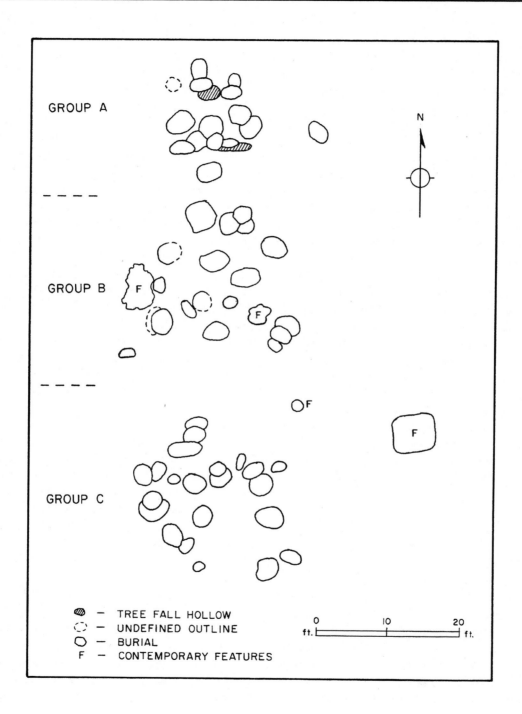

GROUP A

GROUP B

GROUP C

N

⬨ — TREE FALL HOLLOW
⬭ — UNDEFINED OUTLINE
◯ — BURIAL
F — CONTEMPORARY FEATURES

0   10   20
ft.   ft.

FIGURE 24:   THE MIDDLE MARITIME CULTURE CEMETERY AT PORT AU CHOIX, NEWFOUNDLAND The Figure illustrates three clusters of graves in the Locus II cemetery. Such concentrations may relate to family or extended kin burial plots (Tuck 1976: 11). The associated large feature in Group B, marked F, consisted of a layer of whale bone planks while the smaller feature , also indicated by the letter `F´, consisted of two hearths containing fire fractured rock and food refuse. The small feature to the northeast of the Group C cluster contained a concentration of seal bones while the larger feature 4.5 m to the east of Group C consisted of a stone slab pavement lacking cultural materials. Its function is unknown. (Adapted from Tuck 1976: Figure 3. Drawn by Mr. David W. Laverie.)

III. The Maritime Provinces and Adjacent Maine:

The `boneless´ Red Paint cemeteries of Maine were accidentally discovered at the turn of the century (Belcher et al. 1994; Moorehead 1922; Smith 1948; Willoughby 1935). In this work, these cemeteries are regarded as pertaining to Middle Maritime culture. An alternative view holds that the mortuary system was part of the spread of a burial cult from Middle Great Lakes-St.Lawrence culture that cut across different cultural and environmental zones (Sanger 1973: 122). Sanger's central point that it is hazardous to recreate `whole´ cultures from one cultural system, such as the mortuary system, is valid. Sufficient habitation sites, however, have been excavated along the Maine coast to permit examination of more than a single cultural system of Middle Maritime culture in the area.

A small disturbed cemetery in Saint John, New Brunswick, produced gouges, celts, plummets, including one in the form of a fish effigy, abraders, hammerstones, and a stemmed ground slate point (Harper 1956). Unlike the preceding site, the large cemetery at the Cow Point site in the same province was excavated by archaeologists (Sanger 1973). This `boneless´ cemetery contained approximately 65 red ochre burials that, on the basis of grave pit configurations, are inferred to have contained either flexed or bundle burials or both. Dated to 2,000 BC, the cemetery appears to have been used for only a short period of time. No habitation site is present in the vicinity and, in this respect, the cemetery follows the normal pattern of being a sacred place removed from secular activities. Graves were restricted to a 20 m by 6 m area. Both the concentration of graves and the fact that some were superimposed or intersected one another suggests that there were originally some form of surface grave markers. Stratigraphic evidence indicates that the gouges, plummets, and non-functional slate bayonets belonged with the earlier graves while functional slate bayonets and perforated and notched abraders were later in time. The earliest graves occupied the centre of the cemetery whereas later graves occurred on the periphery or were superimposed over the centre. Grave goods in order of frequency were as follows: celts (37.0); ground slate bayonets (23.0); abraders (21.0); plummets (6.0); natural stones that were probably charms (6.0); gouges (3.0), chipped stone points (1.0); and miscellaneous items (3.0) consisting of a gouge /celt combination, a double-bitted celt, strike-a-lights, sharks teeth, unmodified pebbles with four of the 21 examples having natural perforations, and a ground slate pendant. The most common form of ground slate bayonet was the non-utilitarian forms that accounted for 90% of the total of 77 specimens. These particular bayonets appear to have been too fragile to have functioned as lances and were also the only bayonets decorated with

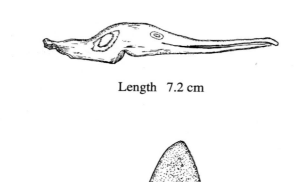

Length   7.2 cm

Length   18.3 cm

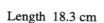

Length   8.9 cm

Length
31.2 cm

FIGURE 25:   GRAVE OFFERINGS FROM THE PORT AU CHOIX CEMETERY, NEWFOUNDLAND AND THE COW POINT CEMETERY, NEW BRUNSWICK   In the left upper corner is a bone pendant depicting the head of a cormorant or merganser while below is a stone killer whale effigy and a bone toggling harpoon head, all from the Port au Choix cemetery. To the right is a decorated ground slate lance from the Cow Point cemetery. The lance is quite delicate and was believed to have been specifically manufactured for placement with the deceased rather than being a functional weapon. (Drawn by Mr. David W. Laverie.)

incised motifs. In every instance the motifs occurred on only one face of the bayonets and were placed in the grave with the motifs `face up´. There is also evidence that the celts, some of which possess lashing grooves on the dorsal face, had been placed in the grave without their wooden handles. None of the stone tools appear to have been manufactured from exotic stone. As with other Middle Maritime culture cemeteries, the mortuary practices at the Cow Point site suggest an egalitarian society in which the grave offerings represented individual gifts premised on ritual devoid of sex or age significance.

Most early investigations of the Red Paint cemeteries of Maine were carried out using excavation and recording methods unacceptable to modern archaeology (Moorehead 1922). An exception was the work of Charles C. Willoughby (1935). A recent re-examination of one site has provided essential information (Snow 1975). The Hathaway site on a tributary of the Penobscot River was first excavated by Warren K. Moorehead in 1912. Despite this earlier work and another excavation in 1947 portions of the site were still intact. It was discovered that a habitation site was situated 150 m away from the cemetery. The Hathaway cemetery was used between 3,750 and 2,000 BC thus spanning the time when such burial practices were common to Middle Maritime culture. Graves were tightly concentrated and, on occasion, superimposed or intersected one another (Snow 1975: Fig.2). In most respects, the site compares closely with the Cow Point site including the nature of the early and late grave offerings. As with the Cow Point site all bone material had been destroyed by the acid soils. Both Snow and Sanger (1973) see the Moorehead or Red Paint burial complex in Maine as a cultic expression of local Middle Great Lakes-St.Lawrence culture (Laurentian Archaic) that was eventually disrupted by ecological change (Snow 1975: 58) or population replacement (Sanger 1973: 133). In this work, the mortuary system is treated as the product of the local Middle Maritime culture and its disappearance from Maine and immediately adjacent New Brunswick relates to population replacement stimulated by environmental change.

Comparing the cemeteries of Middle Maritime culture has been greatly complicated by the absence, in most instances, of organic materials such as bone. Fortunately a capping shell midden at the Nevin site in Maine (Byers 1979) preserved bone and shell and permits a comparison with the Port au Choix site in Newfoundland. In addition to the similarities in stone tool grave offerings, highly specific correspondences existed with reference to the bone tools. Among these correspondences were harpoon foreshafts with identical treatment of the distal and proximal ends, barbed harpoons, points, and small bird darts, daggers, needles with cut eyes, skate teeth beads, tubes with two perforations at one end, modified human bone, similar etched designs, and other items (Tuck 1976a: 110-111). Such correspondences suggest an intimate relationship between widely separated regional expressions of Middle Maritime culture. It is pertinent to note that Middle Maritime culture burial practices differed significantly from those of Middle Great Lakes-St.Lawrence culture (Tuck 1976a: 114-118).

A final element of cosmology from the Maine coast is a dog burial from the Turner Farm site that was apparently associated with a cache of tools (Bourque 1976). This burial is a variation on the situation noted at the Port au Choix cemetery were dog burials appeared to be of symbolic significance as offerings rather than simply reflecting an equivalent burial treatment of humans and dogs.

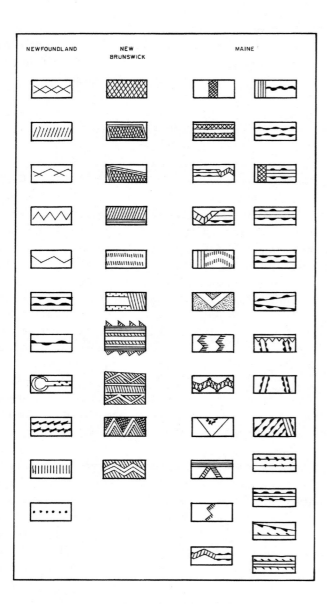

FIGURE 26: MIDDLE MARITIME CULTURE MOTIFS FROM NEWFOUNDLAND, NEW BRUNSWICK, AND MAINE The motifs, engraved on bone and stone implements, are from the Port au Choix site in Newfoundland, the Cow Point site in New Brunswick, and the Nevin Shellheap in Maine. While a number of similarities are apparent between the Newfoundland and Maine motifs, the different patterns of the New Brunswick motifs may relate to the latter being etched on slate rather than bone. A single decorated ground slate point fragment from the Beaches site possessed a motif similar to the lowermost New Brunswick example (Carignan 1975, Plate 8). The symbolic significance of the motifs is unknown but they may relate to ancestor figures (see Carpenter 1986 for an in depth consideration of design symbolism around the world. Drawn by Mr. David W. Laverie.)

IV. The Estuary of the St.Lawrence River:

The only site from this region of possible pertinence is an accidentally discovered burial containing polished stone gouges that was found in the city of Rivière-du-Loup on the southshore of the St.Lawrence River (Dumais 1978: 69).

External relationships:

Neighbouring cultures of Middle Maritime culture were Early Palaeo-Eskimo, Middle Shield, Middle Great Lakes- St.Lawrence, and Susquehanna Archaic. This exceptionally long list of neighbours is a product of both the extensive geographic range and variable environments occupied by Middle Maritime culture and altering environmental conditions such as the progressive release of the interior of the Québec/Labrador Peninsula from the effects of the last glaciation. The impact of some of these neighbouring cultures upon Middle Maritime culture has already been considered and will only be summarized here. The influence of Middle Shield culture is regarded as having been the most disruptive to Middle Maritime culture along the northshore of the St.Lawrence River and Gulf as well as the Labrador coast. Early Palaeo-Eskimo culture contacts with Middle Maritime culture are of significance from the point of view of technological exchanges and how two maritime cultures exploiting the same resources in an area reacted to one another. The relationship between Middle Maritime culture and Middle Great Lakes-St.Lawrence culture was the most pervasive and most difficult to assess. Susquehanna Archaic culture's affect was essentially peripheral, only involving northern Maine and adjacent portions of New Brunswick.

I. Middle Great Lakes-St.Lawrence culture: A close relationship existed between this culture and Middle Maritime culture, so much so that there has been inconsistency in the literature regarding what sites to assign to which culture. The two areas of direct contact were the St.Lawrence River from Québec City to the Ontario border and western New Brunswick and the State of Maine. The intimacy of the relationship between the two cultures is reflected in a wide range of shared traits such as polished stone gouges, ground slate bayonets, points, ulus, rods and plummets. All of the aforementioned traits, except the polished stone rods, have been dated earlier on the coast suggesting a coastal origin with diffusion to the interior. Expansion of Middle Great Lakes-St.Lawrence culture to New Brunswick and New England has been tentatively correlated with the expansion of the hardwood forests at the expense of conifers (Bradstreet and Davis 1975) but the population movement only pertains to the period prior to 3,750 BC. It is speculated that interaction between the two cultures was more influenced by economic and social factors than environmental change. This is reflected in the form of trade objects such as the walrus ivory gouge found at the Brewerton site in northwestern New York state (Beauchamp 1902), the native copper implements of Lake Superior origin via Middle Great Lakes-St.Lawrence culture middlemen on the Ottawa River (Kennedy 1966; n.d.) found along the Gulf of St.Lawrence and Labrador coasts (Fitzhugh 1986) and Newfoundland, and the association of distinctive varieties of stone tools of both cultures, particularly projectile point styles, on sites in the St.Lawrence Valley (Lueger 1977; Marois 1986; Marois et Ribes

1975; Wright 1986; 1994). The presence of Middle Maritime culture as well as Early Maritime culture materials upriver from Québec City probably was the result of seasonal forays into the interior. Such visitations must have had the tacit approval of the resident Middle Great Lakes-St.Lawrence culture bands. A form of developed exchange could possibly account for the cultural mixture apparent in the region. Certainly there is no evidence of a Middle Maritime culture occupation removed from the shores of the St.Lawrence River. A similar culture contact area appears to have existed in western New Brunswick and Maine (Deal 1986:69). In addition to points manufactured from Ramah quartzite, points of apparent Lake Champlain quartzite and chert resembling exceptionally long examples of the Middle Great Lakes-St. Lawrence culture Normanskill point type (Ritchie 1961: 37-38) have been recovered from Middle Maritime culture cemeteries in Maine (Bourque 1994: 26-27).

Although, in most respects, Middle Maritime culture and Middle Great Lakes-St.Lawrence culture are mutually distinct, their overlapping distributions and certain shared traits have blurred differences. This observation pertains to New Brunswick and Maine as well as the St.Lawrence River.

II. Middle Shield culture: The occasional polished stone gouge found as far into the interior as the James Bay drainage (Laliberté 1978) could reflect either Middle Maritime culture or Middle Great Lakes-St.Lawrence culture trade with the Middle Shield culture occupants. While there is little direct evidence of artifact associations or recognized trade items suggestive of contacts between Middle Shield culture and Middle Maritime culture there is settlement pattern evidence that Middle Shield culture was likely the cause of the demise of Middle Maritime culture along the northshore of the Estuary of the St.Lawrence, the Gulf of St.Lawrence, and the Labrador coast. Radiocarbon dates from central Labrador indicate the presence of Middle Shield culture people shortly after 2,000 BC and similar dates pertain to the northern interior of Québec. Further south, in the Chicoutimi region on the Saguenay River, Middle Shield culture sites are estimated to date as early as 3,000 BC (Chapdelaine 1984). It is speculated that Middle Shield culture hunters not only continued to expand to the east and north as areas of the Québec/Labrador Peninsula progressively recovered from the after-affects of glaciation but that in the process they also developed a subsistence strategy requiring seasonal forays to the coast. This would have applied initially to the northshore of the St.Lawrence River and Gulf but would eventually reach the Labrador coast. It is further speculated that this encroachment on Middle Maritime culture territory inhibited the latter access to caribou in sufficient numbers to meet annual clothing and bedding needs. Combined with incursions from the north on the Labrador coast by Early Palaeo-Eskimo culture and deteriorating climatic conditions the situation became untenable for Middle Maritime culture people and they eventually abandoned the entire northshore of the St.Lawrence River and Gulf as well as the Labrador coast. Middle Shield culture settlement pattern evidence from the Labrador coast indicates that they were not seafarers and only made seasonal excursions to the mainland coast (Nagle 1978). A less draconian explanation than the foregoing would be that the entire region had already been abandoned by Middle Maritime culture peoples and Middle Shield culture people simply moved into the void.

III. Early Palaeo-Eskimo culture: The abandonment of the northern and central coast of Labrador by

Middle Maritime culture has generally been attributed to an Early Palaeo-Eskimo cultural incursion from the north around 2,500 BC (Fitzhugh and Lamb 1985: Fig.2). Palaeo-Eskimo descendants would retain a hold on the coast until their replacement around AD 1,000 by Inuit culture. Unlike the Middle Shield culture hunters, Early Palaeo-Eskimo culture hunters were maritimers and would have been in direct competition with Middle Maritime culture people for marine resources. Regardless of the respective roles of Middle Shield culture and Early Palaeo-Eskimo culture in the demise of Middle Maritime culture in the region, it does appear that economic competition with its neighbours ultimately was responsible for the latter's abandonment of the region. An important product of Middle Maritime culture and Early Palaeo-Eskimo culture contact was the exchange of the toggling harpoon technology for the bow and arrow technology (Tuck 1976: 121). It appears that Middle Shield culture also adopted the bow and arrow and, indeed, was the major factor in the western distribution of the new weapon system. Evidence of direct cultural contact is limited to the presence of an Early Palaeo-Eskimo culture burin in direct association with Middle Maritime culture materials at the Rattlers Bight site near Hamilton Inlet.

IV. Susquehanna Archaic culture: In both Maine and adjacent New Brunswick and portions of the St.Lawrence Valley there is evidence of an intrusion by Susquehanna Archaic people (Sanger 1975; Dumais 1978) into former Middle Maritime culture territory. A date of 2,000 BC from a pit feature at the Laforet site near Rivière- du-Loup (Taillon et Barré 1987) on the southshore of the St.Lawrence River is in good agreement with Susquehanna Archaic dates from both coastal and interior sites (Borstel 1982: 79). As noted in the section on **Settlement patterns** the incursion of Susquehanna Archaic people into former Middle Maritime culture territory in northern Maine and adjacent New Brunswick has been attributed to environmental change that favoured their subsistence system over that of the original occupants (Sanger 1975).

Human biology:

The Port au Choix cemeteries in Newfoundland contained more than 90 individuals of all ages and sexes (Anderson 1976; Tuck 1976a). Infant mortality was high with approximately one half of the deceased being less than two years of age. Adult remains were equally divided by gender. General appearance was that of a short people with robust builds and broad foreheads. Males ranged from 159 to 174 cm in height compared to a range of 151 to 166 cm for females. Gum disease leading to tooth loss and jaw bone reabsorption was present but cavities were rare, a pattern resulting from an abrasive, low carbohydrate diet. Female dentition exhibited less attrition but more tooth loss and abscesses than their male counterparts. Arthritis was present in approximately one half of the adults and was particularly common along the spine and on the elbow and finger joints. Healed fractures of head, ribs, and longbones were also identified, some being suggestive of combat. The bone lesions on the skull of a 2 to 4 year old have been diagnosed as possibly being histiocytosis X, a rare disease of unknown cause estimated to have an occurrence of one in two million people a year (Kennedy 1987). A study of both the metric and nonmetric adult skeletal traits from the Port au Choix population indicated a greater degree of genetic variability in females than males. This has been interpreted as evidence that female spouses came to the band from neighbouring bands to reside with their husbands (Kennedy 1981).

Nineteen individuals from the Nevin site cemetery in Maine generally lacked evidence of disease. There was evidence of weaning and immediate post-weaning (up to 5 years after weaning) stress indicated by hypoplasia, a growth disruption of dental enamel formation (Shaw 1988).

Inferences on society:

While ethnographic analogy is an appropriate interpretative aid, particularly where cultural continuity from the archaeological population to a historically recorded population can be demonstrated, the method is still premised upon certain hazardous assumptions. Underestimating the changes wrought by European direct and indirect contact on a native group prior to the time of the ethnographic observations is the greatest single weakness. Prudence would dictate that cultural extrapolations from early historic records to archaeological populations be kept at a most general level. Likely the greatest utility of ethnographic analogy is the sobering light the method throws on the enormous gap in richness of cultural detail between the archaeological evidence and the ethnographic records. In his consideration of Maritime culture in the Hamilton Inlet of Labrador, for example, Fitzhugh (1972) drew analogies with the historically documented Algonquian-speaking Montagnais-Naskapi. Among the comparisons believed to be pertinent were the following: bands range from 50 to 100 people; a general subsistence pattern of caribou hunting in the interior during the winter and fishing, sealing, and waterfowling on the coast or large lakes in the summer although this pattern had many variations determined by resource availability; the majority of the tools made from perishable substances such as bone and antler with stone tools being limited to hammers, netsinkers, abraders, arrowheads, and scrapers or less than one percent of the ethnographic material culture; most animal food bones incinerated, placed on platforms or in trees or disposed of in a body of water to prevent dogs from offending the animal spirits; winter tent camps occupied on average for a few weeks; the winter hunting regions left fallow for approximately 10 years; large quantities of fish stored for fall and winter; mobility required during the winter caribou hunt although the caribou pound with snare openings likely introduced some sedentism under favourable circumstances; and the most dangerous period of the year was in March when stored foods were exhausted but ice crusting made caribou hunting impossible. Subsequent research in the interior of the Québec-Labrador Peninsula has produced only limited evidence of Middle Maritime culture (Samson 1978; 1978a) suggesting that the historically recorded seasonal interior exploitative pattern is not appropriate. The Montagnais-Naskapi analogy is more appropriate to Middle Shield culture.

Middle Maritime culture likely consisted of central-based wandering communities centred on the coast (Tuck 1976a). The probability of band territoriality is supported by the presence of cemeteries representing sacred places used over a prolonged period of time (Cow Point, Port au Choix, Rattlers Bight, Hathaway, etc.) as well as the construction of `land mark´ features such as burial mounds. The evolution of house styles on the Labrador coast from single family dwellings to multiple family partitioned longhouses must reflect some major change in social structure such as the increasing power of lineages or clans and/or the cooperative association with other bands for specific purposes. Such developments could have been task specific, such as mutual defence during hazardous resource exploitation expeditions, rather than being an indication of fundamental changes in the social structure. Whatever the explanation, there is evidence for increasing social complexity that led to seasonal villages likely composed of a number of bands. The evidence of band exogamy in the Port au Choix site skeletal population would imply the existence of a network of blood related bands. These social changes correlated with expanding trade that, among other functions, would be required to strengthen multi-band relationships established through marriage.

Despite the evidence of increasing social complexity in Middle Maritime society individual families still would have related to one another on an egalitarian basis. Evidence of individual or group status differences is not suggested by the grave offerings. At Port au Choix, hunting and fishing equipment and beaver incisor knives were slightly more common with males while skin working tools, needles, and celts (wood gathering) were more frequently found in female graves. Shell beads and pendants were most often found with infants and children and what are thought to be medicine bundles were associated with adults (Tuck 1976a). The evidence in support of an egalitarian society is reinforced by the kinds and quantities of materials found distributed in the individual family cubicles of the Labrador longhouses. These distributions do not indicate specialization or functional/social differences (Fitzhugh 1985). Despite the foregoing, the longhouses may reflect the existence of local leaders with some power who were responsible for territorial defence and the maintenance of the Ramah quartzite trade (Fitzhugh 1984). Such individual authority over the group was probably a temporary expediency required to meet potential threats from Early Palaeo-Eskimo hunters. Given the collective benefits of authority being vested in the captain of a vessel while at sea such temporary lapses from the normal individual egalitarian status may have been more readily acceptable to a maritime people than to mainlanders.

Limitations in the evidence:

The extensive archaeological research which has focused on Middle Maritime culture has permitted a more complete reconstruction than is usually possible. Time and circumstances, however, have assured that even this reconstruction is only complete in a relative sense. The three greatest gaps in the evidence are the paucity of habitation sites in the Maritime provinces due to sinking coastlines, the general absence or paucity of bone preservation, and the strong quarry factor at many sites that complicates the comparative process. Certainly the impact of rising sea levels along the coasts of the Maritime provinces, Maine, and the Island of Newfoundland upon the archaeological record must be regarded as the most serious and irretrievable limitation. The observation that, "All that remains will be the occasional object found in the mud or dragged from the sea floor" (Turnbull 1988: 101) pertains to most parts of the Maritime provinces and Maine. There is also the problem that "...trés peu de sites on livré des pièces que la typologie permittrait d'assigner à une tradition culturelle connue" (Archambault 1987:105).

Some of the questions requiring detailed research involve the eventual fate of Middle Maritime culture after 1,500 BC and the nature of the relationships with Middle Great Lakes- St.Lawrence culture, Middle Shield culture, Early Palaeo-Eskimo culture, and Susquehanna Archaic culture. There is also a need for substantially more information on the technological and social adaptations that permitted this unique culture to flourish in a harsh environment for so many thousands of years. A corollary, of course, is why these same adaptations suddenly failed a large portion of Middle Maritime culture around 1,500 BC.

CHAPTER 15
MIDDLE GREAT LAKES-ST. LAWRENCE CULTURE

Précis:

Middle Great Lakes-St.Lawrence culture occupied the territories now consisting of Southern Ontario, southern Québec, southwestern New Brunswick, and adjacent states. It is a region covered, for the most part, by the mixed hardwood-softwood forests of the Great Lakes-St.Lawrence Forest vegetation province (Rowe 1959). While the origins of Middle Great Lakes-St.Lawrence culture in Period II are poorly defined by 4,000 BC a distinctive and widespread culture is identifiable. The markedly increased archaeological visibility is a phenomenon that occurs throughout eastern North America as a result of population growth and cultural elaboration associated with a more broadly based subsistence pattern including an increasing importance of plants in the diet (Griffin 1978: 231; Mason 1981). Important natural events during Period III were the expansion of the deciduous forest, including nut producing tree species, at the expense of the coniferous forests and an improved fishing potential as a result of the rising waters of the Great Lakes that changed stream gradients (Mason 1981: 145). Undoubtedly the stabilization of the landscape was the major factor responsible for the increasing archaeological visibility of sites. A stable system of rapids in a river with a concentrated seasonal fish resource, for example, would attract recurrent human occupation to specific site locations. This, in turn, resulted in the accumulation of cultural debris creating the partially false impressions of increasing social stability, sedentariness, and population growth. What was likely involved was simply the coalescence of people at particular seasonally rich and now stable locales rather than any fundamental changes in the settlement patterns or social structure.

Despite the richer archaeological record there are a number of problems impeding an understanding of Middle Great Lakes-St.Lawrence culture or Laurentian Archaic as it is commonly known. Foremost among the problems is the fact that the majority of site materials have been recovered from the surface of ploughed fields. Even when excavated, Middle Great Lakes-St.Lawrence culture site material is usually hopelessly intermixed with earlier and later archaeological debris. Single component sites, particularly those pertaining to the earlier portion of Period III and to sites east of the Niagara Escarpment in Southern Ontario, are extremely rare. A taxonomic problem also exists whereby the different emphases placed upon certain facets of the technology can result in a site being assigned to other cultures such as Middle Maritime culture or the Lamoka culture of New York State and the adjacent Niagara Peninsula of Southern

Ontario. Increasing regionalism and the difficulty in distinguishing between the diffusion of technological innovations and population intrusions has further complicated matters, particularly towards the end of Period III. There appears to be significant differences between the societies who occupied either side of the Niagara Escarpment. The richer mast forests to the west with their abundant deer, turkey, and nut resources may have permitted more dispersed settlement patterns lacking the warm month concentrations at favoured fishing locales that tend to characterize contemporary settlement patterns to the east. On the other hand, many potential warm weather fishing locales at the mouths of rivers in the west have probably been drowned. Although the archaeological visibility of sites has improved, this improvement is only relative to the preceding Period II. Water level changes in the Lower Great Lakes, particularly prior to 3,500 BC but as late as 1,000 BC in some regions, drowned many sites while water level fluctuations on Lake Huron and the increased Upper Great Lakes discharge through the Ottawa River resulted in settlement distributions that bear only a partial relationship to present shorelines and river banks. Even in areas of great stability, such as the Upper St.Lawrence River Valley, the fact that people occupied the same site locations over thousands of years has produced hopelessly mixed multi-component sites. This difficulty of isolating single component sites with significant samples has been a major contributor to the current classificatory problems.

The centre of Middle Great Lakes-St.Lawrence culture or Laurentian Archaic, was the mixed hardwood (deciduous) and softwood (coniferous) forests of the Upper St.Lawrence drainage system of Québec and Ontario, the Lower Great Lakes and the northern New England states as far east as interior Maine and New Brunswick. In the words of the originator of the concept of a Laurentian Archaic,"The Laurentian may perhaps best be regarded as an extensive Archaic cultural continuum, widely spread throughout northeastern North America, with its major area of development and diffusion within southeastern Ontario, southern Quebec, and northern New York. Its most diagnostic traits, occurring in considerable morphological variety, comprise the gouge; adze; plummet; ground slate points and knives, including the semi-lunar form or ulu, which occurs also in chipped stone; simple forms of the bannerstone; a variety of chipped-stone projectile points, mainly broad-bladed and side-notched forms; and the barbed bone point" (Ritchie 1965: 79-80).

Around the beginning of Period III Middle Great Lakes- St.Lawrence culture penetrated western New Brunswick and portions of New England. The occupation appears to have been a relatively short-lived foray although later developments in the interior are still poorly understood. People of the interconnecting lake and river networks of the Great Lakes- St.Lawrence Forest vegetation province relied upon deer and fish as well as a wide range of small game and plant foodstuffs. The early technology consisted of large side-notched dart heads, bifacially chipped knives and a number of other less common traits including certain implement categories acquired from Early and Middle Maritime culture populations in the Lower St.Lawrence Valley and the Atlantic coast. These items, represented by bayonets, projectile points and ulus, all in ground slate, and plummets and gouges have come to be regarded as the diagnostic tools of Middle Great Lakes-St.Lawrence culture despite their quantitatively limited occurrence and their origins in another culture. The distribution of these traits progressively weakens as one proceeds to the south and west (Wright 1962). There is, thus, a classificatory problem whereby sites containing typical chipped stone tool inventories are not regarded as `classic' Middle Great Lakes-St.Lawrence culture sites simply because they lack the requisite sprinkling of `diagnostic' ground stone implements. In an effort to accommodate this problem related Period II sites have been called proto-Laurentian (Funk 1988). This nomenclature, however, does not address the issue of widely distributed Period III sites that lack the ground stone tool elements but share in the dominant chipped stone portion of the tool kit (Dragoo 1959; 1966). A number of archaeologists have lumped the assemblages sharing the chipped stone tool technology into a Lake Forest Archaic (Snow 1980; Tuck 1978). In addition to the adoption of Middle Maritime culture traits, Middle Great Lakes- St.Lawrence culture borrowed polished stone spearthrower or atlatl weights from the south. In fact, Middle Great Lakes- St.Lawrence culture stands as an excellent example of how borrowed traits from neighbouring cultures can be grafted onto a predominantly chipped stone tool inventory to produce a tool kit whose spatial variety presents major classificatory problems for archaeologists. Contrary to a restrictive classification of Middle Great Lakes-St.Lawrence culture (Ritchie 1965: 79-80) a broader definition is followed here that places the emphasis upon the dominant, albeit simple, chipped stone tool inventory rather than the relatively rare ground stone tool categories emphasized in the original definition. Consideration of this classificatory problem can be found in a number of articles (Funk 1988; Tuck 1977).

In those rare instances where bone tools have survived they include needles, unilaterally barbed harpoons with or without line holes, conical toggling harpoons with line hole, dart heads, daggers, awls, and beaver incisor tools. Native copper implements, while widely distributed, are only common in the Ottawa Valley that appears to have been a centre of copper implement manufacture and distribution (Kennedy 1962; 1966; 1970). Among the wide range of copper items awls, beads, gorges, dart heads, and knives are most common.

Near the beginning of Period III cemeteries appear in association with the larger seasonal fishing base camps. Although extended and flexed burials are most common the presence of bundle burials and cremations suggest there was some effort made to bring the remains of those who died elsewhere back to specific base camps. This suggests that, in addition to their economic functions, such sites represented `sacred places'. The placement of grave offerings and red ochre with the deceased was variable but became increasingly frequent through time. People were robust, with heavy musculature. Severe dental attrition resulting from eating gritty food frequently led to periodontal disease but most individuals were free of recognizable pathologies excepting fractures and, among older individuals, arthritis. Biological relationships with neighbouring populations traced by physical anthropologists tend to be ambiguous (e.g.Pfeiffer 1977 versus 1979) but given the dispersed nature of the comparative samples and their generally small and fragmented nature the equivocal results are not surprising. When skeletal samples come from the same region but represent different time periods, such as the Morrison's Island-6 and Allumette-1 sites in the Ottawa Valley (Kennedy 1966; n.d.), a close biological relationship is apparent (Pfeiffer 1979). The distribution of certain tool varieties and exotic items indicates that Middle Great Lakes-St.Lawrence culture peoples had contacts not only with related bands but also their Middle Maritime culture and Middle Shield culture neighbours as well as people to the south.

Around 2,000 BC elements of Susquehanna Archaic culture spread up the coast to New Brunswick (Sanger 1975) and into the St.Lawrence Valley (Clermont et Chapdelaine 1982; Dumais 1978) and Southern Ontario (I. Kenyon 1980; Watson 1981). Whether this event was the product of a population movement or a technology transfer is still being debated. It does appear to have been marginal to Middle Great Lakes-St.Lawrence culture that is inferred to have continued to regionally diversify and establish the culture base for the subsequent Late Great Lakes-St.Lawrence culture of Period IV. The archaeological demonstration of this in situ development has been confounded by the difficulty of isolating the single components necessary for the comparative process. A different interpretation of events has appeared in a recent synthesis of the Archaic in Southern Ontario (Ellis et al. 1990). Here, the chronology after 3,250 BC is divided into three sequential units based upon projectile point form, Narrow Point, Broad Point, and Small Point, respectively (Ibid: Fig 4.1, 69). Evidence for this sequence of point styles is predominantly drawn from surface collections from sites west of the Niagara Escarpment in Southern Ontario and by extrapolation from sites in adjacent New York State. Contrasting with this reconstruction is the evidence from the Ottawa Valley where fluctuations in the volume of water discharge altered the local settlement pattern thus permitting some isolation of components. At the Morrison's Island-6 site (Kennedy 1967) in addition to typical Middle Great Lakes-St.Lawrence culture (Laurentian Archaic - Brewerton phase) projectile point types were associated points which would otherwise be classified as either `Narrow Point´ or `Small Point´. `Broad Point´ Archaic (Susquehanna Archaic) is regarded as a `technological diffusion´ into Southern Ontario rather than being the product of a population intrusion (Ellis et al. 1990: 99-100). In a cogent consideration of the Satchell complex, an expression of the widespread Broad Point horizon (I. Kenyon 1980: 18), it is suggested that it may not be "...valid as a taxonomic designation for a phase or archaeological culture..." but rather an expression of a diffused hunting technology which began in the southeastern United States and spread north along the Atlantic coast and west to the lower Great Lakes. The correlation of a number of varieties of broad points with the Deciduous Forest vegetation province in contrast to the Great Lakes-St.Lawrence vegetation province may suggest the richer deer populations of the former region was a factor in the spread of the point types. Conversely, the evidence from the Inderwick site in the Rideau Lakes area of eastern Southern Ontario (Watson 1981) raises the possibility of an actual intruding `Broad Point´ population. At this site an assemblage clearly related to the Susquehanna Archaic is quite distinct from local Middle Great Lakes-St.Lawrence culture materials. Unfortunately the archaeological context at the site was destroyed by elevated water levels and, as with the predominant surface materials in western Southern Ontario (I. Kenyon 1980: 24), leaves the question of technological diffusion or population intrusion an open issue. It is thus felt that until there is considerably more information from demonstrable single components the Middle Great Lakes-St.Lawrence cultural construct should be kept open and flexible.

Cultural origins and descendants:

There currently exists a classificatory problem of what, in technological terms, constitutes Middle Great Lakes-St.Lawrence culture (Laurentian Archaic). Some feel the concept has been over -extended by applying it to cultures lacking the distinctive ground slate tool categories (Funk 1988). Others, basing their comparisons upon the dominant chipped stone tool inventory rather than the ground stone tools, recognize a shared cultural pattern involving a number of regional Archaic populations (Dragoo 1959; 1966). Recognition of the classificatory problems created by placing an emphasis upon certain tool categories is indicated by observations such as, "The Proto-Laurentian groups, with their relatively simple tool kits inherited from older Archaic traditions, evolved into recognizable Laurentian expressions by 3,000 B.C." (Funk 1988: 35; note: this 3,000 BC date was arrived at by subtracting the radiocarbon date from AD 1950 and in terms of the Christian calendar actually calibrates to approximately 3,750 BC). A compromise proposal suggests the existence of two `Laurentian´ traditions, "One is a widespread Middle to Late Archaic manifestation presently recognized only by a chipped stone complex comprising broad-bladed notched projectile points, simple end scrapers and end scrapers with hafting modifications identical to projectile points, and biface `knives´. The second is that confined more or less to the upper St.Lawrence Valley and chronologically of the Late Archaic period that contains the ground stone elements long thought to define Laurentian but which can actually be shown to have originated on the coast from where they were diffused to the upper St.Lawrence drainage" (Tuck 1977: 39). By the `upper St.Lawrence´ Tuck is referring to southeastern Ontario, southern Québec, northern New York as well as northern New England. While the use of two levels of classification, one broadly conceived and the other more narrowly defined, can often be a useful device when attempting to communicate to people at different levels, in this instance it does nothing to address what is essentially a straight forward problem of classification. In this work the term `Middle Great Lakes-St.Lawrence culture´ (née Laurentian) is used in the broadest sense as it pertains to the dominant portion of the technology and the collective evidence from the other cultural subsystems. Membership in this expanded classification, of course, includes assemblages lacking most or all of the ground stone tools. Such a proposal does not deny the considerable regional and temporal variability encompassed within the construct.

A minor classificatory problem relevant to origins involves the `Narrow Point´ construct that is equated with the Lamoka Archaic of New York State and the adjacent Niagara Peninsula of Southern Ontario (Ritchie 1965). With the exception of sites in the Niagara Peninsula region (Lennox 1990; Ramsden 1990) sites assigned to Lamoka culture in the rest of Southern Ontario (Johnston 1984) and the Upper St.Lawrence of Québec (Clermont et Chapdelaine 1982) on the basis of projectile point form are not convincing.

Classificatory problems aside, there appears to be agreement that the ultimate origins of Middle Great Lakes- St.Lawrence culture were to the south. A southeastern Middle Archaic origin has been suggested (Funk 1976; Ritchie 1971a) with the northern and eastward expansion taking place around 4,000 BC (Tuck 1977). While it is agreed that a southern origin is involved in the spread of the technology that eventually becomes recognized as Middle Great Lakes-St.Lawrence culture, the technological introduction would have taken place during Early Archaic times. As noted during the discussion of the Early and Middle Archaic complexes of the Lower Great Lakes in Chapter 4 earlier indigenous populations appear to have been technologically transformed by both the adoption of southern traits and the influence of intruding populations out of the south.

In the original use of the term `Laurentian´ the Vergennes phase is the earliest manifestation from which later Laurentian phases such as Vosburg and Brewerton developed (Ritchie 1965: 84-87). This chronological sequence is supported by both stratigraphy and radiocarbon dates (Funk 1976: 235-238). In fact, on many sites the Vergennes phase represents the earliest evidence of human occupation (Funk 1976; Ritchie 1969). The McCally No.1 site in southern New York (Funk and Hoagland 1972) and similar sites are important for a number of reasons. Typologically the projectile points resemble the typical side-notched Vergennes forms but the ground slate tool categories are totally absent. The 5,500 BC McCally No.1 site either pre-dates the diffusion into the interior of these eastern traits or was situated too far south to participate in the diffusion sphere.

There are differences in the cultural sequences of New York and southern New England when compared to most of Québec and Ontario. In the former region, "...a succession of three vigorous and basic cultural traditions could be postulated for a broad geographic belt extending from western New York to the coast of southern New England. The oldest in the sequence of *identified* cultures would be Laurentian. The second tradition, as yet unnamed, would embrace the narrow point complexes. The third tradition, as defined by Ritchie (1965a, pp.149-177), would be the Susquehanna tradition, closing with the Transitional phases (Frost Island and Orient)" (Funk 1976: 272). In Canada, the `narrow point complexes´, often referred to as Lamoka culture, is absent except for the Niagara Peninsula region. Others, on the basis of what is here regarded as an incomplete comparative approach and questionable application of projectile point typology, however, regard Lamoka culture as being much more widely distributed (Clermont et Chapdelaine 1982; Johnston 1984; Marois et Ribes 1975; Roberts 1985).

The sudden appearance and subsequent disappearance of the `Broad Point´ phenomena in Southern Ontario and Québec remains a perplexing problem. These distinctive projectile points and some of their equally distinctive associated traits, such as stylized preforms, scrapers manufactured from points, soapstone vessels, and zoomorphic pestles, generally do not appear in the region as a demonstrably cohesive entity. The rapid spread of the characteristic point forms throughout much of eastern North America may relate to either some innovation in the weapon system (Cook 1976) or hunting strategies

(I. Kenyon 1980).

The clearest picture of developments at the end of the Archaic period in Ontario comes from a series of sites west of the Niagara Escarpment (Ellis et al. 1990; Kenyon 1959; Lennox 1986; Ramsden 1976; Wright 1972). Contrary to an earlier statement (Wright 1972: 56) I would now include these `Small Point´ sites within the Middle Great Lakes-St.Lawrence culture. This is done on the basis of technological continuities as well as certain correspondences in subsistence, settlement patterns, cosmology, and human biology. Sites across Lake Huron in Michigan exhibit a close relationship to the Southern Ontario sites (Wobst 1968) suggesting a regional Archaic development centred on the Lake. Indeed, an increasing pace of regional diversification appears to have been a general characteristic of terminal Archaic in eastern North America. Where the evidence is substantial, as in the case of the Lake Huron region, a clear transition into subsequent cultures can be traced. This is seen in the number of stone and bone elements of technology that continue into Late Great Lakes-St.Lawrence culture as well as in the settlement patterns, subsistence, and cosmological aspects of the subsequent culture (Wright 1984). The evidence of cultural continuity is supported by stratigraphy (Ritchie 1949).

It has been speculated that Middle Great Lakes-St.Lawrence culture involved people who belonged to the Iroquoian language family (Tuck 1977; Wright 1984). The hypothesis is premised upon continuities in a number of cultural subsystems from Middle Great Lakes-St.Lawrence culture times to historically documented Iroquoian-speaking peoples in the area. Attributing a specific language family to a specific archaeological culture is a hazardous exercise under the best of circumstances. However, there is a reasonable basis for suggesting that unless major cultural discontinuities can be detected in the archaeological record the language documented for the region by European observers in the 16th and 17th centuries can be correlated, **in a general rather than specific linguistic sense**, with the archaeological record. An alternative hypothesis favours an intrusion of Iroquoian peoples from the south (Snow 1980: 258-259; 1993). This controversial matter will be considered in detail in Period IV and Period V. The association of Middle Great Lakes-St.Lawrence culture with the Iroquoian language family would also be complicated if the hypothesis that the Vergennes phase sites in northern Maine and adjacent New Brunswick developed in situ from Middle Archaic complexes (Cox 1991).

Although the picture is far from being clear it appears that between 1,500 and 1,000 BC in Québec and Ontario regional developments out of Middle Great Lakes-St.Lawrence culture established the cultural base for the subsequent culture of Period IV. It was during this time that the manufacturing of clay pottery cooking vessels was introduced from the south. The appearance of pottery on archaeological sites provides a convenient technological basis for distinguishing earlier Archaic (pre-pottery) sites from later Woodland (pottery) sites even though no significant changes in way of life are evident.

Middle Great Lakes-St.Lawrence culture radiocarbon dates from Québec, which include the

Vergennes and Brewerton phases as well as later phases, range from just prior to the beginning of Period III to 1,750 BC (Clermont et Chapdelaine 1982; Marois 1987; Piérard et al. 1987; Rutherford et al. 1984; Wilmeth 1978). Dates from sites east of the Niagara Escarpment in Southern Ontario range from 3,500 to 2,000 BC (Johnston 1984; Johnston and Cassavoy 1978; Wilmeth 1978) while radiocarbon dates pertaining to post Brewerton phase sites west of the Escarpment range from 2,250 to 1,000 BC (Ellis et al. 1990; Kenyon 1959; Lennox 1986; Ramsden 1976; Wilmeth 1978; Wright 1972). Due to the proliferation of radiocarbon dates from Period III sites onward only directly pertinent readings from adjacent states will be included in the text. The dates from the important Frontenac Island site in New York (Ritchie 1965) are excluded due to archaeological context problems.

Technology:

It is convenient to examine Middle Great Lakes-St.Lawrence culture within three segments of time; 4,000 to 3,500 BC, 3,500 to 2,000 BC, and 2,000 to 1,000 BC. These segments of time correlate with what are known as the Vergennes phase, the Brewerton phase, and a Terminal phase with a number of different names.

I. Vergennes phase (4,000 to 3,500 BC): It has been speculated that the early phase of Middle Great Lakes St.Lawrence culture evolved from Early Great Lakes-St.Lawrence culture (Proto-Laurentian Archaic) in response to stress stemming from unspecified environmental change. Technological adjustments involved the adoption of gouges and other wood working implements, ground slate knives, lances, and projectile points, plummets, stone spearthrower weights, and an increasing diversity in the chipped stone tool kit (Funk 1988: 35). Changes in technology were more likely the product of an innate cultural tendency rather than any significant adjustment to environmental change. This cultural tendency of Middle Great Lakes-St.Lawrence culture was a readiness to adopt technological traits from neighbouring cultures. Gouges and points, lances, and knives of ground slate as well as plummets appear to have been adopted from contemporary Middle Maritime culture and, to some extent, Early Maritime culture. The procedures necessary to fashion native copper implements, as well as the specific implement styles, were borrowed from the people of the Upper Great Lakes including Middle Shield culture. From the south came the polished stone spearthrower weights, commonly called bannerstones, and probably manos and pestles.

Vergennes phase sites, such as the Allumette Island-1 site in the Ottawa Valley in Québec (Kennedy 1970), the Otter Creek 2 site in Vermont (Ritchie 1979), and the Hirundo site in Maine (Sanger and MacKay 1979) are often regarded as `classic Laurentian Archaic´ sites because of their relatively high frequencies of `diagnostic´ ground stone tools. As Table 2 illustrates the combined frequencies of these `diagnostic´ tool categories actually represent only a minor element in the total tool kit. The sites compared on the Table, KI and Otter Creek 2, are located in close proximity to one another in western Vermont (Haviland and Power 1981; Ritchie 1968; 1979). High frequencies of hammerstones at both sites correlate with the abundant chipping detritus indicative of stone tool manufacturing. The tool categories adopted from other cultures but regarded as being diagnostic of the Vergennes phase represent 16.9% and 13.5% of the KI and Otter Creek No.2 site tool kits, respectively. It was during the Vergennes phase that these traits became relatively common. The less impressive chipped stone projectile points and knives account for more than half of the total tool kits at both sites. Given the rather parochial nature of the chipped stone component of the tool assemblage it is perhaps understandable why archaeologists have placed an excessive reliance upon the more exotic ground stone tool categories.

The distinctive broad side-notched, concave based, chipped projectile point with strong basal and lateral grinding characteristic of the Vergennes phase is a widely distributed projectile point form "...of the central and northern Mississippi Valley..." (Ritchie 1965: 87). Similar points have been recovered from sites in the Saint John River Valley of New Brunswick, the northern New England states into the Eastern Townships and the Upper St.Lawrence Valley of Québec, and across New York and Southern Ontario. Most of the recoveries are from the surface of sites but in those instances where dates were obtained they generally fall in the 4,000 to 3,500 BC range or earlier. Exposure by the plough of the earliest forms of ground stone implements in the Eastern Townships of Québec (Levesque 1962) and across Southern Ontario (Wright 1962), such as the full-grooved gouge and certain forms of ground slate projectile points, bayonets, and ulus, suggests that a number of the Québec and Ontario sites would qualify for placement within the more restricted classification of Laurentian Archaic (Ritchie 1971a).

The two excavated Vermont sites were practically devoid of bone other than small calcined fragments but the Allumette Island-1 site in the Ottawa Valley was characterized by good bone preservation. In addition to the typical side-notched chipped points, spearthrower weights, ground slate ulus, gouges, chipped stone knives and scrapers, hammerstones, and `numerous abraders´, a large inventory of bone and copper tools were represented among the more than 3,000 artifacts (Kennedy n.d.). Included in the bone tool kit were delicate unilaterally and bilaterally barbed harpoons lacking line holes, beaver incisor tools, gorges, eyed needles, gouges, awls, and bi-pointed projectile points. Of considerable importance at the Allumette-1 Island site were the more than one thousand copper tools exclusive of numerous beads. Abundant copper wastage in the form of flakes and flattened nuggets indicates that copper imported from Lake Superior was being fashioned into tools at the site. The close correspondences in both tool variety and form and the cold hammering- annealing method of manufacture with that of the Upper Great Lakes suggests the existence of an intimate relationship with contemporary Middle Shield culture peoples to the west. Copper items consisted of the following: numerous beads and gorges, the latter being a bi-pointed form of fishhook; 122 projectile points of which the majority were conical in form with the remainder possessing tanged or open-socketed hafting slots for the wooden spear shafts; a unique toggling harpoon with a basal fluke and a line hole somewhat reminiscent of later Middle Maritime culture

ARTIFACT CLASS	KI		OTTER CREEK 2	
	f	%	f	%
Chipped stone points	76	34.7	69	36.1
Chipped stone knives	41	18.7	35	18.3
Ground slate points*	20	9.1	9	4.7
Ground stone rods	20	9.1	2	1.0
Hammerstones	15	6.8	30	15.7
Scrapers	7	3.2	14	7.3
Spearthrower weights*	7	3.2	1	.5
Celts	7	3.2	3	1.6
Ground slate ulus*	4	1.8	6	3.1
Abraders	3	1.4	6	3.1
Gouges*	3	1.4	4	2.1
Anvilstones	3	1.4	-	-
Preforms	2	.9	-	-
Drills	2	.9	1	.5
Pestles	2	.9	-	-
Plummets*	2	.9	1	.5
Hammer/anvil/mano	2	.9	1	.5
Perforated stone	1	.5	-	-
Chopper	1	.5	3	1.6
Copper gorges*	1	.5	5	2.6
Graphite paintstone	-	-	1	.5
TOTALS	219	100.0	191	99.7

TABLE 2: ARTIFACT CLASS FREQUENCIES AT THE KI AND OTTER CREEK 2 SITES, VERMONT Implement categories regarded as Middle Great Lakes-St. Lawrence culture diagnostics but which actually represent borrowed traits from neighbouring cultures are marked with an asterisk.

bone toggling harpoon heads (Tuck 1976: Plate 26); eyeless needles; small knives with hafting tangs; perforators; socketed and unsocketed adzes; composite fishhook barbs; both eyed and eyeless fishhooks; awls; punches; and pendants. Metallurgical examination of two specimens indicated that they had been annealed. The fact that at this early period of copper-working heat would be used to increase the malleability of the metal, which becomes increasingly brittle with cold-hammering, should not come as a particular surprise. From earliest times to the coming of Europeans many siliceous stones, particularly chert, were baked in pit ovens in order to alter the crystal structure in a fashion that improved the chipping characteristics. It appears that a similar procedure was used to offset the copper becoming too brittle as a result of the cold-hammering process.

The Allumette-1 Island site and its descendant Brewerton phase neighbour, the Morrison's Island-6 site, are particularly important to an understanding of Middle Great Lakes-St.Lawrence culture as they represent relatively isolated segments of time within a lengthy cultural development and occur in close proximity to one another. This is unlike most other sites that contain the hopelessly mixed accumulated debris of thousands of years of seasonal occupations. In this instance isostatic uplift eventually blocked the drainage of the Upper Great Lakes via the Ottawa River shortly after 3,000 BC (Hough 1963) and affected water discharge volumes in the River and, thus, the locations of rapids. Summer base camps were generally located at rapids in order to harvest the fish concentrations. The unusual situation on the Ottawa River is indicated by evidence such as, "In the Pembroke region Laurentian sites are at least 14 m above the level of the Ottawa River. Artifacts pertaining to this tradition have not been found on lower terraces nor along present beaches of lakes Allumette, Coulonge, Chats and Deschenes, widenings of the Ottawa River. This situation may be due to greater flow during drainage of the Nipissing Great Lakes into the Ottawa Valley. For example, at the Allumette Island-1 Site, about 14 m above river level, the Indians dug pits through a shallow soil that contains numerous spalled bedrock fragments. If the sand deposit of a slightly lower elevation terrace had been clear of water some 5000 years ago, it would have been much easier for the indians to dig firepits and burial pits there, rather than in the stony soils in which the pits are found" (Barnett and Kennedy 1987: 51).

Another important site with a Vergennes phase occupation is situated at Coteau-du-Lac on the St.Lawrence River 48 km above Montréal (Lueger 1977; Marois 1987). Unfortunately most of the early archaeological remains were disturbed during the construction of a British fort in the early 1800's and became mixed with later cultural debris. The presence of early side- notched projectile points, ridged and unridged ground slate ulus, certain forms of ground slate projectile points, blanks for slate points, ground slate rods, knife forms, bi-pointed bone projectile points, delicate unilaterally barbed harpoons with truncated barbs, and copper fishhooks with attachment eyes, all attest to a Vergennes phase occupation. Some of the stone implements, however, can also be attributed to Middle Maritime culture and are, thus, indicative of culture contact. Of interest is the fact that five of the six plummets are represented by the grooved attachment portion of the implement suggesting that the objects were not only subjected to rough

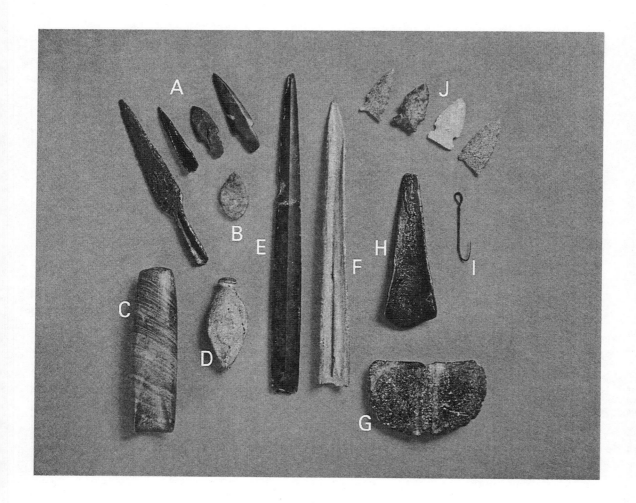

BLACK AND WHITE PLATE XI: TYPICAL MIDDLE GREAT LAKES-ST. LAWRENCE CULTURE TOOLS All of the illustrated specimens are from sites in southern Québec and Ontario and include the following: `a´ - chipped stone projectile points; `b´ - two ground slate points to the left and two copper points to the right; `c´ - a copper fishhook; `d´ - a small sandstone abrader grooved at the top for suspension from a cord; `e´ - a copper gouge; `f´ - a stone plummet; `g´ - a polished slate spearthrower weight; `h´ - a bone dagger; `i´ - a ground slate bayonet; and `j´ - a polished stone gouge. (Reproduced from Wright 1979: Plate 4)

usage but were apparently attached to a line and could be thus retrieved. This indirectly suggests the use of these problematical objects, in this instance, as sinkers attached to fishing lines.

The location of Vergennes phase sites on islands that would only be occupied during the warm months of the year indicates the existence of watercraft. This inference has been reinforced by the recovery of an "...Archaic type ground slate tool..." from the Rideau Lakes area on to which was etched a drawing of a watercraft containing six people (Watson 1990: Figure 9).

II. Brewerton phase (3,500 to 2,000 BC): Brewerton phase evolved directly out of the Vergennes phase through a gradual process of artifact style changes and a decreasing importance of the ground slate industry. The best evidence for this technological transition comes from the comparison of the aforementioned Allumette Island-1 site (Kennedy n.d.) and the Morrison's Island-6 site (Kennedy 1962; 1966) situated less than 1.6 km apart on different islands in the Ottawa River. Calendar adjusted dates for the Allumette Island-1 and Morrison's Island-6 sites are 4,000 BC and 3,500 BC, respectively. Both archaeological and physical anthropological (Pfeiffer 1977: 272) evidence suggests that the two sites represent the same population but removed in time by approximately 500 years. By early Brewerton phase times burial practices had changed as had the following technological traits: the form of the side-notched chipped projectile points; the appearance of a range of corner-notched and stemmed projectile points; the earlier conical copper projectile point form was replaced by stemmed forms; large chipped stone knives and spearthrower weights disappeared although the latter absence is more likely due to non-recovery than non-existence; sandstone abraders used in fashioning copper implements and beaver incisor tools acquire suspension holes and grooves; adze-like scrapers and drills appear; unilaterally barbed harpoons with line holes replaced earlier harpoon forms; the bi-pointed bone projectile point disappeared while the bone fishhook and flute appear for the first time as do incised designs on bone, stone, and copper implements; and copper ornaments, such as bracelets and finger rings, make their first appearance. Other traits, like copper axes, gorges, compound fishhooks, fishhooks, awls, small knives and needles, some with eyes at the later site, ground slate ulus, adzes, plummets, and many of the bone tools, particularly beaver incisor knives, are present on both sites. Allowing for a certain unknown amount of time depth at the two sites the technological conservatism represented in the 500 year interval separating them is impressive.

At a Brewerton phase fishing station on the Richelieu River (Clermont 1974) broad notched projectile points were recovered along with gouges, a ground slate bayonet, a plummet, some choppers, end scrapers, a few drills, and an abundance of flat stone cutting implements believed to have functioned as fish processing knives. The 2,250 BC Cadieux site upriver from Montréal produced ground slate projectile points, a gouge, and Brewerton and Vosburg phase projectile points (Piérard et al. 1987). A pit feature with a dog burial also contained worked beaver and porcupine incisors, a worked bear canine, bone gouges, fishhooks, a harpoon, a worked deer toe bone, and an awl.

In western Southern Ontario Brewerton phase type projectile points have been recovered that were water-tumbled by the Nipissing transgression of Lake Huron. Such specimens can be dated on geological grounds to sometime prior to 3,000 BC when lake waters encroached on former dry land (Ellis and Deller 1986).

The concentration of Brewerton phase sites in New York is in the central, western, and northern regions of the state. As in Canada projectile points tend to become smaller through time and there is an increase in the occurrences of certain ground stone tools such as gouges, adzes, axes, pestles, manos, and anvil stones. Throughout both areas spearthrower weights tend to be represented by a few simple forms although west of the Niagara Escarpment in Southern Ontario the number of different styles rapidly proliferates (Wright 1962). There appears to be an increased use of heated rocks for cooking and hearths composed of firestone pavements become common.

The thirteen dog burials from the Frontenac Island site in New York (Ritchie 1945: 7-8) represented two breeds which, in terms of size, fell into the terrier and shepherd ranges. In addition to the two dog burials from Brewerton in New York near Lake Ontario, dog coprolites or faeces were preserved by the bones in the fish the dogs had been fed.

III. Terminal phase (2,000 to 1,000 BC): The introduction of pottery cooking vessels into the region around 1,000 BC terminates the preceramic period and, for classificatory convenience, initiates Late Great Lakes-St.Lawrence culture. Prior to this event the terminal Archaic or late preceramic phase in Québec, Ontario, and environs is characterized by regional divergence from a Brewerton phase cultural base. Cultural regionalism, of course, existed prior to this time and is most apparent in Southern Ontario as an east-west split on either side of the Niagara Escarpment (Wright 1962). The most striking phenomenon of the Terminal phase is the intrusion of Susquehanna Archaic influences. Originating on the southeastern Atlantic coastal plain this complex with its large, broad stemmed projectile points, distinctive preforms, occasional soapstone cooking vessels and zoomorphic pestles, did penetrate the Upper St.Lawrence Valley and Southern Ontario between 2,000 and 1,500 BC. The nature of the penetration, however, is still a matter of considerable debate. Evidence of a discrete, intrusive Susquehanna Archaic derived complex, often referred to as Broad Point in Ontario or Québec, is not convincing (Clermont et Chapdelaine 1982; I. Kenyon 1980) as it is largely based upon the recovery of the distinctive projectile points from disturbed multi-component sites. An exception to the forgoing may be a Susquehanna Archaic burial in the Gaspé (Dumais 1978). Although the evidence is equivocal it is likely that the sudden appearance of these distinctive broad points pertain to the adoption of an innovative weapon system and an associated hunting strategy by local Middle Great Lakes-St.Lawrence culture people rather than representing an actual penetration into the area of Susquehanna Archaic populations. Unlike the high frequencies of exotic, southern cherts associated with the appearance of the intrusive Southern Early Archaic complex during

Period II most of the chipped stone associated with the appearance of the Broad Point complex are local in origin supporting the likelihood of diffusion of concepts rather than invasion.

Most sites in Québec and Ontario belonging to this time period are situated at favourable fishing and/or hunting locales. As a result it is impossible, in most instances, to isolate individual components. Attempts to use typology or material of manufacture as criterion for cultural separation are fraught with a number of hazardous assumptions (Clermont et Chapdelaine 1982) and inevitably lead to incomplete and potentially misleading cultural reconstructions. Like the partial component isolation of the Vergennes and Brewerton phases at the Allumette Island-1 and Morrison's Island-6 sites on the Ottawa River a happy combination of natural events has resulted in clear component isolation of sites along the coast of Lake Huron (Kenyon 1959; Ramsden 1976; Wright 1972). Seasonally available food at these coastal sites attracted people to the same locales over periods as long as 1,000 years. Sites faced the Lake, usually adjacent to a stream, and wind-blown sands from the exposed beach capped the sequential archaeological deposits to create exceptionally well stratified sites. In addition, the well- drained, neutral soils of the area permitted excellent bone preservation. The technology is characterized by small notched projectile points, triangular knives and/or preforms, end scrapers, bone gorges, composite fishhooks, bone projectile points, beaver incisor knives, birdbone beads, awls, antler flakers, linear flakes, rare native copper items such as fishhooks and awls, anvil stones, wedges, antler shaft-straighteners, and a marked but late increase in the use of large quartzite cobble spall tools. An outstanding characteristic, which is also found on contemporary sites to the south, was the extensive use of cobbles for cooking, much of it coming from large pits used as bake ovens (Ellis et al. 1990: 112). In addition to the evidence of the use of trot and handline fishing in the form of bone gorges and composite hook elements are the abundant stone net sinkers which can be most reasonably interpreted as evidence of the use of gill nets. As the water levels of Lake Huron fell through time and changed the local ecology the importance of fishing decreased relative to hunting (Figure 28).

In addition to a burial of a shepherd sized dog from one site another site contained numerous dog faeces preserved by the bones in the fish the dogs were being fed (Wright 1972). An examination of a sample of this faecal material failed to produce evidence of parasitic tapeworm eggs (Patrick D. Horne: personal communication). Later in time, across Lake Huron at the Schultz site in Michigan, Diphyllobothrium latum eggs were identified in faecal material (McClary 1972). This widespread tapeworm parasite occurs throughout the Great Lakes and can infect humans as readily as dogs (Horne 1985: 305).

At a Terminal phase site in western Southern Ontario, inferred to represent a winter band occupation (Lennox 1986), notched projectile points and utilized flakes dominated the tool kit along with appreciable numbers of scrapers, preforms, and spokeshaves. Drills, denticulates, gravers, and perforators were more weakly represented.

There has been a tendency to restrict comparisons of the Small Point complex of the Terminal phase in the western portion of Southern Ontario to contemporary sites in adjacent Michigan and Ohio (Ellis et al. 1990). While a western relationship is apparent (see Wobst 1968) comparative evidence to the east has been largely ignored. Many of the projectile point styles from the Brewerton phase Morrison's Island-6 site (Kennedy 1966), for example, closely resemble the late notched points found to the west in terms of both form and metrical attributes (I. Kenyon 1989: Table 2). If comparisons had been limited to the chipped stone projectile points from the Ottawa Valley site and the `Small Point´ sites west of the Niagara Escarpment a relationship would undoubtedly have been noted. East-west differences do exist and from earliest times during Period III distributional studies indicate that polished stone gouges are more common east of the Escarpment while stone spearthrower weights are predominantly a western tool category (Wright 1962: Table 1 and Map 2). Other polished stone tool categories, including projectile points, bayonets, ulus, and plummets, while more common to the east of the Niagara Escarpment do have a widespread occurrence in the west. It would appear that the excavation of Vergennes and Brewerton phase sites in the east and Terminal phase sites in the west, compounded by the difficulties of component isolation and the cultural weighting of ground stone tools, are mainly responsible for the impression of a sharp east-west cultural dichotomy. Future excavation will likely reveal closer relationships across the Lower Great Lakes and Upper St.Lawrence Valley.

Subsistence:

Archaeological inferences regarding what people ate and in what quantities during what seasons of the year are affected by a number of factors; acid soils, absent or incomplete faunal analyses, small samples, faunal materials being recovered from mixed cultural deposits where assignment to a specific culture is impossible, insufficient evidence to determine season(s) of occupation, and ritualistic discard of the bones of certain species or as dictated by special circumstances. Ethnographic information indicates that only a portion of the food eaten by people would have left any archaeological record such as bones, shells, or charred plant remains. This is particularly true of the winter food supplies consisting of such archaeologically invisible food stocks as dried and smoked meat, dried berries and roots, animal oils, etc. Attempts to estimate the relative importance of hunting, fishing, and gathering based upon inferred tool function (e.g. projectile points = hunting, grinding tools like metates and manos = plant processing, notched pebbles inferred to be net sinkers = fishing, etc.) (Ritchie 1965) are subject to variables that simply do not permit a simple one-to-one correlation of quantification of tool categories with types of food. Direct faunal and floral evidence and assumptions regarding subsistence inferred from site locations are still the two best indicators of subsistence practices. The vast majority of excavated archaeological sites, however, represent spring to fall occupations and the physical remains of food animals are, in most instances, only a rough indication of the relative importance of various species throughout the year. Due to both preservation and, until recently, inadequate archaeological recovery techniques, the role of plant

BLACK AND WHITE PLATE XII: DOG BURIAL This large male dog was buried in a Terminal phase Middle Great Lakes-St.Lawrence site near the shore of Lake Huron. Dogs probably entered the Western Hemisphere with the first people. As a comrade in the hunt, a guardian of the camp, and, in some instances, a cartage animal, the dog was frequently accorded the same treatment upon death as humans. During times of dire need or ceremonial requirements, however, this first animal to be domesticated by human beings could become food. (Reproduced from Wright 1972: Plate 4.)

---

materials in the diet has been undoubtedly underestimated. The discovery of squash rind (<u>Cucurbita</u> <u>sp.</u>) more than 6,000 years old from the Sharrow site in Maine (Petersen 1991), with an antiquity similar to that of the earliest squash dates from the Mississippi Valley, raises the possibility of the existence of early incipient horticulture among Archaic populations across much of eastern North America including western Southern Ontario. On Period II sites, such as the McCulley No.1 site in southern New York, charred butternut shells and anvil stones interpreted as nut cracking tools, have been reported (Funk and Hoagland 1972). There is also a tentative suggestion that prior to 4,000 BC the oyster beds of the lower Hudson Valley were being exploited (Brennan 1974). Thus, even before Period III there is evidence that people were already exploiting a very wide range of food resources.

I. Vergennes phase (4,000 to 3,500 BC): There is very little direct faunal evidence from sites of this period. A faunal analysis of the important Allumette-1 Island site (Kennedy n.d.) has not been undertaken but the location of the site in a prime fishing area and the abundance of bone gorges, fishhooks, composite fishhook elements, and harpoons, does suggest that fish were likely the major reason for the occupation. Numerous beaver incisor tools also indicate the trapping of this animal with its highly nutritious fatty flesh. Such incisor tools, however, probably do not constitute evidence of beaver hunting at the site from which they are recovered. Deer remains were most common at the Otter Creek No.2 site in Vermont with bear, beaver, muskrat, possible dog, turkey, some birds and turtle being present although bone preservation was poor (Ritchie 1979). While the Hirundo site in Maine lacked bone preservation its location beside a major rapid suggests that anadromous fish, such as shad, alewife, and salmon were the attraction and, if so, the site would have been occupied from spring to fall. There are frequent ethnographic references to northern people establishing the women, children and older people at a favourable fishing location to tend the fish nets and traps and process the fish while the hunters ranged out along the waterways in search of other food resources including big game. A similar pattern appears to have been in place by Vergennes times and likely earlier.

II. Brewerton phase (3,500 to 2,000 BC): The McIntyre site overlooking Rice Lake in eastern Southern Ontario (Johnston 1984) has provided a number of insights into Middle Great Lakes -St.Lawrence culture subsistence. Although a multi-component site the major occupation pertains to the Brewerton phase. This is suggested by both projectile point types and radiocarbon dates that place the occupation at 2,000 BC. Pit fill from features below the plough zone was flotated in order to recover carbonized plant and animal fragments so small that they are generally not recovered using less sophisticated excavation methods. Flotation methods used in the field are variable depending on site characteristics and the preference of the excavator but all use water to float and screen small particles from archaeological deposits including soil fill from features like pits and hearths. Faunal remains from the McIntyre site were limited due to acid soils but quantities of carbonized plant materials were recovered from the pits. A spring to fall occupation is suggested by the food remains as well as the site size, the concentration of cooking pits, and the continuity of occupation. Plant foods consisted of butternut and acorn with lesser frequencies of hickory, hazel, and beech nuts, lambsquarters, grape, raspberry-blackberry, hawthorn, plum, cherry, blueberry, and sumac. There was a particularly high incidence of chenopod (lambsquarters) and cleaver seeds. It has been speculated that selective cutting and clearing of the forest would have encouraged the growth of many of the desirable species and that, "This opening, or rejuvenation, of the forest resulted in some subsistence enrichment" (Yarnell 1984: 109). Butternut, acorn, and *Chenopodium gigantospermum* were the major plant foods used. Butternut is the most nutritious of all local nuts. The abundant bedstraw seeds (*Galium spp.*) are believed to represent bedding material. Wild rice was absent despite the plant's current abundance in the adjacent lake. Either wild rice was not exploited or was not available at the site 4,000 years ago or for unknown cultural reasons or chance has simply not survived in the archaeological record. Given the quantity of plant materials recovered it is difficult to conceive that wild rice remains could have been missed if it were present. The findings from the McIntyre site suggest that although there was a greater variety and abundance of nut bearing trees in western Southern Ontario (Ellis et al. 1990: 91) plant materials were also extensively exploited in the east.

Limited faunal remains from the McIntyre site indicated deer was most important followed by bear, beaver, and possibly dog (Naylor and Savage 1984). In addition, a young dog burial was encountered in one of the pits. Flotated small bone fragments from the pit features identified the importance of fall net fishing for relatively small fish (Waselkov 1984). It has been speculated that the occupants of the McIntyre site may have been responsible for the Atherley Narrows fish weirs 175 km by water to the northwest (Johnston 1984: 81). These weirs, situated in the Narrows between Lake Simcoe and Lake Couchiching, were first documented by Samuel de Champlain in AD 1615 (Biggar 1929). Underwater archaeological reconnaissance of the floor of the original channel of the Narrows encountered an elaborate weir system (Johnston and Cassavoy 1978). Radiocarbon dating of weir stakes provided readings of 3,200 BC. These dates, however, pertain to a single major structure (Figure 27) and there were many other weir stakes on the floor of the channel that belonged to different weir systems. Some stakes had even been cut with iron tools. Under the circumstances the early weir dates and the 2,000 BC estimates from the McIntyre site pit features do not negate the possibility that people from the latter site were involved in some of the weir construction and use. Unfortunately a section of the Narrows was dredged in the 19th century, a process that would have obliterated any archaeological evidence. On the other hand, a band territory exploitation range extending 175 km from a base camp is probably too excessive for the time period and region in question. Weir features would likely have been important in the seasonal rounds of most Middle Great Lakes-St.Lawrence culture bands regardless of which band or bands exploited the weirs at the Narrows.

The aforementioned weir calls for a digression. First, submerged wood is protected from bacterial decomposition by a lack of oxygen thus permitting 5,000 year old wooden weir stakes to survive to this day. Second, Johnston and Cassavoy did little or no underwater excavation but simply plotted the weir stakes that extended above the floor of the channel. Probing did indicate stakes under the mud surface and it can be anticipated that the weir configuration in Figure 27 would be more compact if these stakes had also been recorded. The weir was constructed of maple, birch, cedar, elm, and beech poles ranging from 1.3 to 7.6 cm in diameter with an average of 3.8 cm. Stakes were thrust from 15.2 to more than 61.0 cm into the floor of the channel and extended diagonally for 55 m across the channel. The weir lines began at an underwater constructed stone platform 4.6 m wide intended to prevent the fishermen, likely women, from sinking into the soft mud. A narrow gap existed between the two weir lines and the stone platform where traps and/or nets would be set to intercept fish being channelled to the trap area by the wings of the weir. The wings were oriented to channel fish either travelling with or against the current. Although it is suggested that the weir was used in the spring (Johnston and Cassavoy 1978: 707) when spring spawners such as pickerel, suckers, catfish, perch, and pike were available such an early warm season activity would not contribute to winter food stocks. Fall spawners, such as cisco or lake herring, could have provided much needed high quality protein for the winter. It is a matter of documented record that lake herring were once extremely abundant in the Narrows in late fall and early winter (Hammond 1917: 55). Unfortunately the fish remains from an adjacent land site excavation, dating to a later time period, have not been identified to species. The abundance of fish heads and the scarcity of body parts at this site, however, clearly indicates that the fish were being processed for consumption elsewhere (Wright 1972b). Given the 8 to 12 inch size of the lake herring or cisco (Scott and Crossman 1973: 236) it is not likely much bone could be anticipated in camp refuse as the bones would probably have been consumed along with the dried flesh. If the process of preserving fish by smoking and/or air drying was practiced a major high protein food would have been available as an important part of the winter food requirements. It is known from historically documented accounts that weirs were capable of providing enormous quantities of fish during spawning runs. An innovation, such as fishing weirs, would have had an impact upon settlement distributions and other aspects of culture as well as have contributed to population increase. When weirs were first introduced into the region is unknown. Unfortunately, likely weir site locations are in areas subjected to considerable recent disturbance by channel, dam, and mill construction.

At the disturbed Coteau-du-Lac site upriver from Montréal (Lueger 1977; Marois 1987) the majority of the faunal remains likely pertain to the Brewerton phase occupation. A study of the fish remains from the site (Scott 1977) suggests it owed its existence to the rich fish resources of the area. Channel catfish and redhorse suckers were most common with smallmouth bass, rock bass, and drum also being well represented. In terms of calories all fish species are not equal. Redhorse suckers have between 400 and 500 calories per pound but channel catfish are double this caloric value. The most abundant fish species indicate a spring to early summer occupation but the presence of Atlantic eel (Anquillia rostrata) also suggests summer to fall fishing. It would be a useful archaeological venture to examine the river bed adjacent to the site for possible remnants of weirs and/or traps. The incomplete faunal analysis from this site noted the following occurrences by class: mammal (63.0); fish (30.0); turtle (6.0); bird (1.0); and amphibian (present) (Lueger 1977: 15-16). Among the identified species were muskrat, beaver, otter, deer, bear, canine (likely dog), raccoon, woodchuck, moose, passenger pigeon, geese, ducks, swans, and grouse. The 343 beaver incisor tools constituted the largest single tool category from the site and also imply a large quantity of fat rich meat not to mention cloaks and sleeping robes. At the Cadieux site, a related site further up the St.Lawrence River, a large pit contained a wide range of animal remains consisting mainly of beaver, deer, and fish but also including caribou, molluscs, bear, muskrat, turtle, and mink (Piérard et al. 1987).

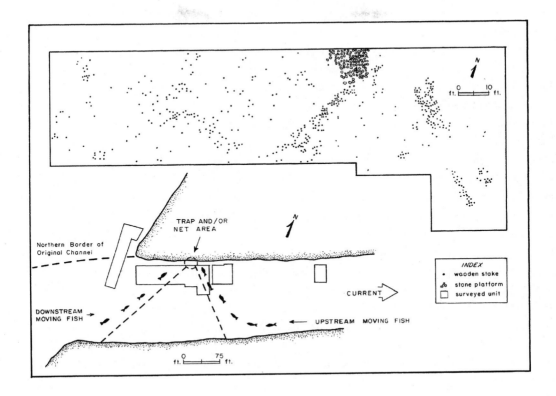

FIGURE 27: A MIDDLE GREAT LAKES-ST.LAWRENCE FISHWEIR AT ATHERLEY NARROWS, ONTARIO Although the underwater floorplan of the wooden stakes of the fishweir in `A´ may appear confusing, this is due to the continuous use and repair of the weirs at this particular location in the channel between Lake Simcoe and Lake Couchiching as well as the fact that stakes covered by mud were not mapped. Sufficient evidence was recorded to recognize a major Middle Great Lakes-St.Lawrence culture weir complex dating to 3,250 BC. The schematic diagram `B´ illustrates how fish moving both upstream and downstream were channelled to the trap area that was provided with a layer of rocks in order that the people tending the trap or net would not sink into the soft mud on the edge of the channel floor. (Adapted, in part, from Johnston and Cassavoy 1978: Figure 3. Drawn by David W. Laverie.)

III. Terminal phase (2,000 to 1,000 BC): Stratified Terminal phase sites on the Lake Huron coast (Kenyon 1959; Ramsden 1976; Wright 1972) span the period from 2,000 BC to shortly after 1,000 BC. Early occupations of these sites exploited spring spawning fish, such as drum, channel catfish, pickerel, and suckers but as falling Lake levels modified the local fish habitat people came to rely increasingly upon land mammals (Figure 28). It is rare that ecological change leaves such a striking record at archaeological sites. In the Ausable River region further south on the Lake Huron coast sites are located "...on or near moraines, major rivers, sand plains and glacial beach lines" (I. Kenyon 1980a: 19). The range of locations is inferred to relate to the ecological diversity of the region. Nuts, such as those of white oak, shagbark hickory, sweet chestnut, and black walnut with their associated deer and turkey populations, are regarded as the major factors determining the location of Terminal phase `Broad Point´ sites although it must be noted that related sites also occur to the east with its more limited nut bearing tree species (Clermont et Chapdelaine 1982; Watson 1981). Throughout much of Southern Ontario the frequent small campsites associated with springs and small streams on well-drained soils have been interpreted as winter deer hunting camps (Roberts 1980). Other sites, like the Surma site in Fort Erie (Emerson and Noble 1966), on the other hand, cannot be associated with a particular portion of the subsistence round and undoubtedly owe their existence to other necessary resources such as, in this instance, the outcrops of high quality Onondaga chert.

While charred walnut shells were recorded from the Davidson site near Lake Huron (I. Kenyon 1980a: 19) and other sites the recovery of plant materials from Terminal phase sites is relatively limited. There are reasons to suspect, however, that plant materials were far more important than the current direct evidence would suggest (Chomko and Crawford 1978; McBride 1978) and that even the possibility of plant husbandry existed (Barber 1977; Petersen 1991: 141-143). Only the flotation of large quantities of feature fill from archaeological sites will throw light on this facet of subsistence.

Settlement patterns:

Although the evidence is equivocal there appears to be a difference between Middle Great Lakes-St.Lawrence culture settlement patterns on either side of the Niagara Escarpment. In eastern Southern Ontario and the Upper St.Lawrence Valley of Québec large, warm weather base camp sites on rivers or large lakes, appear to be the rule while to the west such sites are rare except for the Lake Huron coastal sites of the Bruce Peninsula. Even though the continuously rising waters of the Lower Great Lakes and fluctuations in the water levels of the Upper Great Lakes, with their associated drainage changes (Karrow and Warner 1990: 20-21), have undoubtedly obscured part of the archaeological record, these changes do not appear to be sufficient to totally account for the east-west differences. It may be that the more extensive mast forests of the west, with their greater densities of deer and certain other resources, permitted a more dispersed seasonal settlement pattern that was not as reliant upon fish as in the east.

I. Vergennes phase (4,000 to 3,500 BC): Largely on the basis of the distribution of the distinctive side-notched projectile points it has been suggested that Vergennes phase settlement patterns in New

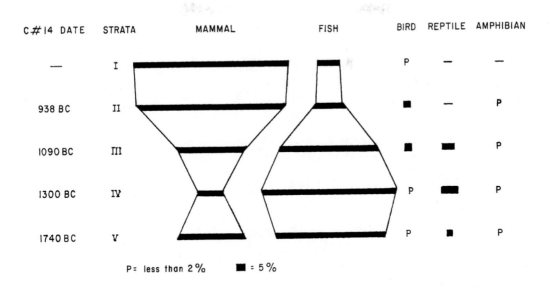

FIGURE 28: CHANGING SUBSISTENCE THROUGH TIME AT THE KNECHTEL I SITE The adage that nothing stays the same is upheld by the evidence from the Knechtel I site on the Lake Huron coast. This stratified Middle Great Lakes-St.Lawrence culture campsite was occupied from 2,000 to after 1,000 BC. The falling water levels of Lake Huron during this period progressively reduced the availability of fish, forcing people to increasingly rely upon land mammals for their sustenance. The earliest and latest strata at the site are Strata V and I, respectively. (Reproduced from Wright 1987: Figure 2)

York involved warm weather fish camps along major streams and lakes followed by interior winter camps (Funk 1976: 238). A similar pattern applies to Québec and eastern Southern Ontario. Sites, such as the Allumette-1 Island site on the Ottawa River, the Coteau-du-Lac site on the St.Lawrence River, the Percy Reach site on the Trent River, and island sites on Rice Lake (Ritchie 1949; personal examination) all represent major warm weather camps or camp areas situated adjacent to excellent fishing and other resources. Such site locations also facilitate mobility, including the portability of goods, through the use of watercraft. The Hirundo site in Maine (Sanger and MacKay 1979) has also been identified as a major spring to summer fishing station. It has been hypothesized that the spread of the Vergennes phase into Maine correlated with the northward shift of a hardwood dominated forest that would have favoured deer over moose or caribou (Sanger 1979: 30). Others have argued for an in situ development of Vergennes out of local Middle Archaic complexes (Cox 1991). The 3,750 BC Vergennes phase sites in interior New

Brunswick and northern Maine are situated on tributaries and headwater lakes frequently adjacent to major marshes. On one of these sites a possible 4 m to 5 m diameter tent ring was recorded (Ibid: 147). In contrast, the KI site in Vermont (Ritchie 1965: 85; Ritchie and Funk 1973: 340) has been interpreted as a winter hunt camp seasonally occupied by a single band. Covering approximately an acre the site also contained a `possible´ house structure 4.6 m in diameter demarcated by post moulds. As the structure was capped with a low mound of earth it has been speculated that it represents the remains of an earth covered lodge. Another probable winter settlement is the small Parrish site in northeastern New York (Weinman and Weinmen 1970). This single component site, situated within 1.6 km of the Fort Ann chert deposits, produced abundant evidence of stone tool manufacturing and a somewhat limited tool kit of the typical side-notched points, some slate scrapers, a knife, a hammerstone, an abrader, and a chipped ulu.

II. Brewerton phase (3,500 to 2,000 BC): Settlement patterns during this period appear to be unchanged from Vergennes times. Indeed, one of the major problems facing archaeologists is the fact that all of these people tended to camp at the same sites as their ancestors. This, in itself, suggests considerable stability through time of at least the warm weather portion of the settlement strategy. The two to three acre Robinson and Oberlander 1 sites, situated at the outlet of Oneida Lake, represent the largest Brewerton phase fishing base camps in New York (Ritchie 1940; Ritchie and Funk 1973: 339-340). Both sites contained the entire record of human occupation in the region except for Palaeo-Indian culture. Within the thick layers of cultural debris patches of sand or gravel 1.8 m to 3.1 m in diameter associated with refuse may represent the remains of house floors. Other features, such as pits and small hearths, were relatively rare. None of the firestone hearths and baking pits recorded at the O'Neil site (Ritchie and Funk 1973) of central New York, were encountered at either Robinson or Oberlander 1. As the 2,500 BC O'Neil site has been interpreted as a fall nut gathering and processing site it is possible feature differences between sites reflect different seasonal activities.

Along the northshore of Lake Ontario the settlement patterns associated with the lakeshore remained unchanged through time (Roberts 1985: 119-120). There is a suggestion of decreasing population density as one advances eastward. Sites are generally located within 40 m of small streams or springs on poor to well-drained soils and average 100 square metres in area with one to three discrete concentrations of debris.

The BiFh-4 site was a fishing camp adjacent to a major rapid on the Richelieu River near Chambly, Québec (Clermont 1974: 46-48). There is tenuous evidence from the site of a 12 m diameter dwelling. Such a large sized structure would indicate a multi-family dwelling but, as noted, the evidence is equivocal. Another base camp on the Richelieu River, the Rapides Fryers site (Hébert 1987), contained mainly locally derived chipped stone materials although 17% of the worked stone was obtained from the Appalachians to the south. A grey quartzite from either the Cheshire quarries of southern Vermont or

Gilman in southern Québec was also represented (Ibid: 96). At the major base camp fishing station of Pointe-de-Buisson 4 (Clermont et Chapdelaine 1982) on the St.Lawrence River house structures were envisioned on the basis of aligned hearths and the distribution of cultural debris. The evidence of dwellings, however, is not convincing. Like the majority of large fishing camp sites multiple occupations and the mixture of cultural debris have confounded the best efforts of archaeologists to demarcate discrete living floors.

A major trading activity throughout Period III and, in particular, during the earlier portions of the Middle Great Lakes -St.Lawrence culture sequence involved the movement of native copper from the Lake Superior region down the Ottawa Valley and, thence, to other areas of northeastern North America (Kennedy 1962; 1966; n.d.; Wright and Carlson 1987). The Allumette Island-1 and Morrison's Island-6 sites, in addition to other activities, functioned as manufacturing centres of copper tools. Detecting other evidence relating to this ancient trade and presumed reciprocity from recipient regions will require a significant increase in research whose focus is the tracing of exotics, particularly lithics, by a range of source identifying or fingerprinting methods. Vergennes phase side-notched projectile points manufactured from the Cheshire quartzite of Vermont (Haviland and Power 1981: 28) recovered from Upper St.Lawrence River sites (personal examination), indicate trade and contact along the tributaries of the St.Lawrence River. Trade from the northeast can be seen in the walrus ivory gouge from the Brewerton site in New York (Beauchamp 1902: 290). Given the cultural mixture at most sites, however, the isolating of such evidence to a particular culture and time will remain a serious problem. A fragment of a walrus ivory implement, for example, was recovered from an island in the Lake St.Francis widening in the St.Lawrence River immediately downriver from Cornwall, Ontario but the item cannot be attributed to a specific portion of the 9,000 years of human occupation at the site.

The disappearance of the hemlock forest due to disease around 2,700 BC was a major botanical horizon marker throughout northeastern North America (Davis 1977). It has led to the speculation that the removal of a favoured deer browse and cover would have required significant adjustments by the contemporary hunting bands (Roberts 1985: 125). Such a suggestion, however, has been countered by the observation that the removal of hemlock would have made room for deciduous trees and, thus, mast foods that would have actually favoured an increase in deer populations (McAndrews 1980). As there does not appear to be any striking disruption in the archaeological record after 2,700 BC it is probably safe to assume that the temporary demise of hemlock did not seriously impact upon deer and, thus, the hunting bands of northeastern North America.

III. Terminal phase (2,000 to 1,000 BC): The base camps of the Terminal phase along the Lake Huron coast (Kenyon 1959; Ramsden 1976; Wright 1972) were situated at favourable fishing locales beside streams entering the Lake. Water transport would have also extended hunting ranges. Falling water

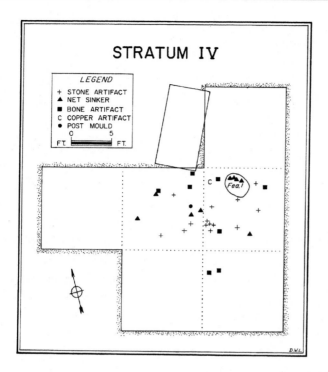

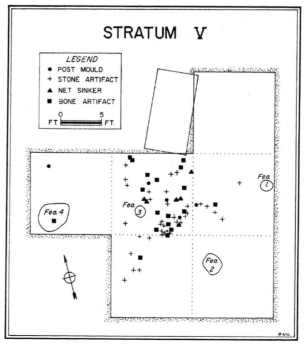

FIGURE 29: REPETITIVE CAMPGROUND USE At the Middle Great Lakes-St.Lawrence culture Knechtel I seasonal camp site people returned consistently to specific locations on the site. This is seen in the distributions of features, tools, and other cultural debris through time as recorded in the different strata of the site. The upper floorplan pertains to the earliest occupation of the site and the lower floorplan to a subsequent occupation. Outside of the areas of concentrated occupation, not shown in the Figure, only a limited amount of cultural debris was encountered although dog faeces, preserved by the bones in the fish the dogs were being fed, were common. This suggests that dogs were probably tethered on the margins of the camp proper. (Reproduced from Wright 1972 c, Figures 5 and 6.)

BLACK AND WHITE PLATE XIII: A MIDDLE GREAT LAKES-ST.LAWRENCE CULTURE COOKING RANGE The photograph from the Knechtel I site excavation on Lake Huron shows a 1,250 BC hearth floor in the right hand corner while to the left, in a lower cultural stratum, is a 1,500 BC pit oven. The black band above the two features represents the 1,000 BC stratum at the site. Concentrations of fire-cracked rock occur in both the hearth and the bottom of the pit. After being exposed to fire rocks slowly release heat and thereby provided an effective means of baking meat or roots. The fragmented rocks resulting from this cooking procedure are frequently the first evidence of an archaeological site. (Reproduced from Wright 1972: Plate 7)

levels eventually drained the original large embayments reducing the fishing potential and forcing a greater reliance on hunting. Fish, such as suckers, still spawn in the adjacent small streams and it can be assumed that fishing continued to be of some importance.

At the Knechtel I site with its 1,000 years of continuous seasonal occupation (Wright 1972) an interesting phenomenon revealed itself. The specific locations of the earliest camps were duplicated by subsequent camps resulting in a series of living floors stratigraphically superimposed over one another. On the margins of these highly local regions of intense occupation numerous dog faeces were found but very little occupational debris. The distributional pattern of cultural debris relative to animal waste

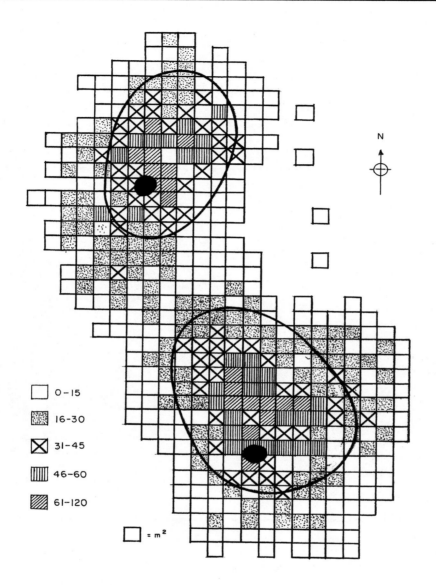

FIGURE 30: MIDDLE GREAT LAKES-ST.LAWRENCE CULTURE WINTER DWELLINGS At the Innes site in Southern Ontario the concentrations of chipping detritus were recorded within each one square metre excavation unit. This recording method, as well as the presence of hearth floors indicated in black, permitted the delineation of the outlines of two dwellings. Artifact distributions mirrored that of the more abundant chipping debris. Such careful field recording methods are able to detect the presence of the ancient dwellings despite the fact that they have been severely disturbed by many years of ploughing. (Adapted from Lennox 1986: Figures 4 and 14. Drawing modified for graphical purposes by Mr. David W. Laverie.)

suggests that the first occupants established the camp site that subsequent descendants re-occupied (Figure 29). The marginal distribution of dog faeces duplicates a current situation in the north where dogs are tethered on the margins of the camp. Such camp sites are clear of undergrowth and, therefore, represent the most convenient camping area for subsequent visitors to a site.

The distribution of artifacts and other cultural debris at the Knechtel I site suggested living floors approximately 4.6 m by 3.0 m. Features, such as firestone hearth pavements, hearth floors made from a layer of clay introduced into the natural sand matrix of the site, and pits including pit ovens (Black and White Plate XIII), tended to be situated along the edges of the concentrations of cultural debris. The post moulds did not form a discernable pattern other than one possible association with a hearth similar to a feature recorded at the related Rocky Ridge site (Ramsden 1976: 34).

In contrast to the warm weather base camps along the Lake Huron coast is the interior 1,500 BC Innes site to the south (Lennox 1986). Although some berries and nut fragments were recovered from the site it is believed to represent a fall through winter camp. The site is situated on a well-drained knoll beside the head of a small rivulet adjacent to a black ash swamp. Tool manufacturing debris was predominantly of the local Onondaga chert although minor amounts of Port Franks chert from the Sarnia area as well as Ohio cherts were present. Two house structures were reconstructed on the basis of artifactual and debris distributions as well as hearth- pits and "As such we can now see the Innes site as representing the remains of two Late Archaic extended family units, similarly composed, each conducting similar activities with the same environs and each contributing like by-products to the accumulation of debris around their respective hearth areas" (Lennox 1986: 234). The two concentrations of cultural debris and their features are interpreted as the remains of extended family ovate structures measuring 11 m by 7 m and 13 m by 10 m. It is the concentration of cultural debris within the units that is suggestive of cold weather activities around a hearth. Such dwellings could have housed between 8 to 10 people for a two dwelling camp of around 20 people. It was this kind of dwelling reconstruction that was attempted at the Pointe-de-Buisson 4 site (Clermont et Chapdelaine 1982) but, unlike the single component Innes site, there the evidence was severely obscured by multiple occupations. Thin but ubiquitous scatterings of debris from the ploughed fields of the interior of Southern Ontario and southern Québec likely represent small winter camp sites. The Innes site is probably a normal type of winter settlement pattern although modified survey and excavation methods will be necessary to recognize them as such. Occasionally remnants survive beneath the plough zone. At the 1,700 BC Thistle Hill site covering an area of 360 square metres two dwellings were encountered. A semisubterranian structure, partially demarcated by posts with a pit in the southern half, was 4 m in diameter. The other dwelling contained a circular hearth and a pit and measured 4.3 m by 3.3 m. The relative scarcity of chipping detritus in the southern half of the dwelling suggested that this area may have been for sleeping (Woodley 1988; 1990: Figure 20). Concentrations of cultural debris within the dwellings would argue for a cold weather occupation rather than the year round occupation favoured by the excavator. In fact, the groupings of two to three concentrations of debris recorded at other contemporary sites in ploughed fields (Roberts 1985) are probably representative of living floors. This increasingly appears to form a general pattern suggestive of the wintering together of two or three related families.

Cosmology:

I. Vergennes phase (4,000 to 3,500 BC): At the Allumette Island -I base camp burials were located at various places on the site rather than being concentrated in a discrete cemetery. Extended and flexed interments were identified as well as a single cremation and a possible partial cremation (Kennedy n.d; Pfeiffer 1977: 28). Plough damage of the shallow archaeological deposits was so severe that it was not possible to determine whether artifacts had been placed with the dead or if they had been dragged into the grave by the plough. Red ochre nodules tended to be concentrated in the burial fill and in two instances powdered red ochre had been added in large quantities. Some of the graves "...were extended a few inches down into the limestone bedrock" (Kennedy n.d.: 7). While cremation can be a culturally preferred method of treatment of the remains of the deceased in certain societies, the practice can also represent a practical method of preparing the remains of deceased kinsmen for transport from remote locales to the desired final place of burial (Pfeiffer 1974; 1977: 121-152). At the KI site in southwestern Vermont (Ritchie 1968) a poorly preserved burial in the floor of a possible house structure was sprinkled with red ochre and then covered with cobbles. Nearby, at the Otter Creek No.2 site, six bundle (?) burials, consisting of two adults, three children, and infant, were recorded (Ritchie 1979). Both grave offerings and red ochre were absent but a dog had been placed in the grave of one of the adults.

Allowing for the limited nature of the evidence it would appear that at this early period in Middle Great Lakes- St.Lawrence culture discrete cemeteries were not the norm. The presence of bundle burials and cremations indicates that the remains of the deceased who died elsewhere were sometimes brought to the summer base camp for final burial. Grave offerings appear to be either absent or rare although the evidence from the Allumette-1 and Coteau-du-Lac sites suggests that this impression may be a product of poor samples.

An elaborately engraved ground slate bayonet from Southern Ontario (Figure 31) that likely pertains to Period III has been interpreted as a shaman amulet with the engravings having some unknown symbolic significance (Johnston 1982: 28). Engraving on stone, bone, and copper tools becomes more common in the following Brewerton phase. Such engravings likely had symbolic significance but there is no reason to suspect a specific association with shamanism. A class of artifact that likely possessed symbolic significance was the elaborately fashioned and polished stone spearthrower weights. Stone spearthrower weights must have been attached to a very small number of the wooden spearthrowers in service at any one time, thus the inference regarding their symbolic and probable status significance. They obviously were not an essential component of the spearthrower in functional terms or there would be a superabundance of such stone weights in the archaeological collections.

II. Brewerton phase (3,500 to 2,000 BC): The 3,500 BC Morrison's Island-6 site was occupied by the descendants of the nearby Allumette Island-1 site (Pfeiffer 1977; 1979). Interments were represented by extended, bundle, and flexed burials. Eight of the 12 graves contained red ochre and two possessed chunks of ochre. The use of red ochre was obviously quite variable as suggested by the observation that "...although burials numbered 12 and 15 each contained a large bevelled, stemmed copper projectile point with a distinctive `fluked´ base (Fig.3, No.6) burial 12 was sprinkled with red hematite but burial 15 contained no hematite" (Kennedy 1966: 102-103). Exclusive of the aforementioned burials 12 and 15, grave offerings by interment were as follows: burial 4 - a stone adze, an eyed bone needle, and a decorated antler object; burial 5 - a small copper projectile point and limestone slabs placed over the lower limbs; burial 6 - a turtle shell rattle, an eyed bone needle, a chunk of copper, and beaver incisor knives and chisels; burial 7 - a stone gouge, a stemmed copper point, and a copper awl; burial 9 - a `killed´ stone plummet-like object; burial 11 - a stone gouge, a bone harpoon, and a copper axe; burial 13 - copper beads and an eyed bone needle; burial 14 - a `killed´ copper axe; burial 16 - a copper spud and two copper axes; burial 17 - copper bracelets on the upper arms and a copper knife; burial 19 - copper bracelets on the lower arms, a decorated bone object, a bone harpoon, and bands of tiny copper beads on the arms and legs that would have fringed clothing. The graves were concentrated in a discrete cemetery. Some knowledge of grave locations, possibly indicated by surface markers, is suggested by one extended burial being placed in a transverse fashion over an earlier extended burial.

Very few of the grave offerings at the Morrison's Island-6 site were `killed´, suggesting that the nature of animistic beliefs operative at the time was not simple. Animism is only one facet of a complex web of religious beliefs among many different peoples. Historically documented native beliefs in Canada appear to have been quite similar to those of the pre-Christian Celtic, Germanic, and Scandinavian peoples of northwestern Europe as well as other parts of the world in the respects that, "Contact, then, with the supernatural world was essential for the community, and in the continual emphasis on methods of divination to discover what was unknown and what the future held, much of the strengths of the old religion lay. Another of its strengths was the efficacy of holy places where prayer and sacrifice might be kept up over centuries. These formed the centres of local communities, symbolising the centre of the world and the inner core of life itself. Others were more secret places to which the family or the individual might turn for reassurance, counsel and the acquisition of skill or wisdom. Such places reflected the wider unity of the divine world of whose powers men might, cautiously and with trepidation, avail themselves" (Davidson 1988: 224). Pre-European natives in Canada and pre-Christian Europeans held much in common regarding the supernatural world and its relationship to humans. Even highly specific and central cosmological symbols were shared, such as the Great Tree that linked the Lower World with the Upper World.

In the approximately 500 years that separated the Allumette Island-1 site and the Morrison's Island-6 site changes in mortuary practices took place. The deceased were now placed in a discrete, repetitively used cemetery and were richly provided with grave offerings. Many of the complete objects found near the graves from the Allumette Island-1 site, however, probably represented grave offerings that were displaced by ploughing over the shallow graves, a possibility reinforced by the offerings found with a Vergennes phase burial at the Coteau-du-Lac site. The Coteau-du-Lac site on the St.Lawrence River above Montréal (Lueger 1977; Marois 1987) contained some severely disturbed graves. Decomposed bones in a small rectangular patch of red ochre containing two beaver incisor tools has been interpreted as the remnants of a flexed burial. An extended female with an infant at her breast was accompanied by two ground bear canines and two fragments of worked turtle shell. A flexed male was placed in a grave with traces of red ochre, two bone daggers, four antler tine flakers, a large antler hook of unknown function, a worked antler object, a polished slate spearthrower weight, a human face effigy pebble, two beaver incisor knives, a chipped stone ulu, three chipped knives, a plummet, a bone point and "...les os d'animaux..." (Marois 1987: 14). A copper fragment also occurred in or near the left hand of this individual and a large bird skull was clasped in the other hand. Another burial with abundant red ochre represented a young man whose head was covered by a large rock slab. Missing parts of the body and rodent gnawing of the bones suggest the body was in an advanced state of decay prior to burial. A fragment of a conical copper point was lodged between the vertebrae indicating the individual had met a violent death. The grave was richly provided with the following offerings exclusive of fragmented items: a bone flesher; two abraders; four bone knives; two antler flakers; two stone plummets; a bent antler object; a weaving needle; a stone adze; four pointed objects inferred to be garment pins; two stemmed points; and a mica slab. In addition to artifacts were the following animal remains: deer bones; a goose ulna; a black bear canine (perforated?) as well as other bear parts; an osprey wing; two raccoon right forearms as well as a raccoon skull clasped in the left hand; a mink upper arm and mandible; snake vertebrae (intrusive?); a groundhog incisor; the vertebrae of a large fish; and beaver teeth (Marois 1987). The pattern of objects occurring in two's undoubtedly had symbolic meaning as well as the range of animals and their particular body parts but this rich symbolism has been forever lost. It will be recalled that the placement of animal body parts with the deceased was a common practice in Middle Maritime culture as well. Beyond the array of grave offerings this particular burial has a special significance. The conical copper projectile point fragment found lodged in his back is typologically characteristic of the Vergennes phase rather than the Brewerton phase. If this early time placement pertains then the finished objects found with the disturbed graves of the Allumette Island-1 site likely do represent offerings rather than accidental inclusions. The 3,500 BC radiocarbon date from the Coteau-de-Lac site grave (Marois 1987) straddles the arbitrary separation of the Vergennes and Brewerton phases. Also of significance is the evidence of either interband hostilities or personal vendettas.

During the excavation of the St.Lawrence Canal at Les Galops Rapids near Brockville, Ontario in 1847 a cemetery was accidentally encountered. While the descriptions of the physical size of the

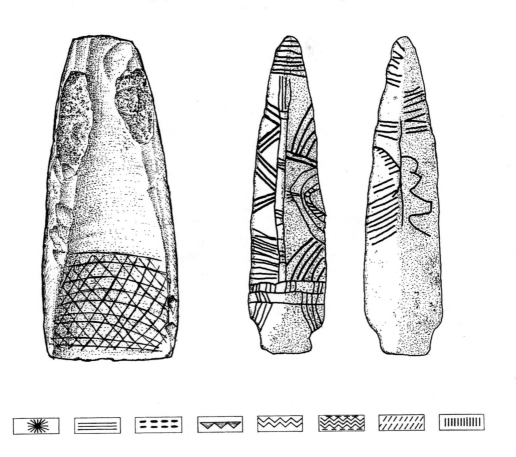

FIGURE 31: MIDDLE GREAT LAKES-ST.LAWRENCE CULTURE ENGRAVED MOTIFS The polished
stone gouge on the left with engraved hatchering was found outside of Sudbury, Ontario while the decorated ground
slate lance to the right was picked-up by a cottager near Peterborough, Ontario. The motifs at the bottom of the
Figure were extrapolated from the written descriptions of engraved bone, stone, and copper tools from the Morrison's
Island-6 site in the Ottawa River, Québec and are, therefore, approximations (Kennedy 1966). A number of parallels
can be seen between these motifs and Middle Maritime culture motifs illustrated in Figure 26. (The lance head was
adapted from Johnston 1982: Figures 1 and 2. Drawings by Mr. David W. Laverie.)

individuals in the cemetery, the depths of the burials, and the arrangement of the bodies, are likely fanciful
recollections of the canal excavators, the recovered copper implements and stone gouges and adzes (Griffin
1961: 118-120; Reynolds 1856) clearly indicate the cemetery pertains to the Brewerton phase. In addition

to a score of presumably extended burials, a cremation was noted. A stone item referred to as a "pipe mouth -piece" was probably a bead. Of particular interest was a small clay (?) human skull effigy. Although the context of the object is uncertain given the circumstances under which it and the other objects were recovered, it does correspond in a general way to the stone pebble human effigy from the Coteau-de-Lac site (Marois 1987: Planche III, 2).

At the Robinson and Oberlander 1 sites at Brewerton, New York the "...random disposition of the dead in the village debris was the customary practice" (Ritchie 1940: 57). Six extended, five flexed, three bundle, a cremation, and two indeterminate burials were represented. Grave offerings were rare and when present were limited in both quantity and variety. In only one instance was red ochre present. Given the multiple occupations of these sites, of course, it is uncertain if all of the burials pertain to Middle Great Lakes-St.Lawrence culture. Indeed, the single cremation has been attributed to the following period. An unusual burial, which can be assigned to Middle Great Lakes-St.Lawrence culture, consisted of a flexed female whose body was place on top of a layer of boulders and then was covered with several more boulders. A hammer/anvil and two side-notched points accompanied the body. The major burial site on Frontenac Island in Lake Cayuga, New York (Ritchie 1945) is not given detailed consideration due to the problem of component mixture. It is of interest, however, to note that a statistical examination of the grave contents (Trubowitz 1977) suggests that chipped and polished stone implements, dogs, antler flakers, and bone awls were found most frequently with extended males while shell ornaments occurred with females.

A problematical class of features are the large pit structures encountered at the Malcolm site on the St.Lawrence River above Cornwall, Ontario (Dailey and Wright 1955: 19-22). The site, sitting adjacent to a rapid and presumably a fishing station, pertained mainly to a Late Great Lakes-St.Lawrence culture occupation although a significant number of the projectile points were Brewerton phase varieties. A radiocarbon date from one of the seven large problematical pits provided a reading of 2,400 BC suggesting the features can be attributed to the Brewerton phase occupation of the site. The pit features (Figure 32), situated on the edge of the river terrace, consisted of oval pits 1.8 m by 1.2 m and .9 m deep. Fire-baked soil lined the sides and bottoms of the features which contained a thick, solid layer of charcoal on the pit floor on top of which rested a layer of severely burnt and fragmented stone. The entire pit was then capped with clay. Refuse of any kind, other than the fire fractured rock and charcoal, was lacking. Although not demonstrable, the most likely function of these features would be as sweat lodges. Sweat lodges are historically documented as being associated with purification and other religious practices.

III. Terminal phase (2,000 to 1,000 BC): The elaboration of mortuary ceremonialism begun during the Brewerton phase and possibly as early as the Vergennes phase acquired cultic proportions during the Terminal phase of Middle Great Lakes-St.Lawrence culture and the early portion of the subsequent Late Great Lakes-St.Lawrence culture. In Southern Ontario, cemeteries have been referred to as the Glacial

Kame complex after a complex first described in the Ohio Valley (Cunningham 1948). The first Glacial Kame cemetery to be excavated by an archaeologist was located near Picton, Ontario (Ritchie 1949). More than 13 graves were encountered that included multiple interments, cremations, flexed, bundle, and extended burials. The tightly concentrated cemetery was situated on the southern and eastern flank of a sand knoll isolated from any habitation site. An earlier discovered grave from the same cemetery contained an extended burial and a cremation covered with red ochre and accompanied by two copper celts, two copper gouges, four copper awls or pikes, two copper beads, cylindrical and discoidal marine shell beads, and circular, semi-circular, and sandal-sole shaped marine shell gorgets (Wintemberg 1928). The pattern of placing objects with the deceased in two's and, to a lesser extent, four's (two pairs?), was noted at the earlier Brewerton phase Coteau-de-Lac site (Marois 1987). The meaning underlying the pairing of objects is unknown but it is speculated that it could symbolize the supernatural Upper World and Lower World between which humans existed. Pairing could also have symbolized the link between the worlds of the dead and the living. Characteristic of the Glacial Kame mortuary complex are copper and marine shell objects. The marine shell is whelk, frequently referred to as conch, that was likely traded into the interior from the Chesapeake Bay area on the Atlantic seaboard (Pendergast 1989: 102). Copper would have come from Lake Superior.

The Picton area excavations revealed a number of interesting aspects of the burial complex such as firestone fragments in the cremations that must have been gathered up at the crematorium along with the remains and carried to the place of final burial in containers. Particularly important from a symbolic standpoint was a green clay-like substance moulded into various sized nodules or formed into thick sheets with which the body of the deceased was either covered or placed upon. This material, most abundant with uncremated remains, has recently been identified as glauconite, a micaceous mineral occurring in marine sediments and probably obtained from the eastern seaboard of the northeastern United States (William S. Donaldson: personal communication). It is speculated that the glauconite may symbolize the aqueous mud associated with the widely distributed Earth-Diver myth of North America (Hall 1979) that accounts for the creation of the Earth and ultimately life and was a central part of the historically documented Iroquoian creation story (Fenton 1962).

Like the accidentally discovered grave from the Picton site reported by Wintemberg (1928), the graves excavated by Ritchie (1949) contained an abundance of marine shell and copper implements and ornaments. Other items consisted of a deposit of muskrat, woodchuck and cottontail skull and longbone parts as well as a hip bone and a fish mandible. Presumably the emphasis on head and longbone parts, as well as the species represented, had symbolic significance as did the head of a pike and a fox mandible in two other graves. This inclusion of specific animal parts with the deceased clearly represents the continuation of a practice most fully recorded at the Coteau-de-Lac site (Marois 1987). Other than a galena nugget and a fragmented stone point all of the other grave offerings consisted of shell and copper items,

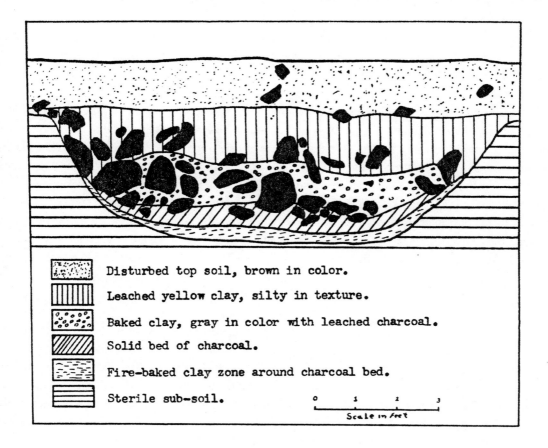

	Disturbed top soil, brown in color.
	Leached yellow clay, silty in texture.
	Baked clay, gray in color with leached charcoal.
	Solid bed of charcoal.
	Fire-baked clay zone around charcoal bed.
	Sterile sub-soil.

Scale in feet

FIGURE 32: PROBLEMATICAL PIT FEATURES FROM THE MALCOLM SITE, ONTARIO Seven large pit features were recorded at this site on the banks of the St.Lawrence River near Cornwall, Ontario. None of the pits contained cultural refuse other than massed layers of highly fragmented large rocks and thick bands of charcoal. The fire-reddened natural clay along the walls and floors of the pits reinforces the evidence of intense heat. The pits were all concentrated in one area of the site adjacent to a gently sloping river terrace overlooking a quiet lagoon at the foot of a major rapid. Contrary to the original conclusion that the features were "...meat baking hearths..." (Dailey and Wright 1955: 22) I would now favour the view that they represent some unusual form of sweat bath. It is historically documented that ceremonial sweat baths were widespread across Canada. A radiocarbon date of 2,500 BC from one of the features suggests they pertain to the Middle Great Lakes-St.Lawrence culture occupation of the site. (Reproduced from Dailey and Wright 1955: Figure 10)

mainly pendants and beads. An unusual specimen was a marine shell human face effigy pendant (Ritchie

1949: Figure 10) that has stone proto-types at the Coteau-de-Lac site and possibly the specimen from Brockville (Reynolds 1856). The aforementioned human face effigy is rendered in a stylized fashion reminiscent of that of much later Iroquoian (Ellis and Ferris 1990: cover illustration; Wright 1974: Plate IX, fig.14) and eastern Algonquian societies (Snow 1978: Figure 3).

The Finlan site near Trenton, Ontario was a Terminal phase Glacial Kame complex cemetery that was totally destroyed by sand pit operations. Like the nearby Picton site, the cemetery appears to have been a concentrated burial area on the south and east flanks of a sand knoll. Quantities of red ochre, cremated and uncremated remains, were scattered about by the earth-moving machinery. Artifacts picked up by local curio seekers consisted of discoidal marine shell beads and pendants, including the characteristic sandal-sole variety, copper beads, two copper celts, abundant chunks of galena, and two left human femurs that had been modified. Galena, a lead sulphide with a very high specific gravity is isotopic specific and can be traced to discrete geological deposits. An analysis of the Finlan site galena revealed that it had come from the headwaters of the Mississippi River in northwestern Illinois (Farquar and Fletcher 1980) more than a 1,000 km to the southwest in a straight line from the Finlan site. The likely water route would have been up the Mississippi River to the Wisconsin River and thence, via the Great Lakes, to the Trenton region. Galena from the related Terminal phase cemeteries at Picton and Isle la Motte in northern Vermont, on the other hand, had been acquired from the relatively close Rossie Mine deposits in New York state.

A number of Terminal phase Glacial Kame cemeteries have been reported in western Southern Ontario (Spence and Fox 1986: 11-15) but unfortunately were destroyed by sand and gravel operations before archaeological examination was possible. An exception to the foregoing is the Hind site overlooking the Thames River. Flexed burials and cremations are reported from this isolated multi-component cemetery (Ellis et al. 1990: 117- 118). The cemetery had been in use for many centuries but most of the graves were assigned to the Glacial Kame complex on the basis of the occurrence of galena, marine shell beads and pendants, copper celts and awls, and Terminal phase projectile point varieties. A grave containing a flexed adolescent and a cremated adult covered with red ochre was richly provided with offerings. A tubular stone pipe, a bear maxilla mask, worked martin, fisher and raccoon mandibles, copper beads, and green clay, probably glauconite, had been placed with the adolescent. The parallels with the Picton site are obvious. A date of 1,000 BC was obtained on this grave. The cremation contained lumps of iron pyrites, which would have been part of a fire- making kit where a spark was produced by striking the iron pyrites nodule against a chunk of chert. Also present were slate and marine shell gorgets and two slate birdstones, the latter likely being symbolic spearthrower weights fashioned in the form of stylized birds. Another isolated Glacial Kame cemetery removed from any habitation site, the Bruce Boyd site (Spence et al. 1979), produced red ochre, notched projectile points and preforms, iron pyrites, copper beads, a copper celt and bracelet, and beaver incisors (Ellis et al. 1990: 115).

At Isle la Morte, on the north end of Lake Champlain in Vermont, gravel operations exposed human bones covered with red ochre as well as evidence of cremations. Salvage excavations (Ritchie 1965: 131) exposed a number of shallow graves. One grave contained a cremation as well as a child's skull and longbone accompanied by a calcined bone awl and a heat-fractured chert flake. Another grave consisted of a concentrated mass of red ochre 38 cm in diameter and 25 cm thick containing the cremated remains of an incomplete adolescent along with two copper gouges, the whole apparently being the contents of a bag brought from the crematorium to the burial site. Other items from the site were another set of copper gouges, thick copper beads, discoidal marine shell beads and pendants, blocks of galena, and a portion of a charred leather shroud. The cemetery was isolated from any habitation site and originally would have contained a half a dozen graves. A radiocarbon date of approximately 1,100 BC (2930 ± 80 BP) was obtained (William A. Ritchie: personal communication 1989).

The Glacial Kame complex shares many traits with the subsequent Period IV Meadowood complex of Late Great Lakes-St.Lawrence culture making the differentiation of the two complexes difficult (Spence and Fox 1986). The Hind site, for example, while considered a Glacial Kame cemetery contains such atypical Glacial Kame traits as marginella shell beads from the East Coast, a stone cylindrical pipe, polished slate birdstones, two to three hole polished slate gorgets, caches of chipped stone projectile points and preforms, and drills. The aforementioned traits are more characteristic of subsequent mortuary elaboration and providing that the 1,000 BC radiocarbon date from the Hind site is accurate, provide evidence of cultural continuity in mortuary practices between the late portion of Period III and the beginning of Period IV.

The mortuary practices of the Terminal phase of the Middle Great Lakes-St.Lawrence culture suggest a cultic involvement in a large area that included Southern Ontario, likely southern Québec, Vermont, likely New York, and Ohio, Michigan, and Indiana. While open to debate regarding definition (Ellis et al 1990: 119), the Glacial Kame complex is regarded as a cult on the basis of a number of shared practices. These include the location and orientation of cemeteries, their isolation from habitation sites, and the range of burial methods. Grave offerings also appear to have been prescribed, unlike the situation earlier in Middle Great Lakes-St.Lawrence culture. Frequent grave accompaniments were copper and marine shell tools and ornaments, often in pairs in the first instance, a green clay-like substance that is probably glauconite, and specific animal parts. The use of the word `cult´, however, must be qualified with the observation that in hunter-gatherer societies individual inclinations often deviated from formally prescribed ritualistic formulae. Evidence from osteological analysis of the Hind site remains indicates that people who died away from the `burial site´ were cremated and their ashes curated until final burial could be arranged (Pfeiffer 1975: 150-151). This suggests that cemeteries were sacred places that also functioned as physical markers validating a specific band's claim to a territory. It has been suggested that the multiple interments in single graves at the Hind site, ranging from two to seven, would presuppose the individuals were related at the family and band level (Spence 1986). None of the Glacial Kame cemeteries provide convincing evidence of social ranking. While infants and young children are underrepresented this was likely a product of cultural practices that had nothing to do with social status. Another characteristic of this Terminal phase mortuary complex is the far-flung trade network that was required to provide grave offerings. This included Lake Superior copper, marine shell and probably glauconite from the Atlantic coast, and galena from as far away as the headwaters of the Mississippi River. The copper and shell sources, for example, involve distances of 1,500 km. The complex was also steeped in symbolism whose meaning is lost; the green clay-like glauconite deposits, the reoccurrence of identical grave offerings in pairs, the offerings of unmodified galena, a lead sulphide with great weight relative to mass, the wide range of body parts from different animal species, etc. Such occurrences should elicit in archaeologists an abiding humility regarding the limitations of their discipline to probe into past matters of the human spirit. A symbolic act most people can readily identify with is the continuing practice of treating deceased dogs in a fashion similar to humans (I. Kenyon 1980a).

Beyond mortuary practices are insights into ritualistic behaviour that can be gleaned from faunal remains. At the Terminal phase Knechtel I site (Wright 1972) the absence of burnt fish bones suggested a taboo against burning such bones but not against feeding fish to dogs. The paucity of mammal skull parts relative to infracranial remains also permits the inference that the skulls were being ritually disposed of away from the camp site. Such practices have frequently been documented among hunting peoples.

External relationships:

The neighbours of Middle Great Lakes-St.Lawrence culture were Middle Maritime culture to the east, Middle Shield culture to the north and west, and various groups to the south.

Middle Great Lakes-St.Lawrence culture adopted a number of categories of polished stone tools from Middle Maritime culture. These included gouges, ground slate bayonets, points and ulus, and plummets. Recent research on deeply stratified sites in central Maine, however, has recovered gouges and ground slate points in late Period II deposits (Petersen 1991: 145-146) suggesting there may have been another point of origin for some of these tool categories. For the moment, the aforementioned ground stone tools are regarded as items that diffused into the interior from the east coast. Only time will tell if the diffusion centre was the Gulf of St.Lawrence and the Maritimes or an earlier as yet poorly defined centre to the south that contributed to the tool kits of both later cultures. Cultural contacts between Middle Great Lakes-St.Lawrence and Middle Maritime culture would likely have taken place along the St.Lawrence River and near the coasts of New Brunswick and northern Maine with the St.Lawrence representing the area of most prolonged contact. The relationship between these two cultures, however, has been confounded by the nature of the evidence as well as the difficulty of isolating single component sites. There is much room for disagreement. Sanger (1979a), for example, regards the `Moorehead´ cemeteries of Maine as being related to Middle Great Lakes-St.Lawrence (Laurentian) culture rather than Middle

Maritime culture, contrary to the association favoured in this study. Sanger has taken this position even though he clearly recognizes the differences between the Vergennes phase material from habitation sites such as Hirundo and that recovered from the Moorehead cemeteries. The Moorehead complex is seen as "...a specialized burial cult..." brought east by Middle Great Lakes-St.Lawrence culture around 3,750 BC which then elaborated into the Moorehead burial tradition (Sanger 1979a: 72). Another opinion is that the Moorehead complex represents a combination of `Small Point´ traits, a complex further south along the Atlantic coast, and certain Vergennes phase traits (Cox 1991). It is also noted that the Vergennes sites in northern Maine had contacts with Middle Maritime culture on or near the coast as indicated by the recovery of a barbed point manufactured from swordfish bill from an interior site. It is further noted that the trade focus of the Maine Vergennes phase sites was with the St.Lawrence River (Cox 1991: 159). There would appear to have been too much emphasis placed on traits shared by both cultures as well as the correlation between the appearance of Middle Great Lakes-St.Lawrence culture in Maine and the northward expansion of the deciduous forest around 3,750 BC. In addition to the ground stone items Middle Great Lakes-St.Lawrence culture and Middle Maritime culture shared a number of other traits such as unilateral single barbed bone harpoons with line hole (Byers 1979: Figure 17; Lueger 1977: Plate 22; Ritchie 1944: Plate 151; Tuck 1976: Plate 27) and single and multiple barbed bone points (Lueger 1977: Plates 20 and 21; Tuck 1976: Plates 28 and 30).

The fingerprinting of exotic items from both Middle Great Lakes-St.Lawrence culture sites and Middle Maritime culture sites is in its infancy. A Brewerton phase projectile point manufactured from Ontario or New York Onondaga chert found at Tadoussac, Lake Superior copper implements in the Gulf of St.Lawrence and environs and Ramah quartzite from northern Labrador and ivory implements in the interior are likely but very dim reflections of a long relationship between these two cultures. Much research, however, is required in order to determine the intensity and the direction of contacts as reflected by the trade in nonperishable goods.

Relationships between Middle Great Lakes-St.Lawrence culture and Middle Shield culture existed but are not clearly documented in the archaeological record. Certainly the trade in Lake Superior copper to Middle Great Lakes-St.Lawrence sites on the Ottawa River (Kennedy 1970: 59-64) would have originated with Middle Shield culture miners. The occasional occurrence of ground slate bayonets and gouges on Middle Shield culture sites, but rarely chipped stone items (Wright 1972c: Plate XII; 17-23) is also indicative of contacts likely based on trade given the selective nature of the tool categories represented. Fingerprinting of exotic quartzite and chert materials from Middle Great Lakes-St.Lawrence culture sites is beginning to highlight relationships between the peoples of the mixed hardwood forests and those of the boreal forest (Wright and Carlson 1987). Evidence from the Lake Temiskaming and Lake Abitibi border area between Québec and Ontario suggests a relatively close relationship between Middle Great Lakes-St.Lawrence culture and Middle Shield culture (Côté 1993; Marois et Gauthier 1989) which is not too surprising given the geographic proximity of these two cultures in the Ottawa River drainage system. There also appears to have been a marginal displacement of the Vergennes phase of Middle Great Lakes-St.Lawrence culture by Middle Shield culture populations due to changes in the climate that favoured Middle Shield culture adaptations over those of Middle Great Lakes-St.Lawrence people (Wright 1983 and unpublished data). A reliance upon a limited number of `index fossils´ to arrive at a cultural identification rather than a consideration of the total technology and other cultural systems has led to the Lake Temiskaming and Lake Abitibi materials frequently being identified as Middle Great Lakes-St.Lawrence culture (Laurentian Archaic) and "...le nébuleux concept d'Archaïque du Bouclier" being rejected (Côté 1993: 21).

Contemporary cultures in Ohio, Michigan, northern Illinois, and Wisconsin shared many attributes of the chipped stone technology with Middle Great Lakes-St.Lawrence culture. Similarities are particularly striking during the Terminal phase (Ellis et al. 1990: 107-109). The shared Terminal phase Glacial Kame mortuary complex also suggests a closely interconnected communication network. Archaeological evidence of a relationship is in agreement with the findings of physical anthropology (Pfeiffer 1979). Fingerprinting exotic lithics are increasingly revealing connections between sites in Southern Ontario and regions of the Ohio Valley (Lennox 1986). In addition to the evidence of exotic chert distributions, the appearance of full-grooved axes on Middle Great Lakes-St.Lawrence culture sites in western Southern Ontario (Wright 1962) indicates contacts with the Ohio Valley. These relationships have long been recognized. "The earliest and longest Archaic occupation of the Upper Ohio Valley was by people possessing a Laurentian-like culture" (Dragoo 1959: 213-214).

Human biology:

Middle Great Lakes-St.Lawrence culture people were robust and generally healthy but did suffer from bone fractures, gum disease related to excessive tooth wear caused by a coarse diet, and minor incidences of arthritis, usually restricted to older individuals (Ritchie 1965). At the Allumette Island-1, Morrison's Island-6, and Hind sites, representing the Vergennes, Brewerton, and Terminal phases, respectively, pathologies were rare other than trauma caused by blows or accidents (Pfeiffer 1977: 155-156). This pattern tends to be common to most hunters and gatherers. There is also some evidence suggesting that people were getting taller as time progressed. The heights of the combined Allumette-1 and Morrison's Island-6 site individuals ranged from 162.4 cm to 165.0 cm for women and 174.8 cm to 178.0 cm for men compared to equivalent measurements of 164.1 cm to 170.0 cm and 177.5 cm and 180.7 cm, respectively, from the Terminal phase Hind site near London, Ontario (Pfeiffer 1977). Infants and juveniles were rare or absent from the Ottawa Valley sites suggesting some form of generational difference in the treatment of the deceased. The presence of hyperdontia or extra teeth in the combined Ottawa Valley sample may indicate a genetic trait and further support the close biological and cultural relationships noted between these two sites. While the sample from the Coteau-de-Lac site was small it did not compare closely with the two Ottawa Valley site samples (Cybulski 1978).

On the basis of discrete morphological skeletal traits (Pfeiffer 1979) rather than cranial measurements (Pfeiffer 1977) it has been suggested that Middle Great Lakes-St.Lawrence populations were distinct from Middle Maritime culture people. Affinities noted between the former culture and the `Old Copper´ culture of Wisconsin are not convincing given the dispersed nature of the comparative collections, the likelihood of cultural mixture at sites such as Frontenac Island, and the Cole site remains being attributed to Middle Great Lakes- St.Lawrence culture rather than Lamoka culture. It has been possible, however, to suggest that local populations were "...involved in broad networks of trade and mate exchange..." (Pfeiffer 1979: 40).

Inferences on society:

The presence of warm weather base camps with long continuous periods of occupation situated at favourable fishing locales, at least in eastern Ontario, southern Québec, and northern New York, suggests territorially based bands. Such bands were likely exogamous. Exogamy, the requirement to obtain a marriage partner outside of one's own band, would imply clusters of interrelated neighbouring bands with females rather than males being the mobile individuals in the marital network. Some of the larger fishing base camps could even have been the result of periodic gatherings of a number of these bands. By extending the rights and obligations of kinship, intermarriage between bands would have facilitated the movement of goods, people, and ideas.

The procedure of fingerprinting exotic lithics and other items to their geological or environmental source, although just beginning to be accepted as an important archaeological interpretative tool, has already demonstrated the existence of extensive trade networks. Networks involved in the distribution of Lake Superior copper, Atlantic coast marine shell, galena, and high quality cherts from a range of sources were well established by Period III throughout eastern North America. These imperishable items must only represent the tip of the iceberg relative to perishable items that have not survived. Perishable goods likely included dried foodstuffs, furs and hides, sinew, medicine, and finished products like fish nets. With such a complex of trade networks in place it can also be speculated that technological and social innovations could be disseminated more readily than in earlier times.

A social-economic pattern of band gatherings at fishing locations on major rivers and lakes in the spring through to the fall, followed by the fall deer and/or elk hunt, and then dispersal of family groupings to the winter hunt camps, seems to best fit the available evidence. Modifications to this generalization would, of course, be determined by local resources and periodic special opportunities. As discussed in the section on settlement patterns the more favourably endowed region west of the Niagara Escarpment may have made major gatherings at favourable fishing locations less important than to the east. A successful fall deer pound hunt could result in the band or a large segment thereof, wintering together, particularly if other stored foods and locally available resources were abundant. The Innes site, for example, has been interpreted as a minimum sized band winter camp (Lennox 1986: 238). At this site the restriction of the exotic Kettle Point or Port Franks chert scrapers to one of the two households has been attributed to a female residence pattern reflecting band exogamy and patrilocality where the men of the household were acquiring their wives from the west and the women were bringing their tools manufactured from locally `exotic´ chert with them.

By Terminal phase times there is increasing evidence of cultural regionalism that could have been, in part, a product of increasing populations and a concomitant contraction in band territory size. The widely based trade and mortuary ceremonialism may have been social devices used to expand relationships between bands beyond direct blood ties (Ellis et al. 1990). Changing mortuary practices thus could reflect changing social systems. The dispersed graves of the 4,000 BC Allumette Island-1 site (Kennedy n.d.) may pertain to individual family burial plots removed from those of other members of the band whereas the cemetery at the Morrison's Island-6 site 500 years later was used by the entire band. By Terminal phase times people were involved in a widespread mortuary cult requiring adherence to at least a certain number of prescribed rituals. Through time, the treatment of the dead appears to have been centred first with the family, then the band, and finally with a number of bands participating in a mortuary cult. The latter practice must relate to some form of symbolic extrasocietal system. If, for example, grave offerings were regarded as a "...social exchange with the land of the dead..." mimicing the role of gift exchange among the living and "...the survivor's reaffirmation of societal endurance..." (Mason 1981: 198) then some significant changes have obviously taken place during this 3,000 year period. Although not totally certain at this time the earliest graves appear to have rarely contained offerings while during the Brewerton phase a wide range of implements, ornaments, and other items appear but their abundance and variety are so variable as to suggest that personal considerations dictated the nature of the offerings. By Terminal phase times the burial procedures and grave offerings are far more prescribed suggesting that social forces external to the nuclear family and, in many respects, the band, were increasingly dictating ritualistic behaviour. Of course, we know nothing of the perishable objects placed with the deceased.

Within Middle Great Lakes-St.Lawrence societies status was likely based upon age, sex, and achievement. The physical anthropological evidence suggesting "...bands of some 35-50 people with no consistent post-marital residential practice, leaving individuals free to respond flexibly to environmental and demographic processes in their choice of band affiliation" (Spence 1986), however, is not totally convincing. It is agreed that `mating networks´ were likely to some degree open-ended (Ibid: 84) but within this flexible structure involving a number of bands males probably remained in the territories of their birth and would, thus, reduce the effect of gene flow allowing from some degree of biological distinctiveness. Attempting to determine the biological relationship both within a band and between bands using osteological evidence is compromised by the likelihood of genetic drift within small breeding populations (Molto 1983: 247). It is inferred that the male function as a hunter in societies such as the one under consideration required both an intimate knowledge of territorial resources and the assistance of male kinsmen in the hunt, thus favouring territorial bonding for life. Female functions permitted them far greater mobility and through marriage and blood ties bonded the larger social unit of a series of bands linked by kinship.

Limitations in the evidence:

The drowning of sites by the rising water levels of the Lower Great Lakes, the isolating of sites in the hinterland by the falling water levels of the Upper Great Lakes, site destruction by a range of natural and recent industrial-economic forces, acid soils, and the generally dispersed settlement patterns of Middle Great Lakes-St.Lawrence culture, have all reduced both the available archaeological record and its visibility (Ellis and Deller 1986; Karrow and Warner 1990). What is probably the greatest single limiting factor, however, is the scarcity of well stratified sites and single component sites. The large warm season base camps are characterized by thin refuse deposits representing the seasonal accumulations of the debris of uncounted generations of people over thousands of years. Isolating discrete cultural components on such sites appears to be impossible regardless of how diligent the excavation techniques. Attempts to isolate components on the basis of typology perpetuate a procedure that can only reinforce a potentially misleading stereotype of technological homogeniety for any particular culture. This difficulty in isolating single components has undoubtedly been responsible for the heavy reliance upon cultural `index fossils´ such as the ground slate and copper components of the technology. For years this dependence upon typological identification of components rather than archaeological context has frustrated efforts to arrive at an accord on the definition of Middle Great Lakes-St.Lawrence culture (Laurentian Archaic). Culture history reconstructions have been further confused by the rudimentary applications of projectile point typology that rely upon the outlines of points rather than a constellation of associated attributes. Finally, the Terminal phase is a time of major but poorly understood change. Influences are apparent from the Susquehanna Archaic culture to the southeast but the nature of the influence is not clear.

If archaeologists had six large stratified sites with long histories of occupation that were strategically distributed throughout the Great Lakes-St.Lawrence vegetation province the resulting information would do more to clarify the present murky picture than the excavation of another 100 multi-component base camps with their thin, mixed mantle of cultural debris. For an useful summary of the problems involved in interpreting the Archaic of Southern Ontario see Ellis et al. (1990: 122-124).

CHAPTER 16 ———————————————
MIDDLE SHIELD CULTURE
———————————————————————————————

Précis:

     Shield culture represented the first significant human occupation of the Canadian Shield, an enormous region encompassing a southwestern portion of the Northwest Territories, most of Manitoba, northern Ontario, northern Québec including a portion of the northshore of the St.Lawrence, and Labrador (Wright 1972; 1981). Shield culture developed out of the Plano culture of southern Keewatin District and eastern Manitoba around 6,000 BC. Elements of this development involved a dependency upon caribou and fish supported by a generalized adaptation to the ecosystems of the Canadian Shield (see Feit 1973). Western bands of Shield culture gradually occupied the Canadian Shield as it was released from the glacial ice and associated bodies of water and was colonized by plant communities and their associated faunas. This incremental process resulted in the occupation of the Canadian Shield following a west to east cline with the Hudson Bay Lowlands of Ontario and much of Québec and Labrador not being settled until around 2,000 BC. The Cree, Ojibwa, Algonkin, Montagnais, and the Beothuck of the time of European contact are regarded as the direct descendants of Shield culture. The close cultural and linguistic affinities between the aforementioned people, exclusive of the Beothuck who became extinct before their language could be properly studied, reflects the exceptional degree to which Shield cultural systems were interconnected throughout a region that covers nearly half of Canada. Factors favouring this `sameness´ were as follows: the association of major food resources with the interconnecting waterways of the Canadian Shield that also functioned as the communication routes in both summer and winter; a broadly adapted subsistence pattern centred on caribou and fish that required considerable territory for small bands of people due to fluctuations in caribou populations compounded by the erratic impact of endemic and often massive forest fires; a flexible social system favouring wide-ranging relationships that was cemented by interband marriages; limited cultural intrusions or influences from neighbouring cultures; and the late colonization of much of the eastern Canadian Shield.

     The technology of Middle Shield culture is characterized by chipped stone knives, scrapers, and projectile points and a general absence of tools formed by stone grinding. As with most cultures, the major tool category was the unmodified flake whose naturally sharp edges could be used for a wide range of cutting, scraping, and slotting tasks. Native copper implements are particularly common on sites in proximity to the copper sources of Lake Superior. There is also evidence of an extensive trade in copper to Middle Great Lakes-St.Lawrence culture populations in the Ottawa Valley. Through time there appears to be an increase in the number of scrapers and side-notched projectile points at the expense of large bifacially flaked knives and lanceolate points. Bone in any form is usually absent except as small calcined fragments. As a result, the inference of a reliance upon caribou and fish must be based upon settlement pattern distributions. A number of caches of stone and copper implements found in Manitoba, Ontario, and Québec are interpreted as `boneless´ graves where acid soils have dissolved the bone. One of the Manitoba sites did contain some human remains. Red ochre, chipped stone tool kits often including items manufactured from Knife River chalcedony from North Dakota and native copper implements, characterizes these features in Manitoba and Ontario suggesting that by 2,000 BC elaborate mortuary ritualism was being practiced by at least those Middle Shield culture populations bordering the more southerly centres of ceremonial elaboration.

Middle Shield culture dwellings ranged from substantial semi-subterranean structures with excavated entrance-ways to very flimsy dwellings that have left little archaeological trace. Settlement pattern distributions do not change in most areas of the Canadian Shield from the earliest human occupation up to the time of European contact indicating that subsistence rounds had been relatively stable over thousands of years. Given the relatively consistent nature of animal behaviour and the stability of the land forms such a situation is not surprising. Unfortunately stratified sites are a rare occurrence and most sites consist of hopelessly mixed cultural debris of untold numbers of campsites representing thousands of years of seasonal occupations. This difficulty of component isolation is the single most serious limitation facing Canadian Shield archaeology.

The Parklands along the southwestern flank of the Middle Shield culture distribution and the Great Lakes-St.Lawrence vegetation province (McAndrews et al. 1987: Plate 4) flanking the southeastern border have acted as major areas of contact between different cultures. These cultural boundaries shifted through time as a result of climatically induced conditions that were either advantageous or disadvantageous to different cultural adaptations. While the cultural homogeneity of Middle Shield culture has been emphasized there is regionalism that is most pronounced along the southern boundaries of the Middle Shield cultural distribution where influences from neighbouring cultures were most intense. Regional differences are to be expected within a cultural construct with the space and time dimensions proposed for Shield culture but these differences would appear to be minor relative to the shared cultural characteristics.

Cultural origins and descendants:

Shield culture developed out of a late Plano culture base on the western and northwestern fringes of the Canadian Shield around 6,000 BC. The transition from Plano culture to Early Shield culture is most apparent at the Sinnock site in southeastern Manitoba (Buchner 1981; 1984). Archaeological evidence between 6,000 and 4,000 BC is sparse but by the end of Period II there is a marked increase in information. A number of Middle Shield culture sites have been dated to the beginning of Period III in the Barrengrounds of the central Keewatin District, Northwest Territories (Gordon 1975; 1976) and to the east as far as the Lake Temiskaming region on the Ontario/Québec border (Knight n.d.; 1974). The eastward spread of Middle Shield culture progressed as the land became habitable (Martijn and Rogers 1969; Parent et al. 1985; Richard 1985) and it was not until sometime around 2,000 BC that Middle Shield culture bands reached the central Labrador coast (Nagle 1978). Similarly, the Hudson Bay Lowlands do not appear to have been occupied prior to 4,000 years ago (Lister 1988; Pilon 1987).

The 2,500 to 2,000 BC Middle Shield culture occupation at the LM-8 site on Manigotagan Lake in southeastern Manitoba "...contained the lanceolate projectile points, boldly side-notched points, large lanceolate and asymmetrical biface forms and crudely fashioned trihedral adzes characteristic of the Caribou Lake complex" (Buchner 1979b: 6). It will be recalled that the Caribou Lake complex is regarded as a transitional phase from late Plano culture to Early Shield culture (Chapter 8). Despite various technological trends and increasing evidence of regionalism there is still a surprising degree of technological homogeniety across the Canadian Shield from central Keewatin District to the Labrador coast. This homogeneity is most apparent in the northern portion of the Middle Shield culture distribution. Sites situated in the more kindly endowed southerly regions reflect a greater degree of regionalism as well as interaction with other cultures to the south.

It has been speculated on the basis of technological, settlement patterns, subsistence, and cosmological evidence (Wright 1972; 1981) that subsequent developments from this common cultural base, spanning much of the Canadian Shield, led directly to the northern Algonquian-speaking peoples who still occupy the territory. These consist of the Cree, the Ojibwa, the Algonkin, and the Montagnais-Nascapi. Included on technological grounds and general way of life within this group of related peoples are the extinct Beothuck of the Island of Newfoundland.

Radiocarbon dates from Middle Shield culture components in Keewatin District, NWT calibrate from approximately 4,000 to 1,000 BC (Gordon 1975; 1976; Wright 1972b). Dated sites in Manitoba currently fall into the late portion of Period III, ranging from 2,500 to 1,000 BC (Buchner 1979; Dickson 1980; Wright 1972a). Northern Ontario dates span the entire Period III but most are towards the end of the period (Arthurs 1980; Knight n.d.; Lister 1988; Pilon 1987; Ridley 1954; Wilmeth 1978). Dated Middle Shield culture sites in north-central Québec consistently fall between 2,000 and 1,000 BC (Chevrier 1986; Denton et al. 1982; Laliberté 1978; Taillon et Barré 1987) while those in Labrador range from nearly 2,000 to 1,000 BC (Nagle 1978). Allowing for the patchy distribution of dated sites and the difficulty of recovering uncontaminated carbon samples from sites in the Canadian Shield, the dates from Keewatin District eastward to Labrador do indicate a west to east decreasing cline that approximately correlates with the regional environmental changes necessary for human occupation.

BLACK AND WHITE PLATE XIV: NORTHERN ALGONQUIAN CAMP   Settlement pattern evidence suggests that Middle Shield culture people followed a way of life essentially the same as that of the Cree, Ojibwa, Algonkin, and Montagnais peoples documented by Europeans observers. With few exceptions only the vaguest evidence of dwellings, such as the bark covered structures in the photograph, has survived in the archaeological record. No trace of the bark canoe, so essential to travel in the vast tracts of the Canadian Shield, has ever been recovered. Manufactured from wood, bark, and leather the majority of the sophisticated technology required for survival has simply vanished from the archaeological record. Note also that the camp is situated on an active beach that would be awash part of the year further dispersing the sparse evidence of human occupation. (Canadian Museum of Civilization, Canadian Ethnology Service, Negative 594: T. L. Weston, 1884, Jackfish River, Lake Winnipeg, Swampy Cree?).

Technology:

Middle Shield culture is a cultural construct of unusually large dimensions that is based predominantly upon a chipped stone technology. The stone tool inventory is dominated by bifacially flaked knives, side-notched and lanceolate projectile points, and large end scrapers. All too often cultural materials come from multi-component sites that defy component separation. Site locations strongly support the inference that the bark canoe was an essential element of the material culture but, of course, no trace of this transportation technology nor the winter equivalents of snow shoes and hand-hauled toboggan, has survived in the archaeological record. Spread across the Canadian Shield from Keewatin District to the coast of Labrador, with a time depth that extends from late Plano culture to the descendants of the present northern Algonquian-speaking peoples, the construct has been criticized as being too all-inclusive and not making allowances for regional developments (Buchner 1979; Hanna 1980; Laliberté 1978; Pollock 1976). This criticism may appear to have some validity when viewed from a regional perspective or relative to the admittedly weak nature of the comparative collections upon which the construct was partially based. On the other hand, the vital contributions of earlier researchers to the eventual formulation of a Shield culture, such as Frank Ridley (1954; 1958; 1966) and Elmer Harp (1961; 1964), have generally been ignored by the construct's critics. The definition of Shield culture was never solely based upon technology. Other cultural systems, such as subsistence, settlement patterns, and cosmology, were essential elements in a formulation of the concept of a distinctive culture adapted to the Canadian Shield that was clearly different from neighbouring cultures. There also appears to be some difficulty among many archaeologists in accepting the use of qualitative and quantitative changes in the basic tool kit through time and space as a valid device to reconstruct culture history rather of relying upon projectile point typology. Archaeological classifications have been plagued by simplistic typological systems that, once entrenched, are extremely difficult to change. Too often these typologies are used as convenient `index fossils´ whereby a handful of traits or even a single specimen will determine a cultural assignment. Certainly if a series of type names had been created for the various Shield culture tool categories it would have made comparisons simpler for other researchers but it would also have added another simplistic scheme to the growing chaos of archaeological nomenclature. Archaeological comparative studies will remain at a rudimentary level until the infant field of archaeosystematics expands along with a greater appreciation for the need of full quantitative and qualitative consideration of all the available evidence and not just selected traits.

In lieu of particularly distinctive `index fossils´ the crudity of the Middle Shield culture chipped stone technology has been used by some as a distinctive cultural trait. The fact that many Middle Shield culture sites are characterized by workshop activity with abundant preforms, bifacial trimming flakes and other rejectage and that massive silicious deposits, such as quartzite, slate, and rhyolite, were exploited, has heightened the impression of overall `crudity´. In truth, the Middle Shield culture chipped stone industry, with its bifacially trimmed core tools and flake implements, is as developed as the technology of any of its neighbours. Stone grinding to fashion tools is generally absent or rare and when present can frequently be attributed to the neighbouring Great Lakes-St.Lawrence culture (Wright 1972: 78). Rare chipped biface blades with a ground bit at one end, however, are present (Storck 1974; Wright 1972: 27).

In order to maintain some control over the enormous area under consideration, as well as the 3,000 years involved, Middle Shield culture technology will be considered within the following regions: the Barrengrounds of Keewatin District; northern and southeastern Manitoba; Northern Ontario; northern Québec; and central and southern Labrador. The decreasing time cline of human occupation from west to east, related to the fact that a large portion of northern Québec and Labrador was uninhabitable until after 4,000 BC, also makes such an arrangement useful.

I. The Barrengrounds of Keewatin District, NWT.:

During the warmer climate between 4,000 and 1,500 BC, when Middle Shield culture sites are most common on the Barrengrounds, the treeline was 160 km further north than it is today (Gordon 1976: 11, 35, and 42). Thus, commuting between the forest and the Barrengrounds would have involved less distance. This all changed with a cold period beginning at 1,500 BC that forced the treeline almost 500 km to the south and led to the eventual abandonment of the region by Middle Shield culture people.

Dates from the Middle Shield culture components of the stratified Migod site (Gordon 1976) and the multi-component Aberdeen site (Wright 1972) indicates that the Thelon and Dubawnt river drainages were occupied seasonally throughout most of the 3,000 years of Period III. As is characteristic of all but the latest sites in this region, bone is absent due to soil acidity. Technological change in the stratified sequence of the Migod site is difficult to detect due to the small samples. The earliest level, dated to just before 4,000 BC, only produced chipping detritus, a few wedges, and a biface knife fragment. The middle level, dated to 3,800 BC, contained side-notched points, wedges, sometimes made on biface fragments, large side and end scrapers, and a range of bifacially flaked knife forms. In the 3,500 BC level both side-notched and stemmed points occur with wedges, end and side scrapers, and lanceolate and ovate-acuminate biface knives. Level 4, dated just prior to 2,000 BC, is likely mixed with the preceding level. It produced side-notched points, lanceolate biface knives, end and side scrapers, wedges, an abrader and a ochre nodule. Although the samples are small one does not receive an impression of significant technological change over the approximately 2000 years that Middle Shield culture people seasonally occupied the Migod site. Allowing for the small samples, there is a decrease in biface knives, an increase in scrapers and, to a lesser extent, wedges (Gordon 1976).

ARTIFACT CLASS	HOUSE STRUCTURE 2		HOUSE STRUCTURE 1	
	f	%	f	%
Projectile points	7	13.7	17	18.7
Scrapers	17	33.3	36	39.6
Biface knives	23	45.1	33	36.3
Flake knives	1	2.0	3	3.3
Linear flakes	2	3.9	-	-
Abraders	-	-	2	2.2
Wedges	1	2.0	-	-
TOTALS	51	100.0	91	100.1

TABLE 3:   COMPARISON OF ARTIFACT CLASS FREQUENCIES FROM HOUSE STRUCTURES 1 AND 2 OF THE ABERDEEN SITE, KEEWATIN DISTRICT.

Although lacking the clearly stratified deposits of the Migod site the Aberdeen site on the Thelon drainage to the north did contain two house structures which are interpreted as single components. The relatively large samples from these houses permit some insights into technological change within Middle Shield culture in the region (Wright 1972b: 10-36). A peat sample from House Structure 1, within which flakes and artifacts were imbedded, gave a reading of 3025 +/- 90 BP (S-506) or a calibrated range of 1,545 to 910 BC. A date of 4,000 to 3,500 BC would appear to be more appropriate when compared to similar dated materials from the Migod site 125 km to the south (Gordon 1976). On the assumption that House Structure 2 is older than House Structure 1 by an uncertain amount, certain trends may be noted on Table 3. Projectile point and scraper frequencies increase slightly at the expense of biface knives. The other artifact class samples are too low to detect trends. A decrease in frequencies of biface knives relative to frequencies of projectile points and scrapers is a widespread Middle Shield cultural technological trend. Lanceolate points predominate in House Structure 2 as opposed to side-notched points in House Structure 1. There are also some minor differences in the attributes of the chipping detritus from the two houses (Wright 1972b: 31-34).

Archaeological evidence of the occupation of the present transitional forest zone of southern Keewatin District and adjacent northern Manitoba by Middle Shield culture people, while present (Irving 1968; Nash 1975), is not nearly as abundant as the evidence from the central Barrengrounds. This limited archaeological evidence could possibly reflect the existence of winter settlements at caribou pounds on frozen lakes or other locales that are difficult or impossible to locate. There are a number of historically documented references to winter caribou pound sites in the region. In AD 1770 Samuel Hearne stayed in a Chipewyan winter camp adjacent to a pound set in the forest at the edge of the Barrengrounds. The camp was occupied by more than 600 people (Hearne 1911). If such large winter aggregations at caribou pound sites were also a Middle Shield culture practice then the resultant sites would be very difficult to locate using standard archaeological survey techniques. The probability that archaeological survey has failed to locate winter pound sites applies throughout those areas of the Canadian Shield where large herds of caribou were hunted. In other words, evidence of limited or non-occupation may well be more a product of limitations in archaeological reconnaissance strategies than an accurate reflection of past human exploitation of a particular region. Sites do occur at caribou crossings in the transitional forest but they appear to represent small, fall campsites in contrast to the large multi-component summer sites of the lower Dubawnt and Thelon rivers. The scattering of distinctive side-notched projectile points in the more southerly Barrengrounds and Manitoba, therefore, probably reflects small family excursions, possibly from unlocated larger base camps.

II. Northern and Southeastern Manitoba:

Middle Shield culture material recovered in northern Manitoba to date have come from the thin deposits of multi-component sites. The Kame Hills site on Southern Indian Lake in the Churchill River system (Dickson 1980) contained Middle Shield culture side- and corner-notched projectile points and hearths lacking diagnostic tools but dated to 1,500 BC. A number of the biface knives, scraper varieties, and wedges could also pertain to the Middle Shield culture occupation of this site. Similar multi-component sites on Gods Lake at the headwaters of the Hayes River drainage have been dated to 1,000 BC. Scrapers, biface and uniface knives, flake knives and wedges dominated the small excavated collections (Wright 1970; 1972: 28-32). A rare occurrence at one of these sites was a mano or hand held grinding stone and a large (41 x 23 x 5 cm) stone metate at another site. Such grinding implements do not necessarily indicate an increasing importance of plant foods as they could equally well have been used to pulverize dried meat or manufacture tools (e.g. anvil). The fact that fire fractured cobble fragments are common on sites in the forest in contrast to their absence on the Barrengrounds sites undoubtedly reflects the availability of fuel. An abundance of these distinctively fractured cobbles indicates the cooking of food by both boiling water with hot rocks and baking on pavements of heated stones, the equivalent to our modern stoves.

Southeastern Manitoba, in contrast to much of the northern part of the province, has been subjected to extensive archaeological survey and excavation (Buchner 1979a; 1982; Steinbring 1980; Wheeler 1978). Throughout this region Middle Plains culture dominated except during Period III when there was an incursion of Middle Shield culture peoples. This occupation, however, was relatively short-lived and correlated with a cooling period when the forests expanded southward and the grasslands contracted to the west (Buchner 1979: 23). A stratified site on Manigotagan Lake in the Caribou Lake region north of the Winnipeg River contained a 2,000 BC Middle Shield culture occupation (Buchner 1979: 33-41; 86-93). The assemblage, with its large side-notched points, end and random flake scrapers, biface knives, some native copper implements, and evidence of ochre, exhibits a close relationship with sites on connecting drainage systems in adjacent Northern Ontario such as the Eaka site on the English River (Wright 1972: 23-27). Similar materials from the Tulibee Falls site (Steinbring 1980: 207-213) in the Winnipeg drainage are also attributed to Middle Shield culture. It should be noted that the aforementioned southeastern Manitoba occupations have been assigned by their excavators to a culture first defined on the prairie edge of southern Wisconsin. Referred to as Old Copper culture or Raddatz, the basis for the Manitoba assignment appears to be the presence of native copper tools and projectile points resembling the Raddatz side-notched point of Wisconsin. While this point type is comparable to Middle Shield culture points the remainder of the Wisconsin and Manitoba assemblages are quantitatively and qualitatively quite different (Wittry 1959; 1959a).

III. Northern Ontario:

It has been suggested (Dawson 1983) that Middle Shield culture in Northern Ontario be divided into northern and southern units with the latter occupying areas near the shores of the Upper Great Lakes and being differentiated from the former by the presence of polished stone and native copper implements. Such use of a limited number of selective tool categories for taxonomic purposes is not well suited to the task of defining cultural constructs. There is no doubt, however, that the more southerly bands of Middle Shield culture in Northern Ontario were closer to the native copper deposits and exposed to greater influences from neighbouring cultures than were their kinsmen to the north.

One of the distinctive characteristics of Middle Shield culture technology in Northern Ontario is the manufacturing of tools and ornaments from native copper. As early as 5,000 BC (Beukens et al. 1992) the native copper deposits of Lake Superior were being exploited by populations living on both the north and south shores of the Lake (Griffin 1961; 34, Map 3). If the density of occurrences of native copper implements reflects the origin of the metal working technology then the centre of the technology was along the western side of Lake Michigan in the state of Wisconsin (Griffin 1961: 90, Map 5). While the native copper deposits were mined for more than 6,000 years the archaeological evidence suggests the peak period of exploitation was between 4,000 and 1,000 BC. Unfortunately thousands of native mining pits were destroyed in the mid-19th and early-20th centuries by mining companies. All that remains of the native workings are a pitifully few recorded accounts (Griffin 1961: 47-76) and a limited number of over-looked native pit shafts. Recent miners appear to have quickly recognized that the most convenient way to the copper was by following the old pre-European workings. Native copper concentrations occur as surface veins. The following comment on a pre-European mining pit in the Upper Peninsula of Michigan provides some appreciation of the capabilities of the ancient miners.

"The depression was twenty-six feet deep, filled with clay and a matted mass of mouldering vegetable matter. When he had penetrated to a depth of eighteen feet, he came to a mass of native copper ten feet long, three feet wide, and nearly two feet thick, and weighing over six tons. On digging around it the mass was found to rest on billets of oak, supported by sleepers of the same material. This wood, specimens of which we have preserved, by its long exposure to moisture, is dark-colored, and has lost all of its consistency. A knife-blade may be thrust into it as easily as into a peat bog. The earth was so packed around the copper as to give it a firm support. The ancient miners had evidently raised it about five feet and then abandoned the work as too laborious. They had taken off every projecting point which was accessible, so that the exposed surface was smooth" (Foster and Whitney 1850: 159-162 in Griffin 1961: 47-48).

Many of the native open pit mines filled with water and organic materials were preserved in the oxygen-depleted or anaerobic environment that inhibits decay. Wooden shovels, leavers, bailing bowls, a wooden ladder made from a tree, and even a leather bag have been recorded (Griffin 1961: 124-129). Copper spear heads, knives, and chisels have also been reported from the pit debris but large grooved and ungrooved hammerstones were by far the most common mining tools. Isle Royale, situated less than 25 km south of the Ontario coast but 70 km from the Keweenaw Peninsula of Michigan, was a major region of copper mining. Copper deposits in fissures and, of greater importance, in lodes of amygdaloids, secondary fillings of cavities, were extensively worked by native miners. It has been estimated that 100 fissures and 1,500 to 2,000 lode mines, usually less than 2.7 m deep but some attaining nearly 6.1 m in depth, once existed on Isle Royale (Bastien n.d.). Support for the popular opinion that the copper was detached from its matrix by the use of fire and water has been either negative or inconclusive.

While eastern Wisconsin has long been regarded as the heartland of a `Old Copper culture´ it is recognized that a number of different cultures participated in the copper technology including Middle Shield culture (Mason 1981: 181-195). In this respect, "It is best to discontinue thinking of the Old Copper culture as a distinct ethnic entity" (Griffin 1978: 238). As copper implements were fashioned by a repetitive process of cold hammering and annealing, the technology cannot be interpreted as the inception of metallurgy, at least, not in the technical sense of the word. Copper becomes brittle with hammering and must be heated (annealed) to re-establish its malleability. Since Palaeo-Indian times heat was used to modify the crystal structure of silicious stones in order to improve their flaking characteristics. Thus, it would appear that long established stone-working methods were simply modified to accommodate the characteristics of native copper.

The Renshaw site near Thunder Bay on the northshore of Lake Superior (Arthurs 1980) represents a Middle Shield culture site that likely exploited the copper on Isle Royale. Nearly 25 km of open water lies between the site and Isle Royale, providing some appreciation of both the seamanship of these people and the capabilities of their watercraft. The probability that the Island was used by northeners is supported by the scarcity of grooved hammerstones in the Isle Royale mines. Such hammerstones were the dominant form on mining sites on the Keweenaw Peninsula of the south shore of Lake Superior (Bastien n.d.; Griffin 1961). Copper implements at the Renshaw site included awls, socketed points, narrow triangular points or parts of composite fishhooks, knives, and single unilaterally barbed harpoons. Abundant copper wastage suggests that copper manufacturing took place. Wood preserved by copper salts in two of the conical copper projectile points was identified as ash and conifer (Arthurs 1980: 5). Also preserved by the copper salts on two other implements were bark and grass remnants of cordage (Beukens et al. 1992: 893). Chipped stone tools were represented by end scrapers, large choppers, biface and uniface knives, and a single side-notched point. Other items were a triple grooved stone interpreted as a netsinker, stone metates, a possible pestle, hammerstones, and two flaked adzes with ground bits. Local cobbles appear to have been the source for the bulk of the stone tool manufacturing.

Of interest is the H. W. Armstrong site on the Pic River to the east on the northshore of Lake Superior (Bell 1928). This suspected pre-Nipissing Lake stage site, geologically dated to 4,000 BC, is named in honour of the divisional engineer in charge of the Canadian Pacific Railways construction of the bridge over the Pic River who, in 1884, recorded the accidental discovery of a copper gaff. The gaff, a tool usually associated with the boating of large fish caught on a line, was associated with a hearth in the bottom of a cavity covered by some 6 m of water-deposited clay capped with gravel. The campsite appears to have been located in a naturally protected bedrock pocket and although now 30 m above Lake Superior, 6,000 years ago it was covered by the Nipissing high water stage and sealed by sediments. For another explanation on how this feature may have become covered with Lake deposits see Quimby and Griffin (1961: 107). Other possible pre-Nipissing Lake stage copper items have been recorded along the northshore of Lake Superior, such as a copper chisel buried under 3.7 m of sediments at Port Arthur (Dawson 1966). Copper gaffs retrieved from the Lake bottom in fishermen's nets could pertain to either the later portion of Period II or Period III (Griffin 1961). Presumably the gaffs were lost while attempting to boat large fish or through boating accidents.

On the height of land north of Lake Superior sites have been excavated that indicate a long period of Shield culture seasonal occupation (Koezur and Wright 1976). On Dog Lake, north of Thunder Bay (McLeod 1980), most of the Middle Shield culture stone and copper items would appear to post date 2,000 BC. Within the Hudson Bay Lowlands recent work has produced evidence of a Middle Shield culture occupation (Lister 1988; Pilon 1987). Another significant site (Adams 1983), located northeast of Lake Nipigon, may represent a terminal Middle Shield culture component. The Fayle site produced a lithic assemblage that foreshadows the Late Western Shield culture (Laurel) of Period IV. A couple of pot sherds were found at the site but as the site location indicates a summer occupation there is no explanation for the scarcity of pottery if the site actually represented a Period IV occupation. It is also of interest to note that the 50 stone tools from the Fayle site were predominantly manufactured from Hudson Bay Lowlands chert nodules. This material was the choice of the late Middle Shield culture and Late Western Shield culture stone knappers of 1,000 BC to AD 500 across much of Northern Ontario. It is speculated that the introduction of bow and arrow technology led to a dramatic switch from the massive siliceous deposits, such as rhyolite and quartzite, to nodular, high quality cherts. The change from massive siliceous rocks to chert nodules to manufacture stone tools resulted in a striking reduction in the size of all tool categories and the total disappearance of some larger forms (Wright 1972). It is suspected that the aerodynamic requirements of the arrow, in contrast to the javelin, required greater precision in stone workmanship and, hence, higher quality stone. Ideological factors involved in the diffusion and adoption of the new technology were also probably important considerations in the dramatic and sudden change in stone varieties used for tool manufacturing. There is evidence to suggest that often when new technologies are adopted there is a concerted effort to carefully replicate the characteristics of the introduced item and that only later, with familiarity, are regional modifications made to the technology. This is probably a pragmatic effort to insure the effectiveness of an unfamiliar technology until it becomes an integral part of a cultural system.

In the Manitoulin Island area of Lake Huron there are three major quarry sites, the Sheguiandah site (Lee 1954; 1955; 1957), the George Lake site (Greenman and Stanley 1943), and the Giant site (Lee 1954a). Level II of the 26 acre Sheguiandah site is dominated by large primary flaked quartzite preforms of predominantly ovate, lanceolate, and semi-lunar form. Scrapers, hammerstones, and linear flakes also occur in this upper level. Two perplexing aspects of the Sheguiandah, Giant, and George Lake sites are the absence of clearly associated projectile points and the relatively limited evidence of a wide distribution of the truly massive amounts of quartzite quarried. If some of the projectile points from Level III of the Sheguiandah site are associated with the Level II preforms and if this occupation does date to the Nipissing Lake stage then a significant portion of the quarry activity would pertain to Middle Shield culture. It is difficult to conceive how people could quarry sites for hundreds, if not thousands, of years, without more of the resulting tools appearing on surrounding sites. Even the scrapers at the Sheguiandah site are predominantly side scrapers rather than the more typical Middle Shield culture end scrapers. Whatever the reasons, the extractive system applied to the massive quartzite deposits of the region was significantly different from most stone tool workshop sites where non-quarry activities leave a more substantial sample of the day-to-day tool kit. Pending the results of ongoing research Level II of the Sheguiandah site, the bifacial preforms of the George Lake site and the Giant site, are tentatively regarded as the products of Middle Shield culture quarry operations that spanned much of Period III. Certainly the large primary flaked bifacial preforms are more characteristic of Middle Shield culture technology than that of adjacent cultures. Perhaps the ultimate resolution of this problem of cultural identification will reside with a detailed consideration of the lithic reduction procedures at these and other sites (Storck 1974).

It was in eastern Northern Ontario that the early work of Frank Ridley laid much of the groundwork for the eventual formulation of the concept of a Shield culture (Ridley 1954; 1958; 1966). The lowest level of the Abitibi Narrows site on the northshore of Lake Abitibi near the Québec border produced large biface and uniface knives and large end scrapers. The only points were stemmed and lanceolate forms. A ground slate point of likely Middle Great Lakes-St.Lawrence culture origin (Laurentian) was also recovered. From the beginning Ridley recognized that other sites in the Canadian Shield, such as those on Lakes Mistassini-Albanel (Martijn and Rogers 1969) and on the headwaters of the St.Maurice River (Burger 1953) of Québec, shared the same percussion flaking technique with its heavy reliance upon bifacial cores and preforms. In contrast to the lower level of the Abitibi Narrows site, the Ghost River sites, also on Lake Abitibi, all appear to represent later Middle Shield culture occupations. A similar sequence of Middle Shield culture occupation has been recorded in the Kirkland Lake District of eastern Northern Ontario (Pollock 1975) and understandably at the eastern end of Lake Abitibi in Québec (Marois et Gauthier 1989). A very late Middle Shield culture occupation was represented in the lowest level of the stratified Frank Bay site on Lake Nipissing (Ridley 1954). Dated to 1,000 BC this occupation contained an abundance of small end scrapers, bifacial and unifacial flaked knives, rare random flake and side scrapers, linear flakes, and a range of notched, stemmed, and trianguloid projectile points. The thinness of the points at the haft (6 mm) suggests that the bow and arrow technology was in use at this time. Measurements of wooden arrow shafts in the ethnographic collections of the Canadian Museum of Civilization indicated that projectile points much over 6 mm in thickness at the notches, where the stone tip would be bound to the wooden arrow shaft, could not possibly be attached to the 9 to 10 mm diameter wooden shafts (Wright 1994: Figure 4).

In his analysis of the stratified Montreal River site on Lake Temiskaming Dean Knight (n.d.; 1974) followed Pollock's regional sequence of Shield culture occupation as represented by the early and late Abitibi Narrows and Mattawan phases. The lowest level of the Montreal River site, dated to 3,800 BC, contained corner-notched and stemmed points, biface knives, abundant slate preforms that may actually represent chitho-like tools rather than unfinished items, end and side scrapers, a hammerstone, a pestle, and a copper awl. Slates, dark chert, and rhyolite in order of frequency characterized the lower level. In the upper level, side-notched, stemmed, and small lanceolate points occurred along with lanceolate knives, slate chithos, abundant end scrapers, side and random flake scrapers, wedges, hammers, drills, and some evidence of stone grinding. Quartz, a range of chert varieties, and some slate, were the common stones used. The heavy use of chert nodules suggests the upper stratum is late, possibly dating around 1,500 BC. From early to late at this important stratified site tools become smaller and biface knives decrease in frequency while projectile points and scrapers increase. These trends appear to generally apply throughout the distribution of Middle Shield culture.

IV. Northern Québec:

Major excavations of multi-component sites at the eastern end of Lake Abitibi (Marois et Gauthier 1989) uncovered a relatively unbroken occupation extending from probable Early Shield culture to European contact. Despite a concerted effort by the excavators to isolate components only a limited degree of superposition of materials was demonstrated. This hopeless mixture of components is unfortunately all too characteristic of sites in the Canadian Shield such as the Middle Shield culture sites further east in the Lac St.Jean area (Fortin 1966). The latter region also produced polished stone gouges and celts. The presence of typical Middle Shield culture artifacts suggests that the gouges were trade items obtained by the Middle Shield culture occupants of the region from their Middle Maritime culture neighbours to the south and east. Surface collections and excavated data from the northshore of the St.Lawrence Estuary indicate the existence of a Middle Shield culture occupation (Chapdelaine 1988; Chevrier 1978; Clermont et al. 1992; Martijn 1974).

Excavations in the Lakes Mistassini-Albanel region of north-central Québec led to the definition of a Wenopsk complex (Martijn and Rogers 1969). Characterized by lanceolate, side-notched, and stemmed points, abundant end scrapers as well as other scraper varieties, a wide range of bifacial knife forms, burinated tools, chipped adzes, linear flakes, uniface knives, and combination tools, there appears to have been relatively little change through time in the basic tool kit although tools become smaller with time. Biface knives, scrapers, and projectile points dominate the assemblage. There is also a general absence of tools fashioned by grinding. The entire sequence is characterized by the use of the local high quality quartzite and undoubtedly a strong `quarry´ factor reflects itself in the assemblage. The Wenopsk complex is regarded as a regional expression of Middle Shield culture with the local Cree bands being its descendants.

The most northerly Middle Shield culture sites in Québec suffer from the chronic problem of thin cultural deposits representing numerous seasonal occupations by small, mobile groups. Indeed, the majority of the sites produce only quartz debitage and very few finished tools (Denton 1988). At Station C of the GaGd-8 site, for example, Middle Shield culture materials were recovered along with an arrowhead made from a brass or copper European trade kettle and some pottery (Laliberté 1982: 69). A hearth, which only contained carbonized bone and dated to AD 1655, was associated with Middle Shield

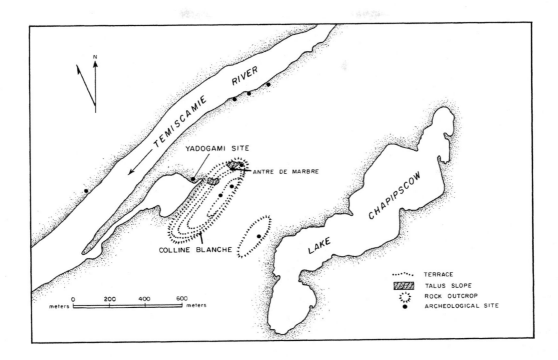

FIGURE 33: A MIDDLE SHIELD CULTURE SITE DISTRIBUTION   Unlike a number of sites along the Temiscamie River in the Lake Mistassini- Lake Albanel region of central Québec, the Yadogami site was situated to exploit the nearby quartzite outcrops immediately to the east. A number of activities would have been carried out at such a site but the most apparent to archaeologists is the evidence of stone tool production that resulted in an enormous quantity of chipping detritus. (Adapted from Martijn and Rogers 1969: Map XII, Figure 36. Drawn by Mr. David W. Laverie.)

culture materials. This all too common inability to isolate components or to be certain of what material is actually being dated by the radiocarbon samples, is an unfortunate archaeological fact of life for researchers working anywhere in the Canadian Shield. Fortunately there are exceptions to this rule, such as the 1,500 BC GaFf-1 site (Chevrier 1986), also in northern Québec. At this site it has been speculated from the excavated evidence that 13 stone knappers produced 300 bifaces and 135 projectile points in a couple of days in preparation for the fall caribou hunt. Actual material recovered consisted of 144 broken preforms and fragments, 12 side-notched projectile points, 18 end and side scrapers, 2 biface knives, 7 utilized flakes, and 3 hammerstones. Of interest was the apparent use of fire to extract the vein quartz from its matrix.

<u>V. Labrador:</u>

The Middle Shield culture penetration to the southern and central coasts of Labrador appears to have occurred around 2,000 BC. This appearance correlates with both the disappearance of Middle Maritime culture from Labrador and the northshore of the Gulf of St.Lawrence and the presence of Early Palaeo-Eskimo culture along the coast. First recognized in Hamilton Inlet and referred to as Brinex culture (Fitzhugh 1972), these small campsites produce side-notched points, end scrapers, and biface knives as well as red ochre nodules. Similarly, the small campsites along the central Labrador coast usually contain small side-notched and triangular points, end scrapers, drills, flake knives, and linear flakes (Nagle 1978). Another distinctive technological feature is the extensive use of heated cobbles in hearths (Ibid: 139), a trait not found on either Middle Maritime culture or Early Palaeo-Eskimo culture sites in the region.

Subsistence:

In most instances all bone is dissolved in the thin, acidic soils of the Canadian Shield. There also appears to have been a practice of not burning animal bones to judge from the relatively few carbonized bones recovered from Middle Shield culture sites. Historically documented ritualistic disposal of the remains or portions thereof of certain animal species may have pertained (Rogers and Rogers 1948). Under the circumstances the location of sites must be used to infer the most likely food resources being exploited. An interesting general settlement pattern characteristic of Middle Shield culture is the repetitive seasonal occupation of sites. Many sites contain evidence of most of the recorded human occupation of a region. Such sites are most frequently associated with good fishing locations. This pattern would suggest that the local food resources that attracted people were relatively stable over many thousands of years. Examples of such sites are to be found in Keewatin District, NWT (Gordon 1976); Manitoba (Dickson 1980); Ontario (Knight n.d.; Ridley 1954; 1966) and Québec (Marois et Gauthier 1989; Martijn and Rogers 1969).

With reference to the sites in the Keewatin District, despite the lack of bone refuse, there is little doubt "... that the prehistory of Keewatin, when it is known in detail, will reflect the history of the caribou,..." (Irving 1968: 30). Sites are strategically situated at caribou interception locations, such as river and lake crossings with good vantage points and high banks and dendritic esker systems to provide cover for the hunters. With few exceptions such caribou interception site locations are also situated adjacent to swift water rich in trout. It is difficult to conceive that the abundant and fat-rich lake trout would have been ignored. Indeed, fish would have been an essential fall-back resource given their predictable availability. Caribou availability, on the other hand, is subject to a range of factors such as forest fires in caribou winter range, crusted snow, and damp and cold weather during calving. Singly or in combination such factors could markedly reduce the numbers of caribou and range patterns. Add to this the fact that, for no reason apparent to humans, the barrenground caribou herds occasionally shift their migratory patterns with

COLOUR PLATE XI: CARIBOU CROSSING   Caribou cows and calves have just reached the south bank of the Thelon River, Keewatin District, on their late summer migration southward from the calving grounds north of the River. The colourful bloom of Arctic cotton in the foreground covers the discarded tools and refuse of hunters who have intercepted the caribou at this site for thousands of years. There was abundant evidence of a Middle Shield culture occupation. People would have moved into the Barrengrounds in the late summer and then drifted southward with the caribou herds as they migrated to their wintering grounds in the forests.   (Reproduced from Wright 1976: Colour Plate II)

potentially dire consequence for the people who depend upon them for survival. A widespread interception network of hunters in combination with alternative resources were likely the most successful counter to such eventualities. The relatively low numbers and dispersed nature of muskox herds would reduce their significance as a major food resource despite the relative ease with which they can be killed. It is further suspected that it would have had to be a very desperate band of hunters to deliberately attack a barrenground grizzly bear. As has been noted in other parts of this work, the importance of fish to the survival of hunting peoples has been almost certainly underemphasized in the historically documented literature. It is perhaps unreasonable to expect a hunter to brag about the number and size of whitefish he captured when his hunting companion has killed a moose, particularly when women were often the major capturers and processors of fish. A subsistence pattern focused on a combination of caribou and fish has likely existed from the beginning of human occupation over much of the Canadian Shield. Further south, beyond the winter range of the large barrenground caribou herds, the food resources become more dispersed and, thus, a more diffuse subsistence pattern prevailed. There would, however, have been a seasonal focus on the rich and predictable and, therefore, dependable fish resources. Examples of a more diffuse subsistence pattern may be seen at the LM-8 site in southeastern Manitoba where, despite poor bone preservation, fish, beaver, and elk remains were associated with the Middle Shield culture occupation of the site (Buchner 1979: 41). In the same general region of Manitoba charred muskrat, beaver, moose and bird remains were recovered from the Tulibee Falls site (Steinbring 1980: 209). In the Lake of the Woods region of Ontario at the Ash Rapids site (Wall n.d.) black bear, moose, deer, beaver, otter, muskrat, hare, turtle, loon, teal, pike, sturgeon, and pickerel were recovered and clearly reflect a diffuse subsistence pattern. Thus, those Middle Shield culture bands who occupied the forests south of the range of the barrenground caribou herds relied upon a "... systematic exploitation of all the resources at differing times. The failure of one resource results in the shift of emphasis to one or more alternate resources" (Dawson 1983a: 57).

Major factors affecting game resources in the Boreal Forest and Lichen Woodland vegetation provinces are forest fires, icing of caribou winter browse, snow depths, wind-chill, natural biological cycles (hare and grouse), and disease, particularly resulting from a parasitic nematode carried by deer that is deadly to moose and caribou populations. The natural cycle of forest fire and forest regrowth results in an initial increase in moose and beaver populations followed by increased woodland caribou populations in the mature forest (Feit 1973; Winterhalder 1981). Within this immense landscape of interconnecting waterways the dispersed and fluctuating animal resources tend to be associated with the water's edge or frozen water systems in winter. Big game like caribou, moose, and beaver was not only important for meat and fat but also essential for hides, sinew, bone and antler (Martijn and Rogers 1969: 52-53). Fish, however, was the most predictable resource which, in combination with big game, permitted survival in the Canadian Shield. There is some indirect evidence to suggest the use of fish weirs in the Hudson Bay Lowlands of Ontario at the Shamattawa Rapids site (Lister 1988). The site, with a likely date of 2,500 BC, was located during an attempt to discover fish weir sites recorded on early 19th century maps. The area in question was recorded to have fish weirs that could produce more than 500 whitefish a day during the fall spawning period (Ibid: 75). Unlike most of the Shield, soil conditions in the Hudson Bay Lowlands sometimes permits bone preservation. Cold weather camps have been identified on the basis of both their sheltered locations and the recovery of beaver, caribou, porcupine, and hare (Pilon 1987). Historic documents indicate that dogs were fed the fish bones thus effectively removing them from the archaeological record (Lister 1988: 79). Despite the absence of direct evidence in the form of bones site locations suggest that fish were critical to survival in the Hudson Bay Lowlands as well as the Canadian Shield in general. Fish captured in the fall would be preserved by smoking and represent an important component of the winter diet.

An adaptable subsistence pattern would have been typical throughout most of the Middle Shield culture distribution excepting the seasonal tundra caribou hunters of Keewatin, northern Manitoba, and northern Québec who, for at least a portion of the year, were able to practice a specialized or focused subsistence economy. By 2,000 BC and probably earlier Middle Shield culture bands began to seasonally exploit the maritime resources along the northshore of the Gulf of St.Lawrence and the central Labrador coast. This maritime adaptation, however, was somewhat tentative with sites only situated along the interior coastal belts unlike the earlier Middle Maritime culture adaptation or that of the contemporaneous Early Palaeo-Eskimo culture (Chevrier 1978; Nagle 1978).

Settlement patterns:

For the northern Ojibwa it has been observed that, "Their lives were oriented largely to the ecotone occurring along the boundary between land and water that constituted so much of their environment" (Rogers and Black 1976: 5). This observation also applies to Middle Shield culture and, indeed, to all the occupants of the Canadian Shield. The summer to fall settlement pattern was a direct reflection of the subsistence strategy. This involved the establishing of a base camp at a good fishing location with surrounding satellite camps that could exploit a large area in order "... to optimize the yield with the least expenditure of energy" (Ibid: 19) (see Figure 37). Winter settlement distributions are largely unknown. On the basis of ethnographic analogy, however, winter settlement could have ranged from dispersed family hunt camps to large gatherings of people at successful caribou pound sites. The latter could even involve a number of neighbouring bands. Although such sites could, on occasion, support hundreds of people throughout the winter, their potential location on frozen swamp lands and lake edges makes their archaeological discovery either impossible or a matter of pure chance.

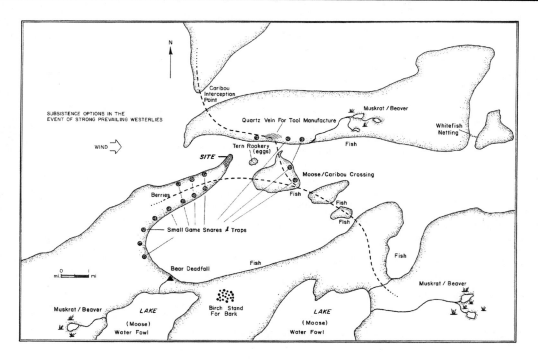

FIGURE 34: MIDDLE SHIELD CULTURE SITE LOCATIONS RELATIVE TO PREVAILING WINDS
With warm weather travel dependant upon canoe transport, it would be inevitable that strong winds would curtail water travel. Middle Shield culture people, like their descendants and their predecessors, favoured camping locales that offered a range of resources as well as alternative routes of travel protected from high winds. This Figure is based upon an actual location on Gods Lake in east-central Manitoba. As illustrated, a wide range of food and raw materials was still accessible to people stranded by strong westerly winds. (Drawn by Mr. David W. Laverie.)

I. The Barrengrounds of Keewatin District, N.W.T.:

The seasonally focused subsistence adaptation of the Barrenground caribou hunters of Keewatin features indicate that caribou was a major focus, locations adjacent to fast water and excellent fishing also suggests that fishing was important. Satellite, small camps in Keewatin District are not nearly as abundant as in the forest proper. A highly focused settlement pattern was adapted to the concentrations of caribou in the Barrengrounds in the summer.

Two Middle Shield culture house structures were excavated at the Aberdeen site on the Thelon River in central Keewatin District (Wright 1972b: 10-36). An ovate 4.6 m by 3 m structure was demarcated by large weight stones and contained a circular, flat bottomed, stone lined pit. A hearth floor was not recognizable. The majority of the tools and cores (82.5%) were concentrated in the eastern half of the house suggesting that the entrance faced west. Such an orientation would overlook a broad expanse of the Thelon River. The house floor consisted of a lower deposit of stained sand and an upper deposit of black-brown peat with both deposits containing artifacts and a large amount of debitage of a distinctive black quartzite suggesting that all of the debris related to a single occupation. Possibly some of the peat in the house represents an accumulation of flooring material. The other house structure was semi-subterranean and measured 4.3 m by 3 m with a 1.8 m long excavated entrance-way (Figure 38). The entrance faced west and slightly north to provide a broad view of the Thelon River. Similar to the situation with the earlier house over 95.0% of the tools and preforms occurred in the eastern half or back of the house along with most of the chipping detritus. In contrast, the western half or front of the house contained only a sparse scattering of flakes as did the entrance-way. It would appear activities, such as stone knapping, were concentrated in the back half of the house while, at the same time, allowing the hunter to periodically scan the Thelon River for crossing caribou. Most of the weight stones around the periphery of the structure were apparently pirated by later occupants of the site. In the centre of the dwelling was a stone-lined pit, similar to the one in the earlier house, and in the eastern sector a 5 cm thick hearth floor of burnt sand and minute fragments of carbonized bone. The southern half of the house was 15 cm higher than the northern half and may have functioned as a sleeping platform. House construction consisted of hollowing-out a shallow basin to a depth of 40 cm where a heavy cobble-gravel floor was encountered. This floor, as well as the excavated entrance-way, was then covered with a thick organic layer that decomposed to a thin greasy-black lense. Artifacts and flakes were incorporated in the peat and fragments of mended specimens ranged from immediately under the surface turf to as much as 30 cm in depth. Even a discrete chipping floor that represented a single event ranged from 13 to 38 cm in depth. This kind of vertical distribution of cultural debris suggests that layers of moss were repeatedly used for flooring and debris simply became incorporated through a process of trampling and other activities. There is some tenuous evidence of two house structures at the Migod site on the Dubawnt River (Gordon 1976: Figs. 9-11). Structures were inferred from concentrations of cultural debris that measured 4 m by 3 m and 4.9 m by 3 m. The dimensions are similar to the clearly demarcated houses at the Aberdeen site 100 km to the north but the total absence of interior features is curious.

There is little evidence of exotic stone being introduced into the central Barrengrounds from the south. Sites are characterized by stone tool kit replenishing activity using locally available quartzite cobbles. As glacial outwash quartzite cobbles were also the major raw material for tools in southern Keewatin District, adjacent Manitoba and eastern Saskatchewan, fingerprinting of lithics will have to focus upon regional differences in quartzites.

Due to a probable shift in caribou calving and migratory patterns in response to the southward retreat of the treeline around 1,750 BC (Gordon 1976: 31-43; Wright 1972b: 42) Middle Shield culture

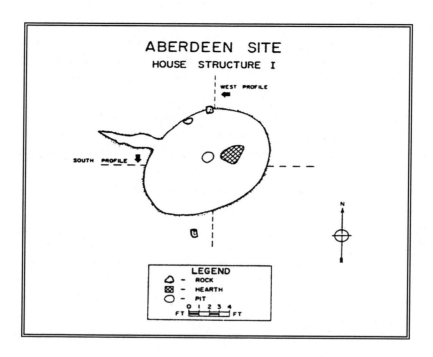

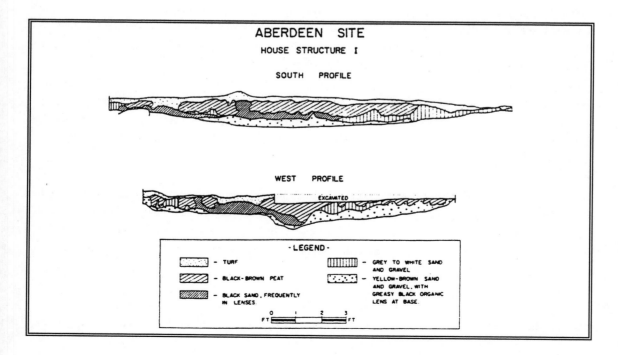

FIGURE 35:   A MIDDLE SHIELD CULTURE DWELLING ON THE BARRENGROUNDS   This semi-subterranean dwelling on the Thelon River overlooked a major caribou crossing. The majority of the cultural debris occurred in the eastern half of the structure suggesting that people worked at a number of tasks in the back of the dwelling while watching through the entranceway for caribou herds swimming across the River from their calving grounds to the north. There was some suggestion of an elevated sleeping platform in the southern half of the structure. A stone-lined central pit, which could have been a central support post hole for holding the skin tent covering in place, was flanked by a cooking hearth. Most of the stone weights that would have held down the edges of the tent covering were apparently removed by subsequent occupants of the site for their own use. At such sites, with thousands of years of seasonal occupation, the only tent rings demarcated by stone weights are usually those of the latest occupants. (Reproduced from Wright 1972b: Figure 2)

---

people abandoned the region. The area was subsequently reoccupied by Early Palaeo-Eskimo hunters from the northwest. It is assumed that the Middle Shield culture hunters shifted southward with the retreating forest boundary but very large sites, equivalent to the Aberdeen Lake site, have not been located in either southern Keewatin District (Irving 1968) or northern Manitoba (Nash 1975).

II. Northern and Southeastern Manitoba:

At the multi-component Kame Hills site on Southern Indian Lake, part of the Churchill River drainage system (Dickson 1980), cobble firestone hearths were associated with the Middle Shield culture occupation but no evidence of house structures per se was detected. This situation is common across the Canadian Shield but as most of the sites would have been warm weather occupations it is presumed that flimsy structures, such as lean-to's and bark sheathed lodges with light pole frames, left no archaeological record or that the record was obscured by subsequent occupations. At the Gods Lake site on the Hayes River drainage of northeastern Manitoba two possible tent rings were indicated by large weight stones that rested on sterile soil (Wright 1972a: 28-29). The possibility that these features represented lodges was unfortunately not recognized at the time of the excavation. If circular in outline the structures would have been approximately 4.6 m or more in diameter. Such dimensions for a nuclear family lodge are quite similar to those noted for related dwellings in Keewatin District. Middle Shield culture distributions along portions of the Winnipeg River in southeastern Manitoba tend to be quite variable with some focus on narrows, islands, and at or near the mouths of tributary rivers (Buchner 1982: Fig.13). A curious feature of the settlement distribution of the brief incursion of Middle Shield culture into a region previously and subsequently occupied by Middle Plains culture is that the settlement patterns of the two cultures duplicate one another. Such duplication raises interesting questions regarding the flexibility of the adaptive systems of Middle Shield culture and Middle Plains culture even allowing for the somewhat cooler conditions that prevailed during the Middle Shield culture occupation (Steinbring 1980).

III. Northern Ontario:

At the Renshaw site on the northshore of Lake Superior (Arthurs 1980: 5) an arc of post moulds associated with a concentration of tools and chipping detritus may have represented some form of temporary shelter or windbreak. Numerous pits and hearths in the more than 20 cm thick cultural deposits built up by windblown sand suggests that the site was repeatedly occupied. At the Smoothwater site in eastern Northern Ontario a tentative 3 m by 3.7 m tent ring with a central hearth pit containing fire fractured rock and concentrated artifacts and debris was identified (Pollock 1975: Fig.12, 55).

Until recently there has been little evidence of a Middle Shield culture occupation in the Hudson Bay Lowlands (Dawson 1976a). Recent reconnaissances (Lister 1988; Pilon 1987) have dispelled the suggestion that the region was not occupied until quite recent times. A rare exception for Middle Shield culture site seasonality is the evidence that two of the Hudson Bay Lowlands sites were cold weather camps (Pilon 1987: 165). Both sites were situated at the junctures of two rivers and as much as 160 km inland from the coast. Earlier failures to detect Middle Shield culture as well as later occupations in the Hudson Bay Lowlands appear to have been the result of a survey strategy that focused upon the major rivers. Sites in such locales would have generally been destroyed by spring flood erosion, ice scouring, and river meandering (Julig 1988).

The relative scarcity of Middle Shield culture sites along the northshores of Lake Superior and Lake Huron is understandable given the falling water levels of the lakes associated with isostatic rebound that have isolated sites well back from the present shoreline in dense bush. To locate such sites survey must be oriented to ancient landforms. A knoll in what is now a long, narrow bog, for example, could represent a Middle Shield culture camp site that once occupied an island in a narrow strait of open water 4,000 years ago. The Renshaw site (Arthurs 1980) and other Middle Shield culture sites along the northshore of Lake Superior occupied the post-glacial Lake Algoma beach but today are situated on ridges overlooking flat land that once was water (see Figure 40 and Saarnisto 1974). Other regions simply appear to have had a limited Shield culture occupation. In contrast to the abundant sites in the English River/Lac Seul region of Ontario and adjacent Manitoba only 3.9% of the 230 components recorded during the West Patricia District survey were Archaic (Reid 1980). This ratio is curiously close to the Archaic assignment of 3.5% of the 85 components recorded on Lake Nipigon (Dawson 1976: 13). There could be a number of explanations for variations in population density across the Canadian Shield during the Middle Shield culture occupation. Specific drainage systems were probably exploited by an individual band. On the Montreal River a Middle Shield culture base camp was situated at the point where the river emptied into Lake Temiskaming. Small camps, however, occurred along the River as far upstream as 32 km (Knight n.d.). The richness of the resources of any particular drainage system would have a direct effect upon the density of settlement. Such areas have been described by anthropologists as hunting ranges with vaguely defined boundaries rather than territories with specific rights of ownership (Rogers 1963). A sense of ownership, however, would have existed at the band level although intermarriage with adjacent bands could alter rights to exclusive use of the land. Many sites were also strategically situated relative to travel routes. The occupants of the multi-component sites at the east end of Lake Abitibi, for example, could travel by inter-connecting river and lake systems to either Lake Temiskaming on the headwaters of the Ottawa River or the headwaters of river systems like the Coulonge and Gatineau (Marois et Gauthier 1989).

IV. Northern Québec:

In the Caniapiscau region of northern Québec sites dating from 1,500 BC to AD 500 are concentrated along the main drainage systems and their tributaries and on top of moraines, knolls, and low terraces (Denton et al. 1982). Caribou were probably the major prey but the dispersed settlement pattern is unlike the seasonal concentrations at major caribou crossings characteristic of Keewatin District. The occurrence of Ramah quartzite from Labrador on the early sites in north-central Québec but the near absence of Mistassini quartzite to the southwest has led to the suggestion that the sites in question were Middle Maritime culture occupations and do not pertain to Middle Shield culture (Denton 1988). Unfortunately, most sites consist of chipping detritus around a hearth with very few diagnostic tools that would permit cultural assignment (Ibid: 148). An intensive field recording effort to delineate lodge floors at Middle Shield culture seasonal camps at the east end of Lake Abitibi in Québec (Marois et Gauthier 1989) did not produce convincing results. As usual, much of the problem related to the seasonal occupation of the same site by earlier and subsequent people resulting in component mixture exacerbated by natural disturbances resulting from treefalls and frost action.

V. Labrador:

Middle Shield culture sites at Hamilton Inlet in southern Labrador frequently contain Seal Lake cherts from the interior of Labrador (Nagle 1978: 121) but virtually no Ramah quartzite from the coast suggesting that the adaptation at this time was to interior caribou hunting in the winter supplemented by a limited use of summer coastal resources (Fitzhugh 1972: 159). Along the central Labrador coast sites are situated in the inlets and on the sheltered side of islands with access to bays and other protected waters. Such site locations suggest spring to summer exploitation of fish, seal, and birds (Nagle 1978: 140). Large cobble firestone hearths with tools in and around them are characteristic of the Middle Shield culture occupation but atypical of the partially contemporary Middle Maritime and Early Palaeo-Eskimo cultures. Both interior (Seal Lake) and central coast (Mugford) cherts are common on the Middle Shield culture sites of the central Labrador coast but very little Ramah quartzite is present suggesting that access to this material on the northern Labrador coast was denied by Early Palaeo-Eskimos (Nagle 1978: 139).

It was at Gods Lake in northeastern Manitoba that a settlement pattern strategy typical of Middle Shield culture occupation of large bodies of water across the Canadian Shield was first recognized. Figure 34 illustrates the strategy that is simply to always be in a position to exploit a range of resources regardless of wind direction and heavy seas. Being unable to move westward by unsafe travelling conditions for three days at the Gods Lake site provided an opportunity for the author to survey in detail the protected areas to the east and north. This pattern of establishing major campsites or camping regions in areas that provide a number of travel alternatives and resource options is a common feature of warm weather settlement across the Canadian Shield. A camping region refers to a base camp area characterized by a dispersed settlement pattern made up of many nearby small campsites rather than a single concentrated large site (Martijn and Rogers 1969: 316). Similarly, survey on the Lake of the Woods in southwestern Ontario found site concentrations along waterways sheltered from the prevailing westerlies and often in association with lithic sources (Reid 1977; Wall n.d.). As the summer big game and fish resources would have been most readily available along the major waterways it is not surprising that concentrations of archaeological sites are associated with these same waterways. Such occupations are often situated at narrows or fast water with good fishing and in proximity to areas with hunting potential. Many of the sites face open water with a westerly to southerly view, presumably for access to any breeze that would reduce the plague of biting insects. Numerous exceptions to this generalization, of course, exist. The Fayle site (Adams 1983) northeast of Lake Nipigon occupied a point of land immediately west of a narrows connecting a chain of lakes that faced northeast but was protected from northwest winds by an esker. This northeast orientation was also the most common pattern for summer fishing sites in the Lakes Mistassini-Albanel region of Québec (Rogers and Rogers 1948). There is little doubt that the voracious swarms of black flies, mosquitos, deer flies, moose flies, and no-seeums of the Canadian Shield influenced summer settlement strategies since time immemorial. The ubiquity and density of biting insects is also probably one of the best explanations for the frequent presence of repetitively used campsites on the smaller islands.

Cosmology:

The only definite Middle Shield culture human remains encountered in the entire Canadian Shield during Period III consist of some tooth enamel and decomposed bone from the LM-8 site in southeastern Manitoba (Buchner 1979: 37-41). A circular burial pit would suggest either a bundle or a flexed burial. A broken ground slate slab, end and random flake scrapers, and a large lanceolate knife had been placed in the grave. All of the artifacts were found in a tight cluster suggesting they were part of a tool kit enclosed in a bag. The body was placed in the grave and covered with a thin layer of soil and ochre after which the tool kit was added followed by an alternating process of burning and filling with ochre, ash, and soil until the pit was filled. Such a sequence of acts obviously had ceremonial significance. The burial has been dated to 2,400 BC. Also in southeastern Manitoba is the Jansson site at Mud Falls on the north bank of the Winnipeg River. Contrary to Steinbring (Steinbring 1970: Fig.25; 1980: 222-233), who assigns the site to Old Copper culture, it is interpreted here as representing either a Middle Shield culture burial from which all bone has disappeared or a votive offering. The materials were collected in 1928 from an eroded river bank and consisted of a bison cranium, a large copper chisel, a socketed copper lance head, a tanged, side-notched copper lance, 2 or 3 side-notched chipped points, and some large fragments of charred wood. The notched points identified by Steinbring as Middle Plains culture Oxbow type points more closely resemble Middle Shield culture side-notched point forms. On the basis of the copper lance heads, which closely resemble specimens from the Allumette -1 site on the Ottawa River, the site is estimated to date to the beginning of Period III.

The McCollum site (Griffin and Quimby 1961; Wright 1972a) is situated at the south end of Lake Nipigon near the Lake's embouchure into the Nipigon River and thence to Lake Superior. Accidentally uncovered by a bulldozer in 1954 the site represents a `boneless´ grave. Disturbed materials occurred "... in an area about 8 feet square..." (Griffin and Quimby 1961: 92). Recollection by the McCollum family suggests that some cordage and wooden spear shaft sections were preserved by the copper salts as well as some human teeth. A number of the artifacts were stained with red ochre. In 1960 a test exploration by the writer encountered an undisturbed portion of the grave pit. The remnant of the grave contained two tightly concentrated deposits of scrapers, utilized flakes, a projectile point, and a number of small copper items, mainly hammered nuggets. A small deposit of red ochre was also present (Wright 1972a: 59-60). Grave offerings in the grave pit, which likely contained a number of individuals, consisted of the following: 29 scrapers; 13 copper discs; 10 copper projectile points; 5 miscellaneous single copper items; 4 bossed copper bracelets; 4 copper triangles; 4 copper beads; 3 copper needles; 3 side to corner-notched chipped points; 2 large biface knives; 2 copper rods; and 2 socketed copper knives. The foregoing are exclusive of the hammered copper nodules, utilized flakes, and red ochre deposits (Colour Plate XII). One of the scraper tools was a linear flake of Knife River chalcedony from North Dakota, a material from which a number of other items in the grave were manufactured. Although not struck from a true blade core such distinctive linear flakes were clearly removed from some form of specialized core to provide long and distinctively laterally curved flakes that were subsequently retouched along the edges. A cache of similar Knife River `blades´ was discovered on the Minnesota side of the Rainy River less than 400 km west of the McCollum site (Stoltman 1971). Typological crossdating suggests this richly endowed grave would date to 2,000 BC.

The Farquar Lake site (Popham and Emerson 1954) was exposed by erosion on the shore of a small bay in the Trent drainage system of Southern Ontario immediately north of the southern terminus of the Canadian Shield. Implements were concentrated in a 2.3 m² area and consisted of 15 scrapers, 1 point?, 5 flakes, 14 copper points, 26 copper awls/gorges/pikes, 5 copper knives, 1 copper adze, a copper wedge,

COLOUR PLATE XII: MIDDLE SHIELD CULTURE OFFERINGS TO THE DECEASED A concentration of copper and stone implements was accidentally exposed during construction of a boat ramp at the southern end of Lake Nipigon, Ontario. The bulldozer cut into a 2,000 BC grave from which bone had disappeared due to the naturally acid soils of the region. This interpretation is supported by the presence of red ochre powder, a common addition to graves during this time period and the observation that some enamel ʻtooth capsʼ were present.

Among the copper items are open socket hafted points and knives, awls, chisels, punches, bossed bracelets, disc pendants, objects of unknown function, and a number of flattened nuggets, the raw material for tool production in the after life. The offerings represent some of the finest examples of native copper craftmanship known from Canada. While the copper would have been mined locally, probably from Isle Royale 145 km to the south in Lake Superior, among the chipped stone scrapers, points, and knives were a number of items manufactured from Knife River chalcedony. This exotic stone would have been traded from its quarry source in North Dakota 1,000 km to the west. (Reproduced from Wright 1972: Colour Plate II)

5 copper beads, and 46 indeterminate copper nuggets and fragments. Most of the stone tools were manufactured from North Dakota Knife River chalcedony (personal examination by the author) and within the scraper grouping were 7 of the distinctive `blade´ flakes noted from Minnesota and the McCollum site to the west. The straight-line distance between the geological source of the chalcedony and the site is in excess of 1,800 km. A red patch of soil associated with the concentration of artifacts may have been ochre but iron oxide staining is a natural phenomenon in the area. Correspondences between copper assemblages of the Farquar Lake site and the Renshaw site on Lake Superior (Arthurs 1980), such as the socketed conical points, single unilaterally barbed harpoons, and crescent knives, suggest a date of around 3,000 BC (Beukens et al. 1992).

A cache excavated at the Ouissinaougouk site in the Hudson Bay Lowlands of Northern Ontario consisted of a 40 cm by 20 cm pile of stone items in a slight depression, possibly resting on a birch bark container (Pilon 1987). Stone items were a side-notched point, three biface knives, five wedges, 4 gravers, 2 cores, 63 scrapers - mainly end scrapers, 16 utilized flakes, 5 spokeshaves, a drill base, and 242 flakes and flake preforms. Use-wear and blood residues on some of the implements were recorded (Ibid: 178) suggesting the cache represented an operational and relatively complete tool kit. It is speculated here that this feature represents either a grave offering in a `boneless´ grave or a votive offering.

Another tentative candidate for a `boneless´ grave is a cache containing "...not less than 200 knives, scrapers, celts, etc..." (Burger 1953: 38) on Lake Manowan on the headwaters of the St.Maurice River in Québec. The artifacts were reported to have occurred in a `heap´ measuring 1.8 m by 3 m. Illustrated specimens include a range of biface knives, a polished stone gouge, and a chipped and ground adze. While the gouge indicates contacts with Middle Great Lakes-St.Lawrence culture populations in the St.Lawrence River Valley the majority of the other implements are characteristic of Middle Shield culture.

Further east in Québec a cluster of tools was recorded at the Abraham site near Schefferville (Denton and McCaffrey 1988). The cache consisted of a typical Middle Shield culture side-notched point, four point preforms, four biface knives, an end scraper, and a side scraper. It is speculated that if a deceased person had been placed on the surface of the ground with grave offerings and then covered with logs or a grave house, such a `cache´ would be the only evidence to survive in the archaeological record.

The presence of tool kits in graves and probable `boneless´ graves appears to be a common feature of Middle Shield culture. Scrapers are a particularly common item in such caches as noted at the LM-8, McCollum, Farquar Lake, and Ouissinaougouk sites. At the McCollum and Farquar Lake sites there was also an abundance of copper implements and nuggets and chalcedony from North Dakota, including large side scrapers made on linear flakes. The variety of grave offerings is distinct from that of contemporaneous neighbouring cultures. Parallels, however, do exist with the mortuary practices of the southern Upper Great Lakes region. Indeed, influences leading to this elaborate ritualism, at least in southern Middle Shield culture, likely stemmed from the south where large cemeteries in eastern Wisconsin, estimated to have contained from 500 to 200 individuals, had an abundance of copper grave offerings, (Mason 1981: 181-194). Large, repeatedly used cemeteries obviously represented sacred places where the deceased were brought over a period of time for final burial. By 3,000 BC and probably earlier burial ritualism had taken on a distinctive character in the Canadian Shield. Burial sites could be either associated with or isolated from habitation sites.

Another class of archaeological site that relates to cosmology are the invocation sites along the northshores of Lake Superior and Lake Huron and as far west as southeastern Manitoba. Sites, generally located on exposed boulder or shingle beaches, contain a range of structures formed by arranging and stacking rocks. They are thought to mainly date between AD 800 and European contact and to pertain to the vision seeking quest of northern Algonquian-speaking peoples (Dawson 1981). Referred to locally along the northshore of Lake Superior as Puckasaw pits, the features on the higher elevated beaches were originally believed to relate to Archaic peoples. However, a copper projectile point found in one such structure, that was used as evidence of antiquity (Emerson 1960) probably pertains to a Late Western Shield culture (1,000 BC-AD 500) occupation (Salzer 1974: 48, Fig.6, J; Wright 1967: 157, Plate VIII, Fig.10). Typological dating of some of these features to the Late Western Shield culture (Laurel) of the Initial Woodland period extends their time depth to an appreciable degree. As there is evidence of the development of Late Western Shield culture out of the preceding Middle Shield culture the possibility of a Middle Shield culture association with some of the features is increased. Diagnostic materials are rarely associated with the Puckasaw pits but when it is the pits tend date to the appropriate elevated beach. This suggests that the features were not randomly scattered about the various beach levels and that beach dating may be appropriate. If this is the case, then many of the pit structures at the Red Sucker Point site near Marathon on the northshore of Lake Superior (Emerson 1960) are associated with the post-glacial Lake Algoma stage and should date to 1,700 BC. If an association of Middle Shield culture with these enigmatic structures can eventually be demonstrated it would reflect a continuity of a cosmological belief system over thousands of years in the region, a situation paralleling that of some of the medicine wheels of the Plains.

The Antre de Marbre at La Colline Blanche site on the Temiscamie River in north-central Quebéc is a unique feature. The cave is the largest of the nearly 50 natural erosional cavities in a quartzite outcrop (Hamelin et Dumont 1964; Martijn and Rogers 1969; 190-204) and was described by Father Pierre Laure in 1730 as follows:

"The aperture is easy to access, and lights up the interior. The vault corresponds, by its brilliancy, to its supports. In one corner is a slab of the same substance, but somewhat rough, which projects, forming a table as if to serve as an alter. Consequently the savages think that it is a house of prayer and council, wherein the spirits assemble. Therefore all do not take the liberty of entering it; but the jugglers who are, as it were, their priests, go there in passing to consult their oracles" (Thwaites 1896-1901: Vol.68, 48).

While there is no evidence of human activity inside the Antre de Marbre less than 90 m to the southwest people had fashioned some of the local quartzite into tools (Martijn and Rogers 1969: 198). Middle Shield culture people occupied the immediate region but the absence of any sign of human activity in or directly in front of the Antre de Marbre suggests that it was a sacred place from earliest times to the present, a place to be avoided by all but the spiritually powerful.

External relationships:

With reference to Canada, the contemporary neighbours of Middle Shield culture were Early Palaeo-Eskimo culture, Middle Plains culture, Middle Maritime culture, and Middle Great Lakes-St.Lawrence culture to the north and east, the west, the east, and south, respectively. There is also evidence of close contacts with the northern regions of what is now the midwestern United States.

Direct evidence of contacts between Middle Shield and Early Palaeo-Eskimo peoples on the central Barrengrounds is absent. The larger size of Early Palaeo-Eskimo tools on the Barrengrounds compared to their diminutive proportions in the Arctic archipelago is probably a product of manufacturing tools from the large and abundant quartzite cobbles of the Barrengrounds rather than an indicator of cultural exchanges with Middle Shield culture. Similarly, the appearance of wedges on Early Palaeo-Eskimo sites on the Barrengrounds (Gordon 1976) probably had more to do with the scarcity of high quality cherts with which to manufacture burins than it did with any cultural exchange. A more likely region for cultural contact between these two cultures would be in the forests of northeastern Manitoba where coastal dwelling Early Palaeo-Eskimos did penetrate the interior in search of caribou (Nash 1969).

In southeastern Manitoba and adjacent Ontario there were almost certainly contacts between Middle Plains culture and Middle Shield culture populations. During the hot and dry weather of the Altithermal, which favoured the expansion of the grasslands at the expense of the forests, Middle Plains culture (Oxbow and McKean complexes) spread into the western margins of the Canadian Shield and penetrated eastward as far as the Rainy River. Conversely, during the Sub-boreal period, cooling conditions favoured the expansion of the forests and with it Middle Shield culture bands who moved into regions formerly occupied by Middle Plains culture people (Buchner 1979). Some impression of the extent of cultural overlap between grasslands/parklands adapted people and forest adapted people can be seen in the cultural distributions along the Winnipeg River (Buchner 1982: 65, Fig.13). Occupations identified as Old Copper and Raddatz are here classified as Middle Shield culture while Oxbow, McKean, and Larter are collectively referred to as Middle Plains culture. It is evident that Middle Shield culture did intrude into former Middle Plains culture territory (Wheeler 1978: 90) and that the territories were eventually reoccupied by Middle Plains culture populations (Larter). Evidence of trade between the two cultures exists in the form of native copper items of eastern origin, such as a copper crescent knife on a site in central

Alberta (Forbis 1970: 17) and Knife River chalcedony from North Dakota on Middle Shield culture sites as far away as 1,800 km to the east.

Polished stone gouges of either Middle Maritime culture or Middle Great Lakes-St.Lawrence culture origins were transported westward by Middle Shield culture people (Dawson 1983: 12, McLeod 1980: 50). Most of these gouges are of the early full grooved variety, thus some could also pertain to Early Shield culture. Gouges appear at the Otter Falls No.7a site on the Winnipeg River and at other sites in the region (Buchner 1982: 26 and 137) and into Minnesota (Johnson 1969: 9). A similar distribution of gouges in northern Québec likely reflects Middle Shield culture contacts with Middle Maritime and Middle Great Lakes-St.Lawrence culture people to the east and south (Burger 1953; Laliberté 1978; Marois et Gauthier 1989). One of the most striking incidences of Middle Shield culture and Middle Great Lakes-St.Lawrence culture economic relationships is to be seen in the abundant native copper working on sites of the latter culture in the upper Ottawa River Valley (Kennedy n.d.; 1967). It appears that a well-established trade network involved the movement of native copper nuggets by Middle Shield culture people to Middle Great Lakes-St.Lawrence culture craftsmen who then fashioned the nuggets into tools and ornaments to be traded to the south and east. It is interesting to note that the Ottawa Valley copper tools are distinctly western in style suggesting there had also been a significant transfer of technology between these two cultures.

There is some tentative evidence of culture contacts among Middle Shield, Middle Maritime, and Middle Great Lakes-St.Lawrence cultures along the St.Lawrence River from Cornwall, Ontario (Wright 1994) to Québec City (Clermont et al. 1992) and on the Saguenay River at Chicoutimi (Chapdelaine 1988). Demonstration of culture contacts along the St.Lawrence and its tributaries that connect the interior of the continent to the Atlantic Ocean will undoubtedly increase as various finger-printing programmes capable of identifying the sources of exotic materials are expanded.

In some respects the relationship between Middle Shield culture and Middle Great Lakes-St.Lawrence culture corresponds to the relationship between Middle Plains culture and Middle Shield culture. There is a marginal geographic overlap of these cultures that changes with time. During a period of warmer climate Early Great Lakes-St.Lawrence and early Middle Great Lakes-St.Lawrence cultures occupied the southern margins of the Canadian Shield as far to the northwest as the Sudbury region including much of the Georgian Bay coast (J.V. Wright: unpublished data). A subsequent cooling trend presumably had a sufficient impact upon this ecotonal zone to favour the adaptation of Middle Shield culture people over that of Great Lakes-St.Lawrence culture. The sequential occupations of the southern margins of the Canadian Shield indicate once again that culturally defined territorial boundaries did fluctuate in response to environmental change. This cultural overlap has also been noted in the Algonquian Park area (Hurley et. al. 1972) and the Kirkland Lake region (Pollock 1976: 167-171). In addition to fluctuating cultural boundaries there is evidence, particularly from Period IV onward, of a broad `buffer zone´ between two neighbouring cultures characterized by a blending of traits from both cultures. In terms of issues relating to both culture change and culture contact such zones of cultural miscegenation will represent an important area of future research.

In the northern interior of Québec at Caniapiscau there is some limited evidence of an initial Middle Maritime culture seasonal occupation followed by a Middle Shield culture occupation beginning about 1,500 BC. There is little evidence of culture contacts to the south or southwest (Denton et. al. 1980: 304; Denton et. al. 1982) and only limited evidence of the acquisition of Ramah quartzite from northern Labrador (Denton et. al. 1982: 190; Samson 1978: 118) suggesting that Early Palaeo-Eskimo occupants of the coast had cut off the source of supply. On the central Labrador coast Middle Shield culture and Early Palaeo-Eskimo culture materials have been found on the same beach (Nagle 1978: 126) but there is no direct evidence of contact. Further to the south, Middle Shield culture eventually prevailed along the northshore of the Gulf of St.Lawrence from Tadoussac to Mingan while Middle Maritime culture was concentrated further east from Tabatière to Blanc Sablon (Chevrier 1978: 83). Problems of temporal overlap, the replacement of Middle Maritime Archaic culture by Middle Shield culture on portions of the Labrador coast and the northshore of the Gulf of St.Lawrence, and the recognition of either culture from the all too often scanty remains, confound a clearer understanding of the relationships between the two cultures. The polished stone gouges from Lac des Commissaires (Laliberté 1978: 92) and Lac St.Jean immediately to the northeast (Fortin 1966) likely represent Middle Maritime culture trade items into Middle Shield culture territory. It is interesting to note that the polished stone gouge of either Maritime culture or Great Lakes-St.Lawrence culture origin is the most common and widespread introduced trait found throughout the Middle Shield culture distribution. Other equally characteristic implements, such as plummets, ground slate lances, points and knives, and bannerstones, are generally absent or rare on Middle Shield culture sites except along cultural boundaries. This prevalence of one tool category would suggest that the polished stone gouge, at least for a period, was a highly prized item by Middle Shield culture people. The distinctive chipped stone industry of Middle Great Lakes-St.Lawrence culture, in contrast, appears to be largely absent from Middle Shield culture sites.

To the south of Canada the only archaeological assemblage that possesses correspondences with Middle Shield culture is the Burnt-Rollways phase (2,000-1,000 BC.) of northern Wisconsin (Salzer 1974). As this phase is both contemporaneous and adjacent to Middle Shield culture and shared a similar lifeway, it is probable that a direct relationship existed.

Human biology:

In terms of Middle Shield culture skeletal remains only the enamel tooth caps of a burial at the LM-8 site in southeastern Manitoba (Buchner 1979) have been recovered. Except in the Hudson Bay

Lowlands or under exceptional circumstances this situation is likely to prevail given the acid soils of the Canadian Shield. In addition, if the McCollum and Farquar Lake sites do represent `boneless´ burials and constitute a common burial pattern of Middle Shield culture then burial sites were often isolated from habitation sites making their location even more difficult. If surface disposal of the deceased along with grave offerings, possibly involving a grave house or some form of log covering, was a normal practice, particularly during the winter when the ground was frozen, then the likelihood of acquiring biological information from skeletal remains is, indeed, remote. Human skeletal material will most likely be discovered by accident.

Inferences on society:

It is inferred that Middle Shield culture society functioned in a very similar fashion to that of the historically documented northern Algonquian-speakers of the Canadian Shield. The fact that subsequent occupations mirror the Middle Shield culture settlement pattern suggests continuity of subsistence rounds and general resource exploitation. As these resources are "...neither evenly nor randomly distributed in space and time..." (Rogers and Black 1976: 21) an intimate knowledge of the floral and faunal resources, the physical environment, seasonal weather patterns that could affect travel, appropriate camp locales and quarry sources, the number of people a certain resource could support and for how long, and knowledge of a host of other lesser factors, were all necessary to survival. The nature of the country and its dispersed resources required a finely-tuned and broadly based exploitive adaptation, "...a definite fluidity of group size, composition, distribution, and movement was required, along with a fine sensitivity to the signs of the coming seasons" (Ibid: 21). Given that family and individual alliances could change through marriage, inter-personal conflicts, and in response to fluctuations in resource availability, flexibility of group size and individual and household mobility between bands would have been an important adaptive strategy. Factors such as freeze-up, break-up, the amount and the character of snow, the amount of water discharge, vary by year but all affect both game availability and hunter mobility (Winterhalder 1981: 72). A major complicating factor would be the endemic forest fires that are estimated to result in significant vegetative changes every 100 to 150 years with a concomitant impact on game availability and diversity (Ibid: 72-81). Within the Shield ecosystem fish have a high degree of stability and predictability while big game is moderately stable and small game tends to be cyclical. This is probably why a consistent settlement pattern was established early on where women were active in fishing and berry gathering and processing activities at the base camps while the hunters ranged over a wide territory in search of game and other resources. There really are no other options to this flexible strategy in most of the Canadian Shield (Martijn and Rogers 1969: 69-139).

Limitations in the evidence:

There are many limitations in the evidence upon which Middle Shield culture is based. The small and dispersed populations of the Canadian Shield have left relatively little trace, many sites have been flooded by dams and most are obscured by heavy bush cover. Compounding the foregoing situation is the limited archaeological survey that has been carried out in most of this enormous and logistically difficult territory. Major sites tend to be concentrated at particularly favourable fishing locations that were exploited on a seasonal basis by people over thousands of years. Such sites are the ones generally excavated by archaeologists despite the fact that it is difficult or impossible to isolate components. Thin, mixed archaeological deposits are the norm in Canadian Shield archaeology. Given the rudimentary state of development of archaeosystematics many archaeologists have relied heavily upon a limited number of so-called diagnostic traits in order to reconstruct culture history. The nature of Middle Shield culture technology is such that full quantitative and qualitative analysis is required including information on tool and flake production procedures in order to achieve an effective comparative base (Stewart 1991). Distinctive tools and styles do exist but they are not sufficiently diagnostic for their cultural significance to be recognized in isolation. The culture history reconstruction problems that stem from reliance on a limited number of tool categories, such as projectile point types, have been commented upon a number of times. Acid soils in the Canadian Shield have dissolved bone so completely that there is virtually no evidence relating to either the bone technology or faunal remains. Lacking a long tradition of archaeological research the Canadian Shield region was first used as a convenient blank area through which various people and/or traits could be moved. While recent archaeological research has filled in the blanks sufficiently to counter certain Asiatic diffusionist schemes there is still a strong tendency for more southerly oriented archaeologists to equate elements in the technology of the Canadian Shield with other cultures. The evidence, in my estimation, stands on its own merits. This great infertile crescent called the Canadian Shield was first occupied by boreal forest and lichen woodland adapted hunters equipped with an efficient and distinctive technology and way of life that prevailed until modified by European influences.

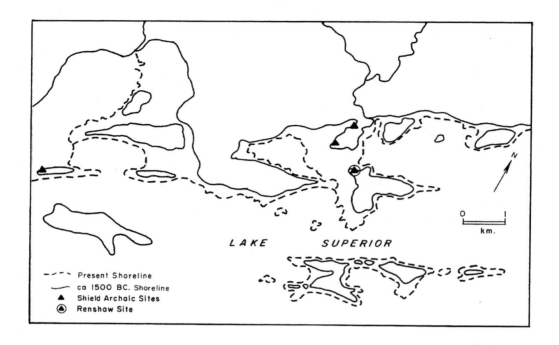

FIGURE 36:   MIDDLE SHIELD CULTURE ARCHAEOLOGICAL VISIBILITY ALONG THE NORTHSHORE OF LAKE SUPERIOR   The dotted line represents the present shoreline of Lake Superior near Thunder Bay, Ontario while the solid line would have been the shoreline around 1,500 BC. Middle Shield culture site locations are, for obvious reasons, oriented to the ancient shorelines. The Figure illustrates the necessity to appreciate past water level fluctuations on large bodies of water. Middle Shield culture sites in this region are now isolated in the interior. Without some understanding of past water levels, archaeological survey along the present shoreline could come to the erroneous conclusion that the area was unoccupied during certain periods. The age of a site such as the Renshaw site, however, cannot be assumed to shortly pre-date the geological age estimate of the beach on which it is located. An original date of 1,500 BC for the Renshaw site agreed well with the 1,750 BC beach age estimate (Arthur 1980). Subsequent AMS dates of more than 3,000 BC (Beukens et al. 1992: Table 2) suggest that the site was actually occupied over a period of more than 1,500 years. (Adapted from Arthurs 1980: Figure 4. Drawn by Mr. David W. Laverie.)

BLACK AND WHITE PLATE XV: MIDDLE SHIELD CULTURE SITE EXCAVATIONS The upper photograph shows the excavation of a site on Lake Abitibi, Québec. The thin archaeological deposits contained evidence of thousands of years of habitation that are often impossible to separate from one another. This is a typical situation on Middle Shield culture sites where subsequent people continued to use the same site locations. (Photograph courtesy of Roger Marois, Archaeological Survey of Canada, Canadian Museum of Civilization.)

The lower photograph, in contrast to the preceding, shows the excavation of a stratified site on the Dubawnt River, Keewatin District, Northwest Territories. Here, the Middle Shield culture occupations were isolated from each other and earlier and later occupations by layers of sterile sediments. Such component separation of Middle Shield culture occupations are extremely rare. (Photograph courtesy of Bryan Gordon, Archaeological Survey of Canada, Canadian Museum of Civilization.)

CHAPTER 17 —————————————————

MIDDLE PLAINS CULTURE

Précis:

Period III falls into the middle of a classificatory unit used on the Northern Plains called the Mesoindian Period (Wormington and Forbis 1965) that extends from the end of Plano culture to the Neoindian Period and involves a time range from 8,000 to 2,000 BP. In a succinct, insightful summary of the Mesoindian Period it has been proposed that the <u>continuous</u> occupation of the short grass Grasslands did not occur until shortly after the beginning of Period III as used in this work and was due to five major factors. These were as follows: the amelioration of the Altithermal droughts; the evolution of the modern bison species from earlier, extinct species; the training of the dog to carry and pull household affects thus markedly increasing mobility; the construction of tipi rings and ceremonial structures using field stones; and the introduction of the method of boiling water with hot rocks in order to produce the grease necessary in the manufacture pemmican (Forbis 1992: 59).

Perhaps to a greater extent than any other region of Canada cultural developments on the Northern Plains has been based upon changes in projectile point styles. Given the general nature of most of the remaining chipped stone technology this emphasis upon one tool category is understandable. In many instances, however, the reliance upon projectile point types to reconstruct culture history has created problems. Even the major archaeological complexes are essentially based on their characteristic point types. The 3,000 years involved in Period III is dominated by three such sequential complexes. The earliest is called Oxbow and was first recognized at the Oxbow Dam site in southeastern Saskatchewan. There is a consensus that the Oxbow complex developed out of earlier, indigenous occupations characterized by side-notched points variously called Mummy Cave, Bitteroot, Salmon River, etc. (see Chapter 9 and Walker 1992: 132-142). The second complex is generally referred to as McKean or as McKean/Duncan/Hanna or some combination of the three different but intergrading and sequential projectile point styles. The McKean complex has been regarded as an intrusive culture on the Canadian Plains with ultimate origins in the Great Basin of Nevada, Utah and adjoining states. Contrary to the preceding, a hypothesis advocating a single unbroken development from Oxbow to McKean is favoured in this work. The third and latest complex is called Pelican Lake and is believed to have developed out of the McKean complex. These three complexes are all included under the rubric Middle Plains culture. If the relationship between the Oxbow and McKean complexes should eventually be demonstrated to be something other than a single, in situ, cultural development then separate cultural designations will be necessary.

Each complex encompasses roughly 1,000 years within Period III (Oxbow - 4,000 to 3,000 BC, McKean - 3,000 to 2,000 BC, and Pelican Lake - 2,000 to 1,000 BC) with the Pelican Lake complex continuing into Period IV (1,000 BC-AD 500). Given the fact that many of the Pelican Lake complex dates fall into Period IV or straddle the Period III/Period IV boundary, the complex will be mainly considered within the Late Plains culture of Period IV in Volume II. The preceding date ranges represent a simplified view of the radiocarbon evidence and substantial overlapping of dates occurs within the linear progression from Oxbow to McKean to Pelican Lake as revealed by stratigraphy. In this respect, the radiocarbon chronology and the stratigraphic chronology are somewhat at odds. As each of the complexes within Period III encompasses approximately the same amount of time, the complex names are retained as useful designations for the early, middle, and late segments of Middle Plains culture development.

Much has been made of the fact that the Oxbow and McKean complexes generally post date the Altithermal. One palaeoclimatic classificatory system (Bryson et al. 1970) suggests that the warm and dry period of the Altithermal, that ended around 3,500 BC, permitted the maximum extension of the grasslands. During a cooler and moister period shortly after 2,000 BC the forests encroached upon the parklands and grasslands by some 50 km to 100 km with the modern climate becoming stabilized around 500 BC. It was after 2,000 BC that significant evidence of mass communal killing of bison herds becomes apparent. This development has been equated with an increase in bison populations (Dyck and Morlan in press). In addition to bison, however, Middle Plains culture people were capable of exploiting the resources of the Boreal Forest and the Mountain/Foothills environmental zones. Both the Kootenay and Peace River regions of British Columbia appear to have been occupied by Middle Plains culture with the Oxbow complex mainly in the north (Fladmark 1981: 131-135) and both the Oxbow and McKean complexes in the south (Choquette 1972; 1973). Any suggestion that Middle Plains culture had a focal economy based solely upon bison underestimates the culture's adaptive capabilities even though the heart of Middle Plains culture was in the Grasslands/Parklands region.

The Middle Plains culture stone tool kit is dominated by projectile points, end scrapers, random flake scrapers, and biface knives. Of interest is the single stone tubular pipe from a McKean complex level at the Cactus Flower site in Alberta that dated to 2,700 BC. If this item actually functioned as a smoking pipe, it would represent the earliest evidence of smoking in Canada. A characteristic Middle Plains culture trait was the use of local stone for tool production although limited amounts of exotic lithics, such as Knife River chalcedony from North Dakota and obsidian from Wyoming, are often present. The bone tool technology appears to be quite rudimentary. What would have been dominant elements in the tool kit, such as objects manufactured from skin and sinew and wood and plant fibres, of course, have not survived in the archaeological record.

Of considerable significance is the probability that all three complexes of Middle Plains culture shared some kind of common belief system. This is suggested by projectile point offerings representative of the point styles of all three complexes in the Majorville Medicine Wheel ceremonial feature (Calder 1977). Current differences in the manner in which the Oxbow, McKean, and Pelican Lake complexes treated their dead may eventually prove to be more a product of limited evidence and precise component identification than being indicative of actual cultural differences.

Cultural origins and descendants:

There is a consensus that the Oxbow complex developed out of the preceding Early Plains culture (Mummy Cave complex) (Dyck 1983; Dyck and Morlan in press; Reeves 1983). The consensus is a vindication of Reeves' (1973) rejection of the proposal that the Northern Plains were largely abandoned by people during the Altithermal. In Saskatchewan, the Oxbow Dam site (Nero and McCorquodale 1958) and the Long Creek site, Level 9, (Wettlaufer and Mayer-Oakes 1960) appear to be near the transition of Early Plains culture into Middle Plains culture (Oxbow complex). Equivalent sites in southern Alberta are Mona Lisa (Wilson 1983), Anderson (Quigg 1984), and the lowest level of the Head-Smashed-In buffalo jump site (Reeves 1978). The chipped stone tool assemblage of the Mummy Cave complex continues into the Oxbow complex with the distinction between the two complexes being based upon the attributes of their respective side-notched projectile points. Indeed, there is considerable overlap in the radiocarbon dates from the two complexes and even some understandable confusion of when Mummy Cave leaves off and Oxbow begins. For example, the basal occupation of the Head-Smashed-In site was initially referred to as Oxbow/McKean (Reeves 1973) but was then changed to terminal Mummy Cave (Reeves 1978). This same classificatory problem appears in Component 5 of the Hawkwood site in Calgary (Van Dyke and Stewart 1985) that is referred to as `Late Mummy Cave/Oxbow´. Technological continuities at this site were noted with the underlying Early Mummy Cave component 4 (Ibid: 109). At the Anderson site in east-central Alberta (Quigg 1984), the 3,500 BC Bitteroot (Mummy Cave) occupation is compared to the Oxbow complex materials from the Long Creek site (Wettlaufer and Mayer-Oakes 1960) and the Gray Burial site (Millar 1981). All of the preceding suggests there are differing views of what constitutes an Oxbow versus a Bitteroot versus a Mummy Cave projectile point. As was the case with the Early and Middle Archaic complexes of eastern North America, the archaeological visibility of the early portion of Middle Plains culture has been obscured by its similarities with much of the technology with Early Plains culture.

While it is generally accepted that the Oxbow complex developed in place out of the indigenous Early Plains culture of Period II, the McKean complex is interpreted as a population intrusion from the Great Basin (Reeves 1974: 1245) that eventually forced Oxbow off the Plains after the two complexes had possibly co-existed with one another for several hundred years. It is a curious fact, however, that while many Oxbow and McKean complex radiocarbon dates do overlap, suggesting the contemporaneity of the two complexes, numerous instances of stratigraphy consistently place the Oxbow complex beneath the McKean complex and their respective projectile point styles are not found in association in such contexts.

Given that both complexes frequently used the same campsites, the probability of an Oxbow occupation occurring above a McKean component or the direct association of the two complexes should be very high if they did, indeed, coexist. An alternative hypothesis and the one favoured here is that the McKean complex developed out of the Oxbow complex and that the major difference between the two complexes was a change from side-notched points to a lanceolate form. This is an acknowledged minority position but it does have other proponents (e.g. Forbis 1992: 49). Such a projectile point style change could simply reflect a modification in point hafting methods whereby the stone tip was attached to the spear shaft with some adhesive rather than sinew lashing. The overlapping radiocarbon dates of the two complexes are probably a reflection of the inherent limitations of the radiocarbon method compounded by problems of clear archaeological context. My inclination is to favour the evidence of stratigraphy over that of radiocarbon dates whenever the two are in conflict. On the other hand, the proposal that the McKean complex entered the northwestern Plains via the mountain regions of Wyoming gains some support from the earlier Wyoming radiocarbon dates (Syms 1970: 131) and the suggestion that the complex developed out of an indigenous late Plano/early Archaic cultural base (Keyser and Davis 1984). Although it has been stated that the Oxbow and McKean complexes are `frequently associated´ (MacNeish 1958; Meyer and Dyck 1968; Syms 1970: 125) the sites in question appear to represent surface and mixed deposits (e.g. Syms 1970: 129). Under either good stratigraphic controls or single component situations the Oxbow and McKean complexes occur as discrete and unassociated entities. Examples are the single component Oxbow complex Harder site (Dyck 1977), the stratified Long Creek site with a dated McKean occupation above a dated Oxbow occupation (Wettlaufer and Mayer-Oakes 1960: 14), and the stratified McKean complex sites of Cactus Flower in Alberta (Brumley 1975) and Crown in Saskatchewan (Quigg 1986).

It has been speculated that the McKean complex discarded its Great Basin plant gathering ways and the people became specialized bison hunters when they entered the Northern Plains (Brumley 1975: 101-102). With reference to the fate of the McKean complex, cumulative frequency graphs of artifact categories at the Cactus Flower site suggest a technological continuity into the subsequent Pelican Lake complex (Brumley 1975: Fig.15, 147), a proposal originally made by Reeves (1970). Certainly the stratigraphic evidence at a number of sites in Alberta, Saskatchewan, and Manitoba indicates that the Pelican Lake complex occurs above the McKean complex just as McKean occurs above the Oxbow complex. While the development of the McKean complex into the Pelican Lake complex represents the most parsimonious explanation (Reeves 1983), there are some major peculiarities of the Pelican Lake complex that need to be explained and not everyone is convinced that a simple cultural transition is involved (Dyck 1983: 104). An alternative hypothesis is that the Pelican Lake complex represented an intrusive population from the western Plains and Mountains (Dyck and Morlan in press; Reeves 1983: 7).This matter will be considered further in Late Plains culture of Period IV (1,000 BC to AD 500).

As noted in Chapter 1, tranquil forms of culture change, such as diffusion of technologies, are favoured over draconian explanations, such as invasion and replacement. This is particularly so when the totality of archaeological evidence only indicates a change in a single or limited number of facets of a single cultural system rather than a drastic alteration to all of the systems. The introduction of a new projectile point style is not regarded as a sufficient basis to posit conquest, eradication, dispersal, and/or absorption when all of the other earlier cultural systems remain essentially intact. This position, that aggressive behaviour would have been rare in the hunting societies making up Middle Plains culture, is also based upon the belief that the economic base of such a culture was ill-equipped to launch and maintain major territorial conquests of neighbouring peoples. Such a proposition is certainly contradicted by the historically documented accounts of the extent of hostilities between such groups as the Cree/Assiniboine versus the Blackfoot/Gros Ventres (Ian Dyck: personal communication) but these developments are regarded as aberrations resulting from the introduction of the horse from the south that increased mobility by as much as eight times (Ewers 1955: 306-308), the spread of the gun from the east with its increased capabilities for mayhem, and the dislocations related to the westward shift of eastern native populations responding to the influence of the European introduced fur trade. The introduction of the horse would have had the most dramatic impact and in a very real sense transformed the native societies of the Plains from pedestrian hunters with dog transport to highly mobile horse pastoralists who exploited the bountiful bison herds much as more traditional pastoralists did their domesticated herds.

In summary, while the Oxbow and McKean complexes in the Northern Plains are regarded by most Plains archaeologists as different cultures representing different ethnic groups (Vickers 1986: 73), with the McKean complex being intrusive (Brumley 1975, 102) and the Oxbow complex being an indigenous development from Early Plains culture (Mummy Cave complex) (Reeves 1973: 1,245), the position favoured here is that the evidence from the various cultural systems of Middle Plains culture, as well as the evidence from stratigraphy, supports an in situ development of Oxbow into McKean and McKean into Pelican Lake. As noted in the Précis, Oxbow complex radiocarbon dates cluster between 4,000 and 3,000 BC, McKean complex dates cluster between 3,000 and 2,000 BC while Pelican Lake complex dates extend from 2,000 BC into Period IV. Many dates attributed to these three complexes, however, have given both earlier and later readings. The outlier dates are regarded as the product of sample contamination and/or context problems. See Morlan (1993: Table 2) for an exemplary consideration of radiocarbon dates from Saskatchewan including the evaluation of their archaeological contexts and validity. For those requiring specific information on the actual radiocarbon dates the following additional references are pertinent: Oxbow complex - Manitoba (Buchner 1979); Saskatchewan (Dyck 1983: Table 10.2); and Alberta (Newton and Pollock 1985; Quigg 1984; Vickers 1986); McKean complex - Manitoba (Haug 1976; Long and Tamplin 1977; Wilmeth 1978); Saskatchewan (Dyck 1983; Quigg 1986); Alberta (Brumley 1975; Calder 1977); and Pelican Lake complex (called Larter in Manitoba) - Manitoba (Buchner 1979); Saskatchewan (Dyck 1983); Alberta (Brumley and Rushworth 1983; Fedje 1986; Reeves 1983).

Technology:

The technology of both the Oxbow complex and its ancestral Mummy Cave complex (Early Plains culture), as well as derivatives, such as the McKean and Pelican Lake complexes, is dominated by chipped stone tools. Figure 38, `A´ provides some impression of the composition of the stone tool kit of both the Oxbow and McKean complexes. One feature that stands out in the Figure is the deviant nature of the

Harder site assemblage (Dyck 1977). This deviation from the other sites is also reflected in the coefficient of similarity figures provided in Figure 38, `B´. With this coefficient, which measures the degree of relationship between any two sites relative to comparable tool categories, projectile point types, or any other body of equivalent data, identical compared sites will have a coefficient of 200 whereas totally different sites will have a coefficient of 0. The following is a comparison of two hypothetical sites provided as a example on how the coefficients are arrived at:

TOOL CATEGORY	ROUSSEAU SITE			RUSSELL SITE		
	f	%		f	%	
Projectile points	41	14.3	Subtract %'s	17	5.8	=8.5
Random flake scrapers	122	42.7	"	149	51.0	=8.3
Biface knives	89	31.1	"	93	31.9	=0.8
Cobble spalls	32	11.2	"	29	9.9	=1.3
Drills	2	0.7	"	0	-	=0.7
Spokeshaves	0	-	"	4	1.4	=1.4
TOTALS	286	100.0		292	100.0	21.0

To arrive at the coefficient of similarity for these two **non-existent** sites the total percentage differences at the bottom of the right hand column is subtracted from 200.0, the total percentages of the other two columns, to obtain the relatively high coefficient of 179.0.

The Harder site is regarded as a winter camp where the stone tool kit was exhausted. This worn-out nature of the tool kit is probably responsible for the Harder site deviation from the other sites on Figure 38. If this should eventually prove to be the case then there will be a basis for distinguishing season of site occupation by the degree of exhaustion apparent in the tool kit. The Harder site aside, both the Oxbow and McKean complexes are dominated by four tool classes; flake scrapers, end scrapers, biface knives, and projectile points in descending order of frequency. The projectile point preforms or triangular projectile points, whichever should be the case, are restricted to the Oxbow complex. However, if these preforms are actually a projectile point style indicative of an alternative hafting method, they would foreshadow the distinctive early point style of the McKean complex (Figure 37, centre). The presence of such triangular points within the exhausted assemblage at the Harder site and the nature of their breakage patterns (Dyck 1977: 90-96) does raise questions regarding their preform classification. For an alternative view regarding this preform-projectile point debate see Dyck (1977: 103).

Even a brief consideration of the tool kits of the Oxbow and McKean complexes helps to explain the heavy reliance placed upon point typology by Plains archaeologists. Despite a general lack of qualitative and quantitative distinctiveness in the non-projectile point portion of the chipped stone technology, there is a greater degree of regional variability in the Oxbow complex. This in itself would appear to be a technological characteristic and not just a product of low samples or variable site function. For example, the six coefficients given on Figure 38, `B´ for the Oxbow complex components range from 45.3 to 141.4 with an average of 95.2. If the exceptionally deviant Harder site is removed, the average rises to 127.9. The 21 coefficients for the McKean complex components, on the other hand, range from 117.4 to 163.6 with an average of 140.7.

The only artifact class frequency trends for the Oxbow complex components are a decrease in the frequency of biface knives and a dramatic drop in flake scrapers at the Harder site. This same trend is apparent within the stratigraphic sequence of the McKean complex Cactus Flower site in Alberta but is reversed in similar stratified deposits at the Crown site in Saskatchewan. There is some indication of a normal distribution through time of cobble tools at the Cactus Flower site but this reflects a local situation as such tools are generally absent from other McKean complex sites. Minor traits, such as hafted spoke-shavers, anvil stones, projectile points modified into scrapers, and a single stone tubular pipe could be diagnostic of the McKean complex but their frequencies are too low to be given much weight. Similarly, rare items such as grooved mauls and native copper tools may be Oxbow complex traits (Dyck 1983: 96) but are, once again, so scarce that they could just as well represent a product of limited sampling. Of considerable interest is the occurrence of an ammonite fossil in the Cactus Flower site (Brumley 1975). Ammonite and baculite fossils were the most common form of `iniskim´, the historically documented Blackfoot word for `buffalo stone´, that were used as medicine for `calling´ bison (Verbicky-Todd 1984: 12-22, 220-224). Similar iniskim were recovered from the Majorville Cairn in Alberta but only in later cultural contexts (Calder 1977: 164-165).

The McKean complex stone tubular pipe from the Cactus Flower site is of interest for a number of reasons. First, with a date of 2,750 BC, it represents the earliest evidence of smoking in Canada. Indeed, tubular pipes do not appear in the northeastern North America until nearly two millennia later. A similar pipe manufactured of bone was recovered from the 2,500 BC McKean complex level of the Mummy Cave site in Wyoming (Wedel 1978). Stone pipes like the one in question are found in the Windmiller culture of the Central Valley of California around this same time period (Aikens 1978). Thus, this single pipe from Alberta would appear to indicate influences from the south and southwest that corresponds with the occurrence of western obsidian on McKean complex sites. Such tubes, of course, could have served other functions than smoking and smoking does not necessarily mean the presence of tobacco. Another stone implement that may have been adopted in the Northern Plains for the first time by Oxbow people is the stone spearthrower weight (Ian Dyck: personal communication) but these rare items are yet to be recovered in good archaeological context. Indeed, they are so rare that their significance is more likely to have been symbolic than functional.

A stone tool category that appears to have been particularly characteristic of the Oxbow complex is fire fractured rock. Until recently, this important element of archaeological debris was not adequately recorded. Fire fractured rock is now believed to be associated on the Plains with the production of bone grease. At the Southridge site in Alberta, for example, more than 2,000 fragments of fire fractured rock was associated with abundant bone fragments (Vickers 1986). Similarly, the frequency of fire fractured rock at the Harder site was only exceeded by bone fragments. In this instance, the 30 kg of rock had to be brought to the site from a locale 9 km away (Dyck 1977: 155). It is assumed that the production of bone grease related to the preservation of meat in the form of pemmican. The impact of such a food storage innovation would have been enormous and yet the archaeological evidence for its existence only consists of fire fractured rock, some bone fragment spoil piles, and less frequently, hearths for heating the stones and pits that would have been lined with hide water containers for boiling the bones to release the fat. The fat would then be skimmed from the surface of the cooled water. It has been speculated that the grooved mauls of the Oxbow complex may have been used for pounding dried bison meat and, thus, were used in pemmican production (Millar 1981a). Pemmican production is believed by some to first appear on the Northern Plains around 3,000 BC with the Oxbow complex (Reeves 1990) as indicated by abundant fire fractured rock, bone boiling pits, the smashing of selected fat and marrow rich bones, and the presence of bone discard piles. It is pertinent to note, however, that fire fractured rock does not appear to be nearly as common on McKean complex sites, such as Cactus Flower (Brumley 1975) and Crown (Quigg 1986). Actually, pemmican can be produced by methods not requiring heated rocks and bone boiling. What may be occurring in the Oxbow complex for the first time is an improvement in methods of grease extraction rather than the innovation of pemmican production per se. It is also worth noting that evidence of bone grease production has been reported from the 5,000 BC Early Plains culture Gowen sites in Saskatchewan (Walker 1992).

Projectile points styles have been used as the commonest method of separating Oxbow from McKean sites. The typical Oxbow complex side-notched point is highly variable in terms of its form attributes just as is the case for its Early Plains culture predecessor. If the triangular points in the Oxbow complex are actually projectile points and not preforms, and there is some basis for this suggestion, then the separation of the Oxbow and McKean complexes on the basis of projectile point styles may not be an entirely valid procedure (Dyck 1977; Vickers 1986). The Oxbow complex triangular points are similar to the earliest of the three point styles that characterize the McKean complex and could represent a prototype.

The McKean complex is characterized by three projectile point styles called McKean Lanceolate, Duncan, and Hanna. These point types tend to grade into one another. There has been some proliferation of regional type names with Hanna points being referred to as Larter points in Manitoba (MacNeish 1958). While it has been argued that the three point types represent sequential styles, the issue does not appear to be quite so simple. All three point types of the McKean complex, for example, occur together in the stratified components of the Cactus Flower site. At the Crown site on the Saskatchewan River, on the other hand, McKean Lanceolate points are stratigraphically earlier than Hanna points (Quigg 1986). In relative terms the three point styles are probably sequential from McKean Lanceolate to Duncan to Hanna with some co-occurrence during periods of stylistic transition. Somehow this sequence appears to have become collapsed at the Cactus Flower site in Alberta. Perhaps the short 300 year sequence represented at the site straddled a critical transition in point style. The most northeasterly McKean complex component, situated on the western margin of the Canadian Shield at the Tailrace Bay site where the Saskatchewan River empties into Lake Winnipeg, contained only McKean Lanceolate point forms (Mayer-Oakes 1970). Both Oxbow and McKean complex point varieties are common in southern Manitoba but are usually recovered from disturbed multi-component sites (Buchner 1979: 80-86; Haug 1976).

The bone and shell technology of the Oxbow and McKean complexes is quite rudimentary in terms of quantity and variety. Bone awls and beads are present in both complexes as are shell beads and pendants. Bone beamers and antler flakers have been reported from Oxbow complex sites (Buchner et al. 1983) and unilaterally barbed harpoons from the McKean complex (Syms 1970). A unique McKean complex specimen is a canine molar gaming piece from the Long Creek site (Wettlaufer and Mayer-Oakes 1960). Simple utilized bone sections and fragments, unrecognized until recently, were likely the most common bone tools in Middle Plains culture.

Although somewhat removed from the usual considerations of technology it has been proposed on the basis of pollen evidence that fire was being used during the Early Plains culture (Mummy Cave complex) and Middle Plains culture (Oxbow and McKean complexes) occupations of the Northern Plains to protect grasslands from encroaching forests and thus encourage browse for the bison herds (Reeves 1990). The use of fire to hold the forest in check and improve grass browse conditions for bison is historically well documented (Grimm 1985). Another important technological element is the evidence of dogs in Middle Plains culture (Brumley 1975: Appendix II; Dyck and Morlan in press; Millar 1978). In a number of instances dog skeletal deformation was likely caused by pulling the travois and/or carrying bundles. In pre-horse times large numbers of dogs would have been required by each family to transport the lodge poles, lodge covering, and other household affects. For a general consideration of the use of dogs as cartage animals during this Period on the Plains see Forbis (1993).

A major workshop and camp site, initially exploited by the Oxbow complex and subsequently by the McKean complex and later groups, is the Strathcona Science Park site on the banks of the North Saskatchewan River outside of Edmonton (Newton and Pollock 1985). Stone cobbles were roughed into shape at some other location before being brought back to the site for final processing. Although this quartzite cobble workshop/living site was used by people for some 4,000 years the various cultural occupations were hopelessly mixed together (Ives 1985). The site location was ideally situated for rejuvenating tool kits while awaiting the return of the bison herds to the Parklands. Workshop procedures were to split a cobble and then produce bifacial and unifacial preforms from the split portions.

Although the McKean complex was able to extend into the margins of the Boreal Forest in northern Manitoba (Mayer-Oakes 1970) it did not spread as far north as its Oxbow predecessor (Gibson 1981; Ives 1981:50; Meyer et al. 1981: 107-129; Millar 1968; Noble 1971; Pollock 1978: Fig.43, 15: 1981; Wright

FIGURE 37: MIDDLE PLAINS CULTURE PROJECTILE POINTS From left to right are an Oxbow side-notched point, a McKean Lanceolate point and a Hanna point. Stratigraphy suggests these three point types represent sequential point style changes although radiocarbon dating would indicate some overlapping from shortly before 3,000 BC to just prior to 1,000 BC. Stratigraphic evidence is given priority over radiocarbon dating because of problems of cultural context and sample contamination with the latter method. Many Plains radiocarbon dates are based on bone that present certain problems for radiocarbon dating. (Drawings by Mr. David W. Laverie. Scale variable.)

1975: Plate XII, fig.29). This would suggest that at least some Oxbow complex bands had developed subsistence strategies that permitted them to exploit a range of ecological zones beyond the Grasslands and Parklands. The extension of the Oxbow complex into the Boreal Forest, however, was apparently weak and should not be overemphasized (Millar 1981a). Despite this caution, there are instances of major sites in the Boreal Forest. The Near Norbert site north of the Churchill River is an Oxbow complex fishing camp site estimated to date to 3,000 BC (Meyer et al. 1981). A series of chipping stations are represented at the site. Side-notched and triangular projectile points and/or preforms, biface knives, bifacial discs or chithos, end scrapers and some minor items were associated with these chipping floors. The paramount stone tool workshop activity at the Near Norbert site makes it difficult to compare the assemblage with other Oxbow complex sites.

As noted in the Précis, the Pelican Lake complex that followed the McKean complex in the Grasslands/Parklands, the Foothills and Mountains to the west, and the Boreal Forest and Canadian Shield to the east, will be considered further in Volume II. While the majority of Pelican Lake complex sites appear to date to Period IV, a number of sites do date to the last 1,000 years of Period III. It is, therefore, appropriate to provide a brief overview of one of these sites. The multi-component LM-8 site in the Boreal Forest/Canadian Shield country of southeastern Manitoba (Buchner 1979) contained a substantial Pelican Lake complex occupation locally referred to as Larter. Seven radiocarbon dates from related components of the Bjorklund site on the Winnipeg River drainage averaged 1,200 BC (Buchner 1982a) and probably

	LONG CREEK 8	SOUTHRIDGE	HAWKWOOD 5-WB	HARDER	C.FLOWER IX	C.FLOWER VIII	C.FLOWER VI	C.FLOWER IV	CROWN LOWER	CROWN UPPER	CEMETERY PT.
LONG CREEK 8		141.4	108.4	87.5	136.5	157.3	120.8	124.9	152.4	172.6	176.4
SOUTHRIDGE	141.4		133.8	54.7	126.1	134.0	109.2	133.9	160.2	139.2	130.4
HAWKWOOD 5-WB	108.4	133.8		45.3	141.4	138.0	118.6	154.9	127.6	112.8	104.4
HARDER	87.5	54.7	45.3		40.2	52.3	53.1	55.4	69.5	33.7	93.3
C.FLOWER IX	136.5	126.1	141.4	40.2		160.5	118.3	138.0	149.9	137.5	131.3
C.FLOWER VIII	157.3	134.0	138.0	52.3	160.5		138.9	153.1	145.0	153.2	148.0
C.FLOWER VI	120.8	109.2	118.6	53.1	118.3	138.9		175.9	130.6	117.4	120.0
C.FLOWER IV	124.9	133.9	154.9	55.4	138.0	153.1	157.9		140.3	119.5	127.1
CROWN LOWER	152.4	160.2	127.6	69.5	149.9	145.0	130.6	140.3		163.6	145.4
CROWN UPPER	172.6	139.2	112.8	33.7	137.5	153.2	117.4	119.5	163.6		159.6
CEMETERY PT.	176.4	130.4	104.4	93.3	131.3	148.0	120.0	127.1	145.4	159.6	

A

	OXBOW				McKEAN						
	LONG CREEK	SOUTHRIDGE	HAWKWOOD 5-WB	HARDER	C.FLOWER IX	C.FLOWER VIII	C.FLOWER VI	C.FLOWER IV	CROWN LOWER	CROWN UPPER	CEMETERY PT.
ARTIFACT CLASS	f %	f %	f %	f %	f %	f %	f %	f %	f %	f %	f %
PROJECTILE PTS.	12 13.5	18 15.3	5 7.6	73 46.2	1 1.6	13 9.8	7 10.3	6 8.7	16 14.8	20 17.4	5 10.0
END SCRAPERS	19 21.3	2 1.7	7 10.6	44 27.8	5 8.1	9 6.8	5 7.4	7 10.1	12 11.1	18 15.6	14 28.0
FLAKE SCRAPERS	30 33.7	68 57.6	39 59.1	7 4.4	25 40.3	48 36.1	23 33.8	33 47.8	46 42.6	37 32.2	17 34.0
BIFACE KNIVES	22 24.7	23 19.5	– –	7 4.4	14 22.6	34 25.6	6 8.8	6 8.7	19 17.6	33 28.7	11 22.0
COBBLE TOOLS	– –	– –	5 7.6	– –	4 6.5	14 10.5	23 33.8	12 17.4	– –	– –	– –
HAMMERSTONES	2 2.2	– –	2 3.0	– –	5 8.1	2 1.5	– –	– –	8 7.4	5 4.3	– –
NOTCHED BIFACES	– –	– –	– –	– –	– –	1 0.8	– –	– –	2 1.9	1 0.9	– –
UNIFACE KNIVES	– –	4 3.4	– –	– –	– –	– –	– –	– –	5 4.6	1 0.9	– –
PT. PREFORMS	2 2.2	3 2.5	– –	22 13.9	– –	– –	– –	– –	– –	– –	– –
DRILL	1 1.1	– –	– –	– –	– –	– –	– –	– –	– –	– –	– –
PERFORATORS	– –	– –	– –	5 3.2	1 1.6	1 0.8	– –	– –	– –	– –	– –
FLAKE KNIVES	– –	– –	8 12.1	– –	7 11.3	6 4.5	2 2.9	3 4.3	– –	– –	– –
SPOKESHAVES	1 1.1	– –	– –	– –	– –	2 1.5	– –	2 2.9	– –	– –	1 2.0
ANVIL STONES	– –	– –	– –	– –	– –	2 1.5	1 1.5	– –	– –	– –	– –
STONE PIPE	– –	– –	– –	– –	– –	1 0.8	– –	– –	– –	– –	– –
SCRAPER ON A PT.	– –	– –	– –	– –	– –	– –	– –	– –	– –	– –	2 4.0
GROUND STONE DISC	– –	– –	– –	– –	– –	– –	1 1.5	– –	– –	– –	– –
TOTALS	89 99.8	118 100.0	66 100.0	158 99.9	62 100.1	133 100.2	68 100.0	69 99.9	108 100.0	115 100.0	50 100.0

B

FIGURE 38:   MIDDLE PLAINS CULTURE STONE TOOL KIT   Table `A´ presents the frequencies of stone tool categories from four Oxbow complex and seven McKean complex sites. The tool categories have been partially modified relative to the classifications in the original publications for the sake of comparability. Despite the fact that these Alberta, Saskatchewan, and Manitoba sites represent a range of settlement varieties as well as time depth, there is a general similarity in the character of the over-all tool kits. Projectile points, end and flake scrapers, and biface knives tend to dominate. Chart `B´ presents the coefficients of similarity derived from the percentage figures in Table `A´ (Brainerd 1951). Only the Harder site in Saskatchewan exhibits consistently low coefficients with the other sites. The Harder site, however, appears to have represented a winter camp whose chipped stone tool inventory was just about exhausted and fragments were utilized to a greater extent than at most of the other sites thus altering the nature of the tool kit.

---

approximate the age of the LM-8 site occupation. The date of the occupation is certainly later than the underlying Middle Shield culture occupation dated to 2,000 BC (Buchner 1979: 128).

The LM-8 site Pelican Lake complex occupation produced the following implements: projectile points - 28 (31.5%); biface knives - 27 (30.3%); end scrapers - 23 (25.8%); side scrapers - 4 (4.5%); flake knives - 3 (3.4%); choppers - 2 (2.3%); a drill - (1.1%); and a hammer/abrader (1.1%) (Buchner 1979). When compared with the Oxbow and McKean complex tool frequencies in Figure 38 the most striking single feature is the absence of flake scrapers from the LM-8 site. LM-8 is most similar to the Harder site with a coefficient of similarity of 125.7. Both the Harder and the LM-8 site have been interpreted as winter hunt camps (Buchner 1979: 26, 100; Dyck 1977) where, relative to the other sites, minimal hide working was carried out. The only other LM-8 site coefficients of similarity over 100 were with the upper McKean complex component of the Crown site (123.4), the Oxbow component of the Long Creek site (121.4), and the McKean component of the Cemetery Point site (113.6). Similarities in the tool kits of the LM-8 site and the Harder site raise the possibility of being able to identify season of occupation of some sites from the composition of their tool kits. The proposition that some of the small projectile points from early Pelican Lake complex sites dating to 1,500 BC may represent evidence of the first appearance of the bow and arrow technology on the Plains (Dyck 1983: 107) will be considered further in Volume II.

It is perhaps appropriate to end the discussion of Middle Plains culture technology with the observation that, in lieu of convenient wood supplies on the Grasslands, dried bison dung was probably widely employed as a fuel (M. J. Wright 1986; 1992).

Subsistence:

The Oxbow complex has been characterized as having an economy focused on bison. This observation pertains mainly to sites on the Grasslands and Parklands. It is becoming increasingly apparent that some bands of the Oxbow complex possessed a broadly based adaptive system and were quite capable of exploiting a wide range of food resources. It would be perhaps more accurate to characterize this adaptive system as opportunistic and flexible. In short, it could be either focal or diffuse as circumstances dictated (Michlovic 1986). There is little question, however, that Oxbow hunters on or near the Grasslands and Parklands concentrated their hunting effort upon bison. Bison, when available in sufficient numbers, simply guaranteed the best return on effort expended (Dyck 1977: 67). This is undoubtedly why Oxbow complex sites are concentrated on the Grasslands and Parklands and the presence of sites in other adjoining environmental zones is comparatively weak. Faunal collections from Grassland/Parkland sites are dominated by bison with canids such as wolf and coyote, a weak second runner up followed by minor evidence of elk, moose, fox, rabbit, martin, goose, frogs, and clams (Dyck 1977). The presence of significant numbers of canids would suggest the use of traps but a large percentage of these remains are also likely domesticated dog. A re-examination of the Harder site faunal remains has determined that the Canis sp. recoveries pertain predominantly to dog and wolf with only rare representations of coyote (Morlan: in press).

An important subsistence consideration would be the necessity of feeding the large number of dogs required to transport camp gear and supplies. Middle Plains culture people were nomads who depended upon dogs for transportation and other services but dogs require meat, either raw or in preserved form. In pre-horse days, it has been estimated that each family required at least 10 dogs. This number of animals would need a substantial quantity of food in the form of meat.

While the basal deposits of the Head-Smashed-In bison jump site (Colour Plate XIII) contained Early Plains culture materials (Mummy Cave complex) no clear evidence of the Oxbow complex was recovered at the site (Reeves 1978) or from any other bison jump site. This situation also applies to the McKean complex despite the single point from the aforementioned site (Dawe and Brink 1991: 155). Common use of the specialized hunting technique of driving bison herds over cliffs does not appear until Pelican Lake complex times. It has been noted with reference to the Head-Smashed-In site that "...the intensive post-kill processing of bison at Head-Smashed-In is an activity primarily, if not exclusively, restricted to the Late Prehistoric Period" (Dawe and Brink 1991: 155). Even the suggestion of the Oxbow complex use of restraining pounds to kill bison in large numbers is being questioned. A reanalysis of the faunal evidence from the Harder winter campsite indicated that both bison nursery herds of cows and their calves and isolated bulls or small bull herds were being exploited (Dyck and Morlan: in press; Morlan: in press). Such evidence does not negate the use of pounds but suggests that if present they were used in conjunction with a number of other hunting techniques. Indeed, the abundance of wolf cranial parts at this site has led to the speculation that wolf pelts with attached skulls were used in stalking bison and that worn out wolf disguises, including the skulls, were discarded at the camp (Dyck and Morlan: in press). The aforementioned re-examination of the Harder site faunal evidence stands as an excellent example of the wide range of information that can be gleaned from even the most fragmented of samples using modern methods of analysis. An important product of this analysis was the evidence that bison limbs were

COLOUR PLATE XIII: HEAD-SMASHED-IN BUFFALO JUMP SITE, ALBERTA   Herds of bison may have been driven over this famous `jump site´ in southern Alberta as early as 4,500 BC until quite recent times as indicated by Piegan native oral tradition and archaeological evidence. Some archaeologists regard the earliest evidence from the site as pertaining to a campsite that does not necessarily constitute evidence of maneuvering bison herds over the cliffs. The photograph provides a view of the initial excavations by the Glenbow-Alberta Institute and the University of Calgary in 1965. Bison herds were once stampeded over the cliff on the right and were dispatched and dismembered on the talus slope where the excavation is taking place. (Photograph provided by B. O. K. Reeves, Department of Archaeology, University of Calgary.)

probably stored on platforms in a frozen state and were subsequently broken into manageable portions by heavy blows that fractured the frozen bone in an atypical fashion.

The impact of the Altithermal on bison availability between 5,500 and 3,000 BC is still a matter of some debate. Earlier arguments for the partial abandonment of the Grasslands during this period, however, have been largely abandoned because of direct archaeological evidence (Reeves 1973). There is also increasing recognition of the impact depositional and erosional forces have had upon archaeological visibility at this time. An inability to accurately identify Early Plains culture side-notched points from later forms when they occur outside of an archaeological context has added to the erroneous impression that people had largely abandoned the Grasslands due to a hypothesized reduction in bison numbers. By the end of this dry climatic episode it is estimated that the Grasslands had expanded as much as 150 km to the north and between 60 and 80 km to the east (Buchner et al. 1983: 48). With reference to Manitoba, it has been suggested that it was not until the end of the Altithermal and the advent of environmental stability that communal bison hunting on the Grasslands became common. This was regarded as a summer activity followed by hunting of scattered bison along the forest margins of the uplands and river valleys in the winter (Buchner et al. 1983: 54). Contrary to the proposal of summer communal bison hunting, the historic documents suggest jump and pound sites were both used during the fall/early winter when bison formed into large and relatively sedentary herds in their winter range. It was during this fall/winter period when the largest human encampments were possible (Arthur 1975). Allowing for local adjustments to a range of fluctuating environmental variables, the historically recorded annual cycle of the Plains tribes was patterned and predictable. A discrete herd/discrete hunting band association on the Northern Plains has even been proposed (Gordon 1979). The supporting evidence for such an intimate relationship between a particular bison herd and a particular band, however, is not convincing. Weaknesses in both the archaeological record and the historic documentation bearing on bison herd movements are simply too pronounced to properly test Gordon's hypothesis.

The McKean complex appears to have followed an essentially similar subsistence pattern as that of the preceding Oxbow complex. This pattern included extensions into the Boreal Forest and the Mountains (Reeves 1974; Syms 1970: 128). Archaeological site distributions indicate that both complexes were concentrated on the Grassland and adjacent Parklands. In the majority of instances, the two complexes are found together at either stratified or mixed sites. There is some suggestion that the McKean complex made greater use of the major river valleys than its predecessor, a proposition supported by the location of the Grand Rapids sites in the Canadian Shield of Manitoba. At the McKean complex Cactus Flower site in Alberta (Brumley 1975) bison remains were most common followed by antelope and minor amounts of mule deer, dog, and traces of kit fox, rabbit, birds, clams, and fish. Among the faunal remains was a butchered 11 month old dog. While the site appears to have been occupied from early spring to late fall, bison tooth eruption patterns and foetal remains indicate that the majority of the bison were fall kills. To judge from the nature of the bison anatomical parts found at the site the bison must have been killed locally as most skeletal elements are present. The antelope, on the other hand, appear to have been killed and butchered some distance from the site proper (Brumley 1975: 83). Direct evidence of butchering was rare at the Cactus Flower site although there was considerable breaking of bones for marrow and grease extraction suggesting the production of pemmican. The reason for the repetitive occupation of this particular site would have been the ease of bison herd access to the river in a region characterized by steep banks. Such a topographic feature would not only channel bison coming to drink or ford the river but would also provide opportunities for ambush. The Crown site, a similar McKean complex stratified site on the Saskatchewan River near Nipawin, contained mainly bison remains followed by moose and minor amounts of elk, dog, beaver, skunk, rabbit, and suckers (Quigg 1986). It appears that entire bison carcasses were brought to the site where they were processed including the production of bone grease.

Faunal evidence from McKean complex sites in the Boreal Forest is virtually non-existent (Mayer-Oakes 1970; Syms 1970) and what does survive generally relates to forest species and not bison. In the Plains/Mountain interface in the Crowsnest Pass of Alberta, however, the winter Foothills sites contained predominantly bison (Driver 1985). Mountain summer sites, on the other hand, are characterized by a decrease in the importance of bison and increasing frequencies of elk, bighorn sheep, and beaver. The continuity of settlement patterns in the eastern slopes of the Rocky Mountains would seem to indicate stability in the subsistence base (Ball 1986; Brink and Dawe 1986; Fedje 1986; Reeves 1974; Ronaghan 1986). Although the small and frequently mixed samples and the poor to non-existent bone preservation in the mountains and foothills have hampered an accurate evaluation of the subsistence patterns, the existing evidence does indicate a shifting focal/diffuse pattern keyed to the seasons and opportunities.

European recorders have noted that native people of the Plains made extensive use of plant foods such as Saskatoon berries, gooseberries, chokecherries, etc. (Graspointer 1981: 84-85). In northeastern Wyoming, at the single component McKean site of Leigh Cave, wild onion, chokecherry, timber pine seeds, buffalo grass, wild rose, juniper bark, yucca fibre, and willow and rye grass were recovered. The use of plant materials on McKean complex sites south of Canada is also suggested by the common occurrences of metates and manos, grinding tools frequently associated with the preparation of plant foods. Metates and manos are either absent or rare in Canada leading to the suggestion that plant use in the north may have been limited (Keyser 1986).

As with most cultures it is difficult to assess the role of plants in Middle Plains culture subsistence given the limited use of appropriate recovery techniques such as flotation and the fact that preservation is usually a product of accidental charring. This is exclusive of those rare instances where dry cave conditions or water saturation has permitted preservation of plant materials. Culinary or preparation accidents, such as burnt meals and over-parching of plant foods for storage, determine if archaeologists are given even a brief glimpse of the use of plants. Excepting most unusual conditions of preservation, it is most unlikely that historically documented important fleshy tubers such as prairie turnip (Psoralea esculenta), biscuit root(Lomtium spp.), bitter root (Leivisia redivivia), Indian potato/Jerusalem artichoke (Helianthus tuberosus), balsam root (Balsamorhiza sagittata), cattail (Typha spp.), wild parsley (Musineon spp.), bush morning glory (Ipomoea leptophylla), and sego/mariposa lily (Calochortus spp.) would be recognizable in the archaeological record (Haberman 1986). Only hackberry, for example, has been identified in the Oxbow complex level of the Long Creek site (Wettlaufer and Mayer-Oakes 1960). Improved field recovery techniques and archaeological survey oriented to plant rich locales may assist in evaluating the role of plants in Middle Plains culture. Any such insights, however, are certain to provide a very incomplete perception of the importance of plants. Even historical documentation of the use of plants is likely incomplete as virtually all of the early European observers were men who were interested in recording native male activities, such as hunting, rather than female plant gathering and processing.

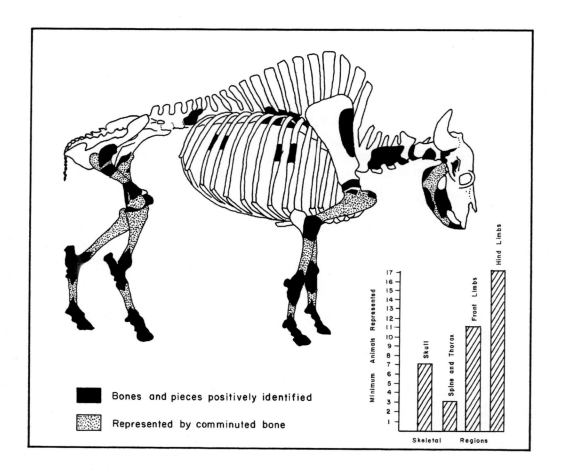

FIGURE 39:   BISON SKELETAL PARTS FROM THE HARDER SITE, SASKATCHEWAN In most instances only selected fat and marrow rich bones were carried back to camp from the kill site. The portion of the head most often found, for example, is the marrow-rich jaw. Limb bones, rich in marrow as well as being a source of raw material for tools, probably were carried back to camp encased in their flesh. As can be seen from the drawing, the spinal column, the pelvic girdle, and skull appear to have been largely abandoned at the kill location. Comminuted bone refers to highly fragmented bone. (Adapted from Dyck 1977: Figs.7 and 8. Drawing by Mr. David W. Laverie.)

Settlement patterns:

It is convenient to view Middle Plains culture settlement patterns relative to three zones, the Grasslands/Parklands, the Mountains/Foothills, and the Boreal Forest. Oxbow and McKean complexes occur in all three zones.

In the Grasslands and Parklands it is not unusual to have sites containing occupations that extend slightly before Period III to the time of European Contact. This suggests that for approximately 6,000 years there was sufficient stability in bison behaviour to permit a repetitive seasonal pattern of site use in certain locales. The historically documented settlement patterns of bands wintering in the Parklands, moving onto the Grasslands in the summer, and then shifting back to the Parklands in fall/winter, would appear to have been practiced by Middle Plains culture hunters. Such a pattern simply reflects the presence of bison herds on the Grasslands during the summer and the shifting of the herds to the Parklands and Parkland margins in the winter. Seasonal migration patterns of bison could, however, be disrupted by a number of factors. Among these were burned-over Grasslands, locust infestations, thaw and freeze cycles, strong winds, heavy snow falls, and mild winters (Buchner et al. 1983). Such factors could shift herds away from normal pasture areas, force herds out of the Grasslands to seek shelter or, conversely, permit the herds to remain on the Grasslands over the winter. People had to adjust to all fluctuations in bison behaviour and thus a wide range of settlement patterns occurs. Despite the foregoing, bison behaviour would have been predictable albeit within a broad spectrum of behaviour altering circumstances. The many multi-component campsites in the Grasslands/Parklands clearly reflect the successful anticipation of bison availability at different seasons of the year.

Topographic relief was a critical settlement consideration with little evidence of occupation on the grassland flats (Adams 1986: 20; Epp 1986). River valleys, valley rims, and coulees were favoured locales whose selection would have been based on a range of interrelated factors such as season, water, animal, plant, and mineral resources, vistas for scanning the country side for game, exposure to wind for relief from mosquitoes, topography for stalking and setting drive lanes and pounds.

Oxbow complex sites in the Grasslands/Parklands typically exhibit heavy utilization of local stone sources for tool manufacture. The presence of native copper implements from Lake Superior and marine shell beads from the Atlantic Coast at the Gray Burial site (Millar 1978) indicates participation in a far flung trade network. This network also included Knife River chalcedony from North Dakota and other exotic stone sources. While local stone was dominant at the Southridge site in southern Alberta there were limited quantities of exotic stone from Montana and/or British Columbia, North Dakota, and the Alberta Foothills (Vickers 1986: 66). The distribution of cultural debris at this summer site, such as flakes, bone fragments, and fire fractured rock, as well as paired hearths and boiling pits, suggested the existence of two residential units. The Harder site was a much larger camp situated in the Parklands of Saskatchewan (Dyck 1977). A winter occupation is premised on the location of the nearest potable water being 20 km away. In winter, of course, snow would have met all the water needs. It is estimated that from six to eight dwellings were present. Evidence for extensive marrow and grease extraction was inferred from the abundance of small bone fragments and fire fractured rock. Located in a dune depression on the edge of a sand plain overlooking grasslands, the Harder site was close to bison pasturage while, at the same time, having the advantages of shelter, fuel, building material, and the rolling topography required by hunters.

Dwellings at the Harder site were demarcated by the distribution of cultural debris in association with hearth and pit features. The most convincing dwelling was a 4 m diameter structure (Dyck 1977: Fig. A1.2, feature 12). More vaguely defined structures ranged up to 6.5 m in diameter. An Oxbow complex tent ring at the EfOp-53 site in Alberta (Quigg 1981: Fig. 9) was also 4 m in diameter. The diameters of historically documented Plains Indian tipis ranged from 4.2 to 6.3 m (Dyck 1977: Fig.9). Tent rings outlined by stone weights to hold the hide covering down first appear on the Northern Plains in association with the Oxbow complex (Quigg 1981: 62). It is of interest to note that these nuclear family Plains dwelling dimensions are essentially the same as those of the Middle Shield culture caribou hunters of the Barrengrounds.

Oval pits at the Harder site, inferred to have functioned as hide smoking pits, occurred both inside and outside of the dwellings. A hearth surrounded by post moulds in an Oxbow complex level of the Long Creek site (Wettlaufer and Mayer-Oakes 1960) was speculated to be a hide curing feature or even a ceremonial structure. Piles of highly broken bison bone were associated with these features. A feature at the Moon Lake campsite (Dyck 1970: Fig.7) may have represented a windbreak demarcated by four post moulds, a hearth, and a scattering of cultural debris to the south of the feature.

McKean complex occupations in the Grasslands and Parklands tend to be situated in the same locations as Oxbow complex sites. Such a settlement distribution is to be expected if, as advocated in this study, McKean is simply the genetic successor of Oxbow and not its replacement. Site locations can range from being adjacent to sloughs (Wormington and Forbis 1965), along major rivers (Adams 1976), on tributaries (Wettlaufer and Mayer-Oakes 1960), on lakes in marsh situations (Haug 1976), and along major moraines (Kelly and Connell 1978). In all instances, settlement was related to the topographic and ecological features that provided maximum return with minimum effort. An excellent example of the foregoing is the stratified McKean complex Cactus Flower site in Alberta (Brumley 1976). The site occurs in one of the rare areas where access to the Saskatchewan River is not barred by steep river banks. Watering or fording bison were, therefore, channelled into a locale that also offered excellent opportunities for ambush. Settlement pattern features at the site consisted of living floors, pit and surface hearths, and bone concentrations. Debris tended to be concentrated around the pit hearths rather than the surface hearths. One living floor, clearly demarcated by cultural debris, consisted of a 4.8 m diameter tipi floor containing a central hearth pit (Figure 44). No post moulds or weight stones were found with this structure but the debris almost appears to have been heaped-up onto the outer edge of the once extant skin tent covering. The presence or absence of stone tent weight stones often relates directly to their availability (Wormington and Forbis 1965: 144). Another 4 m diameter dwelling floor at this site was associated with some scattered and discontinuous weight stones and a pit hearth. The pit hearths were circular features filled with fire fractured rock resting upon a fire-reddened floor. Surface hearths, on the other hand, consisted of ovate, circular, and irregular areas of fire-reddened soil directly on the living floor. An interesting complex of features consisted of a surface hearth associated with four small pits that may have represented stone tempering ovens where siliceous rock was baked to alter the crystal structure and, thus, improve its flaking qualities. One circular pit was associated with a number of very small post moulds that may represent the remains of stakes used for cooking or as drying racks.

McKean complex tent rings at the multi-component Crawford site on the Oldman River of Alberta had inside diameters of slightly less than 5 m and an average of 66 weight stones each (Stuart 1990). While cultural debris was present in the dwellings central hearths were lacking, reinforcing the suggestion that the site represented a summer occupation. Indeed, an extensive outside activity area is believed to have been associated with one to four of the tent rings (Ibid: 105). In the same region of Alberta there is evidence of a marked increase in occupation density in the form of tent rings and bison jumps by 1,500 BC with the appearance of the Pelican Lake complex (Van Dyke et al. 1991: 61-62). River erosion, however, may have obliterated much of the evidence of earlier occupations.

Near Nipawin on the Saskatchewan River, the McKean complex occupation of the stratified Crown site contained several hearths and a bone concentration in the lower levels with one of the hearths being associated with a dog burial. Local cobbles of Swan River chert and quartz were the main source of stone for tools with no evidence of exotic chipping detritus or tools (Quigg 1986: 53). In the upper levels a pit hearth, a fire cracked rock concentration, and a burial were recorded. The ovate pit hearth, filled with 220 fragments of fire fractured rock, was similar to those recorded at the Cactus Flower site.

With reference to the Mountain/Foothills region of Alberta, Early Plains culture (Mummy Cave complex) sites are particularly abundant and have been inferred to have occupied the region while contemporaneous Oxbow and McKean complexes ranged over the Grasslands (Vickers 1986: 63-64). The contemporaneity of the three complexes, however, is not supported by the stratigraphic evidence that indicates they were time segments of a developmental sequence. Unfortunately, a major stratified Foothills site, the Sibbald Creek site (Gryba 1983), with occupations ranging from Palaeo-Indian to European contact, including both the Oxbow and McKean complexes, lacked a Mummy Cave complex occupation and thus issues of contemporaneity could not be addressed. Side-notched and corner-notched Mount Albion points, which are possibly related to the Mummy Cave complex, however, were recovered mainly from below the Oxbow component (Ibid: 62-63). The 11,000 year unbroken seasonal occupation of this probable winter campsite with its southern exposure and access to wood, is one of the characteristic settlement patterns of the Mountain/Foothills zone (Ball 1986; Brink and Dawe 1986; Fedje 1986; Reeves 1974; Ronaghan 1986). Regrettably, many of the sites with a lengthy record of occupation defy effective component separation. This situation will probably be rectified by recently discovered sites in Banff National Park (Fedje 1986). While it has been proposed that the Mountain/Foothills zone represents a unique culture area distinct from either the Plains or the Plateau (Reeves 1974), the evidence can also be interpreted to suggest that the region was either exploited seasonally by both Plains and Plateau adapted cultures, particulary the former, or that certain bands of Middle Plains culture were capable of exploiting the diffuse resources of the Mountain/Foothills while still retaining an essential Plains technology.

Unlike the situation with either the Grasslands/Parklands or the Mountain/Foothills, penetration of Middle Plains culture into the Boreal Forest appears to have been limited. While it has been suggested that the earliest Oxbow complex sites occur on the Plains (Gibson 1981; Spurling and Ball 1981) and are late in the Boreal Forest, the basis for such a conclusion is questionable and the dating is weak (Vickers 1986: 73). Oxbow and Oxbow-like projectile points are found to the north in Manitoba (Gibson 1981), Lake Athabasca (Wright 1975), and even into the southern Northwest Territories (Millar 1968; Noble 1971) but such occurrences are usually stray finds. Actual Oxbow or Oxbow-like sites are rare. One such site is the Near Norbert site north of the Churchill River in northern Saskatchewan (Meyer et al. 1981). Situated near a major waterfall and the confluence of two rivers, the site appears to represent a major base camp at the head of a portage that was occupied in the spring to exploit spawning pickerel (Stizostedion vitreum). Fishing technology and presumably the possession of efficient watercraft hardly fit the image of the Oxbow way of life. The site is important as an indicator of the adaptability of the Oxbow complex. It would appear that the McKean complex possessed the same flexible adaptive capabilities as its predecessor to judge from another probable fishing site in the Canadian Shield at Grand Rapids, northern Manitoba (Mayer-Oakes 1970). As with the Near Norbert site, the location of the Tailrace Bay site provides strong inferential evidence for a sophisticated knowledge of water travel and all the technology such travel entails.

The distributions of Middle Plains culture sites must be viewed relative to changing environments. Until after 3,000 BC the Grasslands and their associated Parklands expanded at the expense of the Boreal Forest. Such change would favour an expansion in the range of the bison herds (Vickers 1986: Fig.2, 11) and a contraction of forest adapted species such as moose. Between 6,500 and 3,000 BC the Grasslands spread into the present day Parklands and, in tandem, the birch dominated Parklands encroached upon the southern Boreal Forest (Meyer n.d.). Although, in part, an ecotone between the Grasslands and the Boreal Forest, the Parklands in terms of its relationship to bison, is more appropriately viewed as an extension of the Grasslands and, hence, more an asset to bison hunters than Boreal Forest hunters. It was probably the wintering bison herds in the Parklands that attracted hunters rather than the more varied resources of an ecotonal region. It would appear that the region of contact between Plains-adapted and Forest-adapted cultures was the shifting ecotone between the Parklands and the Boreal Forest rather than the Parklands proper.

From at least 4,000 BC to AD 500 bison hunters from the Plains dominated the Saskatchewan Parklands as well as the southern edge of the Boreal Forest. These northerly sites represented the winter portion of the seasonal cycle. In order to exploit large areas of both the Parklands and the adjacent Boreal Forest watercraft would have been necessary. Direct evidence of watercraft almost never survives in the archaeological record but Middle Plains culture sites along major river systems in the Canadian Shield/Boreal Forest clearly indicate that the knowledge of water transportation was part of the technological tool-kit.

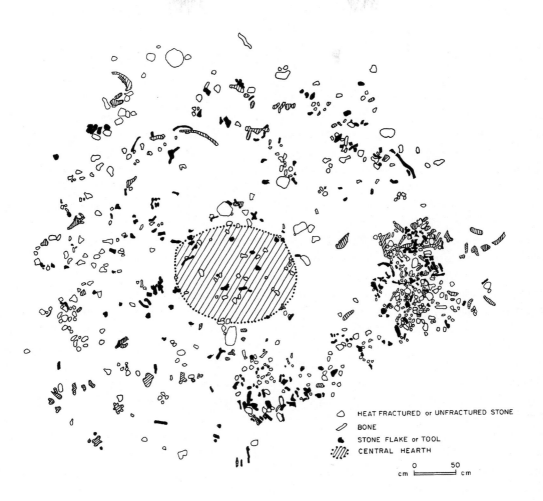

FIGURE 40: MIDDLE PLAINS CULTURE HOUSE FLOOR This 2,750 BC lodge floor at the Cactus Flower site in Alberta is demarcated by stone and bone fragments and tools around a central hearth. The distribution of cultural debris suggests a structure just under 5 m in diameter. Detailed mapping of all cultural evidence is often necessary to delineate house floors, particularly in the absence of stone tent weights or recognizable stains left by pegs used for fastening the edge of the skin tent covering to the ground. (Adapted from Brumley 1976: Fig.7. Drawing by Mr. David W. Laverie.)

In any consideration of the settlement pattern strategies of Middle Plains culture it is necessary, once again, to assess the relationship between the Oxbow and McKean complexes. Stratigraphic evidence suggests that the McKean complex simply followed the Oxbow complex whereas radiocarbon dates indicate that the two complexes were at least partially coeval. As these complexes occupied much of the same territory and the same sites it can be argued that the Oxbow complex was pushed out by the McKean complex and that the stratified sequence is simply reflecting an earlier presence in the area of the Oxbow complex. Or, it could be suggested that the two complexes exploited the same sites at different times of the year but this seems very unlikely given bison behaviour. It could also be hypothesized, on admittedly weak grounds, that Oxbow complex hunting techniques relied upon communal efforts using pounds and other entrapment devices whereas initially the intrusive McKean hunters followed more catch-as-catch-can techniques such as stalking and riverine ambush. If the McKean complex spread out of the Great Basin and southern Foothills into the Northern Plains following the major rivers as has been suggested (Brumley 1975), they may have been able to move into a partial vacuum in the Oxbow complex hunting territories and been tolerated for a period as there was minimal competition. Once established, however, the McKean complex hunters could have expanded at the expense of the Oxbow complex and pushed the latter into less favourable hunting territories. A less draconian explanation for the relationship between these two complexes is favoured here; namely that the McKean complex is a direct in situ descendant of the Oxbow complex as well as being the ancestor of the Pelican Lake complex. In this respect, the three sequential complexes would represent early, middle, and late segments of time within Middle Plains culture. In the Oxbow/McKean replacement hypothesis it is difficult to see what technological advantage the latter had over the former that would have permitted such a major land grab. And where did the expelled Oxbow people go? Hunting and gathering cultures around the world are not renowned for collective military activities. Dead soldiers are also dead hunters that place the survival of the entire band in jeopardy. There is the additional evidence of both complexes contributing to the accretionary construction of the Majorville Medicine Wheel and Cairn suggesting some form of shared cosmological belief system. This type of ceremonial behaviour does not characterize the activity of unrelated cultures. If both Oxbow and McKean complex materials were frequently encountered in direct association with each other under conditions of good archaeological context then there might be a case for arguing that McKean culturally absorbed Oxbow. Such evidence does not appear to exist. Two cultures occupying the same territory and exploiting the same resources but without any apparent cultural interaction would represent not only a unique situation on the Plains but also in the entire archaeological record of Canada.

Cosmology:

There are three aspects of Middle Plains culture that are inferred to relate to how the people viewed their place in the universe, medicine wheels and cairns, symbolic objects such as iniskims or buffalo stones, and the treatment of the deceased.

Along with bison jump sites, medicine wheels represent the most striking archaeological features to be encountered on the Northern Plains. Medicine wheels are predominantly located in Alberta with lesser numbers in Saskatchewan and Montana and a few outliers in Wyoming and South Dakota. They are thus a Northern Plains phenomenon. The term `medicine wheel´ includes a variety of stone alignments composed of boulders and cobbles that can range from accretionary structures representing thousands of years of building stages to burial monuments to great individuals. On the basis of geometry and associated features these structures have been classified into eight major categories (Brumley 1988). To judge from both the artifacts in the medicine wheels and associated radiocarbon dates the construction of a number of medicine wheels first began in Middle Plains culture times.

With the exception of the Early and Middle Maritime culture mound monuments of the northshore of the Gulf of St.Lawrence and the Labrador coast medicine wheels represent the earliest large structural ceremonial features in Canada. The concentrations of such features on the southern Grasslands of Alberta and Saskatchewan suggest that they represent a local innovation of Middle Plains culture (Oxbow) people. All are petroform structures consisting of arranged cobbles and boulders surrounding a cairn situated on top of a prominent hill. Varied in form and size, medicine wheels also had varied functions (Brumley 1988). Some of the smaller, historically documented features are recognized as Blackfoot commemorative tomb structures of respected individuals. Other medicine wheels, generally the larger ones, are accretionary structures whose initial construction was begun by Oxbow people but added to by subsequent people. Intensity of utilization of such features also varied through time. For example, the use of the Majorville Cairn and Medicine Wheel (Calder 1977) was moderate throughout Period III and particularly so relative to the Pelican Lake complex. It was towards the end of Period IV (1,000 BC to AD 500) and throughout Period V (AD 500 to European Contact) that activities at this ceremonial feature were most intense (Ibid: 35-36).

The constellation of beliefs implicit in some of the medicine wheels first made its appearance on the Northern Plains with the Oxbow complex and, with the possible partial exception of the Pelican Lake complex, these beliefs were perpetuated by subsequent occupants up to the time of European contact. This is a continuity of a system of beliefs or religion at geographically specific `sacred sites´ of approximately 5,000 years. The very persistence of the tradition would suggest that the limited evidence for Pelican Lake complex participation is probably fortuitous rather than real. It is difficult to conceive how or why a religious tradition would be broken from approximately 2,000 BC to AD 1 and then be revived with even greater vigour.

The suggestion that elements of medicine wheels, such as the spokes and cairns, were aligned to the summer solstice of the sun and possibly also to certain bright stars (Eddy 1974; Kehoe and Kehoe 1979) has precipitated considerable debate. Despite claims to the contrary, astronomical and statistical evidence does not support the use of these features as astronomical sighting devices for the systematic study of the heavens (Haack 1987; Ovenden and Rodger 1981). This said, it is probable that the alignments are ritualistic approximations related to certain heavenly bodies not requiring an accuracy measurable by statistical means. Other suggested functions of medicine wheels are as memorials to individuals, as vision quest sites for persons seeking a guardian spirit or other spiritual help, as a symbolic lodge for the sun within which the Sundance Ceremony was performed, as directional aids, as a Master symbol, as animal effigies with the associated symbolism, and a range of less likely functions (Wilson 1981). Wilson rejects the calendric function of medicine wheels along with a number of the other hypothetical functions. He does note, however, that the Sundance Ceremony of such importance to the ethnographically observed tribes of the Northern Plains relates to rain and rain to grass and grass to bison. It is further noted that the summer solstice and rainfall peak at the same time, a time of plenty on the Plains (Wilson 1981: 362). Excluding the Blackfoot memorial markers, all that can be said with any confidence is that the medicine wheels performed a range of ceremonial functions. With reference to the large, multi-cultural accretionary medicine wheels, it is likely that the ceremonial function related to the rejuvenation or renewal of the bison herds and thus was associated with the historically documented Sundance rejuvenation ceremony with its circular lodge. Such a proposal cannot, however, be demonstrated by archaeological means.

At the British Block Cairn, an undisturbed Alberta medicine wheel situated on a high hill, the projectile point styles and late pottery was so intermixed throughout the cairn that it was suggested the cairn had acted as a repository for offerings that included early point styles which had been picked up by later people (Wormington and Forbis 1965: 122-125). This point collecting/cairn offering hypothesis is weakened by the total absence of pre-Oxbow and Pelican Lake complex point styles that are both common to the region. The central cairn is 9 m in diameter and 1.8 m in height and is surrounded by a cobble ring 24.4 m in diameter. A human petroform, outlined in cobbles, occurs between the outer ring and the cairn but was impossible to date. The cairn alone is composed of an estimated 100 tons of rock ranging from pebbles to a 180 kg boulder. Tipi rings are typically common in proximity to such cairns suggesting that their sanctity was of such a nature that it was not regarded as a threat to the living.

The Majorville Medicine Wheel (Figure 41), unlike the British Block Cairn, contained evidence of accretionary construction stages. As is typical with such features, the Majorville Medicine Wheel is situated on a prominent hill with a 360• vista. The central Cairn is connected by spokes to an outer surrounding ring and was constructed "...as a series of accretional domes" (Calder 1977: 201) beginning around 3,000 BC and extending to the period of European contact. The Cairn, composed of soil and field stones, is 9 m in diameter and 1.6 m in height. It is surrounded by an oval ring 29 m by 26 m that is connected to the Cairn by 26 to 28 spokes composed of lines of boulders. The closeness in the gross measurements from the British Block Cairn and Majorville Medicine Wheel would suggest that the measurements themselves had some symbolic significance. An estimated 40 tons of rock went into the construction of the Majorville Cairn with the average cobble weighing 4.5 kg. On the basis of the 254 projectile point offerings the history of use of the Cairn begins with both the Oxbow and McKean complexes but was apparently subjected to limited use by the Pelican Lake complex (only five points). Use of the site increased after AD 200. The sequential stages of cairn construction were delineated by point typology supported by obsidian hydration analysis (Calder 1977: 37-41).

The ceremonial nature of the offerings from the Cairn of the Majorville Medicine Wheel is supported by the presence of iniskims, other fossils, concretions, and the painting of artifacts and bones with red

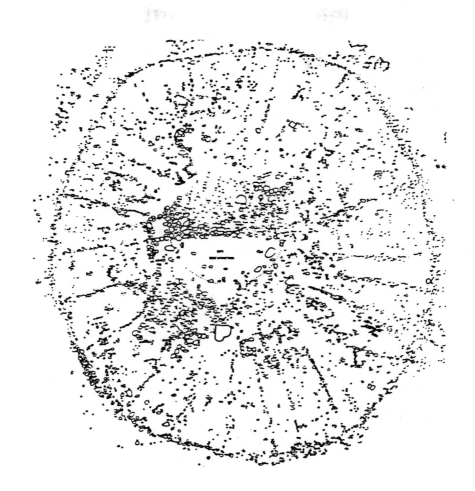

FIGURE 41:   THE MAJORVILLE MEDICINE WHEEL   The Majorville Medicine Wheel in Alberta was initially constructed in 3,000 BC and was added to over the next 5,000 years. Such continuity of use reflects an exceptionally stable ceremonial belief system. (Reproduced from Calder 1977: Figure 2.)

ochre. Some of the artifact clusters may even represent the remains of medicine bundles. Only some of these items, however, can be related to Middle Plains culture use of the Cairn. The iniskims or buffalo stones, for example, all pertain to later periods of the Cairn. It might be suggested that the relatively high frequency of projectile points (17% of the offerings) had some relationship to hunting magic. Nearly half of the points were broken indicating that they were `killed´. Breaking of offerings to release the spirit of the object is a good indicator of animistic beliefs. Only two human bones, a fifth metatarsal and a proximal phalanx, were recovered from the excavations. Of the highly fragmented animal bone offerings in the Cairn a high incidence of young or foetal remains was represented (Calder 1977: 196) supporting the hypothesis that one of the major functions of such features was rejuvenation.It is pertinent to note that archaeological evidence in the immediate vicinity around the Medicine Wheel does not support the speculation of tribal or multiple band ceremonial aggregations (Vickers 1991: 66).

At the time of European contact the Blackfeet and other Northern Plains tribes used `iniskim´ or buffalo stones as medicine for `calling´ bison. Iniskim are usually fossil ammonites or baculites but were sometimes any pebble with an animate form (Verbicky-Todd 1984: 12-22, 220-224). A fossil ammonite and a fragment of another fossil were recovered from the McKean complex Cactus Flower site in Alberta (Brumley 1975). The finding of these objects in such an early context raises the likelihood that the iniskim was a Middle Plains culture trait even though none could be clearly identified to such a context at the Majorville Medicine Wheel.

Considerable information on Middle Plains culture belief systems resulted from the excavation of the Gray Burial site in southwestern Saskatchewan (Millar 1981). More than 300 individuals from 99 burial pits involving from one to 14 individuals were identified. Calibrated radiocarbon dates indicate the use of the cemetery from 3,500 to 1,500 BC. This age spread raises the question of whether the cemetery was solely an Oxbow complex sacred site or whether it was also used by the later Middle Plains culture McKean and Pelican Lake complexes. Certainly some of the grave offerings could be classified as pertaining to the McKean complex (Millar 1981: Fig.3, the two points in the upper right corner). This, once again, brings us back to the question of whether the Oxbow complex triangular chipped bifaces are really preforms or a new projectile point variety hafted without notches, a trait characteristic of the early point form of the McKean complex.

The cemetery is located on a south-facing hill overlooking a major glacial outwash channel. Occupying an area approximately 15 m in diameter the burials were densely concentrated with one burial per square meter (Millar et al. 1972: 11). There appears to have been three distinct areas of burial concentration. Secondary modifications evident in the bundle burials were the removal of the ends of longbones except in the cases of infants, the fragmentation of post-cranial elements, and the painting of bones with red ochre. Some of the bone breakage occurred on site as indicated by surface bone fragments that were mended with fragments from undisturbed burials. A majority of the burials had been exposed prior to final burial, presumably on scaffolds. There is some evidence of defleshing and dismemberment and a single instance of the post-mortem removal of the medial incisors is reported. It has been suggested that the time from death to final burial was quite variable and could have required a number of different scaffold burial sites for some individuals before they reached their final grave in the cemetery. The proposal receives some support from the fact that most of the bundle burials were incomplete and there is evidence of variable weathering of the bones of individuals within the same grave. There was also some

FIGURE 42: THE GRAY BURIAL SITE FLOORPLAN, SASKATCHEWAN The cemetery was in use for nearly 2,000 years between 3,500 and 1,500 BC. As can be seen from the archaeological floorplan, the graves were tightly concentrated and, indeed, a number of graves cut into earlier interments. The site was a sacred burial place where the disarticulated remains of kinsmen were periodically brought for final burial. Although this cemetery has generally been associated with the Oxbow complex there is some evidence to suggest its probable use by the subsequent McKean and Pelican Lake complexes.   (Reproduced from Millar 1978: Figure 28 with permission from Parks Canada.)

minor evidence of burning and the arranging of skeletal elements, such as a circle of skulls being placed around the post-cranial remains and the thrusting of longbones into the foramen magnum of the skull. Even some attempted rearticulation of remains was evident. Not only was the Gray Burial site a Middle Plains culture sacred place where the remains of the deceased were brought for final burial over a period of 2,000 years but the cemetery also likely functioned as a band territorial marker. Its length of use provides some appreciation of the degree of social and territorial stability within the band or bands responsible for the cemetery.

Among the limited grave offerings were projectile points, notched knives, end scrapers, eagle talons, shell gorgets from the Atlantic coast, native copper beads from Lake Superior, and parts of animals, generally the limb bones of canids, bison, antelope, duck, deer, skunk, and jackrabbit. A dog burial was associated with a human bundle burial. There was no correlation of quantity or type of grave offerings with either the age or the sex of the recipient. Red ochre tended to be lavished on the graves. An interesting facet of the Gray Burial site was the probability that graves had been marked with cobble cairns although the direct evidence had been largely destroyed by recent ploughing. Abundant whole and fragmented cobbles that had to be brought to the site occurred in the ploughzone (Millar 1981: 114; Ian Dyck: personal communication). Some graves where the original land surface was intact had cobbles on top of them or, in other instances, cobbles had been included with the grave fill. Grave markers would help to explain the multiple interments in single grave pits. In these instances the graves appear to have been used for successive burials, presumably of kinsmen (Callaghan 1986). The differential weathering of individual burials within the same burial pit also lends support to this proposal (Millar 1981: 104). An intriguing feature was the presence of a purposefully prepared white clay base in some of the graves. Similar coverings of grave floors with a clay-like substance occurred toward the end of Period III in Middle Great Lakes-St.Lawrence culture, in Period V burials mounds of Proto-Plains culture and probably, in a related form, in some Late Plains culture burials in Period IV. The use of clay or marl to line the floor of a grave pit or a mound floor may relate to the widely distributed historically documented Earth-Diver myth that accounted for the creation of the Earth and all its subsequent animate and inanimate entities (Hall: 1979). If this speculation has any credence the examples from the Gray Burial site would be the earliest recorded instances in Canada of this widespread creation legend. Some of the similarities between the Gray Burial cemetery and the unrelated contemporaneous cemeteries of Middle Maritime culture and Middle Great Lakes-St. Lawrence culture is of interest. These similarities include the nature of the grave offerings and their lack or limited correlation with sex or age, offerings of animal parts, the transportation of the dead from temporary graves to a final place of burial at a sacred site often used for prolonged periods with superposition or intrusion of later burials into older grave pits, and with reference to the Middle Maritime culture Port au Choix cemetery, the use of cobbles as grave markers and the concentration of graves into three clusters.

Four other Saskatchewan burial sites have been assigned to the Oxbow complex (Walker 1984). The Greenwater Lake site consisted of an extended adult male burial with a single projectile point and abundant red ochre (Walker 1981). Two other separate burial sites were each represented by extended adults. Both were provided with red ochre. The extended burial position, abundant use of red ochre, and, in one instance, a date of 3,500 BC (Wilmeth 1978) are used to tentatively assign these burials to the Oxbow complex. At the Kisbey site, three bundle burials representing a young adult male, two adolescents, and two children were placed on top of one another in a single grave pit provided with red ochre, some animal skeletal elements, and a stone graver (Walker 1984). A date of 1,500 BC, however, would suggest that the grave is more likely to relate to one of the later complexes of Middle Plains culture.

McKean complex burials have rarely been encountered. Considering that the vast majority of such encounters are purely accidental this is somewhat surprising. At the Crown site in north central Saskatchewan an extended young child burial lacking grave offerings has been reported (Quigg 1986: 114; Walker 1984). In south central Saskatchewan an unusual McKean complex cremation was discovered at the Graham site (Walker 1984). The dismembered bundle burial of a young adult male was burnt in a dry rather than green bone state to judge from the bone fracture patterns. The original bundle burial was apparently retrieved from a scaffold where it had been subjected to animal gnawing and then was cremated in situ in a hearth along with a bison skull fragment. A burnt projectile point and a large side-notched lance or knife were placed in the crematory hearth while 10 stone preforms, a core, 21 flakes, and three bone and antler tools, were deposited adjacent to the crematorium. Although the sample indicative of the McKean complex burial practices is too limited to be given much weight, it is noted that both burials occurred in habitation floors unlike the Oxbow complex cemetery and graves that were isolated from habitation sites.

External relationships:

The most important Middle Plains culture relationship to be resolved is the relationship of the Oxbow complex to the McKean complex. According to radiocarbon dating but not stratigraphy the two complexes were coeval and occupied the same territory. While the projectile point styles of the two complexes are frequently found together at sites (Gibson 1976; 1981; Haug 1976; Reeves 1973: 1,236; Syms 1970: 125) the associations appear to be ones of accidental mixing of archaeological deposits rather than indisputable context. At the Crown site (Quigg 1986: 124) an Oxbow complex projectile point was found between two McKean complex occupation floors. While not indicative of direct contact this occurrence suggests the contemporaneity of the projectile point varieties unless this single instance represents an early case of projectile point collecting or a typological whim. In any respect, a single specimen hardly settles the matter of Oxbow/McKean contemporaneity. It is also pertinent to note that this was the only Oxbow point to appear in the Crown site even though the Oxbow complex is well represented in the area (Meyer 1977: 141-148).

B. O. K. Reeves has proposed that the McKean complex expanded into the Northern Plains and pushed the Oxbow complex into the forest (Vickers 1986: 68). This proposition, as well as the suggestion of a direct association between the two complexes, is compromised by the following: the existence of Oxbow and McKean complex occupations in the same region lacking any evidence of cultural interaction although contemporary according to radiocarbon dating; the existence of a number of stratified sites that consistently have the McKean complex following the Oxbow complex; the lack of evidence of an Oxbow complex exodus into either the Boreal Forest or the Mountain/Foothills at a late date; the occurrence of the McKean complex in these same environmental zones and often with greater frequency than the Oxbow complex; and the absence of any technological or environmental evidence or appropriate analogies to account for such abnormal aggressive/submissive behaviour on the part of two hunting complexes at the same level of technological development. A more parsimonious explanation of the relationship between these complexes is that the Oxbow complex developed into the McKean complex just as the Pelican Lake complex developed out of the latter. The alternative is to have two different cultures occupying the same regions of the Plains, the Mountain/Foothills, and Boreal Forest while competing for the same resources but maintaining their respective cultural purity until the McKean complex somehow replaces the Oxbow complex.

Whether one regards the relationship between the Oxbow and McKean complexes as one of cultural replacement or as temporal phases in a single cultural development as favoured here, there are recognizable differences between the two. An advocate for replacement would point to such differences as being the products of cultural introductions while an in situ advocate would simply regard them as the products of changes through time. Projectile point style changes between the complexes can be viewed either as sudden or gradual depending on whether one accepts or rejects the Oxbow trianguloid points as functioning projectile points that were a prototype of the McKean Lanceolate type or as preforms for Oxbow side-notched points. The remaining tool kit is essentially the same. Evidence relating to burial differences is too limited at this time to be given much significance. Trade network patterns do change where the major evidence of Oxbow complex contacts was with the east and southeast as opposed to the west and southwest for the McKean complex. The preceding observation must be tempered, however, by the observation that both of these complexes were essentially parochial and relied heavily upon local stone for tool manufacturing rather than exotic lithics. Both complexes shared focal and diffuse subsistence adaptive subsistence systems relative to locale, and, thus, shared settlement patterns within the same environmental regions. Both also participated in medicine wheel ceremonialism and probably at sacred burial places if a McKean complex presence is accepted at the Gray Burial site. Do the differences between the two complexes pertain to different cultural origins or changes through time? Much of the evidence is equivocal although when viewed in its totality it suggests a single cultural development and not the replacement of one culture by another. Here I must acknowledge my bias against hunting bands behaving like Asiatic steppe pastoralists; behaviour that would probably have been impossible for their economic level of development to maintain even if inclination for `Lebensraum´ involving the hunting territories of neighbouring peoples had existed.

Most Oxbow complex sites in the Grasslands/Parklands contain at least some Knife River chalcedony from North Dakota. As the latter region was also occupied by Oxbow bands the presence of this material to the north and northwest likely reflects some form of interband trading pattern. The presence of a smattering of native copper implements, however, is evidence of a broader network involving Middle Shield culture in the Canadian Shield to the east. That the trade was reciprocated is suggested by the presence of Knife River chalcedony on Middle Shield culture sites. Other eastern connections are to be seen in the Atlantic coast shell objects recovered from the Gray Burial site (Millar 1978). Such shell items likely proceeded westward through the hands of Middle Great Lakes-St.Lawrence culture traders and other contemporary southern Archaic cultures rather than Middle Shield culture. In contrast, Wyoming obsidian is frequently found on McKean complex sites. A Pacific coast dentalium shell (Dentalium pretiosum) was recovered from the McKean complex Crown site in Saskatchewan (Quigg 1986: 87-89). At the Cactus Flower site in Alberta two Pacific coast shell beads, Natica clausa and Olivella biplicata were retrieved from McKean complex living floors (Brumley 1975: 69). Such west coast marine shell ornaments likely originated with Early West Coast culture people who traded them to Middle Plateau culture people and thence to the Plains. A limited quantity of Montana/Wyoming siltstone, Wyoming obsidian, and Knife River chalcedony was also recovered at this site.

The Winnipeg River and southeastern Manitoba, in general, appears to have been a major culture contact zone between Middle Plains culture and Middle Shield culture, the latter being referred to locally as Raddatz or Old Copper (Buchner 1979: 124; 1982; Wheeler 1978: 90-91). Middle Shield culture people spread westward with the expanding Boreal Forest around 3,000 BC and intruded themselves into the middle of a Middle Plains culture development. At the stratified LM-8 site, for example, a Middle Shield culture occupation occurred above an Oxbow complex living floor and beneath a Pelican Lake complex occupation (Buchner 1979: 10). In this respect, though the area east of the Winnipeg River was a major region of culture contact it was still a region occupied throughout most of Period III by Middle Plains culture. It is most likely that much of the exchange of western Knife River chalcedony and eastern native copper took place in this particular area. Further north, some of the point types and forms from the Tailrace Bay site in Grand Rapids, Manitoba (Mayer-Oakes 1970: 126) likely pertain to Middle Shield culture occupations and raise the probability of exchanges with Middle Plains culture occupations of the same site. Similar contacts could have been made in the eastern portion of the Churchill River in Saskatchewan (Meyer and Smailes 1975: 61; Meyer et al. 1981). In Southern Indian Lake on the Churchill River drainage in northern Manitoba, Middle Plains culture materials have been identified (Kroker 1990: Fig.17) and would have been partially contemporaneous with the indigenous Middle Shield culture (Dickson 1980). Such a Middle Plains culture penetration into the Lichen Woodland vegetation province in the Canadian Shield would be surprising but not impossible. Acceptance of the cultural identification, however, must await a full description of the evidence. Limited evidence of Middle Plains and Middle Shield culture contact occurred at the Crown site on the North Saskatchewan River near Nipawin. Here a single Middle Shield culture side-notched projectile point was recovered from a McKean complex level of the site (Quigg 1986: Fig.6.6, no.20, 122). In a classic instance of the interpretational risks inherent in the use of projectile point typologies, however, the author of the report equated the point with the Mummy Cave complex despite the chronological contradiction such a classification posed for both the archaeological context and radiocarbon dates at the Crown site. The compound the issue, the evidence of similar contemporary side-notched points from Middle Shield culture sites on Southern Indian Lake 500 km to the northeast of the Crown site (Dickson 1980) was ignored.

Human biology:

The most important known Middle Plains culture cemetery is the Gray Burial site in Saskatchewan. The analysis of the remains revealed a population characterized by marked skeletal differences between the sexes. Infant and child mortality was high, representing nearly 60% of the sample as opposed to 8% adolescents and 28% adults. This high incidence of infant and child mortality is similar to that reported from the contemporary Middle Maritime culture Port au Choix cemetery on the Island of Newfoundland (Anderson 1976: 124). Among the adults there was a high incidence of periodontal disease (gum disease affecting the bone surrounding the roots of the teeth that results in tooth loss and other problems) indicative of a diet of coarse foods which prematurely wore-down the teeth. Non-metric skeletal trait studies suggest that the cemetery was used by a single population over a period of 2,000 years. An estimated 500 individuals had been buried indicating that similar cemeteries must exist in other parts of Middle Plains culture territory (Wade 1981). Fluoride analysis of bone samples from multiple burials in single grave pits provided evidence of multiple and separate burial episodes rather than synchronous events (Callaghan 1986). The former study also tended to support the suggestion that the Gray Burial site represented a continuously used cemetery that possessed clear spatial limits. Although referred to as an Oxbow complex cemetery the presence of some McKean complex projectile points and some other traits as well as the radiocarbon date spread would suggest the cemetery was used throughout much of Period III.

A young adult male encountered at a McKean complex site in south-central Saskatchewan appears to represent a bundle burial that was later partially cremated. Some unburned elements were found adjacent to the presumed crematorium hearth (Walker 1984). Cut marks on the bone indicate that the body was dismembered and the fracture pattern of the burnt bone suggests that it was burned when in a dry rather than green or fresh state. There was also some evidence of animal gnawing on the bones suggesting the remains had been retrieved from a scaffold or other surface burial. It is estimated the individual stood approximately 1.8 m in height. The only other reported McKean complex burial from Canada is a three year old child from the Crown site (Quigg 1986). Buried in an extended position beneath a living floor this child exhibited extensive evidence of periostitis of the limbs suggesting that pulmonary hypertrophic osteoarthropathy may have been the cause of death (Walker 1986: 257). In this instance, it is suspected that the cause of the distinctive bone lesions was a non-tuberculous lung abscess.

Inferences on society:

There is merit in the observation that most Plains Indian social and religious institutions observed by Europeans, such as polygamous marriage and the Sundance Ceremony, were in place long before the introduction of the horse and other European influences (Reeves 1990). Reeves has also suggested that the variation in size of tipi rings beginning around 2,300 BC indicate the existence of differential wealth and status. Determining social phenomenon, such as the existence of dog soldiers and polygamous marriage and status and wealth on the basis of the dimensions of tipi rings is, in my opinion, stretching the archaeological evidence. There is evidence from the medicine wheels, however, which warrants the speculation that a ceremony related to the historically documented Sundance Ceremony may have existed as early as Oxbow complex times in southern Alberta and Saskatchewan. A sacred burial locale, like the Gray Burial site, also likely functioned as a physical monument that reinforced band territorial claims. In this respect, in addition to its burial function, such a cemetery in use for 2,000 years, could have stood as a territorial marker consecrated by the presence of generations of deceased kinsmen.

Although the continuity of site occupations, often representing many thousands of years, would suggest some form of societal continuity, the use of multicomponent technological analysis to identify "...a local archaeological population..." and member sites occupied by the same band members (Keyser 1985) is yet to be demonstrated. The data base is also currently insufficient to effectively test the hypothesis that specific bands of hunters preyed upon specific bison herds (Gordon 1979). Intermarriage between bands has been suggested by evidence from the Gray Burial site. In an unpublished M.A. thesis by C. G. Pardoe it is proposed on the basis of a number of non-metric skeletal variables pertaining to the vascular and nervous systems that the Gray Burial site population was a single homogenous group and that "Some evidence indicate female in-migration from outside the population" (in Meiklejohn and Rokala 1986: 353). Band interactions are also reflected in the trade networks (Millar 1981a: 157).

Limitations in the evidence:

The archaeological record of Middle Plains culture is comparatively good despite problems of site destruction and deep burial by the processes of erosion and deposition in many locales (Dyck 1983; Wilson 1983). Both the Grasslands/Parklands and the Mountains/Foothills are characterized by relatively numerous stratified sites. As is normal, the individual components of sites in the Boreal Forest are usually hopelessly mixed together. Bone preservation also tends to be good on sites located in the Grasslands/Parklands but poor to non-existent in the other two environmental zones. One of the major problems in evaluating the archaeological record from the Plains and environs is methodological. There has been an excessive reliance upon projectile point typology and radiocarbon dates to reconstruct the culture history. These tendencies have underemphasized the importance of the frequently excellent stratigraphic record even though most archaeologists would agree that stratigraphy is a more reliable relative gauge of chronology than either typology or radiometric measurements. Certainly confusion has been inserted into the archaeological record by the subjective use of projectile point typology as a means of both estimating and explaining radiocarbon dates. Point types have also been used somewhat indiscriminately to assign specific ethnic and/or linguistic affiliations to sites. This practice has elicited the cautionary retort that "...there is no `Oxbow culture´, but rather a set of sites, components or assemblages that share formally defined Oxbow points. The chances that all Oxbow points were made over the course of 2,000 years by individuals in groups that shared specific aspects of culture - e.g., reckoned themselves as kin, spoke the same language, believed in the same gods, played the same tunes and so forth - are infinitesimally remote " (Forbis 1992: 32, footnote 2). Even though increasingly reports provide relatively complete quantitative and qualitative information on assemblages these data are rarely used for comparative purposes. As a result the classificatory systems are essentially based upon projectile point typology. It would be easier to understand this heavy reliance upon projectile point types if component isolation were difficult or impossible but this is certainly not the case for many sites in the Grasslands/Parklands and the Mountain/Foothills. The methodological limitation in the reconstruction of culture history on the Plains has been compounded by an unfortunate degree of regionalism whereby Alberta archaeologists often look south into Montana and, in particular, Wyoming, for comparisons rather than adjacent Saskatchewan not to mention Manitoba. While this situation is regrettably common to the archaeological comparative process across Canada it has been exacerbated on the Plains by dividing the northern Plains into essentially Alberta/Montana/Wyoming and Saskatchewan/Manitoba/North Dakota units. The preceding criticism is certainly not intended to suggest that archaeologists working in the Canadian Plains lack methodological sophistication or view their evidence through parochial lenses. Rather, it is intended to point out that certain historical developments in the practise of archaeology on the Plains have led to an excessive reliance upon the combined use of projectile point typology and radiocarbon dates in the reconstruction of culture history. This, in turn, has resulted in classificatory schemes that are inconsistent with stratigraphy, other comparative data, and, in some instances, general anthropological theory. Certainly the limitations involved in an over-reliance upon the time/space/culture content assumptions inherent in projectile point types are clearly recognized by some (Forbis 1992; Ronaghan 1986: 290). However, the prevailing epistemology still appears to be best reflected in the following observation, "The cultural sequence in much of northwestern North America has been developed largely on the basis of projectile points. The use of only one artifact category can be justified in many instances because projectile points change technologically and stylistically over relatively short time periods, while other formed artifacts do not undergo the same changes" (Driver 1978: 94) (quoted in Vickers 1986: 9). Such a position begs the question of whether archaeologists are interested in the short term changes in projectile point technology or are concerned with all cultural change and the development of total cultural systems within which technology is but one system and projectile points but one element of that system. Also, to be fair, the relative scarcity of funds to support major archaeological excavations has resulted in a paucity of large scale site excavations. Such excavations with their larger samples and controlled contexts are absolutely necessary if the lean chronological framework erected to date is ever to be fleshed-in.

Recent archaeological research in the Boreal Forest, Canadian Shield, Mountains and Foothills is gradually modifying the earlier impression that Middle Plains culture was essentially a bison oriented culture based in the Grasslands/Parklands. However, though the evidence is becoming increasingly clear that Middle Plains culture had a highly flexible adaptive system that could include either a focused economy or a diffuse economy, most of the current literature still leaves one with the impression that the Grasslands/Parklands bison hunters were the real Middle Plains culture people and not those strange related bands that paddled around in the Boreal Forest catching fish or clambering up the sides of mountains to hunt mountain sheep and goats. For understandable reasons, many archaeologists would prefer their archaeological constructs to fit neatly into nice, tight environmental niches. The survival needs and skills of Middle Plains culture, like other hunting cultures in Canada, however, were obviously unable to accommodate such classificatory neatness.

CHAPTER 18

MIDDLE PLATEAU CULTURE

Précis:

The archaeological record of the Canadian Plateau has elicited a range of conflicting opinions regarding the culture history of the region. It appears that sparse information and cultural regionalism has made syntheses difficult for the interior Pacific Northwest in general and the Canadian Plateau in particular (Leonhardy 1982: 85; Lyman 1985). The Canadian Plateau is composed of the territories between the Coastal Range and the Rocky Mountains, south to the International Boundary and north to the headwaters of the Fraser River at 54• latitude. Influences and/or people could enter the region from the Plains to the east, the Columbia Plateau to the south, the Pacific coast via the major river valleys, and the north through the Cordillera. Limitations in the archaeological record, as well as a heavy reliance upon such criterion as the presence or absence of microblades and the presence of certain projectile point types, have further complicated the situation.

What follows is an outline of the culture history of the region from 4,000 to 1,000 BC. In this work diffusion of technologies and other cultural practices are considered to be mainly responsible for culture change rather than population replacements with their explicit assumptions of invasion and displacement or absorption of earlier people. Technological complexes, such as prepared microblade cores, are regarded as having relative rather than absolute significance in terms of cultural classification. In other words, the presence or absence of such an element of technology is insufficient ground in itself for positing major culture historical events. As noted throughout the volume, all systems of a culture should be considered in any cultural historical reconstruction and not single elements drawn from a single system such as technology. That said, it is readily admitted that there is fertile ground for continuing debate and what follows in one person's viewpoint. For a succinct consideration of the problems facing synthesizers of Canadian Plateau archaeology see Richards and Rousseau (1987).

Middle Plateau culture is the descendant of Early Plateau culture. By 4,000 BC or slightly earlier a gradual change to a seasonal subsistence-settlement pattern economy based upon salmon in conjunction with the introduction of the spearthrower weapon system from the east and/or south, resulted in changes to the cultural pattern. Contrary to the position of cultural continuity taken here, in a recent synthesis of Plateau archaeology these changes are interpreted as evidence of a population intrusion up the Fraser River from the coast by a pre-adapted salmon fishing population unrelated to Early Plateau culture whose descendants they replaced (Stryd and Rousseau in press). The development of the Plateau Pithouse tradition around 2,500 BC, with its riverine pithouse villages and salmon storage technology, established a cultural horizon across the Canadian Plateau. Based upon the appearance of pithouses this tradition, with its three sequential horizons (Richards and Rousseau 1987), represents a practical and flexible way of classifying the archaeological evidence but it need not have involved an intrusive population. Cultural continuities between Early and Middle Plateau cultures suggest that cultural changes were the product of indigenous people in the Plateau adopting a number of innovations, including a subsistence/settlement pattern based upon salmon. The transition to large pit house villages appears to have been a lengthy process. In contrast to the controversy surrounding the origins of Middle Plateau culture there appears to be agreement that it represented the cultural base from which the Salish-speaking peoples encountered by Europeans in the early 19th century developed.

Middle Plateau culture is an admittedly ill-defined cultural construct. The early portion of the cultural development has not been identified in the adjacent Okanagan and Arrow Lakes regions of south-central British Columbia. In the Kootenai region of southeastern British Columbia archaeological evidence is comparable, in a number of respects, to Middle Plains culture. Middle Plateau culture subsistence information is both limited and concentrated in the major river valleys. While salmon and deer appear to have been of greatest importance it is apparent that all resources, ranging from fresh water mussels to skunks, were exploited. It is not possible at this time to assess the role of plant foods that were so important in the diet of people at the time of European contact. Around 2,500 BC subsistence began to focus increasingly upon the harvesting of salmon and other anadromous fish (Kuijt 1989). It is suggested that the change in subsistence pattern was related to environmental factors such as an increasingly cool and moist climate that favoured increased river levels and thus expanding salmon spawning grounds. The use of local stone in tool manufacturing suggests limited relationships with adjacent cultures. Marine shell artifacts and exotic stone do occur but are extremely rare. It is not until the end of Period III and major settlement pattern changes associated with a focused emphasis upon salmon that external contacts become apparent, particularly with the coast.

Some of the preceding comments may be viewed as a criticism of archaeologists working in the Canadian Plateau and this is not the case. The Plateau is an exceptionally difficult region in which to establish syntheses (Richards and Rousseau 1987). Most archaeological excavation has naturally focused on the large, multi-component pit house villages in the river valleys thus providing a biased sample. The topographic extremes of the region, with their associated variable resources, required a dispersed settlement pattern involving innumerable small transitory camp sites containing limited cultural debris. Natural sedimentary processes have obliterated or hidden much of the early archaeological record. Finally, the cul-de-sac topography of the region lends itself to an exceptional degree of cultural regionalism That said, there has been a tendency to link the local culture history too closely to the cultural developments of the Coast, the Plains, the Sub-Arctic, and the Columbia Plateau. As occurs elsewhere, an over-reliance upon microblade technology and projectile point typology to establish cultural constructs and identify cultures has resulted in differing interpretations.

Historically the area was occupied by members of the Salish language family (Kinkade and Suttles 1987). Exceptions were/are a small enclave of Nicola Eyak-Athapascan speakers and the Kootenai or Kootenay. With reference to the Kootenai-speakers, however, there is a possibility of a `distant genetic´ relationship with Salish (Campbell and Mithun 1979: 37-38). Northwestern North America Indian languages, from northern Oregon to Alaska and east to the Foothills of the Rocky Mountains, share many language features suggesting either a shared ancestry or a convergence of language traits due to close contacts over a long period of time. Linguistically the situation is unique in North America. The proposal of an original indigenous population changing its culture through selective adoption of outside innovations appears to be in accord with the linguistic evidence. An in situ origin hypothesis would negate the atypical hunter-gatherer behaviour of territorial conquest explicit in the alternative replacement hypothesis.

There is general agreement that the most important single event in Middle Plateau culture development during Period III was the transition from mobile hunting people to semi-permanent village dwellers increasingly reliant upon stored salmon as the primary winter food (Kuijt 1989). This transition to village life began around 2,000 BC.

Cultural origins and descendants:

In the first synthesis of Plateau archaeology the earliest culture was identified as Southwestern Coastal culture (Cordilleran or Old Cordilleran). It was hypothesized that this culture was replaced by a movement of people out of central British Columbia. The invaders were referred to as the Nesikep tradition (Early and Middle Plateau culture) (Sanger 1970). The foregoing sequence of events has been largely rejected for the following reasons: no antecedents for the Nesikep tradition have been found in the north-central interior of British Columbia (Helmer 1977: 93); the antiquity and even the presence of Southwestern Coastal culture (Cordilleran or Lochnore) in the Plateau is equivocal; and the evidence of cultural continuities during the hypothesized cultural replacement. Relevant to Southwestern Coastal culture there is some evidence that an assemblage, with or without microblades, characterized by bipointed projectile points/knives, cobble tools, and a simple flake industry, may have been present in the Canadian Plateau during Period II (8,000 -4,000 BC). Others would argue that the earliest date for such an occupation was around 4,000 BC (Stryd and Rousseau in press).

The rejection of hypotheses involving territorial conquests from either the north or the west to account for Middle Plateau culture is, in part, based upon the assumption that such militaristic ventures were beyond the economic capability of most hunting and gathering peoples and, indeed, in terms of lifeways would have been unnecessary and even alien to them. Historically documented exceptions to the foregoing generalization are not regarded as being relevant to the pre-European situation as they involved sudden, pervasive, and interrelated `foreign´ influences such as depopulation (disease), increased mobility (horses), weaponry (guns and iron), exceptional increased pressures on resources and land (displacement of eastern native populations to the west), and a ubiquitous economic force (the fur trade). There is also the evidence of cultural continuities between Early Plateau culture and Middle Plateau culture. Based upon the assemblages from the 5,500 BC Lehman site and the 4,250 BC Level VII of the Nesikep Creek site (Sanger 1970) of Period II the stone tool continuities into Period III are microblades, cobble tools, bipointed projectile points/knives, amorphous biface knives, random flake scrapers, end scrapers and other traits.

Middle Plateau culture is regarded as the direct descendant of Early Plateau culture. Cultural changes around 4,000 BC are interpreted as the products of an increasing emphasis upon salmon in the diet as well as the adoption of the spearthrower weapon system. An alternative hypothesis suggests that Middle Plateau culture (Sqlelten tradition) resulted from a population movement of coastal, pre-adapted salmon fishermen up the Fraser River who replaced the resident population (Stryd and Rousseau in press). Although continuities are noted early in Middle Plateau culture, the appearance of the Sqlelten tradition (Lochnore) is stated to initiate a sudden change in technology, subsistence and settlement patterns. The Lochnore phase is treated as a coastal development from Southwestern Coastal culture (Cordilleran) even though it is also considered to be in the interior during Period II. From the Lochnore phase the Shuswap cultural horizon of the Plateau Pithouse tradition developed between 2,500 and 2,000 BC and led through two more cultural horizons to the historically documented Shuswap Salish speakers of the region. The indigenous Nesikep tradition is viewed as speaking a non-Salish language. Both groups co-existed for a period until the Nesikep tradition people were culturally absorbed. It is admitted by the authors of the foregoing scenario that the sequence of events is speculative. Certainly the hypothesis has not yet been demonstrated by archaeological evidence.

As noted on a number of occasions in this Volume the issue of when archaeological evidence reflects an actual population replacement (conquest-dispersal-absorption) or simply the adoption of certain cultural elements by indigenous people often elicits controversy. It is, therefore, useful to consider the basis of opinion regarding the origins of Middle Plateau culture. In the earliest archaeological synthesis of a region of the Canadian Plateau it was noted that the bipointed projectile point was only diagnostic of Southwestern Coastal culture (Cordilleran/Lochnore) when other point styles were absent (Sanger 1969: 192). This qualification has been largely ignored and, indeed, the fact that bipointed projectile points continue to occur throughout the archaeological sequence has been used as a basis from rejecting Sanger's early Lochnore complex (Fladmark 1982: 127). Controversy has also surrounded the origins of the lanceolate, stemmed, and notched projectile points of Middle Plateau culture. Sanger saw parallels with the McKean complex points style of Middle Plains culture (Sanger 1970: 121) but no relationship to the Columbia Plateau (Ibid: 123). Others, also working in the Fraser River drainage (Rousseau and Richards 1985), have associated these same point styles with either the McKean complex or point styles in the Columbia Plateau of southeastern Washington State (Nelson 1969). In contrast, point styles from 2,500 BC to European contact in the central interior of British Columbia have been stated to be more closely related to those of the southwestern Yukon than the Columbia Plateau (Helmer 1977: 95-96). Another opinion sees the "...greatest affinity..." of these point styles with the Columbia Plateau and regards the McKean complex parallels as being a product of cultural interaction (Donahue 1975: 54). The shared attributes of projectile points styles in Middle Plateau culture and Middle Plains culture (McKean complex) appear to be too general in nature to support a direct generic relationship. Stratified sequences like that at the Sunset Creek site in the Columbia Plateau of southwestern Washington (Rice 1969) reveal a Southwestern Coastal culture derived-assemblage dating between 4,000 and 1,000 BC. The stemmed and notched points styles that appear in the sequence between 2,000 and 1,000 BC show little relationship to Middle Plateau culture point styles. At this time period there appears to be a significant cultural division between the drainages of the Fraser River and the Columbia River (Sanger 1968: 113). By 5,000 BC side-notched projectile points resembling Mummy Cave points (see Early Plains culture) associated with bipointed points as well as spearthrower weights and butt spurs (Leonhardy and Rice 1970) mark the appearance of the spearthrower in the region. Whether this weapon system penetrated the Canadian Plateau from the south or across the Rocky Mountains from the Plains is a mute question. The appearance of the new projectile point styles in Middle Plateau culture is regarded as being related to the diffusion of the new weapon system rather than the influx of an alien people.

Microblade technology has been a critical factor in reconstructing Middle Plateau culture history. Initially microblades were used as the diagnostic marker of the Nesikep complex (Sanger 1968; 1970) and were thought to have been of northern origin. Current evidence supports the opinion that the technology most likely entered the Canadian Plateau from the north. Indeed, the dates and distribution of microblades in the Columbia Plateau would suggest that they actually entered that region from the Fraser drainage. The problems with deriving microblade technology from the coast via the Fraser River were considered in Chapter 10. There is an increasing body of evidence to support the opinion that microblade technology is an unreliable element of technology upon which to base culture historical reconstructions. At the stratified Nesikep Creek site, for example, microblades occurred in the lower Level VII but were absent from the upper Level V. With this sole exception the two levels produced related assemblages of tools (Sanger 1968: 113; 170: 67, Table XXXIII). It now appears that microblades were not produced, used, or discarded at all sites of the same culture. Whether this presence and absence of microblades pertains to specific seasonal activities, archaeological sampling, or other factors, cannot be determined at this time. Microblades should simply be regarded as one element of Middle Plateau culture technology that may or may not be represented on all sites of the culture.

Cultural continuities are apparent from Early Plateau culture to Middle Plateau culture, albeit with transitional periods of rapid change as people adapted to a changing environmental conditions and introduced technology. The continuity origin hypothesis is, of course, the antithesis of the conquest/replacement origin hypothesis with its prerequisite of a culture with both exceptional militaristic capabilities and an economy capable of supporting territorial conquest. That internal changes account for the transition of mobile hunters into semi-permanent village dwelling fishermen-hunters is implicit in the observation "Thus, it may be more appropriate to view the appearance of semi-subterranean dwellings in the Canadian Plateau as being an adaptation to changes in availability and reliability of ungulates and salmon resources, rather than as a settlement practice specific to a particular ethnic group" (Kuijt 1989:108).

BLACK AND WHITE PLATE XVI: THE LOCHNORE-NESIKEP LOCALITY   The first archaeological synthesis of a region of the Canadian Plateau of British Columbia was, in large part, based upon sites situated on the tributaries on either side of the Fraser River in this locality. While the altitudinal effect of Plateau topography assured an exceptionally wide range of plant and animal foods, as well as lengthy seasonal availability, deer and migrating salmon appear to have been the major prey sought throughout most of Plateau archaeological history. (Photograph provided by Dr. David Sanger, Department of Anthropology, University of Maine at Orono.)

A factor bearing on the lack of agreement on certain aspects of Middle Plateau culture history has been the relative scarcity of reliable radiocarbon dates. The radiocarbon dating situation has recently improved. Detailed information on Middle Plateau culture radiocarbon dates can be obtained from the following references: Donahue 1975; Fladmark 1976, 1982; Kuijit 1989, Tables 1 and 2; Rousseau and Richards 1985; Sanger 1968, 1970; Turnbull 1977; and Whitlam 1980.

Technology:

After more than two decades the most complete published description of Middle Plateau culture is still that relating to work carried out in the Lochnore-Nesikep locality (Black and White Plate XIII) on the Fraser River (Sanger 1970). The following comments are largely based upon this researcher's descriptions as subsequent workers have not presented their evidence in the same detail. It is cautioned, however, that some component mixture of material from these sites is likely (Richards and Rousseau 1987: 8-11).

The most common artifact classes throughout Middle Plateau culture technology are random flake scrapers and amorphous biface knives. Carefully formed biface knives tend to be rare and some of the triangular specimens could actually be either projectile points or point preforms. An examination of the tool assemblages from the Lochnore III (possible Southwestern Coastal culture), Nesikep VII and Lehman II (Early Plateau culture), Nesikep V (Middle Plateau culture), and Lochnore I (Late Plateau culture) components (Sanger 1970) revealed that approximately 70% of all the assemblages were represented by projectile points, random flake scrapers, and amorphous biface knives except for the Nesikep VII component where nearly half of the small assemblage of 57 specimens were composed of the foregoing artifact categories. Two other major artifact categories, cobble tools and microblades, were not fully quantified in the report and could not be included in the comparisons (see Wyatt 1970, Table XI for microblade information). Microblades were totally absent from the Lochnore III and Nesikep V components. The point to be made is that there appears to be a basic similarity in the tool kits of these components even though they extend from Period II (Lochnore III, Lehman II, Nesikep VII) to Period III

(Nesikep V) and into Period IV (Lochnore I). Minor traits common to all five components are discoidal end scrapers and side scrapers.

Projectile points consisting of two different styles were present; thick, bipointed points lacking edge grinding and thin, corner-notched and triangular points frequently possessing edge grinding. This unusual association of two quite distinctive projectile point styles could reflect the co-existence of two weapon systems; the thrusting spear and the spearthrower. Corner-notched points, often pentagonal in outline, dominate the sequence although bipointed points are ubiquitous. Notched projectile point trends through time are as follows: projectile point neck widths, reflecting the wooden spear shaft width, decrease through time going from an average of 1.7 cm to 1.3 cm; basal and lateral grinding is restricted to the earlier levels; bases tend to be initially concave and to increasingly become straight; basal notching increases; and blade edge serration is early.

Despite the fact that bone preservation ranged from excellent to poor it is apparent that the bone technology of Middle Plateau culture was relatively impoverished. Bone awls, awls or projectile points, antler wedges, beaver and marmot incisor tools, and a few other minor items are represented. Of interest is the single occurrence of a West Coast marine shell (Mytilus californianus) in Level III of the Lochnore site.

In the earliest components of Middle Plateau culture microblades are either rare or absent but tend to increase in numbers through time only to decrease around 1,000 BC. The attributes of the wedge-shaped cores exhibit little change through time. Many microblades derived from these specially prepared cores were modified at one end to function as gravers. The appearance of microblades in the Plateau was originally interpreted as evidence of a southward spread of Athapascan-speaking peoples (Borden 1952; 1962). The lack of other northern traits, however, suggests diffusion was involved rather than a population movement. It has been argued that the Canadian Plateau microblade cores are distinct from those of Early and Middle Northwest Interior culture to the north (Sanger 1968: 114). Indeed, the Plateau blade cores with their natural cortex striking platforms, the general use of one end of the core for blade detachment, and the rarity of core rotation, stand in contrast to contemporary northern microblade cores. Despite the differences, microblade technology in the Canadian Plateau would appear to have its origins in the north. There is the issue of how much the nature of the available stone alter the attributes of the core-blade technology (Fladmark 1985) but this would not appear to pertinent with reference to the Plateau. The suggestion that microblade technology spread into the Plateau via the rivers from the coast (Fladmark 1982: 128; 1986: 49)is rejected on the grounds that an early microblade technology has not been identified along the Southern coast.

The occurrence of microblade technology on sites is erratic. For example, microblades were recovered from the 800 BC Lochnore Creek pit house, the 500 BC Masson Lake site in the Okanagan Valley (Grabert 1974), and the Natalkuz Lake pit house in the central interior of British Columbia (Borden 1952). A short distance to the south of the Natalkuz site, however, the 2,000 BC pit houses of the Tezli site lacked microblades (Donahue 1975). Still further south in the Lillooet region, microblades are stated to be absent after 1,000 BC (Stryd 1973: 24) but a short distance to the west on the Thompson River microblades were absent from the 3,000 BC Rattlesnake Hill site (Fladmark 1986: 49). While microblades appear to disappear from the central interior of British Columbia by 2,000 BC at the Tezli site and the Punchaw Lake site (Fladmark 1985: 203) there is the anomalous situation at Anahim Lake (Wilmeth 1978) where microblades appear as late as AD 400. Regardless of the hazards of component mixture in pit house excavations and the classification problem of linear flakes being interpreted as evidence of a prepared core-blade industry, there is an erratic occurrence of microblades in the Canadian Plateau. As such, this technology may reflect a specific activity that was not performed at all sites of a particular culture (Richards and Rousseau 1987: 57-58). If such should be the case, microblades would be an unacceptable element of technology to use as a key factor in the reconstruction of culture history.

In contrast to microblade technology somewhat less attention has been directed to the rather sudden appearance of notched projectile points in the Plateau. It has been suggested that side-notched projectile points entered the Plateau from the east around 4,000 BC (Fladmark 1986: 46). On the other hand, corner-notched and basally-notched points have been dated between 5,500 and 4,500 BC in Early Plateau culture (Sanger 1970). Regardless of whether these notched points penetrated the Canadian Plateau from the Plains to the east or the Columbia Plateau to the south they likely reflect the spread of the spearthrower into the area and, thus, represent an important technological introduction. As has been noted with reference to other cultures, such projectile points appear suddenly as an addition to the indigenous weapon system. As an example, side-notched points appear suddenly at 5,000 BC along with spearthrower stone weights and butt hooks and are added to the bipointed projectile points of the Cascade phase (6,000 to 3,000 BC) of southeastern Washington State in the Columbia Plateau (Leonhardy and Rice 1970).

An important innovation to appear in the Canadian Plateau around 3,000 BC was the gill or seine net. This possibility is suggested by the stone net sinkers found at the Rattlesnake Hill site on the Thompson River (Fladmark 1986: 51). The acquisition of fish net technology would have had a major effect upon the capability of people to capture large numbers of fish during times of plenty. Around the same time as the appearance of net sinkers there is evidence of increasing cultural regionalism and complexity accompanied by a possible population increase (Fladmark 1986: 21). An increasing ability to exploit the seasonal salmon resource may have led to less dispersed settlement patterns with a greater concentration of people at favoured salmon pools and fillet drying sites. Settlement pattern evidence to date, however, does not support a massive settlement shift to riverine locales much before 1,000 BC when numerous pit house villages appear.

Prior to the end of Period III a number of coastal traits were introduced to the interior. These included ground nephrite adzes and pecked and ground hand mauls, including a zoomorphic example (Fladmark 1986: 136). By the beginning of the Period fire fractured rocks used in cooking are recorded for the first time. It was also during this Period that the first evidence of the domesticated dog is uncovered (Richards and Rousseau 1987: 29). During the 3,000 year span of Period III the three major technological innovations were the adoption of the spearthrower weapon system, the roasting and boiling of food with heated rocks, and the gill-seine net. These innovations appear to have been simply grafted onto an indigenous Early Plateau culture base.

Subsistence:

The range of environmental zones and altitudinally determined seasonality of resources in the Canadian Plateau permitted the exploitation of a wide range of animal and plant resources. Prior to the gradual concentration of people into pit house villages, beginning around 2,500 BC, ungulates like deer, elk, and mountain goats appear to have been the main animal food resources along with freshwater mussels (Kuijt 1989). After 2,500 BC it has been suggested climatic change modified hydrologic conditions that favoured an expansion of salmon numbers at the expense of elk and deer populations. It has been further argued that these climatically induced changes permitted a focused economy based on salmon and its storage that, in turn, allowed the progressive evolution of semi-permanent riverine pit house villages. As a caveat to this scenario it should be noted that stable carbon isotope studies suggest pre-pit house village hunters and gatherers were already consuming large amounts of salmon/steelhead. Stable carbon isotope studies pertaining to the beginning of Period III, for example, suggest that approximately 40% of protein was derived from anadromous fish (Rousseau and Richards 1988: 41). The evidence indicates a steady increase in importance of salmon in the diet (Kuijt 1989: Table 5). River basins always seem to have attracted the largest concentrations of people. Despite the fact that many early sites have either been deeply buried under sediments in the river valleys or destroyed by erosion there is no reason to doubt that this riverine adaptation was a very old one.

The influence of the seasons is reflected in the ethnographically recorded monthly activities of the Chilcotin, Shuswap, Thompson, and Lillooet people. Activities were related to temperature and resource availability and consisted of the following: January - cold; February - some warming; March - people come out of houses; April - lake fish and some roots; May - fish and roots; June - berries; July - lake fish, salmon, and berries; August - salmon; September - salmon processing for storage; October - hunt and trap; November - deer hunting and back into the winter pit houses; and December - cold (extracted from Magne 1985: Table 1). The historically documented importance of stored fish and deer meat, roots, berries, and fungi to carry people through the winter months probably also applied to Middle Plateau culture.

There are always problems with generalizations regarding subsistence patterns, the foremost being the lack of archaeological visibility of much of the potential food. At the time of European contact plant materials were known to be a critical component of the stored winter food. In the Okanagan Valley `root-steaming ovens´ on Period III sites have been recorded (Grabert 1971: 162) and recent research in the highland ecological zones has also produced evidence of root processing ovens (Pokotylo 1981). While it is unfortunately true that archaeology will never be able to accurately assess the importance of plant foods in the diet of past people, it is also probable that archaeological survey and excavation focused on the large winter village sites has presented a biased impression of the importance of various resources.

Without stable carbon isotope studies even the importance of salmon is difficult to assess. If the documented practice of filleting summer caught salmon and discarding or eating the bones prevailed in Middle Plateau culture times there would be no archaeological record of the most important winter stored food. There can be little doubt that the introduction of nets and fish drying techniques revolutionized subsistence but it is uncertain when these techniques were first in place. The Period II Southwestern Coastal culture occupation of the Milliken site in the Fraser Canyon indicates that efficient salmon capturing methods and possibly wind-drying of fish fillets were old practices. But there is no way presently available to determine whether salmon capturing and processing techniques changed dramatically over time or whether their application was simply intensified. Even though the appearance of net sinkers at the Rattlesnake Hill site by 3,000 BC is suggestive of the introduction of the gill net there are a number of ways of attaching stone weights to a net without modifying them. There is also the problem of determining whether larger sites reflect increasing populations that were forced to exploit their environment more intensively or whether more efficient technology permitted increasing large settlements of people. A likely explanation for the appearance of larger sites would be a shift towards the storage of winter foods that led to larger seasonal aggregations of formerly small and more widely dispersed populations.

Faunal remains from most sites in the Canadian Plateau contain elk, bear, mountain sheep and goat, and, most particularly, deer. Deer remains, for example, were most common in the 2,000 BC occupation of the Landels site (Rousseau 1989). Marmot, groundhog, and beaver are also recorded. Fairly typical is the EeRb-10 site on the Thompson River that contained limited quantities of blacktail deer, dog, wolf, red fox, striped skunk, porcupine, snowshoe hare, and beaver (Galdikas-Brindamour 1972). It would appear that just about everything edible was being consumed. Freshwater mussels were extensively exploited at some sites (Mohs 1981: 71) despite ethnographic records that shellfish were regarded as starvation food (Teit 1909: 513).

Given the wide range of micro-environments available for exploitation by people occupying the Canadian Plateau and the probability that a large proportion of the food was processed for winter consumption it is likely that archaeology will never be able to reconstruct the annual diet in a convincing manner. Even major episodes of climatic change, such as prior to 3,000 BC, would have had relatively little impact on the altitudinally sensitive resources that could shift distributions to either lower or upper altitudes as circumstances dictated.

Settlement patterns:

Prior to the first appearance of pit houses around 2,500 BC dwellings must have been flimsy affairs leaving little archaeological trace. Settlement patterns have been described as "...somewhat ephemeral, with no evidence of semi-permanent or permanent dwelling structures, a paucity of lithic and bone refuse and limited evidence for food storage or preparation" (Kuijt 1989: 102). To further complicate settlement pattern studies Middle Plateau culture campsites are not equally visible in all areas of the Canadian

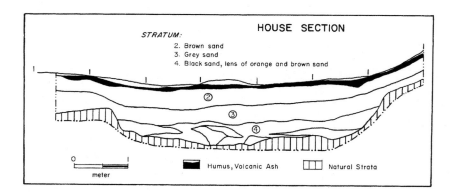

HOUSE SECTION

STRATUM:
2. Brown sand
3. Grey sand
4. Black sand, lens of orange and brown sand

0 ▬▬ 1
meter

■ Humus, Volcanic Ash   ▥ Natural Strata

A

B

C

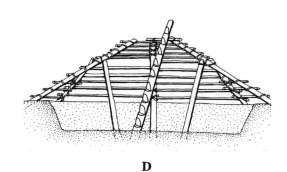

D

FIGURE 43:   MIDDLE PLATEAU CULTURE PIT HOUSE CONSTRUCTION   At the top of the Figure is the crossection of House 4 at the Cayuse Creek site in south-central British Columbia dated to 1,500 BC. Although such semi-subterranean structures are easy to recognize from surface indications it is difficult and often impossible to isolate the cultural debris of the occupants from that of earlier people as the houses were covered with earth often containing earlier artifacts. As the pit house decayed the earth covering the roof and containing the earlier archaeological material would eventually fall into the pit depression. The sequence of cultural occupation at a site is often reversed by such a process. (Adapted from Turnbull 1977: Figure 34. Drawing by Mr. David W. Laverie.)

The photographs illustrate three stages in the restoration of a pit house (A, B, and C). While this particular dwelling is a copy of a recent pit house similar structures have been dated to 2,500 BC (Reproduced from Wright 1976: Plate 26. See Wilmeth 1977). `D´ is a pit house crossection based upon European observations. (Reproduced from Fladmark 1986: Plate 32 with permission).

Plateau. Along the middle Fraser River sites are located near clean water supplied by springs and tributaries rather than being directly adjacent to the silty Fraser River (Sanger 1970: 113). On the nearby South Thompson River, in contrast, sites tend to be situated on the floodplain and, in consequence, the earliest sites are deeply buried beneath sediments. The lower most archaeological deposits of the EeRa-6 site, for example, occur under many meters of river sediments and volcanic ash layers (Mohs 1981: Fig.6.6). Middle Plateau culture sites in this region are so deeply buried that their location presents a major archaeological problem. If the deep burial of early sites by natural depositional forces or, alternatively destruction by bank erosion, was a widespread phenomenon in the Canadian Plateau it would dramatically alter the suggestion that early populations were composed of small groups widely scattered throughout a range of different environmental niches. Instead of a widely dispersed settlement pattern reflecting a diffuse subsistence economy it is possible that an early riverine settlement strategy of Middle Plateau culture has been masked by depositional/erosional forces. Such a possibility would compliment the stable carbon isotope studies that suggest anadromous fish were of considerable importance in the diet by the beginning of Period III.

On the assumption that winter sites required shelter from the wind, fresh water, firewood, and exposure to the winter sun plus good drainage, it has been inferred that the Lochnore site was a winter location. The presence of pit houses, evidence of winter settlement, support the inference. Similarly, the requirement of deep water for salmon pools and an exposed location for the summer drying of salmon has led to the suggestion that the Nesikep Creek site was occupied in the summer (Sanger 1970). If these inferences are correct a comparison of tool assemblages would suggest that there were no significant seasonal alterations to the tool kit. Summer sites, situated close to river pools or river constrictions, stand a high risk of destruction by erosion and placer mining.

Most archaeological excavation in the Canadian Plateau to date has focused on either the floodplain or the first terrace of the major river systems. There is some suggestion that the uplands were exploited but the evidence is sparse and generally consists of a thin scatter of chipping debris. Upland sites of "...brief occupation and limited activity..." (Pokotylo 1981: 382) are characterized by different stages of tool manufacturing and permit certain inferences regarding subsistence and settlement patterns. For example, some appear to represent seasonal extensions from central base camps while others were small extractive base camps. Although rarely dated, it is believed that the upland sites represent a lengthy time span. A similar pattern may have existed in the Kootenai region where historical documents state that the scattered food base forced an equally thin and dispersed record of human activity (Yerbury 1975). Research in the uplands will likely expand with an increase in specific problem oriented research. At the moment such research is in its infancy.

Early in Middle Plateau culture features of any sort are rare. The single pit feature from the 3,500 BC Oregon Jack Creek site has been tentatively identified as a `food boiling pit´ that was subsequently filled with refuse (Rousseau and Richards 1988: 49). Fractured elk bones from the pit may even represent the remnants of a fat extraction process using the boil and skim method. The most characteristic settlement pattern feature of the Canadian Plateau are the remains of the semi-subterranean pit houses. At one time pit houses were believed to have spread into the region from the northern interior via the Cordillera. A major gap in the geographical distribution of northern pit houses relative to the Canadian Plateau, their generally late dates, and significant structural differences compared to more southerly pit houses, has made a northern origin of these dwellings unlikely. It is now believed that pit houses either spread to the north from the Columbia Plateau or up the coastal rivers to the interior or both. On the lower Fraser River the Mauer site pit house has been dated to 3,000 BC (Lohse 1984). This rectangular pit house, with its earth bench and an artifact assemblage related to the local Eayem and Mazama phases (7,500 to 3,000 BC) of the nearby Milliken site (Borden 1960), is unique. Early pit houses in the Columbia Plateau of southwestern Idaho have been dated to about the same time period (Green 1982). Despite the rejection of a northern origin for the pit house there is early evidence for these structures from the central interior. By 2,500 BC a small pit house village began to be established at the Tezli site (Donahue 1975: 39). The site contained 44 house pits and cache pits containing materials dating from 2,500 BC to AD 1710. The two Middle Plateau culture houses at the Tezli site had been subjected to repetitive occupations. One house was 12 m in diameter and less than 1 m deep. To the west of Tezli the Punchaw Lake site 2,500 BC pit house measured 8 m by 6 m and had also been sequentially occupied and rebuilt (Fladmark 1976). The first significant occupation of the Arrow Lakes region of southeastern British Columbia is associated with pit houses (Turnbull 1977). Radiocarbon dates on these pit houses all fall around 1,500 BC. Pit houses also appear at the Shuswap Lakes region around 1,000 BC (Rousseau and Richards 1985). These houses tend to be circular or oval with most structures ranging from 9 m to 12 m in diameter. House floors contain pits, hearths, and posts. Most features occur within the dwellings rather than immediately outside.

The occurrence of the earliest pit houses on the southern, western, and northern margins of the Canadian Plateau leave the ultimate origin of this distinctive style of dwelling in question. Exterior pits adjacent to the pit houses appear by 2,000 BC and are assumed to have been used for the storage of dried salmon (Fladmark 1986: 129). Pits, however, do not ipso facto indicate either the presence or the absence of dried stored foods. In general, pit house villages become most common between 1,500 and 1,000 BC throughout the Canadian Plateau during Period III. The increasing numbers and size of the villages likely reflect an intensification of an earlier subsistence pattern and settlement along with concomitant changes in social structure required by village life, multi-family dwellings, and the cooperative effort required to store large quantities of winter foods.

A common characteristic of Period III in the Canadian Plateau is the limited evidence of trade networks (Fladmark 1986: 49). Local stone is extensively exploited but there is limited evidence of exotic lithics. Obsidian from Oregon has been reported from the Terrace site (Stryd and Rousseau in press) and Mt.Edziza obsidian from northwestern British Columbia does appear in small quantities between 2,500 and 1,000 BC at the Punchaw Lake site more than 600 km to the southeast (Fladmark 1985: 82). Some minor trade in marine shell from the Pacific existed but in most areas exotics are either rare or absent (Sanger 1970: 118).

Cosmology:

There is limited evidence from Middle Plateau culture that can be related to cosmology. At the Nesikep Creek site a cache was discovered consisting of four projectile points, red ochre, marmot incisors, an antler point, a possible bone needle, scrapers, and miscellaneous bird bones (Sanger 1964: 142). The cache could either represent some form of offering or simply be a cache of personal affects that was never retrieved. Toward the end of Period III the earliest known piece of polished stone art work appears in the form of a zoomorphic (frog?) stone pestle handle (Richards and Rousseau 1987: 27). The symbolic significance of the depiction is unknown.

At the Punchaw Lake site a flexed adult burial lacking preserved grave offerings had been placed in an ovate burial pit beneath the earliest central hearth of a sequentially occupied and rebuilt rectangular pit house. The burial is dated to 2,500 BC. Winter burials beneath the central hearth of Plateau houses have been historically documented (Morice 1904: 308). An association of the deceased with the central house hearth suggests that cosmological considerations likely were paramount rather than simply having a convenient locale for interment when the ground was frozen. The fact that subsequent people would occupy the house either suggests that they were ignorant of the burial, an unlikely situation, or that somehow the spirit of the deceased had departed or did not pose a threat to the living.

External relationships:

The sparse evidence of exotic materials in the Canadian Plateau during Period III would lead one to believe that minimal contacts existed with outside groups and that well-developed exchange networks recognizable by archaeological means did not exist. Such an impression may be due to relatively limited research that attempts to relate objects to their geological sources. Major external innovations, such as the spearthrower, the gill net, and the pit house, entered the Canadian Plateau without difficulty. As archaeologists must rely upon those items of trade that survive the passage of time exchange systems involving perishable goods cannot be identified. If significant exchange systems did exist between Middle Plateau culture and its Middle Plains culture, Middle Northwest Interior culture, and Early West Coast culture neighbours, as well as others, they may have been based upon perishable substances such as furs and processed plant and animal foods rather than imperishable items such as exotic stone and shell.

Contacts with Early West Coast culture are indicated by the presence of marine shell but such trade appears to have been limited. Pacific marine shell beads recorded from Middle Plains culture sites likely were obtained via Middle Plateau culture intermediaries. Similarly, there appears to have been little contact with the Columbia Plateau. Contacts to the north also appear to be limited but the occurrence of Mt.Edziza obsidian and a transverse burin from the Tazli site suggest contacts with Middle Northwest Interior culture people.

Two potential areas of contact with the Canadian Plateau are the Peace River region of northeastern British Columbia and adjacent Alberta east of the Rocky Mountains and the Kootenai region of southeastern British Columbia west of the Rocky Mountains but connected to the Alberta Plains by mountain passes. The archaeological record of the Peace River region from earliest times relates to the Plains (Fladmark 1981: 134-135) but Middle Plateau-like projectile points do occasionally find their way into Alberta (Wood 1979: Fig.9) as do obsidian microblades (personal fieldwork in the Peace River Valley of Alberta). Similarly, the Kootenai region shares its culture history with the adjacent Plains and eastern Foothills. In this region the value of finger-printing lithics to geological source has been clearly recognized "The potential value of lithic extractive-utilization patterns as indicators of geographic orientation, seasonal subsistence cycles, and overall territory of aboriginal groups in the Cordilleran region has prompted me increasingly to orient my work towards the location of sources of specific lithic types and the delineation of their spatial and temporal distribution" (Choquette 1973: 119). Detailed descriptive reports of this research are unfortunately not yet available. Major quarry site locales have been discovered such as the Top of the World quarries. The issue of whether the Kootenai region was occupied during Period III by regional variants of Middle Plateau culture, Middle Plains culture, or a distinct Mountain/Foothills culture (Reeves 1974) cannot be resolved at this time. Usually the Kootenai region is equated with Middle Plains culture and especially the McKean complex. Relying upon the culturally `loaded´ implications of imported point typologies has, however, been justifiably questioned (Choquette 1987: 95). At the stratified DjPv-14 site, for example, the post 2,500 BC levels were dominated by stemmed points that could be attributed either to a late McKean complex point style or to a direct development from Period II stemmed points in the region (Ibid: 114). Throughout Period III the Kootenai region occupation is attributed to the Bristow complex that developed out of the indigenous Period II Goatfell complex (Choquette 1987: Fig.3-7). The latter complex is believed to have entered the region from the south. Bristow complex stone technology consisted of reducing local cobbles into biface preforms from which large flakes were detached for immediate use without further modification. Side-notched points, some resembling the Oxbow point type, and stemmed projectile points are typical. The relative scarcity of stratified sites and formal tools has exacerbated the difficulties of establishing a regional culture history (Ibid: 78). Added to these difficulties are the poor bone preservation and dispersed upland settlement pattern. Settlement pattern distributions relate to the movements of the major ungulates of the Kootenai, deer, elk, mountain sheep and goats, and mountain bison, as determined by the availability of browse. As a result, people dependant upon these animals for subsistence would have followed a seasonal shift from the valley lakes to the uplands as browse availability forced the animal herds to move in an altitudinally determined fashion. Such transhumance would naturally require a high degree of mobility and adaptability on the part of human predators. It is not at all clear at this time whether salmon, important in subsequent periods, was a significant element in the diet.

Human biology:

Middle Plateau culture human skeletal evidence is restricted to the single adult burial from the Punchaw Lake site pit house (Fladmark 1976) and two extended burials lacking grave offerings discovered at the EiRm-7 site in the mid Fraser-Thompson River region. The former burial dates to 2,500 BC and the latter to 3,500 BC. Physical anthropological information is not available regarding these three individuals. Carbon isotope studies of the EiRm-7 individuals did suggest that nearly 40% of their protein food was derived from anadromous fish such as salmon and steelhead (Stryd and Rousseau in press).

Inferences on society:

Information on Middle Plateau culture is so incomplete that inferences on society are correspondingly limited. The evidence that salmon were a significant source of protein at the beginning of Period III does raise questions regarding the history of development of the riverine pit house villages so common by the end of Period III. Pit houses appear as early as 2,500 BC but are relatively few in number and cannot be treated as evidence of villages. The early evidence of the importance of salmon in the diet and the likelihood of the destruction or deep burial of many early sites situated in the river valleys suggests that the advent of pit house villages was not a sudden affair but rather a gradual process taking possibly as long as 1,500 years to achieve full-blown village status. The process of changing from a society characterized by small, mobile families organized into bands and practicing a relatively diffuse subsistence pattern to a society centred on large semi-sedentary riverine villages and the storage of salmon would suggest that some significant changes in the social structure must have taken place. Status differentiation cannot be recognized in Period III but such evidence does appear in Period IV. While social organization changes can take place rapidly the processes leading to conditions favourable to such change were likely lengthy and incremental. It would appear that particularly between 1,500 and 1,000 BC significant changes took place in both the subsistence and the settlement pattern systems. On the other hand, there is the possibility that winter pit house villages have made too great an impression upon archaeologists and that pre-pit house village hunters and gatherers, with their comparatively limited archaeological visibility, actually followed an essentially similar way of life orchestrated by a similar social system. Until more is known of the pre-1,500 BC archaeology of the Canadian Plateau it would be fruitless to speculate further on possible changing social systems.

Limitations in the evidence:

The archaeological record of the Canadian Plateau during Period III suffers from more severe limitations than most regions of Canada. These limitations are both physical and methodological. Much of the archaeological record of Middle Plateau culture has been deeply buried by alluvial sediments or destroyed by erosion in many of the river valleys. The archaeological picture has been affected by the concentration of archaeological excavation and survey in the river valleys where the pit house villages are situated. As a result, the archaeological record is dominated by relatively late developments derived from culturally mixed deposits. Recently there has been an increasing focus on human exploitation of the uplands (Magne 1985; Pokotylo 1981). In terms of comparative approaches there has been too great a dependence upon the cultural historical syntheses of adjacent regions such as the Plains and the Columbia Plateau. There has also been a heavy reliance upon specific elements of technology like microblades and projectile point types to reconstruct culture history. As in most regions there is the problem of component mixture at multi-component sites (Richards and Rousseau 1987: 13).There is also a relative paucity of substantive published archaeological reports. Two decades have passed since David Sanger published his synthesis of the Lochnore-Nesikep locality and yet it is only recently that this work has been subjected to critical assessment (Richards and Rousseau 1987; Stryd and Rousseau in press). Unfortunately, the critiques have offered little substantive evidence. Under the circumstances it is not possible to assess the veracity of the observation regarding Canadian Plateau archaeology that "A mosaic of related variant cultures separated by mountain ranges or drainage divides may be the only `typical´ long-standing regional pattern" (Fladmark 1982: 125).

CHAPTER 19

EARLY WEST COAST CULTURE

Précis:

Around 4,000 BC increasing cultural regionalism from the preceding cultural base established by Southwestern Coastal culture and Northwestern Coastal culture is apparent. As noted in Chapters 11 and 12, these two earlier cultures may simply represent geographic variations of a single culture. Stabilization of the coastal environment appears to have encouraged the development of increasingly complex cultural adaptations. As a result of the more or less stable sea levels, riverine deltas and tidal flats were able to support richer coastal and riverine ecosystems. Within these ecosystems, salmon, eulachon, and shellfish were of particular importance. The appearance of large shell middens represents a major difference from the preceding period. Red cedar, so critical to the material culture of the ethnographic West Coast people, also became more available. Progressively larger village sites reflect a settlement pattern approaching the coastal winter villages recorded at the time of European contact. It is only at the end of Period III, however, that direct evidence of plank house villages appears. Art work was still relatively rudimentary and arguments for social structure changes represented by the appearance of certain status objects are not convincing until after 3,000 BC. It is apparent, however, that cultural systems were progressively trending towards the cultural pattern documented by Europeans. A seasonal pattern of coastal winter settlement in the deltas of major rivers, such as the Fraser and Skeena, with summer interior extensions up the rivers to key salmon capturing and processing locations was evolving throughout Period III and would eventually lead to permanent interior settlements. Within a broad cultural pattern sometimes referred to as the Northwest Coast culture type, distinctive regional patterns were already in existence. Not only are there differences which characterize the southern, central and northern coastal regions but both the outer coasts of Vancouver Island and the Queen Charlotte Islands developed in ways distinct from that of the mainland coast. Finer distinctions have been noted within each particular region. Three major subareas, for example, have been identified for the south coast (Mitchell 1990: 357). Indeed, there is a plethora of regional cultural designations. If the Northwest Coast `culture type´ of Period III is considered progressing from north to south along the coast then the following local names by regions pertain: <u>North Coast</u> - Prince Rupert/Skeena River - Prince Rupert III/Haqwilget A, Gitaus VI, and Skeena Complex; Queen Charlotte Islands - Transitional complex and Graham tradition; <u>North-Central Coast</u> - Namu II and III, McNaughton I, and Cathedral phase; <u>South-Central Coast</u> - Bear Cove II and O'Conner II; <u>West Coast of Vancouver Island</u> - Early and part of Middle Yuquot, Shoemaker Bay I; <u>Georgian Strait and Lower Fraser</u> - Maurer,

St.Mungo phase and the early portion of the Locarno Beach phase; Gulf and San Juan Islands - Mayne phase, and the early portion of the Locarno Beach phase; and Fraser Canyon - Eayem and early Baldwin phases (Carlson 1983: Fig.1:2). All of these regional classifications are lumped under the rubric `Early West Coast culture´ in this chapter.

The role of coastal stabilization in cultural developments along the coast cannot be overemphasized. While it has been noted that earlier people already had "... the fundamental technological and economic basis of Northwest Coast culture..." (Fladmark 1982: 132), the cultural elaboration of Period III correlates with resource concentration and accessibility. Thus, the appearance around 4,000 BC of large, semi-permanent settlements coincides with the expanded exploitation of salmon. The emphasis upon salmon, in turn, correlates with the "...attainment of a relatively fixed land-sea interface..." (Fladmark 1975: 288). A simple formulae would be coastal stability = summer/fall salmon fishing and storage = winter villages = winter shellfish exploitation = major shell middens. It should be noted that much of the salmon exploitation actually would have taken place away from the winter villages.

It has been suggested that the West Coast can be viewed as a co-tradition or interaction sphere at this time (MacDonald 1969). Just prior to 1,000 BC there is increasing evidence "... of trade, resource ownership, wealth, and social stratification (suggested by skull deformation, lip labrets, and other ornaments)" (Harris 1987: 3). Technological changes do occur, such as the increasing use of ground slate tools on the south coast around 2,000 BC, but the basic stone tool kit associated with the ethnographically recorded populations appears to have been largely present by the beginning of Period III (Ames 1981: 797; Hobler 1990: 298). Cultural continuities all along the coast clearly extend into Period IV.

Cultural origins and descendants:

There is a consensus that Early West Coast culture developed out of the Southwestern Coastal culture and the Northwestern Coastal culture of Period II. Whether we are dealing with an early maritime adaptation that gradually discarded its prepared core-microblade industry as it spread southward down the coast or two cultures involving a Southwestern Coastal culture advancing northward and meeting and merging with a southward pushing Northwestern Coastal culture are still matters of some debate. Subsequent cultural developments during Period III are generally agreed upon. With reference to the Handbook of North American Indians, Volume 7, Northwest Coast, archaeological articles it has been commented that "...the articles on prehistory show a clear triumph of the continuity model" and that "Gone are the days of evoking repeated population movements to account for cultural changes" (McMillan 1991: 243). The continuity model, however, must still attempt to accommodate the linguistic diversity of the West Coast consisting of five linguistic families composed of forty-five distinct languages (Thompson and Kinkade 1990). This resurrects the old problem regarding the nature of the relationship or lack of relationship between language and culture when applied to tribal and band level societies.

In the Gulf of Georgia region of the south coast earlier technological elements, such as cobble core and spall tools, bipointed projectile points, a range of flake and core tools, bipolar cores, abraders, antler wedges and possibly the unilaterally barbed harpoon, all persist into Period III (Fladmark 1982: Fig.7, 111). Such continuities from a Southwestern Coastal culture base are suggested to have led to the Coast Salish populations encountered by Europeans (Carlson 1990: 67). A similar trend is discernable on the north and central coasts with many traits continuing into subsequent periods. All along the coast cultural developments appear to represent in situ traditions that are characterized by increasing technological complexity. Near the beginning of Period III at the Glenrose cannery site in the Fraser Delta (Bunyan 1978; Matson 1976), for example, the St.Mungo component of Period III developed out of the preceding Southwestern Coastal culture (Cordilleran) occupation but differed in the increased use of shellfish and birds, fewer pebble tools, and a more developed antler/bone industry. Harpoon heads, ground slate points, and drilled beads and pendants also appear for the first time. Cultural continuity at this site continues into the Marpole phase of the Period IV (Matson 1981: 81; Matson et al. 1976). Subsistence at the Glenrose Cannery site reflects an old pattern beginning with Southwestern Coastal culture that simply fluctuated in terms of species used over a period of 6,000 years. Sea mammal and land mammal hunting appear early but shellfish gathering suddenly became important around 3,000 BC.

One of the most complete records of technological continuity from Period II through Period III and on is to be seen in the 9,000 year sequence of the Namu site on the central coast (Carlson 1983a; Hester 1978; Luebbers 1978). In the 4,000 to 1,000 BC levels of this site, microblades, bipointed and lanceolate chipped projectile points, and cobble choppers were only recovered from the early levels while cobble spall flakes of a variety of forms occurred throughout the sequence. Ground celts and abraders, absent from the earliest levels of the site, appear shortly after 4,000 BC. Bone awls, wedges, fishhook barbs, and unilaterally and bilaterally barbed harpoons with guard lines also appear near the beginning of Period III and continue into Period IV (1,000 BC - AD 500). Stone, bone, and shell ornaments, bone projectile points, and some varieties of awls appear late and continue into the upper levels of the site.

While migration was often used in the past to explain culture change (Borden 1975) recent evidence, such as that from the Namu site, suggests that regional cultural continuities are the rule (Mitchell 1971; Murray 1982). This is apparent in the artifact comparisons of the Period II, III, and IV cultural deposits of the Glenrose Cannery site (Matson et al. 1976) provided in Table 4.

When the percentages on Table 4 are reduced to coefficients of similarity (Brainerd 1951) the relationships are as follows: Cordilleran/St.Mungo = 112.4; St.Mungo/Marpole = 106.2; and Cordilleran/Marpole = 68.4. A coefficient of 200.0 means the comparative units are identical and a coefficient of 0.0 means they are totally dissimilar. As would be anticipated, the lowest coefficient is between the two cultures furthest removed from one another in time. Both the qualitative and quantative trends within the technology of the Glenrose Cannery site reflect continuity through time.

Also on the south coast just prior to 1,000 BC a phase called Locarno Beach characterized by toggling harpoons, a range of slate tools fashioned by grinding, and ground stone adzes, is regarded as

ARTIFACT CLASS	PERIOD IV MARPOLE		PERIOD III ST. MUNGO		PERIOD II CORDILLERAN	
Stone	f	%	f	%	f	%
Random flake scraper	22	14.9	116	33.6	81	27.3
Projectile points	14	9.5	15	4.4	5	1.7
Biface knives	5	3.4	8	2.3	6	2.0
Cobble tools	3	2.0	19	5.5	77	25.9
Hammerstones	3	2.0	13	3.8	24	8.1
Cobble spall tools	6	4.1	12	3.5	66	22.2
Denticulates	2	1.4	10	2.9	9	3.0
Abraders	24	16.2	13	3.8	1	0.3
Spokeshave	2	1.4	3	0.9	2	0.7
Wedges	2	1.4	2	0.6	3	1.0
Ground slate knives	22	14.9	----	----	----	----
Ground slate points	8	5.4	2	0.6	----	----
Metate	1	0.7	----	----	----	----
Misc. ground stone	3	2.0	2	0.6	3	1.0
Microblades	4	2.7	----	----	----	----
Drills	1	0.7	1	0.3	----	----
Flake knives	1	0.7	4	1.2	----	----
Anvil stones	----	----	1	0.3	2	0.7
Carved/incised rock	----	----	5	1.5	----	----
Bone						
Awls	12	8.1	40	11.6	2	0.7
Bone/Antler wedges	3	2.0	29	8.4	13	4.4
Flakers	1	0.7	12	3.5	1	0.3
Projectile points	----	----	6	1.7	----	----
Barbs	2	1.4	9	2.6	1	0.3
Needles	1	0.7	1	0.3	----	----

Rings	1	0.7	1	0.3	----	----
Tooth pendants	2	1.4	5	1.5	----	----
Beaver incisors	1	0.7	1	0.3	----	----
Unilat. barb. harpoon	1	0.7	2	0.6	1	0.3
Bilat. barb. harpoon	1	0.7	1	0.3	----	----
Zoomorphic handle	----	----	1	0.3	----	----
Perforated pendants	----	----	9	2.6	----	----
Knife	----	----	1	0.3	----	----
TOTALS	157	100.5	344	100.1	297	99.9

TABLE 4: EARLY WEST COAST CULTURE TOOL ASSEMBLAGE FROM THE GLENROSE CANNERY SITE COMPARED TO THE ASSEMBLAGES OF EARLIER AND LATER OCCUPANTS. (Note: Tool category names are modified from Monks (1976). Cordilleran = Southwestern Coastal culture, St. Mungo = Early West Coast culture, and Marpole = Late West Coast culture.)

developing into the subsequent Marpole phase of the Late West Coast culture of Period IV and, thence, into the Coastal Salish people encountered by Europeans (Mitchell 1971). Similar cultural continuities are noted for the north and central coasts. With reference to the distinctive technology of the Queen Charlotte Islands, a continuity in unifacial tools, a cobble core/spall industry, wedges, abraders, and a general rejection of bifacially flaked tools is maintained until the time of European contact. On the outer coast of Vancouver Island beginning by 2,500 BC at the Yuquot site, "... the archaeological record reflects a single culture in a process of improved adaptation to the outside coastal environment. This process has been, for the most part, one of cultural continuity, with gradual change and some innovations" (Dewhirst 1980: 336) that only ended with the arrival of Europeans in the region. Thus, despite a considerable degree of regional cultural differentiation there appears to be an essential cultural continuity along both the mainland and outer coastlines of the West Coast that lead directly into Period IV. In this respect "It seems likely that when total reconstructed lifeways represented by such prehistoric Northwest Coast assemblages as the Locarno Beach, Marpole, and Gulf of Georgia types are considered, the similarities to other cultures of North America will appear slight. The development of the Northwest Coast way of life would then be seen as a unique attainment, built on a base which has broader affiliations but itself evolving in relative isolation" (Mitchell 1971: 74).

With reference to dating, as with all of the preceding chapters, calendrical dates were extrapolated from dendrochronology adjusted radiocarbon dates following Klein et al. (1982). It is cautioned that this adjustment will differ from calendrical dates provided in many other publications that were derived by subtracting 1950 (AD 1950 is the consensus cut-off date for radiocarbon readings necessitated by atmospheric contamination resulting from the testing of atomic weapons) from the radiocarbon Before Present (BP) date. For readers requiring specific information on radiocarbon dates pertinent to Early West Coast culture much of these data is available in the following publications: North Coast - Coupland 1988; Fladmark 1970; 1975; MacDonald 1969; Severs 1974; Wilmeth 1978; Central Coast - Carlson 1990; Luebbers 1978; and South Coast - Borden 1976; 1976; Calvert 1970; Dewhirst 1980; Eldridge 1981; Fladmark 1975; Matson 1976; McMillan 1981; Mitchell 1971; Mitchell et al. 1981; Wilmeth 1978.

Technology:

Throughout Period III there is progressive elaboration of the technology. With some regional exceptions, the basic tool kit consisted of cobble core and spall tools, core and flake tools, ground slate bipoints, chipped bipoints and contracting stemmed projectile points, ground shell and stone adzes, and unilaterally and bilaterally barbed bone harpoons. The acid neutralizing nature of shell middens has assured the preservation of a much wider range of organic implements (bone and shell) than could otherwise be expected. New traits frequently associated along the entire coast with the shell midden sites are ground and pecked stone implements, a range of ornaments and art work, stone adzes, labrets, beads, pendants, engravings, and sculpture. Some items, such as ground slate knives, projectile points, and pendants, make their appearance together at 4,000 BC along the south coast and into the interior up the Fraser River. While a well-developed flaked stone industry, characterized by chipped leaf-shaped, bipointed, and stemmed projectile points, occurs along the entire inner coast these chipped stone tools are absent from the outer coast of Vancouver Island and the Queen Charlotte Islands (Dewhirst 1980; Fladmark 1970). On the former coast, at Yuquot between 2,500 and 1,500 BC, the technology is dominated by implements produced by grinding rather than chipping and it has been suggested that the Yuquot people "...were comparatively isolated from foreign cultural influences..." (Folan and Dewhirst 1969: 239). Microblade technology appears for the first time along the south coast during this period (Fladmark 1986: 58) but is absent from most of the central and north coasts except at the Namu site on the central coast and up the Skeena River on the north coast where they are abundant early in the local sequence and then steadily decrease in frequency to the end of Period III (Coupland 1988). This erratic occurrence of microblades reflects the situation noted in the Plateau and highlights the hazards of over-emphasizing a single element of technology as a cultural diagnostic when attempting to reconstruct culture history. The extent to which the fashioning of stone tools by grinding was adopted along the coast was also somewhat erratic. Appearing in association with chipped stone implements before Period III on the south coast, by 2,000 BC ground stone tools become increasingly important but still somewhat erratic in their distributions. Stone grinding, for example, was never adopted along the north coast to the same extent as in the south (Fladmark et al. 1990; MacDonald 1969: 250-251) and is even poorly represented on many Gulf of Georgia sites (Matson 1981; Mitchell et al. 1981) as well as the central coast (Carlson 1972: 43-44).

In an early synthesis (Carlson 1970: 115) it was proposed that an assemblage consisting of chipped bipointed and stemmed projectile points, scrapers, knives, pebble choppers, microblades, rare ground slate points and knives, bilaterally and unilaterally barbed harpoons, antler wedges, abraders, labrets, bone pendants, bone points, and red ochre, represented a widespread coastal technology extending from Alaska to the south coast of British Columbia between 3,000 and 1,000 BC. There are, however, undeniable regional quantitative and qualitative variations in technology along the entire coast and particularly on the outer coasts of Vancouver Island and the Queen Charlotte Islands.

It is difficult to determine whether the bone and shell industries became more elaborate during Period III or if they simply have been better preserved in the shell middens. Studies of manufacturing procedures at the Namu site (Luebbers 1978) indicate that bone tool blanks were produced both by splintering and the groove and snap method with the blanks then being ground into the desired shape although whittling was also sometimes used. Bone projectile points, awls, needles, beaver incisor chisels, wedges, and mussel shell adzes, points and knives become common. Unilateral and bilateral barbed harpoons, shouldered to permit a retrieval line to toggle the weapon tip in the prey, appear along the entire coast although they are preceded by simple antler tine harpoons. The limited amount of art work, such as the antler handle from the Glenrose Cannery site, does not anticipate the elaborate art admired by people around the world. As would be expected, the increased manufacture of ground stone, bone, and shell implements is reflected in an increasing abundance of stone abraders.

Based upon the evidence of a distinctive form of human tooth wear along the length of the West Coast it is apparent that shortly after 4,000 BC labrets were being worn by a small proportion of the population. Labrets were ornaments of stone or bone and probably wood that were inserted through a slit in the skin of the mouth. There is some evidence of even earlier use of labrets on the south coast (Carlson 1970). Labrets tend to be rare on the central coast. At the time of European contact the wearing of labrets signified the status of those who wore them. Sometime prior to 3,000 BC on the south coast problematical soapstone and bone spindle-like objects appear for the first time and as early as 2,000 BC stone ear spools may have been present (Fladmark 1982: 120).

It has been hypothesized that the increasing numbers of antler wedges and shell and ground stone adzes late in Period III reflect the importance of woodworking, possibly used in the manufacture of ocean going dugouts and substantial plank houses. There is no evidence, however, for the latter until the end of the period and a total lack of direct evidence of the former. Certainly red cedar became more available around 2,000 BC and would have encouraged the expansion of the wood working industry. In the water-saturated cultural deposits of the Musqueam Northeast site, situated in the Fraser Delta and dating to the end of Period III, wooden plank fragments, wedges, cordage, and fishhooks as well as basketry were recovered. The basketry and cordage styles anticipate the manufacturing procedures of the local Salish people encountered by Europeans (Fladmark 1986: 80-81). This rare assemblage of wooden and bark items revealed a sophisticated technology usually denied to archaeology. It involved basketry with red cedar splits and wrap-around plaiting, open wrapping and open twining, 6 cm to 9 cm gauge netting, cord-lashed unmodified cobble netsinkers, cordage heavy enough to have functioned as sea mammal harpoon lines, a possible plain twined hat fragment, cedar bark bailers, skewers, digging sticks, haft handles, and a probable netting needle (Borden 1976). The basketry and cordage were invariably manufactured from western red cedar (ibid: 251) although the wedges, with attached cord grommets, were generally manufactured from yew.

Towards the end of Period III on the south coast there was a revival of the bifacially fashioned stone tool industry that was either rare or absent along the central and north coasts. Microblades were also still in use although they had disappeared elsewhere (McMillan and St.Claire 1975; Mitchell et al. 1981). These quartz crystal and obsidian pebble core-derived microblades, however, do not resemble either the Plateau microblades or those of the preceding Northwestern Coastal culture (Fladmark 1982: 112). They have been described as the product of a bipolar knapping technique that had nothing to do with earlier microblade industries. It is pertinent to observe that the microblade industry of the Queen Charlotte Islands is replaced prior to 3,000 BC by a bipolar method of producing small microblade-like flakes. Cobble core and spall tools were, however, endemic to the entire region. Labrets, stone sculpture, simple and composite toggling harpoons, adzes, ground slate points and bone needles are some of the more important traits to appear toward the end of Period III on the south coast (Bunyan 1975; Fladmark 1982: Fig.7, 111). Fire fractured rock, indicative of preparing food with heated stones, is also common on sites during this period (Mitchell 1990).

It has been speculated (Coupland 1988) that different seasonal sites of the same people could have significantly different tool assemblages and that some of the earlier noted differences between sites may well pertain to the same people carrying out different tasks at different locales during different seasons of the year. This proposal has yet to be demonstrated for either the interior-coastal Skeena River sites or the interior-coastal Fraser River sites. Indeed, the assemblage from the 3,000 BC deposits of the St.Mungo Cannery site on the Fraser River Delta are stated to most closely resemble the interior Eayem phase deposits from the contemporaneous Esilao site (Calvert 1970: 59). If the interior site represents a summer occupation and the coastal site a winter occupation by the same people then the tool assemblages appear to be essentially the same despite major differences in site locale and function. The dominant position of the cobble core and spall tool category also presents some problems. On the interior Skeena River where bone preservation is absent or poor 14 of the 19 artifact classes pertain to the poorly represented ground and chipped stone categories while the remaining five classes represent the dominant cobble core-spall industry (Coupland 1988: 189). The only exception to this dominate position of cobble tool categories are the microblades from the lower levels of the Paul Mason site. Despite the fact that the cobble-spall industry represents the dominant component of the chipped stone industry of Early West Coast culture it does not, as yet, provide a sensitive vehicle for basing cultural historical interpretations.

The temporal and geographical variability of the stone technology of Early West Coast culture is reflected in Table 5. Frequencies of different artifact categories from five sites are given.   The

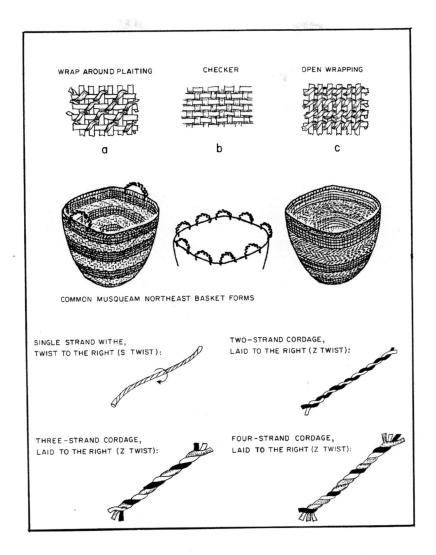

FIGURE 44:   EARLY WEST COAST CULTURE BASKETRY AND CORDAGE   Due to water saturated soil conditions in the lower deposits of the Musqueam Northeast site in the Fraser Delta organic materials were protected from the normal processes of decay. Among the items recovered were sophisticated examples of basketry and a range of cordage varieties. Western red cedar limbs and bark were the raw material used in the manufacture of these items.   (Adapted from Borden 1976: Figures 5, 7, and 11. Drawing by Mr. David W. Laverie.)

ARTIFACT CLASS	GLENROSE		DUKE PT.		MONTAGUE		DiRi-14		P. MASON	
	f	%	f	%	f	%	f	%	f	%
Scrapers	116	51.8	10	20.8	1	1.0*	148	36.0	85	14.3
Proj. pts.	15	6.7	7	14.5	9	8.9	16	3.9	----	----
Biface Knives	8	3.6	10	20.8	18	17.8	4	1.0	32	5.4
Cobble Tools	19	8.5	6	12.5	9	8.9	64	15.6	167	28.0
Hammer-stones	13	5.8	----	----	5	5.0	24	5.8	39	6.5
Cobble Spalls	12	5.4	3	6.3	2	2.0	34	8.3	142	23.8
Abraders	13	5.8	5	10.4	25	24.8	----	----	55	9.2
Grd. stone pts.	2	0.9	1	2.1	4	4.0	----	----	14	2.4
Wedges	2	0.9	1	2.1	----	----	18	4.4	P**	P**
Micro-blades	----	----	3	6.3	2	2.0	28	6.8	25	4.2
Grd. celts	----	----	1	2.1	2	2.0	6	1.5	16	2.7
Ornam. items	5	2.2	----	----	11	10.9	----	----	5	0.8
Grd. slate knives	----	----	----	----	1	1.0	53	12.9	----	----
Saws	----	----	----	----	2	2.0	----	----	12	2.0
Spoke-shaves	3	1.3	----	----	----	----	3	0.7	----	----
Drills	1	0.5	----	----	----	----	4	1.0	----	----
Flake knives	4	1.8	----	----	----	----	3	0.7	----	----
Denticu-lates	10	4.5	----	----	----	----	----	----	----	----
Anvil stone	1	0.5	----	----	----	----	----	----	----	----

Labret	----	----	1	2.1	----	----	----	----	----	----
Earspool	----	----	----	----	1	1.0	----	----	----	----
Stone pendant	----	----	----	----	1	1.0	----	----	----	----
Notched stones	----	----	----	----	3	3.0	----	----	----	----
Mortar	----	----	----	----	1	1.0	----	----	----	----
Red ochre	P	P	----	----	4	4.0	----	----	----	----
Uniface knives	----	----	----	----	----	----	2	0.5	----	----
Edge grd. cobble	----	----	----	----	----	----	3	0.7	----	----
Atlatl weight	----	----	----	----	----	----	1	0.2	----	----
Grinding stone	----	----	----	----	----	----	----	----	4	0.7
Totals	**224**	**100.2**	**48**	**100.0**	**101**	**100.3**	**411**	**100.1**	**596**	**100.0**

TABLE 5: STONE TOOL FREQUENCIES FROM FIVE EARLY WEST COAST CULTURE OCCUPATIONS. (Note: With reference to the single asterisk, while only one scraper is recorded in the appendix it is stated elsewhere that there were "... a relatively great number of stone scrapers..." (Mitchell 1971: 151). The double asterisk indicates that pièces esquillées or wedges were present at the Paul Mason site but were lumped with cores and, therefore, could not be quantified.)

comparative units are the St.Mungo occupation of the Glenrose Cannery site (Matson et al. 1976), occupation I of the Duke Point site (Murray 1982), occupation I of the Eu-1 excavation unit of the Montague Harbour site (Mitchell 1971), occupation 2 of the DiRi-14 site (Eldridge 1981), and the upper levels of the Paul Mason site (Coupland 1988). The first two occupations date to 2,500 BC and both occur in the Gulf of Georgia region of the south coast. The remaining three occupations all date to 1,000 BC and are located in the Gulf of Georgia, the lower Fraser River, and the interior on the Skeena River, respectively. These comparative units were selected on the basis of the integrity of the context of the cultural deposits, the sample size, and the use of descriptive procedures which were amenable to reinterpretation by the writer. Desirable comparative units, such as the Yuquot site on the west coast of

Vancouver Island (Dewhirst 1980), a number of sites in the Prince Rupert area (MacDonald and Inglis 1981), and the Namu site on the central coast, had to be excluded for reasons ranging from sample size to incomplete information. Even though the Cathedral phase on the central coast is believed to span the period between 4,000 and 1,000 BC (Apland 1982; Carlson 1972a) sites attributed to the phase were not used as their dating was based upon equivocal calculations of sea-level changes as well as typology. The artifact categories used in Table 5 represent a reinterpretation of the original descriptions and were necessary in order to accommodate the variable descriptive methods used by different researchers. Other modifications to the original data were also necessary. With reference to the Paul Mason site, for example, the categories cores-pièces esquillées, ground stone fragments, and cores are excluded. Also, retouched cobble flakes and retouched flakes are classified as scrapers and blunted ground stone as celts. Other adjustments involved excluding the 17 stone disc beads from the relatively small sample of the Duke Point site occupation in order to avoid a percentage distortion due to a single broken necklace.

An important technological innovation first identified during Period III are wooden fish weirs. Wooden fish weir stakes preserved underwater and in water saturated mud have been dated between 3,250 and 2,500 BC at the Glenrose Cannery site in the Fraser Delta (Eldridge et al. 1992). These early dates cast doubt on the suggestion that weirs associated with the mass capture and storage of salmon originated in the north and diffused south (Moss et al. 1990) as the earliest weir dates from southeastern Alaska are shortly after 2,000 BC. The Glenrose Cannery site weir stakes were paired suggesting that they originally enclosed horizontal elements such as poles or mats. Weir lines extended into the river at 90• or 45• degree angles with stakes ranging from 2 cm to 21 cm in diameter but predominantly between 3 cm and 6 cm. The suggestion that the weirs were used mainly for the capture of salmon is supported by the masses of salmon bone in the occupational debris of the site. Basketry, cordage, a wooden tray, and a wedge were also recovered during the excavation of the weirs.

Before leaving the technology of Early West Coast culture it is necessary to comment briefly on a somewhat unique practice of questionable utility that is being increasingly applied to the interpretation of West Coast archaeological history. This practice involves taking a particular element or class of technology and endowing it with proxy powers of interpretation which cannot be subjected to objective demonstration. The following are examples of this approach: chipped stone weapon tips are equated with terrestrial big game hunting (Coupland 1988); the manufacture of ground slate implements is seen as a more labour intensive yet `cost effective´ use of raw materials in contrast to the profligate nature of the chipped stone industry and, hence, is interpreted as evidence of increasing sedentism (Fladmark 1986: 60); bone and antler wedges are equated with wooden plank manufacture that is then interpreted as evidence for plank houses (Mitchell 1971: 59); and stone abraders are regarded as evidence of ground stone and bone tools even when there is little or no direct evidence of the latter (Coupland 1988). Such interpretive devices are fraught with hazards and should be used with extreme caution. Too many exceptions to the assumptions underlying such broad, tool class based generalizations exist with reference to both the archaeology of coastal British Columbia, in particular, and North America in general. The total body of evidence from all of the available cultural systems of any particular culture should be used to support broad

BLACK AND WHITE PLATE XVII: EARLY WEST COAST CULTURE ANTHROPOMORPHIC ART
This exceptional 2,500 BC antler carving from the Glenrose Cannery site is less than 11 cm long. The rear view, to the right, reveals a slot that probably once held a beaver incisor knife-chisel. (Photograph provided by Dr. Knut R. Fladmark, Department of Archaeology, Simon Fraser University.)

generalizations. There is also the constant need to maintain a degree of humility relative to the very real limitations of archaeological data. Ethnographic information indicates that terrestrial big game hunters can acquire their prey by means of snares, dead-falls, and other organic traps that leave no archaeological record. Archaeological evidence often provides abundant evidence of the killing of big game animals while producing relatively little direct technological evidence of how the animals were slain.

Subsistence:

Unlike the preceding periods, the stabilization of the coast of British Columbia during Period III permitted deltas and tidal flats to develop and with them the rich coastal and riverine fauna of which salmon, eulachon, and shellfish were most important to people (Fladmark 1986). Although salmon were available earlier it would appear that coastal stabilization permitted the salmon populations to increase. Other important fish species also likely increased in numbers. Coastal stability was a prerequisite for large, stable, shellfish populations, particularly clams and mussels. With shellfish as a predictable winter food in combination with the summer and fall stores of dried salmon conditions favoured sedentary winter settlement on the coast. High protein foods like shellfish (Erlandson 1988) and stored salmon, complemented by the high fat content of eulachon and sea mammal oils along with plant carbohydrates, provided a well-balanced diet that included essential minerals and vitamins as well as calories. Direct evidence of eulachon exploitation is limited but there is evidence that as early as Period II small fish were being captured. It would be surprising if the enormous spawning schools of eulachon in the estuaries of the northern rivers were not harvested using a range of nets and traps. Herring is another small fish that masses into enormous spawning schools and could provide large quantities of food including the highly prized fish eggs.

Regardless of the specific specie source, carbon isotope studies indicate that around the beginning of Period III approximately 90% of protein was obtained from marine sources (Carlson 1990: 65). Similarly, plant foods important for both their carbohydrates and vitamins, must have been harvested despite the largely mute archaeological record. Certainly ethnographic accounts accord a very important role to plant foods (McIlwraith 1948). One of the few cases of an archaeological recovery of plant materials involved skunk cabbage from the 1,500 to 3,000 BC deposits of the Glenrose Cannery site (Mathewes 1976: 99). The importance of fats and/or carbohydrates for healthy nutrition in a high protein diet is only beginning to be appreciated. A balanced diet of protein, fats, and plant carbohydrates may also have been typical of the earliest inhabitants of the coast but it was the coastal stabilization that permitted the shellfish beds to act as magnets to coastal winter settlement.

One of the most striking characteristics of Period III is the appearance of large shell middens between 4,000 and 2,500 BC along the entire coast of British Columbia. There is the possibility, however, that even earlier shell middens have been destroyed by coastal erosion and acid leaching (Fladmark 1986: 112). Shell middens can cover nearly eight acres and be 5 m in depth. It is probable that the appearance of a well-developed bone tool industry during Period III relates to the acid neutralizing affect of the shell that permitted bone preservation rather than to an increased importance of the bone tool industry per se. Hence, it is difficult to assess whether the increase in sea mammal hunting gear, such as harpoons, relates to an actual technological-subsistence adaptation or shift in hunting emphasis (Fladmark 1982: 112) or is simply the product of markedly improved bone survival on sites. In the earliest shell midden deposits of the St.Mungo Cannery site on the south coast (Calvert 1970), dating to 3,000 BC, fish (salmon and sturgeon) and shellfish were the staples. Bay mussel (Mytilus edulis) was the major shellfish species represented. Sea mammal remains were rare but there was abundant evidence of elk, deer, and beaver. Birds were also well represented. Such a faunal record indicates a riverine, land, and intertidal exploitative pattern rather than one with a specific orientation to the sea. In this respect, the faunal evidence mirrors that of the nearby Glenrose Cannery site (Imamoto 1976) except that at this site there is no statistical difference in the ratios of terrestrial and marine faunal materials from the Period II, III, and IV occupations (Matson 1976: 91; 1981: 71). From the Early West Coast culture levels onward at the Glenrose Cannery site shellfish exceed by nearly twice the meat value of all of the mammals (Ham 1976; Matson 1981: 78-79). This would suggest that, at least on a seasonal basis, shellfish were more important than mammals and contrasts with the situation of the Southwestern Coastal culture occupation of the same site during Period II (Figure 49). A study of shell growth rings indicated that the site was being occupied year round during Period III. At the Montague Harbour I component (Mitchell 1971) both bay mussels, which can be gathered from the surface at low tide, and horse and butter clams and rock cockle, which must be dug, represented a `substantial' portion of the diet along with deer, elk, and birds. In contrast, at the Shoemaker Bay I site on Vancouver Island (McMillan 1981: 99), dated between 3,000 and 1,000 BC, clams and mussels do not appear to have been exploited. Relative to the nutritional value of certain shellfish species the following composition of 85 grams of blue mussel meat is pertinent: 73 kilocalories (1 kilocalorie = 4.184 kilojoules); 10.1 grams protein; 1.9 grams fat; 3.1 grams carbohydrates; 0.5 grams polyunsaturated fatty acids; 0.4 grams saturated fatty acid; and cholesterol 24 milligrams. Vitamins are totally absent in contrast to certain other shellfish such as oysters. Mineral content in milligrams is as follows: sodium 243; potassium 272; calcium 22; phosphorus 168; magnesium 29; iron 3.36; zinc 1.36; and copper 0.080 (Pennington 1989: 88).

On the central coast, layers II and III of the Namu site nearly bracket Period III. These two layers are characterized by shellfish remains with particular emphasis being placed upon barnacles and mussels (Hester 1978: 112). Faunal evidence from layer II, beginning shortly before 3,000 BC and extending to after 2,000 BC, suggests an increase in fishing with salmon being the dominant species. Both land and marine mammals are present with the former increasing in frequency through time (Conover 1978). Shellfish and fishing continue to increase in importance in layer III. The early exploitation of rock dwelling shellfish, such as mussels and barnacles, gradually changes to an emphasis on sediment dwelling clams. Exploitation of salmon also increases through time. Throughout the more than 9,000 year occupation of the Namu site deer, dog, seal, sea otter, and mink occur. Dog was only second in importance to deer. Seal included sea lion, fur seal, and harbour seal with the latter being most common. From earliest times large sea mammals, such as dolphins and sea lions, were being taken and clearly indicate the presence of a

BLACK AND WHITE PLATE XVIII: THE NAMU SITE; NEARLY 10,000 YEARS OF OCCUPATION
The relatively unbroken occupation of this important site on the central coast of British Columbia reflects continuity in subsistence practices. Although most major shell middens along the coast do not appear until around 3,750 BC evidence of shellfish exploitation at this site was dated as early as 5,500 BC. (Photograph provided by Dr. Knut R. Fladmark with the permission of Dr. Roy Carlson, Department of Archaeology, Simon Fraser University.)

FIGURE 45:   THE IMPORTANCE OF SHELLFISH THROUGH TIME AT THE GLENROSE CANNERY SITE Kilograms of shellfish meat has been calculated on the basis of shell recovery. Occupation III of this site in the Fraser Delta is a Period II Southwestern Coast culture occupation dating to approximately 5,500 BC. Occupation II is an Early West Coast culture occupation dating to 2,000 BC while Occupation I is a 250 BC Late West Coast culture occupation. Although the Figure suggests a marked increase in the consumption of shellfish during Early West Coast culture times with a subsequent decline, factors such as shell preservation, changing methods of processing shellfish meat (e.g. shells discarded at place of capture and only the meat brought back to the camp), differences in the archaeological samples from the three occupations, and differing seasonal emphases of occupations, could all contribute to leading archaeological interpretations astray. In general, however, the evidence along the coast does indicate an increasing exploitation of shellfish during Early West Coast culture times. (Adapted from Matson 1981: Figure 26. Drawing by Mr. David W. Laverie.)

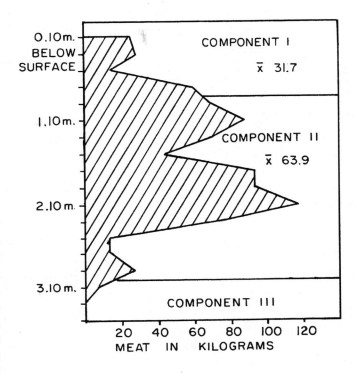

sophisticated maritime adapted technology. A curious discovery at this site was the exceptionally high incidence of porcupine remains. This could suggest trade with the interior given that the species is not usually found in the coast forest. It has been estimated that approximately 80% of the food of the people of Namu came from the coast forest zone with the remainder from the coastal littoral zone (Hester 1978: 101).

On the north coast, in the Prince Rupert Harbour area, small, shallow shell middens begin to appear around 3,000 BC and characteristically contain mussels harvested in winter and spring with some limited evidence of summer-fall exploitation (MacDonald and Inglis 1981: 56). A common settlement pattern seen here, as well as along the entire coast, is site location in sheltered harbours with a reliance upon intertidal resources (MacDonald 1969a: 259). With reference to mammal hunting on the north coast, early in the sequence there appears to be a greater emphasis upon land mammals although seal is present and around

2,000 BC fishing and sea mammal hunting become increasingly important (Fladmark et al. 1990). This increase in the importance of large sea mammals was also noted in the upper levels of the Blue Jacket Creek site on the Queen Charlotte Islands (Severs 1974: 198).

Allowing for regional variation and the poor archaeological visibility of many facets of the subsistence record due to heavy forest cover, eustatic (rising sea levels) and isostatic (rising or sinking land mass) sea level fluctuations, acid soils, and an archaeological bias towards shell midden excavation, it still appears that after 4,000 BC winter villages were being established at favourable shellfish locales on the coast in conjunction with the increasing exploitation and presumably storage of salmon (Fladmark 1975: 249). This combination of a broadly based subsistence pattern, supported by preservation techniques that permitted times of extreme abundance to be exploited, and the use of fish and mammal oil dietary supplements, formed the basis of subsistence from the beginning of Period III to the time of European contact. The uses of the intertidal zone and the evidence of seasonal mobility in subsistence rounds have their origins in the preceding Period II but much of the evidence of continuity has been masked by the effects of fluctuations in sea levels. While there appears to have been a major shift in emphasis in the subsistence system along the entire coast at the beginning of Period III, the developments leading to these changes were likely not quite as sudden as the archaeological record would suggest. Shellfish gathering and large sea mammal hunting were clearly present at earliest times in both Southwestern Coastal culture and Northwestern Coastal culture. The perfection of salmon storage methods that permitted the use of salmon as a winter food in conjunction with coastal stability may have been sufficient to initiate the changes seen in both settlement and subsistence patterns. Sedentism reflected in the shell midden sites would have facilitated population growth, diversified subsistence, and the increasing importance of fish and sea mammals. As has been noted "What is important to recognize here is that the cultural pattern had as its core the subsistence pattern. This base was augmented through time by the addition of new trait complexes" (Hester 1978: 110). Thus, a multiple resource subsistence pattern strategy appears to have been basic to the West Coast from earliest times but as circumstances (coastal stability) and innovations (food storage and oil rendering) permitted, aspects of the basic strategy were elaborated and refined.

Stable carbon isotope studies of human bone collagen suggests that for approximately 5,000 years along the coast of British Columbia more than 85% of the protein ingested by people was of marine origin (Chisholm, Nelson, and Schwarcz 1983). The average amount of marine and terrestrial protein in the diets of people is calculated from the respective values of the stable Carbon 13 isotope in the bone collagen. The atmospheric and marine carbon dioxide reservoirs differ relative to a range of factors that incorporate stable carbons in different manners. Thus the food chains based upon these different reservoirs can be distinguished from one another. It is then possible to detect if a person consumed food related to a terrestrial plant base or a plankton food base or both by the degree of Carbon 13 enrichment in the individual's bone collagen. Another interesting facet of this particular study was the suggestion that children differed in the Carbon 13 values from adults, possibly reflecting a cultural practice whereby children received more terrestrial protein than their elders. A large portion of the marine protein ingested must have been in the form of fatty fish like salmon as a high protein diet bereft of fat is unhealthy for humans (Schwarcz 1991: 269-270). Of importance to archaeological interpretations is the virtual certainty that the quantification of marine versus land animals in faunal analyses is not an accurate reflection of the actual quantities of marine or land foods eaten. A study of the Helen Point site faunal remains from the Gulf of Georgia calculated the intake of marine species to be 55%, a percentage that stood in marked contrast to the 90% intake calculated by the stable carbon technique at the nearby Crescent Beach site (Chisholm, Nelson, and Schwarcz 1983). The question is whether the absolute quantification of marine and land species represents even a rough approximation of the absolute quantities of marine and land protein eaten; historically documented observations regarding methods of food processing, storage and ritual disposal of bones (e.g. Drucker 1951) would clearly suggest that it is not. On the other hand, there are a number of variables that can affect the results of C13 isotope studies, as well as the isotope studies of other elements such as Nitrogen, Hydrogen, Sulphur, Oxygen, and Strontium used in palaeo-diet studies (Schwarcz 1991; Sillen et al. 1989).

Settlement patterns:

With a relatively stabilized coastline and the development of deltas and tidal flats coastal and riverine resources increased in abundance (Fladmark 1986: 53). By the beginning of Period III temperature and rainfall approached modern conditions (Fladmark et al. 1990). As could be anticipated, people were attracted to these seasonally resource-rich locales. As a result, cultural debris like discarded shell valves accumulated at particularly favourable site locations resulting in large shell middens. Such middens represent the accumulated debris of many years of human occupation. In this respect the major difference between the settlement patterns of Period II and Period III relate to a shift from small mobile groups, widely distributed across the land, to a more concentrated pattern of permanent or semi-permanent base camps. Although the sudden appearance of shell middens all along the coast has been interpreted as evidence of a population increase (Fladmark 1975) it is probable that the coalescence of small, formerly more dispersed groups into larger centres has created an erroneous impression of population increase. For the first time, the coastal stability permitted people to gather seasonally at the same locales year after year and for their garbage to accumulate into large middens.

A number of factors coalesced to produce the settlement pattern change to seasonal sedentism. Paramount would have been the increasing reliance upon salmon as a winter food. This presumably was made possible by innovations in food storage and preservation methods. Another factor was coastal stability that both enhanced intertidal resource abundance and permitted settlement in the same locales over periods spanning thousands of years. The extraction of oil from the small, fatty eulachon (candle fish) may have been another important innovation introduced at this time. These beginnings of the semi-permanent villages initiated a process that eventually led to the ethnographically recorded winter villages with their permanent plank houses, art, rituals, and inter-village gatherings (Fladmark 1986: 57). An alternative proposal suggests that while the processing and storage of salmon established the basis for the ethnographically recorded coastal culture, the specialized processing system actually evolved in the Fraser

Canyon and then spread to the coast (Burley 1979). Current evidence, however, suggests that the exploitation of salmon at the canyons of major rivers like the Fraser and Skeena involved seasonal excursions from the coast that only developed into permanent interior winter villages near the end of Period III (Coupland 1988). There is also some indication that by 2,500 BC or earlier the ethnographically identified subareas were becoming recognizable on the north, central, and south coasts. Increasing exploitation of resources on the off-shore islands points to an expanding seasonal round with presumably an elaborating sea mammal hunting system and sea-going water craft. Certainly the multiple component nature of the shell midden sites, as well as sites in the interior on the major salmon rivers (Ames 1979; Borden 1975; Coupland 1988; Kidd 1969), argues for a stability of resource accessibility through time. Site locations both on the coast and in the canyons emphasize the importance of water transportation. Coastal sites are situated near dependable fresh water supplies, in protected harbours, and generally in close proximity to tidal flats rich in shellfish.

The _winter_ occupation of shell midden villages has been emphasized even though this seasonal settlement is basically inferred from ethnographic documents. Actual faunal evidence from sites in the Prince Rupert Harbour and the Fraser Delta, for example, suggest year round occupations by at least a segment of the villagers. Contrary to the faunal evidence (Ham 1976), some have argued that sites such as the Glenrose Cannery site were occupied at varying seasons of the year rather than on a year by year basis (Matson 1976: 300). This conclusion appears to be based, in part, on the absence of recognizable house structures. It has also been speculated that the introduction of the gill net may have led to the fall occupation of such sites (Ibid: 303). A preponderance of salmon vertebrae in the Period III occupation of the Glenrose Cannery site, however, suggests filleting of salmon in preparation for the storage of winter food. On the north coast from 3,000 to 1,000 BC there appears to have been fewer people than during subsequent periods (MacDonald and Inglis 1976: 74). Even at this time, however, the settlement patterns suggest small groups occupying temporary camps from spring to fall who then coalesced into winter coastal villages. The faunal record from these winter villages also indicates some degree of year round occupation. A similar pattern appears to have been in existence by 4,000 BC on the Queen Charlotte Islands (Fladmark et al. 1990). Central coast villages and camps are situated along waterways protected from the open sea. Unlike the situation on both the north and south coast it is possible that the nature of dispersed resources of the region could not support an alternating winter and summer settlement pattern (Simonsen 1973: 23). In the Gulf of Georgia on the south coast Europeans recorded that people travelled up to 480 km during their seasonal rounds (Mitchell 1971: 27). Such mobility must have resulted in numerous small sites but few of the transitory camps have been described in detail. An example of small special purpose camps is represented by the scattered cobble tools along the higher margins of the major rivers. Originally these simple tools were regarded as being as old as the elevated beaches in which they were found (Borden 1975). It has now been determined that most of the cobble core and spall tools relate to the exploitation of forest products and are representative of the entire archaeological record of the British Columbia coast (Inglis and MacDonald 1979: 14). Conversely, the same evidence has been interpreted as the waste products of a cobble tool reduction technology, at least in southern British Columbia (Haley 1988).

Clear evidence of house floors during Period III is scarce. An exception was a house dating to 3,000 BC that sat on a promontory 23 m above the Fraser River and 100 km inland from the coast. The Maurer site dwelling was a semi-subterranean, rectangular structure measuring 11 m by 7 m and 0.3 m in depth (LeClair 1976). A hearth in the south end of the central depression consisted of a 3 m by 5 m pit containing fire fractured rock concentrations at both ends and a charcoal deposit in the centre. Six large, vertical posts along the perimeter, one in each corner and one in the middle of both long axis sides as well as angled posts outside of the bench suggested walls 1.8 to 2.0 m high extending to a flat roof. A side-wall entrance in the east wall was cut through a 1 m wide earth bench that lined the interior and was elevated 30 cm to 40 cm above the floor. This structure, which had been destroyed by fire, still represents a unique form of dwelling in the archaeological record of British Columbia.

One of the best candidates for a house structure on the south coast comes from the 2,500 BC Shoemaker Bay site (McMillan 1981: 98-99). Three large post moulds from 0.8 m to 1.0 m in diameter were arranged in a line with a boulder lined trench 14 m long parallelling the line of posts. In the 1,000 BC level of the same site two 1 m diameter posts were spaced 4 m apart and along with a scattering of smaller posts, hearths, and trenches up to 2 m long, 0.5 m wide and .4 m deep may represent parts of one or more houses. At the St.Mungo Cannery site ash deposits and small hearths in the 3,000 BC occupation were interpreted as living floors (Calvert 1970). Similarly, at the nearby Glenrose Cannery site, fire fractured rock concentrations, scattered post moulds ranging from 10 cm to 20 cm in diameter, and compacted areas, have been cited as evidence of living floors (Gose 1976). The latter tenuous features are believed to pertain to nuclear family dwellings. Numerous wooden wedges at the Musqueam Northeast site have been interpreted as evidence of plank houses in the Gulf of Georgia region by 1,000 BC as such wedges were used at the time of European contact to manufacture wooden house planks (Croes 1976: 293). While this inference may be correct, additional evidence is required before wooden wedges by themselves can be regarded as evidence for the existence of plank houses. In the Prince Rupert Harbour area of the north coast between 3,000 and 1,000 BC stone lined pits filled with fire fractured rocks were identified but not house floors (MacDonald and Inglis 1981). There is, however, some tenuous evidence suggested by post mould patterns of small, flimsy structures lacking subterranean floors. These hypothesized structures appear to have been arranged parallel to the beach (Ibid: 74).

An exception to the limited evidence of house structures during Period III was the discovery of a village of ten dwellings situated at Kitselas Canyon 90 km up the Skeena River from the coast (Coupland 1988). Five radiocarbon dates from house floors suggest that the village was constructed around 1,200 BC. House floors had been cut into a slope overlooking the river and arranged in two rows, a pattern similar to house arrangements recorded much later by Europeans. All of the houses were approximately of the same size with the largest measuring 11 m by 6.6 m. Two or three nuclear families probably occupied each of the rectangular structures. This would represent between 10 and 15 people per house and contrast with the 20 to 25 people per house recorded in the same area by Europeans. It is estimated that between 100 and 125 people occupied the village. Village arrangement indicates corporate planning but the similar size of the houses would suggest an egalitarian rather than a rank or status differentiated community. Such a

FIGURE 46: EARLY WEST COAST CULTURE HOUSE STRUCTURES

The beginnings of village life that would eventually develop into ranked societies appears in the arrangement of the multi-family dwellings of the 1,250 BC Paul Mason site in the Kitselas Canyon of the Skeena River. Here a series of rectangular structures formed two parallel rows with an intervening space or street. The village organization would have required village planning involving supervisory control although the uniformity of house size still suggests an egalitarian society. Built on a slope overlooking the river, the house floors were demarcated by central hearths and post moulds as well as concentrations of cultural debris. Houses were partially cut

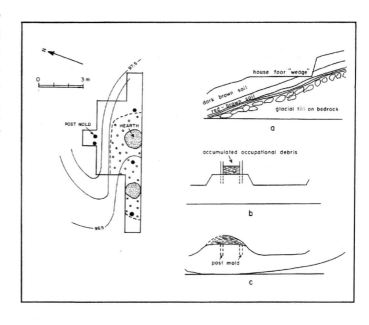

into the slope in the process of levelling the floor (`a´). Soil from this levelling activity was then mounded around the periphery of the living floor as wall support and to form a bench along both sides of the houses. Illustrations `b´ and `c´ schematically show how the house wall would have appeared immediately after abandonment and then after the collapse of the structure. (Adapted from Coupland 1988: Figures 5.4, 5.5, and 5.6. Drawing by Mr. David W. Laverie.)

---

permanent village would require appropriate procedures for salmon preservation and storage. Indeed, numerous storage pits occurred along the east side of the river (Coupland 1988: Fig.8.1, 251) although they cannot be assigned to specific time periods. At the time of European contact the rich salmon resources of the Kitselas Canyon were controlled by specific groups of interior Tsimshian. These people occupied permanent villages, subsisted primarily on salmon, and had a ranked society based upon hereditary. It is suspected that the early village uncovered at the Paul Mason site represents the beginning of the development leading to the villages recorded by Europeans but prior to the development of a ranked society. The Paul Mason village represented a break from previous settlement of the Canyon that began around 3,500 BC; earlier occupations being summer-fall excursions into the interior from the coast for the specific purpose of exploiting salmon (Coupland 1988: 232). Prior to interior villages, settlement patterns consisted of winter occupations in the Prince Rupert region at the mouth of the Skeena River where shellfish gathering was a major activity followed by a shift to the Canyon in the summer to acquire salmon. A similar pattern of seasonal occupations of the interior and the Delta has been proposed for the

Fraser River (Coupland 1988: 300-301; Kidd 1969).

Trade networks along the coast and the interior of British Columbia involved dentalia and other marine shells, obsidian, steatite or soapstone, nephrite, native copper, and amber (Fladmark 1982: 120). Walrus ivory was also traded (Conover 1978) reflecting trade connections with the north. It has even been suggested that regional trade fairs may have been established at the mouths of major rivers during the seasonal fisheries. Such networks were capable of moving items like marine shell beads as far east as the Plains of Alberta by 2,000 BC (Brumley 1975: 69). Interior obsidian from Anahim appears on the Queen Charlotte Islands around the beginning of Period III. At 3,000 BC the small amount of obsidian recovered from both the Kitselas Canyon and the Prince Rupert Harbour region has been identified as coming from the Mt.Edziza deposits of northern British Columbia (Coupland 1988; Fladmark 1985). On the south coast at the Shoemaker Bay site and other sites on the lower mainland and the Gulf Islands, obsidian has been sourced to Glass Buttes in central Oregon (McMillan and St.Claire 1975: 40). Given the geological locations of soapstone and nephrite in the Fraser Canyon and sea mussel shells from the Strait of Juan de Fuca much of the distribution of these materials along the south coast could relate to the seasonal rounds of the various bands as well as trade per se (Mitchell 1971).

Trade networks have not received much attention until recently. Certainly the obsidian sources consisting of Mt.Edziza in the north, Anahim/Mackenzie/Ilgachuz in south-central, and Garibaldi in the south of British Columbia (Figures 47 and 48) as well as sources in Oregon and Wyoming (see Roy L. Carlson 1994 regarding prehistoric obsidian trade) provide an opportunity for determining by trace element analyses probable trade patterns that developed around the high quality silicas from earliest times. Imperishable trade items like obsidian, of course, must also reflect to some degree the trade in perishable goods such as furs, foods, whale and fish oil, and implements.

Cosmology:

The large coastal shell midden village sites created a chemical environment favourable to the preservation of bone including human and animal interments. Most shell midden burials date between 3,750 and 2,500 BC and persist until AD 1300 when, for unknown reasons, above ground burial became the accepted manner of treating the deceased (Cybulski 1992: 165). The fact that burials represent the most common feature in shell middens suggests some form of symbolic association of the deceased with the shell. It has been speculated that midden burials took place when the villages were temporarily abandoned, possibly to permit shellfish populations to recover from human exploitation. During the reoccupation of such villages the locations of the cemeteries were apparently forgotten, unmarked, or unimportant, leading to extensive disturbance of burials due to subsequent village excavation activities (Ibid: 168). Prior to Period III there is little or no evidence of burials from coastal British Columbia and, indeed, precious little bone in any form has survived in the archaeological deposits until the advent of the shell middens. One of the best descriptions of the burial pattern in a major shell midden spanning Period III comes from the Namu site on the central coast.

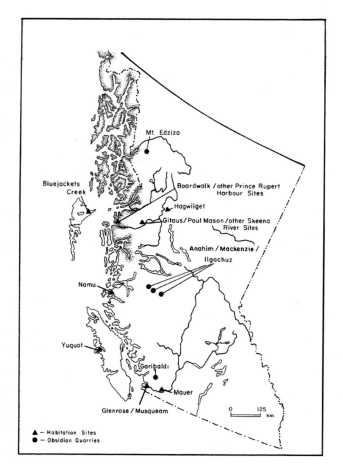

Mt. Edziza

Bluejackets
Creek

Boardwalk / other Prince Rupert
Harbour Sites

Hagwilget

Gitaus / Paul Mason / other Skeena
River Sites

Anahim / Mackenzie /
Ilgachuz

Namu

Yuquot

Garibaldi

Mauer

Glenrose / Musqueam

0   125
km.

▲ — Habitation Sites
● — Obsidian Quarries

FIGURE 47: MAJOR EARLY WEST COAST CULTURE SITES AND INTERIOR OBSIDIAN DEPOSITS From earliest times the volcanic glass referred to as obsidian was a valued item of trade. Used in the manufacture of stone tools, its frequent occurrence on coastal and lower riverine sites is direct evidence of a trading relationship between interior and coastal peoples. Most trade, however, would have been in foodstuffs, furs, and other perishable objects which do not survive in the archaeological record. (Adapted from Fladmark 1986: Map 3. Drawing by Mr.David W. Laverie.)

FIGURE 48: OBSIDIAN TRADE ALONG THE WEST COAST OF NORTH AMERICA BETWEEN 5,000 AND 2,500 BC (Reproduced from Carlson 1983: Fig.1.4 with permission)

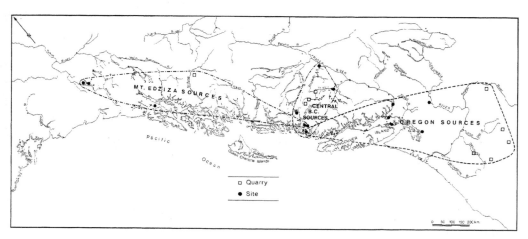

MT. EDZIZA SOURCES

CENTRAL
B.C.
SOURCES

OREGON SOURCES

Pacific

Ocean

□ Quarry
● Site

0   50 100 150 200 km

"Of the 29 individuals uncovered, 19 were located within a 6 metre circle, and of these, 17 occur in multiple interments. Furthermore, assuming that the dating is correct, 24 individuals fall within the 4290-2880 BP time range. These numbers point out that specific burial areas were used and re-used during a relatively short time period. Finally, it seems possible that these were relatives or people known to each other, and that when the last members died, the whole group was buried together. Hence, small interment groupings may have been formed on the basis of the special circumstances surrounding each death and each group. Quite clear is the fact that those individuals who were doing the burying had intimate knowledge of the burial area and were familiar with the history of its occupants" (Luebbers 1978: 34).

While burial mode consisted of flexed, extended, and possible bundle burials the typical pattern was flexed (Curtin n.d.: 19), a form of burial dominant along the entire coast during Period III (Cybulski 1992: 61). An unusual multiple burial at the Namu site involved an intense fire which had been set ablaze on top of the three individuals in the grave cremating two completely and the other in part. Other graves had clusters of cobbles placed near the head and a few bodies were covered with large boulders. Another unusual grave at this site consisted of an adult male and two females. The male had been provided with necklaces and bracelets involving 4,000 shell beads and, in addition to a deposit of red ochre in the neck area, two walrus ivory `gambling pieces´, a possible shell pendant, and two caches of stone and bone tools placed at the shoulder. The tools in the caches consisted of bone points, walrus ivory unilaterally barbed harpoons, and lanceolate and bipointed chipped projectile points. This individual had been killed by a spear that had been propelled from behind with the bone tip of the spear penetrating between the thoracic vertebrae into the spinal column. Aside from the foregoing instance, grave offerings were rare and when present were generally represented by ornaments such as clam shell beads. Of significance was the evidence of a distinctive form of tooth abrasion caused by the wearing of labrets. All three instances of labret wear pertained to males buried in the 3,200 BC layer of the site along with red ochre (Curtin n.d.: 107). The type of labret tooth wear compared closely with that of the contemporaneous Blue Jackets Creek site on the Queen Charlotte Islands (Severs 1974). In addition to the human burials at the Namu site three dog burials were recorded (Conover 1978: 85). It has been speculated that dog skull parts associated with Namu site human burials dating from 3,750 to 2,500 BC may have had ceremonial significance (Cybulski 1992: 66).

In the shell midden of the Blue Jackets Creek site on the Queen Charlotte Islands 28 burials were excavated. An under representation of juveniles, infants, and adolescents suggested young individuals had been buried elsewhere (Murray 1981: 164). Bodies were placed in either a flexed or a sitting position and most dated to 2,000 BC. The significance of the scattered human remains found throughout the midden is unknown (Ibid: 129) although subsequent disturbance of the site was most likely responsible (Cybulski 1992). Red ochre occurred with the three burials placed in a sitting position and most of the flexed burials were oriented north away from the sea (Severs 1974). Grave offerings were represented by etched caribou metapodials and shell disc beads. Buccal abrasion indicative of labret use was present (see Black and White Plates XIX and XX) even though labrets were not recovered from the site (Fladmark et al. 1990). Similar evidence for the use of labrets has been noted along the entire coast (Fladmark 1986).

In the 2,500 to 2,000 BC deposits of the Glenrose Cannery site on the south coast a number of flexed burials with varying orientations were encountered with some the bodies being placed in stone cysts (Styles 1976). Five of the 11 individuals involved had grave offerings including red ochre or limonite nodules and/or powder, a shell necklace, awls, and a bone pendant. In one instance, red ochre had been smeared over the ribs, collar bones, shoulder blades, and hands of the body. After death saw marks on the left parietal of one skull reflects some ceremonial act. The possibility of a bear burial at this site was also noted (Styles 1976: 203). Of interest is an anthropomorphic antler handle resembling a specimen from the Prince Harbour area (Fladmark et al. 1990) thus raising the possibility of some early form of shared symbolism (Black and White Plate XVII). In the 3,000 BC level of the nearby St.Mungo Cannery site, a probable ceremonial feature consisted of a 1.8 m by 2 m rectangular area demarcated by red ochre containing a hearth floor in one corner and a dozen unspecified artifacts on its surface (Clavert 1970: 58). At the end of Period III in the Montague Harbour I site a variable burial pattern was encountered consisting of a flexed burial covered with a stone cairn, a flexed burial, and either bundle or disturbed flexed burials. Scattered human bone included charred adolescent fragments, a child jaw, and a skull (Mitchell 1971: 149). An unusual burial in the sense that it was recovered from a basically shell-free matrix was excavated at the Georgeson Bay site in the Gulf of Georgia (Haggarty and Sendey 1976). Dating to the end of Period III, the burial occurred in a stone cairn accompanied by red ochre, a notched weight, and a ground rectangular nephrite object.

It was during Period III along the south coast as well as up the Fraser River that a fluorescence in a distinctive form of art objects carved out of soft stone and bone took place. The items in question occur in a wide range of forms and may have been ornaments or performed a ceremonial function (Fladmark 1986: 74). With reference to the spindle-shaped category of carvings, which appear as early as 3,750 BC, it has been speculated that these "...carefully crafted creations appear like realistic representations of the larvae of flies or similar insects" (Borden 1983: 134). At the time of European contact insect larvae, grubs, etc. were regarded as possessing supernatural powers that permitted them to change size and form. The objects in question may thus have been symbols of a form of transformational power. Quartz crystal flake tools, which appear late in this region, may have possessed the mystical powers attributed to the crystal and been used as fish knives in order to show respect to the soul of the salmon (Fladmark 1986: 68). On the north coast, stylized human pendants suspended upside down appear by 2,000 BC and are inferred to have had symbolic significance. Near the end of Period III in the same region an art style emphasizing skeletal parts appears. Such items are thought to represent ancestor figures possibly associated with shaman and chief aprons (MacDonald 1983: 104-105). As early as 2,500 BC some art may be related to guardian and shamanic spirits (Carlson 1983a: 204) although art does not elaborate to form lines and interlocking parts until Period IV (Ibid: 203).

External relationships:

Technological correspondences between southwestern Alaska and the Strait of Georgia on the south coast of British Columbia prior to 2,000 BC suggest some form of relationship (Dumond 1978: 89). For example, the toggling harpoon is believed to have come from the north (Fladmark 1982: 120). Ear spools, on the other hand, which appear on the south coast late in Period III, must have been derived from the south. Lip labrets appear along the entire coast at approximately the same time in distinctive northern and southern styles and thus their point of origin is still unclear. Earlier technological similarities noted in Period II involving the San Dieguito complex of the California coast (Aikens 1978) and the Southwestern Coastal culture of British Columbia continues into Period III as seen in certain general correspondences between the Windmiller culture of California and Early West Coast culture, particularly along the south coast. Coastal stability in California, which permitted an earlier development of shellfish harvesting (Erlandson 1988) than was possible to the north, may have led to the development of various shellfish harvesting and storage techniques which eventually diffused northward as coastal conditions became favourable. Such speculative possibilities, however, must await a clearer picture of the archaeological record along the entire west coast of North America.

Certain exotic items, such as the walrus ivory tools from the Namu site (Luebbers 1978), indicate some movement of goods from the north. The clearest evidence of long distance trade from the coast to the interior is represented by the gastropod beads (<u>Natica</u> <u>clausa</u> and <u>Olivella</u> <u>biplicata</u>) found in the 2,000 BC level of the Middle Plains culture Cactus Flower site in Alberta (Brumley 1975: 69). There is little doubt that the major obsidian deposits of Mt.Edziza, Anahim/Mackenzie/Ilgachuz, and Garibaldi hold the greatest promise for tracing trade networks, not only from the interior to the coast but also along the coast (Figure 47 and Figure 48). As could be expected, most of the obsidian on the south coast came from either the nearby Garibaldi source north of the Fraser River or from various locales in eastern Oregon. Similarly, most of the obsidian from the Anahim region occurs on coastal sites immediately to the west. An interesting exception to this pattern is the occurrence of Anahim obsidian in the 3,500 BC occupation of the Paul Mason site at Kitselas Canyon on the Skeena River (Coupland 1988). By 3,000 BC the trade pattern in obsidian in this region had switched to the Mt.Edziza source. Obsidian appearing in occupations at the mouth of the Skeena River and the Queen Charlotte Islands was also derived from the Mt.Edziza source. Such a distribution suggests coastal trade whereby Mt.Edziza obsidian (Fladmark 1985) was moved down the Stikine River to the coast and thence south and north along the coast. Other traits regarded as northern in origin that diffused south along the coast were ground slate points, the technique of sawing hard stone like nephrite with sandstone abraders to produce adzes, and more questionably, labrets (Carlson 1983: 28).

As research into trading networks expands so will understanding of the external relationships of Early West Coast culture with its neighbours, Middle Plateau culture and Middle Northwest Interior culture. It will then be possible to critically evaluate the statement that "...Northwest Coast prehistory is predicated upon the concept that basic to that culture pattern was the multiple resource subsistence strategy. Other elements exhibited in the ethnographic pattern are the result of a complex history of cultural contacts with adjacent regions as well as indigenous developments. Our view is thus that the ethnographic pattern represents an amalgamation and integration of these indigenous and introduced traits. Northwest

Coast prehistory should be viewed as a continuum which included mechanisms for assimilation of new traits" (Hester 1978: 110).

Human biology:

On the basis of dental characteristics it has been argued that West Coast populations represent a homogeneous group related to the Eyak-Athapaskan language family (Na-Dene) who are believed to have migrated into the Western Hemisphere between the first group of migrants and a late Eskimo-Aleut migration (Turner 1983). In addition to other difficulties, the linguistic attribution of this position is highly questionable. While the hypothesis has an appealing parsimony that does concur with some other lines of evidence, its demonstration is far from being achieved. Studies with more modest goals indicate that human skull morphology is quite heterogeneous and that the West Coast does not represent a single breeding population even though there are no sharp genetic boundaries between populations (Cybulski 1990). On the north coast, for example, evidence derived from 17 non-metric cranial traits demonstrated that the outer coast Blue Jacket Creek site population differed markedly from the population of the mainland coast Namu site. The Namu population was far more similar to contemporary people in the Prince Rupert Harbour region and the two populations may have been biologically related (Ibid: 127-128). A close relationship between these two populations was also supported by craniometric characteristics (Cybulski 1992: Table 10, Fig.29, and see his Chapter V, in particular, for a detailed consideration of the skeletal characteristics of the Period III Blue Jacket Creek and Namu sites as well as later populations). Only 77 burials are known from the Early Developmental Stage of Fladmark (1986) covering the period from 3,500 to 1,500 BC. Of these 77 individuals, 61 were recovered from two sites, Blue Jackets Creek on the Queen Charlotte Islands and Namu on the central coast (Cybulski 1994: 76-77). The technological difference apparent between outer and inner coastal sites appears to be, in this instance, duplicated by a similar biological distance.

The 28 individuals from the 2,500 BC occupation of the Blue Jackets Creek site on the Queen Charlotte Islands were characterized by limited sexual dimorphism and moderate narrow crania with high vaults (Murray 1981). Half of the burials consisted of people under 30 years of age and there were exceptionally few infants and adolescents. Six adult males averaged 162.4 cm in height (Cybulski 1990) comparing closely with the seven males from the Namu site. These figures are in close agreement with late 19th century measurements and measurements of living people (Ibid: Table 2).

Excluding the Prince Rupert Harbour population that straddles Period III and Period IV (Cybulski 1992: Fig.11), the following observations concerning pathology pertain to Period III central and north coast populations. At the Namu site there was a 68% incidence of maxillary sinus infection. Evidence of violent trauma, such as healed skull fractures, was most common at Namu and occurred mainly on males (Ibid: Figs. 42 and 43). This suspected evidence of warfare is not nearly as common on the south coast as the central and north coasts. On the other hand, the absence of evidence of violent trauma comparable to the

Namu site at the Blue Jackets Creek site does not support the generalization of a decrease in the incidence of violent trauma from Period III to subsequent periods (Ibid: 158). Cribra orbitalia, an iron-deficiency anemia of complex etiology, was found to occur in higher frequencies on the Queen Charlotte Islands and the Gulf of Georgia than at either Prince Rupert Harbour or Namu (Cybulski 1990: Table 4; 1992: 171). While the presence of cribra orbitalia is relatively consistent through time it is not possible to explain the variability in regional frequencies as the condition can be caused by a number of factors (Cybulski 1992: 57). A rare pathology was identified in a multiple burial at the 1,800 BC Duke Point site on the south coast. The burial contained a number of individuals including a fetus that were infected by treponematosis, an endemic, non-venereal syphilis. A common problem resulting from a gritty meat diet was abscesses caused by excessive wear of the grinding surfaces of the teeth. Approximately half of the adult population was affected by this dental pathology. While arthritis of the elbow, wrist, and knee region was relatively common at the Blue Jackets Creek site on the south coast only a single instance of degenerative arthritis was noted (Beattie 1976). Healed fractures of the vertebral column, the jaw, and lower limbs, were also noted in the latter region (Ibid: 163).

As the largest Period III sample of human skeletal material from the West Coast came from the Namu site it is worthwhile to consider this evidence in some detail. The majority of the burials date to the early portion of Period III. Not only were grave pits shallow permitting them to be ordered within the stratigraphic sequence (Luebbers 1976) but the chronology of burials was upheld by radiocarbon dating (Curtin n.d.). A total of 42 skeletons was identified but some of this number included clusters of remains represented by only a limited number of bones from the same individual. Isolated elements, such as a skull, were not treated as burials. Despite the sample size, the Namu evidence is still regarded as suffering from the problems endemic to shell midden burial evidence, insufficient sample size and incomplete and fragmentary nature of remains. Scattered human remains typically found in shell middens may represent the remains of former above ground burials that became incorporated in the middens (Burley 1989) but it is more likely that such fragments were the result of a number of different activities such as "...digging to retrieve human remains for ritual purposes, other cultural activities (caching material possessions or clearing midden areas for habitation), tree root growth and deadfalls, carnivore and rodent activity, and erosion from sea waves and tides" (Cybulski 1994: 78). A general burial characteristic was a marked under representation of infants (Ibid: Table 1, 83) suggesting that such individuals were buried elsewhere. As a rule, the Namu population appears to have lived a relatively healthy albeit rigorous life. The major causes of death were blows to the head for men, apparently a result of hand to hand combat, and complications in child birth for women. In this respect the female mortality curve peaked significantly earlier than it did for men. Sinus inflammation was endemic. Dental problems appear to have been relatively minor. Despite a high incidence of calculus deposits on tooth surfaces there is limited evidence of periodontal disease (Ibid: 96). Degenerative joint disease (osteoarthritis) and trauma (fractures) were by far the most common problems. In females arthritic lesions typically occurred on parts of the axial skeleton with minor appearances at the elbow and wrist while in males the lower jaw, the shoulder, wrist, hip, and knee were most affected. Degenerative joint disease is `age-progressive´ but can also be `activity-specific´ and a combination of both of these factors was likely involved. Fractures, represented by depressed skull fractures, occurred most frequently on the frontal bone of the skull. Facial injuries, such as broken incisors, nasal bone and eye orbit margin fractures, were largely restricted to males and appear to be related to close quarter combat with clubs. In fact, most of the injuries were to the left frontal portion of the skull as would be anticipated from a blow delivered by a right-handed adversary. Unlike the situation recorded at sites of subsequent periods, there is no evidence of `parrying´ fractures to the forearm (Ibid: 117). Antisocial behaviour, such as lethal combat, would not have been tolerated within a small community and it can be assumed that periodic warfare existed with neighbouring groups. Skeletal robustness characterized both sexes but sexual dimorphism is most apparent in the jaws and upper arms and shoulders of males. The extraordinary development of the trapezium and deltoid muscles required by paddling may account for the rugged characteristics of male upper arms.

Inferences on society:

It has been commented that "We can be confident that, throughout the Middle Development Stage, British Columbia's shores sheltered large populations of nobles, commoners and slaves, of fishermen, hunters, artists and warriors. Here, it is certain, were big plank-house villages boasting monumental art in praise of the material and spiritual wealth of famous families; powerful shamans guarding knowledge of the supernatural realm; and a life humming with feasts, dances, wars and commerce" (Fladmark 1986: 85). Fladmark's Middle Development Stage dates from 2,000 BC to AD 500. A full blown ethnographic pattern by 2,000 BC would appear to be too early. It is largely based upon the increasing frequencies of labrets and art objects, such as bone and tooth pendants, shell and stone disc beads, bird bone and stone tube beads, and spindle-like ornaments (Ibid: 61) and the assumption that such objects reflect rank. Such an assumption is hazardous given the occurrences of quite elaborate grave offerings, including art objects, in early cemeteries in other parts of North America where ranked societies were most unlikely. Extending the ethnographically documented status symbolism of labrets back into Period III when such items were rare and ranked societies were likely in the process of development is probably, to at least some degree, an overextension of the use of ethnographic analogy. Similarly, the speculation that the boulder covered bodies at the Namu site pertained to people of lower status such as slaves is only one of a number of possible explanations.

Evidence of tooth wear from the wearing of labrets (Black and White Plates XIX and XX) but the absence of actual labrets suggests that the objects were not always buried with their owners (family heirlooms?) or were manufactured of perishable materials like wood. Of the 22 instances of distinctive dental abrasion from Prince Rupert Harbour, for example, only two labrets were actually found with their owners. Tooth wear patterns on the central and north coasts during Period III indicates the use of lateral or buccal labrets rather than the medial or labial type which make their appearance in Period IV (Cybuliski 1992: 69). On the south coast, on the other hand, medial labrets appear possibly as early as 3,750 BC. Unlike the situation on the north coast at the time of European contact, when only certain women wore labrets, during Period III both men and women were labret users although they were more common among men. The evidence of labret use on the south coast is more evenly balanced between the genders. If labrets at this time are indicators of ascribed or hereditary status it would suggest a bilateral descent system on the south coast and an initial patrilineal system followed by a matrilineal system of descent on the north coast (Cybulski 1992: 72; Suttles 1990a). Period III labrets along the coast of British Columbia may be indicative of the beginnings of some form of status differentiation but they are not per se evidence of the existence of stratified societies. For a general consideration of labret use and distribution along the West Coast see Keddie (1981). Also historically documented as a mark of family status, although more typical of Period IV, evidence of purposeful skull deformation by binding the heads of infants has been identified in the 1,000 BC level of the Shoemaker Bay site on Vancouver Island (McMillan and St. Claire 1975:65)

More convincing evidence of ranked societies is likely to come from settlement pattern features, such as large house floors in villages that also contain more modest dwellings. The Paul Mason village of 10 equal sized houses arranged in two rows, dated to the end of Period III, would appear to pertain to a corporate society rather than a formally ranked one (Coupland 1988). Such corporate villages were likely a prerequisite to the eventual development of ranked societies but any social transformation from relatively egalitarian societies to stratified societies with lords, nobles, commoners, and slaves probably took time to consolidate and would not have evolved everywhere at the same time or necessarily in the same fashion. Speculating about changing social structure in the archaeological record is a hazardous exercise but the evidence suggests that the development of full-blown ranked societies did not take place until Period IV. The transformation of egalitarian bands into ranked, village-based societies was probably initiated by the desire to exert control over the local salmon resource (Coupland 1988). Control would have required ownership of particularly favourable fishing locations and the authority to organize a labour force in order to produce status enhancing surpluses and maintain a following. Given these requirements for the development of ranked societies one would expect to find the earliest examples of such societies in the coastal villages associated with the canyon regions of major salmon rivers such as the Skeena and the Fraser. Settlement pattern evidence suggests that the process towards ranked societies had only just begun by 1,000 BC. In fact, emergence of ranked societies in the canyon region of the Skeena River does not occur until 500 BC (Coupland 1988), a time coeval with the evidence of ranked societies along the rest of the coast. Matters of rank aside, the evidence from the Namu site of adult males with cranial and facial lesions (Curtin n.d.) indicates the presence of warfare as early as 3,500 BC. It cannot be demonstrated at this early period whether warfare was related to resource acquisition/defence, slave and wealth acquisition, or was simply a heightened pattern of blood revenge and feuding.

With reference to the south coast and the Charles phase that largely encompassed Period III it has been observed "...there is an increasing body of data suggesting social complexity in the Charles period, including intensive salmon harvesting, massive architecture, wealth accumulation, hereditary status, and ranking" (Eldridge et al. 1992: 114). In other words, at least in the Fraser Delta between 3,750 and 2,500 BC incremental changes in the archaeological record appear to be "...critical to the development of the Northwest Coast culture type" (Ibid: 115).

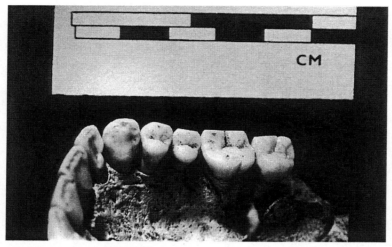

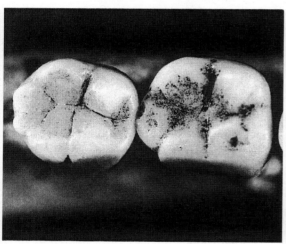
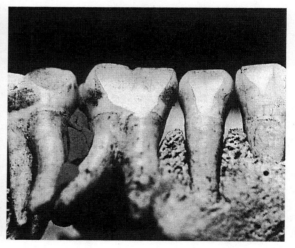

BLACK AND WHITE PLATE XIX: LABRET TOOTH WEAR AT THE BLUE JACKETS CREEK SITE
The photograph presents three views of exterior or labial tooth wear on upper and lower molars and premolars. Such an unusual wear pattern was likely produced by abrasion resulting from the insertion of wooden, stone, or bone labrets into slits made in the cheeks. The Blue Jackets Creek site has been dated to 2,500 BC. As the wearing of labrets at the time of European contact was restricted to people of high rank this particular occurrence has been used to argue for the existence of ranked societies on the Queen Charlotte Islands at an early period. Such a proposition, however, appears to be an overextension of the comparative method called ethnographic analogy. (Photograph courtesy of Dr. J. S. Cybulski, Archaeological Survey of Canada, Canadian Museum of Civilization)

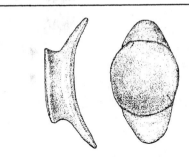

Figure 2. Labret (two views)

BLACK AND WHITE PLATE XX: LABRET USE Poked through a hole in the lower lip a labret of wood, stone, or bone was a mark of beauty and status among women of the north coast at the time of European contact. The practice had nearly died out by the end of the last century. This Haida woman from the Queen Charlotte Islands was still wearing a labret when she was photographed by Richard Maynard in 1884. (Reproduced verbatim from MacDonald and Inglis 1976: Plate 12 and Figure 2. Note: The tooth wear evidence from the Blue Jackets Creek site (Black and White Plate XIX) indicates that at earlier times labrets were worn in the cheeks rather than the lower lip.)

Limitations in the evidence:

Archaeological excavations along the British Columbia coast have naturally tended to focus on shell midden sites located near the present sea level rather than on non-shell sites situated back from the beach in heavy bush. As a result, the last 5,000 years of the archaeological record is the best known (Fladmark 1982: 103-104). Paradoxically, the large shell middens by their very mass make it difficult and expensive to open-up large areas. The normal `telephone booth´ excavation technique produces little information on dwellings that require large areas of sites to be exposed. It is also difficult to recognize house floors in shell middens with all of the disturbances caused by repeated occupations (MacDonald 1969a: 259). Even to obtain adequate samples of artifacts in such middens requires a considerable excavation of shell. At Prince Rupert Harbour, for example, 14,000 cubic feet of shell midden produced 1,000 artifacts, 13 burials and features (Inglis 1973: 142).

On the central coast, river erosion and deposition is likely responsible for the scarcity of sites. It is estimated that nearly half of the mid-19th century historically documented villages in the Bella Coola Valley have already disappeared (Hobler 1990: 304). Occupations of the major deltas have also suffered considerable damage due to recent urban and rural development in places like Vancouver and Prince Rupert. Another limiting factor has been the lower sea levels of the south coast and the higher sea levels of the north coast prior to 3,500 BC (Fladmark 1975) which has created a situation where potential sites were drowned in the south and elevated back into the heavy forest covered hinterland in the north. On the other hand, the earlier, well-exposed elevated beaches in the Prince Rupert Harbour area failed to produce evidence of occupation (MacDonald 1969: 249).

A chronic problem shared with most other areas of the country has been the paucity of detailed descriptive archaeological reports (Abbott 1986: 187). All too frequently preliminary articles are not followed by final reports. A further weakness in the publication record is that an unusually high percentage of important monographs are represented by unpublished manuscripts and theses. While funding is not likely to increase in the foreseeable future much of this inaccessibility of reports required by the Province and universities could be markedly reduced by electronic reproduction. Publication costs and appropriate publication outlets have undoubtedly been major factors effecting the frequency of published monographs. There has also been a "...tendency to accept the presence of one part of an ethnographic pattern as indicating the presence of the full pattern" (Ames 1981: 797) such as shell middens being equated with villages even though there is no direct evidence of houses.

CHAPTER 20 —————————————————————
MIDDLE NORTHWEST INTERIOR CULTURE

Précis:

Early research in northwestern North America (Johnson 1946; Rainey 1940) indicated archaeological connections between Asia and North America and it was this interest in the initial peopling of the Western Hemisphere that led to focused research in the area (MacNeish 1951; 1953; 1954; 1955; 1956; 1959; 1960). Most subsequent work has built upon or attempted to re-interpret R. S. MacNeish's cultural sequences with acknowledged undramatic results (Clark and Morlan 1982). Pertinent to Period III is MacNeish's view that his Northwest Microblade tradition represented a constellation of traits coming from different regions, such as microblade technology from Siberia and notched projectile points from the Plains (MacNeish 1953; 1964). This view would still appear to be partially valid or, at least, more accommodating of the evidence than the major alternative. The alternative view proposes that the indigenous populations of the northwestern interior were replaced by southern Archaic hunters prior to 4,000 BC (Anderson 1970). MacNeish's Northwest Microblade tradition and Anderson's Northern Archaic tradition, or their equivalents, are subsumed within Middle Northwest Interior culture with the Northern Archaic being simply a late phase in the development. Relative to the history of archaeological research the southwest Yukon was the locale of one of the earliest attempts to integrate archaeological evidence with associated environmental information (Johnson and Raup 1964).

Middle Northwest Interior culture must be viewed in relationship to its geographical setting. The region is physiographically dominated by the northwest trending Cordillera consisting of coastal and interior mountain ranges with intervening smaller mountain ranges and plateaus. Major drainages are the Yukon and the Mackenzie, two of the largest river systems in the world. Within this complex mosaic of landforms, small hunting bands relied upon fish and caribou as well as regionally and seasonally available small game, waterfowl, mountain sheep, moose, bison, and berries. To survive in a region with widely dispersed food resources and peak periods of abundance and scarcity has always demanded a broadly based and flexible foraging pattern.

The sparse archaeological remains left by small, mobile groups of people have forced archaeologists to rely upon relatively simple and often equivocal criterion in order to establish cultural constructs. Thus, there is considerable controversy and a proliferation of named constructs including Denali, Northwest Microblade, American Palaeo-Arctic, Tuktu, and Northern Archaic. The last two constructs pertain to assemblages possessing notched points but supposedly lacking microblade technology as distinct from the others. It has been the presence or absence of these two elements of technology, notched projectile points and microblades, which have been the major criteria for distinguishing cultures in the area. For example, it has been proposed that around 4,000 BC Archaic hunters of ultimate eastern North American origin, possessing notched projectile points, spread northward from the Plains with the expanding boreal forest to displace indigenous populations whose tool kits were characterized by microblades (Anderson 1970). Despite the fact that considerable evidence does not support the simple replacement of an earlier microblade-using culture by an alien culture coming out of the northern Plains, it is still generally accepted as a major culture history model for the region (Clark 1987; Dumond 1978) albeit with increasing hesitation and qualification (Clark 1992). In order to accommodate the archaeological evidence, the conquest and assimilation explicit in the hypothesis must have taken place at different times in different areas. The population replacement hypothesis is rejected here on the grounds that a considerable body of archaeological evidence suggests cultural continuity and not cultural replacement. Cultural discontinuity explicit in the replacement hypothesis would appear to be a product of an overly optimistic acceptance of the taxonomic value of notched points and microblades as indicators of total cultures. Rather than representing a population influx, the sudden appearance of notched points is regarded here as evidence of the northward diffusion of the spearthrower weapon system, a process that began 4,000 years earlier in southeastern North America. It has been necessary to create a new name for the culture under consideration in order to avoid a classificatory association with and a reliance upon either microblades or notched projectile points. Middle Northwest Interior culture is an admittedly tentative construct but it is sufficiently open-ended to accommodate the vagaries of an impoverished archaeological record in a region subjected to influences from a number of different areas. It would appear that the difficulties faced by linguists in attempting to classify the northern Athapascan languages of the same region, with their amalgams of regionally shared language characteristics (Krause 1981: 68), is also reflected in the archaeological record.

There is limited archaeological evidence in the central Mackenzie District (Clark 1987: 148) from 5,000 BC to the Early Palaeo-Eskimo culture intrusion into the interior around 2,000 BC. This situation does not apply to the southwestern Mackenzie District, the Yukon Territory, the western Great Bear Lake region and other parts of the Mackenzie Corridor, and northeastern Alberta (Clark 1987; Gordon and Savage 1973; 1974; LeBlanc 1988; Losey et al. n.d.; MacNeish 1954; 1955; Millar 1981). As there is no environmental explanation for the human void in the central Mackenzie District it is likely a problem of archaeological visibility rather than an actual absence of people.

Northwestern North America is geographically situated to receive influences from a number of directions but its major relationships appear to have been to the west with Alaska. There is no evidence of eastern influences from the Barrengrounds of Keewatin District and the eastern Mackenzie District. Despite claims to the contrary, influences from the south out of the Plains appear to be represented by the diffusion of technology, such as the spearthrower, rather than being indicative of population intrusions. For example, the lanceolate point forms from the northwestern interior that are frequently attributed to the Plano culture of the Plains appear on the grounds of dating, the existence of a major hiatus in the geographical distributions of the points in question, and differing point attributes, to be unrelated to those of the Plains and are best regarded as a distinctive northern lance style weapon tip. It is possible that the importance of communal hunting of caribou herds in northwestern North America assured the retention of the thrusting lance long after it had disappeared or was reduced in popularity in other parts of North America. The fact that such lanceolate points are found with or without notched projectile points or microblades highlights the problem of relying upon a limited number of `index fossils´ to classify cultures. Given the chronic problems of small samples of generally non-descript materials recovered from poor contexts that characterize the archaeology of northwestern North America it is not surprising that there are classificatory problems. Such problems are a direct product of limitations in the data base compounded by an overly heavy reliance upon the limited formal tools such as microblades, burins, and notched and lanceolate projectile points.

By the beginning of Period III Middle Northwest Interior culture technology is characterized by microblade production based upon wedge-shaped and tabular-shaped cores, burins of a number of varieties with the notched transverse burin being most distinctive, lanceolate points, a range of scraper and biface knife varieties, gravers, drills, net-sinkers and some other minor items. The most common tools were simple expedient flake tools. As microblade technology began to wane, notched projectile points were introduced. There was also an increase in large biface knives and end scrapers. Notched projectile points appear to have been grafted onto the earlier assemblage but at different times in different regions. Notched points, for example, appear as early as 5,500 BC in northern Alaska but as late as 3,750 BC in the southwest Yukon.

Poor bone preservation restricts direct evidence of subsistence practises. Site distributions indicate that fishing was an important summer to fall activity with the fish camps likely representing the period of the year when the band or bands could gather together at one location to arrange marriages and reaffirm the solidarity of the society. One must qualify such a generalization, however, as a successful caribou pound could have permitted large gatherings of people at single sites in winter but at locations very difficult for current archaeological field reconnaissance techniques to discover. With reference to settlement pattern distributions and pertinent to the hypothesized displacement of microblade-users by notched projectile point-users, the two assemblages appear on the same sites time and again suggesting that there was no significant change in site use and, therefore, subsistence. Such continuity of settlement patterns and presumably subsistence adds support to the argument that a cultural replacement did not take place and that change was a product of technological diffusion and temporal trends. There is a consensus among archaeologists that the late portion of this cultural development led directly to the historic Athapascan-speaking people of northwestern North America.

Cultural origins and descendants:

Middle Northwest Interior culture developed out of the preceding Early Northwest Interior culture, locally referred to as the Palaeoarctic tradition (Anderson 1970; 1984, Dumond 1978). For much of Period III the occupation of the Yukon was attributed to the Northwest Microblade tradition (MacNeish 1964) and, in the northern interior of Alaska, the equivalent Denali tradition (West 1967). Both of these classifications are subsumed under Middle Northwest Interior culture. MacNeish (1964) regarded the Northwest Microblade tradition as an amalgam of an indigenous Plano culture and an Asiatic-derived microblade technology. There is no convincing evidence for the presence of Plano culture although some of the local varieties of lanceolate points do bear a superficial resemblance to southern forms. To the east "...the Mackenzie Basin was a region of the meeting, and in some cases the fusion, of cultures which had long independent histories west and south of the area" (Clark 1974: 55). While the Mackenzie Basin was unlikely to have been some kind of cultural `melting pot´ the region did represent the eastern boundary of Middle Northwest Interior culture. Prior to 4,000 BC notched projectile points appear in the northern interior of Alaska and have been interpreted as evidence of northward spreading Archaic hunters from the Plains. This invasion is believed to have replaced the earlier Northwestern Palaeo-Arctic-derived populations. The hypothesized event occurred in conjunction with an Altithermal warming trend that led to a northward shift of the boreal forest and concomitant changes in animal populations. As noted in the précis, this proposed population movement of Archaic people from the south into northwestern North America and their replacement of the indigenous population is rejected. First, the limited food resources of interior northwestern North America would hardly have provided an economic incentive for one group of hunters to over-run and presumably exterminate another group of hunters. Such warfare is generally alien to hunter-gatherers around the world. Second, the environmental assumptions of the hypothesis are inappropriate for large areas of the region under consideration. Third, microblades and notched points, the so-called cultural markers of the indigenous population and the invading population, respectively, are not mutually exclusive. Notched points can occur within the tool kit of the indigenous population (Northwest Microblade tradition) and microblades in the tool kit of the proposed invading population (Northern Archaic) (see Clark 1981: 115). If notched points do constitute evidence of an intruding population from the south rather than the diffusion of a technological system then the invaders managed to pass through the Mackenzie Corridor without leaving a trace to arrive in northwestern Alaska by 5,500 BC and then arc to the south and the east in order to reach the southwestern Yukon by 3,750 BC (Morrison 1987: 67). Fourth, there are numerous technological, settlement pattern, and subsistence cultural continuities between the two purported alien cultures (MacNeish 1964: 319; Workman 1978: 405). For a more detailed consideration of the problems with the concept of a Northern Archaic intrusion into the Mackenzie Valley see David A. Morrison (1987).

Small samples recovered from poor archaeological contexts, a limited number of trustworthy dates, and the simple nature of the stone tool assemblages, have contributed to the problem of reconstructing the culture history of northwestern North America. The reliance upon notched points and microblades to provide cultural identifications in conjunction with a cavalier importation of certain early Plano culture point typologies, with all of their southern temporal and cultural implications, has further muddied the already murky waters. Poor preservation of bone has not helped matters. Thus, there is a current need for a less technologically constrained culture construct like `Middle Northwest Interior culture´ to incorporate the likely erroneous Northwest Microblade/Northern Archaic dichotomy and to accommodate the whimsical temporal and spatial occurrences of microblades and notched points in assemblages. Problems with the demonstration of the aforementioned cultural dichotomy have been recognized by a number of researchers where "... the logical and probable existence of Northwest Microblade tradition sites without microblades is an insidious problem inasmuch as identification of this tradition is dependent on the recovery of microblades or cores" (Clark 1987: 167). Other inconsistencies arising out of the conquest-replacement scenario have been identified. With reference to the Taye Lake phase, that has been assigned to the Northern Archaic tradition "Although one must assume some technological or adaptive superiority for the new way exemplified by Taye Lake which permitted it to replace old cultures of Plano cast not only in Southwest Yukon but in the District of Mackenzie and elsewhere, I cannot specify in what this superiority lay" (Workman 1978: 428). Such problems are avoided when a cultural construct is based upon all of the available cultural systems such as technology, subsistence, and settlement patterns, and where a cultural continuity rather than cultural replacement model is advocated. This proposal in neither revolutionary nor entirely new. In referring to the Northwest Microblade and Northern Archaic traditions, for example, the question was asked "Are these one and the same culture, or is this situation a case of acculturation..." (Clark and Morlan 1982: 85) and "Under a less restrictive reconstruction stipulating continuity with change instead of intrusion and replacement, the dichotomy between the Northern Archaic and the Northwest Microblade tradition disappears and the former is seen simply as a later phase which in localized cases lacks microblades" (Ibid: 86). Despite such cautions the replacement hypothesis is currently in ascendency (e.g. Dixon 1985) over the original continuity hypothesis proposed by MacNeish (1960: 48) and thus the need for this overly long discussion of the matter. Under the more broadly based definition of Middle Northwest Interior culture the Franklin Tanks site on the Great Bear River (MacNeish 1955) would be an acceptable component and the generally rejected radiocarbon dates (Clark 1987:187-188) appropriate to the period currently under consideration.

Whereas there are two competing origin hypotheses for Middle Northwest Interior culture there is a consensus that subsequent developments led directly to the historically documented northern Athapaskan-speaking peoples of the region. In northwestern Canada these include the Kutchin, Tutchone, Han, Tanana, Hare, Mountain Indians, Kaska, Slavey, and Dogrib.

Calibrated radiocarbon dates from sites in the District of Mackenzie following Klein et al. (1982) are spread throughout the 3,000 years of Period III (MacNeish 1955; 1964; Morrison 1984; Rutherford et al. 1984; Wilmeth 1978). A similar range of dates exists for sites in the Yukon (MacNeish 1964; Wilmeth 1978) as is also the case with northern Alaska (Gal 1982). The single dated Middle Northwest Interior culture site in northern Alberta is 2,750 BC (LeBlanc and Ives 1986). Readers requiring specific information on radiocarbon dates, such as site name, laboratory numbers, material dated, etc., are referred to the above references. All calendrical dates in either BC/AD or `years ago´ are approximations of the mid-points of the statistical age spread provided in calibration tables (Klein et al. 1982) and are not arrived at by the all too common practice of subtracting AD 1950 from the date in radiocarbon years to arrive at BC/AD or `years ago´ age. Such a procedure is mathematically incorrect and results in inaccurate calendrical estimates. For example, following the procedure used in this work a 5,000 +/- 100 BP date (radiocarbon years before present with present meaning AD 1950) has a calibrated calendrical range of 3,950 to 3,640 BC with a mid-point of approximately 3,800 BC. Using the AD 1950 subtraction method the same 5,000 BP radiocarbon date arrives at a 3,050 BC estimate that makes no allowance for the known fluctuations in atmospheric Carbon 14 through time accommodated in the dendrochronology adjusted calibration tables.

To recap, with the caveat that the Northern Archaic tradition is part of Middle Northwest Interior culture, it is agreed that "The Northern Archaic appears to be basically a western tradition that developed primarily out of local Northern Cordilleran and to some degree also from the Palaeo-Arctic culture" (Clark 1991: 49). It is also agreed that this tradition culminated in the northern Athapascan-speaking people encountered in northwestern North America by Europeans (Ibid: 46). While a number of archaeologists see in their data a cultural continuity of at least 6,000 years, Athapascan linguists are not so sanguine. Linguists argue that the proto-Athapascan language homeland was somewhere "...in eastern interior Alaska, the upper drainage of the Yukon River, and northern British Columbia..." (Kraus and Golla 1981: 68) with an expansion eastward into the Mackenzie River Valley and beyond not taking place until sometime after AD 500.

Technology:

It would appear that much of the difficulty involved in arriving at some form of agreement regarding the culture history of northwestern North America during Period III stems from both the nature of the archaeological record and the methods used to interpret that record. Put succinctly, "...much of the confusion concerning the early prehistory of the interior Northwest probably stems from two basic sources: (1) the definition of artifact types (and by extension, historical index types); and (2) the definition, on this uncertain foundation, of traditions" (Gotthardt 1990: 52-53). As is typical throughout the Western Hemisphere and the entire Stone Age world as well, unmodified stone flakes appear to have been the most heavily relied upon tools in Middle Northwest Interior culture. Unlike many other regions, however, a thin scatter of stone flakes and little else appears to be a common characteristic of sites in the interior of northwestern North America. Many of the more finished tool categories, such as scrapers, biface knives, net sinkers, linear flakes, and spoke-shaves are generally not diagnostic in terms of either time or space and are of limited use in identifying the tool assemblage of a particular culture. Even the tool categories treated as diagnostics, projectile points, microblades and burins, often have extensive spatial and temporal distributions. As an understandable outcome of the paucity of distinctive tools there has been a tendency to treat single tool categories as the diagnostic indicators of a particular culture rather than attempting to look at the total assemblage and its relationship to the other cultural systems. One of the most serious abuses of this approach has been the use of early projectile point typologies extrapolated from the Plains. Unfortunately the association of some northwestern interior point forms with post 10,000 year old Plains point types initiated by Richard S. MacNeish in the 1950's is still a common practice. What has been most disruptive to regional interpretations has been the assumption that the time depth demonstrated for certain early projectile point types on the Plains can be directly transferred to sites in the northwestern interior of North America despite both a geographic and temporal hiatus between the sites being compared. The analogy with Plano points from the Plains is often based on something as questionable as point outlines rather than consideration of the constellation of point attributes that can be quite different. There are no compelling reasons to accept any form of direct relationship between the lanceolate projectile points of the Plains and those of northwestern North America. The latter points could very well have been derived from local prototypes that simply persisted through time because of their effectiveness in hunting herd animals like caribou. As has already been discussed, the appearance of the notched projectile point prior to Period III has been attributed to a population invasion and replacement of earlier people (Anderson 1970; Dumond 1978; Workman 1978). The new point style likely represents the continuing northward diffusion of the spearthrower weapon system (Morrison 1987: 65-66). As noted in other regions of Canada, invasion and replacement is often used to account for cultural change. This is a highly questionable explanatory device for most regions of North America. The dispersed food resources available to Middle Northwest Interior culture hunters and gatherers simply could not provide the food surplus necessary to support and maintain a major military operation bent on land acquisition. Environmental change favouring one cultural adaptation over another could result in the expansion of one group at the expense of another group but the cultures would have had to be neighbours and such environmental change was rarely persistent through time or geographically extensive in magnitude. Technological superiority could permit one hunting culture to replace another in regions of limited resources where the superior technology permitted a more efficient harvesting of resources. Possession of a superior weapon system would also have provided an advantage during competition for said resources. If it should eventually develop that an actual cultural replacement took place in parts of the northwestern interior at this time then it would likely relate to the advantages inherent in the spearthrower weapon system over the thrusting lance. Certainly the incursion of Early Palaeo-Eskimo culture into the northern territories of Middle Northwest Interior culture around 2,000 BC would have been aided by their possession of the bow and arrow.

Two central assumptions are made regarding the nature of the Middle Northwest Interior culture technology. First, the notched points represent the diffusion of the spearthrower from the south and, second, the microblade technology is of limited value in reconstructing local culture history. With reference to the latter assumption, microblade technology in Alaska disappeared at sites like Onion Portage around 4,000 BC but lasted until 2,000 BC in the northern interior and until AD 1000 in the subarctic interior of the state. Unlike most previous classification schemes the definition of Middle Northwest Interior culture technology is not dependant upon either microblades or notched projectile points but rather upon the evidence derived from a number of interrelated cultural systems. That said, there is evidence that the popularity of microblades wanes in some areas with the arrival of the notched points. It has been suggested (Richard E. Morlan: personal communication) that microblades, among other functions, were

BLACK AND WHITE PLATE XXI: MIDDLE NORTHWEST INTERIOR CULTURE PROJECTILE POINTS The photograph illustrates the wide variety of projectile point forms that can occur on sites of this culture. Most of the specimens are from sites in the Yukon. (Reproduced from Clark 1991: Plate 14. Photograph provided by Donald W. Clark.)

used as side blades in antler weapon tips and if the notched points do indeed herald the introduction of the spearthrower then some degree of technological replacement could be anticipated. The disappearance of burins or their reduced numbers could also be attributed to the adoption of the spearthrower as burins were likely used in the fashioning of the earlier bone and antler lances and producing the slots for receiving the microblade side blade inserts. Unfortunately the lack of bone preservation does not permit the testing of this possibility. The geographically and temporally variable appearances and disappearances of notched points and microblades makes these tool categories more useful as regional horizon markers rather than culture determinants per se. Expanding the definition of Middle Northwest Interior culture avoids some of the interpretational machinations of previous constructs such as explaining the late persistence of notched burins, microblades, gravers, and lanceolate projectile points in the Tanana Valley of Alaska by suggesting the area was bypassed during the hypothesized Northern Archaic invasion (Workman 1978: 425). Or, conversely, referring to the 600 BC to AD 1000 Minchumina tradition of central Alaska as an "...expanded Northern Archaic tradition" with three sequential phases "...linked by flake burins, microblade technology and lanceolate point forms..." (Holmes 1986: iii). Of interest is the association of lanceolate and notched projectile points, end and side scrapers, microblades, `large blades´, net sinkers, and biface knives at the Tuktu-Naiyak sites in northern Alaska (Campbell 1962; Gal 1982). It is possible that in certain regions of interior northwestern North America circumstances favoured the retention of the older weapon system, either by itself or in combination with the new spearthrower. Such a possibility could account for the highly variable geographic and temporal distribution of side-notched, lanceolate projectile points, microblades, and burins. It is important to appreciate that microblade technology, lanceolate points, and notched points, are simply elements of technological traditions that were adopted by a number of different cultures. They are not tool types in the sense of types that were manufactured by one cultural group for a limited time and were then abandoned (Bryan 1980: 77). In this sense most of the tool categories traditionally regarded as diagnostic in the northwestern interior are not truly `diagnostic´ although certain attribute clusters may constitute culturally distinctive `varieties´.

Paradoxically one of the best examples of a single component Middle Northwest Interior culture site is located on the southeastern-most margin of the culture's distribution near the Athapaska River in northeastern Alberta (LeBlanc and Ives 1986). The Bezya site, a small campsite situated on a small hillock surrounded by muskeg flats, produced a date of 2,500 BC. Cultural debris consisted of wedge-shaped microblade cores, microcore striking platform rejuvenation flakes, microblades, many with secondary edge and/or end modification, a notched transverse burin and burin spalls, side and random flake scrapers, chipping detritus including bifacial trimming flakes, and some other minor items. An exemplary description of the procedures involved in microblade production as well as the distinctions between northern microblade cores and those of the British Columbia Southern Plateau and the coast is provided (Ibid: 86). Temporal and spatial significance of microblade core morphology in northwestern North America and adjacent Asia, however, is still poorly understood (Clark 1992). The Bezya site stands in contrast to a typical Middle Northwest Interior culture site situated at the northeast end of Great Bear Lake. This site produced a microblade core rejuvenation flake, microblades, the tip from a bifacially chipped tool, a spoke-shave, and an abundance of flakes (Clark 1987: 172). The only basis for separating these materials from a subsequent Palaeo-Eskimo culture occupation was the presence of the microblade core rejuvenation flake. Such flakes consist of a tablet-shaped section struck transversely from the top of the microblade core in order to remove the original striking platform and thus change its angle permitting more efficient microblade removal. This distinctive core rejuvenation technique is believed to be characteristic of Middle Northwest Interior culture microblade technology and absent from Palaeo-Eskimo microblade technology. Where the distributions of these two cultures overlapped in the Great Bear Lake region and to the north, Palaeo-Eskimo technology is distinguished by "...many specialized small tools and a distinctive fine flaking style; the Northwest Microblade tradition has many large, rough implements of low characterization and an undistinguished flaking technique" (Clark 1981: 113). As most of the aforementioned materials came from small, surface-collected sites discrete components could not be isolated thus presenting the problem of component mixture. Indeed, the observation that "Notched and lanceolate points, notched burins, microblades, tabular and wedge-shaped microcores, and other traits often appear to be distributed in time and space essentially independent of one another" (Morrison 1984: 53) may be as much a product of the thin archaeological deposits with their small tool samples, poor archaeological contexts, and questionable radiocarbon dates contaminated by humic acids and forest fires, as any exceptionally capricious nature of the tool assemblage. Tool assemblage patterning over a broad area suggests otherwise as do assemblages from rare single component sites. It cannot be denied, however, that quite often sites simply cannot be culturally identified from the thin scatter of stone debris from undatable surface and veneer sites.

Despite the foregoing difficulties there is sufficient evidence distributed throughout the interior of the western Mackenzie District, the Yukon and adjacent Alaska, and northern Alberta and British Columbia to identify two sequential phases of Middle Northwest Interior culture. The early phase is characterized by lanceolate points, notched transverse burins, and less distinctive burinated flakes and bifaces, linear flakes generally called blades (e.g. Dixon 1985: Fig.4, h and i), wedge- and tabular-shaped microblade cores, certain `rough´ tools like hammerstones, chithos, abraders, spall choppers, net sinkers, biface knives, a range of scraper varieties, gravers, spoke-shaves, and some other minor items. The late phase is ushered in with the appearance of the notched points and the gradual but erratic disappearance of microblades. There also appears to an increase in biface knives and end scrapers. Lanceolate points continue to be present along side of the new notched forms as do a large number of the earlier stone tool varieties. The alternative to an in situ technological development is that earlier people and their technology were replaced by an intruding population. This view has been succinctly summarized as follows: "The one significant technological discontinuity in a minimum span of 7-8,000 years of prehistory occurred c.4500-5000 years ago when the early Taye Lake technology with its emphasis on notched, straight and concave base projectiles, a variety of heavy bifaces, endscrapers, and unifaces, lack of microblades and microcores, and sparse and rudimentary burins superseded the Little Arm technology which had been characterized by an emphasis on microblades, a variety of burins, round based projectile points, delicate flake gravers, and unifaces, a simple assortment of heavy thick endscrapers and lack of emphasis on most of the diagnostic characteristics of Taye Lake. The changes appear to have been far-reaching enough that one thinks in terms of movement of peoples rather than diffusion of ideas" (Workman 1978: 414). Despite the preceding, certain technological continuities between the Little Arm and Taye Lake phases are noted (Ibid: 416).

To test the proposed technological discontinuity in the southwest Yukon three components from

Workman's study are compared at the general artifact class level, two components pertaining to the Taye Lake phase or post-invasion technology as represented at the Gladstone site and level 4 of the Little Arm site and one component pertaining to the Little Arm phase or pre-invasion technology as represented by level 5 of the Little Arm site. The Gladstone site is regarded as very early Taye Lake phase and level 4 of the Little Arm site is the component directly above level 5 in the stratified Little Arm site. Both Taye Lake components should be relatively close in time to the preceding Little Arm component and the comparison could be expected to reflect any technological discontinuity. As a certain amount of cultural mixture from the Little Arm phase into the Taye Lake phase at the Little Arm site is suspected (Workman 1978: 398-400, 397) microblades and microblade core frequencies are listed on Table 6 but percentages are not calculated for these particular items. If the scenario favoured here is correct, namely that there was no mixture of earlier Little Arm phase materials in either level 4 of the Little Arm site or the Gladstone site and that the microblade technology was simply a waning element of the assemblage then Table 6 indicates continuity of microblade technology through time. Within this development microblades and burins decrease in frequency while biface knives and scrapers increase. Even when the microblades and microblade cores are removed from consideration the respective tool assemblages from the three components exhibit a relatively close relationship although the very small sample from level 4 of the Little Arms site limits this significance. Relationships reflected in the coefficient of similarity where a coefficient of 200 indicates identical compared units and 0 indicates totally different units (Brainerd 1951) are as follows: Little Arm, level 5 and Gladstone - 120.5; Little Arm, level 4 and Gladstone - 150.1; and Little Arm, level 5 and level 4 - 151.0. If the Little Arm, level 4 and Gladstone components do represent an intruding technology then in its general make-up that technology was strikingly similar to the technology it replaced even to the point of both technologies being dominated by two scraper varieties and sharing minor traits such as net sinkers and the retention of lanceolate points along with the introduced notched points. In many instances across North America the adoption of the spearthrower, as indicated by the appearance of notched projectile points, has been interpreted as a technological and, thus, cultural discontinuity (e.g. Early Archaic complexes, Early Plains culture, etc.). The validity of impressions of cultural discontinuity can only be evaluated by a detailed consideration of the total technologies on both sides of the hypothesized event and its impact upon the other systems of the culture such as subsistence and settlement patterns.

Applying the same descriptive units in Table 6 to the Pointed Mountain site near Fort Liard in southern Mackenzie District (MacNeish 1954), excluding microcores and microblades, the 181 specimens involved produced a high coefficient of similarity of 170.4 with the Gladstone site and a coefficient of 124.3 with the Little Arm, level 5 component. If two of the three radiocarbon dates from the Pointed Mountain site are correct in placing the site at 1,000 BC and the level 5 date of 1,500 BC from the Little Arm site is accurate the two occupations are close to each other in time. Within the local sequence in the Fisherman Lake region of Fort Liard cultural continuities are seen between the Pointed Mountain complex and the following Julian complex (Millar n.d.; 1981). Pointed Mountain has been equated with the Little Arm phase of the southwest Yukon while the Taye Lake phase of the Yukon has been equated with the Julian complex (Millar n.d.; Workman 1978). A restudy of the Julian complex, however, suggests that it

ARTIFACT CATEGORY	LITTLE ARM-5		LITTLE ARM-4		GLADSTONE	
	f	%	f	%	f	%
Projectile points	6	13.1	3	18.8	7	4.5
Biface knives	1	2.2	2	12.5	23	14.8
Burins	12	26.1	2	12.5	3	1.9
End scrapers	7	15.2	3	18.8	36	23.2
Side scrapers	15	32.6	6	37.5	73	47.1
Gravers	3	6.5	-	-	4	2.6
Chithos	-	-	-	-	1	0.7
Cobble spalls	-	-	-	-	2	1.3
Wedge	-	-	-	-	1	0.7
Heavy flaked tool	-	-	-	-	1	0.7
Hammerstones	1	2.2	-	-	1	0.7
Net sinkers	1	2.2	-	-	1	0.7
Ground stone	-	-	-	-	2	1.3
Microcores	11		5		5	
Microblades	405		63		21	
TOTALS	46	100.1	16	100.1	155	100.2

TABLE 6: MIDDLE NORTHWEST INTERIOR CULTURE ARTIFACT ASSEMBLAGES Frequencies and percentages of major tool categories from a Little Arm phase component and two early Taye Lake phase components exclusive of microblades and microcores whose frequencies are, however, presented. Data taken from Workman (1978: 396-404) with the following modifications: unclassifiable, utilized flakes, flake cores, and organic artifact categories excluded; 19 tools recovered from the Gladstone site in 1973 by Richard E. Morlan and 39 tools collected by Douglas Leechman have been added to Richard S. MacNeish's collection upon which William Workman's figures were based; and unifaces were classified as side scrapers and notched cobbles as net sinkers.

is predominantly the product of stone tool reduction processes in quarry site situations rather than being a distinctive cultural complex (Morrison 1984).

Further south in northern Alberta and British Columbia are the Bezya site (LeBlanc and Ives1986) and the Callison site (MacNeish 1960). The Bezya site has already been commented upon as one of the rare examples of a single component Middle Northwest Interior culture site. Wedge-shaped core and microblade technology at this site is regarded as part of a widespread and long-lived `technocomplex´ that crosscut regional and temporal complexes such as Palaeoarctic, Northwest Microblade, Campus-Denali, and Little Arm (Ibid: 88). The Bezya site assemblage compares most closely with the Pointed Mountain and Little Arm sites in the southern Mackenzie District and Yukon, respectively. Relationships are seen between the assemblage from the Callison site in northern British Columbia and the Taye Lake complex (MacNeish 1960: 3) where the "...development from Little Arm to Gladstone to Taye Lake seems to represent a sequence of the Northwest Interior Micro-blade Tradition" (Ibid: 48). In terms of percentages of tool categories the artifacts from the Callison site compare closely to those of both the Gladstone and Pointed Mountain sites with coefficients of similarity of 168.0 and 162.4, respectively, exclusive of microcores and microblades. The probability that the Callison site represents a single component is enhanced by its location on the edge of an extinct (now dry) lake.

A final group of probable Middle Northwest Interior culture sites to be considered are those in the Great Bear Lake region northeast to the Arctic coast. The Franklin Tanks site near the embouchure of the Great Bear River from the Lake (MacNeish 1955) has serious problems of assemblage integrity (Clark 1987). A better candidate for a single component Middle Northwest Interior culture site is the Lapointe site on the Coppermine River 15 km from its embouchure into Coronation Gulf on the coast of the Arctic Ocean (McGhee 1970). In a buried deposit rich in caribou bone and fire fractured cobbles the following items were recovered: collaterally flaked lanceolate points with straight and concave bases; large bifacial knives; blades and a blade core rejuvenation flake; an end scraper on a blade; a possible microblade of quartz crystal; bone awls; and a beaver incisor knife. Two radiocarbon dates span a range of 1,500 to 1,000 BC. Somewhat similar lanceolate points to those from the Lapointe site have been collected from the surface of sites at the east end of Great Slave Lake (MacNeish 1951: 38-39). Surface indications of Middle Northwest Interior culture occur from the Athabasca River area of northern Alberta through to the Coronation Gulf on the coast of the Arctic Ocean. Until more sites are excavated and dated, however, the nature of this eastward distribution will remain poorly understood (Clark 1987: 159-163).

There is little doubt that the general absence of bone preservation has restricted appreciation of the nature of Middle Northwest Interior culture technology. Certainly the perishable artifacts of wood, leather, and bark would have dominated the tool kit. While there is no direct evidence it is difficult to conceive how people could survive in northwestern North America without such essential aids as bark canoes, snowshoes, and snare and dead-fall traps. Heated cobbles used for either boiling water or as hearth stones do not appear to have been a significant element of Middle Northwest Interior culture technology (Losey et al. n.d.; MacNeish 1964; McGhee 1970).

Subsistence:

The people of Middle Northwest Interior culture could exploit an unusual range of habitats within the Boreal Forest, Lichen Woodland, and Tundra vegetation provinces. Subsistence strategies would have been accordingly variable as well as being dictated by the seasons. Given the relative sparse, widely distributed and erratic abundance of resources it is understandable that people had to be highly adaptable and sensitive to every advantage available within their hunting territories. With few exceptions the region in question is characterized by poor to non-existent bone preservation and, therefore, inferences on subsistence must be inferred from site locations. On this basis it would appear that caribou and fish was the most important combination of food animals. Local conditions could result in bison, moose, or mountain sheep being the major big game but it is difficult to understand how people could have survived throughout most the region without its reliable stocks of fish for winter storage and dog food and the relatively predictable caribou herds with their vitally important meat and hides. It can also be assumed that small game and waterfowl were routinely trapped. Prior to 1,500 BC the drier conditions of the Altithermal would have favoured grasslands thus making bison more available. The succeeding wet and cool conditions encouraged the spread of the spruce forest (Workman 1978: Fig.12, 62-63) and with it boreal forest species such as caribou. It was recognized early that subsistence was primarily keyed to the Boreal Forest vegetation province (MacNeish 1964: 381). At the time of European contact stored fish and the hunt were critical to winter survival and settlement pattern evidence suggests that this was a very old pattern. Indeed, the major concentrations of Middle Northwest Interior culture sites are situated adjacent to good fishing whether in the southwest Yukon (MacNeish 1964), the southern Mackenzie District (Millar n.d.), or the Great Bear Lake region (Clark 1987). As with other regions, archaeological visibility in northwestern North America is a problem. Historical documentation, for instance, has noted that the Mackenzie River was an important fishing river but most sites would have been flushed away by the spring floods and their associated ice scouring. It is also difficult to predict where caribou hunting sites, such as the Lapointe site on the Coppermine River (McGhee 1970), are likely to be situated given the range of considerations involved in the location of caribou pounds (Clark 1987: Chapter 7).

Unlike the majority of sites the Lapointe site had good bone preservation. The bulk of the remains were caribou although some evidence of waterfowl was present. A single beaver incisor tool would have been brought to the site from somewhere further south. Concentrations of caribou limb bone mash suggested the production of bone grease (McGhee 1970: 62) and the absence of foot bones indicates that fat-poor bones were not brought back to the camp. More typical in terms of bone preservation are the small calcined fragments from the Bezya site in northeastern Alberta among which only beaver could be identified (LeBlanc and Ives 1986). Although the bone preservation was poor, the burnt fish bones from the Callison site in northern British Columbia (MacNeish 1960: 4) did support the argument that the site was occupied at a time when the ancient lake once contained fish. The limited preservation from southwest Yukon sites does not provide a basis for drawing direct subsistence inferences. While MacNeish (1964: 289) speculated that the Middle Northwest Interior bands of the southwest Yukon dispersed in small, mobile groups during the winter and gathered together as macrobands near lakes in the summer there is no direct evidence of this in the faunal record. For example, the admittedly limited faunal record of bison, caribou, canis sp., moose, black bear, birds, and small mammals does not support the inference that the large base camps were essentially fishing camps. Despite this fact, the inference is likely correct that the aforementioned large sites functioned mainly as fish camps. Bone preservation at the base camps is simply too poor to be relied upon. Historically documented methods of processing fish for winter food and dog food also do not lend themselves to archaeological recovery.

Settlement patterns:

Moreso than with most cultures a full assessment of the settlement patterns of Middle Northwest Interior culture are probably beyond the capabilities of archaeology. The general lack of evidence of settlement along the Mackenzie River except at its delta, for example, appears to be a product of both spring erosion (Clark 1974; MacNeish 1953) and the nature of archaeological reconnaissance (Cinq-Mars 1973: 51) rather than an actual absence of people. Most sites are found inland on large lakes along either side of the Mackenzie River (Ibid: 45). Such sites reflect very sparse populations, particularly when compared to the situation further to the east (Noble 1971) where the Barrengrounds provided exceptional concentrations of caribou and fish. Middle Northwest Interior culture apparently did not exploit these Barrenground resources east of Great Bear and Great Slave lakes (Noble 1981). It does not appear that Middle Northwest Interior culture moved into the Great Bear Lake area until 2,000 BC (Clark 1987: 187). Local situations that permitted exceptional resource concentrations were the major factor leading to site concentrations (Clark 1974: 55). The Fisherman Lake region near Fort Liard represents one such location (Millar n.d.). Subsistence inferences based upon site locations in the Great Bear Lake are biased towards fishing due to survey that focused on the shoreline (Clark 1987). Only at the east end of the lake was there an apparent emphasis upon caribou as well as fish. In this respect, inland settlement patterns are essentially unknown. The extent of the hinterland, the difficulties of foot survey, and the sparse evidence left by small and highly mobile foraging groups will undoubtedly continue to frustrate a fuller understanding of this aspect of Middle Northwest Interior culture settlement pattern distributions. The bulk of archaeological evidence is and will probably continue to be derived from the large summer campsites situated along the shores of the major lakes and rivers. Throughout the interior of northwestern North America the summer to fall settlement patterns reflect the seasonal movements of small groups of people to favoured fishing locations. Such sites tend to be either stratified or otherwise possess evidence of multiple occupations representative of a considerable time span. This evidence, in turn, indicates a relatively stable adaptive pattern practiced over thousands of years. Even the adoption of a new weapon system like the spearthrower did not disrupt the aforementioned pattern of settlement. Fortunately for archaeology the predictable locations of fishing sites concentrated the otherwise small and dispersed hunting groups during the summer (MacNeish 1964: 228) and "...small hunting parties or family units..." appear "...to have congregated in the same favoured places over the years, centuries or millennia..." (Cinq-Mars 1974: 19-20). Large groups of people were also likely associated with winter caribou pounds but the variables involved in determining the locations of such sites have so far defied archaeological survey techniques. It will be necessary to discuss a range of important considerations with native caribou hunters and to make a concerted effort to replicate the topographic features recorded at historically documented caribou pounds (Clark 1987: Chapter 7). Such information could then be used, in conjunction with known caribou behaviour, in an

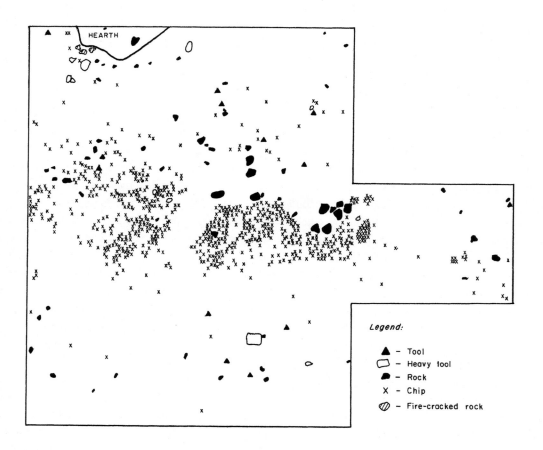

FIGURE 49: MIDDLE NORTHWEST INTERIOR CULTURE SITE FLOOR PLAN This archaeological floorplan from the Gladstone site excavations in the southwest Yukon provides some impression of the difficulty of interpreting the typically limited settlement pattern evidence left by small, transitory groups of people. The floorplan is exceptional for its richness of debris and the presence of a distinct feature. Exclusive of the extension to the right, the excavated block is 4 m x 4 m. (Adapted from Morlan 1974: Fig.3. Drawing by Mr. David W. Laverie.)

attempt to locate pre-European pound sites. Given the undoubtedly subtle variables involved in the decision of where to locate pounds by people with an intimate knowledge of caribou behaviour and a sensitivity to factors that alter said behaviour there is still a `needle in the haystack´ element involved in the search for such sites.

Site types other than camps at favoured fishing locations are lookout sites situated on islands and elevated ridges (Clark 1987: 171; Irving and Cinq-Mars 1974), single occupation caribou hunt camps, and quarry/workshop sites situated at or near a source of desirable stone for tool manufacture (Gotthardt 1990). With reference to the latter site type, one of the largest concentrations is along the lakes close to the welded tuff deposits in the Tertiary Hills 90 km south of Fort Norman in the Mackenzie Valley (Cinq-Mars 1973: Appendix E). This distinctive fused or indurated volcanic ash material with its obsidian-like qualities has been recovered in the form of tools and flakes from sites throughout most of the western District of Mackenzie into Alaska and from the tree-line in the northern Yukon to the Liard River in the south. The major period of use was from 3,000 BC to AD 1. A less widely distributed material, the Barn Mountain chert of northern Old Crow Flats in the northwestern Yukon, has been recovered from the Whirl Lake site some 385 km to the southeast (Gordon and Savage 1973; Gotthardt 1990).

Probably the most common type of site but the most difficult to locate by archaeological survey methods are the small, late fall, winter, and early spring camps (LeBlanc and Ives 1986: 85) composed of refuse left by one or two families. The Bezya site in northeastern Alberta is one such site discovered as part of a major cultural resource management programme associated with the development of the Athapaskan tar sands. Situated on one of the numerous small hillocks surrounded by muskeg, cultural debris was concentrated in a 4 m diameter area. Scattered charcoal flecks, heat fractured chert, and calcined bone fragments suggest the former existence of a hearth. Given the muskeg setting the site must have been occupied when the ground was frozen suggesting that the concentration of debris likely represent the remains of a dwelling. While such a site locale would have been attractive to herbivores like moose it is located 10 km from the Athapaska River and even further from good fishing sites. A diversity of lithic materials was used including the nearby Beaver Creek Sandstone (Fenton and Ives 1982) suggesting that these Middle Northwest Interior culture hunters were familiar with the local geological resources. In addition to the Bezya site other Middle Northwest Interior sites have produced tentative evidence of dwellings. At the Airport site on Colville Lake northwest of Great Bear Lake a 3 m by 4 m concentration of artifacts may demarcate the outline of a structure (Clark 1974). More convincing evidence is the probable lean-to structure from the Otter Falls site in the southwest Yukon (Figure 50). Another possible candidate for a lean-to structure in the same region was uncovered at the Gladstone site (Morlan 1974: Fig.3). This summer occupation involved concentrations of chipping debris and bone fragments that were sharply demarcated on their northern edge by a line of possible weight stones. A hearth was also situated to one side of a possible dwelling and may have been associated (Ibid: Figs. 1 and 2).

Cosmology:

Nil

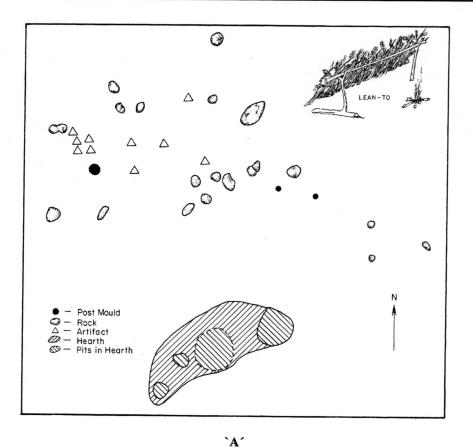

LEAN-TO

● — Post Mould
🖾 — Rock
△ — Artifact
🖾 — Hearth
🖾 — Pits in Hearth

N

`A´

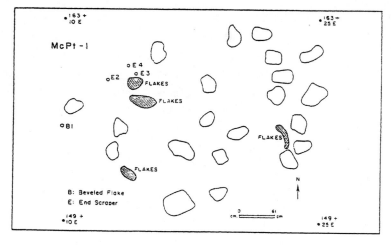

McPt - 1

•163 +
10 E

•163 +
25 E

○ E 4
○ E 3
○ E2
FLAKES

FLAKES

○ B1

FLAKES

FLAKES

N

B: Beveled Flake
E: End Scraper

0   61
cm.   cm

149 +
•10 E

149 +
•25 E

`B´

FIGURE 50:   MIDDLE NORTHWEST INTERIOR CULTURE DWELLINGS Illustration `A´ is an archaeological floorplan from the 3,500 BC Otter Falls site in the southwest Yukon that shows the distribution of cultural debris in relationship to a hearth-pit feature. The distribution of materials is believed to have once represented a flimsy lean-to shelter with associated hearth as reconstructed in the upper right hand corner. (Adapted from Workman 1979: Fig.61. Drawing by Mr. David W. Laverie.)

Illustration `B´ represents a tent floor discovered at a site on Great Bear Lake that may be 3,000 years old. Rocks would have been used to weigh down the outer edge of the tent covering and are shown along with concentrations of chipping detritus. (Reproduced from Clark 1991: Plate 28)

External relationships:

Over 50 years ago certain interior northwestern North American lanceolate projectile points were thought to be the prototypes of similar `Plano culture´ points on the Plains (Hibben 1943: 254-259). MacNeish (1956: 74) turned the direction of this hypothesized relationship around by arguing for a south to north movement. He saw the formation of the Northwest Microblade tradition as an amalgam of an Asiatic-derived microblade technology and southern-derived notched points grafted onto an earlier southern-derived Plano culture assemblage (MacNeish 1964: Fig.84a). The association of some lanceolate point styles in northwestern North America with point styles of Plano culture of the Plains is still a firmly ingrained operating hypothesis. It is used to explain the origins of the northwestern interior lanceolate points and some other traits (Millar 1981: 269) despite temporal and geographical discontinuities as well as major attribute differences between the northwestern interior lanceolate points and those on the Plains. Cautions against relating Plano culture points found 3,200 km away to northwestern interior lanceolate points (Giddings 1963; Irving 1971: 74-75) have, more often than not, gone unheeded. It has even been suggested that the Middle Northwest Interior people (Northwest Microblade tradition) replaced northern Plano people in the southwest Yukon and the western District of Mackenzie around 4,000 BC (Millar 1981: 282). As commented upon in the section on **technology** the temporal and spatial disjunctions between the lanceolate points of the Plains and those of the northwestern interior, as well as the attribute differences between the two groups of points, all suggest that the two styles are unrelated. A more parsimonious explanation for the origin of the northern lanceolates is that they derive from earlier Palaeo-Indian culture occupants of the areas just as Plano culture point styles were derived from the same cultural base in the Plains. The presence of caribou in the north may have encouraged the retention of the earlier weapon system long after it was abandoned on the Plains in favour of the spearthrower. Other relationships with the Plains would appear to be more valid than the foregoing Plano culture association. These pertain to the diffusion of the notched points of Early and Middle Plains culture to the northwestern Interior of North America and the geographical overlap of Middle Northwest Interior culture with Middle Plains culture in northern Alberta. The appearance of notched projectile points in Alaska, the Yukon, and presumably the western District of Mackenzie in the Northwest Territories, is interpreted as the introduction of the spearthrower technology into northwestern North America from the Plains. On the assumption that notched stone projectile points represent the appearance of a spearthrower weapon system that eventually replaced an earlier spear-lance weapon system throughout most of North America the following sequence of diffusion can be proposed. Invented around 8,000 BC in what is now the southeastern United States the spearthrower diffused first to the north and then northwest into what is now Canada. Northwestern North America was one of the last regions to receive the technology. Notched projectile points appear on the Plains around 6,000 BC and reach Alaska near the end of Period II. In his formulation of the Northwest Microblade tradition MacNeish (1954) interpreted the notched points as a diffused element of technology from the Plains.

The overlap of the cultural distributions of Middle Northwest Interior culture and Middle Plains culture in northern Alberta and British Columbia as well as southern Yukon and western Mackenzie District is represented by a veneer of characteristic implements. These consist of the Oxbow point type in the north (MacNeish 1964, Millar n.d.; Noble 1971; 1981) and a correspondingly thin distribution of microblades into Alberta and British Columbia. In addition to a bonafide Middle Northwest Interior culture site like Bezya, microblades occur in a relatively unbroken distribution from the north to southwestern Alberta (LeBlanc and Ives 1986: 85-86). On the basis of stylistic characteristics this evidence of microblade technology is thought to relate to northwestern North America rather than the southern Plateau of British Columbia (Ibid: 89). At a more speculative level it can be suggested that Middle Plains culture and Middle Northwest Interior culture overlapped in the Lake Athabasca area of northern Alberta and Saskatchewan. Side-notched points similar to the Oxbow type are present (Wright 1975: Plate XII, 29) as are probable Northwest Interior culture tools such as a scraper-graver on a blade, the fluted face off a large microblade core, gravers, and what many would call blades (Ibid: Plate VII, 17, 8, 12, and 6 and 7, respectively).

On the northern margins of the distribution of Middle Northwest Interior culture there is evidence of contemporaneity and geographic overlap with Early Palaeo-Eskimo culture (Arctic Small Tool tradition) beginning around 2,000 BC. Early Palaeo-Eskimo culture spread into former Middle Northwest Interior culture territory such as the Great Bear Lake region and northern Yukon (Clark 1987: 1) and south and east of the Mackenzie River (LeBlanc 1991; Pilon 1991). A similar cultural replacement occurred in northern Alaska (McGhee 1988: 373). The likelihood that Early Palaeo-Eskimo culture introduced the bow and arrow weapon system to the Western Hemisphere at this time would have given them an advantage over the indigenous Middle Northwest Interior culture people whose territories they occupied. Despite the apparent contemporaneity and geographical overlap of these two cultures there is no evidence of direct contact (Clark 1991: 102).

Middle Shield culture side-notched points have been identified in the Great Bear Lake region (Clark 1987: 107). While contact between Middle Northwest Interior culture and Middle Shield culture is not inconceivable there is a very large area of archaeologically `terra incognito´ territory between the known distributions of the two cultures with Middle Shield culture being currently confined to Keewatin District of the Northwest Territories (Gordon 1976; Wright 1972). There is a possibility that the resemblance of some western side-notched points to those of Middle Shield culture is fortuitous. Certainly there is no evidence of a significant Middle Shield culture occupation bordering the territory of Middle Northwest Interior culture. Unfortunately the finger-printing of exotic stone materials indicative of contacts between different cultures during Period III is exceptionally limited for the region under consideration.

Human biology:

Nil

Inferences on society:

Throughout Period III Middle Northwest Interior culture people appear to have followed a way of life essentially the same as that of the Athapascan-speaking people of the region at the time of European contact (see Kehoe 1981: 489-492 for a synopsis of this lifeway). Like historically documented practices, numerous deadfall and snare traps for both big and small game animals would have been set in a wide arc around base camps. Settlement pattern evidence suggests the summer gathering of families composing one or two bands at favoured fishing locations. At such times marriages and partnerships, including the establishment of trading partners with neighbouring bands, would be negotiated. Given the small numbers of people involved in these bands intermarriages with neighbouring bands must have existed. In addition to the large summer fish camp gatherings it is possible that the winter could also have been a time of significant socializing around a successful caribou pound. Otherwise, dispersal in small family groups across the hunting territory would be required. Presumably winter residence by large groups of people at a caribou pound would have been the preferred option and dispersal of the band into family groups only occurred when the pounds were unproductive. In summary, these subarctic foragers composed of small, mobile groups of people, responded in a finely balanced manner to what their territories offered and as these offerings were frequently unpredictable and erratic their adaptation was both flexible and opportunistic.

Limitations in the evidence:

A number of factors have combined to severely complicate insights into Middle Northwest Interior culture. These factors are as follows: the prevalence of thin, surface sites representative of many transitory camps; the highly generalized nature of most of the surviving tool kit; poor archaeological contexts of cultural debris including datable materials; humic acid and forest fire contamination of the carbon samples relied upon for dating; poor to non-existent bone preservation; and generally poor archaeological visibility.

With reference to the last limitation there are a number of formidable and, in some instances, irretrievable circumstances that either destroyed or buried the archaeological record. The problems of the erosion and the burying of sites along the major rivers, such as the Mackenzie, have long been recognized (Cinq-Mars 1973a; 1974). Loess and volcanic ash falls have also hidden sites from surface detection. At least the volcanic ash has provided excellent datable horizon markers. In some regions the dispersal of people into extensive muskeg areas during the winter would defy site location except under the most unusual of circumstances. Compounding the aforementioned factors is the frequent heavy forest cover and permafrost conditions where "...it is difficult to locate archaeological sites, and especially buried deposits, in the permanently frozen terrain of the boreal forest or along the soliflucting slopes of the tundra" (Cinq-Mars 1974: 18). Even at the large summer fish camps, with their multiple occupations and relatively abundant cultural debris, archaeological samples are pitifully small. For example, only three sites in the western District of Mackenzie have produced more than 100 artifacts and these sites are all in the Fisherman Lake area of Fort Liard (Morrison 1984: 29). Fisherman Lake has been justly described as "...an oasis in an archaeological desert..." (Ibid: 29). There is also the problem of "...having to read too much from collections that are not very specific, are too small, too mixed, and too often undated..." (Clark 1975: 95). Former cultural constructs, such as British Mountain (MacNeish 1959), which was once thought to be early because of the crudity of the chipped stone technology now appear to represent stone tool manufacturing sites utilized by a number of different cultural groups. In this particular instance a major problem was the lack of clear archaeological context and, thus, the cultural integrity of the collections (Greer 1991).

In addition to the bias inherent in the fact that most archaeological work in the northwestern interior correlates with areas characterized by relative ease of access (Cinq-Mars 1973: 11) there are serious taxonomic problems. The latter problem has been recognized for a long time and has been described as "...a rash of taxonomic measles" (DeLaguna 1962: 169) and "...slipshod typology" (Irving 1971: 74). The concept of a Northern Archaic invasion associated with the appearance of notched points and the purported disappearance of microblades has, indeed, been a `Pandora's box´ (Irving 1971: 75). Fortunately there is an increasing awareness that the culture history of the region is unlikely to be understood by relying solely upon formal tools for analysis. As astutely noted "...much of the uncertainty surrounding present interpretations of the culture-historic sequence in the interior Northwest may relate to a failure to recognize the limits of conventional typology in dealing with expedient or informal technology"(Gotthardt 1990: i).

EARLY PALAEO-ESKIMO CULTURE

Précis:

The origins of Early Palaeo-Eskimo culture were rooted in the Neolithic cultures of northeastern Siberia (Dumond 1984; Irving 1968a; McGhee 1978). Originally the term `Palaeo-Eskimo´ was coined to distinguish a hypothesized early musk-ox hunting culture from the baleen whale hunting culture of the ancestors of the present day Inuit (Steensby 1917). The use of the term to refer to a microlithic technology that spread eastward from Alaska was formulated by Lewis J. Giddings (1951; 1956) and William N. Irving (1953). Whether this culture developed its unique adaptation to the Arctic environment in Siberia or Alaska is a matter of some debate (see McGhee 1978 and 1987a for a consideration of the various origin hypotheses). Early Palaeo-Eskimos were the first people to be able to cope with the environmental constraints of Arctic North America. These constraints included severe cold, a paucity of plant foods, limited seasonal availability of most food animals, limited number of prey species, and scarcity of fuel and raw materials (McGhee 1974: 831-832). Early Palaeo-Eskimos also appear to have been the first people to effectively exploit sea mammals on the open sea ice. A number of regional varieties or subcultures of Early Palaeo-Eskimo culture were originally subsumed under the term `Arctic Small Tool tradition´ (Irving 1968a) but it has recently been agreed to change this name to the shorter and generically implicit term `Palaeoeskimo´ (Maxwell 1976). The name has been hyphenated here in order to be consistent with the spelling of Palaeo-Indian. Paradoxically there is some basis for scepticism regarding a direct generic association of Palaeo-Eskimo culture with the historically documented Inuit of northern Alaska, Arctic Canada, and Greenland (McGhee 1978). The original assumption of an association was premised upon similar ways of life and a perceived cultural continuity extending from the initial appearance of Palaeo-Eskimo culture at about 2,500 BC to the Inuit-speaking peoples of northern Alaska (Anderson 1984). If Early Palaeo-Eskimo culture does represent a late migration from Siberia to Alaska then there are the problems of how it relates to the archaeological record of the Yuit-speaking people of southern and southwestern Alaska and the eastern Siberian coast or to the Aleut-speakers of the Aleutian Islands. Did, for example, Early Palaeo-Eskimo people speak a northeastern Siberian Chukotan language (McGhee 1978: Chapter 2)? The nature of the evidence permits a number of possible views regarding Palaeo-Eskimo and Inuit relationships. A late 3,000 to 2,500 BC migration from Siberia to Alaska and, thence, to the east is favoured in this chapter. The term Palaeo-<u>Eskimo</u> is retained rather than Palaeo-<u>Inuit</u> as the relationship to the Yuit-speaking people of southern Alaska is unclear and even the evidence of cultural continuity to the Inuit-speaking people to the north is compromised by a discontinuity represented by the Old Bering Sea complex.

The rapid spread of Early Palaeo-Eskimo culture throughout the Arctic can be attributed to their ability to exploit lands beyond seasonal commuting ranges of forest dependent Indian cultures. Despite the current absence of a Siberian Bering coast ancestral archaeological culture from which to derive Early Palaeo-Eskimo culture, a western origin is favoured given the absence of potential ancestral cultures in Alaska as well as the sudden appearance of Early Palaeo-Eskimo culture over large areas of both previously unoccupied and marginally occupied lands. In the latter instance, there is a sharp cultural discontinuity with earlier occupations suggesting population replacement rather than cultural change resulting from technological diffusion. Relative to the possible language(s) spoken by Early Palaeo-Eskimo peoples it is noted that some of their direct descendants, the Tunit or Dorset, were Inuit-speakers according to the oral traditions of present day Inuit-speakers in the Canadian Arctic (Rasmussen 1931: 113-114).

The sudden appearance and rapid dispersal of Early Palaeo-Eskimo culture "...provides not only the beginning of the prehistory of most of the American Arctic but also one of its major integrating devices: the first indication of interest in and ability to colonize the High Arctic, that interest so basic to the popular conception of the nature of later Eskimos" (Dumond 1984: 74). Certainly the most unique characteristic of Early Palaeo-Eskimo culture was the ability to maintain viable populations on the vast tundras and the frozen Arctic coastlines of the far north. A flexible economy, based upon the exploitation of land and marine resources and an exceptional technology, permitted these people to be the first to flourish far north of the forest border in regions potentially habitable as early as 5,000 BC (McGhee 1975: 55). Within the archaeological record of the Western Hemisphere the spread of Early Palaeo-Eskimo culture from northern Alaska across Arctic Canada into northern Greenland to form a configuration resembling an asymmetric triangle nearly 5,000 km east by west and 3,000 km north by south was only exceeded by the spread of Palaeo-Indian culture thousands of years earlier. There are parallels with the earlier migration. Early Palaeo-Eskimo technology is strikingly similar from Alaska to Greenland suggesting that the colonizing of new lands was not only a rapid process but that an unusual degree of cultural cohesion and conservatism was maintained through both time and space over vast territories. Like Palaeo-Indian culture, the movement of Early Palaeo-Eskimo peoples was into previously unoccupied territories except along the southern fringes of their territory where they either replaced or reoccupied former `Indian´ territory. It can be assumed that game animals unfamiliar with human predators would initially fall easy victims to the newcomers thus favouring an accelerated spread of people.

Throughout such an enormous and physiographically diversified region as the Arctic an exceptional degree of mobility must have been maintained in order to retain the cultural systems. Cultural homogeneity would have been encouraged by a social organization based upon small bands with very flexible rules of cross membership. Such a system would best meet the marital and social requirements of individual bands and result in a number of interrelated bands. An expansive kinship based collection of bands would then have acted as a social network within which rights and obligations would provide a degree of social security to all the component parts. Undoubtedly the vagaries of Arctic resource availability would assure the maintenance of both physical and social mobility within a broad social network. Many of the factors apparently responsible for the extraordinary degree of cultural homogeneity of the Early Palaeo-Eskimos also pertained to the culture of their Middle Shield culture neighbours to the south (Chapter 16). An exceptional degree of mobility, demanded by the dispersed nature of the animal resources, is reflected in the settlement patterns. In addition to a flexible band affiliation being available to families and individuals, inter-band female residency patterns and other reciprocal insurance devices, such as inter-band trading partners, would have acted as the glue to hold together a geographically extensive social system. In this respect, the constraints faced by the hunting cultures of the treeless Arctic and the forests, while different in degree, would have been similar in kind in that both regions demanded an exceptional degree of mobility and social flexibility supported by a very broad consanguinal and/or fictive kinship network. While such a social network would have accommodated the diffusion of western Arctic traits to the east, such as ground slate tools and stone lamps, local requirements could change the form of the introduced technology thus masking the evidence of diffusion. Insufficient recognition of the role of stimulus diffusion, the diffusion of the knowledge of a technology rather than the direct physical transfer and replication of a technological item or complex, has probably led to the questionable assumption that Arctic cultures represent `closed systems´ (Maxwell 1980: 163).

There is controversial evidence that at least two initial migrations were involved in the occupation of the Canadian Arctic and Greenland. Both migrations would have taken place during the warmer climatic conditions and expanded open water that prevailed between 2,500 and 1,500 BC (McGhee 1978; Nichols 1968; 1972). Apparently spreading across the High Arctic, the first migration by a subculture referred to as Independence I (Knuth 1952) has not been identified in Alaska and has been radiocarbon dated earlier in the east than Palaeo-Eskimo sites in the west. Presumably the earliest sites in Alaska are yet to be discovered. This migration between 2,500 and 2,000 BC may have been followed by a second population movement across the Lower Arctic several centuries later that is assigned to the Pre-Dorset subculture. Pre-Dorset exhibits more specific similarities with the contemporaneous Denbigh subculture of northern Alaska than was the case with Independence I. Subsequent to these initial colonizing movements, populations related to the Independence I subculture appear to have shifted southward down the east coast of Baffin Island and thence to the northern Labrador coast (Cox 1978; Fitzhugh 1976a; Tuck 1975) and as far as the Island of Newfoundland (Tuck n.d.). Similarly, around 1,500 BC some Pre-Dorset people from the Coronation Gulf region of the Arctic Coast moved into the interior in conjunction with a deterioration in the climate and took up residence on the Barrengrounds (Clark 1987; Gordon 1975; Noble 1971). Some of their camps even penetrated as far south as the northshore of Lake Athabasca in Saskatchewan (Wright 1975) and well into northern Manitoba (Irving 1968). These people abandoned the Barrengrounds sometime after 1,000 BC. About the same time as Early Palaeo-Eskimos were moving into the Barrengrounds an apparently small population of coastal oriented Pre-Dorset people spread down both sides of Hudson Bay (Nash 1969; Taylor 1962).

By the end of Period III a number of changes take place in Early Palaeo-Eskimo culture and initiate the Period IV Middle Palaeo-Eskimo culture referred to as Dorset. The most significant of these changes are believed to be the construction of igloos and the establishment of winter sealing villages on the sea ice. Stone oil lamps or possible archaeologically invisible equivalents would have been a necessary element of technology for heating, cooking, and lighting in igloos since open hearths cannot be used in enclosed snow houses. Such lamps, very rare in late Early Palaeo-Eskimo culture, become common after 1,000 BC. What are regarded as special knives for cutting snow blocks for igloo construction also appear. There is indirect evidence, however, that winter sealing villages on the sea ice may have been in existence during Period III.

With few exceptions, the preservation of organic remains in Early Palaeo-Eskimo sites is poor to non-existent. This situation stands in marked contrast to subsequent occupations where increasing perma-frost development assured the preservation of not only bone but other organic materials such as wood. As a consequence, the study of Early Palaeo-Eskimo technology must rely upon the stone tool inventory, a technology dominated by a distinctive class of burins and their resharpening spalls. To judge from use-polish studies of the burins (Gordon 1975; Maxwell 1985) they functioned as a type of draw knife for working hard materials such as ivory and bone. The spalls produced in the process of ˋre-sharpening´ the cutting edge of the burin by removing a single flake may have been used as perforators. Microblades punched from specially prepared cores were another common tool. These major items along with lesser numbers of bipointed and triangular point tips for both arrows and harpoon heads, and gravers are found from the Pacific Ocean across the Arctic to the Atlantic Ocean (Maxwell 1985: Fig.3.4). When bone implements do survive small needles with minute drilled thread holes are generally present. Much rarer are harpoons, initially non-toggling types followed by toggling varieties.

Direct evidence of subsistence is limited. Even when preserved the cultural significance of the refuse bone is questionable, particularly in the High Arctic, given the practices of burning bones as fuel and storing foods acquired in the fall for consumption during the winter. The burning of bones biases the faunal sample in favour of small game remains which were inappropriate as fuel and the storage of seasonal foods confounds efforts to determine seasonality. Early Palaeo-Eskimo culture has generally been described as having a subsistence economy involving the exploitation of both sea and land mammals but the variable nature of the enormous territory involved assured that economies were regionally variable. In some regions, for example, the annual hunting focus could be on caribou and muskox or, in other circumstances, seals. Of all the cultural systems settlement patterns provide the most trustworthy basis for judging subsistence practices rather than the limited faunal remains. Site locations across the territory of Early Palaeo-Eskimo culture indicate that adaptations could be either diffuse or focused depending upon local circumstances. The majority of site locations, however, suggest a balanced seasonal exploitation of both marine and land animals involving open-water seal hunting in the summer, a fall caribou hunt in the interior likely in conjunction with the harvest of char returning to the inland lakes from the ocean, and winter sealing on the sea ice. As indicated, there would be many variations on the aforementioned seasonal subsistence rounds such as the Independence I focus on musk-ox hunting in the northeastern High Arctic. Another deviation from the seasonal sea-land subsistence rounds was the interior adapted caribou hunters and fishermen of the Barrengrounds of Keewatin District although it is not entirely clear whether this interior adaptation was permanent rather than being an annual seasonal event.

There is little evidence to permit inferences on the cosmological beliefs of the Early Palaeo-Eskimo people. A few fragmentary bone maskettes from very late sites in the Igloolik area (Maxwell 1985) hint at some form of shamanistic beliefs. This function is partially inferred from the rich two and three dimensional art of Middle Palaeoeskimo culture during Period IV. A striking maskette from the High Arctic appears to represent a tattooed individual although the symbolism of the design is unknown (Helmer 1986). As with most hunting groups, the Early Palaeo-Eskimos likely believed that all objects and elements had spirit forces. These forces were generally indifferent to humans, who were also an integral part of the system, but could, depending upon either inappropriate or appropriate behaviour on the part of individuals, elicit bad or good responses. Individuals with special powers to manipulate these dangerous spirits were the shamans.

With the exception of western Arctic cultural contacts via diffusion and the mobility of individuals and families, Early Palaeo-Eskimo culture appears to have had relatively little contact with its neighbours. Neighbours in Canada were Middle Northwest Interior culture of the western Subarctic, Middle Shield culture from southern Keewatin District across the Boreal Forest to the central Labrador coast, and Middle Maritime culture along the Labrador coast. As Early Palaeo-Eskimo culture spread into the northern margins of its neighbours it can be assumed that, despite some southward contraction of the latter cultures due to a deteriorating climate, the intruders were regarded as enemies. There is some evidence of direct contact between Early Palaeo-Eskimo and Middle Maritime cultures along the northern Labrador coast in the form of alien diagnostic tools being recovered from the sites of both cultures. More significant is the evidence of technological exchange involving the addition of toggling harpoons to Early Palaeo-Eskimo technology that resemble Middle Maritime culture forms and the appearance of thin, symmetrical side-notched projectile points, believed to be arrowheads, on late Middle Shield culture sites. Such projectile point forms have prototypes in Early Palaeo-Eskimo culture sites. Thus, there appears to have been an exchange of hunting technology, toggling harpoons from Middle Maritime culture and the bow and arrow technology from Early Palaeo-Eskimo culture (Tuck 1976a).

A newborn or premature child recovered from a dwelling floor at the Rocky Point site on Devon Island (Helmer and Kennedy 1986) represents the only skeletal remains in existence that can be definitely attributed to Early Palaeo-Eskimo culture. Given the age of the individual, nothing can be said regarding biological affinities. Both limited preservation of bone during Period III and the possibility that the remains of the deceased were destroyed by exposure to the elements, reduce the chances that samples that could shed light on racial affinities will ever be recovered. With reference to Middle Palaeo-Eskimo culture (Dorset) of Period IV, however, it would appear to "...be safe to predict that the skeletal remains of these cultures will show the Arctic Mongoloid morphological pattern" (Oschinsky 1964: 32).

Despite the exceptional surface exposure of sites, especially in the High Arctic, there are severe limitations in the nature of the evidence on Early Palaeo-Eskimo culture. Limitations include reconnaissance that is often restricted to current population and transportation centres, poor archaeological visibility of the meagre archaeological remains left by highly mobile hunters, soil conditions that destroy all organic material, isostatic rebound isolating early sites from regions of recent human activity, erosion and ice push along rivers, permafrost conditions that destroy or mix stratigraphic deposits, and the build up of peat deposits in the lower and western Arctic which has buried the earliest archaeological remains. Partly compensating for these drawbacks are both the readily recognizable nature of Early Palaeo-Eskimo stone tool technology and its preferential use of high quality and often brightly coloured cherts.

Cultural origins and descendants:

        Early Palaeo-Eskimo culture developed in Siberia from an Eastern Siberian Neolithic cultural base (Giddings and Anderson 1986; Irving 1968a; Mochanov 1969) and may have migrated from Asia to northwestern North America as early as 3,000 BC (Dumond 1968; Irving 1968a). It has been assumed that the Early Palaeo-Eskimos were Eskimo-speakers and the "...ancestors of Eskimos" (Dumond 1984: 75). Early Palaeo-Eskimo culture in Alaska and the northern Yukon is represented by a subculture called the Denbigh Flint complex or simply Denbigh. Cultural continuity extends from Denbigh to Choris to Norton to Ipiutak with a cultural or technological discontinuity appearing within the sequence leading to Birnirk (Anderson 1984: 86). Developments from Birnirk led to the Inuit-speaking people that were encountered by Europeans. The foregoing generally accepted cultural origin and language association poses certain problems such as the nature of the cultural relationship of Early Palaeo-Eskimo culture to the cultures in southern Alaska and Siberia that gave rise to the historic Yuit speakers of the Eskimo language or the relationship to the linguistically more distant Aleut (McGhee 1988: 374). Given the nature of the evidence there are a number of possible scenarios for the origins of the Early Palaeo-Eskimos. These range from an indigenous development in the interior of Alaska out of a cultural base that had it origins in an earlier 8,000 BC Siberian migration to a direct Asiatic migration to Alaska around 3,000 BC (McGhee 1978: Chapter 2; 1987a). The latter hypothesis is most probable for a number of reasons. First, Early Palaeo-Eskimo culture appears suddenly, at approximately the same time, over a territory extending from Alaska to Greenland. Second, while a direct ancestral cultural base for Early Palaeo-Eskimo culture (Irving 1962: 68; MacNeish 1964: 381) is not currently recognized on either the Siberian or Alaskan sides of the Bering Strait (Nash 1969: 144) the extent of archaeological reconnaissance on the Siberian side has been limited. Third, given the land and sea adaptation of Early Palaeo-Eskimo culture it is difficult to understand how it could have originated solely in the Alaskan interior. And, fourth, although Early Palaeo-Eskimo culture spread mainly into unoccupied territories, along its southern margins in both Alaska and Canada it occupied territories formerly exploited by `Indian´ cultures. There is a sharp cultural discontinuity with these earlier cultures (Middle Northwest Interior culture, Middle Shield culture, and Middle Maritime culture) suggesting cultural replacement rather than some form of cultural transformation due to a rapidly diffusing technology. It should be noted that the aforementioned `Indian´ cultures, in at least some instances, likely contracted somewhat from their northern ranges in response to the climatic deterioration of 1,500 BC. Early Palaeo-Eskimo possession of the bow and arrow would have provided a decided combat advantage over the spearthrower and lance of their neighbours should conflict situations arise.

The occupation of northern Alaska, the Canadian Arctic, and Greenland coincided with a warm period and more open water conditions than prevail today. On the basis of slightly differing technologies and house structures and occupations of different beach elevations above sea level two sequential migrations by subcultures of Early Palaeo-Eskimo have been identified in the eastern Arctic (McGhee 1976: 37). The first migration was by Independence I people across the High Arctic into northern Greenland. A series of radiocarbon dates from sites of these first settlers are as early as 2,300 BC. A second migration by the Pre-Dorset subculture through the Lower Arctic appears to have taken place slightly later although the radiocarbon evidence is equivocal. There has been an increasing tendency to lump the Independence I designation under the Pre-Dorset subculture in recognition of the relatively slight differences between the two.

Attempting to establish a sound radiocarbon chronology in the Arctic has been plagued by a number of problems. First, the marine carbon reservoir is different than the atmospheric carbon reservoir in that the erratic welling-up of old carbon in the northern oceans becomes incorporated in the marine biosystem. As a result radiocarbon dated marine mammal organics (bone, fat, and tissue) give older dates than contemporary land mammal bones or plants. It has been suggested that all radiocarbon dates on marine organic matter be discarded (McGhee and Tuck 1976). Second, Siberian drift wood that was used as fuel in the eastern High Arctic can be quite old before being reduced to charcoal and thereby give older than expected dates. This leaves only the Arctic willow and bone dates on land animals to establish a chronology and even here the use of antler for dating presents problems. Unfortunately Arctic willow charcoal or even land mammal bones are not always available on Arctic sites. Although the exclusion of questionable dating materials, such as marine mammal remains, drift wood, and antler, markedly reduces the number of dates in the Arctic it does remove much of the chronological confusion. Given the relative scarcity of stratified sites and the tendency for debris representative of thousands of years of human occupation to occur mixed together, radiocarbon dating in conjunction with isostatically elevated marine strandlines have been heavily relied upon to establish the Arctic chronology. One of the bizarre by-products of the problems with radiocarbon dating archaeological materials in the Arctic is that the earliest radiocarbon dates occur in the northeastern High Arctic rather than in the assumed parental hearth in Alaska. In other words, the radiocarbon cline is the reverse of the proposed migration route from west to east. The problem has also been exacerbated by the paucity of Early Palaeo-Eskimo sites in the western Canadian Arctic (Arnold 1983: 14) although this situation is in the process of being addressed (LeBlanc 1991; Pilon 1991). The early eastern radiocarbon dates for Early Palaeo-Eskimo culture sites have led to the speculation that Early Palaeo-Eskimo culture may have entered northern Greenland and adjacent Canada from the east via an Arctic Ocean sea ice route. This route could have extended from the mouth of the Lena River to Severnaya Zelya and the archipelago of small islands leading to Svalbard and thence across the northern end of the Greenland Sea to northern Greenland (McGhee 1983: 22-23). The 500 km gap between Svalbard and Greenland, with its strong currents and pack ice, would have presented a serious obstacle to foot travellers (Maxwell 1983: 85). Most archaeologists, including McGhee who appears to have been playing the Devil's advocate with his eastern origin hypothesis, anticipate that Early Palaeo-Eskimo ancestral sites will eventually be discovered in Alaska.

A number of dated sites along the northern Labrador coast (Cox 1978; Fitzhugh 1976a; Tuck 1975) are the same age as Independence I sites in northern Ellesmere Island and northern Greenland. Both the technology and the form of dwellings at these Labrador sites and one site on the Island of Newfoundland (Tuck n.d.) more closely resemble the Independence I Early Palaeo-Eskimo subculture pattern than the Pre-Dorset subculture. This may suggest that the initial spread of Independence I was not restricted to the High Arctic but also involved portions of the Low Arctic. There is some evidence of Independence I between the High Arctic and the northern Labrador coast (Maxwell 1985). A significant presence may have been masked by the heavier southern vegetative cover, the isostatic submergence of much of the east coast of Baffin Island, and the fact that both Independence I and Pre-Dorset share so many elements of technology and other cultural traits.

It has been proposed that after the colonization of the Low Arctic elements of the Pre-Dorset subculture shifted back to the west to occupy the Coronation Gulf region of the Central Arctic (Maxwell 1985). The evidence, however, is sufficiently equivocal (Taylor 1964; 1967) that rather than a reoccupation by eastern pioneers it is probable that the area had been continuously occupied. The erroneously early radiocarbon dates on marine mammal remains have been the primary evidence for the hypothesized reoccupation from the east. It was from the Coronation Gulf region, however, that a major Early Palaeo-Eskimo movement into the interior Barrenlands was launched (Gordon 1975; Irving 1968; Noble 1971) that spread as far south as the Lake Athabasca region (Minni 1976; Wright 1975). Around 1,500 BC other Pre-Dorset bands spread down both sides of Hudson Bay (Nash 1969; Taylor 1962).

Despite controversy over the details there is agreement that Middle Palaeo-Eskimo culture developed in situ from Early Palaeo-Eskimo culture. The regional Middle Palaeo-Eskimo subcultures are referred to as Dorset, or the Dorset-like Independence II of the High Arctic (McGhee 1976), and the Groswater Dorset of Labrador (Fitzhugh 1976) and appear around 1,000 BC (Collins 1956; Maxwell 1985; Taylor 1968). This opinion was initially opposed on the grounds that the new traits appearing in Dorset represented Indian influences from the south (Meldgaard 1960: 591-593). While the transformation from Early Palaeo-Eskimo culture to Middle Palaeo-Eskimo culture has been regarded as largely a product of stylistic change (Taylor 1968; Maxwell 1985) it did correlate with a period of increasingly cold climate. The northernmost occupations of Independence I may have been terminated by both game depletion and a deteriorating climate that resulted in the permanent freezing of open water fiords (Fitzhugh 1984: Fig.15). The core area of Middle Palaeo-Eskimo culture (Dorset) development in Period IV was in the Hudson Strait, Foxe Basin, and northern Baffin Island region. Transition from Early to Middle Palaeo-Eskimo culture appears to have involved a large number of bands responding to the climatic deterioration and its impact upon both the environment and society. Dorset people are believed to have spread out from a core area (Fitzhugh 1976: 147) with an adaptation more suitable to the changing environmental circumstances

(Schlederman 1978: 55). Certainly the transition from Early Palaeo-Eskimo to Middle Palaeo-Eskimo culture in the long sequence of cultural development recorded in the Igloolik area of north Baffin Island indicates significant changes in the technology. These included the appearance of polished chert burins, ground slate knives and points, an increase in the use of microblades, the appearance of sled shoes, toy sleds, ice creepers that were attached to foot wear, and snow knives and the apparent abandonment of the bow and arrow and the bow drill (Meldgaard 1980: 169). The sudden technological changes in the Igloolik sequence are at variance with the technological continuities between Early and Middle Palaeo-Eskimo cultures noted in the Lake Harbour area in southern Baffin Island (Maxwell 1985). In the latter instance, however, component mixture posed a serious problem that could mask sudden changes and create an erroneous impression of gradual technological continuity. The pattern of technological change recorded in Igloolik is also supported by the sudden technological break between Early and Middle Palaeo-Eskimo cultures on the Labrador coast (Cox 1978; Fitzhugh 1972). Significant and rapid technological change not only correlates with a period of climatic change but also with equivalent dramatic technological change in northern Alaska. Here, Asiatic pottery, oil lamps, polished slate tools, and new house forms appear within the Choris-Norton portion of the Alaskan sequence as well as evidence of an increasing maritime adaptation in Norton (Maxwell 1980: 174). An important element in the changes resulting in the Dorset subculture of Period IV could have been the transfer of new technologies from Alaska, such as the introduction of stone oil lamps that would assist existence in igloos and, in turn, make winter settlement on the sea ice possible. The probability of the introduction of the igloo is also supported by the appearance of what are believed to be specialized snow knives, an implement documented ethnographically to be used for cutting the snow blocks needed for igloo construction. A chronic difficulty that archaeologists have encountered is trying to identify the winter portion of Early Palaeo-Eskimo settlement patterns. If winter sealing on the sea ice including villages on the sea ice were already in place and not introduced by Middle Palaeo-Eskimo culture it would explain the hiatus in the settlement pattern evidence..

As noted, radiocarbon dating in the Arctic is plagued by a host of problems and yet the radiocarbon chronology has been key to interpretations relating to the culture history of Early Palaeo-Eskimo culture and its relationship to the subsequent Middle Palaeo-Eskimo culture. Calendrical dates drawn from calibrated date ranges for Early Palaeo-Eskimo culture sites are as follows: mainland coastal Northwest Territories - 1,700 to 1,000 BC (McGhee 1975; Pilon 1991; Wilmeth 1978); the Barrengrounds of the Northwest Territories - 1,500 to 1,000 BC (McGhee and Tuck 1976; Wilmeth 1978); the High Arctic archipelago - 2,700 to 2,250 BC (Helmer and Kennedy 1986; Wilmeth 1978); Labrador coast - 2,500 to 1,700 BC (Cox 1978; Wilmeth 1978); and northern Greenland - 2,500 to 1,500 BC (Maxwell 1985; McGhee and Tuck 1976). Specifics concerning the dated sites and the details of the individual date can be obtained from the preceding references and the calendrical calibration ranges from the conversion tables in Klein et al. (1982). All dates on sea mammal organic material, driftwood, and antler are excluded due to a range of factors that cause spurious dates (see McGhee and Tuck 1976; Olsson 1972). A correction formula for sea mammal dates (Arundale 1981) has been rejected on the grounds that there are simply too many uncontrolled factors involved in its formulation (McGhee 1987). It is also cautioned that while Arctic willow charcoal dates are accepted the slow rates of decomposition in the Arctic, as well as the possibility of firewood being obtained from permafrost deposits, could produce earlier dates than the associated archaeological materials. Finally, two dates from the Migod and Migod Island sites on the Dubawnt River in the Barrengrounds (Gordon 1976: 92) are rejected on the grounds of contamination and lack of diagnostic culture context, respectively.

Technology:

Lack of preservation of organic materials over most of the territory occupied by Early Palaeo-Eskimo culture means information on the technology relates mainly to stone tools. The stone tool kit is exceptionally distinctive and readily separable from that of contemporary neighbouring cultures. Implements are not only small but the fine controlled flaking used to fashion them (Gordon 1975: 199) is typical of the chipped stone artifacts from the Pacific to the Atlantic. There was a clear preference to manufacture tools from high quality and often colourful cherts thus adding an aesthetic dimension to the stone tool assemblage (Colour Plate XIV).

Across the Arctic Early Palaeo-Eskimo sites contain burins, microblades, gravers, bipointed and triangular projectile points, the former assumed to be arrowheads and the latter the tips of harpoons, and end scrapers (Maxwell 1985: Fig.3.4). Side blades, inset as the cutting edges of bone or wooden harpoons, lances, and probably arrows, are common as are distinctive concave and straight edged hafted side scrapers. Less common traits are chipped adzes with grinding usually restricted to the bit and ground `burin-like grooving tools´ (Dumond 1984: 74). The most distinctive and common tools are burins and the burin spalls resulting from resharpening the burins, the latter possibly being used as perforating and etching tools. Use-polish studies of burins (Gordon 1975; Maxwell 1985) indicate that they functioned as draw knives used in working hard materials like ivory and bone. Wear is most often observed along the burinated edge rather than the tip (Gordon 1975: 199). In this respect, burins appear to have only been used secondarily for engraving and slotting (Ibid: 231). Microblades have an erratic occurrence. They were struck from small, wedge-shaped cores and increase in popularity toward the end of Period III.

The rare instances where organic materials have survived provide evidence of a sophisticated bone tool technology. Most abundant are delicate bone needles with blunted bases and minute drilled needle eyes for reception of sinew thread. Such implements undoubtedly reflect the importance of tailored skin clothing. The earliest harpoons are non-toggling barbed forms with a pointed base intended to fit into a wooden spear socket. These forms were rapidly replaced by toggling harpoons (Figure 53) that were probably adopted from the Middle Maritime culture hunters of the Labrador coast (Tuck 1976a).

The most economic way of providing an impression of the Early Palaeo-Eskimo culture stone tool kit is presented in Table 7. General artifact category frequencies from the Central and High Arctic, the Barrengrounds, and the Labrador coast are listed. The sites are ordered chronologically rather than geographically and are represented by the following: the East component, (northern locus) on Rose Island in Saglek Bay, northern Labrador (Tuck 1975); Feature 1 of the Gull Cliff site in Port Refuge on Devon

COLOUR PLATE XIV: EARLY PALAEO-ESKIMO TOOLS Like Palaeo-Indian culture thousands of years earlier Early Palaeo-Eskimo tool makers selected brightly coloured cherts for the manufacture of their tools, presumably for aesthetic and, possibly, symbolic reasons. Their tiny chipped stone implements (the dime provides scale) consisted of arrowheads and harpoon tips (upper row), burins (centre), a variety of scraping tools (upper right corner), and microblades that would have been hafted into wooden and bone handles of composite tools (lower right corner). (Picture provided by Robert Mc Ghee, Canadian Museum of Civilization, Hull, Québec.)

Island in the High Arctic (McGhee 1979); the Bloody Falls site where the Coppermine River empties into the Coronation Gulf of the Central Arctic (McGhee 1970); the single feature at the Duc site on the upper Thelon River in the Barrengrounds of the eastern District of Mackenzie (Gordon 1975); and two dwellings from the Seahorse Gully site on the coast of Hudson Bay at Churchill, Manitoba (Meyer 1977). With reference to chronology and context the following information is pertinent: the East component refers to the 2,250 BC stratum situated stratigraphically between Middle Maritime and Middle Palaeo-Eskimo culture occupations; the Gull Cliff site, Feature 1 pertains to a probable living floor and is estimated to date to 1,500 BC (McGhee 1979); the Bloody Falls component represents a single dwelling floor with hearth dated to 1,500 BC; the artifacts from the Duc site came from around a single large hearth and are estimated

FIGURE 51:   EARLY PALAEO-ESKIMO TOGGLING HARPOONS   The two harpoons date to 2,000 BC. Early Palaeo-Eskimo culture probably obtained the toggling harpoon technology from Middle Maritime culture people along the Labrador coast. (Approximately actual size. Drawings by Mr. David W. Laverie.)

to date to 1,250 BC; houses 2 and 5 of the Seahorse Gully site are dated to 1,000 BC on stylistic grounds and both houses are included to illustrate the frequency variability between two contemporary or near contemporary components. The East, Gull Cliff, and Seahorse Gully components represent sea mammal (seal) hunting stations in contrast to the caribou hunt camps represented by the Bloody Falls site and Duc site components. The sites on Table 7 were among the best available in terms of single component reliability, sample size, and dating while, at the same time, being representative of a wide geographical area. It is obvious that a limited number of artifacts are involved. Small samples recovered from all too often questionable archaeological contexts, however, are a fact of life in Arctic archaeology. Only burins, burin spalls, projectiles, and hafted scrapers were represented in all six components. Given the erratic occurrence of most of the tool categories it is not surprising that archaeologists have focused upon the stylistic attributes of certain tool categories to establish temporal and spatial relationships rather than attempting qualitative and quantitative manipulations of total tool kits. Despite the geographic distribution of the components, the time span of more than 1,000 years, and the mix of sea mammal and land mammal hunting stations, the major characteristics of the tool kits are surprisingly similar and certainly quite distinct from that of their southern neighbours. It is apparent, however, that the two subcultures of Independence I (East) and Pre-Dorset (Gull Cliff) in the eastern Arctic exhibit a degree of variability that appears to be absent in Alaska where the Denbigh subculture is seen as a relatively homogeneous cultural expression (Dumond 1984: 75; Giddings and Anderson 1986: 295-300). It should be noted, however, that 750 years separate the aforementioned components. Curiously, the emphasis upon caribou and muskox hunting in the Central Arctic and the Barrengrounds relative to the emphasis upon sealing in the High Arctic and Hudson Bay does not appear to have had much of an impact upon the nature of the chipped stone tool kit. This raises questions regarding Maxwell's (1976a) proposal that the tool kit of any particular site reflects its seasonal activities.

Independence I is characterized by stemmed, bipointed, and lanceolate arrowheads, triangular harpoon tips and stemmed lances, all frequently possessing very fine edge serration. Also common are flake burins, sometimes serrated, and burin spall tools although it has been cautioned with reference to the latter that some of the retouch is actually a product of the detaching blow (McGhee 1979: 44). Other tools are microblades, hafted concave side scrapers, bifacially chipped side blades for insetting into the sides of harpoons and possibly arrows, stemmed and lanceolate knives, stone adzes, spurred end scrapers, drills, retouched flakes, chipped and ground gravers, unilaterally barbed bone darts, delicate bone needles with drilled thread holes, bone chisels and non-toggling, self-armed or tipped harpoons with offset line holes and pointed bases intended for fitting into a socketed lance shaft. This particular variety of harpoon resembles early Asiatic and north Pacific forms (Fitzhugh 1984; Knuth 1967; Maxwell 1985; McGhee 1976; 1979). A number of Independence I chipped stone tools also tend to be large and relatively crude in appearance. Some Early Palaeo-Eskimo culture traits, such as facial grinding of chipped stone arrowheads, stone lamps, and bone lanceheads, appear to be absent from Independence I.

The Pre-Dorset subculture of Early Palaeo-Eskimo culture is characterized by a different form of stemmed point as well as small lanceolate arrowheads and triangular points that are believed to tip toggling harpoons. Other tools are bifacially flaked and ground burins and worked burin spalls, microblades, hafted concave side scrapers, bifacially flaked side blade insets for lances, harpoons, and possibly arrows, symmetrical and asymmetrical stemmed and side-notched knives, chipped and ground stone adzes, end scrapers, drills, retouched flakes, rare oval or round soapstone lamps, ground slate knives, bone and ivory awls and needles with drilled thread holes, bone points and flakers, open socketed toggling harpoons, scrapers made from bear and seal skull parts, needle cases, some with geometric designs, animal carvings and human maskettes that appear late in Period III, and rare native copper items, such as barbs and knives, in the Central Arctic and the Barrengrounds (Maxwell 1984; McGhee 1976; Taylor 1967). Large biface and uniface stone tools of quartzite, quartz and slate also occur in the Central Arctic and the Barrengrounds (Gordon 1975; Taylor 1968: 13-14) but, as a rule, still exhibit the fine flaking pattern typical of Early Palaeo-Eskimo culture. Pre-Dorset is seen as differing from Independence I in possessing smaller microblades, different kinds of projectile points, ovate side blades, distinctive end scrapers, more frequent side scrapers and asymmetric knives, rare circular or ovate soapstone lamps, toggling harpoons, fish spear prongs, bone arrowheads, flaking tools, and more concentrated settlements of circular to ovate dwellings lacking stone passage ways (McGhee 1975).

Although the chronological evidence is equivocal there is a basis for suggesting that the

Artifact category	East		G. Cliff		B. Falls		Duc		S.G. 5		S.G. 2	
	f	%	f	%	f	%	f	%	f	%	f	%
Burin	4	5.3	13	10.6	30	17.9	11	7.4	18	24.7	10	29.4
Burin spalls	6	8.0	45	36.6	84	50.0	45	30.2	40	54.8	12	35.3
Microblades	34	45.3	36	29.3	15	8.9	2	1.3	---	---	---	---
Projectiles	8	10.7	4	3.3	6	3.6	5	3.4	5	6.9	1	2.9
Knives	14	18.7	1	0.8	4	2.4	26	17.4	4	5.5	---	---
H. scraper	1	1.3	1	0.8	2	1.2	?	---	3	4.1	2	5.9
End scraper	2	2.7	---	---	5	3.0	19	12.8	1	1.4	---	---
Side scraper	2	2.7	---	---	6	3.6	?	---	---	---	1	2.9
Flake scraper	2	2.7	13	10.6	---	---	31	20.8	---	---	---	---
Side blade	---	---	2	1.6	12	7.2	9	6.0	2	2.7	1	2.9
Graver	1	1.3	---	---	---	---	---	---	---	---	1	2.9
Drill	1	1.3	2	1.6	---	---	---	---	---	---	---	---
Adze	---	---	---	---	1	0.6	---	---	---	---	---	---
Rough stone	---	---	---	---	---	---	---	---	---	---	5	14.7
Stone lamp	---	---	---	---	---	---	---	---	---	---	1	2.9
Bone needles	NP	---	5	4.1	---	---	NP	---	PP	---	PP	---
Harpoon head	NP	---	1	0.8	---	---	NP	---	PP	---	PP	---
Copper pin	---	---	---	---	3	1.8	---	---	---	---	---	---
Copper ulu	---	---	---	---	---	---	1	0.7	---	---	---	---
Totals	75	100.0	123	100.1	168	100.2	149	100.0	73	100.1	34	99.8

TABLE 7: FREQUENCIES OF ARTIFACT CATEGORIES FROM SIX EARLY PALAEO-ESKIMO CULTURE SITES. Note: knives refer to bifacially flaked tools that are believed to have functioned as cutting implements; scrapers from the Duc site were not subdivided into varieties other than to note that most were end scrapers thus the entire frequency of scrapers at the site was placed in this category while question marks used in the other scraper varieties indicates a possible presence; the graver

from the East site is ground rather than simply chipped; and the rough stone tools from House 2 of the Seahorse Gully site refers to the unique, large chipped adzes, picks, and other rough chopping/cutting tools characteristic of this site; NP = no bone preservation and PP = poor bone preservation; and the hafted scraper category includes hafted scrapers with concave, straight or convex scraping faces.

Independence I and Pre-Dorset subcultures of Early Palaeo-Eskimo culture represent different migrations out of Alaska. Independence I appears to be earlier than either Pre-Dorset or Denbigh but has not been found or recognized in Alaska (McGhee 1975). The distributions of Independence I and Pre-Dorset overlap in areas of the High Arctic, such as Devon Island. A scattering of characteristic Independence I artifacts and house styles have been noted from southern Baffin Island, Mansel Island, Pelly Bay and along the Labrador coast (Maxwell 1985; McGhee 1975: 57; Tuck n.d.) that may indicate an initial occupation of these regions before the carriers of the Pre-Dorset subculture appeared. As the two subcultures shared a majority of technological traits stylistic separation of mixed deposits is often not possible. This probably explains why Independence I sites are frequently referred to as Pre-Dorset (Fitzhugh 1976a) or sites are regarded as a blend of Independence I and Pre-Dorset traits (Bielawski 1982). It has been recommended that the term `Independence I´ be discarded and sites so assigned be placed under the Pre-Dorset designation (Schlederman 1978). The opinion that the temporal and stylistic differences between Independence I and Pre-Dorset are simply too minor to justify separation appears to be gaining an increasing number of adherents (Patricia Sutherland, Canadian Museum of Civilization: personal communication). On the basis of the current evidence, however, a separation into two closely related subcultures still has some utility relative to the culture history of Early Palaeo-Eskimo culture in the eastern Arctic.

Archaeologists are aware of the fact that attempts to trace stylistic change within a technological tradition must take into consideration the constant hazard of component mixture. Not as well recognized is the role of stylistic variability as a product of individual behaviour patterns. Based upon recoveries from individual dwellings and other features at Port Refuge it was found that artifact variability was partially a product of individual manufacturing abilities or attitudes (McGhee 1979: 107). The fact that variability in burin form, for example, reflected the products of specific individuals was reinforced by their associations with right or left handed burins. This discovery led to the rather draconian suggestion that "If the hypothesis ascribing a great deal of stylistic variability in individual ability and preference is correct, typological comparisons of Canadian ASTt stone tool assemblages may be of relatively little use in judging the relationships between components" (McGhee 1980: 443). The evidence upon which this hypothesis is premised, however, lacks convincing temporal controls. It also does not take into account the possibility of multiple knappers in a single dwelling or the eccentric contributions of novice knappers learning the art of stone knapping. Flawed raw materials could also contribute to tool variability. The inability to relate living floors to one another on the basis of burin stylistic attributes could suggest that the site represented a single large occupation rather than a sequential series of temporally distinct living floors and, as such, temporal stylistic randomness has not been demonstrated. What appears to have been demonstrated is that individuals made their own tools rather than specialists and that the average for current populations of 5 to 20 percent left-handedness also applied to Early Palaeo-Eskimo stone tool manufacturers (McGhee 1980: 450).

A totally different approach that attempted to demonstrate regional burin stylistic patterns was similarly flawed because of the nature of the evidence. In this study it was argued that a number of geographically distinct tool kits existed in Early Palaeo-Eskimo sites on the Barrengrounds. The regional tool kits and, specifically, burin styles were seen to correlate with the distributions of the four major caribou herds and were used to support a hypothesis advocating a one to one association of discrete hunting bands of Early Palaeo-Eskimos with discrete caribou herds (the Bluenose, Bathurst, Beverly, and Kaminuriak herds) (Gordon 1975: 295). The major problem with this hypothesis is that only the Beverly herd area has produced sites adequate to test the hypothesis and, thus, the hypothesis has not been demonstrated.

There appears to be agreement that Early Palaeo-Eskimo culture brought the bow and arrow technology with them from Asia. The recovery of tiny projectile points, bone foreshafts, and antler bow braces (Maxwell 1984: 361; Melgaard 1962) not only indicate that this technology was present but that it closely resembled ethnographically documented Inuit bow and arrow technology with its composite, recurved bow construction, bone or antler arrow foreshafts, and blunted, `stunning´ tips. Also included in the weapon system were open-socketed antler lances with stone end and side blades and likely the spearthrower as suggested by the recovery of bone spearthrower hooks (Taylor 1967: Fig.11, g, 228). Reminiscent of later Inuit technology is the antler wound pin from the Menez site on Victoria Island (Ibid: Fig.6, 2). Such pins were used to stop the flow of blood from a slain animal as animal blood soup was an important component of the diet.

The issue of whether Early Palaeo-Eskimo culture possessed watercraft and a capability to hunt sea mammals on the open sea has elicited much speculation. It has been suggested that a lack of maritime hunting technology is the major distinction between Palaeo-Eskimo and the later Inuit cultures (Arnold 1983: 14). This view has been challenged on the grounds of settlement pattern distributions and the evidence of boat parts from Middle Palaeo-Eskimo culture sites (Dorset) (Maxwell 1983). During Erik the Red's exploration of Greenland in AD 982-984 it was mentioned that "They found, both in the eastern and western districts, human settlements with fragments of boats..." (Knuth 1967: 1) and since this reference must pertain to the Late Palaeo-Eskimo culture peoples (Dorset) (McGhee 1978: 26) it could be inferred that their ancestors (Early and Middle Palaeo-Eskimo) also possessed watercraft. This said, it is acknowledged that along the south coast of Devon Island in the High Arctic the close association of Early Palaeo-Eskimo sites with areas that would have had continuous ice in contrast to Inuit site locations in the same general region, may be an indication of the former's less efficient open water hunting capabilities (Sutherland 1991: 141). It is difficult to conceive how Early Palaeo-Eskimo hunters could have survived in most parts of the Arctic without some ability to travel on water and to exploit maritime resources in the water. As with interior Subarctic populations, mobility and adaptability were the keys to survival in the Arctic (Morris 1973: 15) and an inability to effectively exploit maritime resources would likely have been a fatal constraint.

Although there is no evidence of dog team harness technology in Early Palaeo-Eskimo culture there is evidence of the presence of dogs (Harp 1978: 117; Knuth 1967: 32; Meldgaard 1962). Dogs were probably used in a range of hunting functions such as locating seal breathing holes on the sea ice and holding a bear at bay while the hunter manoeuvred into position with his spear. Probably dogs were also used for carrying bundles and, in times of dire need, food.

An element of technology that is often ignored in archaeological reports is the use of heated stones to cook food. Such `hearth stones´ were abundant at the Pre-Dorset Arnapik site (Taylor 1968: 13-14) and in the dwelling hearths of Independence I sites (Knuth 1967). It has been speculated that the vertical stone slab hearth boxes of Independence I dwellings supported skin containers whose liquid contents were cooked with stones heated in the hearth (Harp 1978: 117). Despite the fact that direct evidence of the burning of seal oil in stone lamps for heat, light, and cooking does not appear until near the end of Period III it is possible that lamps made of perishable material, such as hide, could have been used but have left no archaeological trace. It is extremely difficult to envisage how any people could survive the Arctic winter without such an essential element of technology. In the High Arctic, for example, a quarter of the year must be spent in complete darkness and extreme cold.

While the tool kit of Early Palaeo-Eskimo culture is characterized by an essential sameness throughout the Arctic there is at least one major exception to this generalization. The exception is the large chopping and cutting implements classified as gouges, picks, adzes and scraper planes found in some of the Early Palaeo-Eskimo dwellings of the Seahorse Gully site at the mouth of the Churchill River in Manitoba (Meyer 1977). The suggestion that such large flaked implements were adopted from neighbouring Indians (Nash 1969: 110) is not born out by the stone tool technology of the contemporary Middle Shield culture. Such crude implements, roughly flaked from local pyroclastic stone and sometimes possessing bit edge grinding, more likely represent local convenience tools fashioned to take advantage of drift wood coming down the Churchill River.

There is a final note to make regarding Early Palaeo-Eskimo technology. If one is permitted to insert psychological considerations into the discussion then Early Palaeo-Eskimo technology has to be classified as a product of an anal rather than oral culture. The rigid conservatism and conformity that characterize the technology is striking when compared to the stone technologies of all other technological traditions in Canada. It is as if an adult instructor observed every move of the novice stone knapper in order to make certain that the student was doing things in the appropriate "Palaeo-Eskimo-way". One way or the other, there was little tolerance for innovation or deviation. Some individual variability in the production of stone tools, of course, did exist (McGhee 1979) but it appears to have been far more constrained than was the case in the stone working technologies of other stone age cultures.

Subsistence:

Throughout much of the Arctic direct evidence of subsistence in the form of food bones from Early Palaeo-Eskimo sites is rare. In addition, the practice of using large bones as fuel (Schlederman 1978: 48) not only destroyed much of the faunal evidence but also has created the impression that the surviving small mammal and bird remains were more important in the diet than was likely to have been the case. There is the further problem with "...the ethnographically-known propensity of northern peoples to bring home only certain bones, and to store food from season to season or even from year to year" (McGhee 1982: 74). Given these circumstances, site locations are probably a more reliable indicator of subsistence practices than the actual surviving bone although both lines of evidence must be used to reconstruct the subsistence system. In the eastern Arctic from 2,000 to 1,000 BC climatic change trended from warm to cold (Barry et.al. 1977; Maxwell 1985: 46, Fig.3.5). The major cultural changes occurring after 1,000 BC, however, appear to have been mainly the result of technological innovation rather than any significant adjustment of subsistence strategies to a cooling climate.

There are proposals that Early Palaeo-Eskimos were predominantly caribou hunters who supplemented their diet with sea mammals (MacNeish 1959) or were musk-ox hunters (Knuth 1967). Such observations are only pertinent to certain regions. Both the survival requirement of adaptability and its prerequisite mobility and the fact that Early Palaeo-Eskimo culture occupied littoral, open tundra, taiga, and closed boreal forest environments with all of their ecological variations assured that these opportunistic hunters would take full advantage of whatever their hunting territories had to offer. In this respect the subsistence rounds appear to have been remarkably similar to those of the historically documented Inuit. Barring the effects of isostatic and eustatic elevation and submergence of shorelines, Early Palaeo-Eskimo sites were often reoccupied by the ancestors of the present day Inuit. This not only suggests similarities in the subsistence but is also indicative of the finite numbers of rich resource locales in the Arctic.

In the Barrengrounds caribou were undoubtedly the primary prey although fish and musk-ox would also have been important. Due to poor bone preservation there is simply too limited direct evidence to accept the proposal that fish were relatively unimportant (Gordon 1988: 11). It is difficult to conceive that Early Palaeo-Eskimos would ignore the abundance of fat-rich lake trout in the swifts and rapids of the major caribou river crossings. Seasonal berries, such as mountain cranberry, blueberry, crowberry, and cloudberry, rich in vitamins including the all-important Vitamin C, would undoubtedly have been harvested. Lichens were also available as an emergency food (Morris 1972). When bone does survive on Barrengrounds sites, generally in a calcined or charred state, it is almost invariably caribou (Gordon 1975: 150) and likely reflects the use of large mammal bones as fuel. The two main methods of acquiring large numbers of caribou in the Barrengrounds would have been by interception at water-crossing points on rivers and lakes and by the construction of pounds wherein snares were set to entangle and hold the caribou. While interception points are relatively simple for archaeologists to identify, pounds with their complex array of topographical requirements, frequent winter setting, weather, snow, and browse condition determinants, and intimate knowledge of local caribou herd behaviour, present a series of interrelated variables beyond the present skills of archaeologists to determine any patterns useful in locating such sites (Clark 1987). Early Palaeo-Eskimo occupation of the Barrengrounds mimics that of the preceding Middle Shield culture and is maintained by the subsequent Late Northwest Interior culture. Such a repetitive settlement pattern reflects the importance of caribou and fish to all of these cultures. Historically documented practices of caribou hunters in the Barrengrounds are likely pertinent to Early Palaeo-Eskimo culture. Most important of these practices would be the late summer and fall hunt that produced the best hides and the fattest animals. It has been calculated that 50 caribou were required to meet the needs of each person for a single year (Kelsall 1968: 207-208) with 8 to 11 skins per person for clothing and 20 to 30 skins for tent coverings (Morris 1972: 12). There would have been times when much meat was wasted. In the spring and early summer, for example, caribou flesh is very lean and of limited nutritional value and the hides are virtually useless due to warble fly perforations (Ibid: 11). The fat-rich caribou tongue and marrow nevertheless would have been highly prized by fat-deprived people who had just survived a long winter.

Subsistence patterns in the Barrengrounds are somewhat of an anomaly for Early Palaeo-Eskimo culture. A far more typical pattern was a balanced exploitation of both land and marine mammals along with fish and supplementary resources such as small mammals, birds, and eggs. In addition to the Barrengrounds, there are at least four other regions which were somewhat distinctive from one another in terms of subsistence opportunities. These are the Central Arctic, northern Greenland and the High Arctic Islands, the Foxe Basin-Hudson Strait region and immediately adjacent areas such as coastal Hudson Bay, and the Labrador coast, probably including the east coast of Baffin Island. Each of these regions possess different topographical and environmental features that affected such important factors as ice conditions, currents and tidal amplitudes, and plant diversity. All regions were subjected to events that influenced animal numbers and availability such as forest and tundra fires, snow characteristics and depth, icing of winter browse or wet, cold weather during the critical caribou calving period, and sea-ice shifts. The limited capacity of most of the Arctic environments to support large numbers of big game animals, particularly land based species, would have led to regions being periodically `hunted-out´. It is probable that large blocks of land were temporally abandoned to permit game numbers to recover. Mobility would have been the answer of the Early Palaeo-Eskimos to the limited animal carrying capacity of much of the Arctic. Of the preceding regions, southern Baffin Island, the Hudson Strait region, and the Labrador coast possessed the richest sea mammal resources (Maxwell 1985: 16, Fig.2.9).

Faunal remains, on occasion, can reflect a particular seasonal hunting pattern. In the Central Arctic where, contrary to the rule, bone preservation tends to be good, a site such as Umingmak on northern Banks Island was dominated by musk-ox remains while the Buchanan site on adjacent Victoria Island produced predominantly caribou. On the Firth River, near the Yukon coast, the Engigstciak site contained bison, caribou, elk, mountain goat and seal remains (MacNeish 1956) although the actual association of

FIGURE 52: EARLY PALAEO-ESKIMO CULTURE PENETRATION OF THE INTERIOR BARRENGROUNDS
Early Palaeo-Eskimo hunters took advantage of the abandonment of the Barrengrounds by Middle Shield culture hunters during a prolonged cold period beginning around 1,500 BC. Climatic change forced the forests to the south. Middle Shield culture people would have wintered in the forests and their summer seasonal forays into the Barrengrounds would have been forced southward to a practical seasonal commuting range from forest to tundra. The period of cold weather lasted until 700 BC and it is likely that in response the caribou herds would have adjusted their calving areas and wintering ranges. Distributions of Early Palaeo-Eskimo culture sites are believed to indicate the positions of the caribou herds at this time. Oblique lines indicate winter to summer ranges of the major caribou herds. Concentrations of Early Palaeo-Eskimo sites occur in the summer

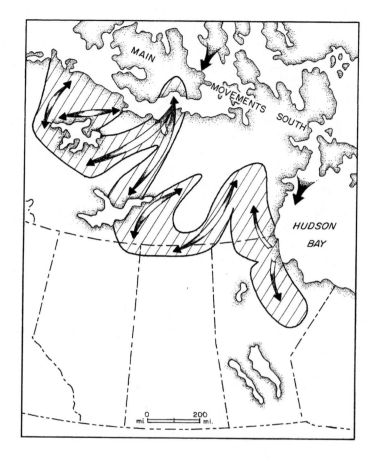

portion of the distribution. With reference to the double arrows in the aforementioned ranges the southern pointing arrows indicate caribou wintering ranges while the northern pointing arrows show the summer ranges and calving grounds. The single arrows in the Arctic Archipelago and along the west side of Hudson Bay represent the points of origin of the Early Palaeo-Eskimo people who occupied the Barrengrounds of Keewatin District and environs for approximately 800 years. (Adapted from Gordon 1981: Fig.5. Drawn by Mr. David W. Laverie.)

this wide array of species with the Early Palaeo-Eskimo occupation of this multi-component site is suspect due to the mixed nature of the deposits. Relatively little evidence of sea mammal hunting by Early Palaeo-Eskimos has been uncovered in the Central Arctic suggesting either that the maritime oriented sites have not been found or that such sites may have been out on the sea ice (Taylor 1964). Another possibility, although an unlikely one, is that marine mammal resources were relatively unimportant in the region.

In northern Greenland and the High Arctic Islands there was considerable variability in what animals were exploited. Musk-ox hunting and coastal and interior lake fishing appear to have been the most important subsistence activities (Fitzhugh 1984: 529; Knuth 1967: 30). The impression that the Early Palaeo-Eskimos of northern Greenland were oriented to the land rather than the sea may simply reflect the limited availability of marine species in the region. Archaeological evidence is also seasonally biased towards the winter settlements and the consumption of stored foods. In the Port Refuge region of northern Devon Island adjacent to a semipermanent open body of water where seal, walrus, bear, beluga, narwhal, and bowhead whale were available, ringed seal was the dominant food remains in the Early Palaeo-Eskimo dwellings although water fowl and Arctic fox bones were common (McGhee 1976; 1979). The scarcity of seal torso remains from these sites suggests that only selected portions of the prey were being brought back to camp (McGhee 1979: 36). Here as elsewhere, however, the use of bone for fuel could confound interpretations based solely upon the surviving direct evidence. The odd fragment of walrus, polar bear, and musk-ox is also recorded as well as the evidence of gnawing on bones suggesting the presence of dogs.

Early Palaeo-Eskimo sites in the Foxe Basin/Hudson Strait region have produced little in the way of faunal remains. What does occur suggests that seal and walrus were important (Taylor 1968a). At the Seahorse Gully site on the coast of Hudson Bay in Manitoba the limited faunal remains were predominantly ringed seal with minor representations of bearded seal, polar bear, wolf, and sea birds (Meyer 1977). At the time the site was occupied there would have been more landfast ice than today thus favouring winter ringed seal hunting. The presence of bearded seal, however, does indicate some open water summer hunting. Thus the occupation appears to span late winter to early summer (Meyer 1977; Nash 1976). Early Palaeo-Eskimo sites in the interior of northeastern Manitoba at Thyazzi (Giddings 1956; Nash 1969) and Shamattawa (Mike Zywina: Parks Canada, Winnipeg, personal communication) on the North Knife and God rivers, respectively, suggests that there was a fall to early winter caribou hunt, possibly supplemented by fishing. Bone preservation was lacking at both sites.

On the Labrador coast migratory animals such as seal, salmon, sea birds, and caribou, would have been the key resources. In this region the behaviour of marine species is relatively predictable but if one of the major prey species became unavailable, for whatever reasons, it would have presented a serious hardship for Early Palaeo-Eskimo people. It has been speculated that sea mammal hunting in the open water fiords of Greenland, Ellesmere and Baffin islands, and the Labrador coast led to the development of a distinct subculture that had only limited contact with the ice choked environment of their kinsmen to the west (Fitzhugh 1976a).

Settlement patterns:

As can be anticipated, a cultural distribution that extended from north of the Alaska Peninsula on the Bering Sea of the Pacific Ocean, eastward across northern Alaska and Canada to Greenland and down the Labrador coast to northern Newfoundland with probes to Lake Athabasca in northern Saskatchewan and into northeastern Manitoba (McGhee 1987a) and that occupied Boreal Forest, Lichen Woodland, and Tundra vegetation provinces in both continental and maritime settings, had considerable settlement pattern variability. The reasons for this variability would be specific to local conditions. For example, the association of Early Palaeo-Eskimo sites with the entrances to bays and fiords along the south coast of Devon Island in the High Arctic are believed to reflect ice conditions favourable to hunting sea mammals (Sutherland 1991). The ground cover characteristic of much of the Arctic has contributed to an unusual richness of information on site settlement patterns involving dwellings and their relationship to one another.

It was once suggested that Early Palaeo-Eskimos were interior caribou hunters who gradually began to exploit maritime resources (MacNeish 1956) or that they were specialized musk-ox hunters and fishermen (Knuth 1967; Steensby 1917). Site locations, however, indicate that these people were quite capable of exploiting marine as well as land resources (Irving 1962). Their occupation of so many different environmental zones is certainly evidence of the Early Palaeo-Eskimo capability to adapt to a wide range of northern environments. The apparent rapidity with which the Arctic territories were occupied may be taken as evidence of the prior existence of a technology, economy, and social system finely tuned to function in a wide range of harsh Arctic and Subarctic conditions.

There is a consensus that Early Palaeo-Eskimo culture rapidly spread throughout both unoccupied lands and the northern territories of their neighbours and then, through isolation, eastern developments became somewhat distinct from those taking place in Alaska and the adjacent Yukon. Although it does appear that east and west parted company a diffusion sphere across the Arctic was retained. In the east, a core area of Palaeo-Eskimo cultural development approximately 1,000 km in diameter existed incorporating Fury and Hecla Strait, Hudson Bay and Hudson Strait (Fitzhugh and Lamb 1985: 359; McGhee 1976). Within this area there is not only evidence of cultural continuity but also settlement concentration and it was from this centre that periodic external settlement forays are believed to have been made. Marginal areas, on the other hand, were only periodically occupied and then abandoned as dictated by circumstances. As has been noted, "One of the striking features of the Paleoeskimo population was its propensity for expanding and retracting its geographical range..." (McGhee 1976: 15). The fringe areas of Early and later Palaeo-Eskimo cultural development were the High Arctic, the Central Arctic coast, the Barrengrounds through to Hudson Bay, eastern Hudson Bay, the Labrador and adjacent Québec coast, and the Island of Newfoundland. Certain aspects of this model of expansion and contraction from a central cultural core can be questioned. Rather than a pulsating model of Arctic settlement from a core area to marginal areas, smaller population centres in the so-called marginal areas likely functioned within an adaptive pattern involving the `hunting out´ of large sections of territory that were then left to recover. It is suspected that such a pattern, involving the exploitation of very large areas and demanding an exceptional degree of mobility, was prevalent outside of the core area and insured contact between regions. Thus it may be that the lack of evidence, in conjunction with the mobility of Early Palaeo-Eskimos, has created the impression of a series of occupational hiatuses which actually consisted of large parcels of lands within an extensive hunting territory that were rapidly harvested by small groups of people and then left fallow for a number of generations. Such apparent hiatuses have also been interpreted as the result of population extinctions (McGhee 1978: 51). Other evidence (McGhee 1987a; Meyer 1977; Tuck 1976a; n.d.) indicates that the only major geographical contraction of Early Palaeo-Eskimo culture took place in the Barrengrounds around 1,000 BC. The abandonment of the interior Barrengrounds probably related to a change in climatic conditions that were initially favourable to the Early Palaeo-Eskimo exploitation of the caribou herds. Otherwise all of the so-called fringe areas appear to have continued to be occupied by the descendants of the Early Palaeo-Eskimos albeit not with the intensity of the occupations evident in the core area.

In order to conveniently handle the land mass involved it is necessary to divide the area into a number of geographical regions. These include (I) Alaska-Yukon, (II) a core area centred on the Foxe Basin including Hudson Bay, Hudson Strait, Baffin Island and west to Prince of Whales and King William islands, (III) the Central Arctic incorporating land adjacent to the Queen Maud, Coronation and Amundsen gulfs, and Victoria and Banks islands, (IV) the interior Barrengrounds, (V) the High Arctic islands, including Devon and Bathurst islands and northern Greenland, and (VI) Labrador and Newfoundland. Before considering aspects of the settlement patterns within these six regions some general observations are in order. The widely spaced and seasonal nature of Arctic and Subarctic resources demanded a high degree of mobility on the part of people dependent upon the hunt (Schledermann 1978). Site locations and the faunal evidence suggest that watercraft and possibly dogs (McGhee 1978: 43) were important elements in this mobility. The archaeological evidence that can be retrieved from the camps left be highly mobile populations is limited. In fact, most Early Palaeo-Eskimo culture sites are characterized by a scarcity or absence of recognizable structural features (Taylor 1962; 1972). The problem of low archaeological visibility has been further exacerbated by the obscuring effects of isostatic and eustatic modification to the land/sea interface central to most Palaeo-Eskimo settlement patterns. While some generalizations on the reasons underlying Early Palaeo-Eskimo culture settlement pattern distributions are probably correct others are premised upon equivocal evidence. The proposition that Indian cultures were seasonally confined by their cultural systems to the forest or shrub zones of the Subarctic whereas Palaeo-Eskimos, like the Inuit, were adapted to marine resources rather than vegetation zones and thus were capable of extensive coastal movements does have merit (Fitzhugh and Lamb 1985: 367). Unlike the ancestors of the neighbouring Indians the cultural adaptations of Palaeo-Eskimos freed them from the necessity of always being within commuting range of the resources of the forest. On the other hand, the proposals that Independence I and Pre-Dorset were distinctive subcultures that represented two temporally discrete migrations into the Arctic or that 500 years after the initial eastward migration there was a swing back to the Central Arctic (Maxwell 1980: 168) are based upon more equivocal evidence. Even the suggestion that the settlement of the Barrengrounds and the abandonment of the High Arctic by Early Palaeo-Eskimos correlated with a deterioration in the climate around 1,500 BC does not necessarily mean that the former population movement represented anything more than seasonal forays into the interior rather than a permanent exodus from the coast or that the appearance of an abandonment of the High Arctic is not a product of limited evidence rather than an indication of a cultural hiatus (Scheldermann 1978). The key to comprehending Early Palaeo-Eskimo culture settlement patterns rests with an appreciation of both the exceptional degree

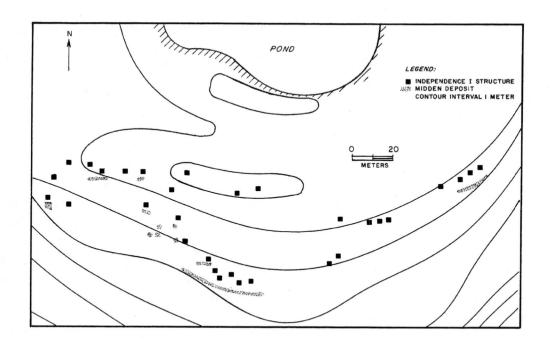

POND

LEGEND:
- ■ INDEPENDENCE I STRUCTURE
- ▨ MIDDEN DEPOSIT
- CONTOUR INTERVAL I METER

N

0   20
METERS

COLD SITE FEATURE 1

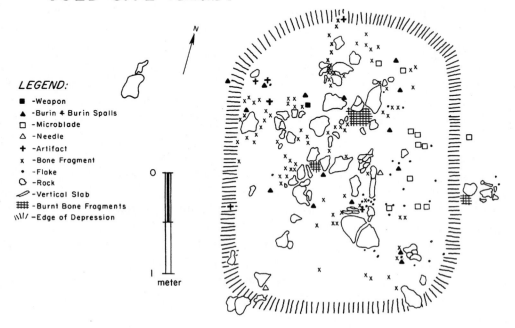

N

LEGEND:
- ■ —Weapon
- ▲ —Burin ✚ Burin Spalls
- □ —Microblade
- △ —Needle
- ✚ —Artifact
- x —Bone Fragment
- • —Flake
- ⟠ —Rock
- ⟋ —Vertical Slab
- ⊞ —Burnt Bone Fragments
- \\\\/ —Edge of Depression

0

I
meter

FIGURE 53: EARLY PALAEO-ESKIMO CULTURE SETTLEMENT PATTERNS ON DEVON ISLAND IN THE HIGH ARCTIC A series of tent floors were recorded at the Cold site. The site has a freshwater pond immediately to the north that would have been the major attraction to the site locale in addition to the broad vista it provided of a bay of the Arctic Ocean and a valley leading into the interior.

At the bottom of the Figure is a detailed floor plan of one of the tent floors. A subrectangular depression had been scraped into the gravel to form the living floor. Cultural debris was concentrated on this floor which also contained a hearth in the north end of the structure. Scattered rock slabs and cobbles likely represent the remains of a destroyed hearth-box. The dwelling would have housed a single family but, to judge from the limited cultural debris, only for a short period of time. (Adapted from McGhee 1979: Figs.4 and 7. Drawing by Mr. David W. Laverie.)

---

of adaptability and mobility of these people with the latter capability strongly implying the existence of water transport. In recent times, the High Arctic islands north of Lancaster Sound were exploited by Inuit from north Baffin Island who apparently treated the region much like a game preserve (Rousselière 1976: 55). Hunters accompanied by their families would move north for a season or several years, often for a specific purpose such as musk-ox or polar bear hunting. There is historic documentation of entire bands moving into the High Arctic islands, eventually shifting to Ellesmere Island or northern Greenland while others, decimated by starvation, returned south of Lancaster Sound. Such mobility by individuals, families or entire bands, stimulated by perceived hunting opportunities or driven by social factors such as feuds, the need for marriageable partners, population pressure, or simply wanderlust, likely characterized Early Palaeo-Eskimo culture as well. Thus, the six regions, Alaska-Yukon, Core area, Central Arctic, Barrengrounds, High Arctic and northern Greenland, and Labrador and Newfoundland, are constructs of descriptive convenience between which there would have been considerable socializing. Despite the aforementioned historically documented incursions from the Core region across Lancaster Sound into the High Arctic islands, the treacherous ice conditions of the Sound must have constituted a considerable barrier. This is suggested by the fact that the Palaeo-Eskimo materials from northern Baffin Island are more like those from the southern end of the same Island than they are to materials from Port Refuge on Devon Island less than half the distance to the north (Rousselière 1976). Although there is evidence of geographical regionalism in Early Palaeo-Eskimo culture interrelationships between the regions existed. "It is as if everyone in the Eastern Arctic had informational contact with everyone else through the interlocking systems of a multitude of small contiguous bands" (Maxwell 1985: 4). Such an interlocking system of reciprocating bands would have represented a very good form of life insurance in the unforgiving Arctic environment.

I. Alaska-Yukon: The Denbigh subculture in Alaska and adjacent northern Yukon while contemporary and, therefore, not ancestral to Early Palaeo-Eskimo culture in Canada, stemmed from the same ancestral stock. A close relationship is not only reflected in the technology but also in elements of the settlement patterns. Settlements in Alaska consisted of interior winter caribou hunting camps, such as the Onion Portage site, followed by spring seal hunting camps on the coast (Giddings and Anderson 1986: 300). At one of the coastal sites on Cape Krusenstern "...tight clusters..." of cultural debris less than 2 m in diameter with associated hearths are interpreted as the remains of tent floors (Ibid: 290). Small, round to subrectangular semi-subterranean dwellings with central hearths are also recorded for interior winter sites on the Alaskan tundra (Irving 1968: 341). As in the situation with the northern distribution of Middle Northwest Interior culture in the Yukon Territory and western Mackenzie District the Denbigh subculture appears in the interior of northern Alaska as an "...intrusive cultural replacement..." (Campbell 1962: 54) of the previous occupants.

II. Core Area: Within the Core area, centred on the Foxe Basin, Early Palaeo-Eskimo occupation was definitely coastal with very few interior sites recorded (Rousselière 1976: 42). Even the coastal settlement patterns are incomplete with the winter segment of the seasonal round appearing to be absent (Maxwell 1976a: 78). This situation, once again, raises the question of whether the appropriate sites have simply not been discovered or whether Early Palaeo-Eskimos, like subsequent populations in the region, had established winter igloo villages on the sea ice. On Somerset Island, however, Palaeo-Eskimo campsites situated in the sheltered minor inlets of Ashton Bay are interpreted as winter sites suggesting that this particular group of people did not live on the ice during the winter (Bielawski 1982). An inland summer occupation has not been identified. Certainly the Ashton Bay coastal settlement pattern stands in marked contrast to the location of sites on southeast facing headlands on southern Baffin Island (Maxwell 1973). This latter settlement pattern is reasonably inferred to represent summer occupations. Although the absence of harpoon float gear has been used to argue for flow edge hunting rather than open water hunting (Maxwell 1985: 86) the highly variable coastal settlement patterns suggest both forms of hunting may well have been practiced. The Ashton Bay settlement pattern also differed from that of the approximately contemporary Port Refuge settlement on Devon Island (McGhee 1979) in the respect that old sites were re-used rather than being avoided as appears to have been the case at Port Refuge. An interesting aspect of the Ashton Bay study was the application of quantitative spatial analysis to the settlement pattern distributions (Bielawski 1982: 39-40). Each settlement pattern hypothesis was evaluated using nearest neighbour indices while contingency table analysis suggested relationships between settlement variables. Regression analyses were also used to test a number of the hypotheses. Such mathematical assessments of a large number of site and site area characteristics can be a valuable tool in any attempt to gain insights into the wide range of factors people must have considered before selecting a site location, particularly a winter site location. Mathematical formulae requiring a random distribution such as most statistical or probability mathematical applications must, however, be used with caution as most archaeological phenomena do not appear to have been randomly distributed. For a succinct summary of both the potential value and the hazards of applying statistical methods to archaeological evidence see Susan R. Wilson (1987).

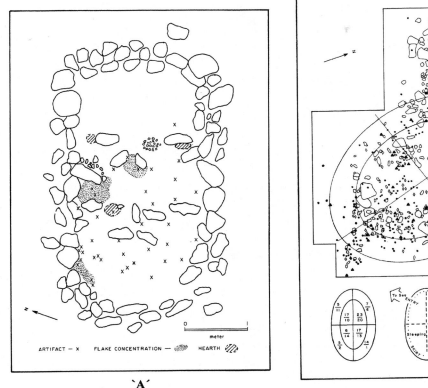

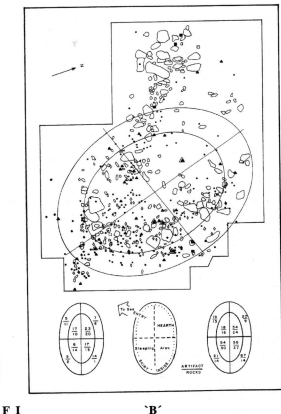

`A`   F I   `B`

GURE 54: EARLY PALAEO-ESKIMO CULTURE DWELLINGS IN THE NORTHWEST TERRITORIES

Floor plan `A´ is from the St.Mary's Hill site in Pelly Bay, a southern inlet of the Gulf of Boothia in the northeastern portion of mainland Northwest Territories. The rectanguloid structure consisted of a slight depression surrounded by relatively large stones that would have once formed a low wall. Three small hearths occurred near the edges of the dwelling. The concentration of cultural debris in the western half of the structure suggest that the eastern half represented the sleeping quarters.

Floor plan `B´ is of a dwelling at the Closure site on the south coast of Baffin Island. Careful plotting of all rocks and cultural debris indicated a sleeping area in the southern half of the structure, a cooking area in the northeastern quadrant, and an entrance way facing the sea in the northwestern quadrant. The two small diagrams on either side of the foregoing reconstruction show the ratios of artifacts to rocks in the outer and inner quadrants of two different dwellings from the same site. Such detailed distributional recording is necessary in order to detect human activity areas within such structures. (Floor plan `A´ adapted from Rousselière 1964: Fig.3 and Floor plan `B´ adapted from Dekin 1976: Figs.2 and 4. Drawings by Mr. David W. Laverie.)

Unlike the situation in the Barrengrounds there does not appear to have been any major penetration of Early Palaeo-Eskimos from the Core Area into the central barrens of Québec (Samson 1978). The seasonal presence of Middle Shield culture hunters in the region at the time likely blocked any deep penetration into the interior. Most major sites, like the Arnapik site on Mansel Island in the northeastern end of Hudson Bay, appear to represent the accumulated debris of a number of centuries. At this site debris was scattered over more than 1,800 m of elevated beach lines removed as much as 1.6 km from the present sea edge by isostatic rebound (Taylor 1968). Relatively few surface features were apparent other than some stone-lined cache pits and the odd dwelling (Ibid: Fig.5).

Tent structures within the Core Area are similar to one another. At the Closure site on south Baffin Island oval summer tent rings 2 m by 1.5 m, with or without weight stones, have been recorded. One of these consisted of an oval tent where the lower flap of the tent skin covering was folded inside of the tent and was then weighted with stones. When the tent was dismantled and the skin covering dragged off the weight stones tended to end up in the middle of the house floor and on top of the cultural debris (Dekin 1976: 82). Based upon the distribution of interior debris and the location of features, the back half of the dwelling represented the sleeping area while the front portion contained a hearth quadrant and an entry quadrant. In contrast, at the Arnapik site (Taylor 1968, Fig.5) an ovate structure 3.7 m by 2.7 m was surrounded by a 1.8 m wide gravel ring that probably represented banking material over the periphery of a tent cover. This structure was not excavated but based upon the distribution of plant growth, which concentrates on even the slightest enriched organic area, and cobble concentrations it can be suggested that the dwelling likely possessed a central hearth and a midden outside of a south facing entrance. A few scattered weight stones were also present. A more fully demarcated structure, measuring 4.25 m by 2 m, (Figure 54) was recorded at the St.Mary's Hill site in Pelly Bay (Rousselière 1964: Fig.3).

In northeastern Manitoba at the Thyazzi site (Nash 1969) a concentration of cultural debris, 9 m by 4 m around a hearth composed of fire fractured rocks likely represents the remains of a summer to fall tent floor. The size of the structure would suggest a multi-family dwelling. A short distance to the south of the Thyazzi site, at the mouth of the Churchill River, the Seahorse Gully site (Meyer 1977) dwellings occurred as clusters of pairs or groups of up to four. Rectangular and square structures, with or without midpassages, tended to be situated on the lower beaches of the site while semi-subterranean, round to oval structures lacking a midpassage, were found on the higher elevations. Rarely could central hearths be recognized. Most tools and other cultural debris were directly associated with the dwellings. Dwelling size and features were quite variable and were represented, in part, by the following: a circular structure 2.4 m in diameter containing very few artifacts or debris; a rectangular 3 m by 3.4 m structure with very large weight stones and a central cluster of stones inferred to be an oil lamp stand; subrectangular structures with dimensions ranging from 2.4 m by 3 m to 3 m by 4.3 m; a large rectangular structure 6.1 m by 3.7 m with a midpassage and a circular hearth; and an oval structure 4 m by 3 m. The larger dwellings were presumably occupied by more than a single family. It has been proposed that the three concentrations of dwellings at this site represent different occupations with each consisting of seven to eight dwellings that would house 50 people, or, in other words, the local band (Meyer 1977). The supporting evidence for this speculation, however, is not convincing and an unknown number of sequential seasonal occupations are likely represented. Limited refuse in the structures suggests that the occupation(s) were relatively short lived. On the basis of location and faunal remains the site is believed to have functioned as a late winter to early spring sealing camp. Evidence of trade, as elsewhere in the Core Area, is limited. This situation is likely due to the current rudimentary knowledge regarding the geological sources of probable exotic varieties of stone used in tool manufacture. The soapstone vessels from the site, however, were likely obtained from somewhere in the central Arctic (Meyer 1977: 272). An interesting aspect of the Early Palaeo-Eskimo site distribution in the Churchill region is the dramatic influence a change in sea levels can have on the local topography and the resources that it was likely to support (Ibid: Map 1).

III. Central Arctic: To date, Early Palaeo-Eskimo culture sites in the Central Arctic have dated later than many of the related sites to the east even though the original migration route was likely through the former area (McGhee 1976: 29). Presumably the earlier sites simply have not been found. A surface collection from the undated Dismal Lake 2 site (Harp 1958) would appear, on stylistic grounds, to be early. Excavated sites pertain to the summer to early fall segment of the seasonal rounds (Taylor 1967) and generally occur at locations used throughout the Palaeo-Eskimo sequence as well as subsequent Inuit occupations. Evidence of winter occupation or sea mammal hunting (McGhee 1975: 64) is absent suggesting the possibility that people wintered on the sea ice. A feature of note is the elaborate inukshuk systems, particularly along the Ehalluk River (Taylor 1972: 72-77). It has been suggested that these stone cairn caribou drive lanes were first constructed by Early Palaeo-Eskimos and then were used by subsequent people (McGhee 1978: 43). While such a proposal is possible it is difficult to prove. Recorded Inuit oral tradition across the central and eastern Arctic, including Greenland, is consistent in observing that the Tunit (Late Palaeo-Eskimo culture) constructed the original inukshuk and saputit (stone fish weirs) (Rasmussen 1931: 43). Such entrapment systems could be expanded and modified by later peoples without leaving any recognizable trace. The co-occurrence of Palaeo-Eskimo occupations and those of later Inuit people at many sites also supports the possibility that Early Palaeo-Eskimos may have been responsible for the original constructions.

IV. Barrengrounds: A number of researchers believe that with the deteriorating climate beginning around 1,750 to 1,500 BC a portion of the Early Palaeo-Eskimo population of the Central Arctic moved into the interior Barrengrounds on a permanent basis (Maxwell 1985: 81). No one, to the best of my knowledge, has raised the equal likelihood that, given the exceptional mobility of Early Palaeo-Eskimos, these interior remains represent summer to fall seasonal forays with a return to the coast in the winter. In other words, some of the Central Arctic Early Palaeo-Eskimo sites and the interior Barrengrounds Early Palaeo-Eskimo sites may simply represent the seasonal camps of the same population. Until the winter settlement pattern of the Central Arctic is determined such a possibility cannot be ruled out. The close relationship between the Early Palaeo-Eskimo technologies of the Central Arctic and the Barrengrounds over a period of at least 500 years suggests some kind of intimate relationship between the two regions that goes beyond simply a common ancestry. Regardless of whether the Early Palaeo-Eskimos of the Barrengrounds were permanent residents or seasonal visitors to this vast region, it appears that a deteriorating climate presented them with an opportunity to penetrate deep into the interior to exploit the rich caribou and fish resources. This also presumes that the changing climate worked to the disadvantage of the Middle Northwest Interior culture and the Middle Shield culture who had formerly occupied large sections of the western and eastern Barrengrounds, respectively. There is the possibility that the bow and arrow weapon system of the Early Palaeo-Eskimos gave them an advantage over their neighbours in conflict situations and that their occupation of the Barrengrounds may have involved some aggression. The most likely route by water transport from the Coronation Gulf into the interior would have been up the Coppermine River (Harp 1958; McGhee 1970) to its headwaters in Clinton-Colden Lake (Noble 1971) and thence to the headwaters of the Thelon drainage (Gordon 1975; Harp 1961) and then up the Dubawnt River (Gordon 1976). There is no evidence yet of Early Palaeo-Eskimo culture on the Back River (J. V. Wright: survey), north of the lower and middle Thelon River (Gordon 1975: 95), or at the embouchure of the Thelon River into Baker Lake despite, in the latter instance, claims to the contrary (Harp 1961). A population movement out of the Coronation Gulf region does not appear to be responsible for Early Palaeo-Eskimo sites in the Barrengrounds of northern Manitoba and the immediately adjacent Keewatin District (Irving 1968; Nash 1969) that are likely the result of seasonal inland excursions from coastal Hudson Bay. Settlement pattern evidence throughout the Barrengrounds (Clark 1987; Gordon 1975; Harp 1958; Irving 1968; Noble 1971) indicates a focus upon the major drainage systems. This suggests that the Early Palaeo-Eskimos relied upon water transportation for mobility and hunting. The concentration of occupations at river and lake caribou crossing locales indicates the lancing of animals from watercraft or as they first emerge from the water (Gordon 1975: 114; 1988: 8). It is difficult to conceive how any people could survive on the Barrengrounds without some form of portable watercraft for travel, hunting, and river crossing. In this respect, Early Palaeo-Eskimo culture site distributions on the Barrengrounds can only be understood as a product of water transportation. Where climatic change has not altered the locations of the calving grounds and wintering ranges of the four major barrenground caribou herds, the sites of all the pre-European cultures who occupied the Barrengrounds are found on the same sites. On the upper Thelon River Early Palaeo-Eskimo site concentrations occur between the calving ground and winter range of the Beverly caribou herd (Gordon 1975). It has generally been assumed that improving climatic conditions permitted the Barrengrounds Palaeo-Eskimos to return to the Arctic coast (Gordon 1975). On the other hand, if they had never left the coast on a permanent basis they may have been pushed out of a large part of their interior hunting range by eastward and northern advancing Late Northwest Interior culture Indians.

In the Barrengrounds of central Mackenzie District north of Great Slave Lake, Early Palaeo-Eskimo sites are usually represented by five to eight hearths clustered in sheltered bays or on points of land and islands (Noble 1971: 107). Presumably the hearths of fire fractured rock and the associated cultural debris represents the remains of small tent structures. At the Junction site on the upper Thelon River a concentration of cultural debris 4 m by 3 m suggests some form of flimsy structure (Gordon 1975: Fig.12, 131). Similarly, at Great Bear Lake concentrations of cultural debris ranging from 1 m by 3 m to 4 m by 5 m and containing central hearths (Clark 1987) were situated several hundred metres inland from the lake

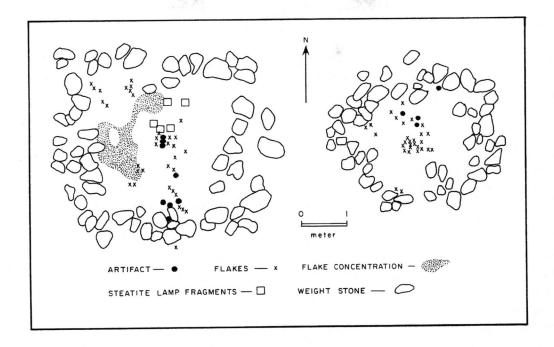

ARTIFACT — ●   FLAKES — x   FLAKE CONCENTRATION — ░

STEATITE LAMP FRAGMENTS — ☐   WEIGHT STONE — ⬭

FIGURE 55: EARLY PALAEO-ESKIMO CULTURE DWELLINGS IN MANITOBA These two dwellings were recorded at the Seahorse Gully site situated on a point of land where the Churchill River empties into Hudson Bay. At the time the site was occupied it would have been located on a small island in the Bay. The site, consisting of as many as 24 house floors, may have represented a late winter to early summer seasonal encampment of an entire band. (Adapted from Meyer 1977: Maps 9 and 10. Drawing by Mr. David W. Laverie.)

and undoubtedly represent the remains of tent shelters.

Most Early Palaeo-Eskimo site clusters in the Barrengrounds occur along the caribou migration routes between the calving grounds and the winter ranges of the herds (Gordon 1981: Fig.5). This has led to the observation that "...man-environment relationships in the barrenland of Canada tend to be man-caribou relationships" (Gordon 1981: 18). The site distribution mimics the historically documented Athapaskan hunting method of `waiting for caribou´ but as caribou behaviour is not entirely predictable (Morris 1972: 10) site areas with the potential for caribou but also rich in fish were particularly favoured (Ibid: 17). Site distributions have also led Gordon (1975; 1988) to speculate that an intimate and specific relationship existed between discrete herds of caribou and discrete hunting bands of humans. Only one herd/man association, the Beverly herd, has a suitable body of evidence and this is insufficient to demonstrate the hypothesis. Also, a basic assumption underlying this hypothesis is that Early Palaeo-Eskimo culture on the Barrengrounds represented a permanent interior adaptation, an assumption that may not be valid. Even though the distance between Central Arctic and interior Barrengrounds Early Palaeo-Eskimo sites is considerable the efficiency of water travel in portable craft and the fact that the northern rivers and lakes abounded with trout and other fish could have made such seasonal trips both feasible in terms of transport and safe in terms of a readily available food.

V. High Arctic: The High Arctic Islands and northern Greenland have provided some of the most detailed settlement pattern evidence. Undoubtedly the smaller populations represented in these harsher regions have resulted in less intermixture with subsequent occupations, a constant problem in the more intensively occupied regions to the south. The classificatory utility of distinguishing between the Independence I and Pre-Dorset subcultures will eventually be determined in this region. There do, however, appear to be certain settlement pattern differences between the two subcultures. Independence I dwellings are generally oval in shape with a central corridor that contains a stone fire-box constructed of vertical stone slabs (Knuth 1954: 377; 1967; Maxwell 1984: 36). In contrast, Pre-Dorset dwellings range from circular to rectangular in outline and generally lack evidence of a distinct hearth floor (McGhee 1979). In northern Greenland, Independence I dwellings are situated on elevated beaches near river mouths and headlands in good fishing and musk-ox hunting locales. To judge from the orientation of the central passage ways the dwellings faced the sea. Rectangular hearth boxes made of vertical stone slabs range from 40 cm to 60 cm in length and contain fire fractured rocks, charcoal, and burnt bone. Some of these structures have a low gravel wall around the perimeter that likely weighted the floor flap of a skin covering (Fitzhugh 1984; Knuth 1967). It has been inferred that the absence of debris or features around the central corridor, excepting the hearth, indicates that the dwellings had skin floors. Further south in the Core Area and along the Labrador coast dwellings similar to the Independence I structures have been recorded raising questions of whether an Independence I occupation preceded the Pre-Dorset occupation in these areas. Increasingly, however, researchers are questioning whether Independence I and Pre-Dorset can really be distinguished from one another on the basis of either technology or house structure features (Maxwell 1985: 74) and suggesting that we are really dealing with a single Early Palaeo-Eskimo culture pattern whose cultural systems change through time. Evidence in support of two sequential Early Palaeo-Eskimo occupations of the Arctic was recorded at Port Refuge on Devon Island where the distributions of the two subcultures overlap (McGhee 1979). If, as has been suggested, "...beach ridge chronology may serve as a reasonably valid dating technique" (Schledermann 1978: 49) then the evidence from the Port Refuge area is compelling. Here the Independence I structures were spaced some 20 m apart along beaches elevated by isostatic rebound and above Pre-Dorset houses that tended to cluster together on a lower beach. House floors facing the sea with associated middens in front were demarcated by growths of saxifrage taking advantage of the minute traces of nutrients left in and around the dwellings.

At the Cold site, situated near a freshwater pond and overlooking the sea and a valley leading to the interior (Figure 53), both the Independence I and Pre-Dorset dwellings were, as a rule, disturbed. One of the best examples of an Independence I dwelling at this site (McGhee 1976) consisted of a rectanguloid depression 3.0 m by 2.2 m and 10 cm in depth with possible remnants of a central corridor and a stone box hearth. An exterior midden on the seaward facing end of the dwelling likely indicates the entrance. The largest rectanguloid structure of this particular string of dwellings measured 3.2 m by 2.8 m. In addition to a number of discrete dwellings at the Cold site there were also less substantial features interpreted as work stations or very temporary dwellings. Some of these stations appear to have functioned as stone tool manufacturing centres. Here as elsewhere, the practice of subsequent people taking weight stones and other structural elements from earlier dwellings for their own needs has obscured dwelling configurations. The Independence I occupation of the Port Refuge area is interpreted as a series of temporary summer hunt camps occupied for a short period to judge from the limited amount of debris. There is no way, however, to determine the contemporaneity of the dwellings and, thus, it is possible that they could represent either sequential seasonal occupations or the contemporary remains of an entire band occupying the site for a single season. Some archaeologists believe the more substantial dwellings with hearths represent the winter structures while the amorphous scatter of stones, lacking discrete hearths, the transitory spring to fall structures of the same community (Maxwell 1985; Schlederman 1978). Given the requirement of mobility Eigel Knuth is probably correct in his view that it may be impossible to distinguish between winter and summer dwellings (Knuth 1967: 42). In northern Greenland and other regions of the High Arctic the 2.5 months of total darkness must have forced Independence I families to stay inside their dwellings and live on stored foods. Therefore, in attempting to identify winter dwellings, associated stone caches may be of greater importance than dwelling structural features per se, particularly when snow block construction may well have been used in these dwellings (Ibid: 44). In this regard, it is worth noting that some of the Port Refuge dwellings were associated with caches and conical pits (McGhee 1976). All of the dwellings at Port Refuge, as in the majority of instances elsewhere in the Arctic and Subarctic, represent nuclear family residences.

Tool concentrations in the Independence I dwellings at Port Refuge tended to occur on the right side of the dwelling as seen looking seaward from the entrance. The concentration of burins, burin spalls, stemmed points, and end blades on this side of the dwelling suggests that it was a tool-use and manufacturing area. In contrast, on the left side of the dwelling microblades and bone needles are commonly found. The difference in the locations of tool varieties has been interpreted as being gender related with tools used by males occurring on the right side of the dwelling while tools used by females are found on the opposite side (McGhee 1979). In northern Greenland, in what are interpreted as Independence I winter dwellings, microblades, burin spall needles, and bone needles were concentrated in the hearth area of the central corridor and are interpreted as reflecting female activities (Knuth 1967: 34). It can be anticipated that artifact distributions within any of these dwellings will be disturbed by processes such as dragging away the tent skin cover while its flap was still weighted down with either stones or gravel and by natural forces such as wind and animal disturbance (e.g. musk-ox browsing on plant growth attracted to the nutrients of the dwelling site) (Knuth 1967: 42).

In contrast to the linear arrangement of the Independence I settlement pattern at Port Refuge, the

Pre-Dorset occupation clustered together. It is unknown if this clustering was a product of multi-season accumulations or the gathering together of a single population (McGhee 1979: 93). Indeed, a short distance to the west of the Port Refuge area both the Independence I and Pre-Dorset occupations were arranged in a linear fashion along the elevated strandlines (Schledermann 1978). It has been suggested that some of the Port Refuge Pre-Dorset circular structures lacking weight stones could actually have been snow houses (McGhee 1978: 40; 1979: 119). Other structures consist of oval depressed tent rings associated with boulder caches (Helmer and Kennedy 1986: 127).

A difference of opinion exists relative to the nature of Early Palaeo-Eskimo settlement of the High Arctic. Based upon the Port Refuge data McGhee (1979) sees the occupation as discontinuous and explains the presence-absence situation by an expansion-contraction-extinction model. Schledermann (1978: 45), using settlement pattern data from another region, argues for cultural continuity. Schledermann's emphasis upon the need for mobility by Early Palaeo-Eskimos relative to resource availability is a more likely scenario than McGhee's periodic extinctions. This is particularly so given the difficulty of locating Early Palaeo-Eskimo sites (Schledermann 1978: 45) and the limited extent of archaeological reconnaissance in the High Arctic. Early Palaeo-Eskimo occupation of the High Arctic might better be conceived of as a matter of intensity rather than a presence or absence (Schledermann 1978: 55). Also, there is the possibility that Early Palaeo-Eskimos had winter villages on the sea ice with the result that in many parts of the Arctic we may simply have lost one entire seasonal segment of the settlement pattern and the segment that likely represented the major seasonal gathering of the band. Thus, in addition to the difficulty of differentiating Independence I from Pre-Dorset using a limited number of `diagnostic traits´, a possible hiatus in the seasonal settlement pattern does not permit placing too much faith on impressions that Pre-Dorset may have represented a significantly larger population than Independence I (McGhee 1975: 63).

VI. Labrador-Newfoundland: Along the northern Labrador coast Early Palaeo-Eskimo sites frequently occupied the same locales as the preceding Middle Maritime culture and subsequent occupants (Tuck 1976: 102). This pattern duplicates the multi-cultural settlement pattern of the Barrengrounds suggesting that, despite different technologies and other cultural systems, all northern hunters shared similar settlement pattern systems, at least for a portion of the year. This push of Early Palaeo-Eskimos into the already occupied territory of northern Labrador correlated with cooling conditions that may have favoured an expansion of sea mammal distributions (Fitzhugh 1972). Not only would the Early Palaeo-Eskimos be competing with Middle Maritime culture hunters on the northern coast but also with incursions from the interior to the central Labrador coast by Middle Shield culture hunters referred locally to as the Charles-Brinex complex (Fitzhugh 1977: Fig.4). The first Early Palaeo-Eskimo settlements were more dispersed and smaller than those of the preceding Middle Maritime culture (Fitzhugh 1977: 490) and would appear to have represented minor seasonal forays. Initially it was thought that Early Palaeo-Eskimos only spread as far south as Hopedale on the central Labrador coast (Fitzhugh 1976a) but there is now evidence that they reached northern Newfoundland (Tuck n.d.). Site locations indicate seal hunting on the sea facing side of the coastal islands in spring, summer base camps in protected bays for fishing, birding, and caribou hunting, and in the fall dispersal of single family groups to exploit seal around the inner islands. As elsewhere, the winter rounds have not been determined (Cox 1978; Fitzhugh 1976b: 135).

Early Palaeo-Eskimos on the Labrador coast made extensive use of the Cape Mugford chert deposits situated on the northern Labrador coast (Gramly 1978) but largely ignored the Ramah quartzite located just to the north of the Cape Mugford deposits. Indeed, the scarcity of local Ramah quartzite at the Rose Island Q site in Saglek Bay (Tuck 1976) suggested that Early Palaeo-Eskimos were either unfamiliar with the source or that the material simply was not an acceptable substitute for the cherts. As Ramah quartzite was the favoured stone of Middle Maritime culture at this time, it might even have been regarded as `enemy stone´. A more technical albeit prosaic explanation would be that a fine-grained cryptocrystalline like Cape Mugford chert was required for the burins that were the most common implement in the stone tool kit.

In the Nain area Independence I-like structures with paved central passage corridors and hearth boxes of vertical stone slabs are recorded as are tent rings (Cox 1978: 98). It has been suggested that the former were fall to winter dwellings and the latter summer dwellings although this seasonal inference appears to be based solely upon the nature of the structures. A central corridor, central hearth dwelling at the Cow Head site in northern Newfoundland, estimated to date to 1,000 BC, has also been recorded (Tuck n.d.). Included with the usual cultural debris from this structure was a reworked Middle Maritime culture celt.

As noted earlier, the eastern portion of the Early Palaeo-Eskimo culture distribution, represented by the High Arctic, Greenland, and Labrador, was distinct from the Core Area (Cox 1978: 114) and, thus, there may actually have been two major core areas. The steep coastline, open water, and seal migration pattern of the eastern region would have favoured north-south movement. Since the eastern coast of Baffin Island, which would have been available to Early Palaeo-Eskimos, is now submerged (Maxwell 1985: 75) it is not possible to determine if this coast was occupied.

Cosmology:

Little is known of Early Palaeo-Eskimo culture cosmology. The premature child remains from the Rocky Point site on Devon Island (Helmer and Kennedy 1986) suggests that disposal of the dead may have been by exposure. This possibility gains some support from the discovery of ellipse-shaped stone alignments measuring 2 m by 1 m situated on isolated elevated beach lines behind Independence I settlements in northern Greenland. It has been speculated that these sterile features represent the remains of burial tents where bodies were laid on the gravel "...within a oval of smaller stones..." (Knuth 1954: 377). In two instances a stone line ran down the centre of the oval, possibly symbolizing the central corridor and thus adding some support to the speculation that the features were symbolic dwellings intended for the deceased (Knuth 1967: 59). This speculation may even be extended to the Independence

I dwellings recorded at Port Refuge where, contrary to normal practice, earlier dwellings were not pilfered of their stones and dwellings were widely separated suggesting purposeful avoidance. While it has been suggested that this pattern may be attributed to unknown social factors or possibly the fear of ghosts (McGhee 1978: 32) if the final function of these dwellings were as repositories of the dead then the observation regarding ghost or spirit avoidance may not be far fetched.

Characteristic of Early Palaeo-Eskimo culture was the use of high quality and frequently very colourful chert in preference to other available silicious materials (Gordon 1975; McGhee 1979). This pattern was so pervasive that it probably reflects some form of unknown symbolically dictated behaviour. It would be an interesting research project to investigate the geographical distributions of cherts used by Early Palaeo-Eskimos in regions where other cryptocrystallines of equal chipping quality were avoided or in regions where the Early Palaeo-Eskimo distribution extended into the former territories of southern Indian cultures in order to determine if the use of such colourful and distinctive cherts functioned as band `badges´ much as has been suggested for the much earlier Palaeo-Indian culture (Ellis 1989). A corollary of such a study would be any indication of avoidance of the favoured chipping materials of displaced earlier alien occupants of regions containing quarries of such materials.

There are two late Early Palaeo-Eskimo culture carved bone maskettes from Igloolik that closely resemble Middle Palaeo-Eskimo (Dorset) Period IV maskettes in being "...incised with an X across forehead and cheek intersecting at the bridge of the nose. There is apparently deep ideological significance to this X since the central forehead on human figurines is often excised, leaving a horned appearance" (Maxwell 1985: 96). In the ethnographic records horned figures often signify personal power or shamanism. A remarkable engraved maskette (Figure 56) from Devon Island (Helmer 1986) would suggest the possibility that tattooing existed in Early Palaeo-eskimo culture. Among the historically documented Inuit tattooing was more common among women than men. The symbolism expressed on this maskette is, of course, unknown.

External relationships:

In addition to contacts with other Early Palaeo-Eskimo people in Alaska suggested by the diffusion of certain technological innovations and by a possible Pre-Dorset harpoon found in a Denbigh subculture site at Point Barrow, Alaska (McGhee 1976: 30), Early Palaeo-Eskimo culture could have come in contact with Middle Northwest Interior, Middle Shield, and Middle Maritime cultures along the southern margins of their territory.

There is no direct evidence of interaction with the Middle Northwest Interior culture even though the two cultures were contemporaries whose distributions overlapped in the Great Bear Lake region (Clark 1987). Shared traits, such as the use of microblades, as well as the general lack of bone preservation, and sites characterized by a thin scatter of multi-component cultural debris, has probably clouded any evidence

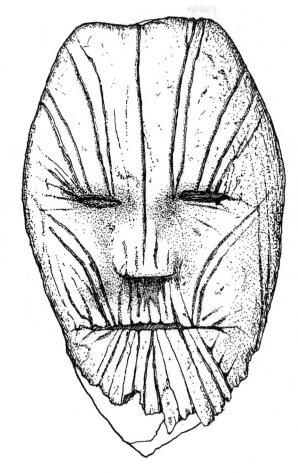

FIGURE 56:   EARLY PALAEO-ESKIMO MASKETTE   This 2,250 BC ivory maskette recovered from a tent floor at the Icebreaker Beach site on Devon Island, N.W.T. is believed to portray a tattooed woman. Measuring only 54 mm by 29 mm, the carving has been executed with great attention to realism in contrast to Middle Palaeo-Eskimo culture anthropomorphic art. It is regarded as an example of a stylistic and symbolic art tradition that extended throughout the development of Palaeo-Eskimo culture and possibly had its roots in Siberia or Alaska. (Adapted from Helmer 1986: 198. Drawing by Mr. David W. Laverie.)

of contact. Contacts likely did take place as suggested by the fact that Early Palaeo-Eskimo culture was intrusive into Middle Northwest Interior culture territory and that both groups exploited the same interior resources, mainly caribou and fish.

It has been speculated that in the Barrengrounds the side-notched projectile point and possibly the chitho of the Timber Point complex of the Canadian Tundra tradition (Pre-Dorset subculture) reflect contacts with Indians (Noble 1971: 109). The `Indian traits´ in the Canadian Tundra tradition, however, are likely a product of component mixture in the small, veneer sites involved (Gordon 1975: 197-199).

Indeed, a short distance to the east in the Barrengrounds of the eastern Mackenzie District and Keewatin District Early Palaeo-Eskimo components have been found sandwiched stratigraphically between Middle Shield and Late Northwest Interior (Taltheilei) culture occupations with no evidence of culture contacts (Gordon 1975; 1976). The Early Palaeo-Eskimo sites on southern Victoria and Banks islands that produced large, atypical, flaked biface knives and preforms were speculated to reflect stimulus diffusion from `southerly Archaic cultures´ (Taylor 1967: 228), a notion that was initially rejected (Taylor 1964). It has since been demonstrated that the closely related Early Palaeo-Eskimos in the Barrengrounds made considerable use of large, rough tools including biface blades (Gordon 1975). These large cutting tools probably performed similar functions as microblades which may explain the scarcity of the latter implements on sites where the former are present.

As Early Palaeo-Eskimo and Middle Shield cultures shared a border from the southern Keewatin District through to the central Labrador coast and as both cultures exploited the same caribou and fish resources there may have been ample opportunities for contact. Not only was Middle Shield culture capable of occupying the tundra on at least a seasonal basis (Gordon 1976; Wright 1972) but Early Palaeo-Eskimos occasionally penetrated into the forests (Gidding 1956; Minni 1976; Nash 1969; Wright 1975). In concert with a deteriorating climate Early Palaeo-Eskimo culture replaced Middle Shield culture on the eastern Barrengrounds around 1,500 BC (Gordon 1975; 1976; Harp 1978: 105-106; Irving 1968; Wright 1972). Whether the Middle Shield hunters were pushed out of their old range while trying to adjust to climatic change is unknown but, if so, the bow and arrow technology of the Early Palaeo-Eskimos would have given them an advantage in a conflict. There is some evidence of a technological transfer whereby Middle Shield culture hunters towards the end of Period III adopted the bow and arrow technology from Early Palaeo-Eskimos. This event likely took place on the central Labrador coast rather than in the Barrengrounds (Nagle 1978).

At the Rose Island Q site in Saglek Bay on the northern Labrador coast an Early Palaeo-Eskimo culture component occurred directly above a Middle Maritime culture occupation (Tuck 1976: 97) with very little time spread between the two occupations. There was no evidence of contact. Early Palaeo-Eskimo specimens, however, have been found in association with Middle Maritime culture sites on the central Labrador coast suggesting "...a southward displacement of Indian peoples as the Paleoeskimos moved southward in some numbers at least as far as the present town of Nain" (Tuck 1976: 97). To judge from the evidence of contact at the Middle Maritime culture Rattler's Bight site in the form of a typical Early Palaeo-Eskimo burin (Fitzhugh 1976a) encounters could have taken place as early as 2,000 BC. An important result of this contact was likely the adoption of the Middle Maritime culture toggling harpoon by Early Palaeo-Eskimos. This probability is suggested by the similarities between early Pre-Dorset toggling harpoons and the earlier Middle Maritime culture harpoon forms (Tuck 1975; 1976a: 87). Some of the small flake points that appear in Middle Maritime culture sites were originally thought to represent the reciprocal transfer of the bow and arrow technology from Early Palaeo-Eskimo culture although the specimens in question may not be arrowheads and date too early to have been obtained from Early Palaeo-Eskimo culture. The Labrador coast presented an ideal situation for culture contacts between Early Palaeo-

Eskimos and both Middle Maritime and Middle Shield cultures as early as 2,000 BC (Fitzhugh and Lamb 1985: Fig.2).

Human biology:

In the intervening 25 years nothing has significantly altered the statement that "Thus far no conclusive skeletal material has been found for the Pre-Dorset, Sarqaq, Choris, Norton, and Denbigh cultural horizons. If the present trend of correlation of Eskimo culture and Eskimo racial morphology continues as new discoveries are made it would be safe to predict that the skeletal remains of these cultures will show the Arctic Mongoloid morphological pattern" (Oschinsky 1964: 32). The only Early Palaeo-Eskimo skeletal remains recovered to date are those of an infant or, more likely, premature birth from the Rocky Point site on Devon Island (Helmer and Kennedy 1986). Situated in one corner of "an amorphous boulder tent ring..." (Ibid: 131) were some human remains mixed with animal bones and a portion of an articulated flexed body partially covered by a rock slab. It is suspected that the slab was accidentally dragged over the body when the skin tent cover was removed. Given the age of the individual nothing can be said concerning biological affinities.

Cultural continuity from Early Palaeo-Eskimo to Middle Palaeo-Eskimo (Dorset) suggests that Early Palaeo-Eskimos were the ancestors of the Middle Palaeo-Eskimos. Given the Middle Palaeo-Eskimo Inuit morphological skeletal features (Harp and Hughes 1968; Oschinsky 1964) it is reasonable to suggest that Early Palaeo-Eskimo people shared the same features. The historically recorded oral traditions of the Inuit of the Central and Eastern Arctic indicate that the Tunit or Dorset (Meldgaard 1960: 594) spoke an Inupik dialect (Rasmussen 1931: 113-114). In contrast to the Indians or `Itqilit´, "We counted the Tunrit a foreign people, yet they spoke our language, lived with us and had the same habits and customs as we had; the Itqilit are quite different. Human beings they are, no doubt, but not at all like us, and they speak in a tongue that we do not understand; and their customs are not ours" (Rasmussen 1931: 121). If there should prove to be continuity from Denbigh to Ipiutak in Alaska (Giddings and Anderson 1986: 316) it may be possible to downstream a relationship back in time from the Ipiutak skeletal morphology which does appear to be Eskimo (Simmons 1986: 359).

Inferences on society:

Early Palaeo-Eskimo society has been described as a highly adapted but conservative system very resistant to change (Maxwell 1976: 5). Such a point of view does not accord well with the rapid changes that took place around 1,000 BC and resulted in the Middle Palaeo-Eskimo culture of Period IV. It is likely that part of the impression of cultural homoeostasis stems from the nature of the southern Baffin Island evidence which appears to be "...inextricably mixed..." (McGhee 1975: 62) and, therefore, incapable of supporting chronologically based perceptions of cultural change. That said, it must be acknowledged that

Early Palaeo-Eskimo culture can be accurately characterized as conservative. One could even go so far as to suggest that it was an `anal´ culture where things had to be done in a specific Early Palaeo-Eskimo way with little tolerance for deviation. In the same vein, while it has been argued that Palaeo-Eskimos possessed a Tightly Constrained System (Nash 1976) where only environmental and economic restraints could force adjustments to an otherwise very conservative and self-perpetuating system, this same statement could be made, with minor qualifications, for all of the hunting peoples of northern Canada.

Critical to any consideration of Early Palaeo-Eskimo society is the fact that it was not initially subject to the controlling forces of a limited territory. During the initial colonizing of the Arctic, Early Palaeo-Eskimos were an expanding population spreading ever onward into new lands. The only approximate analogy with the Early Palaeo-Eskimo occupation of the Arctic was the Palaeo-Indian culture occupation of a large portion of North America. In both instances, the initial homogeneity of technology and other cultural systems was maintained until the populations came into balance with the carrying capacity of the land. It was then, and apparently only then, that a number of regional cultures, or historically what we might call band dialect groups, evolved from their common ancestral cultural base. This impressive migration of a superbly adapted people into an extensive unoccupied territory was the last of its kind for the human species. It was a unique event and there are no historically documented analogies from which to attempt to draw inferences. It is apparent, however, that these widely scattered populations, through some combination of cultural mechanisms, were able to maintain contacts over an enormous territory for a period in excess of 1,000 years. Since the occupation of the Arctic was unique, we can only speculate on the mechanisms that permitted relationships to be maintained initially from Alaska to Greenland and subsequently from the Central Arctic to Greenland. The two cultural mechanisms most capable of maintaining interrelationship over enormous areas of difficult terrain would be an exceptional degree of mobility and the existence of an interconnected network of reciprocally responsible bands that provided an essential social and biological network. It is likely true for both Arctic and Subarctic hunters that "Their most adaptive asset may well have been a small, flexible, band organization constituted of integral economic and egalitarian units" (Maxwell 1980: 181). Although historically documented Inuit band structure was probably somewhat different from that of Early Palaeo-Eskimo society, there were likely a number of parallels given both the nature of the environment and the shared cultural adaptations of Palaeo-Eskimos and the Inuit. For example, "Although there was much fluidity of personnel and the bands within the major regions, it appears that 60 to 70 per cent of the members of one winter's sealing aggregation-band assemblage would return the following year so that a core of members remained from year to year" (Damas 1969: 126). For the Inuit of the Central Arctic, five to eight of these local bands would form a closed connubium at the 90% to 95% level leading to a dialectal tribe of approximately 500. It must be cautioned that drawing ethnographically based analogies between recent Inuit society and Palaeo-Eskimo society is fraught with pit-falls. The preceding caveat aside, there is likely at least some degree of correspondence between the two social systems. If such be the case, bands of 50 to 100 people could have been interconnected in a broad tribal unit or grouping of intermarried bands of between 500 and 1,000 people (McGhee 1976: 37). It can be further speculated that in the case of the Early Palaeo-Eskimos the bands were likely smaller and the tribal structure more spread-out and composed of more bands. Band territories were likely loosely defined with the small bands periodically abandoning large regions in order to permit their resources to recover from human predation. Crisis, such as a late freeze-up, prey reduction due to disease, failure of the caribou to materialize, would force small bands, segments of bands, or families to temporarily affiliate with adjacent bands as the alternative was to perish (McGhee 1976: 39). A network of socially interactive bands with loose or transitory membership rules would be the only real hedge against the many unpredictable hazards of Arctic existence.

With few exceptions, throughout Early Palaeo-Eskimo culture the dwellings were single family structures rather than multiple family dwellings (McGhee 1979: 55). And while it has been speculated that the initial occupation of the Arctic may be regarded "...as a series of small events in which a group of two or three families travelled a few days distance" and that "The cumulative effect of hundreds of such movements over a period of a few centuries must have resulted in the spread of a scattered population throughout arctic Canada, as far north as Pearyland" (McGhee 1978: 33) given a lack of control over the cumulative versus contemporary nature of most Arctic site assemblages, it is unknown if these movements involved a few families or an entire band with the mobility to maintain social contacts with related bands to the west. The nature of the settlement pattern evidence may have led archaeologists astray regarding certain aspects of Early Palaeo-Eskimo society. Assumptions that certain types of dwellings represented winter dwellings and that the absence of oil lamps can be equated with an absence of oil for light and heat have led to improbable scenarios such as Independence I people "... must have lived through the dark period in a kind of stupor. The women were unable to sew, the men could not work up flint articles" (Knuth 1967: 50). Attempts to comprehend the social systems of Early Palaeo-Eskimo culture are compromised by the possibility that these people had a winter settlement pattern on the sea ice that is totally lost to the archaeological record. This segment of the seasonal round would probably have represented the time when the entire band(s) gathered together to reconfirm social solidarity. The fact that Arctic archaeologists have difficulty identifying winter settlements other than through questionable procedures such as inferred winter houses, provides some credence to the speculation that winter igloo villages on the sea ice supported by sealing may have been an integral part of Early Palaeo-Eskimo settlement.

While the nuclear family would have been the most important social unit in Early Palaeo-Eskimo society it can be assumed that a number of families would have closely cooperated with one another. Interior Barrengrounds caribou hunting, for example, was very likely communal as it was with the historically recorded Athapaskans (Morris 1972: 10). Given the requirements of cooperation and strict discipline to successfully operate caribou pounds and water crossing hunts, the aggregate band(s) probably elected hunt leaders with special powers although such status would have been temporary (Gordon 1975: 286).

It cannot be proven but it is likely that Early Palaeo-Eskimo society was patrilineal and patrilocal. Such a descent and residence pattern would have adaptive advantages for hunters who require male kin cooperation in the hunt and an intimate familiarity with the nature of the local territorial resources. Within such a system considerable female inter-band mobility can be expected, which would accommodate the requirement for socially and biologically acceptable marriage partners and hold the safety net represented by the intermarrying bands together with a blood bond. Such envisioned female mobility would also be the major contributing factor to the cultural homogeneity evident over large territorial expanses.

Limitations in the evidence:

Efforts to understand Early Palaeo-Eskimo culture are undoubtedly compromised by the problem of archaeological visibility. Major factors reducing archaeological visibility are reconnaissance biased by logistic convenience to concentrate around modern settlements, sites isolated on elevated beaches by isostatic rebound or submerged beneath the sea, very limited debris left by highly mobile groups, soil and exposure conditions not favourable to the survival of organic materials, erosional forces, dense ground cover in certain locales, and the prevalence of sites that tend to blend into the landscape. Archaeological context in many sites is often obscured by processes such as solifluction (Greer and Le Blanc 1983; MacNeish 1956). There is the academic debate regarding judgemental versus probability sampling (Bielawski 1983: 38-39) and how accurately the archaeological evidence reflects the universe of the Early Palaeo-Eskimo world. It is also an appropriate universal caveat that "The more remote in time the subject of study, the greater the likelihood that even the boundaries of the gap between the archaeological record and those who created it may be unknowable" (Janes 1983: 57). The low archaeological visibility and limited survey may explain why such a subculture as Independence I is only now being tentatively recognized in the western Arctic (LeBlanc 1991; McGhee 1978: 32; Pilon 1991). Such identification is also complicated by the limited differences between the Independence I and Pre-Dorset subcultures that may simply represent temporal variations. A rarely acknowledged problem with archaeological interpretations is that "...eastern Arctic prehistory shares certain patterns with mythological belief: acceptance of prior authority, intolerance of alternative views, and a search for simple explanations for complex phenomena" (McGhee 1983: 21). The exceptional distinctiveness of Early Palaeo-Eskimo culture stone tool technology and the normally small samples has resulted in an overreliance upon a limited number of `diagnostic´ traits when carrying out site comparisons rather than applying rigorous analytical methods (Helmer and Robertson 1990) in conjunction with the analysis of entire assemblages and multiple cultural systems. Finally, as an Arctic culture, there is a likelihood that Early Palaeo-Eskimos constructed dwellings of snow. The possibility of winter sealing villages on the sea ice, has already been raised. In this respect, negative evidence such as the winter seasonal hiatus in the settlement pattern record, may have to be used in innovative ways to fill the gaps possibly created by the uses of snow for construction and the sea ice as a living floor for a portion of the year.

Despite the foregoing problems, exacerbated by the high cost of working in the Arctic, there is no doubt that the lack of dense ground cover has left the archaeological record exceptionally exposed. This compensating factor is clearly seen in the amount of detail available on Early Palaeo-Eskimo culture settlement patterns even though the archaeological debris and remains of dwellings often imperceptibly blend into a monotonous landscape of elevated, grey-white limestone shingle beaches.

EPILOGUE TO VOLUME I AND PROLOGUE TO VOLUME II

Volume I, concerned with the time period of 10,000 to 1,000 BC, has outlined the very incomplete archaeological record of human occupation of the northern part of the Western Hemisphere as represented by Canada. With few exceptions, it is not until after 4,000 BC that the evidence is sufficiently intact to provide some detailed information on the activities of these early populations. Although it was probably around 15,000 years ago that the first small groups of people penetrated the interior of the continent, it is not until 10,000 BC that widely distributed and indisputable archaeological evidence of such a presence is evident. The 7,000 years of Period II and, to a lesser extent, Period III, have left a fragmented record of the human presence and, as a result, there are a number of often contradictory ways to interpret the evidence. Even the matter of when people first entered Beringia and the interior of the Western Hemisphere proper are still issues capable of stimulating heated debate. As such, Volume I and subsequent volumes represent a personal view of the events involved in the human exploration and settling of a large portion of the Western Hemisphere. Evidence from Beringia, which once connected Asia with America, was also evaluated. It is important to *not* regard the people in Beringia as constantly attempting to push out of Asia in some compulsive effort to reach the interior of the Americas. Although much of the evidence is undoubtedly now submerged under the Bering and Chukchi seas, the former land mass that once constituted Beringia is best regarded as a subcontinent in its own right within which there was much moving about in all directions of the various animal species and their human predators. Many of the interpretations in Volume I will undoubtedly be challenged by other archaeologists. Given the incomplete nature of the evidence and the different intellectual propensities of so many scholars working on disparate problems it would be worrisome if many facets of this synthesis did not elicit criticism. Hopefully such criticism will be constructive and eventually contribute to a better synthesis.

The central reason for writing these volumes is the belief that such a synthesis, warts and all, is sorely needed at this time. The myths and stereotypes regarding the native people of the Western Hemisphere, so tenaciously held by the now dominant society (Berkhofer, Jr. 1978; Cooke 1984), are beginning, for the first time, to be seriously attacked by scholars with quite different academic backgrounds (Berger 1991; Jennings 1975; R. Wright 1992). As the discipline of archaeology attempts to reconstruct the record left by the ancestors of the present native people, it has a vital role to play in the ongoing `re-writing´ of the history of the Western Hemisphere. Such an `archaeological´ history is, by the nature of the evidence upon which it must rely, an impersonal version of history when compared to what most people have come to expect from historical studies based upon written documents. It is also true that what is essentially a reference work, where various facets of detailed information can be `looked-up´, does not lend itself to the stimulation of reading of a good novel or mystery. Despite these limitations, an effort has been made to present this dry record of archaeology in a fashion that reinforces the fact that the broken spear point, pottery vessel, fire-cracked rock, and bone fragments are all the products of human activities. There has also been an effort to impart to the mute physical remains pertinent knowledge from other scholarly fields of inquiry in order to provide a more holistic view of past events. Dabbling in other peoples territory and disciplines carry its risks. As has been aptly noted, "One of the problems confronting those who venture to bring together evidence from separate fields is that they are certain to offend those who prefer specialization within a limited and safer pasture" (Davidson 1988: xi). The need to make such a body of evidence available, however, justifies giving offence to some regional or discipline specialists. If the volumes act as a gad fly to stimulate productive responses then so much the better for the next synthesis.

The major cultural events outlined in Volume I include the initial occupation of the lands south of Beringia by Palaeo-Indian culture around 10,000 BC and probably earlier and the settling of the High Arctic and Greenland some 8,000 years later by Early Palaeo-Eskimo culture. In the first instance, people with a technology adapted to northern latitudes occupied the Tundra and Lichen Woodland vegetation provinces that covered Canada at this time (Roberts et al. 1987). In the latter instance, however, the occupation of the High Arctic was only possible because Early Palaeo-Eskimo culture was uniquely adapted to survive in what must be regarded as the most severe and demanding environment to ever challenge human occupation. In addition to the foregoing dramatic population movements there were the more gradual occupations of lands as regions recovered from the effects of the last glaciation. An example is a gradual eastward shift of Shield culture across the Canadian Shield that did not reach the Atlantic coast until 2,000 BC. Another major cultural process apparent throughout Period II and Period III is the evidence of increasing cultural regionalism accompanied by elaboration of technology. Throughout the process of regional cultural differentiation there is also a suggestion of population growth.

A significant innovation during Period II was the invention of the spearthrower in what is now the southeastern United States. This took place around 8,000 BC after which the new weapon system diffused throughout North America only reaching the extreme northwest just prior to Period III. It is of note that the bevelled bladed and serrated edged stone point tips that armed the javelins of the new technology in the east are remarkably similar to recently introduced modifications to steel bread and steak knives in our own technology. Also in Period II there is evidence of the invention of the toggling harpoon on the east coast. Such an occurrence suggests the early existence of a complex large sea mammal hunting technology. Another innovation was the construction of fish weirs across much of Canada and the evidence for the use of both gill nets and dip nets. The bow and arrow weapon system, believed to have been brought to Canada by Early Palaeo-Eskimo culture, appears towards the end of Period III along the Labrador coast from whence it diffused westward to other cultures. Mortuary ceremonialism, appearing as early as Period I, continues to elaborate during Period II and Period III resulting in such impressive structures as some of the medicine wheels of the Plains. To supply the expanding ceremonialism, most often related to mortuary activities, elaborate trade net works were established that moved goods across the continent. Native copper begins to be mined and fashioned into a wide range of tools and ornaments using the cold hammering-annealing procedure as early as 7,000 years ago. By the end of Period III the first hints of cultural developments that would eventually lead to the stratified societies of the West Coast become apparent. Interwoven among these events and developments recognizable from the archaeological evidence are the invisible or nearly invisible facets of technologies which can only be inferred from indirect lines of evidence. Among such technologies would have been the use of watercraft across Canada. Watercraft would have ranged from seaworthy vessels to highly portable bark or skin craft. Winter food supplies, essential to the survival of northern hunting peoples, are almost always invisible in the archaeological record. An exception is the evidence for the production of bone grease on the Plains which was a necessary component of pemmican, one of the most efficient storable food concentrates ever developed.

While the aforementioned cultural events and developments, as well as many other insights, can be gleaned from the archaeological evidence between 10,000 and 1,000 BC, all of the personalities that were the agents and carriers of the changes are mute. The great orators, leaders, inventors, and religious prophets so essential to the writing of documentary history are silent and will remain so. Thus much of the texture which characterizes typical historical presentations is absent from a history based solely upon archaeological evidence; such is the nature of the record. On the other hand, with an archaeological history of preliterate people one does not have to contend with the individual political or religious distortions, conscious or unconscious, present in so many of the documents of the early European explorers and priests. This, of course, is not to deny that there will be many distortions, conscious or unconscious, in an archaeologically based history but such distortions will be mainly errors in interpretation of physical evidence. In a very real sense, an archaeological history is a history of the cultures of past people from which human personalities have been largely excluded.

Volume II considers cultural developments during Period IV (1,000 BC to AD 500). Although only incorporating 1,500 years compared to the more than 9,000 years covered in Volume I, the archaeological information for the period is disproportionately massive compared to what preceded it. The most important cultural characteristic of Period IV is the clear continuity with developments in Period III. Environmental conditions in Canada at this time were similar to the present. Rather than population migrations, diffusion of innovations and concepts appear to have been the major stimulants of cultural change. Around the beginning of Period IV, the technological knowledge needed to produce pottery vessels was introduced from the south into the margins of eastern Canada. The bow and arrow weapon system, which first appeared along the east coast at the end of Period III, continued to be adopted by people further west. Earth burial mound ceremonialism, originating from the Ohio and Illinois valleys and ultimately Mexico, penetrated regions of eastern Canada from Northern Ontario to the Maritime provinces. Among these ceremonial monuments to the deceased were the largest pre-European earthworks to be found in Canada. Situated along the Ontario-Minnesota border, some mounds reached nearly 35 m in diameter, stood more than 7 m in height, and contained over 100 burials. Two thousand years ago the native silver deposits in the Cobalt area of eastern Northern Ontario were mined and traded widely to the south in the form of ear spools and beads. Pottery appears to have been introduced into the Plains from the east around 2,000 years ago at the same time that a burial mound cult of southern origin appeared in southwestern Manitoba. When the bow and arrow weapon system entered the Plains is a more controversial issue. The pit house villages of the Plateau with their specialized focus on salmon as a winter storage food increased in size and number. In Period IV, the main features of West Coast culture recorded by Europeans were in place with plank houses being evident by 2,000 years ago. A concern with status and wealth is also apparent suggesting the development of ranked societies with nobles, free men and women, and slaves. As could be expected, evidence of warfare in the form of fractured skulls and forearms and trophy skulls increases. In the Arctic, Middle Palaeo-Eskimo culture people constructed semisubterranean winter dwellings that were heated and lit with stone oil lamps. The distinctive art style first recognized in Period III becomes increasingly elaborate with clear evidence of shamanism being involved in some instances. Throughout Canada trade networks continued to expand and the increasing number and size of sites suggest population increase in most regions. By the end of Period IV the cultural mosaic of Canada, still firmly anchored in the major environmental zones, provided the foundation for developments which led directly to the majority of the native societies recorded by Europeans as early as the 16th century along the east coast and as late as the 19th century in the north.

REFERENCES

Abbott, Donald N.
1986   A review of `Marpole, anthropological reconstructions of a prehistoric Northwest Coast culture type´ by David V. Burley, Publication No.8, Department of Archaeology, Simon Fraser University, Burnaby, 1980, v + 82 pp., 14 figs., 6 tables. Reviewed in the Canadian Journal of Archaeology, Vol.10:187-191.

Ackerman, Robert E.
1974   Post Pleistocene cultural adaptations on the northern Northwest Coast. In International Conference on the Prehistory and Paleoecology of Western North American Arctic and Subarctic. S. Raymond and P. Schledermann (eds.): 1-20. Archaeological Association of the University of Calgary. University of Calgary.
1980   Microblades and prehistory: technological and cultural considerations for the north Pacific coast. In Early Native Americans, Prehistoric Demography, Economy, and Technology. D.L. Browman (ed.): 189-197. The Hague.
1988   Early subsistence patterns in southeast Alaska. In Diet and Subsistence: current archaeological perspectives. Brenda V. Kennedy and Genevieve M. Le Moine (eds.): 175-189. The Archaeological Association of the University of Calgary, Proceedings of the Nineteenth Annual Conference.

Ackerman, Robert E., T. D. Hamilton, and R. Stuckenrath
1979   Early cultural complexes on the northern Northwest Coast. Canadian Journal of Archaeology, Vol.3:195-209.

Adams, Gary
1976   Prehistoric survey of the Lower Red Deer River 1976. Archaeological Survey of Alberta, Occasional Paper No.3.
1986   Archaeological reconnaissance of Grasslands National Park, 1985. Saskatchewan Archaeology, Vol.7:3-24.

Adams, Nick
1983   An archaeological survey of the Nakina lakes area near Geraldton, Ontario. Ontario Ministry of Citizenship and Culture, Conservation Archaeology Report 15.

Adovasio, J. M., A. T. Boldurian and R. C. Carlisle
1988   Who are those guys?: some biased thoughts on the initial peopling of the New World. In Americans before Columbus: Ice-Age Origins. Ronald C. Carlisle (ed.): 45-61.

University of Pittsburg, Department of Anthropology, Ethnology Monographs No.12.

Adovasio, J. M., J. Donahue, and R. Stuckenrath

1990   The Meadowcroft Rockshelter radiocarbon chronology 1975-1990. American Antiquity Vol.55(2):348-354.

1992   Never say never again: some thoughts on could haves and might have beens. American Antiquity, Vol.57(2):327-331.

Adovasio, J. M., J. D. Gunn, and J. Donahue

1977   Progress report on the Meadowcroft Rockshelter - a 16,000 year chronicle. In Amerinds and their Paleoenvironments in Northeastern North America. The New York Academy of Sciences, 288:137-159.

Adovasio, J. M., J. D. Gunn, J. Donahue, and R. Stuckenrath

1978   Meadowcroft Rockshelter, 1977: an overview. American Antiquity Vol.43(4):632-651.

Agenbroad, Larry D.

1988   Clovis people: the human factor in the Pleistocene megafauna extinction equation. In Americans before Columbus: Ice-Age Origins. Ronald C. Carlisle (ed.): 63- 74. University of Pittsburg, Department of Anthropology, Ethnology Monographs No.12.

Agogino, George A.

1970   Occasional, purposeful fluting of Agate Basin points. Occasional Papers of the New Mexico Academy of Science: 13-15.

Agogino, George A. and W. D. Frankforter

1960   A Paleo-Indian bison-kill in northwestern Iowa. American Antiquity Vol.25(3):414-415.

Aigner, Jean S.

1976   Early Holocene evidence for the Aleut maritime adaptation. Arctic Anthropology XIII(2):32-45.

1978   The lithic remains from Anangula, an 8500 year old Aleut coastal village. Universitat Tubingen, Institut fur Urgeschichte, Urgerchiechtlliehe Materialheflt 3. Turbingen, Germany.

Aigner, Jean S. and Terry DelBene

1982   Early Holocene maritime adaptation in the Aleutian Islands. In Peopling of the New World. Jonathon E. Ericson, R. E. Taylor, and Rainer Berger (eds.): 36-67. Ballena Press Anthropological Papers 23.

Aikens, C. Melvin

    1978   The Far West. In Ancient Native Americans. Jesse D. Jennings (ed.): 131-181. Freeman Press.

    1990   From Asia to America: the first peopling of the New World. In Prehistoric Mongoloid Dispersals. Takeru Akazawa et al. (eds.):1-34. Newsletter of the "Prehistoric Mongoloid Dispersals" Project, No.7, Special Issue.

Alexander, Herbert L.

    1974   The association of Aurignacoid elements with Fluted Point complexes in North America. In International Conference on the Prehistory and Paleoecology of Western North American Arctic and Subarctic. Scott Raymond and Peter Schledermann (eds.), 21-31. Archaeological Association of the University of Calgary. University of Calgary.

    1987   Putu, a Fluted Point site in Alaska. Department of Archaeology, Simon Fraser University, Publication No.17.

Allaire, Louis

    1978   L'archéologie des Kitselas d'après le site stratifié de Gituas (GdTc:2) sur la Rivière Skeena en Columbia Britannique. Musée national de l'Homme, Commission archéologique du Canada, Collection Mercure 72.

    1979   The cultural sequence of Gituas: a case of prehistoric acculturation. In Skeena River Prehistory. Richard Inglis and George MacDonald (eds.): 21-52. National Museum of Man, Archaeological Survey of Canada, Mercury 87.

Ames, Kenneth M.

    1979   Report on excavations at GhSv 2, Hagivilquet Canyon. In Skeena River Prehistory. Richard Inglis and George MacDonald (eds.): 181-218. National Museum of Man, Archaeological Survey of Canada, Mercury 87.

    1981   The evolution of social ranking on the Northwest Coast of North America. American Antiquity, Vol.46(4):789-805.

Anderson, Douglas D.

    1970   Akmak: an early archaeological assemblage from Onion Portage, Northwest Alaska. Acta Arctica 16. Copenhagen.

    1980   Continuity and change in the prehistoric record from north Alaska. In Alaska Native Culture and History. Yoshinobu Kotani and William B. Workman (eds.): 233-252. Senri Ethnological Studies, No.4, National Museum of Ethnology, Senri. Osaka.

    1984   Prehistory of North Alaska. In Handbook of North American Indians. William C. Sturtevant (gen. ed.). Vol.5, Arctic. David Damas (vol. ed.): 80-93. Smithsonian Institution, Washington D.C.

456

Anderson, J. E.
  1976   The human skeletons. Appendix A: 124-131. In Ancient People of Port au Choix by James A. Tuck. Newfoundland Social and Economic Studies No.17, Institute of Social and Economic Research, Memorial University of Newfoundland.

Anderson, T. W., R. W. Mathewes and C. E. Schweger
  1989   Holocene climatic trends in Canada with special reference to the Hypsithermal Interval. In Chapter 7 of Quaternary Geology of Canada and Greenland. R. J. Fulton (ed.): 520-528. Geological Survey of Canada, Geology of Canada No.1.

Apland, Brian
  1982   Chipped stone assemblages from the beach sites of the Central Coast. In Papers on Central Coast Archaeology. Philip M. Hobler (ed.): 13-63. Simon Fraser University, Department of Archaeology, Publication No.10.

Archambault, Marie-France
  1987   L'Archaïque sur la Haute Côte Nord du Saint-Laurent. Recherches amérindiennes au Québec, Vol.XVII(1-2):101-113.

Arnold, Charles D.
  1983   A summary of the prehistory of the western Canadian Arctic. The Musk-ox, 33:10-20.

Arthur, George W.
  1975   An introduction to the ecology of early historic communal bison hunting among the northern Plains Indians. National Museum of Man, Archaeological Survey of Canada, Mercury 37.

Arthurs, David
  1980   The Renshaw site, DaJi-1; an Archaic site on the western Lake Superior shore. Staff Archaeological Reports on File, Historical Planning and Research Branch, Ontario Ministry of Culture and Recreation: 1-20. Ontario.

Arundale, W. H.
  1981   Radiocarbon dating in Eastern Arctic archaeology: a flexible approach. American Antiquity, 46(2):244-271.

Asch, David L. and Nancy B.
  1985   Prehistoric plant cultivation in west-central Illinois. In Prehistoric Food Production in North America. Richard I. Ford (ed.): 149-203. Anthropological Papers No.75, Museum of Anthropology, University of Michigan. Ann Arbor.

Badgley, Ian et Paul Boissonnault
    1985   Le site CeEu-10 - une occupation préhistorique ancienne de la région de Québec. Recherches amérindiennes au Québec, Vol. XV(1-2):151-160.

Ball, Bruce F.
    1986   Site classification and prehistoric settlement systems in the Upper Athabasca River Valley. In Eastern Slopes Prehistory: Selected Papers. Brian Ronaghan (ed.): 133-159. Archaeological Survey of Alberta, Occasional Paper No.30.

Barber, R. J.
    1977   Disjunct plant distributions and archaeological interpretation. Man in the Northeast 13:103-107.

Barnett, Peter J. and Clyde C. Kennedy
    1987   Deglaciation, marine inundation and archaeology of the Renfrew-Pembroke area. In International Union of Quaternary Research, XII International Congress, Quaternary of the Ottawa Region and guide to day excursions. R. J. Fulton (ed.): 45-54.

Barry, R. G., W. H. Arundale, J. T. Andrews, R. S. Bradley, and H. Nichols
    1977   Environmental change and cultural change in the eastern Canadian Arctic during the last 5000 years. Arctic and Alpine Research, 9:193-210.

Bastian, Tyler J.
    n.d.   Prehistoric copper mining in Isle Royale National Park, Michigan. MA thesis, Department of Anthropology, University of Utah, 1963.

Beardsley, R. K., Preston Holder, Alex D. Kreiger, Betty J. Meggers, John B. Rinaldo, and Paul Kutsche

    1956   Functional and evolutionary implications of community patterning. In Seminars in Archaeology: 1955, Robert Wauchope (ed.): 129-157, Society for American Archaeology, Memoir 11.

Beattie, Owen B.
    1972   Salvage archaeology at Bliss Landing. In Reports on Salvage Archaeology in British Columbia in 1971. Roy L. Carlson (ed.): 23-39. Simon Fraser University, Department of Archaeology, Paper No.1.
    1976   Skeletal pathology of prehistoric human remains from Crescent Beach. In Current Research Reports. Roy L. Carlson (ed.): 155-164. Simon Fraser University, Department of Archaeology, Publication No.3.

458

Beauchamp, William M.
   1902   Horn and bone implements of the New York Indians. New York State Museum, Bulletin
            50.

Beaudin, Luc, Pierre Dumais et Gilles Rousseau
   1987   Un site archaïque a la Baie des Belles Amours, Basse-Côte-Nord. Amérindiennes au
            Québec, Vol. XVII(1-2):115-132.

Beaudoin, Alwynne B. and Frances D. Reintjes
   1994   Late Quaternary studies in Beringia and beyond, 1950-1993: an annotated bibliography.
            Provincial Museum of Alberta, Archaeological Survey Occasional Paper No. 35.

Bedwell, S. F.
   1973   Fort Rock Basin prehistory and environment. University of Oregon Books, Eugene.

Bedwell, Stephen Ferguson and L. S. Cressman
   1971   Fort Rock report: prehistory and environment of the pluvial Fort Rock area of
            south-central Oregon. In Great Basin Anthropological Conference, University of Oregon
   1970   Selected Papers. C. Melvin Aikens (ed.): 1-25. University of Oregon Anthropological
            Papers, No.1.

Belcher, William R. David Sanger, and Bruce J. Bourque
   1994   The Bradley Cemetery: a Moorehead Burial Tradition site in Maine. Canadian Journal
            of Archaeology, Vol.18:3-28.

Bell, Charles N.
   1928   An implement of prehistoric man. Appendix to the Report of the Minister of Education
            Ontario, Thirty-sixth annual archaeological report: 51-54.

Benmouyal, Jose
   1976   Archaeological research in the Gaspé Peninsula, preliminary report. In Current Research
            Reports, Roy L. Carlson (ed.): 7-18, Department of Anthropology, Simon Fraser
            University, Publication No.3.
   1987   Des Paléoindiens aux Iroquoiens en Gaspésie: six mille ans d'histoire. Dossiers,
            Soixante-trois. Ministère des Affaires culturelles, Québec.

Berger, Thomas R.
   1991   A Long and Terrible Shadow, white values, native rights in the Americas, 1492-1992.
            Douglas and McIntyre. Vancouver/Toronto.

Beukens, R.P., L.A. Pavlish, R.G.V. Hancock, R.M. Farquhar, G.C. Wilson, P.J. Julig, and William Ross
    1992   Radiocarbon dating of copper-preserved organics. Radiocarbon, Vol.34(3):890-897.

Berkhofer, Jr., Robert F.
    1978   The White Man's Indian, Images of the American Indian from Columbus to the Present. Alfred A. Knopf, New York.

Bielawski, E.
    1982   Spatial behaviour of prehistoric Arctic hunters: analysis of the site distribution on Ashton Bay, Somerset Island, N.W.T. Canadian Journal of Archaeology, Vol.6:33-45.
    1983   Northern archaeology to 1983: a perspective from Arctic prehistory. The Musk-ox, 33:37-41.

Biggar, H. P. (ed.)
    1924   The voyages of Jacques Cartier: published from the originals with translations, notes and appendices. Publications of the Public Archives of Canada, No.11.
    1929   The works of Samuel de Champlain, Vol.III. The Champlain Society.

Bird, J. B.
    1946   The Archaeology of Patagonia. In Handbook of South American Indians, Bureau of American Ethnology, Bulletin 143:17-24.

Boaz, Franz
    1898   Introduction. Memoirs of the Jesup North Pacific Expedition, Vol.I, Part 1.

Bobrowsky, Peter T., Norm R. Catto, Jack W. Brink, Brian E. Spurling, Terry H. Gibson, and Nathaniel W. Rutter
    1990   Archaeological geology of sites in western and northwestern Canada. In Archaeological Geology of North America. N. P. Larca and J. Donahue (eds.): 87-122, chapter 5. Geological Society of America, Centennial Special Volume 4.

Bobrowsky, Peter T. and Nat Rutter
    1990   Geologic evidence for an Ice-Free-Corridor in northeastern British Columbia, Canada. In Current Research in the Pleistocene, Paleoenvironments: Geosciences, Vol.7:133-135.

Boldurian, Anthony T.
    1990   Lithic technology at the Mitchell Locality of Blackwater Draw: a stratified Folsom site in Eastern New Mexico. Plains Anthropologist 35-130, Memoir 24.

Bolian, Charles E.

1980   The Early and Middle Archaic of the Lakes Region, New Hampshire. In Early and Middle Archaic Cultures in the Northeast. David R. Starbuck and Charles E. Bolian (eds.): 115-134. Occasional Publications in Northeastern Anthropology, No.7.

Bonnichsen R. and D. Young

1980   Early technological repertoires: bones to stones. Canadian Journal of Anthropology Vol.1:123-228.

Bonnichsen, Robson and Marcella H. Sorg (eds.)

1989   Bone Modification. Peopling of the Americas Publications, Center for the Study of the First Americans. University of Maine, Orono.

Borden, Charles E.

1952   Results of archaeological investigations in central British Columbia. Anthropology in British Columbia, No.3:31-43.

1960   DjRi 3, an early site in the Fraser Canyon, British Columbia. Contributions to Anthropology 1957, National Museum of Canada, Bulletin 162:101-118.

1961   Fraser River Archaeological Project. National Museum of Canada, Anthropology Papers No.1.

1962   West Coast crossties with Alaska. In Prehistoric Cultural Relations between the Arctic and Temperate Zones of North America. John M. Campbell (ed.): 9-19. Arctic Institute of North America, Technical Paper 11.

1969   Early population movements from Asia into western North America. Syesis 2: 1-14, Provincial Museum of British Columbia.

1975   Origins and development of early Northwest Coast culture to about 3000 B.C. National Museum of Man, Archaeological Survey of Canada, Mercury 45.

1976   A water-saturated site on the South Mainland Coast of British Columbia. In The Excavation of Water-saturated Archaeological Sites (Wet Sites) on the Northwest Coast of North America. Dale R. Croes (ed.): 234-260. National Museum of Man, Archaeological Survey of Canada, Mercury 50.

1979   Peopling and early cultures of the Pacific Northwest. Science 203:963-971.

1983   Prehistoric art of the Lower Fraser region. In Indian Art Traditions of the Northwest Coast. Roy L. Carlson (ed.): 131-165. Simon Fraser University, Department of Archaeology, Publication No.13.

Borstel, Christopher L.

1982   Archaeological investigations at the Young site, Alton, Maine. Occasional Publications in Maine Archaeology No.2, The Maine Historic Preservation Commission.

Bourque, Bruce J.

1975   Comments on the Late Archaic populations of central Maine: the view from the Turner Farm. Arctic Anthropology XII(2):35-45.

1976   The Turner Farm site: a preliminary report. Man in the Northeast 11:21-30.

1994   Evidence for prehistoric exchange on the Maritime Peninsula. In Prehistoric Exchange Systems in North America. Timothy G. Baugh and Johathon E. Ericson (eds.): 23-46. Plenum Press, New York and London.

Bowers, Douglas D.

1982   The Lisburne site: analysis and culture history of a multi-component lithic workshop in the Iteriak Valley, Arctic foothills, northern Alaska. Anthropological Papers of the University of Alaska 20:79-112.

Bradstreet, Theodore E. and Ronald B. Davis

1975   Mid - postglacial environments in New England with emphasis on Maine. Arctic Anthropology XII(2):7-22.

Brainerd, George W.

1951   A place of chronological ordering in archaeological analysis. American Antiquity, Vol.16(4):293- 301.

Brennan, Louis A.

1974   The lower Hudson: a decade of shell middens. Archaeology of Eastern North America, 2(1):81-93.

1979   Propositions concerning the Early Archaic in New York. New York State Archaeological Association, 75:1-14.

Breternitz, David A., Alan C. Swedlund, and Duane C. Anderson

1971   An early burial from Gordon Creek, Colorado. American Antiquity 36(2):170-182.

Brink, John W. and Robert J. Dawe

1986   An introduction to the archaeology of the Grande Cache region in the north Alberta Rocky Mountains. In Eastern Sloples Prehistory: Selected Papers. Brian Ronaghan (ed.): 161-246. Archaeological Survey of Alberta, Occasional Paper No.30.

Broderick, Michael

1988   Residue analysis of Foxie Otter site chipped stone. In The Foxie Otter site, a multicomponent occupation north of Lake Huron. Christopher C. Hanks. Appendix 4. Anthropological Papers No.79, Museum of Anthropology, University of Michigan.

Brose, David S.

462

1989   The Squaw Rockshelter (33CU34): a stratified Archaic deposit in Cayahoga County. Kirklandia No.44: 17-53. The Cleveland Museum of Natural History.

Browman, David L.
1981   Isotopic discrimination and correction factors in radiocarbon dating. In Advances in Archaeological Method and Theory. Michael B. Schiffer (ed.), 4: 241-295. Academic Press, New York.

Broyles, Bettye J.
1971   Second preliminary report: the St.Albans site, Kanawha County, W. Va. Report of Archaeological Investigations No.3. West Virginia Geological and Economic Survey. Morgantown.

Brumley, John H.
1975   The Catus Flower site in southeastern Alberta: 1972-1974 excavations. National Museum of Man, Archaeological Survey of Canada, Mercury 46.
1988   Medicine Wheels of the Northern Plains: a summary and appraisal. Archaeological Survey of Alberta, Manuscript Series No.12.

Bryan, Alan. L.
1969   Early Man in America and the late Pleistocene chronology of western Canada and Alaska. Current Anthropology Vol.10:339-367.
1978   An overview of Paleo-American prehistory from a circum-Pacific perspective. Occasional Paper No.1, Department of Anthropology, University of Alberta. Alan Lyle Bryan (ed.): 306-327.
1979   Smith Creek Cave. D. R. Tuohy and D. Rendall (eds.). The Archaeology of Smith Creek Canyon, Eastern Nevada. Anthropological Papers of the Nevada State Museum, No.17.
1980   The Stemmed Point Tradition: an early technological tradition in western North America. In Anthropological Papers in Memory of Earl H. Swanson, Jr. Special Publication of the Idaho State Museum of Natural History. L. B. Harten et al. (eds.): 77-107.

Bryson, R. A., D. A. Baerreis and W. M. Wendland
1970   The character of late glacial and post-glacial climatic changes. In Pleistocene and Recent Environments of the Central Great Plains. W. Dort Jr. and J. K. Knox Jr. (eds.): 53-74, Department of Geology, University of Kansas Press, Special Publication 3.

Buchner, A. P.
1979   The Shield Archaic: a review. Manitoba Archaeological Quarterly, 3(2):2-11.
1979a   The 1978 Caribou Lake Project, including a summary of the prehistory of east-central Manitoba. Papers in Manitoba Archaeology, Final Report No.8, Department of Cultural

Affairs and Historical Resources, Historic Resources Branch. Manitoba.

1979b   The Caribou Lake Project 1978. Manitoba Archaeological Quarterly, 3(1):5-6. Manitoba.

1980   Cultural responses to Altithermal (Atlantic) climate along the eastern margins of the North American Grasslands 5500 to 3000 BC. National Museum of Man, Archaeological Survey of Canada, Mercury 97.

1980a   A further contribution to the Shield Archaic debate. Manitoba Archaeological Quarterly, 4(1):53-60.

1981   Sinnock: a Paleolithic camp and kill site in Manitoba. Papers in Manitoba Archaeology, Final Report No.10, Department of Cultural Affairs and Historical Resources, Historic Resources Branch, Manitoba.

1981a   The Oxbow Complex and the anomalous winter hypothesis. Canadian Journal of Archaeology, Vol.5:137-144.

1982   An archaeological survey of the Winnipeg River. Papers in Manitoba Archaeology, Final Report No.12, Department of Cultural Affairs and Historical Resources. Manitoba.

1982a   Material culture of the Bjorklund site. Papers in Manitoba Archaeolgy, Miscellaneous Paper No.13. Department of Cultural Affairs and Historical Resources. Manitoba.

1984   Investigations at the Sinnock site, 1980 and 1982. Papers in Manitoba Archaeology, Final Report No.17, Department of Culture, Heritage and Recreation. Manitoba.

1988   The geochronology of the Lockport site. Manitoba Archaeological Quarterly, Vol.12(2):27-31.

Buchner, A. P. and L. F. Pettipas

1990   The early occupations of the Glacial Lake Agassiz Basin in Manitoba; 11,500 to 7,700 BP. In Archaeological Geology of North America. N. P. Lasca and J. Donahue (eds.): 51-59. Geological Society of America, Centennial Special Volume 4.

Buchner, A. P. and L. J. Roberts

1990   Reevaluation of an implement of "Elephant bone" from Manitoba. American Antiquity, Vol.55(3):605-607.

Buchner, A. P., P. Carmichael, G. Dickson, I. Dyck, B. Fardoe, J. Haug, T. & L. Jones, D. Joyes, O. Mallory, M. Mallot, D. Meyer, D. Miller, R. Nash, L. Pettipas, C. T. Shay, E. L. Syms, M. A. Tisdale, and J. P. Whelan

1983   Introducing Manitoba Prehistory. Papers in Manitoba Archaeology, Popular Series No.4, Manitoba Department of Cultural Affairs and Historical Resources.

Buckmaster, Marla M. and James R. Paquette

1988   The Gorto site: preliminary report on a Late Paleo-Indian site in Marquette County, Michigan. The Wisconsin Archaeologist, Vol.69(3):101-124.

464

Bunyan, D. E.
    1978   Pursuing the Past, a general account of British Columbia archaeology. University of British Columbia Museum of Anthropology, Museum Note No.4.

Burger, Valerie
    1953   Indian campsites on Kempt and Manowan lakes in the Province of Quebec. Pennsylvania Archaeologist, XXIII(1):32-45.

Burley, David V.
    1979   Specialization and the evolution of complex society in the Gulf of Georgia region. Canadian Journal of Archaeology, Vol.3:131-144.
    1989   Senewetels: culture history of the Nanaimo Coast Salish and the False Narrows Midden. Royal British Columbia Museum Memoir 2.

Burney, David A.
    1993   Recent animal extinctions: recipes for disaster. American Scientist, Vol.81(6):530-541.

Butler, B. Robert
    1961   The Old Cordilleran culture in the Pacific Northwest. Occasional Papers of the Idaho State College Museum, No.5. Pocatello.
    1962   Contributions to the prehistory of the Columbia Plateau. Occasional Papers of the Idaho State College Museum, No.9
    1963   An Early Man site at Big Camas Prairie, South-Central Idaho. Tebiwa 6:22-33.

Byers, Douglas S.,
    1959   The Eastern Archaic, some problems and hypotheses. American Antiquity, Vol.24(3):233-256.
    1962   New England and the Arctic. In Prehistoric Cultural Relations between the Arctic and Temperate Zones of North America. John M. Campbell (ed.): 143-153. Technical Paper No.11, Arctic Institute of North America.
    1979   The Nevin Shellheap: burials and observations. Papers of the Robert S. Peabody Foundation for Archaeology, Vol.9.

Calder, James M.
    1977   The Majorville Cairn and Medicine Wheel site, Alberta. National Museum of Man, Archaeological Survey of Canada, Mercury 62.

Calkin, Parker E. and Kathleen B. Miller
    1977   Late Quaternary environment and man in western New York. In Amerinds and their Paleoenvironments in Northeastern North America. New York Academy of Sciences

288:297-315.

Callaghan, Richard T.
1986   Analysis of fluoride content of human remains from the Gray site, Saskatchewan. Plains Anthropologist 31(31-114):317-328.

Calvert, Gay
1970   The St.Mungo Cannery site: a preliminary report. B.C. Studies 6-7:54-76.

Campbell, John M.
1962   Cultural succession at Anaktuvuk Pass, Arctic Alaska. In Prehistoric Cultural Relations between the Arctic and Temperate Zones of North America. John M. Campbell (ed.): 39-54. Arctic Institute of North America, Technical Paper No.11.

Campbell, Lyle and Marianne Mithun
1979   Introduction: North American Indian historical linguistics in current perspective. In The Languages of Native America: Historical and Comparative Assessment. Lyle Campbell and Marianne Mithun (eds.): 3-69. University of Texas Press.

Capes, Katherine H.
1964   Contributions to the prehistory of Vancouver Island. Occasional Papers of the Idaho State University Museum, No.15.

Carignan, Paul
1975   The Beaches: a multi-component habitation site in Bonavista Bay. National Museum of an, Archaeological Survey of Canada, Mercury 39.

Carlson, Catherine
1979   The early component at Bear Cove. Canadian Journal of Archaeology No.3:177-194.

Carlson, Roy L.
1970   Excavations at Helen Point on Mayne Island. In Archaeology in British Columbia, New Discoveries. Roy L. Carlson (ed.): 113-125. B.C. Studies 6-7.
1972   Excavations at Kwatna. In Salvage '71, Reports on Salvage Archaeology Undertaken in British Columbia in 1971. Roy L. Carlson (ed.): 41-57. Simon Fraser University, Department of Archaeology, Publication No.1.
1979   The Early Period on the Central Coast of British Columbia. Canadian Journal of Archaeology No.3:211-228.
1983   The Far West. In Early Man in the New World. Richard Shutler Jr. (ed.): 73-96. Sage Publications.

1983a   Prehistory of the Northwest Coast. In Indian Art Traditions of the Northwest Coast. Roy L. Carlson (ed.): 13-32. Simon Fraser University, Department of Archaeology, Publication No.13.

1983b   Change and continuity in Northwest Coast art. In Indian Art Traditions of the Northwest Coast. Roy L. Carlson (ed.): 121-129. Simon Fraser University, Department of Archaeology, Publication No.13.

1988   The view from the north. In Early Human Occupation in Far Western North America: the Clovis-Archaic Interface. Judith A. Willig, C. Melvin Aikens, and Joan L. Fagan (eds.): 319-324. Nevada State Museum, Anthropological Papers No.21.

1990   Cultural antecedents. In Handbook of the North American Indians. William C. Sturtevant (gen. ed.). Vol.7, Northwest Coast. Wayne Suttles (vol. ed.): 60-69. Smithsonian Institution, Washington D.C.

1990a   History of Research in Archaeology. In Handbook of North American Indians. William C. Sturtevant (gen. ed.), Volume 7, Northwest Coast. Wayne Suttles (vol. ed.): 107-115. Smithsonian Institution.

1994   Trade and exchange in prehistoric British Columbia. In Prehistoric Exchange Systems in North America. Timothy G. Baugh and Jonathon E. Ericson (eds.): 307-361. Plenum Press, New York and London.

n.d.   Namu periodization and C-14 chronology. Unpublished manuscript, May, 1990.

Carlson, Roy L. and Aubrey Cannon

1988   Early Namu. Canadian Archaeological Association, 21st Annual Meeting, Abstracts: 33.

Carmichael, P.

1979   The Thunderbird site, EgKx-15: a prehistoric petroform and habitation site in Manitoba. Papers in Manitoba Archaeology, Final Report 6, Manitoba Department of Cultural Affairs and Historical Resources, Historic Resources Branch. Manitoba.

Carpenter, Edmund

1986   Materials for the study of social symbolism in ancient and tribal art, a record of tradition and continuity. Volume 1 (Books 1 to 4), Volume 2 (Books 1 to 5), and Volume 3 (Books 1 to 3). Rock Foundation.

Cavalli-Sforza, L. L.

1986   Population structure. In Evolutionary Perspectives and the New Genetics. H. Gershowitz, D.L. Rucknagel and R. E. Tashian (eds.): 13-30. New York: Liss.

Cavallo, John

1981   Turkey Swamp: a late Paleo-Indian site in New Jersey's Coastal Plain. Archaeology of Eastern North America 9:1-18.

Chapdelaine, Claude

1984   Le site de Chicoutimi, un campement préhistorique au pays des Kakouchaks. Ministère des Affaires culturelles, Dossiers 61.

1987   Le site Jacques à Saint-Roch-de-Richelieu, Archaïque Laurentien ou Post-Laurentien? Recherches amérindiennes au Québec, Vol.XVII(1-2):63-80.

Chapdelaine, Claude et Steve Bourget

1992   Premier regard sur a site Paléoindien récent à Remouski (DcEd-1). Recherches amérindiennes au Québec, Vol.XXII(1):17-32.

Chevrier, Daniel

1978   La Côte Nord de Saint-Laurent. Recherches amérindiennes au Québec VII(1-2):75-86.

1986   GaFf-1: un atelier de taille du quartz en Jamésie orientale. Recherches amérindiennes au Québec, XVI(2-3):57-72.

Childe, V. Gordon

1935   Changing methods and aims in prehistory. Proceedings of the Prehistoric Society, 1:1-15.

Chisholm, Brian S. and D. Erle Nelson

1983   An early human skeleton from north central British Columbia: dietary inference from carbon isotopic evidence. Canadian Journal of Archaeology Vol.7 (1): 85-86.

Chisholm, Brian. S., D. Erle. Nelson and Henry. P. Schwarcz

1982   Stable carbon isotope ratios as a measure of marine versus terrestrial protein in ancient diets. Science 216:1131-1132.

1983   Marine and terrestrial protein in prehistoric diets on the British Columbia coast. Current Anthropology, Vol.23(3):396-398.

Chomko, S. A. and G. W. Crawford

1978   Plant husbandry in prehistoric eastern North America: new evidence for its development. American Antiquity Vol.43(3):405-408.

Choquette, Wayne

1972   Archaeological investigations in the East Kootenay regions, B. C. Canadian Archaeological Association, Bulletin 4:83-84.

1973   Archaeological investigations in the Rocky Mountain Trench and adjacent mountains, southeastern British Columbia, 1973. Canadian Archaeological Association, Bulletin 5: 117-119.

1987   Archaeological investigations in the Middle Kootenai region and vicinity. In Prehistoric Land Use in the Northern Rocky Mountains: a Center for Northwest Anthropology,

Project 4, Perspective from the Middle Kootenai River Valley. A. V. Thoms and G. C. Burtchard (eds.): 57-122.

1987a   A palaeoclimatic model for the Upper Columbia Basin. In Man and the Mid-Holocene Climatic Optimum. Neil A. McKinnon and G. S. L. Stuart (eds.): 311-344. Proceedings of the 17th Annual Chacmool Conference. The University of Calgary Archaeological Association. University of Calgary.

Cinq-Mars, Jacques

1973   An archaeologically important raw material from the Tertiary Hills, Western District of Mackenzie Northwest Territories: a preliminary report. In Preliminary Archaeological Study, Mackenzie Corridor. Jacques Cinq-Mars (ed.): appendix E (E1-E29). Environmental-Social Committee Northern Oil Development Report 73-10. Indian and Northern Development publication number QS-1506-0000-FE-81.

1973a   Preliminary archaeological study, Mackenzie Corridor. Environmental-Social Committee Northern Pipelines, Task Force on Northern Oil Development, Report No.73-10.

1974   Preliminary archaeological study Mackenzie Corridor (second report). Environmental-Social Committee Northern Pipelines, Task Force on Northern Oil Development, Report No.74-11.

1979   Bluefish Cave 1: a Late Pleistocene eastern Beringian cave deposit in the northern Yukon. Canadian Journal of Archaeology No.3:1-32.

1990   La place des Grottes du Poisson- Bleu dans la préhistoirie Beringienne. En Revista de Arqueología Americana, Número 1, Instituto Panamericano de Geografía e Historia: 9-32.

Cinq-Mars, Jacques, C. Richard Harington, D. Erle Nelson and Richard S. MacNeish

1991   Engigstciak revisted: a note on Early Holocene AMS dates from the "Buffalo Pit". NOGAP Archaeology Project: an Integrated Archaeological Research and Management Approach. Jacques Cinq-Mars and Jean-Luc Pilon (eds.): 33-44. Canadian Archaeological Association, Occasional Paper No.1.

Cinq-Mars, Jacques and Richard E. Morlan

n.d.   Bluefish Caves and Old Crow Basin: a new rapport. To appear in the First World Summit Conference publication on Clovis.

Clark, Donald W.

1974   Highlights of archaeological surveys in northern interior District of Mackenzie, N.W.T. Canadian Archaeological Association, Bulletin 6:50-91.

1975   Prehistory of the Western Subarctic. Canadian Archaeological Association, Bulletin 7:76-95.

1981   Prehistory of the Western Subarctic. In Handbook of North American Indians. William

C. Sturtevant (gen. ed.), Vol.6, Subarctic. June Helm (vol. ed.): 107-129. Smithsonian Institution, Washington, D.C.

1983 Is there a northern Cordilleran tradition? Canadian Journal of Archaeology, Vol.7(1):23-48.

1983a Reviews and Book Notes. Canadian Journal of Archaeology, Vol.7(1):93-104.

1983b Mackenzie - river to nowhere? The Musk-ox, No.33:1-9.

1984 Northern fluted points: Paleo-Eskimo, Paleo-Arctic, or Paleo-Indian. Canadian Journal of Archaeology, Vol.4(1):65-81.

1987 Archaeological reconnaissance at Great Bear Lake. Canadian Museum of Civilization, Archaeological Survey of Canada, Mercury 136.

1991 Western Subarctic prehistory. Canadian Prehistory Series, Archaeological Survey of Canada, Canadian Museum of Civilization.

1991a The Northern (Alaska-Yukon) Fluted Points. In Clovis Origins and Adaptations. Robson Bonnichsen and Karen L. Turmise (eds.): 35-48. Corvallis: Center for the Study of the First Americans, Oregon State University.

1992 A microblade production station (KbTx-2) in the south central Yukon. Canadian Journal of Archaeology, Vol.16:3-23.

Clark, Donald W. and A. MacFaden Clark

1975 Fluted points from the Batza Tena obsidian source of the Koyukuk River, region, Alaska. Anthropological Papers of the University of Alaska, 17:31-38.

1983 Paleo-Indians and fluted points: subarctic alternatives. Plains Anthropologist, 28:102(1):283-292.

1993 Batza Tena, Trail to Obsidian, archaeology of an Alaskan obsidian source. Canadian Museum of Civilization, Archaeological Survey of Canada, Mercury 147.

Clark, Donald W. and Richard E. Morlan

1982 Western Subarctic prehistory: twenty years later. Canadian Journal of Archaeology, No.6:79-94.

Cleland, Charles E.

1966 The prehistoric animal ecology and ethnozoology of the Upper Great Lakes region. Museum of Anthropology, University of Michigan, Anthropological Papers 29.

Clermont, Norman

1974 Un site archaïque de la région de Chambly. Recherches amérindiennes au Québec IV(3):33-51.

1987 Les énigmatiques objects piriformes de l'Archaïque. Recherches amérindiennes au Québec, Vol.XVII(1-2):37-46.

470

Clermont, Norman et Claude Chapdelaine

    1982   Pointe - du - Buisson 4: quarante siècles d'archives oubliées. Recherches amérindiennes au Québec, Edition Special.

Clermont, Norman, Claude Chapdelaine, et Jacques Guimont

    1992   L'occupation historique et préhistorique de Place-Royale. Collections Patrimoines, Dossiers, Direction des communications du ministre des Affaires culturelles, Gouvernement du Québec.

Coe, Joffre L.

    1964   The formative cultures of the Carolina Piedmont. Transactions of the American Philosophical Society, n.s. 54(5).

Collins, H. B.

    1963   Palaeo-Indian artifacts in Alaska: an example of cultural retardation in the Arctic. In Early Man in the Western American Arctic: a Symposium. F-H West (ed.): 13-18. Anthropological Papers of the University of Alaska, 12(2).

Collins, Michael B.

    1990   Obeservations on Clovis lithic technology. Current Research in the Pleistocene 7:73-74. A Peopling of the Americas Publication, Center for the Study of the First Americans, University of Maine, Orono.

Conover, Kathryn

    1978   Matrix analyses. In Studies in Bella Bella Prehistory. James J. Hester and Sarah M. Nelson (eds.): 67-99. Simon Fraser University, Department of Archaeology, Publication No.5.

Conway, Thor

    1981   Archaeology in northeastern Ontario, searching for our past. Historical Planning and Research Branch, Ministry of Culture and Recreation, Ontario.

Cook, John P.

    n.d.   The early prehistory of Healy Lake, Alaska. Ph.D. dissertation, Department of Anthropolgy, University of Wisconsin, Madison, Wisconsin, 1969.

    1975   Archaeology of interior Alaska. Western Canadian Journal of Anthropology 5:125-133.

Cook, T. G.

    1976   Broadpoint: culture, phase, horizon, tradition, or knife? Journal of Anthropological Research 32(4):337-357.

Cooke, Katie
1984   Images of Indians held by non-Indians: a review of current Canadian research. Indian and Northern Affairs. Ottawa.

Côté, Marc
1987   Les manifestations Archaïques de la Station 1 du site Hamel. Recherches amérindiennes au Québec, Vol. XVII(1-2):133-138.
1993   Préhistoire de l'Abitibi-Témiscaminque. Recherches amérindiennes au Québec, Vol.XXIII(2-3):5-24.

Cotter, J. L.
1937   The significance of Folsom and Yuma artifact occurrences in the light of typology and distribution. In 25th Anniversary Studies. D.S.Davidson (ed.): 27-36. Philadelphia Anthropological Society.

Coupland, Gary
1988   Prehistoric cultural change at Kitselas Canyon. Canadian Museum of Civilization, Archaeological Survey of Canada, Mercury 138.

Cox, Donald D. and Donald M. Lewis
1965   Pollen studies in the Cruscoe Lake area of prehistoric Indian occupation. New York State Museum, Bulletin 397.

Cox, Steven L.
1978   Palaeo-Eskimo occupations of the north Labrador coast. Arctic Anthropology XV(2):96-118.
1986   A re-analysis of the Shoop site. Archaeology of Eastern North America, Vol.14: 101-170.
1991   Site 95.20 and the Vergennes phase in Maine. Archaeology of Eastern North America, Vol.19:135-161.

Crane, H. R.
1956   University of Michigan radiocarbon dates I. Science 124:3224.

Crawford, Michael H.
1992   When two worlds collide. Human Biology, Vol.64(3):271-279. Wayne State University Press.

Cressman, L. S., D. L. Cole, W. A. Davis, T. M. Newman, and D. J. Scheans
1960   Cultural sequences at the Dalles, Oregon. Transactions of the American Philosophical

Society, n.s. 50(10).

Croes, Dale R.

1976   Resume of five major topic questions concerning the excavation of Northwest Coast wet sites. In The Excavation of Water-saturated Archaeological Sites (Wet Sites) on the Northwest Coast of North America. Dale R. Croes (ed.): 285-302. National Museum of Man, Archaeological Survey of Canada, Mercury 50.

Cunningham, Wilbur M.

1948   A study of the Glacial Kame culture in Michigan, Ohio and Indiana. University of Michigan, Museum of Anthropology, Occasional Contributions 12.

Curran, Mary Lou and John R. Grimes

1989   Ecological implications for Paleoindian lithic procurement economy in New England. In Eastern Paleoindian Lithic Resource Use. Christopher J. Ellis and Jonathan C. Lothrop (eds.): 41-74. Westview Press.

Curtin, A. Joanne

n.d.   Human skeletal remains from Namu (ElSx 1): a descriptive analysis. M.A. thesis in archaeology, Simon Fraser University, Burnaby, B.C. 1984.

Cybulski, Jerome S.

1978   Probable Archaic Period human remains from the Coteau du Lac site. In Essays in Northeastern Anthropology in Memory of Marian E. White, Occasional Publications in Northeastern Anthropology No.5. William E. Engelbrecht and Donald K. Grayson (eds.): 78-95.

1990   Human biology. In Handbook of North American Indians. William C. Sturtevant (gen. ed.), Vol. 7, Northwest Coast, Wayne Suttles (vol. ed.): 52-59. Smithsonian Institution.

1992   A Greenville burial ground, human remains and mortuary elements in British Columbia Coast prehistory. Canadian Museum of Civilization, Archaeological Survey of Canada, Mercury 146.

1994   Culture change, demographic history, and health and disease on the Northwest Coast. In In the Wake of Contact: Biological Responses to Conquest. George Milner and Clark Larsen (eds.): 75-85. New York: Wiley-Liss Inc.

Cybulski, Jerome S., Donald E. Howes, James C. Haggarty, and Morley Eldridge

1981   An early human skeleton from south-central British Columbia: dating and bioarchaeological inference. Canadian Journal of Archaeology No.5:49-59.

Dailey, Robert C. and James V. Wright

1955   The Malcolm site: a late stage of the Middle Point Peninsula culture in eastern Ontario. Transactions of the Royal Canadian Institute XXXI(1):3-23.

Damas, David
     1969   Characteristics of Central Eskimo band structure. National Museum of Canada, Bulletin 228: 116-141.

Damas, David (vol. ed.)
     1984   Handbook of North American Indians, Arctic, Vol.5. William C. Sturtevant (gen. ed.) Smithsonian Institution, Washington.

Davis, E. L., Clark W. Brott, and David L. Weide
     1969   The Western Lithic Co-Tradition. San Diego Museum Papers 6.

Davis, Margaret B.
     1967   Late glacial climate in northern United States: a comparison of New England and the Great Lakes region. In Quaternary Paleoecology. E.J.Cushing and H.E.Wright (eds.): 11-44. Yale University Press.
     1977   Outbreaks of forest pathogens in Quaternary history. Proceedings of the IV International Conference on Palynology, Lucknow, 1976-77, p.21.

Davis, Stanley D.
     1990   Prehistory of southeastern Alaska. In Handbook of the North American Indians. William C. Sturtevant (gen. ed.). Vol 7, Northwest Coast. Wayne Suttles (vol. ed.): 197 -202. Smithsonian Institution, Washington D.C.

Dawe, Bob and Jack Brink
     1991   Preliminary report of the 1988 and 1989 field seasons at Head-Smashed-In buffalo jump. Archaeological Survey of Alberta, Occasional Paper No.33:145-155.

Dawson, K. C. A.
     1966   Isolated copper artifacts from northwestern Ontario. Ontario Archaeology, 9:63-67.
     1976   Algonkians of Lake Nipigon: an archaeological survey. National Museum of Man, Archaeological Survey of Canada, Mercury 48.
     1976a   Albany River Survey, Patricia District, Ontario. National Museum of Man, Archaeological Survey of Canada, Mercury 51.
     1981   Prehistoric stone features on the relic north shore cobble beaches of Lake Superior. In Megaliths to Medicine Wheels: Boulder Structures in Archaeology. Michael Wilson, Kathie L. Road, and Kenneth J. Hardy (eds.): 297-312. Proceedings of the Eleventh Annual Chacmool Conference, the Archaeological Association of the University of

474

Calgary.

1983   Prehistory of Northern Ontario. The
           Thunder Bay Historical Museum Society.

1983a   Prehistory of the interior forest of Northern Ontario. Boreal Forest Adaptations. A.
           Theodore Steegmann Jr. (ed.): 55-84. Plenum Publishing.

1983b   Cummins site: a Late Palaeo-Indian (Plano) site at Thunder Bay, Ontario. Ontario
           Archaeology 39:3-31.

Deal, Michael
    1986   Late Archaic and Ceramic Period utilization of the Mud Lake Stream site, southwestern
           New Brunswick. Man in the Northeast, Vol.32:67-94.

DeJarnette, David L., Edward B. Kurjack, and James W. Cambron
    1962   Stanfield-Worley Bluff Shelter excavations. Journal of Alabama Archaeology, VIII(1 &
           2).

Dekin, Albert A. Jr.
    1976   Elliptical analysis: a heuristic technique for the analysis of artifact clusters. In Eastern
           Arctic Prehistory: Paleoeskimo Problems. Moreau S. Maxwell (ed.): 79-88. Memoirs
           of the Society for American Archaeology, No.31.

    1976a The Arctic Small Tool horizon: a behavioural model of the dispersal of human population
           into an unoccupied niche. In Eastern Arctic Prehistory: Paleoeskimo Problems. Moreau
           S. Maxwell (ed.): 156-163. Memoirs of the Society for American Archaeology, No.31.

DeLaguna, F.
    1962   Intemperate reflections on Arctic and Subarctic archaeology. In Prehistoric Cultural
           Patterns between the Arctic and Temperate Zones of North America. J. M. Campbell
           (ed.): 164-169. Arctic Institute of North America, Technical Paper 11.

Deller, D. Brian
    1976   The Heaman site: a preliminary report on a Paleo-Indian site in Middlesex County,
           Ontario. Ontario Archaeology 27:13-28.

    1979   Paleo-Indian reconnaissance in the counties of Lambton and Middlesex, Ontario. Ontario
           Archaeology 32:3-20.

    1989   Interpretation of chert type variation in Paleoindian industries, southwestern Ontario. In
           Eastern Paleoindian Lithic Resource Use. Christopher J. Ellis and Jonathan C. Lothrop
           (eds.): 191-220. Westview Press.

Deller, D. Brian and Christopher J. Ellis
    1984   Crowfield: a preliminary report on a probable Paleo-Indian cremation in southwestern

Ontario. In New Experiments upon the Record of Eastern Palaeo-Indian Cultures, Archaeology of Eastern North America, 12:41-71.

1992   Thedford II, a Paleo-Indian site in the Ausable River Watershed of Southwestern Ontario. Memoirs, Museum of Anthropology, University of Michigan, No.24.

1992a   The Early Paleo-Indian Parkhill phase in southwestern Ontario. Man in the Northeast, No.44:15-54.

Deller, Brian, Chris Ellis, and Ian Kenyon

1986   The archaeology of the southeastern Huron Basin. In Studies in Southwestern Ontario Archaeology. William A. Fox (ed.): 2-12, London Chapter of the Ontario Archaeological Society, Occasional Publication 1.

Dent, Richard J. and Barbara E. Kauffman

1985   Aboriginal subsistence and site ecology as interpreted from microfloral and faunal remains. In Shawnee Minisink, a stratified Paleoindian - Archaic site in the Upper Delaware Valley of Pennsylvania. Charles W. McNett Jr. (ed.): 55-79. Academic Press.

Denton, David

1988   Long term land use patterns of the Caniapiscau area, Nouveau-Quebec. In Boreal Forest and Sub-Arctic Archaeology. C. S. "Paddy" Reid (ed.): 146-156. Occasional Publications of the London Chapter, Ontario Archaeological Society, No.6.

Denton, David and Moira T. McCaffrey

1988   A preliminary statement on the prehistoric utilization of chert deposits near Schefferville, Nouveau-Quebec. Canadian Journal of Archaeology, Vol.12: 137-152.

Denton, David, Marie Ferdais, Jean-Ives Pintal, Claude Rocheleau, Michel Bouchard, Pierre Richard et Pierre Grégoire

1980   Investigations archéologiques dans la region du futur reservoir Caniapiscau, Rapport Preliminaire - 1979. Interventions Archéologiques - 1, Ministère des Affaires culturelles, Direction générale du patrimoine, Québec.

Denton, David, Nicole Lafrance, Jean-Ives Pintal, Jean-Luc Pilon, et Bertrand Emard

1982   Recherche archéologique dans la region du futur reservoir Caniapiscau, été 1980. Interventions Archéologiques 2, Ministère des Affaires culturelles, Direction générale du patrimoine, Québec.

Dewhirst, John

1980   The indigenous archaeology of Yuquot, a Nootkan outside village. The Yuquot Project, Vol.I, History and Archaeology, No.39, Parks Canada.

476

Diamond, Jared M.

1988   Why was Post-Pleistocene development of human societies slightly more rapid in the Old World than in the New World? In America before Columbus: Ice-Age Origins. Ronald C. Carlisle (ed.): 25-30. University of Pittsburg, Department of Anthropology, Ethnology Monographs No.12.

Dick, Herbert W. and Bert Mountain

1960   The Claypool site: a Cody Complex site in northeastern Colorado. American Antiquity Vol.26(2):223-235.

Dickson, Gary A.

1980   The Kame Hills site. Papers in Manitoba Archaeology, Final Report No.9, Department of Cultural Affairs and Historical Resources, Historic Resources Branch. Manitoba.

Dikov, N. N.

1978   Ancestors of Paleo-Indians and Proto- Eskimo-Aleuts in the Paleolithic of Kamchatka. In Early Man in America from a Circum-Pacific Perspective. A. L. Bryan (ed.): 68 -69. Department of Anthropology, University of Alberta, Occasional Papers 1.

Dillehay, Tom D. and Michael B. Collins

1991   Monte Verde, Chile: a comment on Lynch. American Antiquity, Vol.56(2):333-341.

Dillehay, Tom D. and David J. Meltzer

1991   The first Americans, search and research. CRC Press.

Dincauze, Dena F.

1976   The Neville site, 8,000 years at Amoskeng, Manchester, New Hampshire. Peabody Museum Monographs, No.4.

1984   An archaeo-logical evaluation of the case for pre-Clovis occupations. In Advances in World Archaeology 3. Fred Wendorf and Angela E. Close (eds.): 275-323.

Dincauze, Dena F. and Mitchell T. Mulholland

1977   Early and Middle Archaic site distributions and habitats in southern New England. In Amerinds and their paleoenvironments in northeastern North America. Walter S. Newman and Bert Salwen (eds.): 439-454. New York Academy of Science Bulletin 288.

Dixon, E. James, Jr.

1975   The Gallagher Flint Station, an Early Man site on the North Slope, Arctic Alaska, and its role in relation to the Bering Land Bridge. Arctic Anthropology XII(1):68-75.

1984-85   Review of "Paleoecology of Beringia" by David M. Hopkins, John V. Mathews Jr.,

Charles E. Scheweger, and Steven B. Young (eds.), Academic Press, New York In North American Archaeologist, Vol.6(1):83-94.

1985   Cultural chronology of central interior Alaska. Arctic Anthropology XX(1): 47-66.

Doll, Maurice F. V.

1982   The Boss Hill site (FdPe-4) Locality 2: pre-Archaic manifestations in the Parkland of Central Alberta, Canada. Provincial Museum of Alberta, Human History Occasional Paper 2.

Donahue, Paul F.

1975   Concerning Athapaskan prehistory in British Columbia. The Western Canadian Journal of Anthropology, V(3-4):21-63.

Doyle, Richard A., Nathan D. Hamilton, James B. Petersen, and David Sanger

1985   Late Paleo-Indian remains from Maine and their correlations in northeastern prehistory. Archaeology of Eastern North America 13:1-34.

Dragoo, Don W.

1959   Archaic hunters of the Upper Ohio Valley. Carnegie Museum, Anthropological Series No.3.

1966   The Archaic or hunting, fishing, gathering stage, a review. New York State Archeological Association, The Bulletin 36:5-9.

Drier, Roy W.

1961   The Michigan College of Mining and Technology Isle Royale excavations, 1953-54. In Lake Superior Copper and the Indians: Miscellaneous Studies of Great Lakes Prehistory. James B. Griffin (ed.): 1-7. University of Michigan, Museum of Anthropology, Anthropological Papers No.17.

Driver, Jonathan C.

1982   Early prehistoric killing of Bighorn sheep in the southeastern Canadian Rockies. Plains Anthropologist 27(98):265-271.

1985   Prehistoric hunting strategies in the Crowsnest Pass, Alberta. Canadian Journal of Archaeology, Vol.9(2):109-129.

Drucker, Philip

1951   The Northern and Central Nootkan tribes. Smithsonian Institution, Bureau of American Ethnology, Bulletin 144.

Dumais, Pierre

1978   Le Bas Saint-Laurent. En Images de la préhistoire du Québec. Claude Chapdelaine (ed.). Recherches amérindiennes au Québec VII(1-2):63-74.

Dumais, Pierre et Gilles Rousseau

1985   Trois sites paléoindiens sur la côte sud de l'estuaire du Saint-Laurent. En La Période Paléoindienne. Claude Chapdelaine (ed.): 135-149. Recherches amérindiennes au Québec XV(1-2).

1986   Menagoesenog, ou les Îles de la Madeleine: contexte environnmental. En Les Micmacs et la Mer. Charles A. Martijn (ed.): 67-98. Recherches amérindiennes au Québec.

Dumond, Don E.

1969-1970   Eskimos and Aleuts. Proceedings of the 8th International Congress of Anthropological and Ethnological Sciences. Tokyo and Kyoto, Vol.3:102-104.

1977   The Eskimos and Aleuts. London: Thames and Hudson.

1978   Alaska and the Northwest Coast. In Ancient Native Americans. Jesse D. Jennings (ed.): 42-94. Freeman Publications.

1981   Archaeology on the Alaska Peninsula: the Naknek region, 1960-1975. University of Oregon Anthropological Papers No.21.

1984   Prehistory: summary. In Handbook of North American Indians. William C. Sturtevant (gen. ed.), Vol.5, Arctic. David Damas (vol. ed.): 72-79. Smithsonian Institution, Washington D.C.

Dumond, Don E., Winfield Henn and Robert Stuckenrath

1976   Archaeology and prehistory on the Alaska Peninsula. Anthropological Papers of the Unversity of Alaska 18(1):17-29.

Dumont, Elizabeth M. and Lewis A. Dumont

1979   Of paradigms and projectile points: two perspectives on the Early Archaic in the Northeast. New York State Archaeological Association, The Bulletin 75:38-52.

Dumont, John

1981   The Paleo-Indian - Early Archaic continuum, an environmental approach. Archaeology of Eastern North America 9:18-37.

Dunnell, Robert C.

1982   Science, social science, and common sense: the agonizing dilemma of modern archaeology. Journal of Anthropological Research 38(1):1-25.

1991   A review of "A history of archaeological thought" by Bruce G. Trigger. American Scientist, January-February, Vol.79(1):87-88.

Dyck, Ian G.

1970   Two Oxbow settlement types in central Saskatchewan. Napao II(2):1-29.

1977   The Harder site: a Middle Period bison hunter's campsite in the northern Great Plains. National Museum of Man, Archaeological Survey of Canada, Mercury 67.

1983   The prehistory of southern Saskatchewan. In Tracking Ancient Hunters: Prehistoric Archaeology in Saskatchewan. H. T. Epp and I. Dyck (eds.): 63-139. Saskatchewan Archaeological Society, Regina.

Dyck, Ian and Richard E. Morlan

(in press)   Hunting and gathering traditions: Canadian Prairies. In Handbook of North American Indians. William C. Sturtevant (gen. ed.), Vol.13, Plains, Raymond J. DeMallie (vol. ed.). Smithsonian Institution.

Ebell, S. Biron

1980   The Parkhill site: an Agate Basin surface collection in south central Saskatchewan. Pastlog 4, Manuscript Series in Archaeology and History, Saskatchewan Culture and Youth, Regina.

Eddy, John A.

1974   Astronomical alignments of the Big Horn Medicine Wheel. Science 184(4141): 1035-1043.

Edwards, Robert L. and K. O. Emery

1977   Man on the Continental Shelf. In Amerinds and their paleoenvironments in northeastern North America, Annals of the New York Academy of Sciences, 288: 245-256.

Eiseley, Loren C.

1955   The Paleo-Indians: their survival and diffusion. In New interpretations of aboriginal American culture history. Betty J. Meggers and Cliffor Evans (eds.): 1-11. 75th Anniversary Volume of the Anthropological Society of Washington, D.C.

Eldridge, Morley

1981   The Hope Highway Archaeological Salvage Project. In Annual Research Report No.1, Activities of the Heritage Conservation Branch for the Year 1978. Bjorn Simonsen, Ray Kenny, John MacMurdo, and Pauline Rafferty (eds.): 53-110.

Eldridge, Morley and Steven Acheson

1992   The antiquity of fish weirs on the Southern Coast: a response to Moss, Erlandson, and Stuckenrath. Canadian Journal of Archaeology, Vol.16:112-116.

480

Ellis, Christopher J.

1989   The explanation of Northeastern Paleoindian lithic procurement patterns. In Eastern Paleoindian Lithic Resource Use. Christopher J. Ellis and Jonathan C. Lothrop (eds.): 139-164. Westview Press.

Ellis, C. J. and D. Brian Deller

1982   Hi-Lo materials from southwestern Ontario. Ontario Archaeology 38:3-22.

1986   Post-glacial Lake Nipissing waterworn assemblages from the southeastern Huron Basin area. Ontario Archaeology 45:39-60.

1991   Paleo - Indians. In Prehistory of Southern Ontario to A.D. 1650, Chapter 3. Neil Ferris and Chris Ellis (eds.): 37-64 , Ontario Archaeological Society, London Chapter.

1991a   A small (but informative) Early Archaic component at the Culloden Acres site, Area B. Kewa 91-8:2-17. Newsletter of the London Chapter of the Ontario Archaeological Society.

Ellis, Chris J, Ian T. Kenyon and Michael W. Spence

1990   The Archaic. In The Archaeology of Southern Ontario to A.D. 1650. Chris J. Ellis and Neal Ferris (eds.): 65-124. Ontario Archaeological Society, London Chapter, Occasional Publication No.5.

Ellis, Christopher J. and Jonathan C. Lothrop

1989   Preface. In Eastern Paleoindian Lithic Resource Use. Christopher J. Ellis and Jonathan C. Lothrop (eds.): xix-xxi. Westview Press.

Ellis, Chris J., Ian T. Kenyon, and Michael W. Spence

1990   The Archaic. In The Archaeology of Southern Ontario to A.D. 1650. Chris J. Ellis and Neal Ferris (eds.): 65-124. Occasional Publication of the London Chapter, Ontario Archaeological Society, No.5.

Ellis, Chris J., Stanley Wortner, and William A. Fox

1991   Nettling: an overview of an Early Archaic "Kirk Corner-notched Cluster" site in southwestern Ontario. Canadian Journal of Archaeology, Vol.15: 1-34.

Emerson, J. Norman

1960   The Puskasaw Pits and the religious alternative. New Pages in Prehistory, 1959. Ontario History LII(1):2 pages.

Emerson, J. N. and William C. Noble

1966   The Surma site, Fort Erie, Ontario. Ontario Archaeology 9:68-88.

Emperaire, J., A. Laming-Emperaire et H. Reichlen

1963   La Grotte Fell et Autres sites de la région volcanique de la Patagonie Chilienne. Journal de la Société des Américanistes 52:167-254. Paris.

Epp, Henry T.

1986   Prehistoric settlement response to the Harris Sand Hills, Saskatchewan, Canada. Plains Anthropologist 31(111):51-64.

1990   Human effect: dynamical extinction- expansion process. Canadian Journal of Archaeology Vol.14:93-105.

Epp, Henry T. and Ian Dyck (eds.)

1983   Tracking ancient hunters, prehistoric archaeology in Saskatchewan. Saskatchewan Archaeological Society, Regina.

Erlandson, Jon M.

1988   The role of shellfish in prehistoric economies: a protein prespective. American Antiquity, Vol.53(1):102-109.

Ewers, John C.

1955   The horse in Blackfoot Indian culture. Bureau of American Ethnology, Bulletin No.159, Smithsonian Institution, Washington D.C.

Farquhar, R. M. and I. R. Fletcher

1980   Lead isotope identification of sources of galena from some prehistoric Indian sites in Ontario, Canada. Science 207:640-643.

Fedirchuk, Gloria

1970   Recent archaeological investigations at Fisherman Lake: the Julian site. In Early Man and Environments in Northwest North America. R. A. Smith and J. W. Smith (eds.): 105-116. University of Calgary Archaeological Association.

Fedje, Daryl

1984   Archaeological investigations in Banff National Park-1983. In Archaeology in Alberta 1983. David Burley (ed.): 77-95, Archaeological Survey of Alberta, Occasional Paper No.23.

1986   Banff archaeology 1983-1985. In Eastern Slopes Prehistory: Selected Papers. Brian Ronaghan (ed.): 25-62. Archaeological Survey of Alberta, Occasional Publication No.30.

Feit, Harvey A.

1973   The ethno-ecology of the Waswanipi Cree: or, how hunters can manage their resources.

In Cultural Ecology: Readings on the Canadian Indians and Eskimos. Bruce A. Cox (ed.): 115-125.

Fenton, M. M. and J. W. Ives
1984   The stratigraphic position of Beaver River Sandstone. In Archaeology in Alberta 1983. David Burley (ed.): 128-136. Archaeological Survey of Alberta, Occasional Paper 23.

Fenton, William N.
1962   "This Island, the world on the turtle's back". Journal of American Folklore 75(298):283-300.

Figgins, J. D.
1927   The antiquity of man in America. Natural History 27:229-239.

Fisher, Daniel C.
1984   Taphonomic analysis of Late Pleistocene mastodon occurrences: evidence of butchery of North American Paleo-Indians. Paleobiology 10(3):338-357.
1984a   Mastodon butchery by North American Palaeo-Indians. Nature 308(5956): 271-272.

Fitting, James E.
1963   The Hi-Lo site: a late Palaeo-Indian site in western Michigan. The Wisconsin Archeologist, 44(2):21-24.
1968   Environmental potential and the postglacial readaptation in eastern North America. American Antiquity 33(4):441-445.
1970   The Archaeology of Michigan. The Natural History Press.

Fitting, James E., Jerry DeVisscher, and Edward J. Wahla
1966   The Paleo-Indian occupation of the Holcombe Beach. University of Michigan, Museum of Anthropology, Anthropology Papers 27.

Fitzhugh, William W.
1972   Environmental archeology and cultural systems in Hamilton Inlet, Labrador. Smithsonian Contributions to Anthropology No.16.
1975   A Maritime Archaic sequence from Hamilton Inlet, Labrador. Arctic Anthropology XII(2):117-138.
1976   Preliminary culture history of Nain, Labrador: Smithsonian Fieldwork, 1975. Journal of Field Archaeology 3:123-142.
1976a   Environmental factors in the evolution of Dorset culture: a marginal proposal for Hudson Bay. In Eastern Arctic Prehistory: Paleoeskimo Problems. Moreau S. Maxwell (eds.): 139-149. Memoirs of the Society for American Archaeology, No.31.

1976b   Paleoeskimo occupations of the Labrador coast. In Eastern Arctic Prehistory: Paleoeskimo Problems. Moreau S. Maxwell (ed.): 103-118. Memoirs of the Society for American Archaeology, No.31

1977   Population movement and culture change on the central Labrador coast. Annals of the New York Academy of Sciences, Vol.288:481-497.

1978   Maritime Archaic cultures of the central and northern Labrador coast. Arctic Anthropology XV(2):61-95.

1981   Smithsonian archaeological surveys, central and northern Labrador, 1980. Archaeology in Newfoundland and Labrador, 1980. Jane Sproull Thomson and Bernard Ransom (eds.), Annual Report 1:26-47.

1984   Residence pattern development in the Labrador Maritime Archaic: longhouse models and 1983 surveys. Archaeology in Newfoundland and Labrador 1983. Jane Sproull Thompson and Callum Thompson (eds.), Annual Report 4:6-47.

1984a   Paleo-Eskimo cultures of Greenland. In Handbook of North American Indians. William C. Sturtevant (gen. ed.), Vol.5, Arctic, David Damas (vol. ed.): 528-539. Smithsonian Institution.

1985   Early Maritime Archaic settlement studies and central coast surveys. Archaeology of Newfoundland and Labrador, 1984. Annual Report 5:48-85.

1985a   The Nulliak pendants and their relation to spiritual traditions in Northeast prehistory. Arctic Anthropology XXII(2):87-109.

Fitzhugh, William W. and H. F. Lamb

1985   Vegetation history and culture change in Labrador prehistory. Arctic and Alpine Research, Vol.17(4):357-370

Fladmark, Knut R.

1970   Preliminary report on the archaeology of the Queen Charlotte Islands: 1969 field season. B.C. Studies 6-7:18-45.

1975   A paleoecological model for Northwest Coast prehistory. National Museum of Man, Archaeological Survey of Canada, Mercury Series 48.

1976   Punchaw village: a preliminary report, archaeology of a prehistoric settlement. Current Research Reports, No.3. Roy L. Carlson (ed.): 19-32. Simon Fraser University, Department of Archaeology.

1978   A guide to basic archaeological field procedures. Department of Archaeology, Simon Fraser University, Publication No.4.

1979   Routes: alternate migration corridors for Early Man in North America. American Antiquity Vol.44(1):55-69.

1979a   The Early Prehistory of the Queen Charlotte Islands. Archaeology 32(2): 38-45.

1981   Paleo-Indian artifacts from the Peace River District. BC Studies, No.48, Winter 1980-81:124-135.

1982   An introduction to the prehistory of British Columbia. Canadian Journal of Archaeology No.6:95-156.

1983   Times and places: environmental correlates of Mid-to-Late Wisconsinan human population expansion in North America. In Early Man in the New World. Richard Shutler Jr. (ed.): 13-42, Sage Publications, Beverly Hills / London / New Delhi.

1985   Glass and ice, the archaeology of Mt. Elziza. Department of Archaeology, Simon Fraser University, Publication No.14.

1986   The prehistory of British Columbia. National Museum of Man, Canadian Prehistory Series, National Museums of Canada.

1990   Possible early human occupation of the Queen Charlotte Islands, British Columbia. Canadian Journal of Archaeology, Vol.14:183-197.

Fladmark, Knut R., Kenneth M. Ames, and Patricia D. Sutherland

1990   Prehistory of the Northern Coast of British Columbia. In Handbook of North American Indians. William C. Sturtevant (gen. ed.). Vol.7, Northwest Coast. Wayne Suttles (vol. ed.): 229-239. Smithsonian Institution.

Fladmark, Knut R., Jonathan C. Driver, and Diana Alexander

1988   The Paleoindian component at Charlie Lake Cave (HbRf39), British Columbia. American Antiquity Vol.53(2):371-384.

Folan, William J. and John T. Dewhirst

1969   Yuquot, British Columbia: the prehistory and history of a Nootkan village. Northwest Anthropological Research Notes 3(2):217-239.

Forbis, Richard G.

1961   Early point types from Acasta Lake, Northwest Territories. American Antiquity Vol.27(1):112-113.

1968   Fletcher: a Paleo-Indian site in Alberta. American Antiquity 33(1):1-10.

1970   A review of Alberta archaeology to 1964. Publications in Archaeology, No.1, National Museum of Man.

1992   The Mesoindian (Archaic) Period in the Northern Plains. Revista de Arqueología Americana, Número 5:27-70. Instituto Panamericano de Geografía e Historia.

1993   Dogs and the Post-Altithermal reoccupation of the Plains. In The Palliser Triangle, a region in space and time. R. W. Barendregt, M. C. Wilson, and F. J. Jankunis (eds.): 215-221.

Fortin, J. Henri

1966   Archéologie au Saguenay: un site Royaume du Saguenay. Rapport Préliminaire Site O (Section 4) - Lac St.Jean, P.Q. Société d'Archéologie du Saguenay, Métabetchouan,

Québec.

Foster, J. W. and J. D. Whitney
1850 Report on the geology and topography of a portion of the Lake Superior Land District in the State of Michigan. Copper Lands, House Executive Documents No.69, Part I, Washington D.C.

Fowler, Melvin L.
1959 Summary report of Modoc Rock Shelter, 1952, 1953, 1955, 1956. Illinois State Museum. Report of Investigations 8. Springfield.

Fox, William A.
1975 The Palaeo-Indian Lakehead complex. Canadian Archaeological Association, Collected Papers, March 1975b: 29-53. Division of Parks, Historical Sites Branch. Toronto.
1977 The trihedral adze in northwestern Ontario. Data Box 350, Research Manuscript Series, Ministry of Culture and Recreation, Ontario.

Frison, George C.
1976 Cultural activity associated with prehistoric mammoth butchering and processing. Science 194:728-730.
1978 Prehistoric hunters of the High Plains. Academic Press.
1980 Man and bison relationships in North America. In The Ice-free corridor and peopling of the New World, Proceeds of the Fifth Biennial Conference of the American Quaternary Association, Edmonton, September 2-4, 1978, Canadian Journal of Anthropology, 1(1):75-76.
1983 The Western Plains and Mountain Region. In Early Man in the New World. ed. Richard Shutler, Jr.: 109-124, Sage Publications. Beverely Hills.
1988 Paleoindian subsistence and settlement during Post-Clovis times on the Northwestern Plains, the adjacent mountain ranges, and intermontane basins. In Americans before Columbus: Ice-Age Origins. Ronald C. Carlisle (ed.): 83-106, Department of Anthropology, University of Pittsburg, Ethnology Monograph No.12.
1989 Fenn Clovis Cache. Abstract of The First World Summit Conference of the Peopling of the Americas. John Tomenchuk and Robson Bonnichesen (eds.). Center for the Study of the First Americans.
1990 The North American High Plains Paleoindian: an overview. In Revista de Arqueología Americana, Número 2:9-54, Instituto Panamericano de Geografía e Historia.
1974 (ed.),The Casper site, a Hell Gap bison kill on the High Plains. Academic Press.

Frison, George C., R. L. Andrews, J. M. Adovasio, R. C. Carlisle, and Robert Edgar
1986 A late Paleoindian animal trapping net from northern Wyoming. American Antiquity

51(2):352-360.

Frison, George C. and Bruce A. Bradley
1980   Folsom tools and technology at the Hanson site, Wyoming. University of New Mexico Press, Albuquerque.

Frison, George C. and M. Huseas
1968   Leigh Cave, Wyoming, Site 48WA304. The Wyoming Archaeologist 11(3):20-33.

Frison, George C. and Dennis. J. Stanford
1982   The Agate Basin site, a record of the Paleoindian occupation of the northwestern High Plains. Academic Press, New York.

Funk, Robert E.
1965   The Archaic of the Hudson Valley: new evidence and new interpretations. Pennsylvania Archaeologist XXXV(3-4):139-160.
1976   Recent contributions to Hudson Valley prehistory. New York State Museum, Memoir 22.
1978   Post-Pleistocene adaptations. In Handbook of North American Indians. William C. Sturtevant (gen. ed.), Vol.15, Northeast. Bruce G. Trigger (vol. ed.): 16-27.
1979   The Early and Middle Archaic in New York as seen from the Upper Susquehanna Valley. New York State Archaeological Association, The Bulletin 75:23-37.
1983   The Northeastern United States. In Ancient Native Americans, Vol.1. Jesse D. Jennings (ed.): 303-371. W. H. Freeman.
1988   The Laurentian concept: a review. Archaeology of Eastern North America, Vol.16:1-42.

Funk, Robert E. and Howard Hoagland
1972   An Archaic camp site in the Upper Susquehanna drainage. New York State Archaeological Association, The Bulletin 56:11-22.

Funk, Robert E., George R. Walters, William F. Ehlers, Jr., John E. Guilday, and G. Gordon Connally
1969   The archaeology of Dutchess Quarry Cave, Orange County, New York. Pennsylvania Archaeologist XXXIX(1-4):7-22.

Gal, Robert
1982   Appendix I: An annotated and indexed roster of archaeological radiocarbon dates from Alaska, north of 68 latitude. In Archaeological Investigations in the National Petroleum Reserve in Alaska. Anthropological Papers of the University of Alaska, 20(1-2):159-180.

Galdikas-Brindamour, Birute

1972   Faunal material from eight archaeological sites: a preliminary report. Salvage'71, Reports on salvage archaeology undertaken in BC in 1971. Roy L. Carlson (ed.): 199-205. Simon Fraser University, Department of Archaeology, Publication No.1.

Gardner, William M.

1977   Flint Run Paleo-Indian complex and its implications for eastern North American prehistory. In Amerinds and their Palaeoenvironments in Northeastern North America. W. S. Newman and B. Salwen (eds.), Annals of the New York Academy of Sciences, 288:257-263

1983   Stop me if you've heard this one before: the Flint Run Paleoindian campsite revisted. Archaeology of Eastern North America, 11:49-64.

Garland, Elizabeth B. and James W. Cogswell

1985   The Powers mastodon site, Van Buren County, Michigan. The Michigan Archaeologist, 31(1-2):3-39.

Gibson, Terrance H.

1976   The Cherry Point site: a multi-component lake-prairie habitation on the north eastern Plains. Western Canadian Journal of Anthropology 6(4):62-98.

1981   Remnant Oxbow on the Northern Plains: the evidence and its implications for regional prehistory. Canadian Journal of Archaeology No.5:131-136.

Giddings, J. Louis

1951   The Denbigh Flint complex. American Antiquity, Vol.16(3):193-203.

1956   A flint site in northern most Manitoba. American Antiquity, Vol.21(3):255-268.

1963   Some Arctic spear points and their counterparts. In Early Man in the Western Arctic: a Symposium. F. H. West (ed.): 1-13. Anthropological Papers of the University of Alaska, 10 (1).

1964   The archaeology of Cape Denbigh. Brown University Press.

Giddings, J. Louis and Douglas D. Anderson, 1986. Beach ridge archaeology of Cape Krusenstern. National Park Service, U.S. Department of the Interior, Publications in Archaeology 20.

Goebel, Ted, Roger Powers, and Nancy Bigelow

1991   The Nenana Complex of Alaska and Clovis origins. In Clovis origins and adaptations. Robson Bonnichsen and Karen L. Turnmire (eds.): 49-79. Peopling of the Americas Publication, Center for the Study of the First Americans. Oregon State University.

Goodyear, Albert C.

488

1989   A hypothesis for the use of cryptocrystalline raw materials among Paleoindian groups of North America. In Eastern Paleoindian Lithic Resource Use. Christopher J. Ellis and Jonathan C. Lothrop (eds.): 1-9. Westview Press.

Gordon, Bryan H. C.
1970   Recent archaeological investigations on the Arctic Yukon coast: including a description of the British Mountain Complex at Trout Lake. In Early Man and Environments in Northwest North America. R. A. Smith and J. W. Smith (eds.): 67-86. University of Calgary Archaeological Association.

1975   Of men and herds in Barrenland prehistory. National Museum of Man, Archaeological Survey of Canada, Mercury 28.

1976   Migod - 8,000 years of Barrenland prehistory. National Museum of Man, Archaeological Survey of Canada, Mercury 56.

1979   Of men and herds in Canadian Plains prehistory. National Museum of Man, Archaeological Survey of Canada, Mercury 84.

1981   Man-environment relationships in Barrenland prehistory. Institute for Northern Studies, The Musk- Ox, No.28:1-19.

1988   Of men and reindeer herds in French Magdalenian prehistory. BAR International Series 390. Oxford.

Gordon, Bryan C. and Howard Savage
1973   Mackenzie Delta archaeology - 1972. In Preliminary Archaeological Study, Mackenzie Corridor. J. Cinq-Mars (ed.): Appendix D, Environmental-Social Committee Northern Pipelines, Task Force on Northern Development, Report No.73-10.

1974   Whirl Lake: a stratified Indian site near the Mackenzie Delta. Arctic, 27(3):175-188.

Gose, Peter
1976   Chapter 10: the features at Glenrose. In The Glenrose Cannery site. R. G. Matson (ed.): 190-202. National Museum of Man, Archaeological Survey of Canada, Mercury 52.

Gotthardt, Ruth Margrit
1990   The archaeological sequence in the Northern Cordilleran: a consideration of typology and traditions. Heritage Branch, Government of the Yukon, Hude Hudan Series, Occasional Papers in Archaeology No.1.

Grabert, Garland F.
1971   Some implications of settlement variation in the Okanagan region. In Aboriginal Man and Environments on the Plateau of Northwest America. Arnoud H. Stryd and Rachel A. Smith (eds.): 153-167. University of Calgary Archaeological Association.

1974   Okanagan archaeology. Syesis 7, Supp.2, Provincial Museum of British Columbia.

1979 Pebble tools and time factoring. Canadian Journal of Archaeology No.3: 165-175.

Graham, R. W.
1982 Clovis peoples in the Midwest: the importance of the Kimmswick site. The Living Museum, 44(2):27-29.

Graham, Russell W., C. V. Haynes, D. L. Johnson, and M. Kay
1981 Kimmswick: a Clovis-mastodon association in eastern Missouri. Science 213:1115-1117.

Gramly, Richard M.
1978 Lithic source areas in northern Labrador. Arctic Anthropology XV(2): 36-47.
1982 The Vail site: a Palaeo-Indian encampment in Maine. Bulletin 30 of the Buffalo Society of the Natural Sciences. Buffalo.
1984 Kill sites, killing ground and fluted points at the Vail site. In New Experiments upon the Record of Eastern Palaeo-Indian Cultures, Archaeology of Eastern North America, 12: 110-121.
1988 Discoveries at the Lamb site, Genesee County, New York 1986-7. Ohio Archaeologist Vol.38(1):4-10.
1988a Palaeo-Indian sites south of Lake Ontario, Western and Central New York State. In Late Pleistocene and Early Holocene Paleoecology and Archeology of the Eastern Great Lakes Region. R. S. Laub, N. G. Milles and D. W. Steadman (eds.): 265-280. Bulletin 33 of the Buffalo Society of the Natural Sciences.
1988b The Adkins site: a Palaeo-Indian habitation and associated stone structure. Persimmons Press Monographs in Archaeology, Buffalo N.Y.
1990 Guide to the Palaeo-Indian artifacts of North America. Persimmon Press Monographs in Archaeology, Buffalo N.Y.
1991 Blood residues upon tools from the East Wenatchee Clovis site, Douglas County, Washington. Ohio Archaeologist, Vol.41(4):4-9.
1993 The Richey Clovis Cache. Persimmon Press Monographs in Archaeology. Buffalo.

Gramly, Richard, Michael and Robert E. Funk
1990 What is known and not known about the human occupation of the Northeastern United States until 10,000 B.P. Archaeology in Eastern North America, Vol.18:5-31.

Graspointner, Anreas
1981 Southern Alberta-the nomadic culture. In Alberta Archaeology: Prospect and Retrospect. T. A. Moore (ed.): 83-95.

Grayson, Donald K.
1984 Archaeological associations with extinct Pleistocene mammals in North America. Journal

of Archaeological Science 11:213-221.

1987 An analysis of the chronology of Late Pleistocene mammalian extinctions in North America. Quaternary Research 28:281-289.

1988 Perspectives on the archaeology of the first Americans. In Americans before Columbus: Ice-Age Origins. Ronald C. Carlisle (ed.): 107-123. Department of Anthropology, University of Pittsburg, Ethnology Monographs No.12.

Green F. E.

1963 The Clovis blades: an important addition to the Llano Complex. American Antiquity Vol.29(2):145-165.

Green, Thomas J.

1982 Pit house variability and associations at Givens Hot Springs, southwestern Idaho. Northwest Anthropological Research Notes, 16(1):77 (abstract).

Greenberg, Joseph H.

1987 Language in the Americas. Stanford University Press.

Greenberg, Joseph H., Christy G. Turner II, and Stephen L. Zegura

1986 The settlement of the Americas: a comparison of the linguistic, dental, and genetic evidence. Current Anthropology 27(5): 477-497.

Greengo, Robert E.

1982 Observations on Central Plateau prehistory. Northwest Anthropological Research Notes, 16(1):77-78 (abstract).

Greenman, E. F. and George M. Stanley

1940 A geologically dated camp site, Georgian Bay, Ontario. American Antiquity Vol.5(3):194-199.

1943 The archaeology and geology of two early sites near Killarney, Ontario. Papers of the Michigan Academy of Science, Arts and Letters, Vol.28:505-530.

Greer, Sheila C.

1991 The Trout Lake archaeological locality and the British Mountain problem. In NOGAP Archaeology Project: an Integrated Archaeological Research and Management Approach. Jacques Cinq-Mars and Jean-Luc Pilon (eds.): 15-31. Canadian Archaeological Association, Occasional Paper 1.

Greer, Sheild C. and Raymond J. LeBlanc

1983 Yukon culture history: an update. The Musk-ox, 33:26-36.

Griffin, James B.

1977   A commentary on Early Man studies in the Northeast. In Amerinds and their Environments in Northeastern North America. Walter S. Newman and Bert Salwen (eds.): 3-15. Annals of the New York Academy of Sciences, Vol.288.

1978   The Midlands and northeastern United States. In Ancient Native Americans. Jesse D. Jennings (ed.): 221 -280.

Griffin, James B. (ed.)

1961   Lake Superior copper and the Indians: miscellaneous studies of Great Lakes prehistory. Museum of Anthropology, University of Michigan, Anthropological Papers No.17.

Griffin, James B. and George I. Quimby

1961   The McCollum site, Nipigon District, Ontario. In Lake Superior Copper and the Indians: Miscellaneous Studies of Great Lakes Prehistory. James B. Griffin (ed.): 91-102. University of Michigan, Museum of Anthropology, Anthropological Papers No.17.

Grimes, John R., W. Eldridge, B. G. Grimes, A. Vaccaro, F. Vaccaro, J. Vaccaro, N. Vaccaro, and A. Orsini

1984   Bull Brook II. In New Experiments upon the Record of Eastern Palaeo-Indian Cultures, Archaeology of Eastern North America, 12:159-183.

Grimm, Eric C.

1985   Vegetation history along the prairie-forest border in Minnesota. In Archaeology, Ecology and Ethnohistory of the Prairie-Forest Border Zone of Minnesota and Manitoba. Janet Spector and Eldon Johnson (eds.): 9-30. Reprints in Anthropology 31.

Groison, Dominique

1985   Blanc-Sablon et le Paléo-Indien au détroit de Belle-Isle. Recherches amérindiennes au Québec Vol.XV(1-2):127-133.

Gruhn, Ruth

1965   Two early radiocarbon dates from the lower levels of Wilson Butte Cave, south-central Idaho. Tebiwa 8:57.

Gryba, Eugene M.

1976   The early side-notched component at site DjOn-26. Archaeological Survey of Alberta, Archaeology in Alberta 1975, Occasional Paper 1. J. Michael Quigg and W. J. Bryne (eds.): 92-107.

1980   The early side-notched point tradition on the central and northern Plains. Directions in Manitoba Prehistory, Papers in Honour of Chris Vickers. Leo Pettipas (ed.): 37-63.

1983   Sibbald Creek: 11,000 years of human use of the Alberta Foothills. Archaeological Survey of Alberta, Occasional Paper 22, Alberta Culture.

Gustafson, Carl E., Delbert Gilbow, and Richard D. Daugherty
1979   The Manis Mastodon site: Early Man in the Olympic Peninsula. Canadian Journal of Archaeology No.3:157-164.

Guthrie, R. D.
1980   Bison and Man in North America. In The Ice-free Corridor and Peopling of the New World, Proceeds of the Fifth Biennial Conference of the American Quaternary Association, Edmonton, September 2-4, 1978. Canadian Journal of Anthropology, No.1(1):55-74.
1982   Mammals of the mammoth steppe as paleoenvironmental indicators. In Paleoecology of Beringia. D. M. Hopkins, J. V. Matthews Jr., C. E. Scheweger, and S. B. Young (eds.): 307-326. Academic Press, New York.
1984   Mosaics, allelochemics and nutrients: an ecological theory of Late Pleistocene megafaunal extinctions. In Quaternary Extinctions: a Prehistoric Revolution. P. S. Martin and R. G. Klein (eds.): 259-298. University of Arizona Press.

Haack, Steven C.
1987   A critique of Medicine Wheel astronomy. Archaeological Survey of Alberta, Occasional Paper 31:129-139.
1987a   A critical evaluation of medicine wheel astronomy. Plains Anthropologist 32 (115):77-82.

Haberman, Thomas W.
1986   Comment on McKean plant food utilization. Plains Anthropologist 31 (113):237-240.

Haggarty, J. C. and John H. W. Sendey
1976   Test excavation at the Georgeson Bay site, Gulf of Georgia region. Occasional Papers of the British Columbia Provincial Museum, 19. Victoria.

Haley, Shawn D.
1983   The South Yale site: yet another point. The Midden, Publication of the Archaeological Society of British Columbia, 15(5):3-5.
1988   The Pasika Complex revisted. Canadian Archaeological Association, 21st Annual Meeting, Abstracts: 38.

Hall, Robert L.
1979   In search of the ideology of the Adena-Hopewell climax. In Hopewell Archaeology, the Chillicothe Conference. David S. Brose and N'omi Greber (eds.): 256-265.

Ham, Leonard C.
  1976   Chapter 3: Analysis of shell samples. In The Glenrose Cannery site. R. G. Matson (ed.):
            42-78. National Museum of Man, Archaeological Survey of Canada, Mercury 52.

Hamelin, Louis-Edmond et Benoit Dumont
  1964   La Colline Blanche au nord-est de Mistassini: géomorphologie et sciences humaines.
            Trevaux Divers 6, Centre d'Etudes Nordiques, Université Laval.

Hamell, George R.
  1983   Trading in metaphors: the magic of beads. In Proceedings of the 1982 Glass Trade Bead
            Conference. Rochester Museum and Science Center. Research Records No.16. Charles
            F. Hayes (ed.):5-28.

Hamilton, Scott
  1991   Archaeological investigations at the Wapekeka Burial site (FlJj-1). Cultural Resource
            Management Report.

Hammatt, Hallett H.
  1970   A Paleo-Indian butchering kit. American Antiquity Vol.35(2):141-152.

Hammond, J. Hugh
  1917   The Narrows between Lake Simcoe and Lake Couchiching. Province of Ontario,
            Twenty-ninth Annual Archaeological Report: 53-58.

Hanks, Christopher C.
  1988   The Foxie Otter site, a multicomponent occupation north of Lake Huron. Anthropological
            Papers No. 79, Museum of Anthropology, University of Michigan.

Hanna, Margaret
  1980   Trends and traditions in the Boreal Forest: an appraisal of the Shield Archaic as defined
            by J. V. Wright. In Directions in Manitoba Prehistory, Papers in Honour of Chris
            Vickers. Leo Pettipas (ed.): 65-88. Manitoba Archaeological Society.

Hannus, L. Adrien
  1989   Flaked mammoth bone from the Lange/ Ferguson site, White River Badlands area, South
            Dakota. In Bone Modification. Robson Bonnichsen and Marcella H. Sorg (eds.): 395
            -412. Peopling of the Americas Publications, Center for the Study of the First Americans,
            University of Maine, Orono.

Hanson, Jeffery R.

1984   Bison ecology in the Northern Plains and a reconstruction of bison patterns for the North Dakota region. Plains Anthropologist 29(104):93-113.

Harington, C. R.
1978   Quaternary vertebrate faunas of Canada and Alaska and their suggested chronological sequence. Syllogeus No.15, National Museum of Natural Sciences. Ottawa.
1980   Climatic change in Canada. Syloogeus No.26. National Museum of Natural Sciences. Ottawa.
1981   Climatic change in Canada 2. Syllogeus No.33. National Museum of Natural Sciences. Ottawa.
1983   Climatic change in Canada 3. Syllogeus No.49. National Museum of Natural Sciences. Ottawa.
1985   (ed.), Climatic change in Canada 5 (critical periods in the Quaternary climatic history of northern North America). Syllogeus 55. National Museum of Natural Sciences. Ottawa.

Harington, C. R. and G. Rice (eds.)
1984   Climatic change in Canada 4 (annotated bibliography of Quaternary climatic change in Canada). Syllogeus 51. National Museum of Natural Sciences. Ottawa.

Harp, Elmer Jr.
1952   An archaeological survey in the Strait of Belle Isle area. American Antiquity, Vol.16(3):203-220.
1958   Prehistory in the Dismal Lake area, N.W.T., Canada. Arctic 11(4):219-249.
1961   The archaeology of the Lower and Middle Thelon, Northwest Territories. Arctic Institute of North America, Technical Paper No.8. Montreal.
1964   Evidence of Boreal Archaic culture in southern Labrador and Newfoundland. National Museum of Canada, Bulletin 193:184-261.
1978   Pioneer cultures of the Sub-Arctic and Arctic. In Ancient Native Americans. Jesse D. Jennings (ed.): 94-129. W. H. Freeman, New York.

Harp, Elmer Jr. and David R. Hughes
1968   Five prehistoric burials from Port au Choix, Newfoundland. Polar Notes, No.VIII:1-47.

Harper, J. R.
1956   Portland Point, cross roads in New Brunswick history. Historical Studies No.9, New Brunswick Museum, Saint John.

Harris, R. Cole (ed.) and Geoffrey J. Matthews (carto.)
1987   Historical Atlas of Canada, Volume I, From the Beginning to 1800. University of

Toronto Press.

Haug, James K.

1976   The 1974-1975 excavations at the Cherry Point site (DkMe-10): a stratified Archaic site in southwest Manitoba. Papers in Manitoba Archaeology, Final Report No.1, Department of Tourism, Recreation and Cultural Affairs, Historic Resources Branch, Manitoba.

1981   Analysis of a Paleo-Indian occupation floor at the Black Duck site, ElMb-10, Manitoba. Papers in Manitoba Archaeology, Miscellaneous Paper No.11, Department of Cultural Affairs and Historical Resources, Historic Resources Branch. Winnipeg, Manitoba.

Haury, Emil W.

1953   Artifacts with mammoth remains, Naco, Arizona. American Antiquity, Vol.19(1):1-14.

Haury, Emil W., E.B. Sayles and William W. Wasley

1959   The Lehner Mammoth site, southeastern Arizona. American Antiquity, Vol.25(1):2-30.

Haviland, William A. and Marjory W. Power

1981   The Original Vermonters, native inhabitants, past and present. University Press of New England. Hanover.

Hayden, Brian

1982   Interaction parameters and the demise of Paleo-Indian craftsmanship. Plains Anthropologist 27:109-123.

Haynes, C. Vance

1980   The Clovis Culture. In Proceedings of the Fifth Biennial Conference of the American Quaternary Association, Edmonton, September 2-4, 1978, Canadian Journal of Anthropology, No.(1):115-121.

1982   Were Clovis progenitors in Beringia? In Paleoecology of Beringia. David M. Hopkins, John V. Matthews Jr., Charles E. Schweger, and Steven B. Young (eds.): 383-398. Academic Press, New York.

Haynes, C. Vance, D. J. Donahue, A. J. T. Jull, and T. H. Zabel

1984   Application of accelerator dating to Fluted Point Paleoindian sites. In New Experiments upon the Record of Eastern Palaeo-Indian Cultures, Archaeology of Eastern North America, 12: 184-191.

Hearne, Samuel

1911   A journey from Prince of Wales' Fort in Hudson's Bay to the Northern Ocean, in the years 1769, 1770, 1771 and 1772. J. B. Tyrrell (ed.), The Champlain Society.

496

Hebda, R. and R. Mathewes
1984   Holocene history of cedar and Native Indian cultures of the North American Pacific Coast,   Science 225:711-712.

Hébert, Bernard
1987   Un regard nouveau sur le Site Rapides- Fryers. Recherches amérindiennes au Québec, Vol.XVII(1-2):89-100.

Helgason, Gail
1987   The First Albertans, an archaeological search. Lone Pine Publishing, Edmonton.

Helm, June
1968   The nature of Dogrib socioterritorial groups. In Man the Hunter. R. B. Lee and I. DeVore (eds.): 118- 125.

Helm, June (vol. ed.)
1981   Handbook of the North American Indians, Subarctic, Vol.6. William C. Sturtevant (gen. ed.), Smithsonian Institution, Washington.

Helmer, James W.
1977   Points, people and prehistory: a preliminary synthesis of culture history in north central British Columbia. In Prehistory of the North American Sub-Arctic, the Athapascan Question. J. Helmer, S. Vandyke, and F. Kense (eds.): 90-96. University of Calgary Archaeological Association.
1986   A face from the past: an early Pre-Dorset ivory maskette from Devon Island, N.W.T. Etudes Inuit Studies, Vol.10(1-2):179-202.

Helmer, James W. and Brenda V. Kennedy
1986   Early Palaeo-Eskimo skeletal remains from north Devon Island, High Arctic Canada. Canadian Journal of Archaeology, Vol.10:127-143.

Helmer, James W. and Ian G. Robertson
1990   A quantitative shape analysis of Early Palaeo-Eskimo endblades from northern Devon Island. Canadian Journal of Archaeology, Vol.14:107-122.

Henn, Winfield
1978   Archaeology on the Alaska Peninsula: the Ugashik drainage, 1973-1975. University of Oregon Anthropological Papers No.14.

Hester, James J.

1978   Conclusions: early tool traditions in Northwest North America. In Studies in Bella Bella Prehistory. James J. Hester and Sarah M. Nelson (eds.): 101-112. Department of Archaeology, Simon Fraser University, Publication No.5.

1979   Comments: The Early Period in Northwest Coast prehistory. Canadian Journal of Archaeology, No.3:229-231.

Hibben, F. C.

1943   Evidence of Early Man in Alaska. American Antiquity, Vol.8(3):254-259.

Hinshelwood, A. and E. Webber

1987   Testing and excavation of the Ozbolt property, part of the Biloski site (DcJh-9), a late Palaeo-Indian archaeological site, Thunder Bay, Ontario. Ontario Department of Citizenship and Culture, Ontario Conservation Archaeology, North Central Region, Report 25.

Hlady, W. M.

1969   A Scottsbluff projectile point from Arden, Manitoba. Manitoba Archaeological Newsletter 6(1-2):3-6.

1970   Manitoba - the Northern Woodlands. In Ten Thousand Years Archaeology in Manitoba. Walter M. Hlady (ed.): 93-121. Manitoba Archaeological Society.

Hobler, Philip M.

1978   The relationship of archaeological sites to sea levels on Moresby Island, Queen Charlotte Island. Canadian Journal of Archaeology No.2:1-13.

1990   Prehistory of the Central Coast of British Columbia. In Handbook of North American Indians. William C. Sturtevant (gen. ed.). Volume 7, Northwest Coast. Wayne Suttles (vol. ed.): 298-305. Smithsonian Institution.

Holmes, Charles E.

1986   Lake Minchumins prehistory, an archaeological analysis. Alaska Anthropological Association, Monograph Series 2.

Hopkins, David M.

1967   The Cenozoic history of Beringia: a synthesis. In The Bering Land Bridge. D.M. Hopkins (ed.): 451-484. Stanford University Press.

Hopkins, David M., John. V. Matthews Jr., Charles. E. Schweger, and Steven. B. Young, (eds.),

1982   Paleoecology of Beringia. Academic Press.

Horne, Patrick D.

1985 A review of the evidence of human endoparasitism in the pre-Columbian New World through the study of coprolites. Journal of Archaeological Science 12:299-310.

Hough, Jack L.
1963 The prehistoric Great Lakes of North America. American Scientist, Vol.51 (1):84-109.

Howley, James P.
1915 The Beothucks or Red Indians. Cambridge University Press.

Huckell, Bruce B.
1979 Of chipped stone tools, elephants, and the Clovis hunters: an experiment. Plains Anthropologist, 24(85):177-189.
1982 The Denver elephant project: a report on experimentation with thrusting spears. Plains Anthropologist, 27(97):217-224.

Hurley, W. M., I. T. Kenyon, F. W. Lange and B. M. Mitchell
1972 Algonquin Park Archaeology 1971. University of Toronto, Department of Anthropology, Anthropological Series, No.10.

Husted, Wilfred M.
1969 Bighorn Canyon archaeology. Smithsonian Institution River Basin Surveys, Publications in Salvage Archaeology, No.12.

Husted, Wilfred M. and Robert Edgar
n.d. The Archaeology of Mummy Cave, Wyoming: an introduction to Shoshonean prehistory.

Immamoto, Shirley
1976 Chapter 2: An analysis of the Glenrose faunal remains. In The Glenrose Cannery site. R. G. Matson (ed.): 21-41. National Museum of Man, Archaeological Survey of Canada, Mercury Series No. 52.

Inglis, Richard
1973 Contact salvage 1973: a preliminary report on the salvage excavations of two shell middens in the Prince Rupert Harbour, N. C. GbTo-33/36. Canadian Archaeological Association, Bulletin 5:140-144.

Inglis, Richard I. and G. F. MacDonald
1979 Introduction. In Skeena River Prehistory. National Museum of Man, Archaeological Survey of Canada, Mercury 87:2-17.

Irving, William N.
1953   Evidence of early tundra cultures in northern Alaska. Anthropological Papers of the University of Alaska, 1(2):55-85.
1962   A provisional comparison of some Alaskan and Asian stone industries. In Prehistoric Cultural Relations between the Arctic and Temperate Zones of North America. John M. Campbell (ed.): 55-69. Arctic Institute of North America, Paper 11.
1968   The Barren Grounds. In Science, History and Hudson Bay, Vol.I. C. S. Beals and D. A. Shenstone (eds.): 26-54. Department of Energy, Mines and Resources, Ottawa.
1968a   The Arctic Small Tool Tradition. Eighth International Congress of Anthropological and Ethnological Sciences, Proceedings, Vol.3:340-342. Tokyo and Kyoto.
1971   Recent Early Man research in the North. Arctic Anthropology VIII(2):68-82.

Irving, William N. and J. Cinq-Mars
1974   A tentative archaeological sequence for Old Crow Flats, Yukon Territory. Arctic Anthropology XI:65-81.

Irwin-Williams, Cynthia, Henry Irwin, George Agogino and C. Vance Haynes
1973   Hell Gap: Paleo-Indian occupation of the High Plains. Plains Anthropologist 18:40-53.

Irwin, Henry T. and H. M. Wormington
1970   Paleo-Indian tool types in the Great Plains. American Antiquity Vol.35 (1):24-34.

Ives, John W.
1981   The prehistory of the Boreal Forest of northern Alberta. In Alberta Archaeology: Prospect and Retrospect. T. A. Moore (ed.): 39-58, Archaeological Society of Alberta. Lethbridge.
1983   Evaluating the effectiveness of site discovery techniques in Boreal Forest environments. In Directions in Archaeology: a Question of Goals. P. D. Francis and E. Poplin (eds.): 95-114. Proceedings of the Fourteenth Annual Conference, 1981, the Archaeological Association of the University of Calgary.
1985   The results of mitigative excavations during the fall of 1979, Strathcona Science Park archaeological site (FjPi-29). Archaeological Survey of Alberta, Manuscript Series No.3.

Ives, John W., Alwynne B. Beaudoin, and Martin P. R. Magne
1989   Evaluating the role of a western corridor in the peopling of the Americas. Paper presented at the Circum-Pacific Prehistory Conference, Seattle, August 1989.

Jackson, Lawrence J.
1987   Ontario Paleoindians and proboscidians: a review. Current Research in the Pleistocene 4:109-112. A Peopling of the Americas Publication, Center for the Study of Early Man,

500

University of Maine, Orono.

1990   Sandy Ridge - a Gainey occupation in south-central Ontario. Current Research in the Pleistocene 7: 23-27. A Peopling of the Americas Publication, Center for the Study of the First Americans, University of Maine, Orono.

1990a   Interior Paleoindian settlement strategies: a first approximation for the Lower Great Lakes. Research in Economic Anthropology, Supplement 5:95-142. JAI Press Inc.

Jackson, Lawrence J. and Heather McKillop

1987   Early Paleoindian occupation in interior southcentral Ontario. Current Research in the Pleistocene 4:11-14. A Peopling of the Americas Publication, Center for the Study of Early Man, University of Maine, Orono.

1991   Approaches to Palaeo-Indian economy: an Ontario and Great Lakes perspective. Midcontinental Journal of Archaeology, Vol.16(1):34-68.

Janes, Robert R.

1983   Ethnoarchaeological observations among the Willow Lake Dene, Northwest Territories, Canada. The Musk-ox, 33:56-67.

Janusas, Scarlett Emilie

1984   A petrological analysis of Kettle Point chert and its spatial and temporal distribution in regional prehistory. National Museum of Man, Archaeological Survey of Canada, Mercury 128.

Jelinek, A.J.

1967   Man's role in the extinction of Pleistocene fauna. In Pleistocene Extinctions: the search for a cause. P.S. Martin and H.E. Wright Jr. (eds.): 193-200. Yale University Press.

1992   Perspectives from the Old World on the habitation of the New. American Antiquity, Vol.57(2):345-347.

Jenks, Albert E.

1937   Minnesota's Browns Valley Man and associated burial artifacts. American Anthropological Association, Memoirs No.49.

Jenness, Diamond

1932   The Indians of Canada. National Museum of Canada.

Jenning, Francis

1975   The invasion of America, Indians, colonialism, and the cant of conquest. The University of North Carolina Press.

Jennings, Jesse D.

  1957   Danger Cave. Society for American Archaeology, Memoir 14.

  1989   Prehistory of North America (3rd edition). Mayfield Publishing Company, Mountain View, California.

Jerkic, Sonja M.

  1975   Description of skeletal material. In An Archaic sequence from the Strait of Belle Isle, Labrador. Robert McGhee and James A. Tuck: 93-94. National Museum of Man, Archaeological Survey of Canada, Mercury 34.

Johnson, Elden

  1969   The prehistoric peoples of Minnesota. Minnesota Prehistoric Archaeology Series, the Minnesota Historical Society.

Johnson, D. L., P. Kawano, and E. Ekker

  1980   Clovis strategies of hunting mammoth (Mammuthus columbi). In The Ice-Free Corridor and Peopling of the New World, Proceedings of the Fifth Biennial Conference of the American Quaternary Association, Edmonton, Sept. 2-4, 1978, Canadian Journal of Anthropology, Vol.1, No.1, N. W. Rutter and C. E. Schweger (eds.): 107-114.

Johnson, Frederick

  1946   An archaeological survey along the Alaska Highway, 1944. American Antiquity, Vol.11:183-186.

Johnson, Frederick and Hugh M. Raup

  1964   Investigations in southwest Yukon: geobotanical and archaeological reconnaissance. In Investigations in Southwest Yukon, Papers of the R. S. Peabody Foundation of Archaeology 6(1):1-198.

Johnson, Frederick et al.

  1949   The Boylston Street Fishweir II, a study of the geology, palaeobotany, and biology of a site on Stuart Street in the Back Bay District of Boston, Massachusetts. Papers in the Robert S. Peabody Foundation, Vol.4, No.1.

Johnston, Richard B.

  1968   Archaeology of Rice Lake, Ontario. Anthropology Papers No.19, National Museum of Canada.

  1982   An engraved slate point from Southern Ontario. Ontario Archaeology 38:23 -30.

  1984   Archaeology of the McIntyre site. In The McIntyre site: archaeology, subsistence and environment. Richard B. Johnston (ed). National Museum of Man, Archaeological

Survey of Canada, Mercury 126:7-86.

Johnston, Richard B. and Kenneth A. Cassavoy
1978   The fishweirs at Atherley Narrows, Ontario. American Antiquity Vol.43(4):697-709.

Julig, P. J.
1984   Cummins Paleo-Indian site and its paleoenvironment, Thunder Bay, Canada. In New Experiments upon the record of Eastern Palaeo-Indian cultures. Archaeology of Eastern North America, Vol.12. Richard Michael Gramly (ed.): 192-209.

1988   Burins from the Cummins Paleoindian site, Thunder Bay, Ontario. Current Research in the Pleistocene 5:29-30.

1988a   Prehistoric site survey in the western James Bay Lowlands, Northern Ontario. In Boreal Forest and Sub-Arctic Archaeology. C. S. "Paddy" Reid (ed.): 121-145. Ocassional Publications of the London Chapter, Ontario Archaeological Society, No.6.

n.d.   The Cummins site complex and Paleoindian occupations in the northwestern Lake Superior region. PhD. thesis, Department of Anthropology, University of Toronto, 1988.

Julig, P. J., J. McAndrews, and W. C. Mahoney
1986   Geoarchaeological investigations at the Cummins Paleoindian site, Thunder Bay, Ontario. Current Research in the Pleistocene 3:79-80.

Julig, P. J., L. A. Pavlish, and R. G. V. Hancock
1989   Aspects of Late Pleistocene lithic technological organization in the northwestern Lake Superior region of Canada. In Eastern Paleoindian Lithic Resource Use. Christopher J. Ellis and Jonathan C. Lothrop (eds.): 293-322. Westview Press.

Karrow, P. F., J. R. Clark, and J. Terasmae
1961   The age of Lake Iroquois and Lake Ontario. Journal of Geology, Vol.69(6):659-667.

Karrow, P. F. and B. G. Warner
1990   The geological and biological environment for human occupation in Southern Ontario. In Prehistory of Southern Ontario to A.D. 1650. Neal Ferris and Christopher J. Ellis (eds.): 5-35, Ontario Archaeological Society, London Chapter.

Katzenberg, M. Anne
1992   Advances in stable isotope analysis in prehistoric bones. In Skeletal Biology of Past Peoples: Research Methods. Shelley R. Saunders and M. Anne Katzenberg (eds.): 105-120. Wiley-Liss Inc.

Katzenberg, M. Anne and Norman C. Sullivan

1979 A report on the human burial from the Milton-Thomazi site. Ontario Archaeology 32:27-34.

Keddie, G. R.
1981 The use and distribution of labrets on the North Pacific Rim. Syesis 4:59-80.

Keenlyside, David L.
1984 The Prehistory of the Maritimes. Canada's Visual History, No.65. National Museum of Man.

1985 La période Paléoindienne sur l'Île-du-Prince-Édouard. Recherches amérindiennes au Québec Vol.XV(1-2):119-126.

1985a Late Palaeo-Indian evidence from the southern Gulf of St.Lawrence. Archaeology of Eastern North America, 13:79-92.

1991 Paleoindian occupations of the Maritimes region of Canada. In Clovis Origins and Adaptations. Robson Bonnichsen and Karen L. Turnmire (eds.): 163-173. Corvallis: Center for the Study of the First Americans, Oregon State University.

Kehoe, Alice B.
1981 North American Indians, a comprehensive account. Prentice-Hall Inc.

Kehoe, Alice B. and Thomas F. Kehoe
1979 Solstice-aligned boulder configurations in Saskatchewan. National Museum of Man, Canadian Ethnology Servie, Mercury 48.

Kelley, Robert L. and Lawrence C. Todd
1988 Coming into the country: early Paleoindian hunting and mobility. American Antiquity Vol.53(2):231-244.

Kelly, Michael E. and Barbara E. Connell
1978 Survey and excavations of The Pas Moraine: 1976 field season. Papers in Manitoba Archaeology, Final Report 4, Department of Tourism, Recreation and Cultural Affairs, Historic Resources Branch,Manitoba.

Kelsall, J. P.
1968 The migratory Barren-ground caribou of Canada. Canadian Wildlife Service.

Kennedy, Brenda
1981 Marriage patterns in an Archaic population, a study of skeletal remains from Port au Choix, Newfoundland. National Museum of Man, Archaeological Survey of Canada, Mercury 104.

504

1987   A possible case of Histiocytosis X in an Archaic Indian from Port au Choix, Newfoundland. Canadian Journal of Archaeology, Vol.11:109-117.

Kennedy, Clyde C.
1962   Archaic hunters in the Ottawa Valley. New Pages of Prehistory, 1961. Ontario History, LIV(2):6 pp.- no pagination.
1966   Preliminary report on the Morrison's Island - 6 site. National Museum of Canada, Bulletin 206, Contributions to Anthropology, 1963-64, Part 1:100-124.
1970   The Upper Ottawa Valley. Renfrew County Council.
n.d.   The Allumette Island-1 (AL1) site. Field Report to the National Museum of Canada, 38pp. (Canadian Museum of Civilization, Archaeological Survey of Canada, Manuscript 1344).

Kenyon, Ian T.
1980   The Satchell Complex in Ontario: a perspective from the Ausable Valley. Ontario Archaeology 34:17- 43.
1980a   The George Davidson site: an Archaic "Broadpoint" component in southwestern Ontario. Archaeology of Eastern North America, Vol.8:11-28.
1989   Terminal Archaic projectile points in southwestern Ontario: an exploratory study. Kewa, Newsletter of the London Chapter, Ontario Archaeological Society, Vol.89(1):2-21.

Kenyon, Walter A.
1959   The Inverhuron site. The Royal Ontario Museum, Art and Archaeology Division, Occasional Paper 1.

Kenyon, W. A. and C. S. Churcher
1965   A flaked tool and a worked antler fragment from Late Lake Agassiz. Canadian Journal of Earth Sciences 2:237-246.

Keyser, James D.
1985   The archaeological identification of local populations: a case study from the northwestern Plains. Plains Anthropologist 30(108):85-102.
1986   The evidence for McKean plant utilization. Plains Anthropologist 31(113):225-235.

Keyser, J. D. and C. M. Davis
1984   Lightning Spring: 4000 years of pine parkland prehistory. Archaeology in Montana, 25(2-3):1-64.

Kidd, Robert S.
1969   Archaeological survey in the Lower Fraser River Valley, British Columbia, 1963.

National Museum of Canada, Contributions to Anthropology VI: Archaeology and Physical Anthropology, Bulletin 224:208-247.

Kinkade, M. D. and Wayne Suttles

1987   Plate 66. Historical Atlas of Canada, from the beginning to 1800. Volume I, R. Cole Harris (ed.).

Klein, Jeffrey, J. C. Lerman, P. E. Damon, and E. K. Ralph

1982   Calibration of radiocarbon dates: tables based on the consensus data of the Workshop on Calibrating the Radiocarbon Time Scale. Radiocarbon Vol.24(2):103 -150.

Knight, Dean H.

n.d.   The Montreal River and the Shield Archaic. PhD. thesis, Department of Anthropology, University of Toronto 1977.

1974   Montreal River salvage project progress report: 1972. National Museum of Man, Archaeological Survey of Canada, Mercury 15. W. J. Byrne (ed.): 74-87.

Knuth, Eigil

1952   An outline of the archaeology of Peary Land. Arctic, 5(1):17-33.

1954   The Paleo-Eskimo culture of northeast Greenland elucidated by three new sites. American Antiquity, Vol.19(4):367-381.

1967   Archaeology of the musk-ox way. École Pratique des Hautes Études, Contributions du Centre d'Études Arctiques et Finno Scadinaves, No.5:1-78. Paris.

Koezur, Polly and J. V. Wright

1976   The Potato Island site, District of Kenora, Ontario. National Museum of Man, Archaeological Survey of Canada, Mercury 51:1-51.

Kraft, H. C.

1975   The archaeology of the Tocks Island area. Seton Hall University Museum, South Orange, N.J.

Krauss, Michaeol E. and Victor K. Golla

1981   Northern Athapaskan languages. In Handbook of North American Indians. William C. Sturtevant (gen. ed.). Vol.6, Subarctic. June Helm (vol. ed.): 67-85. Smithsonian Institution.

Kroker, Sid

1990   Archaeology and Hydro-Electric Development in Northern Manitoba: a retrospective on the Churchill River Diversion and Nelson River Power Development. Manitoba

Archaeological Quarterly, Vol.14(1-4).

Kuijt, Ian
1989   Subsistence resource variability and culture change during the Middle-Late prehistoric cultural transition on the Canadian Plateau. Canadian Journal of Archaeology, Vol.13:97-118.

Lahren, Larry A.
1971   Archaeological investigations in the Upper Yellowstone Valley, Montana: a preliminary synthesis and discussion. In Aboriginal Man and Environments on the Plateau of Northwest America. Arnoud H. Stryd and Rachel A. Smith (eds.): 168-176. The University of Calgary Archaeological Association.

Lahren, Larry and Robson Bonnichsen
1974   Bone foreshafts from a Clovis burial in southwestern Montana. Science 186:147-150.

Laliberté, Marcel
1978   La forêt boréale. En Images de la préhistoire du Québec. Claude Chapdelaine (compilateur): 87-97. Recherches amérindiennes au Québec, Vol.VII(1-2):87-97.
1982   La préhistoire du Lac Kanaaupscow (Réservoir LG-2, Baie James). Dossier 53, Ministère des Affaires culturelles, Direction générale de patrimoine.

Larsen, Helge
1968   Trail Creek: the final report on the excavation of two caves on Seward Peninsula, Alaska. Acta Artica, 15. Copenhagen.

Laub, Richard S.
1990   The Hiscock site (Western New York): recent developments of Pleistocene and Holocene interest. Current Research in the Pleistocene 7: 116-118. A Peopling of the Americas Publication, Center for the Study of the First Americans, University of Maine, Orono.

Laughlin, W. S., J. B. Jorgensen and B. Frohlich
1979   Aleuts and Eskimos: survivors of the Bering Land Bridge coast. In The First Americans: Origins, Affinities and Adaptations. W. S. Laughlin and A. B. Harper (eds.): 91-104. New York: Gustav Fischer.

Lazenby, M. E. Colleen
1980   Prehistoric sources of chert in northern Labrador: field work and preliminary analyses. Arctic 33 (3):628-645.

LeBlanc, Raymond J.
    1991   New data relating to the prehistory of the Mackenzie Delta region of the NOGAP
                Archaeology Project. In NOGAP Archaeology Project: an Integrated Archaeological
                Research and Management Approach. Jacques Cinq-Mars and Jean-Luc Pilon (eds.):
                65-76. Canadian Archaeological Association, Occasional Publication No.1.

LeBlanc, Raymond J. and John W. Ives
    1986   The Bezya site: a wedge-shaped core assemblage from northeastern Alberta. Canadian
                Journal of Archaeology, Vol.10:59-98.

LeBlanc, Raymond J. and Milton J. Wright
    1990   Macroblade technology in the Peace River region of northwestern Alberta. Canadian
                Journal of Archaeology, Vol.14:1-11.

LeClair, Ronald
    1976   Investigations at the Maurer site near Agassiz. Current Research Reports. Roy L. Carlson
                (ed.): 33-42. Simon Fraser University, Department of Archaeology, Publication No.3.

Lee, Thomas E.
    1954   The first Sheguiandah expedition, Manitoulin Island, Ontario. American Antiquity,
                Vol.20(2):101-111.
    1954a   The Giant site, Manitoulin Island, 1951. National Museum of Canada, Bulletin 132:66-
                71.
    1955   The second Sheguiandah expedition, Manitoulin Island, Ontario. American Antiquity,
                Vol.21(1):63-71.
    1957   The antiquity of the Sheguiandah site. The Canadian Field Naturalist 71(3): 117-137.

Leechman, Douglas
    1950   An implement of elephant bone from Manitoba. American Antiquity, Vol.2:157-160.

Lennox, Paul A.
    1986   The Innes site: a plow-disturbed Archaic component, Brant County, Ontario.
                Midcontinental Journal of Archaeology 11(2):121-168.
    1990   The Canada Century site: a Lamoka component located on the Niagara Peninsula,
                Ontario. Ontario Archaeology, No.51:31-52.
    1993   The Karsel and Blue Dart sites: two components of the Early Archaic bifurcate base
                projectile point tradition, Waterloo County, Ontario. Ontario Archaeology No.56:1-31.

Leonhard, Frank C. and David G. Rice
    1970   A proposed culture typology for the Lower Snake River region, southeastern Washington.

508

Northwest Anthropological Research Notes, 4(1):1-29.

Leonhardy, Frank C.

1982   Archaeology of the Canadian Plateau, the view from the south. Northwest Anthropological Research Notes, 16(1):85 (abstract).

Levesque, René

1962   Les richesses archéologiques du Québec. La société d'archéologie de Sherbrooke. Presses de l'Université de Sherbrooke.

1980   Initiation à l'archéologie. Leméac.

n.d.   Cadre géographique des gisements archéologiques de la région de Blanc Sablon. Memoire presente a l'Université de Sherbrooke pour l'obtention de la maitrise des arts, 1977.

Levine, Mary Ann

1990   Accommodating age: radiocarbon results and fluted point sites in northeastern North America. Archaeology of Eastern North America, Vol.18:33-63.

Levson, Vic M.

1990   Late glacial paleoenvironments in the Rocky Mountain, Jasper, Canada: implications for human habitation sites. Current Research in the Pleistocene 7:138-140. A Peopling of the Americas Publication, Center for the Study of the First Americans, University of Maine, Orono.

Linnamae, Urve

1975   The Dorset culture: a comparative study in Newfoundland and the Arctic. Technical Papers of the Newfoundland Museum, No.1.

Lister, Kenneth R.

1988   Provisioned at fishing stations: fish and the native occupation of the Hudson Bay Lowland. In Boreal Forest and Sub-Arctic Archaeology. C. S. "Paddy" Reid (ed.): 72-99. Occasional Publications of the London Chapter, Ontario Archaeological Society, No.6.

Logan, Wilfred D.

1952   Graham Cave, an Archaic site in Montgomery County, Missouri. Missouri Archaeological Society, Memoir No.2.

Lohse, E. S.

1984   45-OK-11: a 5000 year old housepit site. Northwest Anthropological Research Reports, Abstracts of papers presented at the 36th annual Northwest Anthropological Conference,

18 (1):65 (abstract).

Long, Austin and Morgan Tamplin
1977   University of Arizona radiocarbon dates from archaeological sites in Manitoba. Papers in Manitoba Archaeology, Miscellaneous Papers 4:43-54. Department of Tourism, Recreation and Cultural Affairs, Historic Resources Branch. Manitobal.

Losey, Timonthy C., G. Conaty, and Dale S. Slater
n.d.   Archaeological investigations at the Esker Bay site, N.W.T. Manuscript No.1455, Records Section, Archaeological Survey of Canada, Canadian Museum of Civilization.

Lowther, G. R.
1962   An account of an archaeological site on Cape Sparbo, Devon Island. National Museum of Canada, Bulletin 180:1-19.

Loy, Thomas H.
1987   Recent advances in blood residue analysis. In Archaeometry: Further Australasian Studies. W. R. Ambrose and J. M. J. Mummery (eds.): 57-65. The Australian National University and Australian National Gallery. Canberra.

Luebbers, Roger
1978   Excavations: stratigraphy and artifacts. In Studies in Bella Bella Prehistory. James J. Hester and Sarah M. Nelson (eds.): 11-66. Simon Fraser University, Department of Archaeology, Publication No.5.

Lueger, Richard
1977   Prehistoric occupations at Coteau-du-Lac, Quebec: a mixed assemblage of Archaic and Woodland artifacts. Parks Canada, History and Archaeology No.12:3-100.

Lundelius, Ernest L. Jr.
1988   What happened to the mammoth? the climatic model. In America before Columbus: Ice-Age Origins. Ronald C. Carlisle (ed.): 75-82. Department of Anthropology, University of Pittsburg, Ethnology Monographs No.12.

Luternauer, J. L., John J. Claque, K. W. Conway, J. V. Barrie, B. Blaise, and R. W. Mathewes
1989   Late Pleistocene terrestrial deposits on the continental shelf of western Canada: evidence for rapid sea-level change at the end of the last glaciation. Geology, Vol.17:357-360.

Lynch, Thomas F.
1990   Glacial-age man in South America? a critical review. American Antiquity

510

Vol.55(1):12-36.

MacDonald, George.F.

1968   Debert: a Palaeo-Indian site in central Nova Scotia. Anthropology Papers, No.16,
            National Museum of Canada.

1969   Preliminary culture sequence from the coast Tsimshian area, British Columbia. Northwest
            Anthropological Research Notes 3(2):240-254.

1969a   Discussion. Current archaeological research on the Northwest Coast. Symposium
            presented at the 22nd Annual Northwest Anthropological Conference, Northwest
            Anthropological Reseach Notes 3(2):225-263.

1983   Eastern North America. In Early Man in the New World, ed. Richard Shutler, Jr., Sage
            Publications, Beverly Hills. pp. 97-108.

1983a   Prehistoric art of the Northern Northwest Coast. In Indian Art Traditions of the
            Northwest Coast. Roy L. Carlson (ed.): 99-120. Simon Fraser University, Department
            of Archaeology, Publication No.13.

MacDonald, George F. and Richard I. Inglis

1976   The Dig, an archaeological reconstruction of a west coast village. Canadian Prehistory
            Series, National Museum of Man.

1981   An overview of the North Coast Prehistory Project (1966-1980). B. C. Studies 48:37-63.

MacLeod, Donald

n.d.   A Red Paint burial site in northeastern Newfoundland. Paper presented at the 32nd
            Annual Meeting of the Society for American Archaeology, Ann Arbor.

MacNeish, Richard S.

1951   An archaeological reconnaissance in the Northwest Territories. National Museum of
            Canada, Bulletin 123:24-41.

1952   A possible early site in the Thunder Bay District, Ontario. National Museum of Canada,
            Bulletin 120:23-47.

1953   Archaeological reconnaissance in the Mackenzie River drainage. National Museum of
            Canada, Bulletin 128:23-29.

1954   The Pointed Mountain site near Fort Liard, Northwest Territories, Canada. American
            Antiquity, Vol.19:234-253.

1955   Two archaeological sites on Great Bear Lake, N.W.T.. National Museum of Canada,
            Bulletin 136:54-84.

1956   The Engigstciak site on the Yukon Arctic coast. Anthropological Papers of the University
            of Alaska 4:91-111.

1956a   Archaeological reconnaissance of the Delta of the Mackenzie River and Yukon coast.
            National Museum of Canada, Bulletin 142:46-69.

1958	An introduction to the archaeology of southeastern Manitoba. National Museum of Canada, Bulletin 142.

1958   An introduction to the archaeology of southeastern Manitoba. National Museum of Canada, Bulletin 142.

1959   A speculative framework for northern North American prehistory as of April 1959. Anthropologica, N.S. 1(1):7-23.

1959a   Men out of Asia; as seen from the northwest Yukon. Anthropological Papers of the University of Alaska, 7(2):41-70.

1960   The Collison site in the light of archaeological survey of southwest Yukon. National Museum of Canada, Bulletin 162:1-51.

1964   Investigations in Southwest Yukon: archaeological excavations, comparisons, and speculations. Papers of the Robert S. Peabody Foundation of Archaeology, Vol.6(2):201-471. Phillips Academy, Andover.

MacNeish, Richard S. and K. H. Capes

1958   The United Church site near Rock Lake in Manitoba. Anthropologica No.6:119-155.

Magne, Martin P. R.

1985   Lithics and livelihood: stone tool technologies of central and southern interior British Columbia. National Museum of Man, Archaeological Survey of Canada, Mercury 133.

Marois, Roger

1987   Souvenirs d'antan: les sépultures archaïques de Coteau-du-Lac, Québec. Recherches amérindiennes au Québec, XVII(1-2):7-35.

Marois, Roger et Pierre Gauthier

1989   Les Abitibis. Musée canadien des civilisations, commission archéologique du Canada, Dossier Mercure No.140.

Marois, Roger et Rene Ribes

1975   Indices de manifestations culturelles de l'Archaique: la region de Trois- Rivieres. Musée National de l'Homme, Commission Archéologique du Canada, Collection Mercure, Dossier 41.

Martijn, Charles A.

1974   Archaeological research on the lower St.Lawrence North Shore, Quebec. National Museum of Man, Archaeological Survey of Canada, Mercury 15. W. J. Byrne (ed.): 112-130.

1985   Le Complexe Plano de Témiscamie est-il une illusion? Recherches amérindiennes au Québec Vol.XV(1-2):161-164.

Martijn, Charles A. and Edward S. Rogers

512

1969 Mistassini-Albanel, contributions to the prehistory of Quebec. Centre d'Etudes Nordiques, Travaux Divers 25, Université Laval.

Martin, Paul S.
1973 The discovery of America. Science 179(4077):969-974.
1982 The pattern and meaning of Holarctic mammoth extinction. In Paleoecology of Beringia. David M. Hopkins, John V. Matthews Jr., Charles E. Schweger, and Steven B. Young (eds.): 399-408. Academic Press, New York.

Mason, Owen
1993 News from north of the Alaska Range. Alaska Anthropological Association Newsletter, Vol.18(2).

Mason, Ronald J.
1981 Great Lakes Archaeology. New World Archaeological Record, Academic Press.

Mason, Ronald J. and Carol Irwin
1960 An Eden-Scottsbluff burial in northeastern Wisconsin. American Antiquity, Vol.26(1):43-57.

Mathews, W. H.
1979 Late Quaternary environmental history affecting human habitation of the Pacific Northwest. Canadian Journal of Archaeology, No.3:145-156.

Matson, R. G.
1976 The Glenrose Cannery site. National Museum of Man, Archaeological Survey of Canada, Mercury Series No. 52.
1981 Prehistoric subsistence patterns in the Fraser Delta: the evidence from the Glenrose Cannery site. B. C. Studies 48:86-102.
n.d. The Old Cordilleran component at the Glenrose Cannery site and the origins of the Northwest Coast Pattern. Paper presented at the Canadian Archaeological Association Symposium on Early Man in British Columbia, 1988.

Matthewes, Rolf W.
1976 Chapter 7: Pollen analysis at Glenrose. In The Glenrose Cannery Site. R. G. Matson (ed.): 98-103. National Museum of Man, Archaeological Survey of Canada, Mercury 52.

Matthews, J. V. Jr.
1982 East Beringia during Late Wisconsin time: a review of the biotic evidence. In

Paleoecology of Beringia. David M. Hopkins, John V. Matthews Jr., Charles E. Schweger, and Steven B. Young (eds.): 127-150. Academic Press, New York.

Maxwell, Moreau S.

1962   Pre-Dorset and Dorset sites in the vicinity of Lake Harbour, Baffin Island, N.W.T. National Museum of Canada, Bulletin 180:20-55.

1973   Archaeology of the Lake Harbour District, Baffin Island. National Museum of Man, Archaeological Survey of Canada, Mercury 6.

1976   Introduction. In Eastern Arctic Prehistory: Paleoeskimo Problems. Moreau S. Maxwell (ed.): 1-5. Memoirs of the Society for American Archaeology, No.31.

1976a   Pre-Dorset and Dorset artifacts: the view from Lake Harbour. In Eastern Arctic Prehistory: Paleoeskimo Problems. Moreau S. Maxwell (ed.): 58-78. Memoirs of the Society for American Archaeology, No.31.

1980   Archaeology of the Arctic and Subarctic zones. Annual Review of Anthropology, 9:161-185.

1983   Discussant's comments: Northern Archaeology Symposium, Part One - Regional Overviews. The Musk-ox, 33:83-85.

1984   Pre-Dorset and Dorset prehistory of Canada. In Handbook of North American Indians. William C. Sturtevant (gen. ed.), Vol.5, Arctic, David Damas (vol. ed.): 359-368. Smithsonian Institution.

1985   Prehistory of the Eastern Arctic. New World Archaeological Record. Academic Press.

Mayer-Oakes, W. J.

1970   Archaeological investigations in the Grand Rapids, Manitoba, Reservoir 1961-1962. Occasional Paper No.3, Department of Anthropology, University of Manitoba.

McAndrews, J. H.

1980   Ontario forest and prehistory: a miscellany. Ontario Archaeological Society, Arch Notes 6:7-9.

McAndrews, J. H., K. -B. Liu, G. C. Manville, V. K. Prest, and J. - S. Vincent

1987   Environmental change after 9000 BC. Plate 4, Historical Atlas of Canada, from the beginning to 1800, Vol.I, Plate 4. R. Cole Harris (ed.) and Geoffrey J. Mathews (cartographer/ designer). University of Toronto Press.

McBride, K. A.

1978   Archaic subsistence in the lower Connecticut River Valley: evidence from Woodchuck Knoll. Man in the Northeast 15-16:124-132.

McCaffrey, Moira T.

514

1986   La préhistoire des Îles de la Madaleine: bilan préliminaire. En Les Micmacs et la Mer. Charles A. Martijn (ed.): 99-162. Recherches amérindiennes au Québec.

McClary, Andrew
1972   Notes on some Late Middle Woodland coprolites. In The Schultz site at Green Point: a stratified occupation area in the Saginaw Valley of Michigan. James E. Fitting (ed.): 131-136. Univerisity of Michigan, Museum of Anthropology, Memoir 4.

McCracken, Harold, Waldo R. Wedel, Robert Edgar, John H. Moss, H. E. Wright, Wilfred M. Husted, and William Mulloy
1978   The Mummy Cave Project in northwestern Wyoming. The Buffalo Bill Historical Center.

McGhee, Robert
1970   Excavations at Bloody Falls, N.W.T. Canada. Arctic Anthropology, VI(2): 53-65.
1974   The peopling of arctic North America. In Arctic and Alpine Environments. Jack D. Ives and Roger G. Barry (eds.): 831-855.
1975   An individual view of Canadian Eskimo prehistory. Canadian Archaeological Association, Bulletin 7:55-75.
1976   The Burial at L'Anse Amour. Canadian Prehistory Series, National Museum of Man.
1976a   La sepulture de L'Anse - Amour. Musée national de l'Homme, Collection la préhistoire du Canada.
1976b   Paleoeskimo occupations of Central and High Arctic Canada. In Eastern Arctic Prehistory: Paleoeskimo Problems. Moreau S. Maxwell (ed.): 15-39. Memoirs of the Society for American Archaeology, No.31.
1976c   Parsimony isn't everything: an alternative view of Eskaleutian linguistics and prehistory. Canadian Archaeological Association, Bulletin 8:62-81.
1978   Canadian Arctic prehistory. Canadian Prehistory Series, National Museum of Man and Van Nostrand Reinhold.
1979   The Palaeoeskimo occupations at Port Refuges, High Arctic Canada. National Museum of Man, Archaeological Survey of Canada, Mercury 92.
1980   Individual stylistic variability in Independence I stone tool assemblages from Port Refuge, N.W.T. Arctic, 33(3):443-453.
1982   The past ten years in Canadian Arctic prehistory. Canadian Journal of Archaeology, No.6:65-77.
1983   Eastern Arctic prehistory: the reality of a myth? The Musk-ox, 33:21-25.
1987   Invited review: Archaeology of the Eastern Eskimo. The Quarterly Review of Archaeology, Fall Issue.
1987a   The Peopling of the Arctic. Plate 11, Vol.I, Historical Atlas of Canada, from the Beginning to 1800. R. Cole Harris (ed.). University of Toronto Press.
1988   A scenario for Eskimo-Aleut prehistory. In The Late Prehistoric Development of

Alaska's Native People. Robert D. Shaw, Roger K. Harritt and Don E. Dumond (eds.): 369-377. Alaska Anthropological Association Monograph Series 4.

1989   Ancient Canada. Canadian Museum of Civilization and Libre Expression (available in French under the title "Le Canada au temps des envahisseurs").

1991   Canada Rediscovered. Canadian Museum of Civilization and Libre Expression (available in French under the title "Le Canada au temps des aventuriers").

McGhee, Robert and James A. Tuck

1975   An Archaic sequence from the Strait of Belle Isle, Labrador. National Museum of Man, Archaeological Survey of Canada, Mercury 34.

1976   Up-dating the Canadian Arctic. In Eastern Arctic Prehistory: Paleoeskimo Problems. Moreau S. Maxwell (ed.): 6-14. Memoirs of the Society for American Archaeology, No.31.

McIlwraith, T. F.

1948   The Bella Coola Indians. (two volumes), University of Toronto Press.

McKenna, Robert A. and John P. Cook

1968   Prehistory of Healy Lake, Alaska. VIIIth Congress of Anthropological and Ethnological Sciences, Vol. III:182-184. Science Council of Japan, Tokyo.

McLeod, Mike

1980   The archaeology of Dog Lake, Thunder Bay - 9000 years of prehistory. Report submitted to the Ontario Heritage Foundation (two volumes).

McMillan, Alan D.

1981   Archaeological research in Nootka territory: Barkley Sound to the Alberni Valley. B. C. Studies, 48:86-102.

1988   Native Peoples and Cultures of Canada, an anthropological overview. Douglas and McIntyre.

1991   Review of "Handbook of North American Indians, Volume 7, Northwest Coast. Wayne Suttles (vol. ed.), William C. Sturtevant (gen. ed.). Smithsonian Institution. In Canadian Journal of Archaeology, Vol.15:237-247.

McMillan, Alan D. and Denis E. St.Claire

1975   Archaeological investigations in the Alberni Valley. B. C. Studies, 25:32-77.

McNett, Charles W. Jr., Barbara A. McMillan, and Sydne B. Marshall

1977   The Shawnee-Minisink site. In Amerinds and their paleoenvironments in northeastern North America, Annals of the New York Academy of Science, 288:282-296.

Mehringer, Peter J. Jr.
    1988   Clovis cache found, weapons of ancient Americans. National Geographic, Oct.: 500-503.

Meiklejohn, C. and D. A. Rokala
    1986   The Native Peoples of Canada: an annotated bibliography of population biology, health, and illness. Canadian Museum of Civilization, Archaeological Survey of Canada, Mercury 134.

Meldgaard, Jorgen
    1960   Prehistoric culture sequences in the Eastern Arctic as elucidated by stratified sites at Igloolik. Selected Papers, 5th International Congress of Anthropological and Ethnological Sciences, Philadelphia 1956: 588-595.
    1962   On the formative period of the Dorset culture. In Prehistoric Cultural Relations between the Arctic and Temperate Zones of North America. John M. Campbell (ed.): 92-95. Arctic Institute of North America, Technical Paper 11.

Meltzer, David J.
    1984-85   On stone procurement and settlement mobility in eastern Fluted Point groups. North American Archaeologist 6:1-24.
    1988   Late Pleistocene human adaptations in Eastern North America. Journal of World Prehistory 2(1):1-52.
    1989   Was stone exchanged among eastern North American Paleoindians? In Eastern Paleoindian Lithic Resource Use. Christopher J. Ellis and Jonathan C. Lothrop (eds.): 11-39. Westview Press.
    1989a   Why don't we know when the first people came to North America? American Antiquity, Vol.54(3):471-490.
    1990   Review of "Americans before Columbus: Ice-Age Origins. Ronald C. Carlisle (ed.), 1988, Department of Anthropology, University of Pittsburgs, Ethnology Monographs No.12. In Geoarchaeology: an international journal 5(4):387-390.
    1993   Pleistocene peopling of the Americas. Evolutionary Anthropology, Vol.1(5): 157-169.

Meltzer, David J. and Robert C. Dunnell
    1987   Fluted points from the Pacific Northwest. Current Research in the Pleistocene 4: 64-67. A Peopling of the Americas Publication, Center for the Study of Early Man, University of Maine, Orono.

Meltzer, David J. and J. I. Mead
    1983   The timing of late Pleistocene mammalian extinctions in North America. Quaternary Research 19:130-135.

Meyer, David

1970   Plano points in the Carrot River Valley. Saskatchewan Archaeology Newsletter 29:8-21.

1977   The Nipawin archaeological survey. Saskatchewan Research Council, Publication No.C-77-6.

1977a   Pre-Dorset settlements at the Seahorse Gully site. National Museum of Man, Archaeological Survey of Canada, Mercury 57.

1983   Review of The Boss Hill site (Fd Pe 4) Locality 2: Pre-Archaic manifestations in the Parkland of central Alberta, Canada by Maurice F. V. Doll, Human History Occasional Paper No.2, Provincial Museum of Alberta. Canadian Journal of Archaeology, Vol.7(2):247-249.

1985   A component in the Scottsbluff Tradition: excavations at the Niska site. Canadian Journal of Archaeology Vol.9(1):1-37.

n.d.   North-south interactions in central Saskatchewan: evidence from the southern forest region. Unpublished manuscript.

Meyer, David and Ian Dyck

1968   The Connell Creek Site FhMu-1. Saskatchewan Archaeology Newsletter 23:2-9.

Meyer, David and Henri Liboiron

1990   A Paleoindian drill from the Niska site in southern Saskatchewan. Plains Anthropologist, 35-129:299-302.

Meyer, David and S. J. Smailes

1975   Churchill River study (Missinipe Probe) - Archaeology. Saskatchewan Museum of Natural History, Final Report 19.

Meyer, David, James S. Wilson, and Olga Kleinko

1981   Archaeological mitigation along the Key Lake Access Road. Saskatchewan Research Council, Publication No.C-805-11-E-81.

Michels, J. and I. F. Smith

1967   Archaeological investigation of the Sheep Rock Shelter, Huntington County, Pennsylvania. Vols. 1 and 2, Department of Sociology and Anthropology, Pennsylvania State University.

Michlovic, Michael G.

1986   Cultural evolution and Plains archaeology. Plains Anthropologist 31 (113):2207-2218.

Millar, James F. V.

1968   Archaeology of Fisherman Lake, Western District of Mackenzie, N.W.T. PhD.

1978   dissertation, Department of Archaeology, University of Calgary.

1978   The Gray site: an early Plains burial ground. Parks Canada, Manuscript Report No.304 (2 volumes).

1981   Interactions between the Mackenzie and Yukon basins during the early Holocene. In Networks of the Past: regional interactions in archaeology. Peter Francis, F. J. Kense and P. G. Duke (eds.): 259-294. Archaeological Association of the University of Calgary.

1981a   Introduction to the Oxbow Complex in time and space. Canadian Journal of Archaeology, No.5:83-88.

1981b   Mortuary practices of the Oxbow Complex. Canadian Journal of Archaeology, No.5:103-117.

1981c   The Oxbow Complex: 1980 perspectives. Canadian Journal of Archaeology, No.5:155-160.

Millar, James F. V., H. Epp, T. W. Foster, J. S. Wilson, and G. Adams
1972   The Southwestern Saskatchewan Archaeological Project. Napao 3(2):1-39.

Miller, Norton G.
1973   Late-glacial and postglacial vegetation change in southwestern New York state. New York State Museum, Bulletin 420.

Miller, S. J.
1990   Characteristics of mammoth bone reduction at Owl Cave, the Wasden site, Idaho. In Bone Modification: proceedings of the First International Conference on bone modification. R. Bonnichsen and M. Sorg (eds.): 381-394. Center for the Study of the First Americans, University of Maine, Orono.

Minni, Sheila Joan
1976   The prehistoric occupations of Black Lake, Northern Saskatchewan. National Museum of Man, Archaeological Survey of Canada, Mercury 53.

Mitchell, D. H.
1969   Site survey in the Johnstone Strait region. Northwest Anthropological Research Notes 3(2):193-216.

1971   Archaeology of the Gulf of Georgia area, a natural region and its culture types. Syesis 4, Supp.1, Provincial Museum of British Columbia.

1990   Prehistory of the coasts of Southern British Columbia and northern Washington. In Handbook of North American Indians. William C. Sturtevant (gen. ed.). Vol.7, Northwest Coast. Wayne Suttles (vol. ed.): 340-358. Smithsonian Institution.

Mitchell, Donald H., Rebecca Murray, and Catherine Carlson

1981   The Duke Point archaeological project: a preliminary report on fieldwork and analysis. Annual Research Report No.1:21-51, Province of British Columbia.

Mochanov Iurii A.

1969   The Dyuktai Upper Paleolithic culture and certain aspects of its genesis. Sovetskaya Arkheologiya 4:236-239. (in Russian).

1969a   The Bel'kachinsk Neolithic culture of the Aladan. Arctic Anthropology, VI(2): 104-114.

1978   Stratigraphy and absolute chronology of the Paleolithic of northwest Asia, according to the work of 1963-73. In Early Man in America from a Circum-Pacific Perspective. A. L. Bryan (ed.): 54-66. Occasional Papers of the Department of Anthropology, No. 1, University of Alberta, Edmonton.

1980   Early migrations to America in the light of a study of the Dyuktai Paleolithic culture in northeast Asia. In Early Native Americans. D. L. Browman (ed.): 119-133. The Hague.

Mohs, Gordon

1981   An assessment and evaluation of heritage resources in the South Thompson River Valley of British Columbia. Ministry of Provincial Secretary and Government Services, Occasional Paper No.8, Province of British Columbia.

Molto, J. E.

1983   Biological relationships of Southern Ontario Woodland peoples: the evidence of discontinuous cranial morphology. National Museum of Man, Archaeological Survey of Canada, Mercury 117.

Monks, Gregory

1976   Chapter 16: Quantitative comparison of the Glenrose components with the Marpole component from DhRt-3.In The Glenrose Cannery Site. R. G. Matson (ed.): 267-280. National Museum of Man, Archaeological Survey of Canada, Mercury 52.

Moorehead, Warren K.

1922   A report on the archaeology of Maine. Phillips Academy, Department of Anthropology, Andover, Massachusetts.

Morice, A.

1904   The history of the northern interior of British Columbia. Ye Galleon Press, Farfield (1971).

Morlan, Richard E.

1974   Gladstone: an analysis of horizontal distributions. Arctic Anthropology, XI(suppl.):82-

520

        93.

1980   Taphonomy and archaeology in the Upper Pleistocene of the Northern Yukon Territory:
            a glimpse of the peopling of the New World. National Museum of Man, Archaeological
            Survey of Canada, Mercury 94.

1987   The Pleistocene archaeology of Beringia. In The Evolution of Human Hunting. Matthew
            H. Nitecki and Doris V. Nitecki (eds.): 267-307. Plenum Publishing Corporation.

1988   Pre-Clovis people: early discoveries of America? In Americans Before Columbus: Ice-age
            Origins. Ronald C. Carlisle (ed.): 31-43. Ethnology Monographs 12, Department of
            Anthropology, University of Pittsburg.

1991   Peopling of the New World: a discussion. In Clovis Origins and Adaptations. Robson
            Bonnichsen and Karen L. Turnmire (eds.): 303-307. Corvallis: Center for the Study of
            the First Americans, Oregon State University.

1992   Appendix 2: 203-208. Bison size and gender at the Gowen sites. In The Gowen sites,
            cultural responses to climatic warming on the Northern Plains (7500-5000 BP). Ernest
            G. Walker. Canadian Museum of Civilization, Archaeological Survey of Canada,
            Mercury 145.

1993   A compilation and evaluation of radiocarbon dates in Saskatchewan. Saskatchewan
            Archaeology, Vol.13:3-84.

(in press) Oxbow bison procurement as seen from the Harder site, Saskatchewan. Journal of
            Scientific Archaeology.

Morlan, Richard E. and Jacques Cinq-Mars
1982   Ancient Beringians: human occupation in the Late Pleistocen of Alaska and the Yukon
            Territory. In Paleoecology of Beringia. D.M. Hopkins, J.V. Matthews Jr., C.E.
            Schweger, and S.B. Young (eds.): 353- 381. Academic Press, New York.

1989   Canada's oldest known artifacts. In Abstracts of The First Peopling of the Americas.
            John Tomenchuk and Robson Bonnichsen (eds.). Center for the Study of the First
            Americans. University of Maine, Orono.

Morlan, R. E., D. E. Nelson, T. A. Brown, J. S. Vogel, and J. R. Southon
1990   Accelerator Mass Spectrometry dates on bone from Old Crow Basin, northern Yukon
            Territory. Canadian Journal of Archaeology, Vol.14:75-92.

Morlan, Richard E. and William B. Workman
1980   Prehistoric man in the southwest Yukon. In Kluane Pinnacle of the Yukon. John B.
            Theberge (ed.): 97-107.

Morris, Margaret W.
1973   Great Bear Lake Indians: a historical demography and human ecology, Part I: the
            situation prior to European contact. The Musk-ox, 11:3-27., Institute for Northern

Studies.

Morrison, David A.
1984   A reassessment of the Julian Complex, Fisherman Lake, N.W.T. Canadian Journal of Archaeology, Vol.8(1):29-56.

1987   The Middle Prehistoric Period and the Archaic concept in the Mackenzie Valley. Canadian Journal of Archaeology, Vol.11:49-74.

Morse, Dan F.
1982   A Paleo-Indian/Early Archaic cemetery possibility in Arkansas. In Peopling of the New World. Jonathan E. Ericson, R. E. Taylor and Rainer Berger (eds.): 147-162. Ballena Press, Anthropological Papers No.23.

Moss, Madonna L., Jon M. Erlandson, and Robert Stuckenrath
1990   Wood stake weirs and salmon fishing on the Northwest Coast: evidence from southeast Alaska. Canadian Journal of Archaeology, Vol.14:143-158.

Muller-Beck, Hansjurgen
1967   On migrations of hunters across the Bering Land Bridge in the Upper Pleistocene. In The Bering Land Bridge, D.M.Hopkins ed., pp.373-408. Stanford University Press.

1982   Late Pleistocene man in Northern Alaska and the mammoth - steppe biome. In Paleoecology of Beringia. David M. Hopkins, John V. Matthews Jr., Charles E. Schweger and Steven B. Young (eds.): 329-352. Academic Press, New York.

Mulloy, William
1958   A preliminary historical outline of the Northwestern Plains. University of Wyoming Publications 22(1). Laramie.

Murray, Jeffery S.
1981   Prehistoric skeletons from Blue Jackets Creek (Fl Ua 4), Queen Charlotte Islands, British Columbia. In Contributions to Physical Anthropology, 1978-1980. Jerome S. Cybulski (ed.): 127-175. National Museum of Man, Archaeological Survey of Canada, Mercury 106.

Murray, Rebecca Anne
1982   Analysis of artifacts from four Duke Point area sites near Nanaimo, B. C.: an example of cultural continuity in the southern Gulf of Georgia region. National Museum of Man, Archaeological Survey of Canada, Mercury 113.

Nagle, Christopher

1978   Indian occupations of the intermediate period on the central Labrador coast: a preliminary synthesis. Arctic Anthropology XV(2):119-145.

Nash, Ronald J.

1969   The Arctic Small Tool Tradition in Manitoba. Occasional Paper 2, Department of Anthropology, University of Manitoba.

1975   Archaeological investigations in the transitional forest zone: northern Manitoba, southern Keewatin, N.W.T. Manitoba Museum of Man and Nature.

1976   Cultural systems and culture change in the Central Arctic. In Eastern Arctic Prehistory: Paleoeskimo Problems. Moreau S. Maxwell (ed.): 150-155. Memoirs of the Society for American Archaeology, No.31.

1978   Prehistory and cultural ecology - Cape Breton Island, Nova Scotia. Canadian Ethnology Society, Papers from the Fourth Annual Congress. Richard J. Preston (ed.): 131-155. National Museum of Man, Canadian Ethnology Service, Mercury 40.

Naylor, Larry J. and Howard G. Savage

1984   Analysis of the macro - faunal remains from the McIntyre site, Peterborough County, Ontario. In The McIntyre site, archaeology, subsistence and environment. Richard B. Johnston (ed.): 115-134. National Museum of Man, Archaeological Survey of Canada, Mercury 126.

Nelson, Charles M.

1969   The Sunset Creek site (45-KT-28) and its place in plateau prehistory. Report of Investigations, No.47, Washington State University, Laboratory of Anthropology. Pullman.

Nelson, Charles M.

1990   Prehistory of the Puget Sound region. In Handbook of North American Indians. William C. Sturtevant (gen. ed.), Vol.7, Northwest Coast. Wayne Suttles (vol. ed.): 481-484. Smithsonian Institution.

Nero, Robert W.

1959   An Agate Basin point site in Saskatchewan. The Blue Jay 17(1):32-40.

Nero, Robert W. and B. A. McCorquodale

1958   Report on an excavation at the Oxbow Dam site. The Blue Jay, 16(2):82-90.

Newman, M. and P. Julig

1989   The identification of protein residues on lithic artifacts from a stratified Boreal Forest site. Canadian Journal of Archaeology, Vol.13:119-132.

Newton, Barry M. and John W. Pollock

1985   FjPi-29, a prehistoric workshop site in the Alberta Parklands. Archaeological Survey of Alberta, Manuscript Series, No.2.

Nichols, H.

1968   Pollen analysis, paleotemperature, and the summer position of the Arctic front in the post-glacial history of Keewatin. Bulletin of the American Meteorological Society, 49(4):387-388.

1972   Summary of the palynological evidence for Late-Quaternary vegetational and climatic change in the Central and Eastern Canadian Arctic. In Climatic Changes in Arctic Areas during the Last Ten Thousand Years. Y. Vasari, H. Hyvarinen, and S. Hicks (eds.): 309-338. Acta Universititas Ouluensis, Series A Scientiae Resum Naturaluim 3, Geologica 1.

Noble, William C.

1971   Archaeological surveys and sequences in central District of Mackenzie, N.W.T. Arctic Anthropology VIII(1):102-135.

1972   One hundred and twenty - five years of archaeology in the Canadian provinces. Canadian Archaeological Association, Bulletin 4:1-78.

1981   Prehistory of the Great Slave Lake and Great Bear Lake region. In Handbook of North American Indians. William C.Sturtevant (gen. ed.), Vol.6, Subarctic. June Helm (vol. ed.): 97-106. Smithsonian Institution, Washington D.C.

Olsson, Ingrid

1972   The pretreatment of samples and the interpretation of the results of C-14 determinations. In Climatic Changes in the Arctic Area during the Last Ten Thousand Years. Y. Vasari, H. Hyvarinin, and S. Hicks (eds.): 8-37. Acta Universititas Ouluensis, Series A (3).

Oschinsky, Lawrence

1964   The most ancient Eskimos. The University of Ottawa Press.

Ossenberg, N. S.

n.d.   Native people of the American Northwest: population history from the perspective of skull morphology. Paper presented at the University of Tokyo symposium on "The Evolution and Dispersal of Modern Humans in Asia". November 1990.

Ovenden, Michael W. and David A. Rodger

1981   Megaliths and medicine wheels. In Megaliths to Medicine Wheels: Boulder Structures in Archaeology. The Archaeological Association of the University of Calgary, Proceedings of the Eleventh Annual Conference. Michael Wilson, Kathie L. Road, and

524

Kenneth J. Hardy (eds.): 371-386.

Palmer, Gary B.
1975   Cultural ecology in the Canadian Plateau: pre-contact to the early contact period in the territory of the Southern Shuswap Indians of British Columbia. Northwest Anthropological Research Notes, 9(2):199-245.

Parent, M., J. -M. M. Dubois, P. Bail, A. Larocque et G. Larocque
1985   Paleogeographie du Québec méridional entre 12500 et 8000 ans B.P. Recherches amérindiennes au Québec, XV(1-2):17-37.

Peacock, William
1976   Chapter 13: Analysis of variance of the Glenrose artifact assemblage. In The Glenrose Cannery Site. R. G. Matson (ed.): 231-241. National Museum of Man, Archaeological Survey of Canada, Mercury 52.

Pei, Gai
1985   Comment on "The `Dyuktai Culture' and New World Origins" by Sembok Yi and Geoffrey Clark, Current Anthropology 26(1):14-15.

Pennington, Jean A. T.
1989   Food values of portions commonly used. Harper and Row, New York (15th edition).

Petersen, James B.
1991   Archaeological testing at the Sharrow site: a deeply stratified Early to Late Holocene cultural sequence in Central Maine. Maine Archaeological Society and the Maine Historic Preservation Commission, Occasional Publications in Maine Archaeology, No.8.

Petersen, James B., Nathan D. Hamilton, David E. Putnam, Arthur E. Spiess, Robert Stuckenrath, Cynthia A. Thayer and Jack A. Walford
1986   The Piscataquis Archaeological Project: a Late Pleistocene occupational sequence in northern New England. Archaeology of Eastern North America, Vol.14:1-18.

Petersen, James B. and David E. Putnam
1987   Another Holocene sequence and recent programs of the Piscataquis Archaeological Project in central Maine. Current Research in the Pleistocene Vol.4: 23-24.

Pettipas, Leo F.
1969   Early Man in the Swan River Valley. Manitoba Archaeological Newsletter 6(3):3-22.
1975   The Paleo-Indian prehistory of Saskatchewan. Saskatchewan Archaeology Newsletter

50:1-32.

1980   The Little Gem Complex. Saskatchewan Archaeology 1:3-81.

1985   Recent developments in Paleo-Indian archaeology in Manitoba. In Contributions to Plains Prehistory, David Burley (ed.): 39-63. Archaeological Survey of Alberta, Occasional Publication No.26

Pettipas, Leo F. (ed.)

1983   Introducing Manitoba prehistory. Papers in Manitoba archaeology, Popular Series No.4, Manitoba Department of Cultural Affairs and Historical Resources. Manitoba.

Pettipas, Leo F. and Anthony P.Buchner

1983   Paleo-Indian prehistory of the Glacial Lake Agassiz region in southern Manitoba, 11 500 to 6500 B.P. In Glacial Lake Agassiz. J.T.Teller and Lee Clayton (eds.): 421-451, Geological Association of Canada Special Paper 26.

Pfeiffer, Susan

1974   Analysis of cremations from two Late Archaic burial sites: Riverside and Hind. The Wisconsin Archaeologist 55(4):302-308.

1977   The skeletal biology of Archaic populations of the Great Lakes region. National Museum of Man, Archaeological Survey of Canada, Mercury 64.

1979   Archaic population affinities as determined by analysis of cranial morphology. Ontario Archaeology 32:35-41.

Pielou, E. C.

1991   After the Ice Age, the return of life to glaciated North America. University of Chicago Press.

Piérard, Jean, Marc Côté et Lyn Pinel

1987   Le chien de l'occupation archaïque du site Cadieux. Recherches amérindiennes au Québec, Vol.XVII(1-2):47-61.

Pilon Jean-Luc

1982   Le site Neskuteu au Mushuau Nipi (Nouveau - Québec): manifestation de la période archaïque. Collection Nordicana, No.46: 1-38., Centre d'études nordiques, Université Laval, Québec.

1987   Washahoe Inninou Dahtsuounoaou: ecological and cultural adaptation along the Severn River in the Hudson Bay Lowlands of Ontario. Ontario Conservation Archaeology Report, No.10. Ontario Ministry of Citizenship and Culture.

1991   Insights into the prehistory of the Lower Mackenzie Valley, Anderson Plain region, Northwest Territories. In NOGAP Archaeology Project: an Integrated Archaeological

Research and Management Approach. Jacques Cinq-Mars and Jean-Luc Pilon (eds.): 89-111. Canadian Archaeological Association, Occasional Paper No.1.

Plumet, Patrick, Jean-François Moreau, Hélène Gauvin, Marie-France Archambault, et Verginia Elliott,
1993   Le site Lavoie (DbEj-11), L'archaïque aux Grandes Bergeronnes Haute Côte-Nord du Saint-Laurent, Québec. Paléo-Québec No.20. Recherches amérindiennes au Québec.

Pokotylo, David L.
1981   Towards an understanding of prehistoric upland settlement behaviour in the British Columbia southern interior plateau. In Networks of the Past: Regional Interaction in Archaeology. Peter D. Francis, K. J. Kense, and P. G. Duke (eds.): 379-396, The Archaeological Association of the University of Calgary.

Pollock, John W.
1976   The culture history of Kirkland Lake District, northeastern Ontario. National Museum of Man, Archaeological Survey of Canada, Mercury 54.
1978   Early cultures of the Clearwater River area. Archaeological Survey of Alberta, Occasional Paper 6.
1981   Plains Archaic complexes in the Alberta Parkland and Boreal Forest. Canadian Journal of Archaeology, Vol.5:145-153.

Pollock, John W. and W. C. Noble
1975   Archaeology of the Hawley Lake area, Hudson Bay Lowlands, Ontario. Canadian Archaeological Association - Collected Papers March 1975. Ontario Historic Site Branch Research Report 6:74-98.

Popham, Robert E. and J. N. Emerson
1954   Manifestations of the Old Copper Industry in Ontario. Pennsylvania Archaeologist, XXIV(1):3-19.

Porter, Stephen C.
1988   Landscapes of the last Ice Age in North America. In Americans before Columbus: Ice-Age Origins. Ronald C. Carlisle (ed.): 1-24. Department of Anthropology, University of Pittsburg, Ethnology Monographs No.12.

Powers, Wm. Roger
1973   Palaeolithic man in northeast Asia. Arctic Anthropology, X(2):1-106.
1978   Early man in America from a Circum- Pacific perspective. A. L. Bryan (ed.): 72-77. Occasional Paper No. 1, Department of Anthropology, University of Alberta, Edmonton.
1985   North Alaska Range Early Man Project. National Geographic Society Research Reports,

Vol 19:1 -6.

1990   The peoples of Eastern Beringia. In Prehistoric Mongoloid Dispersals, No.7: 53-74, Prehistoric Mongoloid Dispersals Project, The University Museum, The University of Tokoyo.

Powers, Wm. Roger, F.E. Goebel and N.H. Bigelow

1990   Late Pleistocene occupationat Walker Road: new data on the central Alaska Nenana Complex. Current Research in the Pleistocene 7: 40 -43. A Peopling of the Americas Publication, Center for the Study of the First Americans, University of Maine, Orono.

Powers, Wm. Roger and John F. Hoffecker

1989   Late Pleistocene settlement in the Nenana Valley, central Alaska. American Antiquity, Vol.54(2):263-287.

Powers, Wm. Roger, R. Dale Gutherie, and John F. Hoffecker

n.d.   Dry Creek, archaeology and paleoecology of a Late Pleistocene Alaskan camp. National Park Service unpublished manuscript.

Prest, V. K.

1970   Quaternary geology of Canada. In Geology and Economic Minerals of Canada. R. J. W. Douglas (ed.): 675-764. Geological Survey of Canada, Economic Geology Report No.1, Part B.

Prufer, Olaf H. and Raymond S. Baby

1963   Palaeo-Indians of Ohio. Ohio State Historical Society.

Quigg, J. Michael

1976   A note on the Fletcher site. In Archaeology in Alberta 1975. J. Michael Quigg and W. J. Byrne (eds.): 108-110. Archaeological Survey of Alberta, Occasional Publication No.1.

1981   Stone circle excavations in Alberta to 1978: a summary. In Megaliths to Medicine Wheels: Boulder Structures in Archaeology. Proceedings of the Eleventh Conference, The Archaeological Association of the University of Calgary. Michael Wilson, Kathie L. Road, and Kenneth J. Hardy: 47-68.

1981a   Stone alignments. In Alberta Archaeology: Prospect and Retrospect. T. A. Moore (ed.): 59-68. The Archaeological Society of Alberta. Lethbridge.

1984   A 4700-year-old assemblage from east-central Alberta. Plains Anthropologist, 29(104):151-159.

1986   The Crown site (FhNa-86) excavation results. Nipawin Reservoir Heritage Study, Vol.8. David Meyer (ed.). Saskatchewan Research Council/Saskatchewan Power Corporation.

528

Quimby, George I. and James B. Griffin

1961   Various finds of copper and stone artifacts in the Lake Superior Basin. In Lake Superior Copper and the Indians: Miscellaneous Studies of Great Lakes Prehistory. James B. Griffin (ed.): 103-117. University of Michigan, Museum of Anthropology, Anthropological Papers No.17.

Rainey, F. C.

1940   Archaeological investigations in central Alaska. American Antiquity, Vol.5:299-308.

Ramsden, Peter

1976   Rocky Ridge: a stratified Archaic site. Ontario Ministry of Culture and Recreation, Historical Planning and Research Branch, Research Report 7.

1990   The Winter site (AkHb-2): a Late Archaic component near Guelph, Ontario. Ontario Archaeology 50:27-38.

Rasmussen, Knud

1931   The Netsilik Eskimos, social life and spiritual culture. Report of the Fifth Thule Expedition 1921-24, Vol.VIII, Nos.1-2. Copenhagen.

Reagan, Michael J., Ralph M. Rowlett, Ervan G. Garrison, Wakefield Dort Jr., and Chris J. Johannsen

1978   Flake tools stratified below Paleo - Indian artifact. Science 200:1272-1275.

Reanier, Richard

1990   Natural environment. In The 1989 Exxon Valdez cultural resource program. Charles M. Mobley et al.: 13- 48. Exxon Shipping Company and Exxon Company.

Reeves, Brian O. K.

1969   The southern Alberta paleo-cultural and paleo-environmental sequence. In Post-Pleistocene Man and his Environment on the Northern Plains, the University of Calgary Archaeological Association. R. G. Forbis, L. B. Davis, O. A. Christensen, and G. Fedirchuk (eds.): 6-46.

1970   Cultural dynamics in the Manitoba Grasslands 1000 BC - AD 700. In Ten Thousand Years, Archaeology in Manitoba. Walter A. Hlady (ed.): 153-174. Manitoba Archaeological Society.

1972   A partial Holocene pedological and archaeological record from the southern Alberta Rocky Mountains. Arctic and Alpine Research 4(4):325-336.

1973   The concept of an Altithermal cultural hiatus in northern Plains prehistory. American Anthropologist Vol.75(5):1221-1253.

1974   Prehistoric archaeological research on the eastern slopes of the Canadian Rocky Mountains 1967-1971. Canadian Archaeological Association Bulletin 6:2-31.

1975   Early Holocene (ca. 8000 to 5500 B.C.) prehistoric land/resource utilization patterns in Watertown Lakes National Park, Alberta. Arctic and Alpine Research 7(3):237-248.

1978   Head-Smashed-In: 5500 years of bison jumping in the Alberta Plains. Plains Anthropologist, Memoir 14, 23(82) Pt.2:151-174.

1983   Culture change in the Northern Plains: 1000 BC-AD 1000. Archaeological Survey of Alberta, Occasional Paper No.20.

1990   Communal bison hunters of the Northern Plains. In Hunters of the Recent Past. Leslie B. Davis and Brian O. K. Reeves (eds.): 168-194. Unwin Hyman, London.

Reid, C. S. "Paddy"

1977   Environment, Man, and Maymaygwasphi: the dimensions of past human cultural impact in the Lake of the Woods area, Part I-1976, Part II-1977. Ministry of Culture and Recreation, Research Manuscript Series, Data Box 311, 312. Ontario.

1980   Approaches to the archaeology of West Patricia: a preliminary statement. In Studies in West Patricia Archaeology. C. S. Paddy Reid (ed.): 215-230. Ministry of Culture and Recreation, Archaeological Research Report 15. Ontario.

Renfrew, Colin and Paul Bahn

1991   Archaeology, Theories, Methods, and Practice. Thames and Hudson Inc., New York.

Renouf, Priscilla

1977   A late Paleo-Indian and Early Archaic sequence in southern Labrador. Man in the Northeast No.13:35-44.

Reynolds, Thomas

1856   Discovery of copper and other Indian relics, near Brockville. The Canadian Journal N. S., Vol.1(4):329-334, Toronto.

Ribes, René

1964   Les stations Archaïques de Red Mill. Cahiers d'archéologie Québécoise 1(1) 1-24, Musée d'archéologie, Le Centre des Etudes Universitaires de Trois-Rivières.

1966   Pieces de la périod Archaïque trovees vers 1700 dans la région de Bécancour. Cahiers d'archéologie Québécoise 2(1): 22-33, Musée d'archéologie, Le Centre des Etudes Universitaires de Trois-Rivières.

Rice, David G.

1972   The Windust Phase in Lower Snake River region prehistory. Washington State University, Laboratory of Anthropology, Report of Investigations No.50. Pullman.

Richard, Pierre J.H.

1977   Histoire post-wisconsinienne de la végétation du Québec méridional par l'analyse pollinique. Service de la recherche, Publications et rapports divers. Direction générale de forêts, ministère des terres et forêts du Québec. Québec.

1985   Couvert végétal et paléoenvironnements du Québec entre 12 000 and 8000 ans BP, l'habitabilité dans un milieu changeant. Recherches amérindiennes au Québec, XV(1-2):39-56.

Richards, Thomas H. and Michael K. Rousseau

1987   Late prehistoric cultural horizons on the Canadian Plateau. Simon Fraser University, Department of Archaeology, Publication No.16.

Ridley, Frank

1954   The Frank Bay site, Lake Nipissing, Ontario. American Antiquity, Vol.20(1): 40-50.

1958   Sites on Ghost River, Lake Abitibi. Pennsylvania Archaeologist, XXVIII(1):39-56.

1966   Archaeology of Lake Abitibi, Ontario-Quebec. Anthropological Journal of Canada, 4(2):2-50.

Ritchie, J. C.

1976   The Late-Quaternary vegetational history of the western interior of Canada. Canadian Journal of Botany 54(15):1793-1818.

1980   Towards a Late-Quaternary Palaeoecology of the Ice-Free Corridor. In The Ice-Free Corridor and Peopling of the New World, Proceeds of the Fifth Biennial Conference of the American Quaternary Association, Edmonton, September 2-4, 1978, Canadian Journal of Anthropology, 1(1):15-28.

1984   Past and present vegetation of the Far Northwest of Canada. University of Toronto Press.

1987   Postglacial vegetation of Canada. Cambridge University Press.

Ritchie, James C. and Les C. Cwynar

1982   The Late Quaternary vegetation of the North Yukon. In Paleoecology of Beringia. David M. Hopkins, John V. Matthews Jr., Charles E. Schweger, and Steven B. Young (eds.): 113-126. Academic Press, New York.

Ritchie, J. C., L. C. Cwynar, and R. W. Spear

1983   Evidence from north-west Canada for an early Holocene Milahkovitch thermal maximum. Nature 305:126-128.

Ritchie, William A.

1940   Two prehistoric village sites at Brewerton, New York. Researches and Transactions of the New York State Archaeological Association, IX(1).

1944   The pre-Iroquoian occupations of New York State. Rochester Museum of Arts and

Sciences, Memoir No.1.

1953   A probable Paleo-Indian site in Vermont. American Antiquity Vol.18(3): 249-258.

1965   The Archaeology of New York State. Natural History Press.

1969   The archaeology of Martha's Vineyard: a framework for the prehistory of southern New England, a study of coastal ecology and adaptation. Natural History Press.

1971   The Archaic in New York. New York State Archaeological Association, The Bulletin 52:2-12.

1979   The Otter Creek No.2 site in Rutland County, Vermont. The Bulletin and Journal of the Archaeology of New York State 76:1-21.

Ritchie, William A. and Robert E. Funk

1971   Evidence for Early Archaic occupation on Staten Island. Pennsylvania Archaeologist XXXX1(3):45-59.

1973   Aboriginal settlement patterns in the Northeast. New York State Museum and Science Service, Memoir 20.

Roberts, Arthur

1980   A geographic approach to Southern Ontario Archaic. Archaeology of Eastern North America, Vol.8:28-45.

1984   Ice free corridor Paleoindian survey. Current Research 1:15-17. A Peopling of the Americas Publication, Center for the Study of Early Man, University of Maine, Orono.

1985   Preceramic occupations along the north shore of Lake Ontario. National Museum of Man, Archaeological Survey of Canada, Mercury 132.

Roberts, Arthur and J.H. McAndrews

1987   Southern Ontario, 8600 BC. Plate 3, Historical Atlas of Canada from the beginning to 1800, Vol. I. R.Cole Harris (ed.) and Geoffrey J. Matthews (carto./design), University of Toronto Press

Roberts, Arthur, J. H. McAndrew, V. K. Prest, and J. - S. Vincent

1987   The Fluted Point People, 9500 - 8200 BC. Plate 2, Historical Atlas of Canada, from the beginning to 1800, Vol. I. R. Cole Harris (ed.) and Geoffrey J. Matthews (carto./ design.). University of Toronto Press.

Roberts, Arthur, J. V. Wright, V. K. Prest, and J. -S. Vincent

1987   The Plano People, 8500-6000 BC. Historical Atlas of Canada, from the beginning to 1800, Vol.I, Plate 5. University of Toronto Press.

Rogers, Edward S.

1963   The hunting group-hunting territory complex among the Mistassini Indians. National

Museum of Canada, Bulletin 195.

Rogers, Edward S. and Mary B. Black
1976   Subsistence strategy in the fish and hare period, Northern Ontario: the Weagamow
            Ojibwa, 1880-1920. Journal of Anthropological Research, 32(1):1-43.

Rogers, Edward S. and Marray H. Rogers
1948   Archaeological reconnaissance of Lakes Mistassini and Albanel, Province of Quebec,
            1947. American Antiquity, Vol.14(2):81-98.
1950   Archaeological investigations in the region about Lake Mistassini and Albanel, Province
            of Quebec, 1948. American Antiquity, Vol.15(4):322-337.

Rogers, Richard A. and Larry D. Martin
1986   Replication and the history of Paleoindian studies. Current Research in the Pleistocene
            3: 43-44. A Peopling of the Americas Publication, Center for the Study of Early Man,
            University of Maine, Orono.

Rogers, Richard A., Larry D. Martin and T. Dale Nicklas
1990   Ice-age geography and the distribution of native North American languages. Journal of
            Biogeography 17:131-143.

Romanoff, Steven
1985   Fraser Lillooet salmon fishing. Northwest Anthropological Research Notes, 19(2):119-
            160.

Ronaghan, Brian
1986   The status of prehistoric research in Alberta's eastern slopes. In Eastern Slopes
            Prehistory: Selected Papers. Brian Ronaghan (ed.): 269-352. Archaeological Survey of
            Alberta, Occasional Paper No.30.

Roosa, William B.
1977   Great Lakes Paleoindian: the Parkhill site, Ontario. In Amerinds and their
            paleoenvironments in northeastern North America, Annals of the New York Academy
            of Sciences, 288: 349-354.
1977a   Fluted points from the Parkhill, Ontario site. In For the Director: Research Essays in
            Honor of James B. Griffin. Charles E.Cleland (ed.): 87-122. Anthropological Papers,
            Museum of Anthropology, University of Michigan, 61.

Rousseau, Mike K.
1989   Upper Oregon Jack Creek Valley heritage resources. The Midden, Vol.21 (2): 6-11.

1991   Landels, an 8500 year-old deer hunting camp. The Midden 23(4):6-9.

Rousseau, Mike K. and Thomas H. Richards
1985   A culture-historical sequence for the South Thompson-Western Shuswap Lakes region
            of British Columbia: the last 4000 years. Northwest Anthropological Research Notes,
            19(1):1-32.
1988   The Oregon Jack Creek site (EdRi-6): a Lehman Phase site in the Thompson River
            Valley, British Columbia. Canadian Journal of Archaeology, Vol.12:39-63.

Rousselière, G. -M.
1964   Palaeo-Eskimo remains in the Pelly Bay region, N.W.T. Contributions to Anthropology
            1961-62, Part I, National Museum of Canada, Bulletin 193:62-183.
1976   The Paleoeskimo in northern Baffinland. In Eastern Arctic Prehistory: Paleoeskimo
            Problems. Moreau S. Maxwell (ed.): 40-57. Memoirs of the Society for American
            Archaeology, No.31.

Rowe, J. S.
1959   Forest regions of Canada. Department of Northern Affairs and Natural Resources,
            Forestry Branch, Bulletin 123.

Ruhlen, Merritt
1989   Linguistic evidence for the peopling of the Americas. In Abstracts of The First World
            Summit Conference on the Peopling of the Americas. John Tomenchuk and Robson
            Bonnichsen (eds.): 13-14. Center for the Study of the First Americans, University of
            Maine, Orono.
1990   Phylogenetic relations of Native American languages. In Prehistoric Mongoloid
            Dispersals, No.7: 75 - 96. Prehistoric Mongoloid Dispersals Project, The University
            Museum, The University of Tokyo.

Runnings, Anna L., Carl E. Gustafson and Dave Bentley
1989   Use-wear on bone tools: a technique for study under the scanning electron microscope.
            In Bone Modification. Robson Bonnichsen and Marcella H. Sorg (eds.): 259-266.
            Peopling of the Americas Publications, Center for the Study of the First Americans,
            University of Maine, Orono.

Rutherford, A. A., Jurgen Wittenberg, and B. C. Gordon
1984   University of Saskatchewan Radiocarbon Dates X. Radiocarbon Vol.26(2):241-292.

Saarnisto, Matti
1974   Stratigraphical studies on the shoreline displacement of Lake Superior. Canadian Journal

of Earth Sciences, 12:300-319.

Salzer, R. J.
  1974   The Wisconsin North Lakes Project: a preliminary report. In Aspects of Upper Great
          Lakes Anthropology. Elden Johnson (ed.): 40-54. Minnesota Prehistoric Archaeology
          Series 11, Minnesota Historical Society..

Samson, Gilles
  1978   Preliminary cultural sequence and palaeo -environmental reconstruction on the Indian
          House Lake region, Nouveau-Quebec. Arctic Anthropology XV(2):186-205.
  1978a   Le Nord-Est de la péninsule Québec- Labrador. Recherches amérindiennes au Québec,
          VII(1-2):111-124.

Sanders, Thomas N.
  1990   Adams: the manufacturing of flaked stone tools at a Palaeoindian site in western
          Kentucky. Persimmon Press Monographs in Archaeology. Buffalo.

Sanger, David
  1964   Excavations at Nesikep Creek (EdRk:4), a stratified site near Lillooet, British Columbia:
          a preliminary report. Contributions to Anthropology 1961-62, Part I. National Museum
          of Canada, Bulletin 193:130-161.
  1967   Prehistory of the Pacific Northwest Plateau as seen from the interior of British Columbia.
          American Antiquity Vol.32(2):186-197.
  1968   Prepared core and blade traditions in the Pacific Northwest. Arctic Anthropology
          V(1):92-120.
  1968a   Seven thousand years of prehistory in the interior of British Columbia. The Beaver,
          Spring Issue.
  1969   Development of the Pacific Northwest Plateau Culture Area: historical and environmental
          considerations. Contributions to Anthropology: Ecological Essays. National Museum of
          Man, National Museums of Canada, Bulletin 230:15-23.
  1969a   Cultural traditions in the interior of British Columbia. Syesis, 2:189-200
  1970   The archaeology of the Lochnore-Nesikep locality, British Columbia. Syesis, Vol.3,
          Supplement 1. British Columbia Provincial Museum.
  1973   Cow Point: an Archaic cemetery in New Brunswick. National Museum of Man,
          Archaeological Survey of Canada, Mercury 12.
  1975   Culture change as an adaptive process in the Maine - Maritimes region. Arctic
          Anthropology XII(2):60-75.
  1979   Some thoughts on the scarcity of archaeological sites in Maine between 10,000 and 5,000
          years ago. In Discovering Maine's Archaeological Heritage. David Sanger (ed.): 23-34.
  1979a   Who were the Red Paints? In Discovering Maine's Archaeological Heritage. David

Sanger (ed.): 67-73.

1988   Maritime adaptations in the Gulf of Maine. Archaeology of Eastern North America, Vol.16:81-99.

Sanger, David and Robert G. MacKay

1979   The Hirundo archaeological project - preliminary report. In Discovering Maine's Archaeological Heritage. David Sanger (ed.): 35-48.

Saunders, J.J.

1980   A model for man-mammoth relationships in Late Pleistocene North America. In The Ice-free Corridor and Peopling of the New World, Proceeds of the Fifth Biennial Conference of the American Quaternary Association, Edmonton, September 2-4, 1978, Canadian Journal of Anthropology, 1(1):87-98.

Saylor, Stanley

1977   The 1976 excavations at EgKx-1, Wanipigow Lake. Papers in Manitoba Archaeology, Preliminary Report 4, Department of Tourism, Recreation and Cultural Affairs, Historic Resources Branch. Manitoba.

Schalk, R.

1977   The structure of an anadromous fish resource. In For Theory Building in Archaeology. L. R. Binford (ed.): 207-249. Academic Press, New York.

Schledermann, Peter

1978   Prehistoric demographic trends in the Canadian High Arctic. Canadian Journal of Archaeology, No.2:43-58.

Schneider, Fred

1982   The Pelland and Moe site blades: Paleo-Indian culture history in the Upper Midwest. Plains Anthropologist Vol.27(96):125-135.

1984   (ed.) North Dakota's first excavated and dated Paleo-Indian spearpoints. North Dakota Archaeological Association Newsletter 5: 5.

Schroedl, Alan R. and Ernest G. Walker

1978   A preliminary report on the Gowen site: an Early Middle Prehistoric site on the northwest Plains. Napao 8(1&2):1-5.

Schurr, Theodore G., Scott W. Ballenger, Yik-Yuen Gan, Judith A. Hodge, D. Andrew Merriwether, Dale N. Lawrence, William C. Knowles, Kenneth M. Weiss, and Douglas C. Wallace

1990   Amerindian mitochondrial DNAs have rare Asian mutations at high frequencies, suggesting they derived from four primary maternal lineages. American Journal of Human Genetics 46:613-623.

Schwarcz, Henry P.
1991   Some theoretical aspects of isotope paleodiet studies. Journal of Archaeological Science, Vol.18:261-272.

Schweger, C. E.
1987   A critical appraisal of the Altithermal and its role in archaeology. In Man and the Mid-Holocene Climatic Optimum. Proceedings of the 17th Annual Chacmool Conference, The Archaeological Association of the University of Calgary. Neil A. McKinnon and G. S. L. Stuart (eds.): 371-377.

1989   Paleoecology of the western Canadian ice - free corridor. In Chapter 7 of Quaternary Geology of Canada and Greenland. R.J. Fulton (ed.): 491-498, Geological Survey of Canada, Geology of Canada No.1.

Schweger, C.E. and M. Hickman
1989   Holocene paleohydrology of central Alberta: testing the general circulation model climate simulation. Canadian Journal of Earth Sciences 26:1826-1833.

Schweger, C. E., J. V. Matthews Jr., D. M. Hopkins, and S. B. Young
1982   Paleoecology of Beringia-a synthesis. In Paleoecology of Beringia. David M. Hopkins, John V. Matthews Jr., Charles E. Schweger, and Steven B. Young (eds.): 425-444. Academic Press, New York.

Schweger, Charles, Thelma Habgood, and Michael Hickman
1981   Late glacial-Holocene climatic changes in Alberta: the record from lake sediment studies. In The Impacts of Climatic Fluctuations in Alberta's Resources and Environment: Proceedings of the Workshop and Annual Meeting of the Alberta Climatological Association, February 1981. K. R. Leggat and J. T. Kolylak (eds.): 47-60. Atmospheric Environmental Service, Environment Canada, Edmonton, Report No. WAES-1-81.

Scott, W. B.
1977   Fish remains from the Cloverleaf Bastion of the Fort at Coteau-du-Lac, Quebec. Parks Canada, History and Archaeology No.12:121-157.

Scott, W.B. and M.G. Scott
1988   Atlantic fishes of Canada. University of Toronto Press in cooperation with the Minister of Fisheries and Oceans and the Canadian Government Publishing Centre. Supply and Services Canada.

Sellards, E. H.
 1952   Early Man in America, a study in prehistory. Texas Memorial Museum Publication, University of Texas Press, Austin.

Severs, Patricia D. S.
 1974   Archaeological investigations at Blue Jackets Creek, FlUa-4, Queen Charlotte Islands, British Columbia, 1973. Canadian Archaeological Association, Bulletin No.6:165-205.

Shaw, Leslie C.
 1988   A biocultural evaluation of the skeletal population from the Nevin site, Blue Hill, Maine. Archaeology of Eastern North America Vol.16:55-77.

Shay, C. Thomas
 1971   The Itasca bison kill site, an ecological analysis. Publications in the Minnesotal Historical Society, Minnesota Prehistoric Archaeology Series.

Shipman, Pat, Daniel C. Fisher, and Jennie J. Rose
 1984   Mastodon butchery: microscopic evidence of carcass processing and bone tool use. Paleobiology 10(3):358-365.

Short, Susan K.
 1978   Palynology: a Holocene environmental perspective for archaeology in Labrador-Ungava. Arctic Anthropology XV(2):9-35.

Shreeve, James
 1990   Argument over a woman, science searches for the mother of us all. Discover, the World of Science 11(8):52-59.

Sillen, Andrew, Judith C. Sealy, and Nikolaas J. van der Merwe
 1989   Chemistry and paleodietary research: no more easy answers. American Antiquity, Vol.54(3):504-512.

Simmons, William S.
 1986   Appendix II - Human skeletal material from Cape Krusenstern and Battle Rock. In Beach Ridge Archaeology of Cape Krusenstern by J. Louis Giddings and Douglas D. Anderson. National Park Service, US Department of Interior, Publications in Archaeology 20:356-361.

Simonsen, Bjorn O.
 1973   Archaeological investigations in the Hecate Strait-Milbanke Sound area of British

Columbia. National Museum of Man, Archaeological Survey of Canada, Mercury 13.

1979   Attrition of coastal archaeological resources in the Maritime Provinces of Canada. Council of Maritime Premiers, Reports in Archaeology, No.3.

Smith, B. L.

1948   An analysis of the Maine Cemetery Complex. Bulletin of the Massachusetts Archaeological Society 9(2-3):19-71.

Smith, J. G. E.

1975   The ecological basis of Chipewyan socio-territorial organization. In Proceedings of the Northern Athabascan Conference 1971, Vol.2. A. McFadyen Clark (ed.): 389-461. National Museum of Man, Canadian Ethnology Service, Mercury 27.

Smith, Jason W.

1974   The Northeast Asian-Northwest American Microblade Tradition (NANAMT). Journal of Field Archaeology 1(3/4):347-364.

Smith, Jason W. and V. Harrison

1978   An early unifacial technology in northern British Columbia. Journal of Field Archaeology 5:116-120.

Smith, Jason W. and Rachel A. Smith

1982   New light on early sociocultural evolution in the Americas. In Peopling of the New World. Jonathon E. Ericson, R. E. Taylor, and Rainer Berger (eds.): 229-261. Ballena Press, Anthropological Papers No.23.

Snow, Dean R.

1969   A summary of excavations at the Hathaway site in Passadumkeag, Maine, 1912, 1947, and 1968. University of Maine at Orono, Department of Archaeology.

1978   Late prehistory of the East Coast. In Handbook of North American Indians, Vol.15, Northeast. Willian C. Sturtevant (gen. ed.), Bruce G. Trigger (vol. ed.): 58-69. Smithsonian Institution.

1980   The Archaeology of New England. Academic Press.

1992   L'augmentation de la population chez les groupes Iroquoiens et ses conséquences sur l'Étude de leurs origines. With introduction by Claude Chapdelaine and commentary by Hubert Charbonneau, Norman Clermont, W.E. Englebrecht, Peter G. Ramsden, Gary Warrick, Ronald F. Williamson, and J.V. Wright with reply by Dean R. Snow. Recherches amérindiennes au Québec, Vol.XXII(4):3-36.

Spence, Michael W.

1986 Band structure and interaction in Early Southern Ontario. Canadian Journal of Anthropology, Vol.5(2):83-95.

Spence, Michael W., W. D. Finlayson, and R. H. Pihl
1979 Hopewellian influence on Middle Woodland cultures in Southern Ontario. In Hopewell Archaeology: the Chillicothe Conference. D. Brose and N. Greber (eds.): 115-121. Kent State University Press.

Spence, Michael W. and William A. Fox
1986 The Early Woodland occupation of Southern Ontario. In Early Woodland Archaeology. Kenneth B. Farnsworth and Thomas E. Emerson (eds.): 1-46, Center for American Archaeology, Kampsville Seminars in Archaeology, No.2.

Spiess, Arthur E.
1984 Arctic garbage and New England Paleo-Indians: the single occupation option. In New Experiments upon the Record of Eastern Palaeo-Indian Cultures. Archaeology of Eastern North America, 12:280-285.

Spiess, Arthure E., Bruce J. Bourque and Steven L. Cox
1983 Cultural complexity in maritime cultures: evidence from Penobscot Bay, Maine. In The Evolution of Maritime Cultures on the Northeast and the Northwest Coasts of America. Ronald J. Nash (ed.): 91-108. Simon Fraser University, Department of Archaeology, Publication No.11.

Spiess, Arthur and Deborah Brush
1987 Patterning in Paleoindian behavior: the Michaud site. Current Research in the Pleistocene 4: 34-35. A Peopling of the Americas Publication, Center for the Study of Early Man, University of Maine, Orono.

Spiess, Arthur E. and Peter L. Storck
1990 New faunal identifications from the Udora site: a Gainey-Clovis occupation site in Southern Ontario. Current Research in the Pleistocene 7: 127-129. A Peopling of the Americas Publication, Center for the Study of the First Americans, University of Maine, Orono.

Spurling, Brian E. and Bruce F. Ball
1981 On some distributions of the Oxbow Complex. Canadian Journal of Archaeology, No. 5:89-101.

Steele, D. Gentry and Joseph F. Powell

1992   Peopling of the Americas: paleobiographical evidence. Human Biology, Vol.64(3):303-336. Wayne State University Press.

Steensby, H. P.
1917   An anthropogeographical study of the origin of Eskimo culture. Meddelelser om Gronland 53:39-288.

Steinbring, Jack
1966   A Scottsbluff projectile point from Manitoba. The Wisconsin Archaeologist 47(1):1-7.
1970   Evidence of Old Copper in a northern transitional zone. In Ten Thousand Years, Archaeology in Manitoba. Walter M. Hlady (ed.): 47-74. Manitoba Archaeological Society.
1974   The preceramic archaeology of Northern Minnesota. In Aspects of Upper Great Lakes Anthropology. Elden Johnson (ed.): 64-73. Prehistoric Archaeology Series 11, Minnesota Historical Society.
1980   An introduction to the archaeology of the Winnipeg River. Papers in Manitoba Archaeology, Miscellaneous Paper No.9. Department of Cultural Affairs and Historical Resources. Manitoba.

Stewart, Andrew
1984   The Zander site: Paleo-Indian occupation of the southern Holland Marsh region of Ontario. Ontario Archaeology 41:45-79.
1991   Recognition of Northern Plano in the context of settlement in the Central Northwest Territories: developing a technological approach. Canadian Journal of Archaeology, Vol.15: 179-191.

Stewart, Ian
1989   Does God play dice? the mathematics of chaos. Oxford Basil Blackwell.

Stoltman, James B.
1971   Prismatic blades from northern Minnesota. Plains Anthropologist, 16(52): 105-110.
1978   Temporal models of prehistory: an example from eastern North America. Current Anthropology Vol.19(4):703-746.

Stoltman, James B. and David Baerreis
1983   The evolution of human ecosystems in the eastern United States. In Late-Quaternary Environments of the United States, Vol.2. Henry Wright (ed.): 252 -268. University of Minnesota Press.

Storck, Peter L.

1974 Two probable Shield Archaic sites in Killarney Provincial Park, Ontario. Ontario Archaeology No.21:3-36.

1978 The Coates Creek site: a possible Late Paleo-Indian-Early Archaic site in Simcoe County, Ontario. Ontario Archaeology 3:25-46.

1979 A report on the Banting and Hussey sites: two Paleo-Indian campsites in Simcoe County, Southern Ontario. National Museum of Man, Mercury Series, Archaeological Survey of Canada, No.93.

1982 Palaeo-Indian settlement patterns associated with the strandline of Glacial Lake Algonquin in southcentral Ontario. Canadian Journal of Archaeology, No.6:1-31.

1984 Research into the Paleo-Indian occupations of Ontario: a review. Ontario Archaeology 41:3-28.

1988 Recent excavations at the Udora site: a Gainey/Clovis occupation site in Southern Ontario. Current Research in the Pleistocene 5: 23-24. A Peopling of the Americas Publication, Center for the Study of the First Americans, University of Maine, Orono.

1988a The Early Palaeo-Indian occupation of Ontario: colonization or diffusion? Bulletin of the Buffalo Society of Natural Sciences, Vol.33:243-250.

1994 Case closed: the Fisher File. Rotunda, The Magazine of the Royal Ontario Museum, Vol 27(10):34-40.

Storck, Peter L. and John Tomenchuk

1990 An Early Palaeoindian cache of informal tools at the Udora site, Ontario. Research in Economic Anthropology, Supplement 5:45-93. JAI Press Inc.

Storck, Peter L. and Peter H. von Bitter

1989 The geological age and occurrence of Fossil Hill Formation chert: implications for Early Paleoindian settlement patterns. In Eastern Paleoindian Lithic Resource Use. Christopher J. Ellis and Jonathan C. Lothrop (eds.): 165-189. Westview Press.

Stothers, David M.

1982 Earliest man in the Western Lake Erie Basin. Man in the Northeast, No.23:39-46.

Stothers, David M. and Timothy J. Abel

1991 Earliest Main in the southwestern Lake Erie Basin: a 1990 perspective. North American Archaeologist Vol.12(3):195-242.

Struiver, M. and G.W. Pearson

1986 High-percision calibration of the radiocarbon time scale, AD 1950-500 BC. Radiocarbon 28:805-838.

Stryd, Arnoud H.

1971   A speculative framework for Plateau prehistory. In Aboriginal man and environments on the plateau of northwest America. Arnoud H. Stryd and Rachel A. Smith (eds.): 7-13. The University of Calgary Archaeological Association.

1973   The later prehistory of the Lillooet area, British Columbia. Unpublished Ph.D. thesis, University of Calgary.

Stryd, Arnoud H. and Michael Rousseau

(in press)   The Early Prehistory of the Mid-Fraser-Thompson River area of British Columbia. Simon Fraser University, Archaeology Department.

Stuart, Glenn S. L.

1990   The Cranford site (DlPb-2), a multicomponent stone circle site on the Oldman River. Archaeological Survey of Alberta, Manuscript Series No.17.

Stuiver, Minze and Bernd Becker

1986   High precision calibration of the radiocarbon time scale, AD 1950-2500 BC. Radiocarbon 28(2B):863-910.

1993   High-precision decadal calibration of the radiocarbon time scale, AD 1950-6000 BC. Radiocarbon, Vol.35(1):35-65.

Styles, Norla

1976   Chapter 11: Preliminary report on the burials at Glenrose. In The Glenrose Cannery Site. R. G. Matson (ed.): 202-213. National Museum of Man, Archaeological Survey of Canada, Mercury 52.

Sutherland, Patricia D.

1991   Archaeological site distributions on the south coast of Devon Island, High Arctic Canada. In NOGAP Archaeology Project: an Integrated Archaeological Research and Management Approach. Jacques Cinq-Mars and Jean-Luc Pilon (eds.): 131-142. Canadian Archaeological Association, Occasional Paper No.1.

Suttles, Wayne (vol. ed.)

1990   Handbook of the North American Indians, Northwest Coast, Vol.7., William C. Sturtevant (gen. ed.). Smithsonian Institution, Washington.

1990a   Introduction. Handbook of the North American Indians, Northwest Coast, Vol.7. William C. Sturtevant (gen. ed.) and Wayne Suttles (vol. ed.): 1-15. Smithsonian Institution.

Swanson, E. H. Jr.

1962   Early cultures of northwestern North America. American Antiquity Vol.28:151-158.

Syms, E. Leigh
  1970   The McKean Complex in Manitoba. In Ten Thousand Years, Archaeology in Manitoba. Walter M. Hlady (ed.): 123-138. Manitoba Archaeological Society.
  1980   The co-influence sphere model: a new paradigm for Plains developments and Plains-Parkland-Woodland processual inter-relationships. In Directions in Manitoba Archaeology, Papers in Honour of Chris Vickers: 111-140. Association of Manitoba Archaeologists and the Manitoba Archaeological Association.

Szathmary, E. J. E. and N. S. Ossenberg
  1978   Are the biological differences between North American Indians and Eskimos truly profound? Current Anthropology, Vol.19:673-701.

Taillon, Hélène et Georges Barré
  1987   Datations au 14C des sites archéologiques du Québec. Dossiers cinquante-neuf, Ministère des Affaires culturelles, Québec.

Tamplin, Morgan J.
  n.d.   Prehistoric occupation and resource exploitation on the Saskatchewan River in the Pas, Manitoba. PhD. thesis, University of Arizona, 1977.

Tankersley, Kenneth B.
  1989   A close look at the big picture: Early Paleoindian lithic resource procurement in the Midwestern United States. In Eastern Paleoindian Lithic Resource Use. Christopher J. Ellis and Jonathan C. Lothrop (eds.): 259-292. Westview Press.

Tankersley, Kenneth B. and Cherl Ann Munson
  1992   Comments on the Meadowcroft Rockshelter radiocarbon chronology and the recognition of coal contaminants. American Antiquity, Vol.57 (2):321-326.

Tauber, H.
  1981   13C evidence for dietary habits of prehistoric man in Denmark. Nature 292: 332-333.

Taylor, R. E.
  1987   Radiocarbon dating: an archaeological perspective. Academic Press.

Taylor, R. E., L. A. Payen, C. A. Prior, P. J. Slota, Jr., R. Gillespie, J. A. Gowlett, R. E. M. Hedges, A. J. T. Jull, T. H. Zabel, D. J. Donahue, and R. Berger
  1985   Major revisions in the Pleistocene age assignments for North American human skeletons by C-14 accelerator mass spectrometry: none older than 11,000 C-14 years B.P. American Antiquity, Vol.50(1):136-140.

544

Taylor, William E. Jr.

1962   Pre-Dorset occupations at Ivugivik in northwestern Ungava. In Prehistoric Cultural Relations between the Arctic and Temperate Zones of North America. John M. Campbell (ed.): 80-90. Arctic Institute of North America, Technical Paper 11.

1964   Interim account of an archaeological survey in the Central Arctic, 1963. Anthropological Papers of the University of Alaska, 12(1):46-55.

1965   The fragments of Eskimo prehistory. The Beaver, Spring.

1967   Summary of archaeological field work on Banks and Victoria islands, Arctic Canada, 1965. Arctic Anthropology, IV(1):221-243.

1968   The Arnapik and Tyara sites: an archaeological study of Dorset culture origins. Memoirs of the Society for American Archaeology, No.22.

1968a   Eskimos of the north and east shores. In Science, History and Hudson Bay, Vol.I. C. S. Beals and D. A. Shenstone (eds.): 1-26. Department of Energy, Mines and Resources, Ottawa.

1972   An archaeological survey between Cape Perry and Cambridge Bay, NWT, Canada in 1963. National Museum of Man, Archaeological Survey of Canada, Mercury 1.

Teit, James

1909   The Shuswap. American Museum of Natural History Memoirs, Vol.2, Part 7: 447-758.

Thomas, Peter A. and Brian S. Robinson

1980   The John's Bridge site: VT-FR-69, an Early Archaic period in northwestern Vermont. Report 28, Department of Anthropology, University of Vermont.

Thompson, Laurence C. and M. Dale Kinkade

1990   Languages. In Handbook of North American Indians. William C. Sturtevant (gen. ed.). Vol.7, Northwest Coast. Wayne Suttles (vol. ed.): 30-51. Smithsonian Institution.

Thomson, Callum

1984   Maritime Archaic occupation of Big Island, Saglek Bay: a preliminary report. Archaeology in Newfoundland and Labrador, 1983, No.4. Jane Sproull Thomson and Callum Thomson (eds.): 48-54.

Thwaites, Reuben Gold

1896-1901   Jesuit Relations and Allied Documents, Vols.1-73. Cleveland.

Trigger, Bruce G.

1989   A history of archaeological thought. Cambridge University Press.

Trigger, Bruce G. (vol. ed.)

1978   Handbook of North American Indians, Northeast, Vol.15, William C. Sturtevant (gen. ed.). Smithsonian Institution, Washington.

Trubowitz, Neal L.

1977   A statistical examination of the social structure of Frontenac Island. Current perspectives in Northeastern Archaeology, Researches and Transactions of the New York State Archaeological Association XVII(1):123-147.

1979   The Early Archaic in western New York. Archaeological Association of New York State, The Bulletin 75:52-57.

Tuck, James A.

1971   An Archaic cemetery at Port au Choix, Newfoundland. American Antiquity Vol.36(3):343-358.

1974   Early Archaic horizons in eastern North America. Archaeology of Eastern North America, 2(1):72-80.

1975   Prehistory of Saglek Bay, Labrador: Archaic and Palaeo-Eskimo occupations. National Museum of Man, Archaeological Survey of Canada, Mercury 32.

1975a   The northeastern maritime continuum: 8000 years of cultural development in the far Northeast. Arctic Anthropology XII(2):139-147.

1976   Newfoundland and Labrador prehistory. Canadian Prehistory Series, National Museum of Man.

1976a   Ancient people of Port-au-Choix, the excavation of an Archaic Indian cemetery in Newfoundland. Newfoundland Social and Economic Studies, No.17. Institute of Social and Economic Research, Memorial University of Newfoundland.

1976b   Paleoeskimo cultures of northern Labrador. In Eastern Arctic Prehistory: Paleoeskimo Problems. Moreau S. Maxwell (ed.): 89-102. Memoirs of the Society for American Archaeology, No.31.

1977   Early cultures on the Strait of Belle Isle, Labrador. In Amerinds and their Paleoenvironments in Northeastern North America. Walter S. Newman and Bert Salwen (eds.): 472-480. The New York Academy of Sciences, Bulletin 288.

1977a   A look at Laurentian. In Current Perspectives in Northeastern archaeology, Essays in Honor of William A. Ritchie. Robert E. Funk and Charles F. Hayes III (eds.): 31-40. Researches and Transactions of the New York State Archaeological Association, XVII(1).

1978   Regional cultural development, 3000 to 300 BC. In Handbook of North American Indians, Vol.15, Northeast. Smithsonian Institution, William C. Sturtevant (gen. ed.) and Bruce G. Trigger (vol. ed.): 28-43.

1978a   Archaic burial ceremonialism in the `Far Northeast'. Occasional Publications in Northeastern Anthropology No.5. Essays in Northeastern Anthropology in Memory of Marian E. White. William E. Engelbrecht and Donald K. Grayson (eds.): 67-77.

1982   Prehistoric archaeology in Atlantic Canada since 1975. Canadian Journal of Archaeology

No.6:201- 218.

1984   Maritime provinces prehistory. Canadian Prehistory Series, National Museum of Man.

(n.d.)   The archaeology of Atlantic Canada. Manuscript in possession of author.

Tuck, James A. and Ralph T. Pastore

1985   A nice place to visit, but...prehistoric human extinctions on the Island of Newfoundland. Canadian Journal of Archaeology Vol.9 (1): 69-80.

Turnbull, Christopher J.

1977   Archaeology and ethnohistory in the Arrow Lakes, southern British Columbia. National Museum of Man, Archaeologicial Survey of Canada, Mercury 65.

1988   Reflections on a ground slate bayonet fragment from the Tantramar Marsh, Upper Bay of Fundy. Canadian Journal of Archaeology Vol.12:87-108.

Turner, C. G. II

1983   Dental evidence for the peopling of the Americas. In Early Man in the New World. R. Shutler Jr. (ed.): 147-157. Sage Press, Beverly Hills.

Van Dyke, Stanley, Sharon Hanna, Wendy Unfreed, and Barbara Neal

1991   That Dam Archaeology: campsite archaeology in the Oldman River Reservoir. Archaeological Survey of Alberta, Occasional Paper No.33:26-65.

Van Dyke, Stan and Sally Stewart

1985   Hawkwood site (EgPm-179): a multicomponent prehistoric campsite on Nose Hill. Archaeological Survey of Alberta, Manuscript Series No.7.

Verbicky-Todd, Eleanor

1984   Communal buffalo hunting among the Plains Indians. Archaeological Survey of Alberta, Occasional Paper 24.

Vickers, J. Roderick

1986   Alberta Plains prehistory: a review. Archaeological Survey of Alberta, Occasional Papers Nos. 27 and 28:1-139.

1991   Seasonal round problems on the Alberta Plains. Canadian Journal of Archaeology, Vol.15:55-72.

Voorhies, M. R. and R. G. Corner

1986   The giant bear Arctodus as a potential breaker and flaker of Late Pleistocene megafaunal remains. Current Research in the Pleistocene. A Peopling of the Americas Publication 3:49-51.

Wade, William D.
1981   Temporal and biological dimensions of the Gray site population. Canadian Journal of Archaeology, Vol.5:119-130.

Walker, D. N. and G. C. Frison
1982   Studies on Amerind dogs, 3: prehistoric wolf/dog hybrids from the Northwestern Plains. Journal of Archaeological Science 9:125-172.

Walker, Ernest G.
1981   The Greenwater Lake site (FcMv-1): an Archaic burial from Saskatchewan. Napoa 11(1&2):8-12.
1984   The Graham site: a McKean cremation from southern Saskatchewan. Plains Anthropologist, 29(104):139-150.
1986   Human skeletal remains from the Crown site. Appendix A In The Crown site (FhNa-86) Excavation Results. Saskatchewan Research Council, Vol.8. David Meyer (ed.).
1992   The Gowen sites, cultural responses to climatic warming on the Northern Plains (7500-5000 B.P.). Canadian Museum of Civilization, Archaeological Survey of Canada, Mercury 145.

Wall, Robert D.
n.d.   The preceramic period in the southwest Canadian Shield: an initial model formulation. PhD. thesis, Catholic Univesity of America, 1980.

Warnica, James M.
1966   New discoveries at the Clovis site. American Antiquity Vol.31(1): 345-357.

Waselkov, Gregory A.
1984   Small faunal remains from the McIntyre site. In The McIntyre site: archaeology, subsistence and environment. Richard B. Johnston (ed.). National Museum of Man, Archaeological Survey of Canada, Mercury 126:137-158.

Watson, Gordon D.
1981   A Late Archaic Broadpoint phase in the Rideau Lakes area of Eastern Ontario. The Ottawa Archaeologist, Newsletter of the Ottawa Chapter, Ontario Archaeological Society, Vol.10(9):2-15.
1990   Palaeo-Indian and Archaic occupations of the Rideau Lakes. Ontario Archaeology, 50:5-26.

Wedel, Waldo R.
1978   The prehistoric Plains. In Ancient Native Americans. Jesse D. Jennings (ed.): 183-220.

548

Weinman, Paul L. and Thomas P. Weinman

1970 The Parrish site - a Vergennes component. New York State Archaeological Association, Bulletin 49:30-32.

Wellman, Beth

1974 Prehistoric site survey and salvage in the Upper Schoharie Valley, New York. Eastern States Archaeological Federation, Bulletin 34:15.

West, Frederick Hadleigh

1967 The Donnelly Ridge site and the definition of an early core and blade complex in central Alaska. American Antiquity, Vol.32(3):360-382.

1981 The archaeology of Beringia. Columbia University Press, New York.

1983 The antiquity of man in America. In Late Quaternary Environments of the United States. H. E. Wright Jr. (ed.), Vol.I, The Late Pleistocene. Stephen C. Porter (ed.): 364-382. University of Minnesota Press.

Wettlaufer, Boyd

1955 The Mortlach site in the Besant Valley of central Saskatchewan. Department of Natural Resources, Anthropological Series No.1.

1981 The Oxbow Complex in time and space - Forward. Canadian Journal of Archaeology, No.5: 79-81.

Wettlaufer, B. N. and W. J. Mayer-Oakes

1960 The Long Creek site. Department of Natural Resources, Anthropological Series No.2.

Wheat, Joe Ben

1972 The Olsen-Chubbuck site, a Paleo-Indian bison killn. American Antiquity Vol.37 (1-2), Memoirs of the Society for American Archaeology, No.26.

1979 The Jurgens site. Plains Anthropologist 24-84 (2), Memoir 15.

Wheeler, Clinton, J.

1978 The Caribou Lake Project 1977. Papers in Manitoba Archaeology, Preliminary Report 5. Department of Tourism, Recreation and Cultural Affairs. Manitoba.

Whitlam, Robert G.

1980 Archaeological investigations at Cache Creek (EeRh 3). Heritage Conservation Branch, Occasional Papers 5, Province of British Columbia.

Willey, Gordon R.

1966   An introduction to American Archaeology, Volume I, North and Middle America. Prentice-Hall Inc.

Willey, Gordon R. and Jeremy A. Sabloff
1974   A history of American archaeology. Thomas and Hudson.

Williams, R.C., A.G. Steinberg, H. Gershowitz, P.H. Bennett, W.C. Knowles, D.J. Pettitt, W.J. Butler et al.
1985   GM allotypes in native America: evidence for three distinct migrations across the Bering land bridge. American Journal of Physical Anthropology 66:1-19.

Willig, Judith A. and C. Melvin Aikens
1988   The Clovis-Archaic Interface in Far Western North America. In Early Human Occupation in Far Western North America: the Clovis-Archaic Interface. Judith A. Willig and C. Melvin Aikens (eds.): 1-40. Nevada State Museum, Anthropological Papers No.21.

Willoughby, Charles C.
1935   Antiquities of the New England Indians. Peabody Museum of Archaeology and Ethnology.

Wilmeth, Roscoe
1968.   A fossilized bone artifact from southern Saskatchewan. American Antiquity, Vol.33(1):100-101.
1977   Pit-House construction and the disturbance of stratified sites. Canadian Journal of Archaeology, No.1:135-140.
1978   Canadian archaeological radiocarbon dates (revised version). National Museum of Man, Archaeological Survey of Canada, Mercury 77.
1978a   Anahim Lake archaeology and the early historic Chilcotin Indians. National Museum of Man, Archaeological Survey of Canada, Mercury 82.

Wilmsen, Edwin N.
1965   An outline of Early Man studies in the United States. American Antiquity Vol.31(2-1):172-192.

Wilmsen, E.N. and F.H.H.Roberts, Jr.
1978   Lindenmeier, 1934- 1974: concluding report on investigations. Smithsonian Contributions to Anthropology 24.

Wilson, Michael C.
1981   Sun dances, thirst dances, and medicine wheels: a search for alternative hypotheses. In

Megaliths and Medicine Wheels: Boulder Structures in Archaeology. Michael Wilson, Kathie L. Road, and Kenneth J. Hardy (eds.): 333-370. Proceedings of the Eleventh Annual Chacmool Conference, The Archaeological Association of the University of Calgary.

1983   Once upon a river: archaeology and geology of the Bow River Valley at Calgary, Alberta, Canada. National Museum of Man, Archaeological Survey of Canada, Mercury 114.

Wilson, Robert L.

1976   Archaeological investigation near Kamloops, B. C. MA thesis, Simon Fraser University.

Wilson, Susan R.

1987   Statistics and archaeology. In Archaeometry: further Australian Studies. W. R. Ambrose and J. M. J. Mummery (eds.): 261-267. The Australian National University and the Australian National Gallery. Canberra.

Wintemberg, W. J.

1928   Artifacts from ancient graves and mounds in Ontario. Transactions of the Royal Society of Canada, Third Series XXII(II):175-202.

1943   Artifacts from ancient workshop sites near Tadoussac, Saguenay County, Quebec. American Antiquity Vol.8(4):313-340.

Winterhalder, Bruce

1981   Foraging strategies in the Boreal Forest: an analysis of Cree hunting and gathering. In Hunter-Gatherer Foraging Strategies, Ethnographic and Archeological Analyses, Prehistoric Archeology and Ecology Series. Bruce Winterhalder and Eric Smith (eds.): 66-98. University of Chicago Press.

Witthoft, John

1952   A Paleo-Indian site in eastern Pennsylvania: an early hunting culture. Proceedings of the American Philosophical Society, Vol.96(4):464-495.

Wittry, Warren L.

1959   The Raddatz Rockshelter, Sk5, Wisconsin. The Wisconsin Archaeologist Vol.40(2):33-69.

1959a   Archaeological studies of four Wisconsin rockshelters. The Wisconsin Archaeologist Vol.40(4):137-267.

Wobst, Martin H.

1968   The Butterfield site, 20 BY 29, Bay County, Michigan. Anthropological Papers, Museum of Anthropology, University of Michigan, No.32:173-275.

Wood, William J.
1979   The Upper Peace River, Alberta, Permit Number 78-10, Archaeology in Alberta 1978. J. M. Hillerud (ed.): 26-33, Archaeological Survey of Alberta, Occasional Paper No.14.

Woodley, Philip J.
1988   Thistle Hill (AhGx-226): a Late Archaic house pit feature from Southern Ontario. Canadian Journal of Archaeology, Vol.12:197.
1990   The Thistle Hill site and Late Archaic adaptations. Occasional Papers in Northeastern Archaeology, No.4. Copetown Press.

Workman, William B.
1978   Prehistory of the Aishihik-Kluane area, southwest Yukon Territory. National Museum of Man, Archaeological Survey of Canada, Mercury 74.

Wormington, H.M.
1957   Ancient Man in North America. Denver Museum of Natural History. Denver, Colorado.

Wormington, H. M. and Richard G. Forbis
1965   An introduction to the archaeology of Alberta, Canada. Denver Museum of Natural History, Proceeding No.11.

Wortner, Stan and Chris Ellis
1993   The Snary early Paleo-Indian site. Kewa 93-2. Newsletter of the London Chapter, Ontario Archaeological Society.

Wright, J. V.
1962   A distributional study of some Archaic traits in Southern Ontario. National Museum of Canada, Bulletin 180: 124-142.
1967   The Laurel tradition and the Middle Woodland period. National Museum of Canada, Bulletin 217.
1970   The Shield Archaic in Manitoba - a preliminary statement. In Ten Thousand Years, Archaeology in Manitoba. Walter M. Hlady (ed.): 29-45. Manitoba Archaeological Society.
1972   Ontario prehistory, an eleven-thousand- year archaeological outline. Canadian Prehistory Series, National Museum of Man.
1972a   The Shield Archaic. National Museum of Man, Publications in Archaeology, No.3.
1972b   The Aberdeen site, Keewatin District, N.W.T. National Museum of Man, Archaeological Survey of Canada, Mercury 2.

| 1972c | The Knechtel I site, Bruce County, Ontario. National Museum of Man, Archaeological Survey of Canada, Mercury 4. |

1972c   The Knechtel I site, Bruce County, Ontario. National Museum of Man, Archaeological Survey of Canada, Mercury 4.

1972d   The Dougall site. Ontario Archaeology, 17:3-23.

1974   The Nodwell site. National Museum of Man, Archaeological Survey of Canada, Mercury 22.

1975   The prehistory of Lake Athabasca: an initial statement. National Museum of Man, Archaeological Survey of Canada, Mercury 29.

1976   Six chapters of Canada's prehistory. Canadian Prehistory Series, National Museum of Man.

1976a   The Grant Lake site, Keewatin District, N.W.T. National Museum of Man, Archaeological Survey of Canada, Mercury 47.

1978   The implications of probable Early and Middle Archaic projectile points from southern Ontario. Canadian Journal of Archaeology No.2:59-78.

1979   Quebec prehistory. Canadian Prehistory Series, National Museum of Man and Van Nostrand Reinhold.

1979a   The Shield Archaic: a critique of a critique. Manitoba Archaeological Quarterly, 3(3-4):30-35.

1981   Prehistory of the Canadian Shield. In Handbook of the North American Indians. William C. Sturtevant (gen. ed.), Vol.6, Subarctic. June Helm (vol. ed.): 86-96. Smithsonian Institution.

1982   La circulation de biens archéologiques dans le bassin du Saint-Laurent au cours de la préhistoire. Recherches amérindiennes au Québec, 12(3):193-205.

1983   Prehistoric cultural distributions as an indicator of environmental change. In Critical Periods in the Quaternary Climatic History of Northern North America, an International Meeting sponsored by the National Museum of Natural Sciences, Climatic Change in Canada Project. Ottawa. (a 2 page abstract).

1984   The cultural continuity of the northern Iroquoian-speaking peoples. In Extending the Rafters: Interdisciplinary Approaches to Iroquoian Studies. M. K. Foster, J. Campisi, and M. Methun (eds.): 283-299. State University of New York Press, Albany.

1985   The development of prehistory in Canada, 1935-1985. American Antiquity, Vol.50(2):421-433.

1987   Archaeological evidence for the use of furbearers in North America. In Wild Furbearer Management and Conservation in North America. Milan Novak, James A. Baker, Martyn E. Obbard, and Bruce Mulloch (eds.): 3-12. Ontario Ministry of Natural Resources.

1990   Archaeology of Southern Ontario to A.D. 1650: a critique. In The Archaeology of Southern Ontario to A.D. Chris J. Ellis and Neal Ferris (eds.): 493-503. Occasional Publication of the London Chapter, Ontario Archaeological Society, No.5.

1994   The prehistoric transportation of goods in the St. Lawrence River Basin. In Prehistoric Exchange Systems in North America. Timothy G. Baugh and Jonathon E. Ericson (eds.): 47-71. Plenum Press, New York and London.

Wright, J. V. and Roy Carlson

1987   Prehistoric Trade. Plate 14, Historical Atlas of Canada, Vol.I: from the beginning to 1800. R. Cole Harris (ed.) and Geoffrey J. Mathews (cartographer and designer), University of Toronto Press.

Wright, Milt

1986   Le Bois de Vache: this chip's for you. Saskatchewan Archaeology, Vol.7:25-31.

1992   Le Bois de Vache II: this chip's for you too. In Buffalo. John Foster, Dick Harrison, and I. S. MacLaren (eds.): 225-244. Alberta Nature and Culture Series.

Wright, Ronald

1992   Stolen continents, the Americas through Indian eyes since 1492. Houghton Mifflin Co.

Wyatt, David

1970   Statistical analysis of Lochnore-Nesikep locality microblades. An appendix in Archaeology of the Lochnore-Nesikep Locality by David Sanger, Syesis 3:130-146.

Yarnell, Richard A.

1984   The McIntyre site: Late Archaic plant remains from Southern Ontario. In The McIntyre site: archaeology, subsistence and environment. Richard B. Johnston (ed.). National Museum of Man, Archaeological Survey of Canada, Mercury 126:87-111.

Yerbury, J. C.

1975   Nineteenth century Kootenay settlement patterns. Western Journal of Anthropology, IV(4):23-35.

Yi, Sembok and Geoffrey Clark

1985   The "Dyuktai Culture" and New World Origins. Current Anthropology 26(1):1-20.

Ministère des Affaires culturelles, Québec

1985   L'Archéologie au Québec.

1986   Archaeology in Quebec.

GLOSSARY

ablating continental glacier - melting and contracting glaciers of the Laurentide Ice Sheet which at one time covered most of Canada east of the Continental Divide.

adze - a polished stone woodworking celt with a bevelled cutting bit; the gouge, with a U-shaped crossection at the bit end, is a form of adze.

Altithermal - a period of exceptionally warm climate in North America between 6,500 and 3,500 BC; a geographically variable phenomenon whose impact appears to have been most intense on the Plains.

ammonite - a fossil mollusc used on the Plains as an amulet.

anadromous - fish species that ascend rivers from the sea to spawn.

animism - the attribution of a living soul or spirit to inanimate objects and natural phenomenon, such as stone and wind, as well as animate objects, such as animals and plants.

anvil - a stone slab upon which objects were broken (nuts) or fashioned into tools with a hammerstone.

Archaic - a general archaeological classificatory term used in a number of different ways but generally to describe the hunting and gathering cultures that followed Palaeo-Indian culture until the appearance of pottery which introduced the Woodland period.

arris - the sharp ridge that occurs between two flake scars on chipped stone tools; multiple parallel arrises on long, narrow flakes are used as evidence of the presence of specialized microblade cores.

arroyo - a steep banked erosion gully of a small stream; use limited to western North America where they were sometimes used as natural bison traps.

artifact - any object either modified or used by humans; an arrowhead and a natural stone cobble used as either a hammer or heated to boil water are both artifacts.

Aurignacian lithic industry - an ancient Eurasian stone tool industry based upon large linear flakes and blades, the latter being struck or punched from specially prepared cores.

awl - a sharply pointed object, usually of bone or copper, used to perforate leather in the manufacturing of clothing, tent covers, etc.

band exogamy - the requirement of all members of a band to find spouses outside of their own band community.

Beringia - the landmass that once joined Asia and North America and by which the first people are believed to have reached the Western Hemisphere.

biface knife - a cutting implement of stone, chipped on both faces to produce sharp marginal edges.

biface preform - an unfinished chipped biface that can be readily modified into a number of different types of tools.

bioturbation - the disturbance of the soil, including archaeological deposits, by biological agencies such as burrowing rodents, tree-falls, root disturbance, insects and later human activities.

bipolar cores - stone cores where flakes were removed from both ends of the core, frequently by placing the core on an anvil and striking the other end with a hammerstone.

blank - a roughed-out stone object for eventual manufacture into a tool or ornament; occasionally used as an equivalent term for a biface preform.

bolastone - a grooved, round stone resembling the stones used as part of a historically documented hunting implement consisting of a number of stone weights attached to thongs that was thrown through the air in order to entangle birds and other animals.

burin - a cutting and slotting implement of stone occurring in a number of forms that is believed to have been used mainly in the fashioning of stone and ivory objects; it most distinctive characteristic is the resharpening procedure which involves the striking off of a small flake to create a sharp edge and corner.

burin spall - the flake detached from a burin in order to resharpen the burin edge; the spall sometimes used as a needle.

butt hook or spur - the bone hook at the butt end of a spearthrower that engages the end of the spear.

cairn - any constructed mound of rocks or boulders whether covering a burial, a food cache, or to act as a navigational aid or marker.

calcined bone - bone reduced to a friable state by burning.

canids - members of the Family Canidae that includes dog, coyote, wolf, and fox.

celt - a polished stone woodworking implement, more rarely of chipped stone, which includes adzes with asymmetrical bits and axes with symmetrical cutting bits.

Cervids - members of the Family Cervidae that includes deer, caribou, moose, and wapiti or elk.

chalcedony - a fine grained variety of silica used in stone tool manufacture.

chert - a general term for all crypotcrystalline silica varieties that can be chipped into tools by percussion and/or applied pressure; unlike some geological definitions, its use in archaeology always implies that chert must fracture in the conchoidal fashion required for chipped stone tool production.

chitho - an Athapaskan word for a specialized form of stone scraper used in hide preparation that is characterized by bifacial retouch restricted to the tool edge; usually fashioned from flat sheets of quartzite or slate.

chopper - a large and roughly formed chipped stone implement, often manufactured from a cobble, with either a bifacially or unifacially flaked cutting edge.

cist - a container of vertically set stone slabs usually associated with a burial chamber.

Clovis culture - a name of the early portion of Palaeo-Indian culture, named after the original discovery near Clovis, New Mexico.

coefficient of similarity - a method of mathematically arriving at a degree of relationship between any two comparable bodies of data from two different sites (see Brainerd, George W. 1951).

collagen - the organic fraction of bone, now judged to be more accurate in radiocarbon dating than the apatite or mineral fraction of bone.

Continental Ice Sheet - for archaeological purposes, this refers to the last glacier to cover most of Canada except the Cordillera of western North America; also called the Laurentide Ice Sheet.

core - a stone from which flakes were detached either to be used as such or further modified into tools; cores come in a wide range of forms.

cryoturbation - disturbance of the soil, including archaeological deposits, by freeze and thaw cycles and features associated with permafrost.

delphinids - the numerous species of dolphins and porpoises of the Family Delphinidae including killer whales.

dendritic esker system - eskers are elevated depositional features of sorted sand and gravels formed by rivers running under the glacial ice that take on the form of a river drainage system; such areas were favoured by hunters for ambushing prey.

dendrochronology - an absolute dating method based upon the counting of the annual growth rings in trees and extending the resulting patterns back in time by overlapping distinctive modern growth configurations with the progressively older patterns found in logs recovered from both archaeological and geological deposits; by radiocarbon dating the dendrochronology dated tree rings from longlived trees like the bristle cone pines of Nevada and California and the bog oaks of Northern Ireland it has been possible to calibrate radiocarbon years into calendrical years.

denticulate - a flake or chipped stone cutting implement with one or more edges chipped in the form of a saw edge.

detritus - usually used to refer to the waste flake products resulting from stone chipping.

drill - a hand-held or hafted chipped stone tool with a long and narrow working bit used to drill holes into different materials.

effigy - an object or feature fashioned to replicate the form of an animal, including humans.

eustatic - refers to absolute changes in sea level that were/are world-wide rather than being a product of local land or sea floor movements.

exogamous - the reverse of endogamous in that marriage partners must be drawn from outside of the immediate community rather than from within.

finger printing - a blanket term involving a range of petrographic and chemical analyses to relate the material from which a particular archaeological specimen was manufactured to its geological source (e.g. a specific deposit of quartzite) and includes biological origins (e.g. a shark tooth or marine shell pendant from an interior site).

fire fractured rock - sometimes called `firestone´, fire fractured rock is often the first archaeological evidence of human activity; the heating of usually igneous rock to bake food or place in water containers to boil food or render fat results in the heated rock shattering into distinctive shaped fragments.

flake knife - as used in this work, a flake with one or more edges bifacially flaked to perform a cutting function.

flesher - the bone flesher is a specialized hide working implement used for removing hair and excess fat and tissue from an animal hide.

Folsom culture - a name for late Palaeo-Indian culture derived from the site of initial discovery near Folsom, New Mexico.

gaming disk - a round disc of stone, bone, or pottery, believed to be a token in some game of chance.

gill net - a net whose mesh is designed to catch in the gills of fish.

graphite - a black, naturally occurring carbon used as paint.

graver - a flake with one or more spurs unifacially flaked into the edges and used for delicate cutting and engraving work.

hammerstone - a naturally occurring hard variety of rock of appropriate size and weight used to hammer objects including breaking chert in manageable pieces; the process of hammering leaves pitting as evidence that the stone had been used as a tool.

hematite - a natural occurring bright red coloured iron oxide used as paint and frequently associated with burials.

Holocene - pertains to the post-galcial portion of the Quaternary Period that is preceded by the Pleistocene; generally assigned to the time period from 8,000 BC to the present.

hypoplasia - a distinctive grooving in human teeth indicative of nutritional stress; particularly after weaning.

hypothesis - a reasoned assumption whose validity is to be tested; a starting point in seeking truth.

Hypsithermal - see Altithermal.

impoundment - a pound or corral, usually constructed of poles and brush, used to contain herd animals such as bison and deer until they can be killed.

incise - a form of decoration on stone, bone, or pottery whereby lines are cut into the object to produce a design.

index fossil - in archaeology, the expression is used to describe an artifact whose form is believed to be so diagnostic of a particular time and place that its presence alone is regarded as sufficient evidence to make a cultural identification and time estimate for an otherwise undated site; effective in certain instances, its use nevertheless has frequently been abused.

iniskim or inisk'im - a Blackfoot expression for `buffalo stones´, these fragments of fossil ammonites and bacculites resemble the bison form and were believed to be important in hunting magic.

intermontane - between mountains.

isostatic rebound - relates to the tendency of the Earth's crust to maintain a state of equilibrium with the result that when the crust is depressed by the weight of glacial ice it will recover or `rebound´ when the weight is lessened or removed.

javelin - a light throwing spear propelled with a spearthrower.

kill site - a site where a large animal or a herd has been killed and butchered.

knapping - stone chipping.

Levallois core - a specialized core from which large flakes were struck to be manufactured into tools; specifically the tortoise-shaped core that first appeared during the Upper Pleistocene.

limonite - a yellow to brownish-yellow mineral used as a pigment.

linear flake - a long, narrow flake with a single medial arris resulting in a triangular crossection that was used unaltered or modified into a scraper or knife; unlike blades, linear flakes were not detached from specialized cores whose specific purpose was the production of numerous long, narrow flakes that, as a result, invariably contained multiple arrises on their dorsal faces.

linguistic family - all those languages, including mutually incomprehensible ones, affiliated by general linguistic structure such as the Montagnais, Ojibwa, Cree, and Blackfoot speakers of the Algonquian language family.

lithic - stone.

littoral - the area along a shoreline; particularly the shallow water equatic region.

maddock - a hoe-like tool, usually used for digging.

mano - derived from the Spanish word for `hand´ these circular stones with flat grinding faces were used to process food, particularly dried corn, on a larger stone called a metate.

marmot - a large member of the rodent family.

mast forest - a hardwood forest characterized by numerous nut bearing trees occuring in clusters of the same age and size, especially oak trees; attractive to deer and turkeys.

matrilocal - a residency pattern whereby the husband lives in the residence of his wife; the opposite of patrilocal residency.

Mazama ash - a volcanic ash or tephra that blanketed a wide area of western North America after a volcanic explosion in Oregon shortly after 6,000 BC; provides an important geological time marker for archaeologists and geologists.

medicine wheel - a general term applied to a wide range of features on the Plains that were produced by arranging cobbles on the surface of the ground; some features were accretionary structures involving ceremonial centres that were used for thousands of years.

megafauna - the large and now extinct mammals of the end of the Pleistocene, such as mastodon, mammoth, horse, and large forms of bison, that were hunted by Palaeo-Indians.

micro (-flake, -blade, -lithic) - used in a number of different ways but always denoting something small as opposed to macro or large.

mortuary ritualism - ceremonies associated with human burial.

mustelidae - members of weasel family including marten, fisher, ermine, mink, wolverine, badger, skunk, and otter.

obsidian - a form of volcanic glass greatly prized for its chipping qualities; also used with limited success as a dating method based upon the degree of hydration of the obsidian.

pastoralist - people whose economy is based upon domesticated livestock requiring grazing range.

patrilineal - the tracing of one's descent through the male rather than the female line; the opposite of matrilineal.

patrilocal - where the wife takes up residency in her husband's community; the opposite of matrilocal.

pedological - relating to the study of soils.

petroform - a feature, usually in animal form, realized by arranging cobbles on a flat bedrock or ground surface; related to cosmological beliefs.

petrograph - a picture carved into a stone face on a cliff, boulder, or artifact

petrographic analysis - a microscopic method used to measure the crystalline and other structural features of thin, sliced sections of stone; a major method in archaeology to link archaeological specimens with specific geological deposits of stone.

pit - any hole dug into the ground for purposes that can range from cooking to burial.

pit house - a semi-subterranean dwelling.

Pleistocene - the early, glacial portion of the Quaternary period; generally regarded as extending from 1,600,000 to 10,000 years ago.

plummet - a tear-drop shaped stone with a lashing groove at the narrower end that probably functioned as some kind of fishing sinker or jigging lure.

pluvial lake - the abnormally high rainfall that occurred to the south of the major glaciations, as well as the runoff from the melting glaciers, was responsible for exceptionally large bodies of freshwater at the end of the Pleistocene with, for example, lakes such as Winnipeg, Winnipegosis, and Manitoba being only surviving remnants of the much larger glacial Lake Agassiz.

pollen profile - tree and other plant pollen deposited in small lakes and wet areas can, under certain circumstances, be retrieved as a core and the record of plant species changes plotted through time and related to climatic change.

pre-fluted point sites - pre-Palaeo-Indian sites.

preform - a rudimentary chipped stone biface that can be readily fashioned into finished tools.

proboscidian - elephant; mammoth or mastodon in the Western Hemisphere.

projectile point - the stone or, more rarely, bone or copper weapon tip that was propelled through the air by hand, spearthrower or bow; also applied to the tips of hand thrusted spears.

quartzite - a metamorphized sandstone that fractures in a conchoidal manner and, thus, can be chipped into tools.

radiocarbon dating - a dating method based upon the principle that all living organisms take in the radioactive Carbon 14 isotope which decays in a measurable rate upon the death of the organism, whether animal or plant, a rate that can be measured and thus provide a statistical estimate of the time of death of the organism.

radiocarbon dating (AMS) - accelerator mass spectrometry introduced an improvement to radiocarbon dating by providing the capability to measure individual Carbon 14 atoms, thus permitting the rapid dating of samples of a only a few milligrams.

radiocarbon years (AD 1950) - radiocarbon years cannot be directly equated with calendar years but must first be calibrated using dates arrived at by radiocarbon dating samples that were first absolutely dated by the dendrochronology method; thus, uncalibrated radiocarbon dates are recorded as BP (Before Present) rather than BC or AD with Before Present meaning before AD 1950 when atomic bomb testing in the atmosphere made it impossible to accurately date materials after this time.

refugia - restricted areas where plant and animal species can survive to eventually repopulate lands when environmental conditions improve.

scaffold burial - many societies buried there kinsmen either permanently or temporarily on a platform elevated above the ground; often the disarticulated skeletal remains would subsequently be gathered into a bundle for final burial in some selected sacred place.

scraper - a common tool on most archaeological sites, the scraper was a chipped stone cutting and scraping implement used for fashioning implements and preparing hides; it comes in a wide variety of forms usually designated by adjectives such as end, side, random flake, etc.

semilunar knife - also called an ulu if made in polished slate, this distinctive type of knife is half-moon in shape and thus the name.

serration - appearing for the first time around 8,000 BC, the much improved cutting capabilities of the serrated edges of Early Archaic projectile points and knives resembles that of our modern serrated steel bread knives.

settlement patterns - this term includes how people distributed themselves across the landscape, the living floor characteristics of their camp sites and villages, and the specific details of their individual dwellings.

siliceous deposit - the geological deposit of any siliceous stone (chert, obsidian, basalt, quartzite, quartz, etc.) that will take a conchoidal fracture and can thus be fashioned into tools.

spearthrower - a device that permitted a javelin to be thrown further with greater force and accuracy than hand thrown spears; also called an atlatl after the Aztec word for the weapon.

spearthrower weights - also called atlatl weights, these polished stone objects were attached to the wooden spearthrower; their relative scarcity and elaborate forms, particularly in eastern North America, suggest that they were predominantly of symbolic importance rather than being a necessary component of the spearthrower technology.

spokeshave - flakes or biface knives with unifacially flaked concavities in their edges used to fashion objects with circular crossections such as wooden spear and arrow shafts.

stable carbon isotope studies - the stable or non radioactive carbon isotopes are Carbon 12 and Carbon 13; the ratios of the two isotopes can be recorded in human bone and indicate whether the food past people ingested was derived from a specific type of environment such as marine or desert.

stratigraphy - the law of superposition states that lower strata in a stratigraphic column are progressively older than the upper strata; this applies to archaeological deposits as well as geological formations and is the most important of all the relative dating methods.

systematics - refers to the logical classification of data following agreed upon principles that permit others to use said data without being subjected to logical inconsistencies such as the use of the same term for different phenomenon; archaeological systematics is still in its infancy.

tephra - highly fragmented volcanic debris generally distributed by wind in the form of ash; an important datable horizon marker for archaeology wherever it occurs.

theory - an assumption based upon principles independent of the phenomenon under investigation e.g. the fact that the lowest most deposit in an archaeological site is the oldest in the site is supported by the law of superposition which was established by geological evidence.

thermoluminescence - the radioactive decay of trace minerals in pottery clay or temper and heated chert dislodge electrons of other minerals, some of which become trapped but release photons (light) when heated; the intensity of the light can be measured and a calculation made of the date when either the clay was fired or the chert tempered by baking.

toggling harpoon - a specialized form of harpoon head with retrieving line that detaches from the harpoon shaft upon impact and under tension turns or toggles under the hide of the prey to hold it fast; an important element of technology for sea mammal hunters.

travois - a triangular device made from three poles whose apex was attached with a harness to the back of a dog who then would transport the load by dragging; characteristic of pre-horse transportation on the Plains.

typological cross-dating - certain artifact categories defined in terms of form attributes and dated at one site, such as projectile point or pottery types, are identified at another site where the age and cultural affiliation are assumed to be the same as that of the dated site; a useful dating method in many instances but often abused by inappropriate application.

ulu - see semilunar knife.

vegetation province - the general classification unit indicative of different plant communities such as the latitudinal or altitudinal relationship of the Tundra, Lichen Woodland, and Boreal Forest vegetation provinces.

votive - a ceremonial offering to a God or Spirit or deceased kinsman.

wedge - also called pièce esquillée, these small square to rectangular bipolar chipped stone implements have been interpreted as cores, wedges for splitting bone, and burins; use-wear studies indicate that they functioned as simple graving, slotting, and scraping tools and, therefore, are most appropriately classified as burins.

Woodland - a general time period that follows the Archaic period, particularly in eastern North America, that is initiated by the appearance of pottery manufacturing which provides a convenient temporal `index fossil´ for archaeologists.